management

AN ASIA–PACIFIC PERSPECTIVE

John R. SCHERMERHORN Jr | John CAMPLING

David POOLE | Retha WIESNER

WILEY

John Wiley & Sons Australia, Ltd

First published 2004 by
John Wiley & Sons Australia, Ltd
33 Park Road, Milton, Qld 4064

Offices also in Sydney and Melbourne

Authorised adaptation of the seventh edition by John R. Schermerhorn Jr,
Management (ISBN 0 471 43570 8), published by John Wiley & Sons,
Inc., New York, United States of America. Copyright © 2002 in the
United States of America by John Wiley & Sons, Inc. All rights reserved.

US edition © John Wiley & Sons, Inc. 2002
Australian edition © John Wiley & Sons Australia, Ltd, 2004

National Library of Australia
Cataloguing-in-Publication data

Management: an Asia–Pacific perspective.

Includes index.
For tertiary students.
ISBN 0 470 80104 2.

1. Management — Asia — Textbooks. 2. Management —
Pacific Area — Textbooks. I. Schermerhorn, John R.

658.0095

Cover and internal design images: copyright 2002 Digital Vision;
copyright 1999 PhotoDisc, Inc.

Printed in Singapore by
Kyodo Printing Co (S'pore) Pte Ltd

10 9 8 7 6 5 4 3 2 1

ABOUT THE AUTHORS

John R. Schermerhorn Jr

John Schermerhorn Jr, PhD, MBA (distinction), BS, is professor of management in the College of Business at Ohio University, where he teaches graduate and undergraduate courses in management. He is dedicated to serving the needs of practising managers in all types of organisations and has written comprehensively on management to help others bridge the gaps between theory and practice. At Ohio University, John has been named a University Professor, the university's highest campus-wide honour for excellence in undergraduate teaching. He is committed to instructional excellence and curriculum innovation, and is working extensively with technology use and Internet applications in the classroom. John's vast international experience adds a unique global dimension to his textbooks. He has worked in China, Egypt, Indonesia, Thailand, Malaysia, Vietnam, the Philippines, Poland, Hungary, Venezuela and Tanzania. He has also served as a Visiting Professor of Management at the Chinese University of Hong Kong, as on site Coordinator of the Ohio University MBA and Executive MBA programs in Malaysia, and as Director of the Interdisciplinary Center for Southeast Asia Studies at Ohio University. He is also a member of the graduate faculty at Bangkok University, Thailand, and serves as adviser to the Lao-American College in Vientiane, Laos. John is the author of the US edition of this textbook, *Management, seventh edition*, and senior co-author of *Managing Organizational Behavior, seventh edition*, *Introducing Management* and *Basic Organizational Behavior, second edition*.

John Campling

John Campling, BA Hons, MA, MIR, PhD (Cambridge), is a senior lecturer in management and the director of the Master of Business Administration program at the School of Business, James Cook University, Cairns. John has lectured, researched and published extensively on human resource management, industrial relations and organisational change in Australia, Europe and North America. He is the co-author of *Bargained Out: Negotiating Without Unions in Australia*, and his current research focuses on sustainable business strategies, innovation and the management of technology.

David Poole

David Poole, BBus, MBA, MEdAdmin, PhD, is senior lecturer in management within the School of Management at the University of Western Sydney. His research interests include public sector management, university management, organisational behaviour and business strategy. David's research has been published in journals such as *Management Today, Leading and Managing, Higher Education* and the *International Journal of Public Sector Management*. During 2001, he served as Visiting Professor of Management at Utah State University. David has also taught in the MBA programs of the Macquarie Graduate School of Management (MGSM), Australian Graduate School of Management (AGSM) and Sydney Graduate School of Management (SGSM).

Retha Wiesner

Retha Wiesner is associate professor in the Faculty of Business and head of the Department of Management and Organisational Behaviour at the University of Southern Queensland. Before entering academia in 1989, she gained extensive human resource management and organisational behaviour experience as an industrial psychologist and HR manager. Retha has taught human resource management and organisational behaviour courses in Australia and overseas, and is still actively involved as a consultant to many Australian organisations. She is the co-author of *Management & Organisational Behaviour*, and her current research interests include a major national and international study on employee management practices and organisational change in small and medium-sized enterprises.

BRIEF CONTENTS

CONTENTS

CHAPTER 6
Ethical behaviour and social responsibility 146

Getting connected: **Goldman Environmental Prize** —
help make this world a better place 147
What is ethical behaviour? 148

PART 3 ▸ *Mission*

CHAPTER 7
Planning and controlling 172

Getting connected: **Australian Art Resources** —
expanding in an uncertain market 173
How and why managers plan 174

CHAPTER 8
Strategic management   204

Getting connected: **Virgin Blue** — think global but act local   205

CHAPTER 9
Entrepreneurship and new ventures   240

Getting connected: **Wizard** — the new kid on the home loan block   241

CHAPTER 17
Communication and interpersonal skills   462

CHAPTER 18
Change leadership   492

CAREER READINESS WORKBOOK

Career advancement portfolio   W-4

Research and presentation projects   W-8

Cross-functional integrative case   W-15

Exercises in teamwork   W-20

Management skills assessments W-32

INTRODUCTION

Welcome to the first edition of *Management: An Asia–Pacific Perspective*! This text has been designed to be enjoyable and includes many easy-to-use features.

Managing an organisation in the Asia–Pacific region has never been more demanding. There is the aim of getting the most from diverse workforces, when members are diverse in terms of age, gender, ethnicity or any of the many other characteristics that make us unique. There is also the challenge of managing the organisation's approach to ethics and social responsibility. In the wake of the corporate collapses of companies like HIH and One.Tel, a renewed focus on ethics alerts us to the need to once again consider the values of our organisations.

Many organisations throughout the region are exporting products, establishing international offices, or developing links with other organisations in the region via alliances and joint ventures. International management entails developing an understanding of other cultures and markets with a view to ensuring that organisations respond positively to the great potential of international business.

In this era of empowerment and flatter organisation structures, managers must come to terms with the challenge of working with people who desire as much responsibility, autonomy and freedom as they do. Often the role of the manager has become more of a coach and mentor than a traditional supervisor.

Organisations seem to be rising and falling at a greater rate than has occurred in the past. Managers need to think entrepreneurially to ensure that evolving and entirely new products and services are created to meet the changing needs of customers. The entrepreneurial imperative is a competency few managers can ignore.

Technology is continuing to develop at such a rate that simply keeping up is becoming increasingly difficult. Significant consequences arise from the organisation's choice of technology, whether it is used to produce key outputs or for internal information management and communication. Managers are under pressure as a result of the increasing legislative requirements and sociopolitical pressure for sustainable businesses and industrial development in the Asia–Pacific region. Sustainability is driving technological change in many organisations. Those companies who innovate to meet this challenge will be the ones to survive and prosper in the 21st century. The text introduces students to the important sustainability and innovation developments that have an impact on contemporary organisations.

Rather than viewing these many challenges as negative and overwhelming, management students should be encouraged to regard them with a positive focus. With the necessary management theories, concepts, tools and examples, students will be able to meet these demands. It is with this goal in mind that *Management: An Asia–Pacific Perspective* has been written.

Building on the best management writing we could find, we have created a text that aims to be engaging, relevant, challenging and useful. By *engaging*, we hope that readers will do more than just 'read' the text, and instead will analyse, critique and reflect on its contents. We have aimed for an easy-to-read style of writing and are delighted with the use of colour and design that encourage students to gain the maximum value from the book. We also hope that students will engage with *Management: An Asia–Pacific Perspective* by applying the concepts covered to their own careers. In particular, the career connection features found in each chapter describe career competencies associated with the topic being discussed, and ask students to consider whether they have the skills demanded of effective 21st-century managers. Each chapter also includes reality checks with a slightly different perspective on the topic.

We have also made the text as *relevant* as possible to the experiences and aspirations of our student cohorts. While the vast majority of management students are relatively young, a growing number of more experienced people are taking university and college studies in management. Variations in age are compounded by differing competencies in communication and general awareness of the organisational world. In responding to this diversity, we have provided a significant number of contemporary examples of management in practice found in Australia, New Zealand, South-East Asia and the United Kingdom. Organisations such as Virgin Blue, Flight Centre, Aussie Home Loans, BHP Billiton, Masport, BridgeClimb and Skyrail ITM feature in chapter examples or case studies; while the management and leadership approaches of prominent managers of the last decade, such as Michael Chaney, Dick Smith, Poppy King, Richard Branson and Gerry Harvey, find a place throughout the text. The key managerial tasks discussed above, including globalisation, entrepreneurship, technology and ethics, are brought to life through practical examples and case studies.

We have provided numerous examples of companies undertaking various Internet activities. Web sites are referred to in the opening case studies in each chapter, as well as in the many themed elements found throughout the text. In the sidebars of each chapter, we have provided brief examples of organisations, from SC Johnson to McDonald's, and suggested further research and investigation at their web sites.

Management: An Asia–Pacific Perspective is a *challenging* text, incorporating critical comments about management practices that should stimulate greater student appreciation of the complexities and paradoxes of contemporary organisational life. In particular, each chapter contains a counterpoint that poses an alternative view on the topic and requires students to think about the relevance and cultural reliability of the theoretical frameworks that bound the topic. The counterpoints are particularly useful for tutorial discussions, class debates or assignment questions. In addition, questions for reflection are attached to other key features, such as reality check and career connection. A number of integrated cases from Australasian and international contexts are also provided so that students learn to develop a multidisciplinary approach to management issues and problems. As management is, to paraphrase Mintzberg, 'a messy task involving multiple pressures and roles', the integrated cases provide students with an opportunity to consider the ways in which concepts, theories and frameworks flowing from a range of chapters might fit together.

We have made *Management: An Asia–Pacific Perspective* as *useful* as possible, recognising that there are usually broader aims associated with foundational management subjects than just imparting key concepts and theoretical frameworks. In our experience, it is also critical that we develop relevant career-linked competencies in our students. The skills required to write effectively, make professional and interesting presentations, undertake effective research and develop abilities in teamwork are among the more important of these competencies. By encouraging their development in our students, we promote the kinds of self-management skills so critical for effective management in all types of organisational contexts. With this in mind, the text includes a Career Readiness Workbook with exercises in teamwork and a managerial skills assessment inventory that can be used in association with many of the chapters to build competencies in these areas. A list of thought-provoking research and presentation projects is also included, providing a number of relevant and interesting assignment topics. Perhaps one of the more useful features is the career advancement portfolio, supplying diagnostic tools, templates and tips for students considering their careers and seeking to develop a better understanding of their career-relevant competencies. Practical advice will assist students to promote their strengths and develop their areas of weakness as they target management jobs in any industry. We hope that many students will be encouraged to take advantage of this feature.

For the reasons discussed above, we believe you will enjoy using *Management: An Asia–Pacific Perspective*. However, like good managers, we are also interested in continual improvement; so please send us any questions, comments or suggestions you have for future editions.

We would like to sincerely thank Janine Spencer-Burford and the John Wiley & Sons publishing team for their outstanding contribution to this book, and the many organisations and people in Australia, New Zealand and overseas who agreed to be interviewed and who supplied information for the numerous and various case studies for this book. We are also grateful to the following reviewers for their insightful comments and suggestions:

   Meredith Jackson, Queensland Department of Employment and Training
   Veronica Powers, Swinburne University of Technology
   Ray Hingst, University of Southern Queensland
   Bill Smith, Eastern Institute of Technology, New Zealand
   Peter Bryar, Netlink (Australia Wide Internet Services)
   Ravi Bhat, UNITEC Institute of Technology, New Zealand
   Leonie Timmerman, Queensland Department of Employment and Training
   Patricia Tuckett, Queensland Department of Employment and Training

John Campling would also like to thank his family — Joyce, Marilyn and Susan — for their support and encouragement with this book and with all his previous academic endeavours, and dedicates this book to his late father, Derek J. Campling.

David Poole would like to thank the love of his life, Wendy, his three great kids — Bethany, Samuel and Chloe — and his mum, Jean, who provided an office and many cups of tea, facilitating much of the writing on this project.

Retha Wiesner thanks Johan and Anchen for their patience and support, and her dear friends Karebo, Belinda, Liza, Nicci, Pat, Marlene and Alet for their encouragement.

John R. Schermerhorn Jr
John Campling
David Poole
Retha Wiesner

May 2003

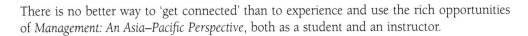

There is no better way to 'get connected' than to experience and use the rich opportunities of *Management: An Asia–Pacific Perspective*, both as a student and an instructor.

For students

An extensive student web site has been developed in support of Management: An Asia–Pacific Perspective both for classroom applications and for distance learning environments. This site is available at www.johnwiley.com.au/highered/management. It includes the following special resources for enrichment of the student learning experience:

- interactive practice tests, e-flashcards and crossword puzzles for every chapter
- interactive online versions of cases for critical thinking
- interactive online information on the companies featured in the chapters
- interactive online versions of all in-chapter career connections
- interactive online versions of management skills assessments, exercises in teamwork, research and presentation projects, and cross-functional integrative cases
- links to organisations and information sites relevant to chapter materials
- full electronic version of the career advancement portfolio.

For instructors

Management: An Asia–Pacific Perspective is supported by a comprehensive resource package that assists the instructor in creating a motivating and enthusiastic learning environment.

- A complete instructor's resource guide, comprising a unique, comprehensive inventory of resources for building a system of customised instruction is available. The guide offers helpful teaching ideas, advice on course development, sample assignments, chapter-by-chapter text highlights, learning objectives, lecture outlines, class exercises, lecture notes, answers to all end-of-chapter material and tips on using cases.
- An updated comprehensive test bank is available, consisting of 2700 multiple-choice, true–false and essay questions categorised by pedagogical element (margin notes, key terms or general text knowledge), page number and type of question (factual or applied).
- A PowerPoint presentation outlines key concepts from each chapter and contains data from the text. Designed as a complete course support in its own right, this presentation can be customised or modified to suit the particular requirements of any instructor or used in its entirety.
- An extensive instructor's web site supports *Management: An Asia–Pacific Perspective* for classroom applications and distance learning settings. This site is available at www.johnwiley.com.au/highered/management. It includes the following special resources to support instructors in their commitments to rich and stimulating student learning environments:
  - complete online instructor's resource guide containing teaching support for the textbook, for all features in the Career Readiness Workbook, and with additional recommendations for course enrichment
  - supplementary in-class exercises and activities, with supporting PowerPoint downloads and presentations
  - PowerPoint downloads for text figures
  - instructor's versions of online cases
  - access to the Author's Classroom.
- The Author's Classroom, a special online resource designed by John Schermerhorn Jr, brings to all instructors the activities, approaches and materials from his classroom. This

unique feature enables instructors to enrich their courses. By going on line with the Author's Classroom, instructors find additional teaching ideas and resources for each chapter, including John's personal PowerPoint presentations, special in-class activities, preferred web sites for browsing during class and more. By using *Management: An Asia–Pacific Perspective* you get more than a textbook, and you get more than your students' access to a complete learning resource with integrated text, Career Readiness Workbook and student web site. You can also join the author's classroom!

- Web CT and Blackboard support for *Management: An Asia–Pacific Perspective* is available for online teaching and learning designs supported by these systems. John Wiley & Sons Australia will provide basic content based on material accompanying the text. Instructors have the option of uploading additional material and customising existing content to fit their needs.

HOW TO USE THIS BOOK

Management: An Asia-Pacific Perspective has been written and designed as an integrative and interactive learning resource. The chapter features have been chosen to enhance the clear learning objectives, integrated textual examples, useful end-of-chapter study guides and extensive online activity and support.

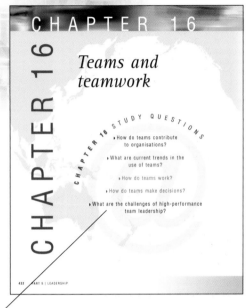

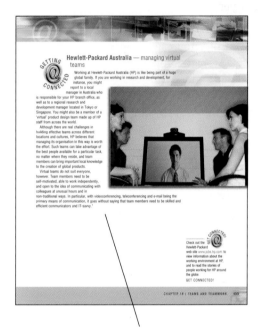

Each chapter opens with two very helpful sections:
study questions that provide students with the learning objectives of the chapter, and a brief **introduction** offering a real-world example that highlights the chapter themes.

Each chapter concludes with an integrated **study guide**. Designed for self-study, it includes a summary of responses to the study questions first posed in the chapter opening section, a list of key terms, applied activities and suggested career readiness activities found in the Career Readiness Workbook and online.

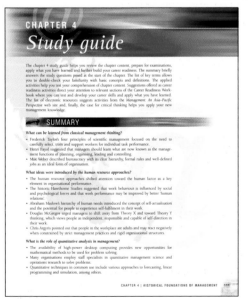

Individual **cases for critical thinking** bring to life the decisions managers must make every day on both a national and global level.

Thematic boxes with photo-illustrated examples of organisations are embedded as part of the general text discussion for each chapter. Additional brief real-world examples are featured as **margin photo** essays in each chapter.

The theme of this book is career development, and the **get connected!** sidebars link text material to online companies and web resources, encouraging students to explore, research and keep up to date with management practices.

Each chapter includes a **career connection** that links text material to realities and developments in the new workplace. These features pose questions that are relevant to your career development and professionalism.

Innovative **reality checks** in each chapter introduce a key fact or survey result relevant to text discussion.

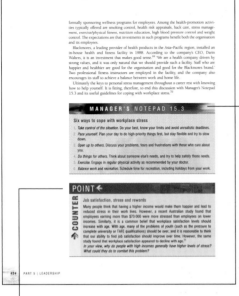

To assist in developing practical applications, **manager's notepads** provide concise lists of helpful hints that describe the dos and don'ts of managerial behaviour.

The **counterpoint** feature stimulates critical thinking and classroom discussion by offering a different point of view or asking students to question the theory presented in the text.

Special **margin notes** call attention to important lists of information as they are presented throughout the text.

Bold **key terms** are called out and defined in the margins. They form a running glossary of key concepts from the chapter discussion.

The innovative **Career Readiness Workbook** provides many ways to take full advantage of the management course and advance your career readiness.

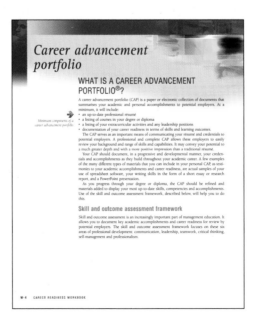

The **career advancement portfolio** provides templates for student portfolios to document academic and personal accomplishments. This resource allows the students to frame and summarise their credentials for external review in the search for employment. It also offers a way for course assignments to be inventoried for academic assessment and competency demonstration.

Research and presentation projects help students gain familiarity with important real-world issues while further building their skills in using the Internet, gathering and interpreting information, and making written and oral presentations.

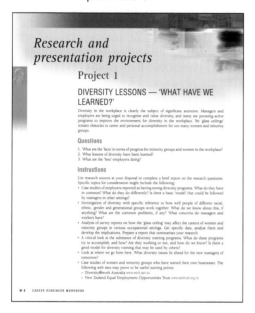

A **cross-functional integrative case** on Sarina Russo reinforces the importance of functional integration, technology use and strategic thinking in management today.

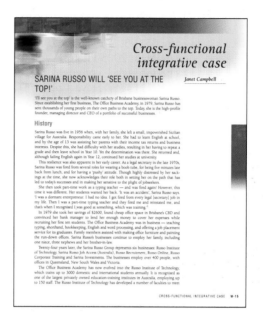

A rich portfolio of **exercises in teamwork** offers opportunities to explore, in a team setting, a variety of issues and topics from chapter and class discussions. Through participation in the exercises, students can gain a better understanding of how text concepts and ideas are put into practice.

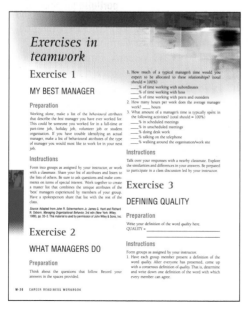

Self-awareness and insight are critical to continued personal and professional development. The workbook provides a diverse set of **management skills assessments** for students to analyse their knowledge of management issues and their possession of the skills necessary to tackle issues.

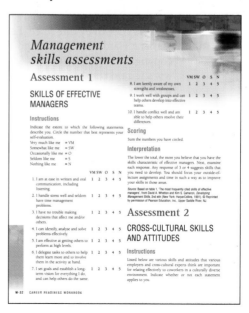

ACKNOWLEDGEMENTS

The authors and publisher would like to thank the following copyright holders, organisations and individuals for their permission to reproduce copyright material in this book.

© SEEK Communications Ltd. www.seek.com.au: p. 3 • Digital Vision: pp. 5 and 153, copyright 2002 Digital Vision • PhotoDisc, Inc.: pp. 6, 71, 99, 136, 188, 267 (left), 317, 417, 467, 494, 502, copyright 1999 PhotoDisc, Inc.; pp. 21, 22, 35, 46, 68, 433, copyright 2002 PhotoDisc, Inc.; pp. 63, 267 (bottom right), 270, 320 (bottom), 478, copyright 1998 PhotoDisc, Inc.; pp. 65, 95, 278 (top), 283, 380, 455, 463, copyright 2000 PhotoDisc, Inc.; pp. 96 and 439, copyright 2003 PhotoDisc, Inc.; p. 228 (margin), copyright 1995 PhotoDisc, Inc.; p. 267 (centre and top right), copyright 1997 PhotoDisc, Inc.; p. 329, © PhotoDisc, Inc.; p. 404, © PhotoDisc/ Getty Images/ Steve Cole • © Australian Business Ethics Network. www.bf.rmit.edu.au/Aben: p. 9 • AAP: p. 31, © AAP Image/ Paul Sakuma; p. 40, © AAP Image/ Geert Vanden Wijngaert; p. 205, © AAP Image/ Dave Hunt; p. 244 (top), © AAP Image/ Silvia Duplain; p. 377, AAP Image/ Lisa Davies; p. 521, © AAP Image/ Damian Dovarganes • EyeWire Images: pp. 37, 104, 148, 278 (bottom), 332, 383, 406, 471, copyright 2002 EyeWire; pp. 168 and 313, copyright 2003 EyeWire • Amacom: p. 51 (figure 2.6), *Beyond Race And Gender* by R. Roosevelt Thomas Jr. Copyright 1991 By Am Mgmt Assn / Amacom (B) in the format. Textbook via Copyright Clearance Center • Corbis Images: p. 57, Australian Picture Library/ Corbis/ Paul A. Souders; pp. 122 and 127, copyright 1999 Corbis Corporation • Newspix: p. 67, © Newspix/ Toru Yamanaka; p. 155, © Newspix/ Paul Burston; p. 186, © Newspix/ John Feder; p. 243 (top), © Newspix/ Frank Violi; p. 243 (middle), © Newspix/ Troy Bendeich; pp. 244 (bottom), 346, 391, 460, © Newspix; p. 291, © Newspix / Craig Greenhill; p. 351, © Newspix/ Andy Baker; p. 429, © Newspix/ Brett Faulkner • Getty Images: p. 88, © Getty Images/ Justin Sullivan; p. 114, © Getty Images/ Junko Kimura; p. 243 (bottom), © Getty Images/ Robert Mora; p. 251, © Getty Images/ Stone/ David Woolley; p. 355, © Getty Images/ Bryan Mitchell; p. 512, © Getty Images/ Sam Sargent • © SPSS Australasia Pty Ltd. www.spss.com.au: p. 106 • Courtesy of NTT DoCoMo: p. 117 • © Reebok. www.reebok.com: p. 131 • © Cadbury Schweppes Pty Ltd: p. 143 • Courtesy of Goldman Environmental Prize: p. 147 • Hubbards Foods Ltd: p. 157, © Hubbards. www.hubbards.co.nz • © Artville/ Getty Images/ Russell Thurston: p. 160 • © Coo-ee Picture Library: p. 173 • © Dyson. www.dyson.com: p. 177 • © Ocean Spirit Cruises. www.oceanspirit.com.au: p. 179 • © Skyrail ITM. www.skyrail.com.au: p. 202 • © Gippsland Aeronautics: p. 207 • Simon & Schuster, Inc.: p. 218 (figure 8.4). Reprinted with the permission of the Free Press, a division of Simon & Schuster Adult Publishing Group, from *Competitive Strategy: Techniques For Analysing Industries And Competitors* by Michael E. Porter. Copyright © 1980, 1998 by the Free Press • Courtesy of Dendy Cinema Pty Ltd: p. 224 (margin) • Mariana Hardwick: p. 226, photograph by Joseph Koprek • Procter & Gamble Pty Ltd: p. 237, copyright © 2003 Procter & Gamble • © IKEA: p. 210 • © Wizard Financial Services. www.wizard.com.au: p. 241 • © Tjapukai Aboriginal Cultural Park. www.tjapukai.com.au: p. 247 • Digital Stock: pp. 248 and 399, copyright 1998 Digital Stock/ Corbis Corporation • © Vitasoy: p. 252 • © Masport Ltd: p. 262 • © LG Electronics. www.lge.com.au: p. 295 • © PricewaterhouseCoopers: p. 297 • © Shopfast. www.shopfast.com.au: p. 307 • © McDonalds. www.mcdonalds.com.au: p. 320 (top margin) • © George Holman. www.ezypay.com.au: p. 361 • Image Addict: p. 374, copyright 2002 www.imageaddict.com.au • © BridgeClimb. www.bridgeclimb.com: p. 403 • Pearson Education US: p. 413 (figure 15.4), *Work Redesign*, by Hackman and Oldham. © Reprinted by permission of Pearson Education, Inc., Upper Saddle River, NJ • © Geyer Pty Ltd. www.geyer.com.au: p. 468 • APL: p. 489, Australian Picture Library/ Corbis/ Jose Fuste Raga • © Fisher & Paykel: p. 493 • © Ballard Power Systems: p. 495 • © Rivers. www.rivers.com.au: p. 508.

MANAGEMENT
TODAY

PART 1

CHAPTER 1

The dynamic new workplace

CHAPTER 1 STUDY QUESTIONS

▸ What are the challenges of working in the new economy?

▸ What are organisations like in the new workplace?

▸ Who are managers and what do they do?

▸ What is the management process?

▸ How do you learn the essential managerial skills and competencies?

SEEK — create your own future

SEEK is one of the most popular online destinations for job seekers in Australia and New Zealand. More than 600 000 job seekers check in each month to view what jobs are on offer locally and around the world and to use SEEK's career resources. More than 30 000 new jobs are listed each month. Job candidates and employers can connect easier and faster by using online job services like SEEK www.seek.com.au, Monster www.monster.com.au and others.

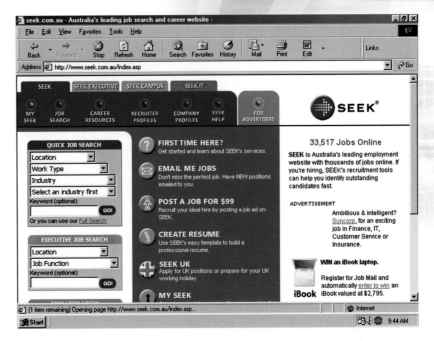

SEEK offers a range of services, including Job Mail, which e-mails suitable job opportunities to job seekers; My Résumé, where job seekers can use an easy résumé building tool; and the Application Tracker, which logs the details of online job applications. SEEK designed its site with distinct zones, reflecting the diversity of its users. Most jobs appear in the SEEK zone, but executive, graduate and IT positions appear in their own zones. SEEK Executive includes senior and managerial positions for people who have substantial experience. SEEK Campus lists jobs and job information for university students and recent graduates. SEEK IT has IT jobs and resources for IT workers.

Potentially, students could use SEEK for many of their career development needs. For example, they could build their résumés and apply for their first job online, research what employers are looking for from graduates, find a professional position in the SEEK Campus zone once they graduate, and then find new positions to help their career advance throughout life in the SEEK Executive zone.

Since its inception in 1997, SEEK has been recognised as one of Australia's fastest growing businesses and one of the most successful start-up companies in the country.[1]

The 21st century has brought with it a new workplace, one in which everyone must adapt to a rapidly changing society with constantly shifting demands and opportunities. Learning and speed are *in*; habit and complacency are *out*. Organisations are fast changing, as is the nature of work itself. The economy is global, driven by innovation and technology. Even the concept of success, personal and organisational, is evolving as careers take new forms and organisations transform to serve new customer expectations. Such developments affect us all, offering both 'unparalleled opportunity and unprecedented uncertainty'. In this age of continuous challenge, a compelling message must be heard by all of us — smart people and smart organisations create their own futures![2]

Speaking about the future, what do companies like Flight Centre, Macquarie Bank, Deloitte Touche Tohmatsu, Lion Nathan and Star City have in common? They represent very different industries, but together they are ranked as the top five employers to work for in Australia (with over 1000 staff).[3] They are all companies with futures.

In the quest for the future the best employers share an important commitment to people. Amidst high performance expectations, they offer supportive work environments that allow people's talents to be fully utilised while providing them with both valued rewards and respect for work-life balance. At the best of the best, for example, employees benefit from flexible work schedules, onsite child care, onsite health and fitness centres, domestic partner benefits, as well as opportunities for profit sharing, cash bonuses and competitive salaries. In short, the best employers are not just extremely good at attracting and retaining talented employees. They also excel at supporting them in a high-performance context so that their talents are fully utilised and their contributions highly valued.

Visit www. bestemployersaustralia.com and learn about the latest companies to win the much sought after 'best employer in Australia' award.
GET CONNECTED!

After studying high-performing companies like those just mentioned, management scholars Charles O'Reilly and Jeffrey Pfeffer conclude that success is achieved because they are better than their competitors at getting extraordinary results from the people working for them. 'These companies have won the war for talent', they say, 'not just by being great places to work — although they are that — but by figuring out how to get the best out of all of their people, every day.'[4] This, in large part, is what *Management: An Asia–Pacific Perspective* and your management course are all about. Both are designed to introduce you to the concepts, themes and directions that are consistent with career success and organisational leadership in today's high-performance work settings. As you begin, consider further the challenge posed by the title of O'Reilly and Pfeffer's book: *Hidden Value: How Great Companies Achieve Extraordinary Results with Ordinary People*. Let your study of management be devoted to learning as much as you can to prepare for a career-long commitment to getting great things accomplished through working with people.

WORKING IN THE NEW ECONOMY

Yes, we now live and work in a new economy ripe with challenging opportunities and dramatic uncertainty.[5] The new economy is a networked economy in which people, institutions and nations are increasingly influenced by the Internet and continuing developments in information technology.[6] The chapter opener on SEEK is but one example of how the Web and its vast networking capabilities are changing our lives. The new economy is a global economy, whose scope increases daily. The nations of the world and their economies are increasingly interdependent, and with this globalisation comes great challenges as well as opportunities. The new economy is knowledge driven. We must all accept that success must be forged in workplaces reinvented to unlock the great potential of human intelligence. The high-performance themes of the day are 'respect', 'participation', 'empowerment', 'involvement', 'teamwork', 'self-management' and more.

Undoubtedly, too, the new economy is performance driven. Expectations of organisations and their members are very high. Success must be earned in a society that demands nothing less than the best from all its institutions. Organisations are expected to continuously excel on performance criteria that include concerns for innovativeness, employee development and social responsibility, as well as more traditional measures of profitability and investment value. When they fail, customers, investors and employees are quick to let them know. For individuals, there are no guarantees of long-term employment. Jobs are increasingly earned and re-earned every day through one's performance accomplishments. Careers are being redefined in terms of 'flexibility', 'free agency', 'skill portfolios' and 'entrepreneurship'. Today, it takes initiative and discipline and continuous learning to stay in charge of your own career destiny. Tomorrow's challenges are likely to be even greater.

Just what are the challenges ahead?

www.volunteer.com.au

Not all work is 'for-pay work'. In today's complex society not-for-profit organisations fulfil important roles, and they depend on volunteers to make it all possible. SEEK Volunteer helps match volunteers across Australia with not-for-profit organisations needing their services.

Intellectual capital

The dynamic pathways into the future are evident among new benchmarks being set in and by progressive organisations everywhere. Many will be introduced throughout *Management: An Asia–Pacific Perspective* and on its special student web site. You should follow developments at companies like General Electric, for example, where former CEO Jack Welch has been viewed by some as one of the great corporate leaders of our time. In a highly competitive, fast-paced and high-technology business environment, he claims that the essential dimension of organisational success rests with the talents of people. 'We have to get everybody in the organisation involved', Welch says about GE. 'If you do that right, the best ideas rise to the top.'[7]

Welch is not alone in his views on executive leadership. Paul Simons, former chairman of Woolworths Limited, rates the training and development of any company's people as a 'ten'. He sees ongoing personal development as essential in keeping an industry competitive, and he views the promotion of leading-edge skills and knowledge in people to the extent where they become leaders in their fields as critical.[8]

At Lion Nathan Australia, Australasia's biggest beverages business, a growth-oriented ethos is expressed as 'we all grow, financially and professionally'. The underlying aim is to create a work environment in which people really want to perform.[9]

The point of these examples is clear. People — what they know, what they learn and what they do with it — are the ultimate foundations of organisational performance. They represent an **intellectual capital** defined as the collective brain power or shared knowledge of a workforce that can be used to create value.[10] Indeed, the ultimate elegance of the new workplace may well be its ability to combine the talents of many people, sometimes thousands of them, to achieve unique and significant results.

This is the new age of the **knowledge worker** — someone whose mind is a critical asset to employers and who adds to the intellectual capital of the organisation.[11] If you want a successful career in the new economy you must be willing to reach for the heights of personal competency and accomplishment. You must be a self-starter willing to continuously learn from experience, even in an environment that grows daily more complex and challenging.

Intellectual capital is the collective brain power or shared knowledge of a workforce.

A **knowledge worker** is someone whose knowledge is a critical asset to employers.

Globalisation

Japanese management consultant Kenichi Ohmae suggests that the national boundaries of world business have largely disappeared.[12] At the very least we can say that they are fast disappearing. Who can state with confidence where their favourite athletic shoes or the parts for their personal computer were manufactured? More and more products are designed in one country, while their component parts are made in others and the assembly of the final product takes place in still another. Top managers at Ford, IBM, Sony and other global corporations, for example, have no real need for the word 'overseas' in everyday business vocabulary. They operate as global businesses that view themselves as equidistant from customers and suppliers, wherever in the world they may be located.

Globalisation is the worldwide interdependence of resource flows, product markets and business competition.

This is part of the force of **globalisation**, the worldwide interdependence of resource flows, product markets and business competition that characterises our new economy.[13] In a globalised world, countries and peoples are increasingly interconnected through the news, in travel and lifestyles, in labour markets and employment patterns, and in business dealings. Government leaders now worry about the competitiveness of nations just as corporate leaders worry about business competitiveness.[14] The world is increasingly arranged in regional economic blocs, with North and Latin America, Europe and the Asia–Pacific Region (inluding Australia and New Zealand) as key anchors, and with Africa fast emerging to claim its economic potential. Like any informed citizen, you too must understand the forces of globalisation and be prepared to participate in them.

HIGH PERFORMANCE

BRL Hardy • www.brlhardy.com.au

A responsible, global business

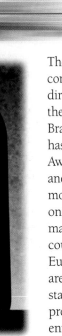

The BRL Hardy wine group, 2001 Australian Exporter of the Year, is confident in its strategy to enter the key US market. Managing director Stephen Millar has forecast 'superb' times ahead, following the establishment of a US business in partnership with Constellation Brands, the large wine and liquor group in the USA. The company has also been awarded the 2002 Ramsar Wetland Conservation Award. Ramsar is the world's peak wetland conservation organisation and this is the first ever award to an Australian company for promoting the conservation and wise use of wetlands. Hardy counts as one of its major strengths its large and professional sales and marketing teams in Australia and overseas. It exports to over 60 countries including the major markets of the United Kingdom, Europe, Canada, the USA and New Zealand. Achievements like these are only possible through its commitment to its mission of understanding and satisfying customer needs, by encouraging creative production and marketing skills, and through providing a stimulating environment in which to work and grow.[15]

Technology

The global economy isn't the only beneficiary of developments with new technology. Who hasn't been affected by the Internet and the World Wide Web? It's part of the theme of *Management: An Asia–Pacific Perspective* — 'Getting Connected' — and the Internet support for the book greatly enriches your learning opportunities. Just join in and get connected . . . the paths are endless, ever changing and exciting to explore. If you aren't willing to become a participant in the still-exploding world of the information superhighway, you'll be left behind. It's not an option anymore — it's an entry requirement in the new workplace.

'With computers and high technology,' someone once said, 'work will never be the same.' It has already changed and you had better be ready. For better or worse, we now live in a technology-driven world increasingly dominated by bar codes, automatic tellers, computerised telemarketing campaigns, electronic mail, Internet resources, electronic commerce and more. Computers and information technology help organisations of all types and sizes, locally and internationally, to speed transactions and improve decision making.[16] From the small retail store to the large multinational firm, technology is an indispensable part of everyday operations — whether one is checking inventory, making a sales transaction, ordering supplies or analysing customer preferences.

These lessons of 'e-business' are also being transferred to 'e-government', as local and national governments rush to take advantage of the Internet revolution. And when it comes to communication, within the many parts of an organisation or between the organisation and its suppliers, customers and external constituents, geographical distances hardly matter anymore. Computer networking can bring together almost anyone from anywhere in the world at the mere touch of a keyboard. In 'virtual space' people in remote locations can hold meetings, access common databases, share information and files, make plans and solve problems together — all without ever meeting face to face.

As the pace and complexities of technological change accelerate, the demand for knowledge workers with the skills to use technology to full advantage is increasing. The shift to an information-based economy is dramatically changing employment. The fastest growing occupations are computer related. Skilled help is in demand — low-skill workers displaced from declining industries find it difficult to find new jobs offering adequate pay. In a world where technological change is occurring at an accelerating rate, computer literacy must be mastered and continuously developed as a foundation for career success. For example, 9.2 million adults, or 66 per cent of all adults in Australia, used a computer during 2001. Some 42 per cent used a computer at work and this percentage is increasing every day. In New Zealand, 47 per cent of households had a home computer, and 37 per cent had access to the Internet in 2001. Eighty-eight per cent of New Zealand businesses regularly used a computer, and 36 per cent operated a web site.[17]

CAREER CONNECTION

Technology

Centrelink

A model for web services?
www.centrelink.gov.au

By moving many government services on line, the stereotypes of long lines and poor service are being tested. Centrelink's web service is one example. Centrelink delivers services, programs and payments for Australian government departments. During the Ansett Airlines collapse, thousands of employees lost their jobs. Centrelink immediately set up a site to assist former Ansett employees and contractors. This ranged from service requests, which could be processed on the Web, to access to Job Network services, which are provided nationally by a network of organisations dedicated to helping job seekers find and keep a job. This indicates a change in the relationship between the government's services and its constituents.

Another example of how Centrelink is branching out to a system of client self-service using online facilities was the range of assistance it offered to the victims and families directly affected by the Bali bomb disaster in 2002. Centrelink provided hotline services which were open seven days, 24 hours a day, for people within Australia and from Indonesia inquiring about possible services and payments. This changing relationship between the government and its customers/clients could bring with it the next online and Internet revolution — e-government.

Questions

How will the Internet alter the relationship between the government and its constituents?

What changes in e-government could be expected in the next five years?

Is there a career for you in the government service?

How might online services affect client service jobs?

Diversity

Labour-force projections indicate that in 2011 the Australian workforce will consist of a large proportion of employees aged over 45 years. The Australian Bureau of Statistics predicts that major gains will occur in the 45–54 year age group with a projected increase of 36 per cent for men and 75 per cent for women; growth rates for 55–64 year olds will result in a 79 per cent increase, with that group becoming 10.8 per cent of the workforce in 2011. Consequently, as increasing numbers of the workforce belong to these older age groups it could be expected that the primary dimension of age could become an important basis for the development of diversity management initiatives. Statistics New Zealand's projections indicate that half the labour force will be older than 42 years by 2051, compared with the median age of 37 years in 1996. It is estimated that the 45–64 year olds will make up 40 per cent of the labour force in 2051.[18]

 **Workforce diversity** describes differences among workers in gender, race, age, ethnic culture, able-bodiedness, religious affiliation and sexual orientation.

The term **workforce diversity**, discussed further in chapter 2, is used to describe the composition of a workforce in terms of differences among the members.[19] These differences include gender, age, race, ethnicity, religion, sexual orientation and able-bodiedness. In Australasia the legal context of human resource management, described in chapter 12, is very strict in prohibiting the use of demographic characteristics for staffing decisions such as hiring and promotion. However, discrimination against older employees is rife. Australasian organisations have been reluctant to hire older staff in spite of evidence to indicate beliefs in their lessened capacity are false. Likewise, other forms of discrimination persist despite laws designed to prevent it.

The issues of managing workforce diversity, however, extend beyond legal considerations alone. Today's increasingly diverse and multicultural workforce offers great opportunities with respect to potential performance gains.[20] By 'valuing diversity' organisations can tap a rich talent pool and help everyone work to their full potential. But what does this really mean? It should mean 'enabling every member of your workforce to perform to his or her potential'. A female vice-president at Avon once posed the challenge of managing diversity this way: 'consciously creating an environment where everyone has an equal shot at contributing, participating, and most of all advancing'.[21]

Although easy to say, meeting societal responsibilities to truly value diversity has proven harder to accomplish. Even though progress in equal opportunity continues to be made, lingering inequalities remain in the workplace. However, not only will the composition of the workforce change in the future, but the nature of the relationships people have with organisations will also continue to change. The 1990s were characterised by an upward trend in all kinds of non-standard forms of employment which undermine people's job security. There has been increasing use of casual work, temporary work, outsourcing and the use of agencies and other labour-market intermediaries. Given the continuing need for organisations to respond quickly in the marketplace, we could expect these forms of flexible employment to increase; but differences in approaches to pay, conditions of employment and opportunities for development are ready examples of the inequality this can involve.[22]

Diversity bias can still be a limiting factor in too many work settings. Managing a diverse workforce needs to take into account the different needs of members of different identity groups. This latter point is illustrated very clearly by Fiona Krautil, who makes reference to wild animals in the zoo. She says:

> Imagine your organisation is a giraffe house. Equal opportunity has been very effective widening the door of the giraffe house to let the elephant in, but home won't be best for the elephant unless a number of major modifications are made to the inside of the house. Without these changes the house will remain designed for giraffes and the elephant will not 'feel at home'.[23]

REALITY CHECK

Barriers to employment of older workers

According to the National Seniors Association there are many mature-age workers who want to stay in work, but employers will not hire them. The truth behind Australasia's trend toward early retirement is that workers over 50 are the first to be retrenched and last to be rehired.

Why do you think employers might be reluctant to hire older workers?

Prejudice, or the holding of negative, irrational opinions and attitudes regarding members of diverse populations, sets the stage for diversity bias in the workplace. This bias can take the form of **discrimination** that actively disadvantages them by treating them unfairly and denying them the full benefits of organisational membership. It can also take the form of what some call the **glass ceiling effect** — the existence of an invisible barrier or 'ceiling' that prevents women and minority groups from rising above a certain level of organisational responsibility.[24] Scholar Judith Rosener suggests that the organisation's loss is 'undervalued and underutilised human capital'.[25]

Ethics

When a well-known business executive goes to jail for some misdeed, we notice. When a major environmental catastrophe occurs because of a business misdeed, we notice. Increasingly, too, we notice the 'moral' aspects of the everyday behaviour by organisations, their executives and employees.[26] Society is becoming strict in its expectation that social institutions conduct their affairs according to high moral standards. A global recession, coupled with a spate of corporate collapses in Australia, has put the spotlight on the quality and moral standards of Australian boards and managers. It is not a pretty picture. The collapses of Ansett Australia, HIH Insurance, Harris Scarfe and One.Tel had one thing in common — bad management. In the case of One.Tel, rumours of falsified accounts and misleading statements to shareholders and directors were investigated by the corporate regulator, the Australian Securities and Investments Commission. Evidence was mounted that the poor shape of the company was known long before the administrators were called in, and some creditors had noticed a slowdown in payments during the final quarter of 2000. The collapse of One.Tel has destroyed fortunes, reputations, companies and consumer faith in competition in the telecommunications industry — and left 1600 One.Tel staff unemployed.[27]

The pressure for ethical and socially responsible conduct is on, and justifiably so. Organisations and their managers are responding. They have to. Organisations won't be able to keep customers if they don't treat them right and act in ways that are consistent with society's values. The expectations characteristic of this new century include sustainable development and protection of the natural environment, protection of consumers through product safety and fair practices, and the protection of human rights in all aspects of society, including employment.[28] Workplace concerns include equal employment opportunity, equity of compensation and benefits, participation and employee involvement, privacy and due process, job security, occupational health and safety, and freedom from sexual harassment. Employees are demanding more self-determination on the job — they want to be part of everyday decisions on how and when to do their jobs, and they expect real opportunities to participate in job-related decisions. Job security is a concern at a time when many organisations are cutting back their full-time workers and hiring more part-time or 'contingency' workers.

Ethical and social responsibility issues involve all aspects of organisations, the behaviour of their members and their impact on society. You must be ready to understand the ethical context of working in the new economy and you must be prepared to perform in ways that fulfil your ethical commitments as well as those of your employer. Consider, for example, the ethical framework set by this statement from the credo of Johnson & Johnson:

> We are responsible to the communities in which we live and work and to the world community as well. We must be good citizens — support good works and charities and bear our fair share of taxes. We must encourage civic improvements and better health and education. We must maintain in good order the property we are privileged to use, protecting the environment and natural resources.[29]

⚙ Prejudice is the display of negative, irrational attitudes toward women or minority groups.

⚙ Discrimination occurs when someone is denied a job or a job assignment for reasons not job relevant.

⚙ The **glass ceiling effect** is an invisible barrier limiting the advancement of women and minority groups.

www.bf.rmit.edu.au/ Aben/

The Australian Business Ethics Network was established to promote ethical practices in business, advocate the need for ethics as part of business courses and to provide a forum for ethicists to discuss and exchange ideas on teaching, training and consulting in the field of business ethics.

Careers

The nature of work has changed in the new economy, and the challenges of change make personal initiative and self-renewal hallmarks of the day. The career implications of the new employment patterns characteristic of this dynamic environment are extremely significant. British scholar Charles Handy suggests the analogy of the Irish shamrock to describe and understand them.[30]

Picture an organisation as a shamrock with three leaves. Each leaf has a different career implication. In one leaf are the core workers. These full-time employees pursue traditional career paths. With success and the maintenance of critical skills, core employees can advance within the organisation and may remain employed for a long time. In the second leaf of the shamrock organisation are contract workers. They perform specific tasks as needed by the organisation and are compensated on a contract or fee-for-services basis rather than by a continuing wage or salary. Contract workers sell a skill or service to employers — they will likely service many different employers over time. In the third leaf are the casual and part-time workers who are hired only as needed and for only the number of hours needed. Employers expand and reduce their casual staffs as business needs rise and fall. Casual and part-time work can be a training ground for full-time work in the first leaf, when openings are available.

You must be prepared to prosper in any of the shamrock's three leaves. The typical career of the 21st century won't be uniformly full-time and limited to a single large employer. It is more likely to unfold opportunistically and involve several employment options over time. 'Free agency' is a term increasingly used to describe career management in the new workplace.[31] What it means is that not only must you be prepared to change jobs and employers over time, but your skills must be portable and of current value in the employment markets. Skills aren't gained once and then forgotten — they must be carefully maintained and upgraded all the time. One career consultant suggests that you approach this career scenario with the analogy of a surfer: 'You're always moving. You can expect to fall into the water any number of times, and you have to get back up to catch the next wave.'[32]

Handy's advice is that you maintain a 'portfolio of skills' that are always up to date and valuable to potential employers. The end-of-text Career Readiness Workbook includes templates for you to build a personal Career Advancement Portfolio® that directly responds to Handy's challenge. By following the instructions provided, you can build either a paper or electronic portfolio that includes a professional résumé and work samples that demonstrate your critical managerial skills and competencies. A well-constructed student portfolio can be an important source of advantage in competitive markets as you search for apprenticeships and jobs. Consider what a career advancement portfolio can do for you!

ORGANISATIONS IN THE NEW WORKPLACE

The new world of work is a 'wired' world, one tied to the connectivity made possible by information technology. Management consultant Tom Peters described work in new organisations this way:

> In the next few years, whether at a tiny company or behemoth, we will be working with an eclectic mix of contract teammates from around the globe, many of whom we'll never meet face-to-face. Every project will call for a new team, composed of specially tailored skills ... Every player on this team will be evaluated ... for the quality and uniqueness and timeliness and passion of her or his contribution.[33]

Take a look ahead. Visit www.gradlink.edu.au to learn more about Gradlink, the one-stop shop for graduate careers information.
GET CONNECTED!

Portfolio careers, in which you carry and develop a portfolio of skills and a portfolio of current projects, will be the reality of the future. Check out www.attain-ed.com/career_center/tableofcontents.html and see what Attain recommends as the steps to achieving career and life planning success.
GET CONNECTED!

Organisations in the new workplace are challenging settings, but exciting for their great opportunities and possibilities. Peters calls it a 'wired, wild new age of work'. Whether these organisations are large or small, business or not-for-profit, each should make real and positive contributions to society. We each have a stake in making sure that they perform up to expectations. For individuals, organisations are also the principal source of careers and one's economic livelihood. In his article 'The company of the future', Harvard Professor Robert Reich says: 'Everybody works for somebody or something — be it a board of directors, a pension fund, a venture capitalist or a traditional boss. Sooner or later you're going to have to decide who you want to work for.'[34]

In order to make good employment choices and perform well in a career, you must have a fundamental understanding of the nature of organisations in the new workplace. Manager's Notepad 1.1 provides a first look at some of the critical survival skills that you should acquire to work well in the organisations of today . . . and tomorrow.[35]

MANAGER'S NOTEPAD 1.1

Critical survival skills for the new workplace

- *Mastery.* You need to be good at something; you need to be able to contribute something of value to your employer.
- *Contacts.* You need to know people; links with peers and others within and outside the organisation are essential to get things done.
- *Entrepreneurship.* You must act as if you are running your own business, spotting ideas and opportunities, and stepping out to embrace them.
- *Love of technology.* You have to embrace technology; you don't have to be a technician, but you must be willing and able to fully utilise IT.
- *Marketing.* You need to be able to communicate your successes and progress, both yours personally and those of your work group.
- *Passion for renewal.* You need to be continuously learning and changing and updating yourself to best meet future demands.

What is an organisation?

Formally stated, an **organisation** is a collection of people working together to achieve a *common purpose*.[36] It is a unique social phenomenon that enables its members to perform tasks far beyond the reach of individual accomplishment. This description applies to organisations of all sizes and types, from businesses such as Harvey Norman and eBay, to not-for-profit organisations such as a government agency or community hospital. From society's perspective they all share a broad purpose — providing useful goods or services. Each in its own way should return value to society and satisfy customers' needs in order to justify continued existence.

Having a clear sense of purpose that is tied to 'quality products' and 'customer satisfaction' is increasingly viewed as a source of organisational strength and performance advantage. Belief in a strong and compelling organisational purpose is one of the reasons given by employees who remain very loyal to their employers. In the words of Don Argus, managing director of the National Australia Bank: 'At the end of the day, integrity is the big one. If people trust you, then you can get where you want to. But if people don't, you have no chance.'[37]

An **organisation** is a collection of people working together in a division of labour to achieve a common purpose.

Organisations as systems

Organisations are systems composed of interrelated parts that function together to achieve a common purpose.[38] It is helpful to view them as **open systems** that interact with their environments in the continual process of transforming resource inputs into product outputs in the form of finished goods and/or services. As shown in figure 1.1, the external environment is a critical element in the open-systems view of organisations. It is both a supplier of resources and the source of customers, and it has a significant impact on operations and outcomes. Both the boundaries of any organisation — the supply side and the customer side — and its internal operations must be well managed for performance success.

Open systems transform resource inputs from the environment into product outputs.

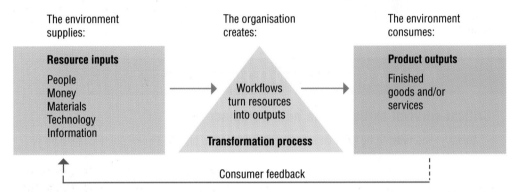

Figure 1.1 ▸ Organisations as open systems

In the open-systems view of organisations, the customer truly reigns supreme. Feedback from the environment tells an organisation how well it is doing. Without customer willingness to use the organisation's products, it is difficult to operate or stay in business over the long run. The ultimate test for any organisation rests with the marketplace — once someone uses a product, the question becomes: Will they do so again … and will they recommend that others do the same?

Organisational performance

Resources and customers are two critical elements in the open-systems view of organisations. For an organisation to perform well, resources must be well utilised and customers well served. The notion of *value creation* is very important in this context. If operations add value to the original cost of resource inputs, then a business organisation can earn a profit — that is, sell a product for more than the cost of making it (e.g. fast-food restaurant meals); or a not-for-profit organisation can add wealth to society — that is, provide a public service that is worth more than its cost (e.g. fire prevention services in a community). Value is created when an organisation's resources are used in the right way and at the right time and at minimum cost to create high-quality goods and services for customers.

The best organisations use a variety of performance measures. On the customer side, high-performing organisations measure customer satisfaction and loyalty, as well as market share. On the employee side, they measure retention, career development, job satisfaction and related issues.[39] One of the most common indicators of overall organisational performance is **productivity**, a summary measure of the quantity and quality of work performance with resource utilisation taken into account. Productivity can be measured at the individual and group as well as organisational levels.

Productivity is the quantity and quality of work performance, with resource utilisation considered.

Figure 1.2 links productivity with two terms commonly used in management — effectiveness and efficiency. **Performance effectiveness** is a measure of task output or goal accomplishment. If you are working in the manufacturing area of a computer firm, for example, performance effectiveness may mean that you meet a daily production target in terms of the quantity and quality of keyboards assembled. By so doing, you allow the company as a whole to maintain its production schedule and meet customer demands for timely delivery and high-quality products.

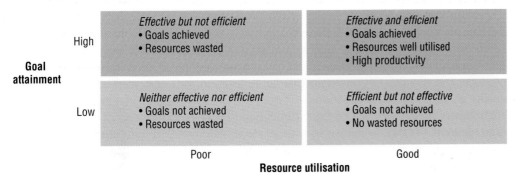

Figure 1.2 ▸ Productivity and the dimensions of organisational performance

Performance efficiency is a measure of the resource cost associated with goal accomplishment. Cost of labour is a common efficiency measure. Others include equipment utilisation, facilities maintenance and returns on capital investment. Returning to the example of computer assembly, the most efficient production is that accomplished at a minimum cost in materials and labour. If you were producing fewer computer keyboards in a day than you were capable of, this would contribute to inefficiency in organisational performance; likewise, if you made a lot of mistakes or wasted materials in the assembly process this is also inefficient work that raises costs for the organisation.

Changing nature of organisations

Change will be a continuing theme of this book, and organisations are certainly undergoing dramatic changes today. Among the many forces and trends in the new workplace, the following organisational transitions set an important context for the study of management:[40]

- *Pre-eminence of technology.* New opportunities appear with each new development in computer and information technology; they continually change the way organisations operate and how people work.
- *Demise of 'command-and-control'.* Traditional hierarchical structures with 'do as I say' bosses are proving too slow, conservative and costly to do well in today's competitive environments.
- *Focus on speed.* Everything moves fast today; in business those who get products to market first have an advantage, and in any organisation work is expected to be both well done and timely.
- *Embrace of networking.* Organisations are networked for intense real-time communication and coordination, internally among parts and externally with partners, contractors, suppliers and customers.
- *Belief in empowerment.* Demands of the new economy place premiums on high-involvement and participatory work settings that rally the knowledge, experience and commitment of all members.

⚙ **Performance effectiveness** is an output measure of task or goal accomplishment.

⚙ **Performance efficiency** is a measure of resource cost associated with goal accomplishment.

How organisations are changing

- *Emphasis on teamwork.* Today's organisations are less vertical and more horizontal in focus; they are increasingly driven by teamwork that pools talents for creative problem solving.
- *New workforce expectations.* A new generation of workers brings to the workplace less tolerance for hierarchy, more informality and more attention to performance merit than to status and seniority.
- *Concern for work-life balance.* As society increases in complexity, workers are forcing organisations to pay more attention to balance in the often-conflicting demands of work and personal affairs.

There are many forces driving these changes in organisations. Along with the pressures of competition, globalisation and emerging technologies, there also has been a revolution of sorts among modern-day consumers. They are unrelenting in their demand for quality products and services. Organisations that fail to listen to their customers and fail to deliver quality goods and services at reasonable prices will be left struggling in a highly competitive environment. References will be made throughout this book to the concept of **total quality management (TQM)** — managing with an organisation-wide commitment to continuous improvement and meeting customer needs completely.[41] For the moment, the quality commitment can be recognised as a hallmark of enlightened productivity management in any organisation.

> **Total quality management (TQM)** is managing with commitment to continuous improvement, product quality and customer satisfaction.

COUNTERPOINT

The more things change, the more they stay the same

The cynics will argue: 'The more things change, the more they stay the same' and 'Management has stuffed it up again'. The polarisation of cultural perspectives between those at the coalface and those managing the changes is often enforced by uncontrollable external factors. Very often, as an organisation allocates more of its resources into managing the organisation, it is removing them from the front end. Work units are left feeling disenfranchised and neglected. Managers finding themselves in difficult positions rationalise decisions, develop slogans and shroud themselves behind management speak. Inevitably this creates division, conflict, inertia and chaos. This happens, for example, when employees are not consulted regarding decisions affecting them directly.

MANAGERS IN THE NEW WORKPLACE

In an article entitled 'Putting people first for organisational success', Jeffrey Pfeffer and John F. Veiga argue forcefully that organisations perform better when they treat their members better. However, they also point out that too many organisations fail to operate in this manner and, as a consequence, suffer performance failures. Pfeffer uses the term 'toxic workplaces' to describe organisations that treat their employees mainly as costs to be reduced. True high-performing organisations, he points out, treat people as valuable strategic assets that should be carefully nurtured.[42] The themes and concepts set forth in *Management: An Asia–Pacific Perspective* support this view that high-performing organisations operate with a commitment to people as their most important assets. Importantly, in the day-to-day flow of events in any workplace, those who serve in managerial roles have a special responsibility for ensuring that this commitment is fulfilled.

What is a manager?

You find them in all organisations. They work with a wide variety of job titles, such as team leader, department head, project manager, unit supervisor, senior executive, administrator and more. They also always work directly with other persons who are dependent on them for critical support and assistance in their own jobs. We call them **managers**, persons in organisations who directly support and help activate the work efforts and performance accomplishments of others.

For those serving as managers, the responsibility is challenging and substantial. Any manager is responsible not just for his or her own work, but for the overall performance accomplishments of a team, work group, department, or even the organisation as a whole. Whether they are called direct reports, team members, work associates, subordinates or something else, these are the essential human resources whose tasks represent the real work of the organisation. Those persons working with and reporting to managers are, in short, the critical human capital upon whose intellects and efforts the performance of any organisation is ultimately built. How well the manager performs in supporting them makes a critical difference in their performance and that of the organisation.

Every manager's job thus entails a key responsibility — to help other people achieve high performance. As pointed out by management theorist Henry Mintzberg, being a manager in this sense is a most important and socially responsible job:

> No job is more vital to our society than that of the manager. It is the manager who determines whether our social institutions serve us well or whether they squander our talents and resources. It is time to strip away the folklore about managerial work, and time to study it realistically so that we can begin the difficult task of making significant improvement in its performance.[43]

Managers are responsible for and support the work of others.

Levels and types of managers

The nature of managerial work is evolving as organisations change and develop with time. A *Wall Street Journal* report describes the transition as follows: 'Not so long ago they may have supervised ten people sitting outside their offices. Today they must win the support of scores more — employees of different backgrounds, job titles and even cultures'. The report goes on to say that 'these new managers are expected to be skilled at organising complex subjects, solving problems, communicating ideas and making swift decisions'.[44]

LEVELS OF MANAGERS

At the highest levels of organisations, common job titles are chief executive officer, chief operating officer, managing director and director. These **top managers** are responsible for the performance of an organisation as a whole or for one of its larger parts. They pay special attention to the external environment, are alert to potential long-run problems and opportunities, and develop appropriate ways of dealing with them. The best top managers are future-oriented strategic thinkers who make many decisions under highly competitive and uncertain conditions. Top managers scan the environment, create and communicate long-term vision, and ensure that strategies and performance objectives are consistent with the organisation's purpose and mission. Managing Director of TNT Logistics Asia, Meredith Hellicar, maintains that without vision, leadership is only half realised. She asserts that there is no one else than the top manager who can really impart it, and although she thinks it should be developed in a cooperative manner, the leader needs to be the one who's imparting it and being seen to be living and doing it.[45]

Top managers guide the performance of the organisation as a whole or of one of its major parts.

Middle managers oversee the work of large departments or divisions.

Middle managers are in charge of relatively large departments or divisions consisting of several smaller work units. Examples are clinic directors in hospitals; deans in universities; and division managers, plant managers and branch sales managers in businesses. Middle managers work with top managers and coordinate with peers to develop and implement action plans consistent with organisational objectives. They should be team oriented and able to work well with people from all parts of an organisation to get work accomplished. An important example is the job of **project managers**, people who coordinate complex projects with task deadlines while working with many persons of different expertise both within and outside the organisation. At General Electric, for example, corporate trouble-shooters or 'black belts' have been organised to manage groups that solve problems and create change across divisions and geographic boundaries within the company. One of them, Wendell Barr, recruited a cross-functional team from marketing, human resources and field operations staff to design a new compensation system.[46]

Project managers coordinate complex projects with task deadlines and people with many areas of expertise.

Team leaders or **supervisors** report to middle managers and directly supervise non-managerial workers.

First jobs in management typically occur as assignments as **team leaders** or **supervisors** — people in charge of small work groups composed of non-managerial workers. Even though most people enter the workforce as technical specialists, sooner or later they advance to positions of initial managerial responsibility. Job titles for these *first-line managers* vary greatly but include such designations as department head, group leader and unit manager. For example, the leader of an auditing team is considered a first-line manager, as is the head of an academic department in a university. Managers at this level of responsibility ensure that their work teams or units meet performance objectives that are consistent with higher-level organisational goals. Manager's Notepad 1.2 offers advice on the performance responsibilities of team leaders and supervisors.[47]

MANAGER'S NOTEPAD 1.2

Nine responsibilities of team leaders

1. Plan meetings and work schedules.
2. Clarify goals and tasks, and gather ideas for improvement.
3. Appraise performance and counsel team members.
4. Recommend pay increases and new assignments.
5. Recruit, train and develop team to meet performance goals.
6. Encourage high performance and teamwork.
7. Inform team members about organisational goals and expectations.
8. Inform higher levels of team needs and accomplishments.
9. Coordinate with other teams and support the rest of the organisation.

Line managers directly contribute to the production of the organisation's basic goods or services.

Staff managers use special technical expertise to advise and support line workers.

TYPES OF MANAGERS

In addition to serving at different levels of authority, managers work in different capacities within organisations. **Line managers** are responsible for work activities that make a direct contribution to the organisation's outputs. For example, the general manager, retail manager and department supervisors of a local department store all have line responsibilities. Their jobs in one way or another are directly related to the sales operations of the store. **Staff managers**, by contrast, use special technical expertise to advise and support the efforts of line workers. In a department store, the director of human resources and the chief financial officer would have staff responsibilities.

In business, **functional managers** have responsibility for a single area of activity, such as finance, marketing, production, human resources, accounting or sales. **General managers** are responsible for more complex units that include many functional areas. An example is a plant manager who oversees many separate functions, including purchasing, manufacturing, warehousing, sales, personnel and accounting. It is common for managers working in public or not-for-profit organisations to be called **administrators**. Examples include hospital administrator, public administrator, city administrator and human-service administrator.

Managerial performance

Managers everywhere face a common problem. They must all set the conditions through which others, working individually and in groups, can contribute their talents to the accomplishment of organisational goals. Furthermore, managers must do this while being held personally 'accountable' for results achieved. The team leader reports to a middle manager, the middle manager reports to a top manager, and even the most senior top manager typically reports to a board of directors. In these reporting relationships, **accountability** exists as the requirement of one person to answer to a higher authority for performance results achieved in his or her area of work responsibility. These results will typically be measured in terms of team or work unit productivity, including the accomplishment of both performance effectiveness and performance efficiency.

But the concept of performance accountability alone does not tell the whole story. Managerial performance is multidimensional. Effective managers help others to both achieve high performance outcomes and experience satisfaction in their work. This dual concern for performance and satisfaction is a central theme in the new workplace, and it runs throughout *Management: An Asia–Pacific Perspective*.

The emphasis on satisfaction helps focus attention on **quality of work life (QWL)** issues as an indicator of the overall quality of human experiences in the workplace. A 'high-QWL' workplace expresses a true respect for people at work by offering such things as fair pay, safe working conditions, opportunities to learn and use new skills, room to grow and progress in a career, protection of individual rights, and pride in the work itself and in the organisation. Part of any manager's accountability is to achieve high-performance outcomes while maintaining a high-quality work-life environment.[48] Simply put, in the new workplace, performance, satisfaction and a high-quality work life can and should go hand in hand.

Changing nature of managerial work

Managerial work in the organisations of today is also changing. The words 'coordinator', 'coach' and 'team leader' are heard as often as 'supervisor' or 'manager'. The work managers perform is less directive and more supportive than in the past. It has to be in a world where high performance comes only to those who truly value and sustain human capital. There is little tolerance or need in today's organisations for those who simply sit back and tell others what to do. The best managers are well informed regarding the needs of those reporting to or dependent on them. They can often be found working alongside those they supervise. They will always be found providing advice and developing the support needed for others to perform to the best of their abilities. High-performing managers are good at building

Functional managers are responsible for one area of activity, such as finance, marketing, production, human resources, accounting or sales.

General managers are responsible for complex organisational units that include many areas of functional activity.

Administrators are managers who work in public or not-for-profit organisations.

Accountability is the requirement to show performance results to a supervisor.

Quality of work life (QWL) is the overall quality of human experiences in the workplace.

working relationships with others, helping others develop their skills and performance competencies, fostering teamwork, and otherwise creating a work environment that is both performance-driven and satisfying to those who do the required work.

An emphasis on customers increasingly drives managerial work in these new settings. Among the many changes taking place, the concept of the 'upside-down pyramid' is one of the most descriptive. As shown in figure 1.3, it offers an alternative and suggestive way of viewing organisations and the role played by managers within them. The operating workers are at the top of the upside-down pyramid, just below the customers and clients they serve. They are supported in their work efforts by managers located at the bottom. These managers aren't just order-givers, they are there to mobilise and deliver the support others require to best serve customer needs. The implications of this notion are dramatic, and they are consistent with the adage that people are an organisation's most important asset. Each member of the upside-down pyramid is a value-added worker — someone who creates eventual value for the organisation's customers or clients. The whole organisation is devoted to serving the customer, and this is made possible with the support of managers.

Many trends and emerging practices in organisations, such as the upside-down pyramid, require new thinking from people who serve as managers. As noted earlier, we are in a time when the best managers are known more for 'helping' and 'supporting' than for 'directing' and 'order-giving'. Even in an age of high technology and 'smart' machines, the human resource is indispensable. Worker involvement and empowerment are critical building blocks of organisational success. Full human resource utilisation increasingly means changing the way work gets done in organisations by pushing decision-making authority to the point where the best information and expertise exist — with the operating workers.[50]

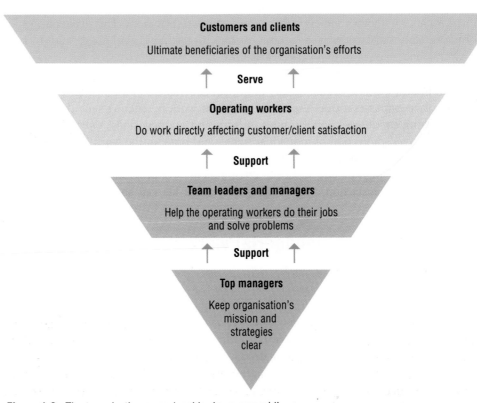

Figure 1.3 ▸ The organisation as an 'upside-down pyramid'

THE MANAGEMENT PROCESS

The ultimate 'bottom line' in every manager's job is to succeed in helping an organisation achieve high performance by using all of its human and material resources. If productivity in the form of high levels of performance effectiveness and efficiency is a measure of organisational success, managers are largely responsible for ensuring its achievement. It is their job to successfully mobilise technology and talent by creating work environments within which others work hard and perform to the best of their abilities.[51]

Functions of management

All managers in daily events must have the capabilities to recognise performance problems and opportunities, make good decisions and take appropriate action. They do this through the process of **management** — planning, organising, leading and controlling the use of resources to accomplish performance goals. These four functions of management and their interrelationships are shown in figure 1.4. All managers, regardless of title, level, type and organisational setting, are responsible for the four functions.[52] However, it is important to know that they most often do not accomplish these functions in linear step-by-step fashion. Rather, the reality of managerial work is that the functions are being continually engaged as a manager moves from task to task and opportunity to opportunity in the process of mobilising resources to accomplish goals.

Management is the process of planning, organising, leading and controlling the use of resources to accomplish performance goals.

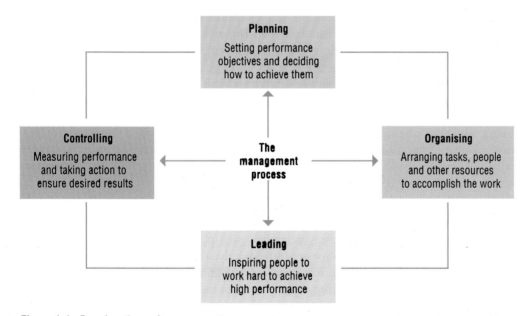

Figure 1.4 ▶ Four functions of management

PLANNING

In management, **planning** is the process of setting performance objectives and determining what actions should be taken to accomplish them. Through planning, a manager identifies desired work results and identifies the means to achieve them. In the USA, for example, Ernst & Young developed an initiative to better meet the needs of the firm's female professionals.[53] Top management grew concerned about the firm's retention rates for women and by a critical report by the independent research group Catalyst. Ernst & Young

Planning is the process of setting objectives and determining how to accomplish them.

responded by setting a planning objective to reduce turnover rates for women. Rates at the time were running at 22 per cent per year and costing the firm about 150 per cent of each person's annual salary to hire and train new staff.

ORGANISING

Organising is the process of assigning tasks, allocating resources and arranging activities to implement plans.

At Ernst & Young, chairman Phil Laskawy believes that the best plans will fail without strong implementation. This begins with **organising**, the process of assigning tasks, allocating resources and arranging the coordinated activities of individuals and groups to implement plans. Through organising, managers turn plans into actions by defining jobs, assigning personnel and supporting them with technology and other resources. Continuing with the example, Laskawy prepared to meet his planning objective by first organising a new Office of Retention and hiring Deborah K. Holmes as a director to head it. As retention problems were identified in various parts of the firm, Holmes further convened special task forces to tackle them and recommend location-specific solutions. A Woman's Access Program was started to give women access to senior people for mentoring and career development.

LEADING

Leading is the process of arousing enthusiasm and directing efforts toward organisational goals.

Speaking at a forum of corporate leaders, Phil Laskawy said: 'At Ernst & Young, the firm has been focused on the need to attract and retain the best by building a leadership and family culture. The firm wants all of our people to be committed to the same goal.' In management, **leading** is the process of arousing people's enthusiasm to work hard and direct their efforts to fulfil plans and accomplish objectives. Through leading, managers build commitments to a common vision, encourage activities that support goals, and influence others to do their best work on the organisation's behalf. In respect to the goals of Ernst & Young's Office of Retention, Deborah Holmes identified a core issue — work at the firm was extremely intense and women often felt strain because their spouses also worked. She became a champion for improved work-life balance and pursued it through the special task forces. Although admitting that 'there's no silver bullet' in the form of a universal solution, new initiatives from the office included 'call-free holidays' where professionals do not check voice mail or e-mail on weekends and holidays, and 'travel sanity' that limits staff members' travel to four days a week so they can get home for weekends.

CONTROLLING

Controlling is the process of measuring performance and taking action to ensure desired results.

Phil Laskawy recognises that a key issue in how well plans get implemented is how well the organisation adapts to rapid change. In today's dynamic times, things don't always go as anticipated and plans must be modified and redefined with the passage of time. The management function of **controlling** is the process of measuring work performance, comparing results to objectives, and taking corrective action as needed. Through controlling, managers maintain active contact with people in the course of their work, gather and interpret reports on performance, and use this information to plan constructive action and change. At Ernst & Young, Laskawy and Holmes knew what the retention rates were when they started the new program, and they have been able to note improvements as the program's work progresses. Through measurement they were able to track progress against objectives. Yearly results indicate that retention is up at all levels. The initiative remains alive at the firm and Laskawy's original planning objectives are being accomplished. Lasting and significant change is contributing to improved work-life balance and better retention rates.

Breaking the glass ceiling in corporate leadership

When Jo Anne Collier became the chief operating officer for one of Australia's largest recruitment firms, she had earned her way to the top. Formerly managing director of Adecco, she worked to deliver flexible solutions to Adecco's blue-chip clients. At 36 she became the company's youngest chief operating officer and first female head. She would often see companies recruiting casual employees with little training, from a queue at the factory gate. Under Jo Anne Collier's leadership, Adecco is becoming a leading provider in flexible workforces. As the official staffing services supporter to the 2000 Olympic and Paralympic games, it recruited the largest flexible workforce ever assembled in Australia.[54] Another woman to watch is Gail Kelly, a former Latin and history teacher in her native South Africa. She worked her way up the corporate ladder to chief executive of St.George Bank, Australia's fifth-largest bank. She commenced her banking career as a teller in 1980 at the South African bank Nedcor. Before coming to Australia in 1997, Gail Kelly became general manager, personal banking at Nedcor. After joining the Commonwealth Bank as general manager of strategic marketing, she quickly became part of the key executive team. In January 2002, Gail Kelly joined the St.George Bank. She argues that women should believe in themselves and try, test and stretch themselves.[55]

Managerial activities and roles

Although the management process may seem straightforward, things are more complicated than they appear at first glance. In his classic book, *The Nature of Managerial Work*, Henry Mintzberg offers this observation on the daily activities of corporate chief executives: 'There was no break in the pace of activity during office hours. The mail . . . telephone calls . . . and meetings . . . accounted for almost every minute from the moment these executives entered their offices in the morning until they departed in the evenings.'[56] Today we would have to add ever-present e-mail to Mintzberg's list of executive preoccupations.[57]

In trying to systematically describe the nature of managerial work and the demands placed on those who do it, Mintzberg offers the set of ten roles depicted in figure 1.5. The roles involve managing information, people and action. They are interconnected, and all managers must be prepared to perform them.[58] In Mintzberg's framework, a manager's *informational roles* involve the giving, receiving and analysing of information. The *interpersonal roles* involve interactions with people inside and outside the work unit. The *decisional roles* involve using information to make decisions to solve problems or address opportunities.

Mintzberg is also careful to note that the manager's day is unforgiving in intensity and pace of these role requirements. The managers he observed had little free time because unexpected problems and continuing requests for meetings consumed almost all the time that became available. Importantly, the responsibility of executive work was all-encompassing in the pressure it placed on the executives for continuously improving performance results. Says Mintzberg: 'The manager can never be free to forget the job, and never has the pleasure of knowing, even temporarily, that there is nothing else to

www.ey.com.au

The Equal Opportunity for Women in the Workplace Business Achievement Awards recognised Ernst & Young Australia's chief executive officer, Brian Schwartz, as the 'Leading CEO for the Advancement of Women'. The number of female partners doubled in his first three years as chief executive, and the firm is committed to further improve the gender balance at senior levels within the firm. Regular Women's Leadership meetings are conducted nationally to discuss issues and build informal networks across the firm.[59]

do ... Managers always carry the nagging suspicion that they might be able to contribute just a little bit more. Hence they assume an unrelenting pace in their work.'[60]

Interpersonal roles	Informational roles	Decisional roles
How a manager interacts with other people • Figurehead • Leader • Liaison	How a manager exchanges and processes information • Monitor • Disseminator • Spokesperson	How a manager uses information in decision making • Entrepreneur • Disturbance handler • Resource allocator • Negotiator

Figure 1.5 ▸ Mintzberg's ten managerial roles

Managerial work is busy, demanding and stressful not just for chief executives but for managers at all levels of responsibility in any work setting. A summary of research on the nature of managerial work offers this important reminder[61] — managers work long hours. They work at an intense pace, at fragmented and varied tasks, with many communication media, and they accomplish their work largely through interpersonal relationships.

Managerial agendas and networks

It is not only the complexity and pace of managerial work that makes it challenging. There are subtle intricacies in the day-to-day flow of events and interactions that must also be mastered. Consider this description of a brief incident in the day of the general manager of a business.

> On his way to a meeting, a GM bumped into a staff member who did not report to him. Using this opportunity, in a two-minute conversation he (a) asked two questions and received the information he needed, (b) reinforced their good relationship by sincerely complimenting the staff member on something he had recently done, and (c) got the staff member to agree to do something that the GM needed done.[62]

The description provides a glimpse of an effective general manager in action. It portrays two activities that management consultant and scholar John Kotter considers critical to a general manager's success in mastering two critical challenges — agenda setting and networking. Through *agenda setting*, good managers develop action priorities for their jobs that include goals and plans that span long and short time frames. These agendas are usually incomplete and loosely connected in the beginning, but become more specific as the manager utilises information that is continually gleaned from many different sources. The agendas are kept always in mind and are 'played out' whenever an opportunity arises, as in the example given above.

Good managers implement their agendas by working with a variety of people inside and outside the organisation. In Kotter's example, the GM was getting things done through a staff member who did not report directly to him. This is made possible by *networking*, the process of building and maintaining positive relationships with people whose help may be needed to implement one's work agendas. Since networks are indispensable to managerial success in today's complex work environments, excellent managers devote much time and effort to network development. In the case of this general manager, for example, the networks included relationships with peers, higher-level executives, subordinates and members of their work teams, as well as with external customers, suppliers and community representatives.

MANAGERIAL LEARNING

British educator and consultant Charles Handy calls today's turbulent times 'the age of unreason'.[63] Above all, it is an era of high performance expectations for organisations and their members. Change is a way of life, and it demands new organisational and individual responses. And along with all this, the quest for high performance is relentless. Everywhere new workers are expected to use new ways to achieve high productivity under new and dynamic conditions. They are expected to become involved, fully participate, demonstrate creativity, and find self-fulfilment in their work. They are expected to be team players who understand the needs and goals of the total organisation and who use new technologies to their full advantage.

All of this, of course, places a premium on *your* commitment to learning — not just formal learning in the classroom, but also **lifelong learning**. This is the process of continuously learning from our daily experiences and opportunities. Especially in a dynamic and ever-changing environment, a commitment to lifelong learning helps us build portfolios of skills that are always up to date and valuable in the labour markets. A critical part of job-related learning, furthermore, comes from 'learning by doing'. This means that you must always look for good job opportunities that make such learning possible.

Lifelong learning is continuous learning from daily experiences and opportunities.

Essential managerial skills

A **skill** is an ability to translate knowledge into action that results in desired performance. Obviously, many skills are required to master the challenging nature of managerial work. The most important ones are those that allow managers to help others become more productive in their work. Harvard scholar Robert L. Katz has classified the essential skills of managers into three categories: technical, human and conceptual.[64] Although all three skills are essential for managers, he suggests that their relative importance tends to vary by level of managerial responsibility as shown in figure 1.6.

A **skill** is the ability to translate knowledge into action that results in desired performance.

Lower-level managers	Middle-level managers	Top-level managers

Conceptual skills — the ability to think analytically and achieve integrative problem solving

Human skills — the ability to work well in cooperation with other persons

Technical skills — the ability to apply expertise and perform a special task with proficiency

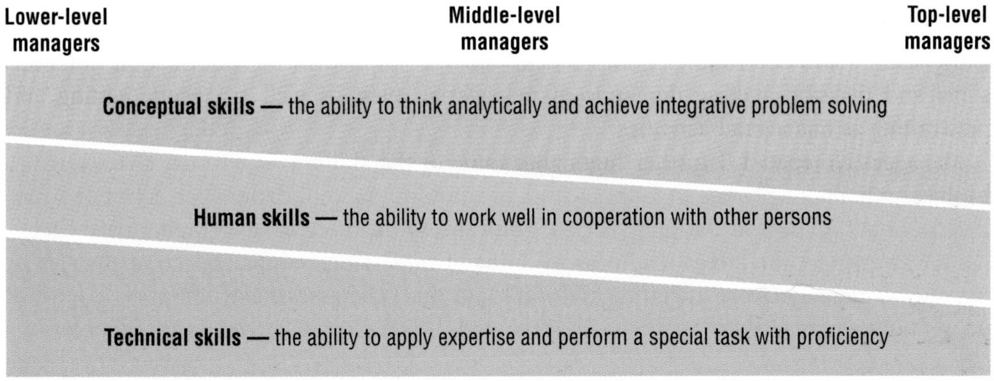

Figure 1.6 ▸ Essential managerial skills

A **technical skill** is the ability to use a special proficiency or expertise to perform particular tasks. Accountants, engineers, market researchers, business planners and computer scientists, for example, possess technical skills. These are initially acquired through formal education and are further developed by training and job experience. Technical skill in the new network economy is also increasingly tied to computer literacy and utilisation of the latest information technology. Figure 1.6 shows that technical skills are very important at

A **technical skill** is the ability to use a special proficiency or expertise in one's work.

career entry levels. The critical question to be asked and positively answered by you in this respect, and in preparation for any job interview, comes down to this simple test: 'What can you really do for an employer?'

The ability to work well in cooperation with other persons is a **human skill**. It emerges in the workplace as a spirit of trust, enthusiasm and genuine involvement in interpersonal relationships. A manager with good human skills will have a high degree of self-awareness and a capacity to understand or empathise with the feelings of others. An important component of the essential human skills is **emotional intelligence**.[65] Discussed in chapter 13 for its leadership implications, emotional intelligence is defined by scholar and consultant Daniel Goleman as the 'ability to manage ourselves and our relationships effectively'.[66] Given the highly interpersonal nature of managerial work, human skills are critical for all managers. Figure 1.6 shows that they are consistently important across all the managerial levels. Again a straightforward question puts you to the test of interpersonal skills and emotional intelligence: 'How well do you work with others?'

All good managers ultimately have the ability to view situations broadly and to solve problems to the benefit of everyone concerned. This ability to think critically and analytically is a **conceptual skill**. It involves the ability to break down problems into smaller parts, to see the relations between the parts, and to recognise the implications of any one problem for others. As we assume ever-higher responsibilities in organisations, we are called upon to deal with more ambiguous problems that have many complications and longer-term consequences. Figure 1.6 shows that conceptual skills gain in relative importance for top managers. At this point, you should ask: 'Am I developing critical thinking and problem-solving capabilities for long-term career success?'

Skill and outcome assessment

Business and management educators are increasingly interested in helping people acquire the essential skills and develop specific competencies that can help them achieve managerial success. A **managerial competency** is a skill-based capability that contributes to high performance in a management job.[67] A number of these competencies have been implied in the previous discussion of the management process, including those related to planning, organising, leading and controlling. Competencies are also implicit in the information, interpersonal and decision-making demands of managerial roles, as well as agenda setting and networking as managerial activities.

Manager's Notepad 1.3 further highlights some of the skills and personal characteristics business schools emphasise in helping students develop the foundations for continued professional development and career success. You can use this notepad as a preliminary checklist for assessing your career readiness in terms of professional skills and competencies. A format for more formally including this skill and outcome assessment template as part of your study of management is provided in the end-of-text Career Readiness Workbook.

GETTING CONNECTED WITH *MANAGEMENT: AN ASIA–PACIFIC PERSPECTIVE*

Management: An Asia–Pacific Perspective is designed to facilitate your learning about management, organisations and the new workplace. When the chapter discussions are combined with the activities and resources in the Career Readiness Workbook, the book offers a unique opportunity to establish your career readiness.

A **human skill** is the ability to work well in cooperation with other people.

Emotional intelligence is the ability to manage ourselves and our relationships effectively.

A **conceptual skill** is the ability to think analytically and solve complex problems.

A **managerial competency** is a skill-based capability for high performance in a management job.

Management: An Asia–Pacific Perspective chapter organisation

As described in figure 1.7, the chapters are divided into five parts:

- *Part 1: Management today* focuses on the new workplace, environment and diversity, as well as information and decision making. Chapters on these topics introduce important developments and forces that impact the emergence of the new management in this age of globalisation and the new economy.

Chapter organisation of Management: An Asia–Pacific Perspective

- *Part 2: Context* describes the historical and contemporary context for modern management. The chapters examine the historical foundations of management, the global economy, cultural dimensions, ethics and social responsibility.

- *Part 3: Mission* addresses the purpose and goals of organisations and the action foundations for their accomplishment. The chapters focus on management functions of planning and controlling, with special emphasis on strategic management, entrepreneurship and new ventures.

- *Part 4: Organisation* examines the nature of organisations as work systems and processes. The chapters describe approaches to organisation structures, high-performance designs and the all-important human resource management systems.

- *Part 5: Leadership* introduces the great opportunities of leadership in organisations, with special emphasis on understanding the personal skills and competencies requisite to leadership success. Chapter topics include motivation and rewards, individual performance, stress, communication, teamwork and group performance, and the processes of innovation and change leadership.

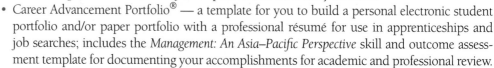

Part 1 **Management today**
• The dynamic new workplace
• Environment and diversity
• Information and decision making

Part 2 **Context**
• Historical foundations of management
• Global dimensions of management
• Ethical behaviour and social responsibility

Managerial skills and competencies

Career Readiness Workbook

Part 3 **Mission**
• Planning and controlling
• Strategic management
• Entrepreneurship and new ventures

Part 4 **Organisation**
• Organising
• Organisational design and work processes
• Human resource management

Part 5 **Leadership**
• Leading
• Motivation and rewards
• Individuals, job design and stress
• Teams and teamwork
• Communication and interpersonal skills
• Change leadership

Figure 1.7 ▸ *Management: An Asia–Pacific Perspective* — a learning framework

Career Readiness Workbook

Management: An Asia–Pacific Perspective includes a unique and exciting end-of-text Career Readiness Workbook that provides resources to extend your learning in relevant career directions. Components in this workbook are also provided in enhanced electronic versions on the *Management: An Asia–Pacific Perspective* web site. They include:

Features in the Career Readiness Workbook

• Career Advancement Portfolio® — a template for you to build a personal electronic student portfolio and/or paper portfolio with a professional résumé for use in apprenticeships and job searches; includes the *Management: An Asia–Pacific Perspective* skill and outcome assessment template for documenting your accomplishments for academic and professional review.
• Research and presentation projects — a rich set of unique activities to help consolidate your learning about management through Internet research.
• Cross-functional integrative case — a real-life example to reinforce concepts introduced in each chapter.
• Exercises in teamwork — exercises designed to improve your familiarity with real management situations and help you gain insight into your skills and capabilities in interpersonal relations and teamwork.
• Management skills assessments — self-assessment inventories designed to help identify your strengths and developmental needs in the essential managerial skills and competencies.

When this book declares GET CONNECTED!, you should take notice. If you read and study the chapters in *Management: An Asia–Pacific Perspective*, explore and use the accompanying online learning resources, and take full advantage of your class discussions and activities, you will surely benefit by strengthening your foundations for career success. In the changing world of work today and with all the challenges of a new economy, the premium is on continuous learning and professional development. *Management: An Asia–Pacific Perspective* and its online resources were designed to help you gain advantage through improved career readiness. Go for it. Get connected!

CHAPTER 1
Study guide

The chapter 1 study guide helps you review the chapter content, prepare for examinations, apply what you have learned and further build your career readiness. The summary briefly answers the study questions posed at the start of the chapter. The list of key terms allows you to double-check your familiarity with basic concepts and definitions. The applied activities help you test your comprehension of chapter content. Suggestions offered as career readiness activities direct your attention to relevant sections of the Career Readiness Workbook where you can test and develop your career skills and apply what you have learned. The list of electronic resources suggests activities from the *Management: An Asia–Pacific Perspective* web site and, finally, the case for critical thinking helps you apply your new management knowledge.

SUMMARY

What are the challenges of working in the new economy?

- Today's turbulent environment challenges everyone to understand and embrace continuous change and developments in a new information-driven and global economy.
- Work in the new economy is increasingly knowledge based, and people, with their capacity to bring valuable intellectual capital to the workplace, are the ultimate foundation of organisational performance.
- The forces of globalisation are bringing increased interdependencies among nations and economies as customer markets and resource flows create intense business competition.
- Ever-present developments in information technology and the continued expansion of the Internet are reshaping organisations, changing the nature of work, and increasing the value of people capable of performing as knowledge workers.
- Organisations must value the talents and capabilities of a workforce whose members are increasingly diverse with respect to gender, age, race and ethnicity, able-bodiedness and lifestyles.
- Society has high expectations for organisations and their members to perform with commitment to high ethical standards and in socially responsible ways, including protection of the natural environment and human rights.
- Careers in the new economy require great personal initiative to build and maintain skill 'portfolios' that are always up to date and valuable to employers challenged by intense competition and opportunities of the information age.

What are organisations like in the new workplace?

- Organisations are collections of people working together to achieve a common purpose.
- As open systems, organisations interact with their environments in the process of transforming resource inputs into product outputs.
- Productivity is a measure of the quantity and quality of work performance, with resource utilisation taken into account.

- High-performing organisations are both effective, in terms of goal accomplishment, and efficient, in terms of resource use.
- Organisations today continue to emphasise total quality management in a context of technology utilisation, more empowerment and teamwork, and concern for work-life balance, among other trends.

Who are managers and what do they do?

- Managers directly support and facilitate the work efforts of other people in organisations.
- Top managers scan the environment, create vision and emphasise long-term performance goals; middle managers coordinate activities in large departments or divisions; team leaders and supervisors support performance at the team or work-unit level.
- Functional managers work in specific areas such as finance or marketing; general managers are responsible for larger multifunctional units; administrators are managers in not-for-profit organisations.
- A key aspect of managerial work is accountability to higher levels for performance results that the manager depends on other persons to accomplish.
- The upside-down pyramid view of organisations shows operating workers at the top and responsible for meeting customer needs, while being supported from below by various levels of management.
- A key aspect in the changing nature of managerial work is emphasis on being good at coaching and supporting others, rather than simply directing and order-giving.

What is the management process?

- The management process consists of the four functions of planning, organising, leading and controlling.
- Planning sets the direction; organising assembles the human and material resources; leading provides the enthusiasm and direction; controlling ensures results.
- Managers implement the four functions in daily work that is intense and stressful, involving long hours and continuous performance pressures.
- Managerial success in this demanding context requires the ability to perform well in interpersonal, informational and decision-making roles.
- Managerial success in this demanding context also requires the ability to utilise interpersonal networks to accomplish well-selected task agendas.

How do you learn the essential managerial skills and competencies?

- Career success in the new economy requires continual attention to the process of lifelong learning from all aspects of daily experience and job opportunities.
- Skills considered essential to managerial success are broadly described as technical (ability to utilise knowledge and technology), human (ability to work well with other people) and conceptual (ability to analyse and solve complex problems).
- *Management: An Asia–Pacific Perspective* offers skill and outcome assessment activities considered by business schools and employers as basic foundations for managerial success. These are communication, teamwork, self-management, leadership, critical thinking and professionalism.
- *Management: An Asia–Pacific Perspective* focuses attention on your career potential through a special end-of-text Career Readiness Workbook, including a template for building print and electronic versions of your personal Career Advancement Portfolio®.
- *Management: An Asia–Pacific Perspective* enriches your learning experience with an online study guide and e-resource centre for each chapter.

KEY TERMS

accountability (p. 17)

administrators (p. 17)

conceptual skill (p. 24)

controlling (p. 20)

discrimination (p. 9)

emotional intelligence (p. 24)

functional managers (p. 17)

general managers (p. 17)

glass ceiling effect (p. 9)

globalisation (p. 6)

human skill (p. 24)

intellectual capital (p. 5)

knowledge worker (p. 5)

leading (p. 20)

lifelong learning (p. 23)

line managers (p. 16)

management (p. 19)

managerial competency (p. 24)

managers (p. 15)

middle managers (p. 16)

open systems (p. 12)

organisation (p. 11)

organising (p. 20)

performance effectiveness (p. 13)

performance efficiency (p. 13)

planning (p. 19)

prejudice (p. 9)

productivity (p. 12)

project managers (p. 16)

quality of work life (QWL) (p. 17)

skill (p. 23)

staff managers (p. 16)

supervisors (p. 16)

team leaders (p. 16)

technical skill (p. 23)

top managers (p. 15)

total quality management (TQM)
(p. 14)

workforce diversity (p. 8)

APPLIED ACTIVITIES

Short-response questions

1. List and explain the importance of three pressures in the areas of ethics and social responsibility that managers must be prepared to face in the future.

2. Explain how 'accountability' would operate in the relationships between (a) a manager and her subordinates and (b) the same manager and her boss.

3. Explain how the 'glass ceiling effect' may work to the disadvantage of female middle managers in a large corporation.

4. What is 'globalisation' and how does it relate to Kenichi Ohmae's notion of the borderless world?

Application question

5. You have just been hired as the new supervisor of an audit team for a national accounting firm. With eight years of experience, you feel technically well prepared for the assignment. However, this is your first formal appointment as a 'manager'. Things are complicated at the moment since the team should have 12 members, but there are five vacancies to be filled. Your boss wants the new team to be as 'diverse' as possible. How will this situation challenge you to use and develop managerial skills and related competencies so that you can successfully manage diversity on the audit team?

CAREER READINESS ACTIVITIES

Recommended individual and group learning activities from the end-of-text Career Readiness Workbook for this chapter include:

Career advancement portfolio   *WB*

Update your career advancement portfolio to reflect your new skills and experiences. Include skills and personal insights you gain from the following projects and exercises.

Research and presentation project   *WB*

• Project 1 — Diversity lessons — 'what have we learned?'

Cross-functional integrative case   *WB*

Read the integrative case on Sarina Russo and answer the following questions:

1.1   Check out the Sarina Russo Group web site www.sarinarusso.com.au. In what ways can you identify that the businesses are working in the new econoomy?

1.2   Do you think that Sarina Russo would be a supporter of globalisation? Why or why not?

1.3   In her early career, do you think Sarina Russo experienced the glass ceiling effect?

Exercises in teamwork   *WB*

• Exercise 1 — My best manager
• Exercise 2 — What managers do
• Exercise 3 — Defining quality
• Exercise 13 — The future workplace

Management skills assessment   *WB*

• Assessment 1 — Skills of effective managers

ELECTRONIC RESOURCES

Don't forget to take full advantage of the online support for *Management: An Asia–Pacific Perspective* at www.johnwiley.com.au/highered/management: chapter 1 practice tests, e-flashcards, crossword puzzles, interactive management skills assessments, interactive cases, the online career advancement portfolio and much more!

CASE FOR CRITICAL THINKING

Read the following case for critical thinking on Apple Computer. While you are reading the case keep in mind what you have learned in this chapter, then answer the questions.

Apple Computer:
passion, design and the future

Apple Computer paradoxically exists as both one of the computer industry's greatest successes as well as one of its greatest failures. It single-handedly created the personal computer industry, bringing such behemoths as IBM and Digital Equipment almost to their knees. At the same time, Apple is an example of opportunities lost due to large personal egos and poor management decisions. It offers a fascinating look at business and management.

Corporate history

The history of Apple Computer is a history of passion among its founders, employees and loyal users. The company was established by Steven Wozniak and Steven Jobs in 1976. Both had an interest in electronics from an early age, with Wozniak working at Hewlett-Packard and Jobs at Atari. The company's first personal computer was built by Wozniak and named the Apple I.[68]

Things started to take off for Apple in 1977 when it introduced the Apple II, which featured a plastic case and colour graphics. The addition of a floppy drive in early 1978 added to the popularity of the new computer. By 1980, the release of the Apple III found the company with several thousand employees and Steven Jobs at the helm.

Early on, Apple Computer exhibited an extreme emphasis on new and innovative styling in its computer offerings. Jobs's eccentric personality pervaded the culture of Apple and all the people who worked there. He took a personal interest in the development of new products, including the Lisa and the legendary Macintosh with its graphical interface and 3.5-inch floppy disk.

The passion Apple is so famous for was clearly evident in the design of the Macintosh. Project teams worked around the clock to develop the machine and its innovative graphical user interface (GUI) operating system (Mac OS). Based loosely on a design developed by the Xerox Palo Alto Research Center, the use of graphical icons to create simplified user commands was immensely popular.[69]

With the entrance of IBM into the personal computer market in 1981, Jobs realised that it was time for Apple to 'grow up'. In early 1983, he was able to persuade John Sculley, then president of Pepsi-Cola, to join Apple as president. The two men clashed almost from the start, with Sculley eventually ousting Jobs from the company.

After struggling early, the launch of the Mac II — with its increased speed, Motorola chip and expandability — reinvigorated Apple's sales. 'The twin introductions of the LaserWriter, the first affordable PostScript laser printer for the Mac, and PageMaker, one of the first desktop publishing programs ever', also helped lift sales. 'These two in tandem made the Mac an ideal solution for inexpensive publishing.'[70]

However, a saturated personal computer market, due largely to IBM PC-clones of every variety, caused Apple huge problems in the early 1990s. In addition, the launch of Microsoft's Windows 3.0, a greatly improved version of the Wintel operating system, proved a major obstacle for Apple. A major turning point occurred in 1991, when Apple contemplated licensing its Mac operating system to other computer manufacturers and making it run on Intel-based machines. Had the firm chosen this strategy, it may well be that Apple would be the present-day Microsoft. However, Apple's chief operating officer at the time, Michael Spindler, quashed the idea, saying that it was 'too late to license'.[71]

Innovative design to the rescue

In the 1990s, Apple introduced the very popular PowerBook notebook computer line, along with the unsuccessful Newton personal digital assistant (PDA). Sculley, having lost interest in the day-to-day operations of Apple, was eventually forced out and replaced with Michael Spindler.

Spindler oversaw a number of innovations, including the PowerMac family — 'the first Macs to be based on the PowerPC chip, an extremely fast processor co-developed with IBM and Motorola. The PowerPC processor allowed Macs to compete with, and in many cases surpass, the speed of Intel's newer processors.'[72] In addition, Apple was successful in licensing its operating system to a number of Mac-cloners, but never with the necessary numbers to extend its market share.

After a difficult time in the mid-1990s, Spindler was replaced with Gil Amelio, the former president of National Semiconductor. This set the stage for one of the most famous returns in corporate history.

After leaving Apple, Steven Jobs started a company to develop the NeXT computer, an advanced personal computer with a sleek, innovative design. However, with its proprietary software, the device never caught a large following.

Jobs's return

In late 1996, Apple announced the purchase of NeXT. Jobs returned to Apple in an unofficial capacity as adviser to the president. However, with the resignation of Gil Amelio, Jobs eventually accepted the role of 'interim CEO' (iCEO) of Apple Computer. He wasted no time in making his return felt.

Jobs announced an alliance with former rival Microsoft. In exchange for US$150 million in Apple stock, Microsoft and Apple would have a five-year patent cross-licence for their graphical interface operating systems. He revoked licences allowing the production of Mac clones, and started offering Macs for sale over the Web through the Apple Store.

In addition to a slew of new product offerings, Jobs introduced the iMac, with a revolutionary see-through design that has proved popular among consumers. This was followed shortly by the iBook, a similar-type portable computer. Apple once again was viewed as an industry innovator, with its revolutionary designs and innovations.[73]

Unfortunately, Apple remains a relatively small player in the computer industry. While its products are wildly popular among a dedicated set of users, it still commands just a little over 5 per cent of the total computer market. It remains locked in constant boom-or-bust cycles dependent on its ability to turn out a stream of new product hits.

What does the future hold?

Apple is faced with a stark reality: Can it continue to offer both hardware and software solutions in a rapidly changing technology environment? Its decision early on to keep its technology proprietary, as opposed to IBM's decision to support an open architecture system, has proved to be a costly strategy to support in the long run.

There are those who argue that Apple should reinvent itself once again, and this time concentrate on software. Although existing Apple users are fiercely loyal, the company has always had problems winning over non-Mac users.[74]

Apple is betting that its new operating system, Mac OS X, will be a big hit. Mac OS also offers features that make the Macintosh a more attractive platform for businesses than it has been in the past. It is the largest update in the operating system since it was first released in the mid-1980s. Once again, will this attract new buyers, or just recycle present Apple enthusiasts? Apple launched an advertising campaign called 'Switch' targeted squarely at getting Windows users to move to the Macintosh platform.

One aspect of Apple's new corporate strategy is to take advantage of the explosion of personal electronic devices — for example, CD players, MP3 players, DVD players and digital cameras — by adding value to these devices with Mac-only applications, such as iTunes, iMovie and iDVD. Apple hopes to make the Mac the 'digital hub of the new digital lifestyle', revitalising sales and guaranteeing the long-term security of the company.[75]

Source: © Glen Sanford www.apple-history.com.

QUESTIONS

1. Why is Apple not a dominant provider of personal computers?
2. Can Apple continue as an independent concern with such a small share of the computer market?
3. Should the company provide its operating system to run on both Apple and PC systems?
4. What would you suggest Steven Jobs do to popularise the Apple computer line?

Environment and diversity

CHAPTER 2 STUDY QUESTIONS

▶ What is the external environment of organisations?

▶ What is a customer-driven organisation?

▶ What is a quality-driven organisation?

▶ What is the internal environment and organisational culture?

▶ How is diversity managed in a multicultural organisation?

Agilent Technologies — company of your dreams

GETTING @ CONNECTED

Agilent Technologies www.agilent.com is a global communications, electronics and life sciences company with approximately 41 000 employees in 40 countries. Headquartered in the USA, Agilent also has major product development and manufacturing sites in Australia, China, Japan, Korea, Malaysia, Singapore, Germany and the United Kingdom.

A study by Hewitt Associates recognised Agilent as a 'Best Employer to Work For in Australia'. Hewitt found that Agilent attracted and retained talented workers by providing a workplace and culture (the 'beAgilent' culture) that engages its employees' intellectual and emotional commitment. The company seeks to closely align the performance of employees with the company's business goals as part of its strategy. Sydney-based employee Hadley Richardson said: 'I stay because I love the work! Agilent is one of the most flexible companies I have worked for or with. By that I mean Agilent is swift to resolve any issues and often addresses all of the needs of its employees. It's not a question of why I stay but why would I leave? I have made long-term plans in my life and Agilent is in them.'

Australia's Equal Opportunity for Women in the Workplace Agency recognised Agilent's diversity policies by naming it one of Australia's top female-friendly companies in the 'Employer of Choice for Women' awards.[1]

GET CONNECTED!
@

Learn more about diversity in the workplace by visiting the web sites of the Equal Opportunity for Women in the Workplace Agency www.eeo.gov.au or the Equal Employment Opportunities Trust www.eeotrust.org.nz.

GET CONNECTED!

Once a benchmark for science fiction writers, the 21st century is now placing unrelenting new demands on organisations and their members. Managers today are learning to operate in a world that places a premium on information, technology use, quality, customer service and speed. They are learning how to succeed in a world of intense competition, continued globalisation of markets and business activities, and rapid technological change. This chapter introduces the external and internal environments of organisations as two important considerations in the quest for high performance in demanding and dynamic times. The chapter opening example of Agilent Technologies sets the stage. It introduces the importance of core values and the belief in people. It raises the question: What must organisations do to remain successful in the dynamic, complex and ever-changing environment of today?

ENVIRONMENT AND COMPETITIVE ADVANTAGE

Time magazine's choices for person of the year have reflected the transition from the industrial age to the information era. Between the 1920s and 1990, the magazine recognised only Walter Chrysler (1928) and Harlow Curtice (1955), chief executive of General Motors, from the commercial world. Both men were captains of an industrial age that is now in the throes of deep transformation. In the last decade of the 20th century, however, *Time* featured a business representative as the magazine's person of the year on three separate occasions: Ted Turner (1991) of CNN, whose television news empire helped to bring the world closer to its global village status; Andrew Grove (1997) of Intel, whose computer chips helped to change the world and its economy; and Jeff Bezos (1999) of Amazon.com, who has changed the way the world shops. Turner, Grove and Bezos all represent the dawning of the information age, along with its profound impact on the global economy and the world of work. This change represents major challenges to organisations and individual career seekers.[2] When looking at things from a business vantage point, IBM's CEO Louis V. Gerstner Jr once described the challenge this way: 'We believe very strongly that the age-old levers of competition — labor, capital and land — are being supplemented by knowledge, and that most successful companies in the future will be those that learn how to exploit knowledge — knowledge about customer behavior, markets, economies, technology — faster than their competitors'.[3] Knowledge and speed are indispensable to success in this new economy. Even as Gerstner and other executives strive to lead their organisations toward a high-performance edge, they cannot afford for a minute to rest on past laurels. The world is too uncertain and the competition too intense for that. 'In order to survive,' Reich points out, 'all organizations must dramatically and continuously improve — cutting costs, adding value, creating new products.'[4]

What is competitive advantage?

Astute executives understand the management implications in the prior observations. They are ever-alert to environmental trends that require adjustments in the ways their organisations operate and that offer opportunities to achieve **competitive advantage**.[5] This term refers to the use of a core competency that clearly sets an organisation apart from its competitors and gives it an advantage over them in the marketplace. Simply put, competitive advantage comes from an ability to do things better than one's competitors. An organisation may achieve competitive advantage in many ways, including through its products, pricing, customer service, cost efficiency and quality, among other aspects of operating excellence.

A **competitive advantage** allows an organisation to deal with market and environmental forces better than its competitors.

But regardless of how the advantage is achieved, the key result is the same — an ability to consistently do something of high value that one's competitors cannot replicate quickly or do as well.

ENTREPRENEURSHIP

Blueprint Management Group •
www.blueprintmg.com.au

Blueprint for success

Andrew Price and a colleague, Trevor Folsom, heard the call to competitive advantage. They also followed the pathways of entrepreneurship. They left their jobs at an American financial services company and started their Sydney-based call centre, called Blueprint Management Group, with only $5000. They identified a gap in the market for outbound telemarketing. They believed that companies could build relationships with their customers by talking to them and extracting information from them, in order to up-sell and cross-sell their products. Rather than handling inbound calls on behalf of customers including other call centres at the time, Price and Folsom offered 'marriage marketing' — ringing a company's customers to sell them new products or services (cross-selling) or more expensive products or services (up-selling). It took two years for the market to understand the concept.

To prove the concept to customers, in March 1997 Price and Folsom started the Sydney Beer Club, a loyalty program on behalf of pubs offering discounts and incentives, including free beer. They built the club's membership to 2500 using telemarketing. In April 1998, Cable & Wireless Optus became Blueprint's first big customer. They started a trial of ten staff for Optus, but within two months this had grown to 280 staff. Other customers now include organisations such as Westpac, Quicken and AMP. In 1998–99, Blueprint turned over $4.7 million, 60% of which came from Optus. In March 1999, Optus took its call centre in-house but, despite the loss of that business, Blueprint turned over $6.5 million in 1999–2000 and $14.6 million in 2000–01.[6]

The general environment

Business excellence in organisations is only possible when business leaders understand the interdependencies between their organisation and the external environment. Comparisons by the Organisation for Economic Co-operation and Development (OECD) have highlighted the importance that Australia improves its world competitiveness. The Karpin Report in 1995 also focused on Australia's poor track record when compared with other OECD members such as the USA, Sweden, Japan, Germany and New Zealand.[7] Competitive advantage in the demanding global economy can be achieved only by continuously scanning the environment for opportunities, and taking effective action based on what is learned.[8] The ability to do this begins with the answer to a basic question: What is in the external environment of organisations?

The **general environment** consists of all the background conditions in the external environment of an organisation. This portion of the environment forms a general context for

◆ The **general environment** is comprised of cultural, economic, legal–political and educational conditions.

managerial decision making. The major external environmental issues of our day include factors such as the following:

Elements in the general environment

- *economic conditions* — general state of the economy in terms of inflation, income levels, gross domestic product, unemployment and related indicators of economic health
- *sociocultural conditions* — general state of prevailing social values on such matters as human rights, trends in education and related social institutions, as well as demographic patterns
- *legal–political conditions* — general state of the prevailing philosophy and objectives of the political party or parties running the government, as well as laws and government regulations
- *technological conditions* — general state of the development and availability of technology, including scientific advancements
- *natural environment conditions* — general state of nature and conditions of the natural environment, including levels of public concern expressed through environmentalism.

If we take the natural environment as an example, Australian power stations seem to be finding the potential for competitive advantage. For example Alstrom Power was awarded the Australian Engineering Excellence Award for developing a cost-effective technology that allows waste products from coal washeries to be used to generate electricity. Historically, the waste has been left to decompose and generate methane.[9]

Manager's Notepad 2.1 highlights important diversity trends in the sociocultural environment of organisations.[10] It is also important to note that differences in any and all general environment factors are especially noticeable when organisations operate internationally. External conditions vary significantly from one country and culture to the next. Managers of successful international operations understand these differences and help their organisations make the operating adjustments needed to perform within them.

MANAGER'S NOTEPAD 2.1

Diversity trends in the sociocultural environment

- People from a non-English-speaking background are an increasing percentage of the workforce.
- More women are working.
- People with disabilities are gaining more access to the workplace.
- Workers are increasingly from non-traditional families (e.g. single parents, dual wage earners).
- Average age of workers is increasing.
- Religious diversity of workers is increasing.

🗸 The **specific environment** includes the people and groups with whom an organisation interacts.

🗸 **Stakeholders** are the individuals, groups and institutions directly affected by an organisation's performance.

The specific environment

The **specific environment** consists of the actual organisations, groups and persons with whom an organisation interacts and conducts business. These are environmental elements of direct consequence to the organisation as it operates on a day-to-day basis. The specific environment is often described in terms of **stakeholders** — the individuals, groups and institutions who are affected in one way or another by the organisation's performance.

Figure 2.1 shows multiple stakeholders as they may exist in the external environment of a typical business.

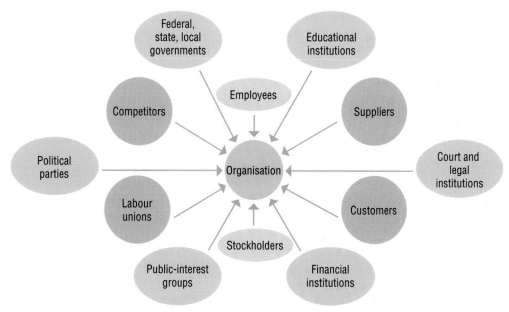

Figure 2.1 ▸ Multiple stakeholders in the environment of organisations

Sometimes called the *task environment*, the specific environment and the stakeholders are distinct for each organisation. They can also change over time according to the company's unique customer base, operating needs and circumstances. Important stakeholders common to the specific environment of most organisations include:

- *customers* — specific consumer or client groups, individuals and organisations that purchase the organisation's goods and/or use its services
- *suppliers* — specific providers of the human, information and financial resources and raw materials needed by the organisation to operate
- *competitors* — specific organisations that offer the same or similar goods and services to the same consumer or client groups
- *regulators* — specific government agencies and representatives, at the local, state and national levels, that enforce laws and regulations affecting the organisation's operations.

Components of the specific or task environment

Environmental uncertainty

The fact is that many organisations today face great uncertainty in their external environments. In this sense, **environmental uncertainty** means that there is a lack of complete information regarding what developments will occur in the external environment. This makes it difficult to predict future states of affairs and to understand their potential implications for the organisation. Figure 2.2 describes environmental uncertainty along two dimensions — complexity, or the number of different factors in the environment, and the rate of change in these factors.[11]

In general, the greater the environmental uncertainty, the more attention that management in an organisation must direct toward the external environment. It has to be continually studied and monitored to spot emerging trends. Also, the greater the environmental uncertainty the more need there is for flexibility and adaptability in organisational designs

Environmental uncertainty is a lack of complete information about the environment.

and work practices. Because of this uncertainty, organisations must be able to respond quickly as new circumstances arise and information becomes available. Throughout this book you will find many examples of how organisations are becoming more flexible in the attempt to better deal with the high amounts of environmental uncertainty that so often prevail in today's dynamic times.

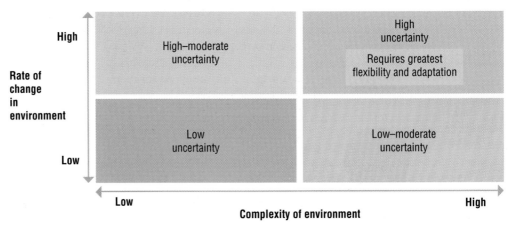

Figure 2.2 ▸ Dimensions of uncertainty in organisational environments

CUSTOMER-DRIVEN ORGANISATIONS

Question: What's your job?
Answer: I run the cash register and pack groceries.
Question: But isn't it your job to serve the customer?
Answer: I guess, but it's not in my job description.

The customer is 'captain' of the supply chain for Dell Computer. Founder and chairman Michael Dell firmly believes that competitive advantage can be found by focusing supply chain management on meeting customer preferences. The company is a leader in using information technology to create operating efficiencies that deliver products and services meeting customer preferences.

This conversation illustrates what often becomes the missing link in the quest for total quality and competitive advantage — customer service.[12] Contrast this conversation with the following testimony from a customer of an organisation selling teddy bears, who called to report that her new mail-order teddy bear had a problem. The company responded promptly, she said, and arranged to have the bear picked up and replaced. She wrote to say 'thank you for the great service and courtesy you gave me'.[13]

Who are the customers?

Figure 2.3 expands the open-systems view of organisations introduced in chapter 1 to now depict the complex internal operations of the organisation as well as its interdependence with the external environment. In this figure, the organisation's *external customers* purchase the goods produced or use the services provided. They may be industrial customers, that is, other firms that buy a company's products for use in their own operations; or they may be retail customers or clients who purchase or use the goods and services directly. *Internal customers*, by contrast, are found within the organisation. They are the individuals and groups who use or otherwise depend on the results of others' work in order to do their own jobs well. Any job or function is both a supplier and a customer. Customers have the right to expect high-quality and on-time inputs from the earlier points in the workflow; suppliers, in turn, have the responsibility to deliver high-quality and on-time inputs to the next point. The notion of customer service applies equally well to workflows within the organisation as well as to the relationship between the organisation and its ultimate consumers in the external environment.

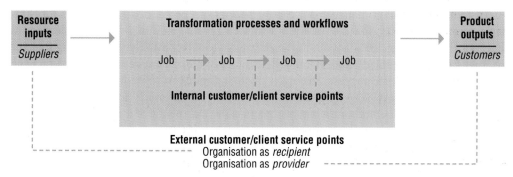

Figure 2.3 ▸ The importance of external and internal customers

What customers want

Customers sit at the top when organisations are viewed as the upside-down pyramids described in chapter 1. And without any doubt, customers put today's organisations to a very stiff test. They primarily want three things in the goods and services they buy — high-quality, low-cost and on-time delivery. Offering them anything less is unacceptable.

Organisations that can't meet these customer expectations suffer the market consequences — they lose competitive advantage. Some time ago, for example, Intel Corporation faced a crisis in customer confidence when a defect was found in one of its Pentium chips. At first, top management of this highly regarded company baulked at replacing the chips, suggesting that the defect wasn't really important. But customers were angry and unrelenting in their complaints. Eventually the customers won, as they should. Intel agreed to replace the chips without any questions asked. The company also learned two important lessons of successful businesses today: (1) always protect your reputation for quality products — it is hard to get and easy to lose, and (2) always treat your customers right — they, too, are hard to get and easy to lose.

Customer relationship management

When pursued relentlessly as a goal, customer service can be an important source of competitive advantage. Just imagine the ramifications if every customer or client contact for an organisation was positive. Not only would they return again as members of a loyal customer base, but they would also tell others and expand the size of that base. Progressive managers understand this concept and work hard to establish and maintain high standards of customer service. They try to provide every customer with goods and services that are high in quality and low in cost, meet their needs and require only short waiting times. Operating a business or other type of organisation with a customer-centred focus that strategically tries to build relationships and add value to customers is known as **customer relationship management (CRM)**.

The use of CRM in pursuit of competitive advantage is rapidly evolving with the support of information technology that allows organisations to maintain intense communication with customers as well as to gather and use data regarding their needs and desires. At Marriott International, for example, CRM is supported by special customer management software that tracks information on customer preferences. When you check in, the likelihood is that

⚙ **Customer relationship management (CRM)** strategically tries to build lasting relationships and add value to customers.

your past requests for things like a king-size bed, no smoking room and computer modem access will already be entered in your record. Says Marriott's chairman: 'It's a big competitive advantage'.[14]

Customer relationship management clearly belongs on the list of any manager's top strategic priorities. *Business Review Weekly* interviewed several prominent business leaders to find out the big issues for Australia in the next few years. Leonie Clyne, managing director of Angus Clyne, identified expectations of customers for excellent service as a major issue for all organisations. She suggests that even small and medium-size companies will need to introduce customer-service programs to manage these expectations.[15] To meet the challenge, organisations must first find out what customers want and then give it to them. This simple prescription is at the heart of a comprehensive strategy for CRM.

Just as organisations need to manage customers on the output side, they are also customers of their suppliers. Supplier relationships must be well managed too. The concept of **supply chain management** involves strategic management of all operations relating an organisation to the suppliers of its resources, including purchasing, manufacturing, transportation and distribution.[16] The goals of supply chain management are straightforward — achieve efficiency in all aspects of the chain while ensuring the necessary flow and on-time availability of quality resources for customer-driven operations.[17]

> **Supply chain management** strategically links all operations dealing with resource supplies.

QUALITY-DRIVEN ORGANISATIONS

If managing for high performance and competitive advantage is the theme of the day, 'quality' is one of its most important watchwords. Customers want quality whether they are buying a consumer product or receiving a service. The achievement of quality objectives in all aspects of operations is a universal criterion of organisational performance in manufacturing and service industries alike. The competitive demands of a global economy are an important force in this race toward total quality operations. The **ISO certification** standards set by the International Organization for Standardization in Geneva, Switzerland, have been adopted by many countries of the world as quality benchmarks. Businesses that want to compete as 'world-class companies' in delivering consistent quality are increasingly expected to have ISO 9000 certification at various levels. To gain certification in this family of standards, they must refine and upgrade quality in all operations and then undergo a rigorous assessment by outside auditors to determine whether they meet ISO requirements. Increasingly, the ISO 'stamp of approval' is viewed as a necessity in international business — the ISO certification provides customers with assurance that a set of solid quality standards and processes are in place. In respect to quality of environmental management systems, for example, the new ISO 14000 series is now setting international standards.

> **ISO certification** indicates conformance with a rigorous set of international quality standards.

Total quality management

The term **total quality management** (TQM) was introduced in chapter 1. It describes the process of making quality principles part of the organisation's strategic objectives, applying them to all aspects of operations, committing to continuous improvement, and striving to meet customers' needs by doing things right the first time. The quality movement around the world has been strongly influenced by the pioneering work of W. Edwards Deming and Joseph M. Juran. Interestingly, their ideas became popular in Japan starting in the early 1950s and gained prominence in Western countries only after the Japanese became so successful in world markets by competing with a product quality advantage.[18] The commitment

> **Total quality management** is managing with commitment to continuous improvement, product quality and customer satisfaction.

to total quality operations is now a way of life in world-class organisations everywhere. The Australian Business Excellence Awards are the showcase for Australian organisations that have achieved high performance across 12 principles in business excellence according to a quality framework.

There are many quality improvement approaches being tested and used around the world. Most begin with an insistence that the total quality commitment applies to everyone in an organisation and to all aspects of operations, right from resource acquisition through to the production and distribution of finished goods and services.[19] One well-known consultant, Philip Crosby, became quite famous for offering these 'four absolutes' of management for total quality control: (1) *quality means conformance to standards* — workers must know exactly what performance standards they are expected to meet; (2) *quality comes from defect prevention, not defect correction* — leadership, training and discipline must prevent defects in the first place; (3) *quality as a performance standard must mean defect-free work* — the only acceptable quality standard is perfect work; and, (4) *quality saves money* — doing things right the first time saves the cost of correcting poor work.[20]

Quality and continuous improvement

Among the many approaches to quality commitment, the work of W. Edwards Deming is another useful benchmark. The story begins in 1951 when he was invited to Japan to explain quality control techniques that had been developed in the USA. The result was a lifelong relationship epitomised in the Deming prize, which is still annually awarded in Japan for excellence in quality. 'When Deming spoke', we might say, 'the Japanese listened'. The principles he taught the Japanese were straightforward ... and they worked: tally defects, analyse and trace them to the source, make corrections, and keep a record of what happens afterward.[21] Deming's '14 points to quality' emphasise constant innovation, use of statistical methods and commitment to training in the fundamentals of quality assurance.[22]

The search for quality is closely tied to the emphasis on **continuous improvement** — always looking for new ways to improve on current performance.[23] A basic philosophy of total quality management is that one can never be satisfied — something always can and should be improved on. Continuous improvement must be a way of life. Another important aspect of total quality operations is cycle time — the elapsed time between receipt of an order and delivery of the finished product. The quality objective here is to reduce cycle time by finding ways to serve customer needs more quickly.

One way to combine employee involvement and continuous improvement is through the popular **quality circle** concept.[24] This is a group of workers (usually no more than ten) who meet regularly to discuss ways of improving the quality of their products or services. Their objective is to assume responsibility for quality and apply every member's full creative potential to ensure that it is achieved. Such worker empowerment can result in cost savings from improved quality and greater customer satisfaction. It can also improve morale and commitment, as the following remarks from quality circle members indicate: 'This is the best thing the company has done in 15 years ... The program proves that supervisors have no monopoly on brains ... It gives me more pride in my work.'[25]

Quality, technology and design

This is the age of technology, and technology utilisation has a major role to play in the quality aspects of operations. In retailing, for example, Levi Strauss & Company has a program called 'Personal Pair' which uses flexible manufacturing systems to offer jeans made to

GET CONNECTED!

Learn more about the standards for business and quality excellence in Australia and New Zealand at the web sites www.businessexcellence australia.com.au and www.businessexcellence.co.nz.

GET CONNECTED!

Continuous improvement involves always searching for new ways to improve operations quality and performance.

A **quality circle** is a group of employees who periodically meet to discuss ways of improving work quality.

CONNECTION

Diversity

University of Southern Queensland

Promoting multiculturalism
www.usq.edu.au

Managing diversity is a pathway to competitive advantage. This is evident at an organisation such as the University of Southern Queensland (USQ), which has proven itself as a world leader in actively promoting multiculturalism on and off campus. It has launched a Register of Languages to help overcome any cultural and language difficulties that may present a barrier to understanding or learning. USQ has won two marketing awards from the Ethnic Affairs Commission of New South Wales for its success in attracting foreign students. USQ has a strong organisational culture of incorporating the appreciation of cultural diversity into its policies and practices. It also promotes and advances the development of multiculturalism and improved community relations, and provides substantial assistance in the settlement process of individuals and groups who have migrated to Australia from overseas. USQ is committed to significantly contributing to the support of harmony, the reduction of prejudice and the combat of discrimination in the community. These values create value for its multicultural staff and students.

Questions

Are you ready for a career working in, and helping to lead, a truly multicultural organisation?

How can managing diversity lead to competitive advantage?

someone's personal measurements. Tamawood Homes is another organisation that uses the latest developments in computer-aided design, computerised estimating and project management to provide numerous plans from which clients can choose. These plans can then be customised to the specifications of potential homeowners. And the Tin Box Asia Pacific's web site means that businesses all over the world can order unique tin box packaging on line.

These are all examples of how new technologies are changing the nature of manufacturing and improving both quality and efficiency of operations. Among the terms describing these developments, *lean production* uses new technologies to streamline systems and allow work to be performed with fewer workers and smaller inventories. The use of *flexible manufacturing* allows processes to be changed quickly and efficiently to produce different products or modifications to existing ones. Through such techniques as *agile manufacturing* and *mass customisation*, organisations are able to make individualised products quickly and with production efficiencies once only associated with the mass production of uniform products.[26] All such systems use computer-based technologies to better integrate the various aspects of manufacturing with customer preferences. They allow modifications to be made quickly, with high quality and in a cost-efficient fashion.

Another timely and important contribution to quality management is found in product design. We are all aware of design differences among products, be they cars, computers, mobile phones, stereos, watches, clothes or whatever. But what may not be recognised is that design makes a difference in how things are produced and at what level of cost and quality. A 'good' design has eye appeal to the customer and is easy to manufacture with productivity. In today's competitive global economy, such designs are strategic weapons. 'Design is it', says consultant Tom Peters, arguing that it will be the key to competitive advantage in the future.[27]

Progressive manufacturers now emphasise *design for manufacturing*. This means that products are styled to lower production costs and smooth the way toward high-quality results in all aspects of the manufacturing processes.[28] Styling is now often developed on the computer and then tested via simulation for its manufacturing implications. Teamwork among engineering, production, marketing and other functional areas is also improving the design process. A manufacturing approach that shows respect for the natural environment is *design for disassembly*. The goal is to design products taking into account how their component parts will be reused at the end of product life. For example, automakers are using more parts that can be recycled — computer makers are now more willing to take back obsolete machines, disassemble them and recycle the parts.

INTERNAL ENVIRONMENT AND ORGANISATIONAL CULTURE

Culture is a popular word in management these days. Important differences in national cultures will be discussed in chapter 5 on the global dimensions of management. Now it is time to talk about cultural differences in the internal environments of organisations. **Organisational culture** is defined by noted scholar and consultant Edgar Schein as the system of shared beliefs and values that develops within an organisation and guides the behaviour of its members.[29] Sometimes called the *corporate culture*, it is a key aspect of any organisation and work setting. Whenever someone, for example, speaks of 'the way we do things here', they are talking about the culture.

⚙ Organisational culture is the system of shared beliefs and values that develops within an organisation and guides the behaviour of its members.

What strong cultures do

Although it is clear that culture is not the sole determinant of what happens in organisations, it is an important influence on what they accomplish … and how. The internal culture has the potential to shape attitudes, reinforce common beliefs, direct behaviour and establish performance expectations and the motivation to fulfil them. A widely discussed study of successful businesses concluded that organisational culture made a major contribution to their long-term performance records.[30] Importantly, the cultures in these organisations provided for a clear vision of what the organisation was attempting to accomplish, allowing individuals to rally around the vision and work hard to support and accomplish it. In these and related ways, organisational culture is a bond that further mobilises resources for action.[31]

Strong cultures, ones that are clear and well defined and widely shared among members, discourage dysfunctional work behaviours and encourage positive ones. They commit members to do things for and with one another that are in the best interests of the organisation, and then they reinforce these habits. The best organisations have strong cultures that show respect for members and encourage adaptability and continuous improvement in all areas of operations. They are likely to have cultures that are performance-oriented, emphasise teamwork, allow for risk taking, encourage innovation and make the wellbeing of people a top management priority.[32] Honda is a good example. The firm's culture is tightly focused around what is known as 'The Honda Way' — a set of principles emphasising ambition, respect for ideas, open communication, work enjoyment, harmony and hard work.

Levels of organisational culture

Organisational culture is usually described from the perspective of the two levels shown in figure 2.4 — the 'observable' culture and the 'core' culture.[33] The *observable culture* is visible — it is what one sees and hears when walking around an organisation as a visitor, a customer or an employee. In strong culture organisations the observable culture will be readily apparent. It can be seen in the way people dress at work, how they arrange their offices, how they speak to and behave toward one another, the nature of their conversations and how they talk about and treat their customers. More formally stated, the observable culture includes the following elements of daily organisational life — through them, new members learn the organisation's culture and all members share and reinforce its special aspects over time:

- *stories* — oral histories and tales, told and retold among members, about dramatic sagas and incidents in the life of the organisation
- *heroes* — the people singled out for special attention and whose accomplishments are recognised with praise and admiration among members; they include founders and role models

Elements in the observable culture of organisations

www.hp.com.au
www.hp.co.nz

With the boundaries between work and home blurring, innovative employers are redesigning the work community. Hewlett-Packard helps employees achieve a work-life balance. Most employees are free to choose their working and office hours as long as management objectives are met. The company supports this by providing mobile phones, laptops and home modem connections.[34]

⚙ **Core values** are underlying beliefs shared by members of the organisation and that influence their behaviour.

- *rites and rituals* — the ceremonies and meetings, planned and spontaneous, that celebrate important occasions and performance accomplishments
- *symbols* — the special use of language and other non-verbal expressions to communicate important themes of organisational life.

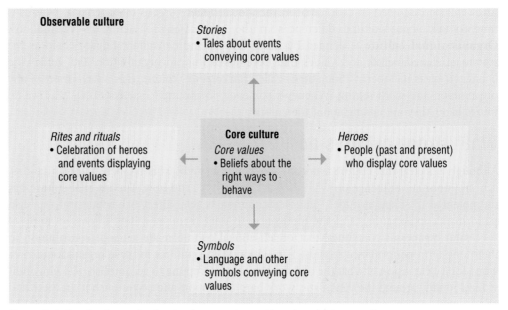

Figure 2.4 ▸ Levels of organisational culture — observable culture and core culture

Standing at the foundation of what one directly observes in the daily life of an organisation is a second and deeper level of culture. This is the core culture, and it determines why things are this way. It consists of **core values** or underlying assumptions and beliefs that influence behaviour and actually give rise to the aspects of observable culture just described. Values are essential to strong culture organisations and are often widely publicised in formal statements of corporate mission and purpose. Strong culture organisations operate with a small but enduring set of core values. Researchers point out that the enduring commitment to core values is a major ingredient of organisations that achieve long-term success. Highly successful companies typically emphasise the values of performance excellence, innovation, social responsibility, integrity, worker involvement, customer service and teamwork. Examples of core values that drive companies such as Australian Postal Corporation, winner of the Australian Good Reputation Index, include: to act with integrity and fairness, to recognise the needs of the community, to be commercially competitive, to foster a performance-driven culture, to create a safe, challenging and fun workplace, to encourage innovation and technological leadership. The reputation index examines, through the perceptions of stakeholders and experts, activities that directly contribute to reputation.[35]

Leadership and organisational culture

Leadership of the organisational culture involves establishing and maintaining appropriate core values. Whereas this is most often considered a top management job, the same definition holds for any manager or team leader at any level of responsibility. Just like the organisation as a whole, any work team or group will have a culture. How well this culture operates to support the group and its performance objectives will depend in part on the strength of the core values. At any level, these values should meet the test of these three criteria: (1) *relevance* — core values should support key performance objectives; (2) *pervasiveness* — core values should be known by all members of the organisation or group; and (3) *strength* — core values should be accepted by everyone involved.[36]

Attention is now being increasingly given to the concept of a **symbolic leader**, someone who uses symbols well to establish and maintain a desired organisational culture. Symbolic managers and leaders talk the 'language' of the organisation. They are always careful to use spoken and written words to describe people, events and even the competition in ways that reinforce and communicate core values. *Language metaphors* — the use of positive examples from another context — are very powerful in this regard. For example, Lend Lease, a fully integrated global real estate group, maintains that 'we are always looking at the stars, even as we keep our eyes on budgets, time and other rigorous metrics'.[37]

Good symbolic leaders highlight the observable culture. They tell key *stories* over and over again, and they encourage others to tell them. They often refer to the 'founding story' about the entrepreneur whose personal values set a key tone for the enterprise. They often talk about organisational *heroes*, past and present, whose performances exemplify core values. They often use symbolic rites and rituals that glorify the performance of the organisation and its members. At Mary Kay Cosmetics, gala events at which top sales performers share their tales of success are legendary. So too are the lavish incentive awards presented at these ceremonies, especially the pink luxury cars given to the most successful salespeople.[38]

DIVERSITY AND MULTICULTURAL ORGANISATIONS

At the very time that we talk about the culture of an organisation as a whole, we must also recognise the presence of diversity. Organisations are made up of people, each of whom comes as a unique individual. An important key to competitive advantage is respecting this diversity and allowing everyone's talents to be fully utilised.

As first introduced in chapter 1, **diversity** is a term used to describe differences among people at work. Primary dimensions of diversity include age, race, ethnicity, gender, physical ability and sexual orientation. But workplace diversity is a broader issue still, including also such things as religious beliefs, education, experience and family status, among others.[39] In his book, *Beyond Race and Gender*, consultant R. Roosevelt Thomas Jr makes the point that 'diversity includes everyone'. He says: 'In this expanded context, white males are as diverse as their colleagues'.[40] Thomas also links diversity and organisational culture, believing that the way people are treated at work — with respect and inclusion, or with disrespect and exclusion — is a direct reflection of the organisation's culture.

Thomas's diversity message to those who lead and manage organisations is straight to the point. Diversity is a potential source of competitive advantage, offering organisations a mixture of talents and perspectives that is ready and able to deal with the complexities and uncertainty in the ever-changing 21st-century environment. If you do the right things in organisational leadership, in other words, you'll gain competitive advantage through diversity. If you don't, you'll lose it.

What is a multicultural organisation?

A key issue in the culture of any organisation is *inclusivity* — the degree to which the organisation is open to anyone who can perform a job, regardless of their race, sexual preference, gender or other diversity attribute.[41] The term **multiculturalism** refers to pluralism and

A **symbolic leader** uses symbols to establish and maintain a desired organisational culture.

The term **diversity** describes race, gender, age and other individual differences.

Multiculturalism involves pluralism and respect for diversity.

A **multicultural organisation** is based on pluralism and operates with respect for diversity.

Characteristics of multicultural organisations

respect for diversity in the workplace. There is no reason why organisational cultures cannot communicate core values and encourage common work directions that respect and empower the full demographic and cultural diversity that is now characteristic of our work-forces. The 'best' organisational cultures in this sense are inclusive. They value the talents, ideas and creative potential of all members. The model in this regard is the truly **multicultural organisation** with these characteristics:[42]

- *Pluralism*. Members of both minority cultures and majority cultures are influential in setting key values and policies.
- *Structural integration*. Minority-culture members are well represented in jobs at all levels and in all functional responsibilities.
- *Informal network integration*. Various forms of mentoring and support groups assist in the career development of minority-culture members.
- *Absence of prejudice and discrimination*. A variety of training and task force activities continually deal with the need to eliminate culture-group biases.
- *Minimum intergroup conflict*. Diversity does not lead to destructive conflicts between members of majority and minority cultures.

Organisational subcultures

 Subcultures are common to groups of people with similar values and beliefs based on shared work responsibilities and personal characteristics.

Like society as a whole, organisations contain a mixture of **subcultures** — that is, cultures common to groups of people with similar values and beliefs based on shared work responsi-bilities and personal characteristics. There are *occupational cultures* in organisations, and they must be understood for their work and managerial implications.[43] For example, salaried professionals such as lawyers, scientists, engineers and accountants have been described as having special needs for work autonomy and empowerment that may conflict with tra-ditional management methods of top-down direction and control.[44] Unless these needs are recognised and properly dealt with, salaried professionals may prove difficult to integrate into the culture of the larger organisation.

There are also *functional subcultures* in organisations, and people from different functions often have difficulty understanding and working well with one another. For example, employees of a business may consider themselves 'systems people' or 'marketing people' or 'manufacturing people' or 'finance people'. When such identities are overemphasised, there is a tendency to separate in-group members from the rest of the organisation. Members of the functional groups may spend most of their time with each other, develop a 'jargon' or technical language that is shared among themselves, and view their role in the organisation as more important than the contributions of the other functions.

Differences in *ethnic or national cultures* are discussed in chapter 5 on the global dimen-sions of management.[45] Although it is relatively easy to recognise that people from various countries and regions of the world may represent different cultural backgrounds, it is far harder to turn this awareness into the ability to work well with persons whose ethnic cultures differ from our own. The best understanding is most likely gained through direct contact and a personal commitment to remain open-minded when working with persons from different ethnic backgrounds. As imprecise as our understanding of ethnic subcultures may be, things seem even less clear on matters of race. Importantly, a key question remains largely unanswered: Where can we find frameworks for understanding ethnic and racial subcultures? If improved cross-cultural understandings can help people work better across national boundaries, why can't improved cross-cultural understandings help people from different racial subcultures work better together?

A matter of trust

A joint study by the Australian Institute of Management and Monash University shows that many managers don't feel their staff trust them. Caring for colleagues and active involvement in the company's vision seem to be very important.[46]

If you are currently working, do you trust your boss?

We live at a time when the influence of *generational subcultures* at work is of growing importance. But the issues are more subtle than young–old issues alone. It is possible to identify 'generational gaps' among 'baby boomers' now in their 50s, 'generation Xers' now in their 30s and early 40s, 'nexters' now in their 20s, and the 'millennial generation' in high school at the turn of the century. Members of these generations grew up and are growing up in quite different worlds — they have been and are being influenced by different values and opportunities. Their work preferences and attitudes tend to reflect the influence of those differences. Someone who is 60 years old today, a common age for senior managers, was 15 in the 1950s. They may have difficulty understanding, supervising and working with younger managers who were teenagers during the 1970s, 1980s and even the 1990s. And if you are one of the latter generations — perhaps the millennial generation, you'll need to ponder how well you will do in the future when working with colleagues who grew up in the early years of the 21st century.[47]

Issues of gender relationships and gender discrimination also continue to complicate the workplace. Some research shows that when men work together, a group culture forms around a competitive atmosphere, in which the games and stories deal with winning and losing in various situations. It also often involves the use of sport metaphors.[48] When women work together, a rather different culture may form, with more emphasis on personal relationships and collaboration. One can reasonably ask: What happens when *gender subcultures* mix in the organisation?

Challenges faced by minority groups and women

The very term *diversity* basically means the presence of differences. But what does it mean when those differences are distributed unequally across organisational levels or among work functions? What difference does it make when one subculture is in 'majority' status while others become 'minorities' in respect to representation with the organisation? For example, even though organisations are changing today, it is still the case that most senior executives in large organisations are older, white and male. There is still likely to be more workforce diversity at lower and middle levels of most organisations than at the top. Take a look at the situation described by figure 2.5. What are the implications for members of minority groups such as women, disabled people, people from non-English-speaking backgrounds or people of colour in organisations traditionally dominated by a majority culture, such as white males? Consider disability discrimination. This type of discrimination occurs when a person is treated unfairly or badly compared with others as a result of their having an impairment or disability. Very often this happens because people have unfair, old-fashioned, stereotypical or prejudiced ideas or beliefs about people with disabilities. Discriminations could also occur indirectly when a condition, rule or policy that seems to be fair or neutral has a negative impact on people with a particular disability or impairment. For example, it would be indirect discrimination against those with visual impairments if everyone were required to provide a drivers licence for identification, because a visually impaired person is ineligible for such a licence and therefore would not be able to comply with the requirement.[49]

The daily work challenges faced by minority cultures or populations in organisations can range from having to deal with misunderstandings and lack of sensitivity on the one hand to suffering harassment and discrimination, active or subtle, on the other. *Sexual harassment* in the form of unwanted sexual advances, requests for sexual favours, and sexually laced communications is a problem female employees in particular may face. Minority-group workers can also be targets of cultural jokes — one survey reports some 45 per cent of respondents had been the targets of such abuse. Discrimination against pregnant women is another issue. All parties to the employment relationship should be well informed about their rights and

GET CONNECTED!

Explore the workforce projections, statistics and other reports for New Zealand, Australia and Singapore. For New Zealand, the data could be found at Statistics New Zealand www.stats.govt.nz; for Australia, at the Australian Bureau of Statistics www.abs.gov.au; and for Singapore, at Statistics Singapore www.singstat.gov.sg.

GET CONNECTED!

REALITY CHECK ✔

How does age affect attitude?

Data collected from 4000 executives show correlations between age and personality traits related to work effectiveness. Patience improves with age, blossoming (the data say) after the age of 45.

Is this your experience?

responsibilities with regards to workplace discrimination. During the National Pregnancy and Work Inquiry this was repeatedly voiced. The inquiry was provided with information indicating that discrimination on the basis of pregnancy and the inability to obtain paid maternity leave are significant factors contributing to Australian women and their partners deciding to not have children or to limit the size of their families. The EEO Trust in New Zealand advises employers on how to avoid discriminatory practices and improve good workplace relationships. It recommends employers adopt a flexible policy in relation to parental leave. In 2002, New Zealand introduced government-funded paid maternity leave — Australia and the USA are the only OECD countries with no paid maternity leave.[50] Minority-group members may also face *job discrimination*. Microsoft, for example, has been criticised as treating the firm's 5000 or more temporary workers unfairly in terms of access to benefits and work assignments. Some temporaries (who wear orange identification badges at work) claim that they are treated as second-class citizens by the permanent employees (who wear blue badges).[51]

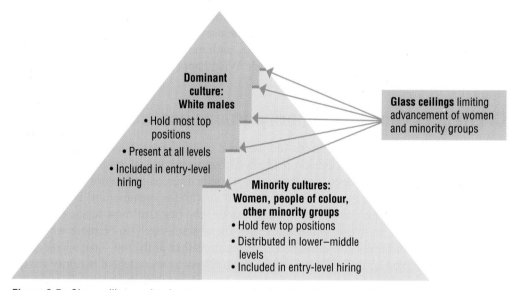

Figure 2.5 ▸ Glass ceilings as barriers to women and minority cultures in traditional organisations

Sometimes the adaptation of minority groups to organisations dominated by a majority culture takes the form of tendencies toward *biculturalism* — the display by members of minority cultures of characteristics of the majority culture that seem necessary to success in the organisational environment. For example, one might find gays and lesbians hiding their sexual orientation from coworkers out of fear of prejudice or discrimination. Similarly, one might find a person from a non-English-speaking background carefully training herself to not use at work certain words or phrases that might be considered part of her cultural slang.

The special economic and work challenges faced by minority groups are not always highly visible. We all know, for example, that the last decade was one of global economic expansion. But how many of us know that disabled workers largely failed to share in the gains? At the same time that demand for workers in general rose, the employment rate of the disabled fell. For example, in 2000 the representation of people with a disability in the New South Wales public sector was estimated at 6 per cent (a decline from 7 per cent in 1999) and people with a disability requiring work-related adjustments as 1.9 per cent (a decline from 2.2 per cent in 1999).[52] While debate continues on the causes of the decline, the need to do more to improve work opportunities for the disabled is indisputable.

Managing diversity

There's no doubt today what minority-group workers want.[53] They want the same thing everyone wants. They want respect for their talents and a work setting that allows them to achieve to their full potential. It takes the best in diversity leadership at all levels of organisational management to meet these expectations. R. Roosevelt Thomas Jr defines **managing diversity** as the process of comprehensively developing a work environment that is for everyone. He says that it involves creating an internal environment that allows 'all kinds of people to reach their full potential' in the pursuit of organisational objectives.

> **Managing diversity** is building an inclusive work environment that allows everyone to reach their full potential.

POINT ← / ↑ COUNTER

The downside of affirmative action

There has been a steady push for equality in countries such as Australia and New Zealand over the past decades. However, forums, such as the Endeavour Forum www.endeavourforum.org.au are increasingly voicing concerns about issues like affirmative action. They argue that in the drive to create equality for women in the workplace, men are slowly being marginalised, and that those who may not be deserving of benefits are being rewarded. The view is also being held that affirmative action actually disadvantages innocent men for the alleged 'crimes' of past generations and that two wrongs do not make a right. Furthermore, it is felt that women who have not been the 'victims' of past discrimination are being rewarded. In a submission to the Affirmative Action Agency, the Endeavour Forum argued that men are too busy helping women and are therefore disadvantaging themselves in the process.[54]

What is your view on this very controversial issue?

Figure 2.6 describes managing diversity as the most comprehensive of three leadership approaches to diversity. The first is **affirmative action**, in which leadership commits the organisation to hiring and advancing minority groups and women. The second is *valuing diversity*, in which leadership commits the organisation to education and training programs designed to help people better understand and respect individual differences. The third is *managing diversity*, in which leadership commits to changing the organisational culture to empower and include all people. For Thomas, managing diversity offers the most value in respect to competitive advantage.[55]

> **Affirmative action** commits the organisation to hiring and advancing minority groups and women.

Affirmative action
Create upward mobility for minority groups and women

Valuing differences
Build quality relationships with respect for diversity

Managing diversity
Achieve full utilisation of diverse human resources

Figure 2.6 ▸ Multicultural organisations — from affirmative action to managing diversity

Source: Developed from R. Roosevelt Thomas Jr, *Beyond Race and Gender* (New York: AMACOM, 1992), p. 28.

A diverse workforce offers a rich pool of talents, ideas and viewpoints useful for solving the complex problems of highly competitive and often uncertain environments. When well managed, this diversity becomes a major asset. A diverse workforce is best aligned with the needs and expectations of a diverse customer and supplier base, including those increasingly distributed around the world and among its cultures. For example, Lucent Technologies' clients come from diverse markets throughout the world. To help understand the needs of the global marketplace, Lucent Technologies has developed a workforce that reflects that diversity through all areas of its business.[56]

Organisations that Thomas calls 'diversity mature' are well positioned to derive these and other sources of competitive advantage. In these organisations there is a diversity mission as well as an organisational mission — diversity is viewed as a strategic imperative and the members understand diversity concepts.[57] Ultimately, however, he considers the basic building block of a diversity-mature organisation to be the *diversity-mature individual*. This is someone who can positively and honestly answer questions such as those posed in Manager's Notepad 2.2.[58]

MANAGER'S NOTEPAD 2.2

Are you mature on diversity?

- Do you accept responsibility for improving your performance?
- Do you accept responsibility for improving the performance of your organisation?
- Do you understand yourself and your organisation?
- Do you understand important diversity concepts?
- Do you make decisions involving differences based on ability to meet job requirements?
- Do you understand that diversity is complex and accompanied by tensions?
- Are you able to cope with tensions when dealing with diversity?
- Are you willing to challenge the way things are?
- Are you willing to learn continuously?

Managing diversity is both a personal and organisational challenge. On a personal level, it means accepting the goal of diversity maturity as described in the notepad. As an organisation, it means committing leadership to making fundamental changes in the organisational culture and its guiding mission and practices. Managers and people working at all levels of responsibility must benefit from a strong organisational culture based on true participation, involvement and empowerment. Such cultures value the talents, ideas and creative potential of all members, not just the majority members.

Perhaps the most important word in human resource management today is 'inclusiveness'. By valuing diversity and building multicultural organisations that include everyone, we can strengthen organisations and bring them into better alignment with the challenges and opportunities of today's environment. Importantly, the foundations of future success will be built on the foundations of diversity. As Michael R. Losey, president of the Society for Human Resource Management (SHRM) says: 'Companies must realise that the talent pool includes people of all types, including older workers; persons with disabilities; persons of various religious, cultural and national backgrounds; persons who are not heterosexual; minorities; and women'.[59]

GET CONNECTED!

@ Visit Window on the World www.windowontheworldinc.com for business tips on diversity among the world's cultures.

GET CONNECTED!

CHAPTER 2
Study guide

The chapter 2 study guide helps you review the chapter content, prepare for examinations, apply what you have learned and further build your career readiness. The summary briefly answers the study questions posed at the start of the chapter. The list of key terms allows you to double-check your familiarity with basic concepts and definitions. The applied activities help you test your comprehension of chapter content. Suggestions offered as career readiness activities direct your attention to relevant sections of the Career Readiness Workbook where you can test and develop your career skills and apply what you have learned. The list of electronic resources suggests activities from the *Management: An Asia–Pacific Perspective* web site and, finally, the case for critical thinking helps you apply your new management knowledge.

SUMMARY

What is the external environment of organisations?

- Competitive advantage and distinctive competency can only be achieved by organisations that deal successfully with dynamic and complex environments.
- The external environment of organisations consists of both general and specific components.
- The general environment includes background conditions that influence the organisation, including economic, sociocultural, legal–political, technological and natural environment conditions.
- The specific or task environment consists of the actual organisations, groups and persons an organisation deals with, including suppliers, customers, competitors, regulators and pressure groups.
- Environmental uncertainty challenges organisations and their management to be flexible and responsive to new and changing conditions.

What is a customer-driven organisation?

- Any organisation must develop and maintain a base of loyal customers or clients, and a customer-driven organisation recognises customer service and product quality as foundations of competitive advantage.
- Customer service is a core ingredient of total quality operations, and it includes concerns for both internal customers and external customers.
- The 'upside-down pyramid' is a symbol of how organisations of today are refocusing on customers and on the role of managers to support work efforts to continually improve quality and customer service.
- Operations management is specifically concerned with activities and decisions through which organisations transform resource inputs into product outputs.
- Today, operations management is increasingly viewed in a strategic perspective and with close attention to the demands of productivity, quality and competitive advantage.

What is a quality-driven organisation?

- To compete in the global economy, organisations are increasingly expected to meet ISO 9000 certification standards of quality.
- Total quality management involves making quality a strategic objective of the organisation and supporting it by continuous improvement efforts.
- The commitment to total quality operations requires meeting customers' needs — on time, the first time and all the time.
- The use of quality circles — groups of employees working to solve quality problems — is a form of employee involvement in quality management.

What is the internal environment and organisational culture?

- The internal environment of organisations includes organisational culture, which establishes a personality for the organisation as a whole and has a strong influence on the behaviour of its members.
- The observable culture is found in the rites, rituals, stories, heroes and symbols of the organisation.
- The core culture consists of the core values and fundamental beliefs on which the organisation is based.
- In organisations with strong cultures, members behave with shared understandings that support the accomplishment of key organisational objectives.
- Symbolic managers are good at building shared values and using stories, ceremonies, heroes and language to reinforce these values in daily affairs.

How is diversity managed in a multicultural organisation?

- The organisational culture should display a positive ethical climate or shared set of understandings about what is considered ethically correct behaviour.
- Multicultural organisations operate through a culture that values pluralism and respects diversity.
- Organisational cultures typically include the existence of many subcultures, including those based on occupational, functional, ethnic, racial, age and gender differences in a diverse workforce.
- Challenges faced by organisational minority groups include sexual harassment, pay discrimination, job discrimination and the glass ceiling effect.
- Managing diversity is the process of developing a work environment that is inclusive and allows everyone to reach their full work potential.
- Diversity leadership helps mobilise the full talents of an organisation to achieve and sustain competitive advantage.

KEY TERMS

affirmative action (p. 51)

competitive advantage (p. 36)

continuous improvement (p. 43)

core values (p. 46)

customer relationship management (CRM) (p. 41)

diversity (p. 47)

environmental uncertainty (p. 39)

general environment (p. 37)

ISO certification (p. 42)

managing diversity (p. 51)

multicultural organisation (p. 48)

multiculturalism (p. 47)

organisational culture (p. 45)

quality circle (p. 43)

specific environment (p. 38)

stakeholders (p. 38)

subcultures (p. 48)

supply chain management (p. 42)

symbolic leader (p. 47)

total quality management (p. 42)

APPLIED ACTIVITIES

Short-response questions

1. What operating objectives are appropriate for an organisation seeking competitive advantage through improved customer service?
2. What is the difference between an organisation's external customers and its internal customers?
3. What is the difference between the observable and core cultures of an organisation?
4. Why is it important for managers to understand subcultures in organisations?

Application question

5. Two businesswomen, former university classmates, are discussing their jobs and careers over lunch. You overhear one saying to the other: 'I work for a large corporation, while you own a small retail business. In my company there is strong corporate culture and everyone feels its influence. In fact, we are always expected to act in ways that support the culture and serve as role models for others to do so as well. This includes a commitment to diversity and multiculturalism. Because of the small size of your business, things like corporate culture, diversity and multiculturalism are not so important to worry about.' Do you agree or disagree with this statement? Why?

CAREER READINESS ACTIVITIES

Recommended individual and group learning activities from the end-of-text Career Readiness Workbook for this chapter include:

Career advancement portfolio   **WB**

Update your career advancement portfolio to reflect your new skills and experiences. Include skills and personal insights you gain from the following projects and exercises.

Research and presentation projects   `WB`

- Project 1 — Diversity lessons — 'what have we learned?'
- Project 2 — Changing corporate cultures

Cross-functional integrative case   `WB`

Read the integrative case on Sarina Russo and answer the following questions:

2.1 Undertake a search on the Internet and/or in the Yellow Pages.

(a) What organisations would you identify as key competitors to Sarina Russo Job Access?

(b) What competitive advantages do they have in comparison to Sarina Russo Job Access?

2.2 Identify one point from the following factors in the general environment that could relate to Sarina Russo Job Access: economic, sociocultural, legal–political and technological conditions.

2.3 What might be the key areas of environmental uncertainty faced by Sarina Russo Job Access?

Exercises in teamwork   `WB`

- Exercise 3 — Defining quality
- Exercise 20 — Gender differences in management

Management skills assessment   `WB`

- Assessment 2 — Cross-cultural skills and attitudes

ELECTRONIC RESOURCES

Don't forget to take full advantage of the online support for *Management: An Asia–Pacific Perspective* at www.johnwiley.com.au/highered/management: chapter 2 practice tests, e-flashcards, crossword puzzles, interactive management skills assessments, interactive cases, the online career advancement portfolio and much more!

CASE FOR CRITICAL THINKING

Read the following case for critical thinking on The Coca-Cola Company. While you are reading the case keep in mind what you have learned in this chapter, then answer the questions.

As one of the world's best-known brands, Coca-Cola endured some important changes in the latter half of the 1990s. Chief executive of 17 years Roberto Goizueta passed away in 1997. During Goizueta's tenure at Coca-Cola, the market value dramatically increased from US$4 billion in 1981 to nearly US$150 billion today. This makes him one of the greatest value creators in history. Former chief financial officer Douglas Ivester was appointed as his replacement. Many investors wondered if Coke could continue its incredible pace in the global soft drink market.

Coca-Cola's global dominance

The larger a company is, the harder it is to continue to grow at a steady pace. This was the major challenge facing The Coca-Cola Company in the late 1990s. The US market had already been well developed, with an average of 296 servings of Coke products consumed by every man, woman and child.[60] But the company had not introduced a major new product in nearly ten years. Demand for diet drinks — the fastest growing soft drinks of the 1980s — had levelled off, and demand for cola-flavoured drinks had begun to decrease.[61] According to a former Coke executive: 'The problem was that Diet Coke was driving the engine and everybody was living off that'.[62]

Meanwhile, the competition had not been sleeping. Pepsi was test-marketing a colourless cola, Crystal Pepsi, in response to consumer interest in clear flavoured waters and seltzers. Pepsi had also come out with a new advertising campaign and slogan. Neither company appeared to be particularly concerned about competition from other soft drink manufacturers. However, consumers were drinking more and more new types of beverages and, in the USA, traditional juice companies such as Very Fine and Ocean Spray had begun to package their products in single-serving cans in addition to the traditional bottles or juice boxes. Snapple, once owned by Quaker Oats and now by Triarc Beverage Group, developed a new process for bottling tea that required no preservatives and expanded its product line from juices into seltzers and other natural sodas.[63]

Then chief executive Roberto Goizueta recognised the problem. He challenged his new chief operating officer, company president Douglas Ivester, to rejuvenate the Coke brand. Under Ivester's direction, Coke's advertising agency was given the freedom to develop different messages and marketing campaigns aimed at different groups of consumers. Previously, Coke had been advertised with a single theme and image, intended to appeal to everyone. Ivester also rehired Sergio Zyman as head of marketing. This surprised many people, since Zyman had been largely responsible for New Coke, a reformulation of Coca-Cola with a new taste designed to compete more closely with Pepsi but which had proved highly unpopular among Coke drinkers.

Zyman led the introduction of new packaging — the plastic contour bottle based on Coke's traditional glass shape.[64] He also emphasised the importance of marketing the product in ways other than just traditional advertising. One new idea was 'fast-lane merchandisers' — coolers of Coke at the end of checkout counters designed to attract people standing in line.[65] The company also signed an agreement with Rutgers University, paying the school US$10 million for ten-year rights to be the exclusive supplier of soft drinks and juices, including to vending machines, cafeterias, convenience stores and student centres.[66] A similar Pepsi contract with Pennsylvania State University was expected to earn Pepsi US$14 million over ten years. In addition to their sales, both companies valued these contracts because of their ability to reach and influence younger cola drinkers.

The Coca-Cola Company also actively began to develop new products.[67] It introduced POWERADE, challenging Gatorade in the US$1.2 billion sports drink market, and promoted it with free samples at the World Cup soccer matches throughout the USA. OK Soda, a lightly carbonated drink was targeted at generation X. The company also developed Fruitopia drinks, mixtures of fruit flavours such as cranberry lemonade, for the alternative beverage market.

Chief executive Goizueta and president Ivester were also concerned with expanding Coke's international base. In 1993, more than 6.3 billion unit cases of Coke and Coke Classic were sold worldwide, in more than 195 countries. Diet Coke, also known as Coke Light, was the number one low-calorie soda in the world, available in 117 countries. However, 80 per cent of these cases were sold in only four markets, all English speaking. Fanta was the only global brand in orange sodas, available in 170 countries; and Sprite, available in 168 countries, was the fifth-largest selling brand in the world. Coke was also the largest marketer of juice and juice-drink products in both the USA (with brands including Minute Maid and Hi-C) and the world. However, Goizueta felt that there was still room to grow.

To manage the scope of its business, The Coca-Cola Company is divided into two soft drink business sectors — the North America Business Sector and the International Business Sector. The North America Business Sector is made up of Coca-Cola USA, which operates in the USA; Coca-Cola Ltd, which is responsible for soft drink operations in Canada; and Houston-based Coca-Cola Foods, which produces and markets juices and juice drinks.

The International Business Sector is divided into four operating groups, each of which is responsible for a geographic region of the globe. The Greater Europe Group manages the countries of the European Union, Central and Eastern Europe, Scandinavia and the former Soviet Union. The Latin America Group oversees Mexico and Central and South America. The Middle and Far East Group manages the countries of the Pacific and the Middle East. The Africa Group is responsible for sub-Saharan Africa.

Traditionally, The Coca-Cola Company's main technique for entering and building foreign markets had been through independent bottlers, to whom it sold its 'secret formula' in the form of syrup or concentrate. However, this meant relying on the local bottlers to distribute and market Coke products. Soon after he became chief executive, Goizueta was asked by John Hunter, his regional manager in the Philippines, to consider becoming an active partner in the Philippine bottler, which had been neglecting Coke and concentrating on the beer it bottled. Coke invested US$13 million, becoming the controlling partner in a joint venture with the bottler. Goizueta and his managers made this their model for international expansion. When entering a new market, the company would seek to establish distribution of Coke products in key population centres and develop relationships with the important retail channels. It would look for 'well capitalised business partners with local know-how and visibility'. The workforce would come from the local area and would be extensively trained and eligible for promotion.

These strong, experienced partner companies helped Coke move quickly into Eastern Europe in the 1990s. On one tour, Goizueta attended the opening of plants in Prague (with anchor bottler Coca-Cola Amatil of Australia), Warsaw (with anchor bottler Ringnes of Norway) and Bucharest. When the USA ended its ban with Vietnam in 1994, Coca-Cola had already signed a joint venture agreement for at least two plants and was prepared to start operations within weeks. Coke re-entered the market in India in late 1993, having left the country many years earlier when the Indian government pushed for local ownership. This time, Coke formed a strategic alliance with Parle Exports, a local company with its own soft drink brands and a network of 60 bottling plants. The company saw India's 896 million people and fast-growing middle class as a significant growth opportunity. Coke also began a joint venture with the Swiss company, Nestlé, to produce and market canned coffee and tea drinks.[68]

Coke's dominance

The Coca-Cola Company is the global soft drink industry leader. Every day consumers enjoy an average of more than 773 million servings of Coca-Cola (known as Coca-Cola Classic in the USA and Canada), Diet Coke (known as Coca-Cola Light in some countries), Sprite, Fanta and other products of The Coca-Cola Company. Syrups, concentrates and beverage bases for Coca-Cola, the company's flagship brand, and other company soft drinks are manufactured and sold by The Coca-Cola Company and its subsidiaries in more than 195 countries around the world.

One of Ivester's first threats was the currency crisis across South-East Asia in late 1997. Rather than viewing the situation as a setback, the new chairman saw it as an opportunity to bolster its business in these areas. The strength of the dollar against other major currencies is a primary concern, as Coke receives 80 per cent of its profit from overseas — 15 per cent to 17 per cent from Japan alone. Coca-Cola learned from the peso crisis in Mexico in 1994 and used that situation to build its business there — with a market share much larger than it was in 1994. Ivester's decision to restructure Coca-Cola's global bottling system by lashing together hundreds of small bottlers into a handful of well-capitalised 'anchor' bottlers with strong local ties and distribution systems is paying off handsomely.[69]

In a continued sign of its global emphasis, Coca-Cola signed an agreement in December 1997 to purchase the Orangina brands and four bottling and concentrate plants in France from Pernod Ricard SA for a value of US$700 million. However, both Pepsi and the French government have worked to overturn the agreement. With its addition of Surge and Citra, Coke is acknowledging the movement of the US market away from colas (72 per cent in 1990 to 64 per cent in 1996), with the fastest growing brands including Sprite, Mountain Dew and Dr. Pepper.[70]

With global opportunity goes global risk. In the third quarter of 1998, Coke suffered a drop in its unit shipments from 11 per cent to 3 per cent growth compared to the previous year's quarter, as a result of the Asian currency crisis and global recessionary effects. System-wide revenue slipped 4 per cent, although Coke still showed a profit of US$888 million.[71] However, unit shipment growth remained slow in 1999, causing analysts to question whether Ivester could continue the fantastic growth of the Coca-Cola franchise.

In addition, Coke experienced some embarrassing problems with its brands in Europe in June 1999, including a contamination scare that caused more than 200 people to become sick in Belgium. Coke was forced to recall 14 million cases of its drinks at a loss of over US$60 million.[72] Coke was soundly criticised for its slow reaction to the crisis.

As a result of this and other problems, Douglas Ivester announced in December 1999 that he would be stepping down as chief executive of Coca-Cola in April of 2000. 'After reflection and thought, I have concluded that it is time for me to move on to the next stage of my life.'[73] Coke's board named Douglas Daft as Ivester's replacement.

Daft came to the position facing a host of problems, including slowing unit growth, an ugly class action racial discrimination suit which resulted in a US$195.2 million settlement offer from the firm to over 2000 of its employees, and an aborted takeover offer for Quaker Oats and its Gatorade sport drink brand. Losing out to PepsiCo in the Gatorade battle leaves Coke with a weakened strategy of beefing up its 'fizz-less' soft drink products, which include the Nestea line of drinks and Fruitopia fruit drinks, as well as introducing new products.[74]

But it is exactly these drinks on which Coke is pinning its hopes for a dramatic turn-around. Daft is attempting to change the highly bureaucratic, slow-moving, centralised structure of Coke to promote a change to 'thinking local, acting local'. He was able to develop just such a strategy in his former post in Asia, where Coke now sells over 250 different drinks.[75] As one of his first acts as chief executive, he axed 6000 employees, many of them middle and senior managers in Atlanta.

Coke plans to introduce its own energy drink, KMX. In addition, it will develop a bottled coffee drink, Planet Java. This gives Coke its first US coffee brand and pits it against Frappuccino, a venture between PepsiCo and Starbucks Corporation, which currently faces no significant competition in the category. 'Planet Java is a great way for us to get into the market', said Susan McDermott, a spokeswoman for Coca-Cola North America. 'It's got a distinctive brand personality and it's performing well in areas where it's available.'[76]

QUESTIONS

1. What are the management functions performed by Roberto Goizueta, John Hunter and Douglas Ivester? How do their responsibilities differ?
2. Describe the changes in Coca-Cola's environment once Roberto Goizueta became CEO and then after his death.
3. How has the discrimination suit hurt Coke?
4. How has The Coca-Cola Company changed to adapt to its environment?

CHAPTER 3

CHAPTER 3

Information and decision making

CHAPTER 3 STUDY QUESTIONS

- How is information technology changing the workplace?

- What are the current directions in information systems?

- How is information used for decision making?

- How do managers make decisions?

- Why are knowledge management and organisational learning important?

Infocomm Development Authority of Singapore — support for smart companies to pursue e-futures

GETTING @ CONNECTED

Singapore is in a unique position to offer itself as a home base for companies seeking to launch into Asia. To help capitalise on this opportunity, Singapore provides world-class business infrastructure, including an open telecommunications market, a crucial part of any economy in the information and e-business age.

Telecommunications and information policy and development is the domain of the Infocomm Development Authority of Singapore (IDA) www.ida.gov.sg. IDA's vision is to create a 'digital future' for Singapore. The IT2000 vision put Singapore on the world map for becoming the first nation to connect all households onto a broadband network called SingaporeONE ('one network for everyone'). Beginning in 2000, the e-Government Action Plan was initiated to better serve Singaporeans (individuals and businesses) through the exploitation of technology. More than 1500 public services had been e-enabled by 2002. Services deemed feasible for e-delivery were accessible or could be transacted on line by the end of 2002. Accenture ranked Singapore number two for three consecutive years in overall maturity in realising the e-government vision among the 23 countries surveyed. Singapore was honoured with the Explorer Award for its innovative online program at the E-Gov 2002 Show.

The Singapore Supreme Court is one good example. It is able to combine the business needs of the court and the innovative use of technology to transform the once traditional paper-based litigation system into a comprehensive innovative e-litigation system. The IDA has called for industry collaboration in a home-networking project to test out new capabilities in home environments and innovative online services.[1]

GET CONNECTED! @

Singapore is already seeing tremendous results from its vision of a digital future. You can learn more about the IDA at www.ida.gov.sg. What could countries such as Australia and New Zealand learn from the collaborative e-ventures between the government and businesses in Singapore?

GET CONNECTED!

Information is data made useful for decision making.

Intellectual capital is the collective brain power or shared knowledge of a workforce.

Computer competency is the ability to understand and use computers to advantage.

Information competency is the ability to use computers and information technology to locate, retrieve, evaluate, organise and analyse information for decision making.

Information technology (IT) is computer hardware, software, networks and databases supporting information use.

Just as technology is changing governments and businesses, it is also dramatically and continually changing the nature of work and organisations themselves. We are in what futurist Alvin Toffler calls the third wave of development, characterised by an information-driven society that is digital, networked and continuously evolving.[2] The key to performance in this new world is **information** and the way it flows and is used by people in organisations. We live and work at a time when more information about more things is being made available to more people more quickly than ever before. The question is: How well do we as individuals and as organisations take full advantage of it?[3]

Our increasingly networked and global economy has been described by Peter Drucker as one in which 'the productivity of knowledge and knowledge workers' will become the decisive competitive factor.[4] In this era of information, there is no doubt that **intellectual capital** is a major source of competitive advantage. As first defined in chapter 1, it is the collective brain power or shared knowledge of a workforce that can be used to create wealth.[5] Knowledge is an irreplaceable organisational resource, and the goal should always be to grow and create it. The information from which knowledge is created increasingly moves at high speed through electronic computer and telecommnication networks that link each of us to the world at large with an access and intensity never before possible. Thus, the foundations for knowledge building increasingly rest with two core competencies: **computer competency** — ability to understand computers and use them to best advantage personally and professionally; and **information competency** — ability to use computers and information technology to locate, retrieve, evaluate, organise and analyse information for decision making.

INFORMATION TECHNOLOGY AND THE NEW WORKPLACE

The future is *now* when it comes to the rapidly evolving state of **information technology (IT)**, the combination of computer hardware, software, networks and databases that allows information to be shared, stored and manipulated. Organisations are changing as continuing new developments in IT exert their influence. Information departments or centres are appearing on organisation charts. The number and variety of information career fields is rapidly expanding. Job titles such as chief information officer and chief knowledge officer are appearing in the senior ranks of organisations. All of this, and more, is characteristic of the great opportunities of our new age of information. At the software firm PeopleSoft, for example, a vice-president once faced the problem of trying to meet expectations for an early release of a sophisticated software package. His team used web-based tools and a Lotus Notes database to facilitate a process that could have taken months if done any other way. The PeopleSoft team consolidated information from employees around the world and provided the needed feedback within two weeks. 'It was really amazing', said the vice-president, who added, 'Then again, it's how we do things around here.'[6]

Work and the electronic office

That's the way things are done at any progressive workplace these days. A good example of the everyday impact of information technology on work is the *electronic office*. This term refers to the use of computers and related technologies to electronically facilitate operations in an office environment. The electronic office that you may soon enter may well look like the one described opposite.

People work at 'smart' stations supported by computers that allow sophisticated voice, image, text and other data-handling operations. Many of these stations are temporary spaces that telecommuters 'visit' during those times when they are in the main office; otherwise they work from virtual offices — on the road, anywhere. Voice messaging uses the voice recognition capabilities of computers to take dictation, answer the telephone and relay messages. Databases are easily accessed and shared to solve problems, and to prepare and analyse reports. Documents drafted via word processing are stored for later retrieval and/or sent via electronic mail or facsimile transmission to other persons. Filing cabinets are few, and little paper is found. Meeting notes are written on electronic pads or jotted in palm-held electronic diaries. All are easily up-loaded into computer files. Mail arrives and is routed to its destination via computer, where it is electronically prioritised according to its importance and linked to relevant databases to speed problem solving. Computer conferencing and videoconferencing are commonplace. E-meetings allow people separated by great distances — distributed even around the world — to work together on projects every day without meeting personally face to face.

www.itawards.com

Information communication technology facilitates knowledge-based cultures in the new economy. Check out the Asia Pacific ICT Awards to learn more about how the sharing of knowledge is achieved across participating communities and countries.

This is not fantasy. It's real. Progressive organisations are doing all they can to utilise computers and information technology to streamline work, improve operating efficiencies and make overall performance improvements. Such work settings are designed for high performance in a workplace dominated by concerns for speed — of decision making and action. Organisations exist in dynamic and turbulent environments where 'speed to market', 'quick response', 'fast cycle time' and 'time-based competition' are priority topics in any executive suite. They are continually investing in IT in the quest for competitive advantage through lower costs, better quality and improved customer services.

How information technology is changing organisations

Without a doubt, the most significant way in which IT is changing organisations today can be summed up in one sentence: *Information technology is breaking down barriers.*[7] It breaks barriers by making communication easy, immediate, inexpensive and important. The benefits are important and the impact far reaching. As indicated in figure 3.1, IT use is breaking down barriers within organisations and it is breaking down barriers between the organisation and its environment. It is making the organisations more efficient and effective, and much more competitive in the process.[8]

Within organisations the increasing use of IT means that individuals and teams, working in different departments, levels and physical locations, can more easily communicate and electronically share information with one another. It also means that the organisation can operate with fewer middle managers whose jobs otherwise would be to facilitate these information flows. Instead of people moving information among and across levels, computers do the job for them. This means that IT-intensive organisations are 'flatter' and operate with fewer levels than their more traditional organisational counterparts. It brings them opportunities for competitive advantage in increased speed of decision making, use of better and more timely information for decision making, and more coordination of decision making and action among relevant components. It also offers the advantage of increasing flexibility in reconfiguring operations and organising special projects in response to competitive needs and opportunities.

The best organisations also take advantage of IT in managing their relationships with key elements in the external environment. IT plays an important role in customer relationship management by quickly and accurately providing information for decision makers regarding

The digital divide

People who are on low incomes, without tertiary education, living in rural and remote areas, of Maori, Aboriginal and Torres Strait Islander heritage, with disabilities, with a language background other than English, or aged over 55 are less likely to use the Internet.

How might this affect their job chances?

customer needs, preferences and satisfactions. IT helps manage and control costs in all aspects of the supply chain from initiation of purchase to logistics and transportation to point of delivery and ultimate use. IT also helps build and manage relationships with strategic partners. It enables business contracts to be continuously maintained and efficiently fulfilled regardless of physical location.

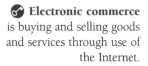
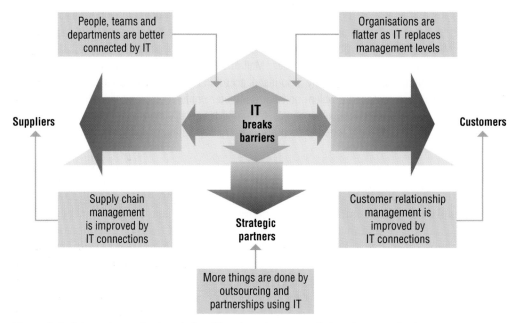

Figure 3.1 ▸ Information technology is breaking down barriers and changing organisations.

How information technology is changing business

Electronic commerce is buying and selling goods and services through use of the Internet.

Welcome to the world of one of the most significant business developments of all time — **electronic commerce**, or 'e-commerce'. This is the process of buying and selling goods and services electronically through use of the Internet and related information technologies.[9] Business transactions between buyers and sellers are completed on line rather than face to face. In *business-to-consumer e-commerce*, or B2C, businesses like Amazon.com and Dell.com sell directly to customers over the Internet. In *business-to-business e-commerce*, or B2B, businesses use the Internet to collaborate and make transactions with one another. The chapter opening example shows how e-collaboration can build positive e-futures.

Companies that pursue e-commerce models are often called 'dot-coms', due to the presence of the '.com' designation in their web site addresses. One of the prominent companies in web site registrations, Network Solutions, describes the stages of development in the 'dot-com life cycle' as follows:[10]

Steps in developing an e-business

1. *Secure an online identity.* Organisations at this stage have a web address and most likely a posted home page.
2. *Establish a Web presence.* Organisations at this stage use their home page for advertising or promotional purposes; it offers company and/or product information, but does not allow visitors online queries or ordering.
3. *Enable e-commerce.* Organisations at this stage are viable e-commerce businesses whose web sites allow visitors to order products on line.

4. *Provide e-commerce and customer relationship management.* Organisations at this stage use their web sites to develop and maintain relationships with customers by serving key processes, such as checking status of orders or inventory levels on line.
5. *Utilise a service application model.* Organisations at this stage use advanced web site capabilities to fully serve business functions and processes such as financial management and human resources.

The domain of electronic commerce is developing rapidly, and it is one of the forces of globalisation that opens the world at large to competition and business opportunity. An emerging force in Australasia and Europe that will make a major worldwide impact is known as *m-commerce* — the use of mobile phones to act as electronic wallets that allow users to perform banking transactions, purchase goods and services, and pay bills. In the future, for example, Virgin Mobile customers could use their Internet-enabled mobile phones to book Virgin Blue flights through the Virgin Blue web site.

GLOBALISATION

Amazon.com • www.amazon.com

In the information age, 'dot-com' means business

Amazon invites you to shop in their bookstore any time you want, day or night, 365 days a year. After all, it's on line — e-business with a capital 'E'. It has established a new level and form of competition in the bookstore industry. And the growth goes on. Log onto Amazon.com today and you can also buy everything from health and beauty aids to tools and hardware, to toys and videogames and more. You can shop Amazon.com in Australia, New Zealand, Singapore and many other countries. What began as a firm advertising 'Your next book is only a click away', may now be the world's biggest consumer marketplace.

INFORMATION AND INFORMATION SYSTEMS

Formally defined, *information* is data in the form of raw facts or descriptions that are meaningful and useful for decision making. People in any work setting, large or small, must have available to them the right information at the right time and in the right place if they are to perform effectively. This is made possible by **information systems** that use the latest in information technology to collect, organise and distribute data in such a way that they become meaningful as information.

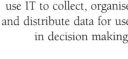

Information systems use IT to collect, organise and distribute data for use in decision making.

What is useful information?

IT and the information systems that support work and decision making in organisations must provide information that is truly useful. The five essential characteristics of useful information are:

Characteristics of useful information

1. *Timeliness.* The information is available when needed; it meets deadlines for decision making and action.
2. *Quality.* The information is accurate and it is reliable; it can be used with confidence.
3. *Completeness.* The information is complete and sufficient for the task at hand; it is as current and up to date as possible.
4. *Relevance.* The information is appropriate for the task at hand; it is free from extraneous or irrelevant materials.
5. *Understandability.* The information is presented in proper form easily understood by the user; it is free from unnecessary detail.

Information needs of organisations

The availability of advanced IT has made information more readily available and useful than ever before. This information serves the variety of needs described in figure 3.2. At the organisation's boundaries, information in the external environment must be accessed and used to successfully manage relationships with key stakeholders. Managers need this *intelligence information* to deal effectively with such outside parties as competitors, government agencies, creditors, suppliers and stockholders. As Peter Drucker says about the information age, 'a winning strategy will require information about events and conditions outside the institution'. He goes on to add that organisations must have 'rigorous methods for gathering and analyzing outside information'.[11] In addition to the gathering of intelligence information, organisations also provide to the external environment many types of *public information*. This serves a variety of purposes ranging from image building to product advertising to financial reporting for taxes.

Within organisations, people need vast amounts of information to make decisions and solve problems in their daily work. These vertical and horizontal information flows are shown also in figure 3.2. Higher-level managers tend to emphasise information use in strategic planning, whereas middle and lower managers focus more on operational considerations involving the implementation of these plans. The information needs of workers centre on accomplishing tasks. This involves gathering, storing, sharing and using information to solve operating problems in order to best meet the needs of internal and external customers. Organisations that are best able to facilitate the fast and easy sharing of information internally are well positioned for competitive advantage.

One of the greatest advantages of IT use within organisations is its contribution to empowerment. The ability to gather and move information quickly, and from top to bottom, allows top levels to stay in control while freeing lower levels to make speedy decisions and take the actions they need to best perform their jobs. This helps build competitive and customer-responsive

www.cisco.com.au
www.cisco.co.nz

Network solutions are mainstream business at Cisco Systems. So are strategic alliances. The firm owns only two of the 38 plants that assemble its products.

organisations. Silicon Valley pioneer and Cisco Systems CEO John Chambers, for example, points out that he always has the information he needs to be in control from the top — be it earnings, expenses, profitability, gross margins and more. He also says, importantly: 'Because I have my data in that format, every one of my employees can make decisions that might have had to come all the way to the president … Quicker decision making at lower levels will translate into higher profit margins … Companies that don't do that will be non-competitive.'[12]

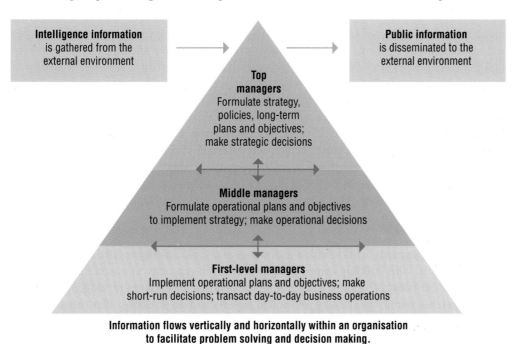

Figure 3.2 ▸ External and internal information needs of organisations

Developments in information systems

You will encounter many types of information systems in your career. At times you may be the designer of a new system and you may serve on an information steering committee, but you will always be an end user. In this sense, your task will be to use information systems well to make good decisions, to master the performance requirements of complex projects, and more generally to contribute regularly to enhanced organisational productivity. As you look ahead, keep in mind the advice in Manager's Notepad 3.1.

MANAGER'S NOTEPAD 3.1

Avoiding common information systems mistakes

- Don't assume more information is always better.
- Don't assume that computers eliminate human judgement.
- Don't assume the newest technology is always best.
- Don't assume nothing will ever go wrong with your computer.
- Don't assume that everyone understands how the system works.

DECISION SUPPORT SYSTEMS

A **decision support system** (DSS) allows users to interact directly with a computer to organise and analyse data for solving complex and sometimes unstructured problems. Decision support systems are now available to assist in such business decisions as mergers and acquisitions, plant expansions, new product developments and stock portfolio management, among many others.

A fast-growing technology involves group decision support systems (GDSSs), which are interactive computer-based information systems that facilitate group efforts to solve complex and unstructured problems. GDSS software, called *groupware*, allows several people to simultaneously work on a file or database and work together on computer networks. It facilitates information exchange, group decision making, work scheduling and other forms of group activity without the requirement of face-to-face meetings. Groupware is especially useful in facilitating work by team members who work different shifts or are spread over large geographic distances, even globally. The willingness and skills needed to participate effectively in these *virtual teams* are increasingly essential to one's personal career portfolio. The Lotus Development Corporation offers a variety of groupware products that are popular in the business setting. WebCT or Blackboard offer additional versions popular in many universities.

> ✔ A **decision support system** allows a computer to help organise and analyse data for problem solving.

EXPERT SYSTEMS

Another developing area of information technology is *artificial intelligence* (AI), a field of study that is concerned with building computer systems with the capacity to reason the way people do, even to the point of dealing with ambiguities and difficult issues of judgement. These **expert systems** mimic the thinking of human experts and, in so doing, offer consistent and 'expert' decision-making advice to the user. Some expert systems are rule-based and use a complicated set of 'if . . . then' rules to analyse problems. These rules are determined by specialists who work with actual human experts in a certain problem area and then build their problem-solving rules into a computer program. One complaint about the technology is that the use of expert systems 'de-skills' work by requiring the employee to know less because the computer does more.[13] Advocates, however, point out that expert systems make it easier to concentrate one's attention and problem-solving skills on the more complex matters.

> ✔ **Expert systems** allow computers to mimic the thinking of human experts for applied problem solving.

INTRANETS AND EXTRANETS

Central to the electronic office is the integration of computers and software into *networks* that allow users to easily transfer and share information through computer-to-computer linkages. **Intranets** are networks of computers that use special software, such as Lotus Notes, to allow persons working in various locations for the same organisation to share databases and communicate electronically. The goal is to promote more integration across the organisation and improve operations efficiency and quality. At Ford, for example, more than 120 000 workstations scattered in company offices around the world are linked by an intranet. Using a technology called the Concentric Network, moreover, Ford integrates voice, data and video in a single network that allows employees to share information and work together in real time.[14]

A related trend is the emergence of fully integrated **enterprise-wide networks** that move information quickly and accurately from one point to another within an organisation. For example, a field salesperson may pass on a customer's suggestion for a product modification via electronic mail. This mail arrives at the computer used by a product designer at company headquarters. After creating a computer-assisted design for the product, the designer

> ✔ **Intranets** are computer networks used for communication and data sharing within an organisation.

> ✔ **Enterprise-wide networks** use IT to move information quickly and accurately within an organisation.

passes it on simultaneously to engineering, manufacturing, finance and marketing experts for their preliminary analysis. Working as a virtual team, everyone including the field salesperson may then further consider the design and agree on its business potential.

Extranets are computer networks that use the public Internet to allow communication between the organisation and elements in its external environment. IT that allows information transfers between two or more organisations is a basic foundation for the fast-paced developments occurring in electronic commerce. Through electronic data interchange (EDI), companies communicate electronically with one another to move and share documents such as purchase orders, bills, receipt confirmations and even payments for services rendered.

Extranets are computer networks for communication between the organisation and its environment.

TECHNOLOGY

The Wesley Hospital • www.wesley.com.au

Implementing an enterprise-wide network to improve patient care

The Wesley private hospital in Brisbane has rolled out a hospital-wide, computerised clinical information system to improve patient care and assist doctors. Eventually the system will connect five hospitals and two or more other facilities, providing staff with access to read and update patient records that will be kept in a single file. According to Dr Jennifer King, general manager of the Wesley Hospital:

> Research shows a doctor's ability to correctly diagnose a problem increases by as much as 50 per cent when they have information on the patient's history … In a hospital, you may interact with many people, so the information about you is dispersed around the institution, with different people and different systems. Consolidating all of that into one place makes all the information the hospital has about you available wherever it is needed and reduces the risk of transcription errors.[15]

INFORMATION SYSTEMS AND THE MANAGER'S JOB

 A **management information system** uses IT to meet the information needs of managers in daily decisions.

Specific to the management context, a **management information system** (MIS) is specifically designed to use information technology to meet the information needs of managers as they make a variety of decisions on a day-to-day basis. For example, a long-haul refrigerated trucking company might use a computerised MIS to monitor organisational performance. The system could track everything from billing accuracy to arrival times to driver satisfaction with company maintenance on their vehicles. Pay bonuses and extra annual leave days could be awarded based on driver performance on such goals as safety and fuel consumption.[16]

All of the critical managerial roles identified by Henry Mintzberg and discussed in chapter 1 (see figure 3.3) involve communication and information processing.[17] To be effective, any manager must act as a nerve centre of information flows — gathering, giving and receiving information from many sources. Today's developments in IT support all aspects of the management process, making possible performance levels that are truly extraordinary. Among the advantages of appropriate MIS use in the manager's job are:

Advantages of appropriate MIS use in the management process

- *Planning advantages*. MIS use allows for better and more timely access to useful information, as well as for the involvement of many people in the planning process.
- *Organising advantages*. MIS use allows for more ongoing and informed communication among all parts of the organisation, helping ensure better coordination and integration.
- *Leading advantages*. MIS use allows for better and more frequent communication with all organisation members and key environmental stakeholders.
- *Controlling advantages*. MIS use allows for more immediate and complete measurement of performance results and real-time solutions to performance problems.

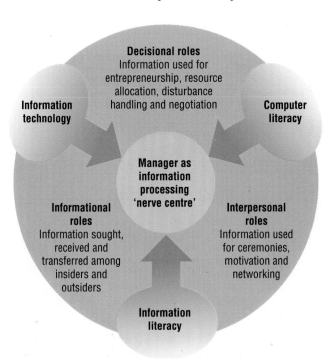

Figure 3.3 ▸ Information systems and the nature of managerial work

INFORMATION AND DECISION MAKING

Information sets the foundations for management and organisational success. The work of managers can be described as engaging in planning, organising, leading and controlling in the process of solving a continuous stream of daily problems. The most obvious problem situation is a *performance deficiency* — that is, when actual performance is less than desired. For example, a manager faces a possible problem when turnover or absenteeism suddenly increases in the work unit, when a subordinate's daily output decreases, or when a higher executive complains about something that has been said or done. However, another important problem situation emerges as a *performance opportunity* when an actual situation either turns out better than anticipated or offers the potential to be so. The challenge in dealing with a performance deficiency or performance opportunity is to proceed with effective **problem solving** — the process of identifying a discrepancy between an actual and desired state of affairs and then taking action to resolve the deficiency or take advantage of the opportunity.

> **Problem solving** involves identifying and taking action to resolve problems.

The entire problem-solving process is dependent on the right information being available to the right people at the right times so that they can make good problem-solving decisions. A **decision**, to be precise, is a choice among alternative possible courses of action. The process of decision making is driven in part by the quality of information available. Information systems assist managers to gather data, turn them into useful information, and use that information to make effective problem-solving decisions.

> A **decision** is a choice among possible alternative courses of action.

Types of managerial decisions

Managers resolve problems by making different types of decisions in their day-to-day work. Some are **programmed decisions** — that is, solutions already available from past experience to solve problems that are familiar, straightforward and clear with respect to information needs. These decisions apply best to problems that are matters of routine; although perhaps not predictable, they can at least be anticipated. This means that decisions can be planned or programmed in advance to be implemented as needed. In human resource management, for example, problems are common whenever decisions are made on pay rises and promotions, leave requests, committee assignments and the like. Knowing this, proactive or forward-looking managers plan ahead on how to make decisions on such issues when and if they should arise.

> **Programmed decisions** apply solutions from past experience to a routine problem.

Managers must also deal with new or unexpected situations that present unstructured problems full of ambiguities and information deficiencies. These problems are typically unanticipated and must be dealt with as they occur. Unstructured problems require **non-programmed decisions** that specifically craft novel solutions to meet the demands of the unique situation at hand. Most problems faced by higher-level managers are of this type, with the problems often involving choice of strategies and objectives in situations of some uncertainty.

> **Non-programmed decisions** apply specific solutions crafted for a unique problem.

An extreme type of non-programmed decision must be made in times of **crisis** — the occurrence of an unexpected problem that can lead to disaster if not resolved quickly and appropriately. The growing dependence of organisations on technology raises many such opportunities. Any organisation maintaining a web site, for example, may face occasional crisis shutdowns due to server failures. 'Hacker' attacks on web sites are also increasingly common, as firms like Microsoft, eBay and Amazon know only too well.[18]

> A **crisis** is an unexpected problem that can lead to disaster if not resolved quickly and appropriately.

The ability to handle crises may be the ultimate test of a manager's problem-solving capabilities. Unfortunately, research indicates that managers may react to crises by isolating themselves and trying to solve the problem alone or in a small 'closed' group.[19] This tendency actually denies them access to crucial information and assistance at the very time they are most needed. The crisis may even be accentuated if more problems are created because critical decisions are made with poor or inadequate information and from a limited perspective. Managers in progressive organisations anticipate that crises will occur and plan ahead on how to deal with them. Consider growing concerns about workplace bullying in Australia and New Zealand. The National Occupational Health and Safety Commission (NOHSC) of Australia and the Occupational Safety and Health Service of the Department of Labour, New Zealand, offer guidelines for employers on how to recognise situations that are prone to violence and how to prepare for such crises.

Decision conditions

People in organisations make decisions under each of the three conditions described in figure 3.4 — decisions in environments of certainty, risk and uncertainty. Although managers make decisions in each environment, the conditions of risk and uncertainty are common at higher management levels where problems are more complex and unstructured. Former Coca-Cola CEO Roberto Goizueta, for example, was known as a risk taker. Among his risky moves were introducing Diet Coke to the market, changing the formula of Coca-Cola to create New Coke, and then reversing direction after New Coke flopped.[20] More recently, top management at H. J. Heinz Company took an unusual risk with the introduction of EZ Squirt, a 'green' ketchup.

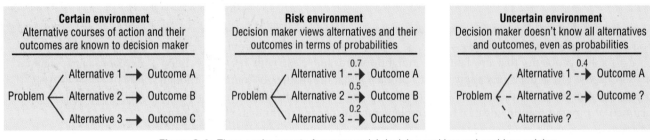

Figure 3.4 ▶ Three environments for managerial decision making and problem solving

🔘 **Certain environments** offer complete information on possible action alternatives and their consequences.

🔘 A **risk environment** lacks complete information, but offers 'probabilities' of the likely outcomes for possible action alternatives.

🔘 An **uncertain environment** lacks so much information that it is difficult to assign probabilities to the likely outcomes of alternatives.

The decisions to market New Coke and green ketchup are quite different from the relative predictability of those made in a certain environment, one where sufficient information is available about possible alternative courses of action and their outcomes. This is an ideal decision condition where the task is simply to study the alternatives and choose the best solution.

Very few managerial problems occur in **certain environments**, but steps can sometimes be taken to reduce uncertainty. In the case of Heinz's green ketchup, for example, the firm made the go-ahead decision only after receiving favourable reports from kids participating in special focus groups testing the new product. However, this still left the firm with a **risk environment**, one where information on action alternatives and their consequences is incomplete, but some estimates of 'probabilities' can be made. A *probability*, in turn, is the degree of likelihood (e.g. four chances out of ten) that an event will occur. Risk is a common decision condition for managers. It is especially typical for entrepreneurs and organisations that depend on ideas and continued innovation for their success.

When information is so poor that managers are unable even to assign probabilities to the likely outcomes of alternatives that are known, an **uncertain environment** exists. This is the most difficult decision condition.[21] The high level of uncertainty forces managers to rely heavily on creativity in solving problems; it requires unique, novel and often totally innovative alternatives to existing patterns of behaviour. Groups are frequently used for problem solving in such situations. In all cases, the responses to uncertainty depend greatly on intuition, judgement, informed guessing and hunches — all of which leave considerable room for error.

How managers approach decisions

In practice, people display three quite different approaches or 'styles' in the way they deal with problem situations. Some are *problem avoiders* who ignore information that would otherwise signal the presence of an opportunity or performance deficiency. Such persons are *inactive* and do not want to make decisions and deal with problems. *Problem solvers*, by contrast, are willing to make decisions and try to solve problems, but only when forced to by the situation. They are *reactive* in gathering information and responding to problems after they occur. As a result they may deal reasonably well with performance deficiencies, but they miss many performance opportunities. *Problem seekers* actively process information and constantly look for problems to solve or opportunities to explore. True problem seekers are *proactive* and forward thinking; they anticipate problems and opportunities and take appropriate action to gain the advantage. Success at problem seeking is one of the ways exceptional managers distinguish themselves from the merely good ones.

Another distinction in the way managers approach decisions contrasts tendencies toward 'systematic' and 'intuitive' thinking. In **systematic thinking** a person approaches problems in a rational, step-by-step and analytical fashion. This type of thinking involves breaking a complex problem into smaller components and then addressing them in a logical and integrated fashion. Managers who are systematic can be expected to make a plan before taking action and then to search for information to facilitate problem solving in a step-by-step fashion.

Someone using **intuitive thinking**, by contrast, is more flexible and spontaneous and also may be quite creative.[22] This type of thinking allows us to respond imaginatively to a problem based on a quick and broad evaluation of the situation and the possible alternative courses of action. Managers who are intuitive can be expected to deal with many aspects of a problem at once, jump quickly from one issue to another and consider 'hunches' based on experience or spontaneous ideas. This approach tends to work best in situations of high uncertainty where facts are limited and few decision precedents exist.[23]

Managers should feel confident in approaching decisions from the perspectives of both systematic and intuitive thinking. Senior managers, in particular, must deal with portfolios of problems and opportunities that consist of multiple and interrelated issues. This requires *multidimensional thinking*, or the ability to view many problems at once, in relationship to one another and across long and short time horizons.[24] The best managers also 'map' multiple problems into a network that can be actively managed over time as priorities, events and demands continuously change. And importantly, they are able to make decisions and take

CONNECTION

CAREER

Entrepreneurship

Café Bones

Cappuccino or Pupaccino?
www.cafebones.com.au

Some very innovative ideas are rewarded by the Yellow Pages® Business Ideas Grants. Mary-Anne Danaher and Lynne Blundell from Café Bones were among the winners in 2001. The pair established Café Bones in Sydney in March 2000. It is an outdoor dog-friendly café, offering food and beverages for humans and dogs. The menu for dogs includes the beverage Pupaccino™ and gourmet dog biscuits Bone Bix®. Café Bones will even prepare birthday cakes for customers' dogs. Danaher and Blundell came up with the idea after meeting while walking their dogs.[25]

Question

The originators of ideas like this one found a niche for their products using their special talents. Do a personal 'talent' inventory. In what entrepreneurial directions might your special talents take you?

Systematic thinking approaches problems in a rational and analytical fashion.

Intuitive thinking approaches problems in a flexible and spontaneous fashion.

actions in the short run that benefit longer-run objectives. It is important not to be sidetracked from long-run goals while making decisions and sorting through a shifting mix of daily problems. Somehow a consistent long-term direction must be retained, even as each short-term problem is being resolved. This requires skill at **strategic opportunism** — the ability to remain focused on long-term objectives while being flexible enough to resolve short-term problems and opportunities in a timely manner.[26]

Strategic opportunism focuses on long-term objectives while being flexible in dealing with short-term problems.

THE DECISION-MAKING PROCESS

The specific act of **decision making** involves making a choice among alternative courses of action. However, the decision-making process involves a cycle of activities and events that begins with identification of a problem and ends with the evaluation of implemented solutions.[27]

Decision making is the process of making choices among alternative courses of action.

Steps in decision making

The common steps in a rational approach to decision making are described in figure 3.5. They are (1) identify and define the problem, (2) generate and evaluate possible solutions, (3) choose a preferred solution and conduct the 'ethics double-check', (4) implement the solution, and (5) evaluate results. Importantly, Step 3 in this model includes a built-in 'checkpoint' as a way to verify the ethical aspects of a decision before any action is taken. Working with the following case will help put all five steps into perspective.[28]

> *The Heinz Wattie's case.* Heinz Wattie's Australasia decided to close its Dandenong factory (one of four manufacturing sites in Australia) and to move production to Echuca, Wagga Wagga and New Zealand. This would enable consolidation of its regional corporate office into Melbourne. This closure would affect 192 workers. The Dandenong factory was scheduled to close in November.

This case reflects how competition, changing times and the forces of globalisation can take their toll on organisations, the people that work for them and the communities in which they operate. Think about how you would feel as one of the affected employees. Think about how you would feel as the mayor of this city. Think how you would feel as a senior manager having to make the required decisions.

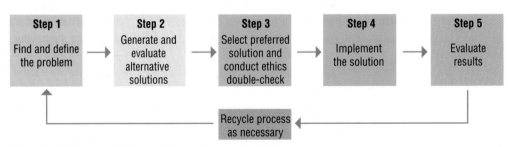

Figure 3.5 ▸ Steps in decision making and problem solving

DECISION-MAKING STEP 1: IDENTIFY AND DEFINE THE PROBLEM

The first step in decision making is to find and define the problem. This is a stage of information gathering, information processing and deliberation.[29]

The way a problem is originally defined can have a major impact on how it is eventually resolved. Three common mistakes may occur at this critical first step in decision making.

Mistake number 1 is defining the problem too broadly or too narrowly. To take a classic example, the problem stated as 'build a better mousetrap' might be better defined as 'get rid of the mice'. That is, managers should define problems so as to give themselves the best possible range of problem-solving options. *Mistake number 2* is focusing on symptoms instead of causes. Symptoms are indicators that problems may exist, but they shouldn't be mistaken for the problems themselves. Managers should be able to spot problem symptoms (e.g. a drop in performance). But instead of treating symptoms (such as simply encouraging higher performance), managers should deal with their root causes (such as discovering the worker's need for training in the use of a complex new computer system). *Mistake number 3* is choosing the wrong problem to deal with. Managers should set priorities and deal with the most important problems first. They should also give priority to problems that are truly solvable.

> *Back to the Heinz Wattie's case.* Closing the Dandenong plant would put a substantial number of people from the city out of work. The unemployment created would have a negative impact on individuals, their families and the community as a whole. The local financial implications of the plant's closing would be great. The problem for Heinz Wattie's management is how to minimise the adverse impact of the plant closing on the employees, their families and the community.

DECISION-MAKING STEP 2: GENERATE AND EVALUATE POSSIBLE SOLUTIONS

Once the problem is defined, it is possible to formulate one or several potential solutions. At this stage, more information is gathered, data are analysed, and the pros and cons of possible alternative courses of action are identified. This effort to locate, clarify and evaluate alternative solutions is critical to successful problem solving. The involvement of other people is very important here in order to maximise information and build commitment. The end result can only be as good as the quality of the alternative solutions generated in this step. The better the pool of alternatives, the more likely a good solution will be achieved.

Common errors in this stage include selecting a particular solution too quickly and choosing an alternative that, although convenient, has damaging side effects or is not as good as others that might be discovered with extra effort. The analysis of alternatives should determine how well each possible course of action deals with the problem while taking into account the environment within which the problem exists. A very basic evaluation involves **cost-benefit analysis**, the comparison of what an alternative will cost in relation to the expected benefits. At a minimum, the benefits of a chosen alternative should be greater than its costs. Typical criteria for evaluating alternatives include the following:

 Cost-benefit analysis involves comparing the costs and benefits of each potential course of action.

- *Benefits.* What are the 'benefits' of using the alternative to solve a performance deficiency or take advantage of an opportunity?
- *Costs.* What are the 'costs' of implementing the alternative, including resource investments as well as potential negative side effects?
- *Timeliness.* How fast will the benefits occur and a positive impact be achieved?
- *Acceptability.* To what extent will the alternative be accepted and supported by those who must work with it?
- *Ethical soundness.* How well does the alternative meet acceptable ethical criteria in the eyes of the various stakeholders?

Criteria for evaluating alternatives

> *Back to the Heinz Wattie's case.* In the words of chief executive Neville Fielke: 'We were initially hopeful of securing investment and expansion for Dandenong but regrettably the factors

aligned against that option were fundamental and compelling'. The Heinz Wattie's plant would be closed. Among the possible options were: to close the plant on schedule and be done with it; to delay the plant's closing until all efforts had been made to secure investment and expansion for Dandenong; to close the plant and offer transfers to other Heinz Wattie's plant locations; or to close the plant, offer transfers and help employees to find new jobs in and around Dandenong.

DECISION-MAKING STEP 3: CHOOSE A SOLUTION

The **classical decision model** describes decision making with complete information.

An **optimising decision** chooses the alternative giving the absolute best solution to a problem.

At this point in the decision-making process an actual decision is made to select a particular course of action. Just how this is done and by whom must be successfully resolved in each problem situation. Management theory recognises differences between the classical model and the behavioural model of decision making, as shown in figure 3.6. The **classical decision model** views the manager as acting in a certain world. Here, the manager faces a clearly defined problem and knows all possible action alternatives as well as their consequences. As a result, he or she makes an **optimising decision** that gives the absolute best solution to the problem. The classical approach is a very rational model that assumes perfect information is available for decision making.

Classical model
Views manager as acting with complete information in a certain environment

- Clearly defined problem
- Knowledge of all possible alternatives and their consequences
- Optimising decision — choice of the 'optimum' alternative

Behavioural model
Views manager as having cognitive limitations and acting with incomplete information in risk and uncertain environments

- Problem not clearly defined
- Knowledge is limited on possible alternatives and their consequences
- Satisficing decision — choices of 'satisfactory' alternative

Judgemental heuristics approach
Heuristics are adopted to simplify managerial decision making

Decisions are influenced by:
- Information readily available in memory — the availability heuristic
- Comparisons with similar circumstances — the representativeness heuristic
- Current situation — the anchoring and adjustment heuristic

Figure 3.6 ▸ Classical, behavioural and judgemental heuristics approaches in decision making

Behavioural scientists question these assumptions. Perhaps best represented by the work of Herbert Simon, they recognise the existence of *cognitive limitations*, or limits to our human information-processing capabilities.[31] These limitations make it hard for managers to become fully informed and make perfectly rational decisions. They create a *bounded rationality* such that managerial decisions are rational only within the boundaries defined by the available information. The *administrative* or **behavioural decision model**, accordingly, assumes that people act only in terms of what they perceive about a given situation. Because such perceptions are frequently imperfect, the decision maker has only partial knowledge about the available action alternatives and their consequences. Consequently, the first alternative that appears to give a satisfactory resolution of the problem is likely to be chosen. Simon, who won a Nobel Prize for his work, calls this the tendency toward **satisficing decisions** — choosing the first satisfactory alternative that comes to your attention. This model seems especially accurate in describing how people make decisions about ambiguous problems in risky and uncertain conditions.

The **behavioural decision model** describes decision making with limited information and bounded rationality.

Satisficing decisions choose the first satisfactory alternative that comes to your attention.

Back to the Heinz Wattie's case. Management at Heinz Wattie's decided to follow the fourth alternative as described in step 2 of the decision-making process. 'This has been a particularly difficult decision. For the last 12 months we have been examining Dandenong's potential, but ultimately the age of the factory, the prohibitive cost of modernising the factory, continued low productivity — and the recent success of the Hastings operation — led to this decision [to close the factory]'. The closure enabled Heinz Wattie's to 'consolidate operations at the company's new $10 million baby food factory at Echuca in Victoria and the existing manufacturing sites at Wagga Wagga in New South Wales and Hastings in New Zealand'.

DECISION-MAKING STEP 4: IMPLEMENT THE SOLUTION

Given the choice of preferred solution, appropriate actions must be taken to fully implement it. This is the stage at which directions are finally set and problem-solving actions are initiated. Nothing new can or will happen according to plan unless action is taken. Managers not only need the determination and creativity to arrive at a decision, they also need the ability and willingness to implement it.

The 'ways' in which previous steps have been accomplished can have an additional and powerful impact at this stage of implementation. Difficulties at this stage often trace to the *lack-of-participation error*, or the failure to adequately involve those persons whose support is necessary to ensure a decision's complete implementation. Managers who use participation wisely get the right people involved in decisions and problem solving from the beginning. When they do, implementation typically follows quickly, smoothly and to everyone's satisfaction. Involvement not only makes everyone better informed, it also builds the commitments needed for implementation.

> *Back to the Heinz Wattie's case.* Heinz Wattie's went ahead with the consolidation of the regional corporate office in Melbourne, which created about 30 new jobs. 'There will be additional jobs created in Echuca associated with the transfer of production from Dandenong … we have created more than 120 jobs in Australia in the last eight months, with more jobs to be created in Echuca in coming months.' Heinz Wattie's identified positions at other sites for relocation offers, and set up counselling and career advisory services on site at Dandenong. Redundancy packages were available for employees who left the company.

DECISION-MAKING STEP 5: EVALUATE RESULTS

The decision-making process is not complete until results are evaluated. If the desired results are not achieved, the process must be renewed to allow for corrective actions. In this sense, evaluation is a form of managerial control. It involves a continuing commitment to gather information on performance results. Both the positive and negative consequences of the chosen course of action should be examined. If the original solution appears inadequate, a return to earlier steps in problem solving may be required to generate a modified or new solution. In this way, problem solving becomes a dynamic and ongoing activity within the management process. Evaluation is also made easier if the solution involves clear objectives that include measurable targets and timetables.

> *Back to the Heinz Wattie's case.* The Echuca plant created 70 jobs, and the regional transaction centre, which relocated to Melbourne, created a further 20 jobs. You can look back on the case and the problem-solving process just described and judge for yourself how well the management at Heinz Wattie's did in dealing with this very difficult problem. Would you have approached the situation and the five steps of decision making differently?

Behavioural influences on decision making

The manager's decision-making world is most often imperfect, subject to the influences of cognitive limitations, risk and uncertainty. As a result, the behavioural model is more common in decision-making practice than the rational model. Faced with complex environments, limited information and cognitive limitations, people also tend to use simplifying strategies for decision making. These strategies, shown in figure 3.6, are called **heuristics**, and their use can cause decision errors. An awareness of judgemental heuristics and their potential biases can help improve your decision-making capabilities.[32]

The *availability heuristic* occurs when people use information 'readily available' from memory as a basis for assessing a current event or situation. An example is deciding not to invest in a new product based on your recollection of how well a similar new product performed in the recent past. The potential bias is that the readily available information may be fallible and represent irrelevant factors. The new product that recently failed may have been a good idea that was released to market at the wrong time of year.

The *representativeness heuristic* occurs when people assess the likelihood of something occurring based on its similarity to a stereotyped set of occurrences. An example is deciding to employ someone for a job vacancy simply because he or she graduated from the same school attended by your last and most successful new employee. The potential bias is that the representative stereotype may fail to discriminate important and unique factors relevant to the decision. For instance, the abilities and career expectations of the newly hired person may not fit the job requirements.

The *anchoring and adjustment heuristic* involves making decisions based on adjustments to a previously existing value or starting point. An example is setting a new salary level for an employee by simply raising the prior year's salary by a reasonable percentage. The potential bias is that this may inappropriately bias a decision toward only incremental movement from the starting point. For instance, the individual's market value may be substantially higher than the existing salary. A simple adjustment won't keep this person from looking for another job.

Good managers are also aware of another behavioural tendency and source of potential decision-making error called **escalating commitment**. This is a decision to increase effort and perhaps apply more resources to pursue a course of action that is not working.[33] In such cases, managers let the momentum of the situation overwhelm them. They are unable to decide to 'call it quits', even when experience otherwise indicates that this is the most appropriate thing to do. Manager's Notepad 3.2 offers advice on avoiding this tendency.

Heuristics are strategies for simplifying decision making.

Escalating commitment is the continuation of a course of action even though it is not working.

MANAGER'S NOTEPAD 3.2

How to avoid the escalation trap

- Set advance limits on your involvement and commitment to a particular course of action; stick with these limits.

- Make your own decisions; don't follow the lead of others since they are also prone to escalation.

- Carefully determine just why you are continuing a course of action; if there are insufficient reasons to continue, don't.

- Remind yourself of what a course of action is costing; consider the saving of such costs as a reason to discontinue.

- Watch for escalation tendencies; be on guard against their influence on both you and others involved in the course of action.

Individual and group decision making

One of the important issues in decision making is the choice of whether to make the decision individually or with the participation of a group. The best managers and team leaders don't limit themselves to just one way. Instead, they switch back and forth among individual and group decision making to best fit the problems at hand. A managerial skill is the ability to choose the 'right' decision method — one that provides for a timely and quality decision, and one to which people involved in the implementation will be highly committed. To do this well, however, managers must understand both the potential assets and potential liabilities of moving from individual to more group-oriented decision making.[34]

The *potential advantages of group decision making* are highly significant, and they should be actively sought whenever time and other circumstances permit. Team decisions make greater amounts of information, knowledge and expertise available to solve problems. They expand the number of action alternatives that are examined; they help to avoid tunnel vision and consideration of only limited options. Team decisions increase the understanding and acceptance of outcomes by members. And importantly, team decisions increase the commitments of members to work hard to implement final plans.

The *potential disadvantages of group decision making* trace largely to the difficulties that can be experienced in group process. In a team decision there may be social pressure to conform. That is, individual members may feel intimidated or compelled to go along with the apparent wishes of others. There may be minority domination, where some members feel forced or 'railroaded' to accept a decision advocated by one vocal individual or small coalition. Also, there is no doubt that the time required to make team decisions can sometimes be a disadvantage. As more people are involved in the dialogue and discussion, decision making takes longer. This added time may be costly, even prohibitively so, in certain circumstances.[35]

Ethical decision making

Chapter 6 is entirely devoted to ethics and social responsibility issues in management. For the present, however, it is important to recognise that any decision should be ethical. It should meet the test described in step 3 of decision making as the 'ethics double-check'. This involves asking and answering two straightforward but powerful questions: How would I feel if my family found out about this decision? and How would I feel if this decision were published in the local newspaper?

Although it adds time to decision making, the ethics double-check is increasingly necessary to ensure that the ethical aspects of a problem are properly considered in the complex, fast-paced and often-uncertain decision conditions so common in today's organisations. It is also consistent with the demanding moral standards of modern society. A willingness to pause to examine the ethics of a proposed decision may well result in both better decisions and the prevention of costly litigation. Again, chapter 6 will explore these and related issues in depth.

KNOWLEDGE MANAGEMENT AND ORGANISATIONAL LEARNING

Management theorist Peter Drucker considers knowledge the principal resource of a competitive society and warns that 'knowledge constantly makes itself obsolete'.[36] This is an age in which intellectual capital counts highly, and knowledge workers — the people who have the knowledge — are critical assets. It is an age of transformation that places increasing value on learning and knowledge management.[37]

What is knowledge management?

A new term is earning a significant place in management theory and practice. The concept of **knowledge management** is used to describe the processes though which organisations develop, organise and share knowledge to achieve competitive advantage.[38] It is a mobilisation of intellectual capital. The significance of knowledge management as a strategic and integrating force in organisations is represented by the emergence of a new executive job title — chief knowledge officer (CKO). This position of CKO is responsible for energising learning processes and making sure that an organisation's portfolio of intellectual assets and pool of knowledge are well managed and continually enhanced. The intellectual assets, furthermore, include such things as patents, intellectual property rights, trade secrets and special processes and methods, as well as the accumulated knowledge and understanding of the entire workforce. John Peetz, chief knowledge officer at Ernst & Young USA, considers knowledge management one of four core processes — 'sell work, do work, manage people and manage knowledge'.[39]

GET CONNECTED!

Learn how to register a domain name for your own dot-com business. For a .au domain name, visit the Australian Domain Registration Services at www.domainregistration.com.au

GET CONNECTED!

Knowledge management involves the understanding of and commitment to the information technology described in this chapter. It requires the creation of an organisational culture in which information sharing, learning and knowledge creation are part of the norm. It requires a special form of organisational leadership that recognises that intellectual capital is an invaluable asset in this age of transformation. And at the bottom of it all, knowledge management requires managerial and leadership respect for people and their wonderful creative potential in organisations. According to Jack Welch, former CEO of General Electric:

> All we are talking about is human dignity and voice — giving people a chance to speak, to have their best idea. That is a global desire of all people who breathe ... My job is allocating capital, human and financial, and transferring best practice. That's all. It's transferring ideas, constantly pushing ideas, putting the right people in the right job and giving them the resources to win.[40]

Organisational learning

'Learning', says BP's CEO in the USA John Browne, 'is at the heart of a company's ability to adapt to a rapidly changing environment.' He goes on to add: 'In order to generate extraordinary value for its shareholders, a company must learn better than its competitors and apply that knowledge throughout its businesses faster and more widely than they do'.[41] Like other progressive organisations today, BP is striving to build the foundations of a true **learning organisation**. This is an organisation that 'by virtue of people, values and systems is able to continuously change and improve its performance based upon the lessons of experience'.[42] Consultant Peter Senge, author of the popular book, *The Fifth Discipline*, identifies the following core ingredients of learning organisations:[43]

Ingredients of learning organisations

1. *Mental models.* Everyone sets aside old ways of thinking.
2. *Personal mastery.* Everyone becomes self-aware and open to others.
3. *Systems thinking.* Everyone learns how the organisation works.
4. *Share vision.* Everyone understands and agrees to a plan of action.
5. *Team learning.* Everyone works together to accomplish the plan.

Senge's concept of the learning organisation places high value on developing the ability to learn and then make that learning continuously available to all organisational members. BP's CEO Browne says that organisations can learn from many sources. They can learn from their own experience. They can learn from the experiences of their contractors, suppliers, partners and customers. And they can learn from firms in unrelated businesses.[44] All of this, of course, depends on a willingness to seek out learning opportunities from these sources and to make information sharing an expected and valued work behaviour. In addressing the challenges of competing in a global economy, for example, General Electric's former CEO Jack Welch says: 'The aim in a global business is to get the best ideas from everywhere … Our culture is designed around making a hero out of those who translate ideas from one place to another, who help somebody else.' During his leadership, GE was transformed into a learning organisation in which information and ideas are quickly shared across its many diverse components. By combining a strong culture with the support of the latest in information technology, Welch pursued his goal of creating a truly 'boundaryless' company that values knowledge as a critical resource for competitive advantage.[45]

POINT ⇐

COUNTER

Judgement requires more than information

There are many definitions of knowledge management but there is one point that arises from all these definitions — to enable judgement. Comprehensive data and timely information are not enough for those who need to make day-to-day or even minute-to-minute decisions. When there exists a lack of trust among team members, and decisions emerge that are not based on a shared understanding of the business needs but rather on internal politics, the best information in the world would mean very little.[46]

Can you think of a business leader that made a 'bad' decision even though he or she had sound information at his or her disposal?

CHAPTER 3

Study guide

The chapter 3 study guide helps you review the chapter content, prepare for examinations, apply what you have learned and further build your career readiness. The summary briefly answers the study questions posed at the start of the chapter. The list of key terms allows you to double-check your familiarity with basic concepts and definitions. The applied activities help you test your comprehension of chapter content. Suggestions offered as career readiness activities direct your attention to relevant sections of the Career Readiness Workbook where you can test and develop your career skills and apply what you have learned. The list of electronic resources suggests activities from the *Management: An Asia–Pacific Perspective* web site and, finally, the case for critical thinking helps you apply your new management knowledge.

SUMMARY

How is information technology changing the workplace?

- Continuing advances in computers and information technology (IT) bring many opportunities for improving the workplace by better utilising information.
- Anyone entering the modern workplace, with its premium on intellectual capital and knowledge workers, must possess both computer competency and information competency.
- Today's 'electronic' offices with e-mail, voice messaging and networked computer systems are changing the way work is accomplished in and by organisations.
- A major and rapidly growing force in the economy are e-businesses, which use the Internet and computer networking to engage in business-to-consumer and business-to-business electronic commerce.

What are the current directions in information systems?

- A management information system (MIS) collects, organises, stores and distributes data in a way that meets the information needs of managers.
- Decision support systems (DSSs) provide information and help managers make decisions to solve complex problems.
- Group decision support systems use groupware to allow the computer-mediated exchange of information and decision making by group members.
- Intranets and computer networks allow persons within an organisation to share databases and communicate electronically; extranets and the Internet allow for communication between the organisation and its environment.

How is information used for decision making?

- Information is data that are made useful for decision making and problem solving.
- A problem is a discrepancy between an actual and a desired state of affairs.
- Managers face structured and unstructured problems in environments of certainty, risk and uncertainty.
- The most threatening type of problem is the crisis, which occurs unexpectedly and can lead to disaster if it is not handled quickly and properly.

How do managers make decisions?

- The steps in the decision-making process are find and define the problem, generate and evaluate alternatives, choose the preferred solution, implement the solution and evaluate the results.
- An optimising decision, following the classical model, chooses the absolute best solution from a known set of alternatives.
- A satisficing decision, following the administrative model, chooses the first satisfactory alternative to come to attention.
- Judgemental heuristics — such as the availability heuristic, the anchoring and adjustment heuristic and the representativeness heuristic — can bias decision making.
- Group decisions offer the potential advantages of greater information and expanded commitment, but they are often slower than individual decisions.

Why are knowledge management and organisational learning important?

- The old ways of management aren't good enough anymore; an age of transformation demands that the best of the past be combined with new thinking so organisations can be competitive in the 21st century.
- Knowledge management is the process of capturing, developing and using the knowledge of an organisation to achieve competitive advantage.
- A learning organisation is one in which people, values and systems support continuous change and improvement based on the lessons of experience.

KEY TERMS

behavioural decision model (p. 78)

certain environments (p. 74)

classical decision model (p. 78)

computer competency (p. 64)

cost-benefit analysis (p. 77)

crisis (p. 73)

decision (p. 73)

decision making (p. 76)

decision support system (p. 70)

electronic commerce (p. 66)

enterprise-wide networks (p. 70)

escalating commitment (p. 80)

expert systems (p. 70)

extranets (p. 71)

heuristics (p. 80)

information (p. 64)

information competency (p. 64)

information systems (p. 68)

information technology (IT) (p. 64)

intellectual capital (p. 64)

intranets (p. 70)

intuitive thinking (p. 75)

knowledge management (p. 82)

learning organisation (p. 82)

management information system (p. 72)

non-programmed decisions (p. 73)

optimising decision (p. 78)

problem solving (p. 73)

programmed decisions (p. 73)

risk environment (p. 74)

satisficing decisions (p. 78)

strategic opportunism (p. 76)

systematic thinking (p. 75)

uncertain environment (p. 74)

Short-response questions

1. In any organisation, what is the purpose of an information system?
2. What three factors are most important to the success of an information system and what are three common information system mistakes that managers should avoid?
3. What is the difference between problem solving and decision making?
4. How would a manager use systematic thinking and intuitive thinking in problem solving?

Application question

5. As a participant in a new 'mentoring' program between your university and a local high school, you have volunteered to give a presentation to a class of final year students on the challenges in the new 'electronic workplace'. The goal is to sensitise them to developments in office automation and motivate them to take the best advantage of their high school program so as to prepare themselves for the workplace of the future. What will you say to them?

CAREER READINESS ACTIVITIES

Recommended individual and group learning activities from the end-of-text Career Readiness Workbook for this chapter include:

Career advancement portfolio   WB

Update your career advancement portfolio to reflect your new skills and experiences. Include skills and personal insights you gain from the following projects and exercises.

Research and presentation project   WB

• Project 2 — Changing corporate cultures

Cross-functional integrative case   WB

Read the integrative case on Sarina Russo and answer the following questions:

3.1 At what stage of development in the dot-com life cycle are Sarina Russo Job Access and the Russo Institute of Technology?

3.2 Find an example in the integrative case of a non-programmed decision made by Sarina Russo. What was the related unique situation that resulted in the non-programmed decision?

Exercises in teamwork   WB

• Exercise 4 — What is your propensity for taking risks?
• Exercise 13 — The future workplace
• Exercise 14 — Dots and squares puzzle

Management skills assessment   WB

• Assessment 3 — Decision-making biases

ELECTRONIC RESOURCES

Don't forget to take full advantage of the online support for *Management: An Asia–Pacific Perspective* at www.johnwiley.com.au/highered/management: chapter 3 practice tests, e-flashcards, crossword puzzles, interactive management skills assessments, interactive cases, the online career advancement portfolio and much more!

CASE FOR CRITICAL THINKING

Read the following case for critical thinking on Sun Microsystems. While you are reading the case keep in mind what you have learned in this chapter, then answer the questions.

CASE FOR CRITICAL THINKING

Sun Microsystems: will Sun rule the Web?

What does it take to foster a computer revolution? Bill Gates's Microsoft model, based on distributed personal computers with software (largely Microsoft's) loaded on each individual machine, may be slowly giving way to a networked system long championed by Scott McNealy's Sun Microsystems. In fact, McNealy has been one of the few computer industry leaders to take on Microsoft directly, with a zeal and tenacity that is legendary. Steven M. Milunovich, an analyst with Merrill Lynch, argues: 'If you want to know where the computer industry is going, ask Sun'.[47]

Corporate history

Sun Microsystems was founded by Andreas Bechtolsheim, Bill Joy, Vinod Khosla and Scott McNealy in 1982. The first Sun system, the Sun-1, was a high-performance computer based on readily available, inexpensive components and the UNIX operating system largely developed by Joy while in graduate school at the University of California, Berkeley. From the very start, Sun resisted the so-called Microsoft Windows/Intel (Wintel) model and concentrated on high-end workstations, suitable for engineering, designers, Wall Street traders and CAD/CAM applications.

Scott McNealy took over as president of Sun in 1984 and since then has waged a constant war with Bill Gates and Microsoft. At first, Sun's market niche of high-end workstations kept it from competing directly with personal computers. However, over time PCs acquired more and more computing power, putting them in more direct competition with workstations. As a consequence, Sun has branched out into other computer areas, with an emphasis on the Internet.

Sun is the only major company that builds an entire line of computers based exclusively on its own designs, its own chips ('Sparc') and its own software, a version of the Unix operating system known as Solaris. As such, Sun stands alone as the 'pure' alternative to the Wintel world.[48] This strategy is not without its detractors, who point out that Sun handicaps itself by requiring huge research and development expenses compared to those firms relying on Windows and Intel. 'Sun spends 10.4 per cent of its sales on [research and development], compared to 4.5 per cent at Compaq and 1.6 per cent at Dell', who rely on Intel and Microsoft for much of their research.[49]

McNealy boasts that 'there are three technology companies left in the computer world. Intel, Microsoft and Sun'.[50] 'They [Sun] are beginning to be viewed as much more credible as an end-to-end solution provider', says Joe Ferlazzo, an analyst at Technology Business Research. Sun offers an attractive alternative with the same operating system on everything from a $2500 workstation with a single Sparc chip to a $1 million server with 64 parallel chips delivering as much computing power as an IBM mainframe. 'That's what's needed in the ISP environment and in corporate computing', he adds. In the opposite camp, Susan Whitney of IBM argues: 'To believe that a single architecture will address all the business requirements is not a sound strategy'.[51]

Undeterred, McNealy stays convinced of his mission, which is no less than to overthrow the personal computer. 'The PC is just a blip. It's a big, bright blip, but just a blip', says McNealy. 'Fifty years from now, people are going to look back and say: "Did you really have a computer on your desk? How weird."'[52] Analyst C. B. Lee of Sutro and Company and a former Sun manager argues that 'McNealy shoots off his mouth too much. At some point, you've gotta be more mature.'[53]

Offsetting McNealy's brashness is Ed Zander, chief operating officer for Sun, who exhibits a more conservative aura. 'I think McNealy and Zander are kind of like Yin and Yang', says Milunovich from Merrill Lynch. 'McNealy is the high priest of the religion. Ed is much more pragmatic. Having both is very good for Sun.'[54]

One thing McNealy has been able to accomplish is the constant re-invention of Sun as times and external conditions change. Starting with workstations and their various components, he has now positioned the firm to offer top-of-the-line servers that power the Internet. With the development of Java and Jini, Sun is evolving into a powerful software machine that serves to drive the Internet and future 'information appliances'.

To do this, Sun recognises the need for talented people. Many observers rate Sun's employees among the most talented in Silicon Valley. To keep them in a competitive marketplace, Sun emphasises the following perks.

- *Family care*. Adoptive parents receive financial assistance of up to $2000. Lactation rooms help new mothers return to work. In the San Francisco Bay Area, parents can take sick children to a special day care centre that cares for children with minor illnesses. Sun also offers a dependant-care spending account, a consultation and referral program, and an employee-assistance program providing short-term professional counselling.
- *Private workspace*. When Sun designed its Menlo Park campus, the company asked employees for suggestions — and found that engineers prefer private offices to Dilbert-like cubicles. The engineers got the space they demanded for quiet development time.
- *Respecting employee time*. Flexible hours and telecommuting help accommodate busy schedules and keep employees from wasting time on Californian freeways. Train travellers can catch a special shuttle to Sun facilities, and the company reimburses some commuting costs.[55]

Hard to find where the Sun don't shine

As early as 1987, Sun coined the phrase 'the network is the computer'.[56] But it has only been recently, with the full advent of the Internet coupled with Sun's Java programming language, that all the pieces may actually be falling into place to make this vision a reality. 'Microsoft's vision was to put a mainframe on everybody's desktop', claims McNealy. 'We want to provide dial tone for the Internet. We couldn't have more different visions.'[57]

In 1995, Java was introduced as the first universal software designed from the ground up for Internet and corporate intranet developers to write applications that run on any computer, regardless of the processor or operating system.[58] Most recently Sun has introduced Jini, a promising technology that lets computers and appliances connect to a network, as simply as a telephone plugs into the wall.[59] Sun's objective is to make access to the Internet and computing as simple as picking up a phone and hearing a 'webtone'.

Even Microsoft yielded to Java's appeal, licensing a version to develop its own line of software. Java's appeal is its ability to lower companies' IT costs because it runs unchanged on any device with a computer chip, enabling everything from wallet-sized cards to trucks to communicate over a network. However, Microsoft and Sun immediately got into a battle when Microsoft made a proprietary version of Java to run only on Windows programs. Sun sued and has won an initial ruling against Microsoft.

Sun claims that network computing will herald a shift away from personal computers to more friendly appliances such as phones, digital assistants and televisions. It hopes Java will provide the link to its powerful network servers with these new network devices.[60] Microsoft prefers its Windows CE operating system to provide this link. In addition, it views web appliances as 'companions' rather than replacements to today's PCs.

The allure of a host of Internet devices is their ability to bring in more users. Their convenience and ease of use promotes a more ubiquitous presence for the Web and the information located there. Java goes after this 'embedded' software market by powering the programs that run everything from phone switches to factory automation equipment.

Network computers	Stripped-down desktop computers run programs downloaded from the Internet.
TVs and pay television set-top boxes	TCI will distribute 20 million Java-equipped set-top boxes to encourage communication over cable.
Screenphones	Simple devices for straightforward services such as grocery ordering
Mobile phones and pagers	Mobile phone manufacturers plan to use Java to offer new services through their devices.
Smart cards	Java smart cards program routine processes, such as airline ticket purchases, directly on the cards.
Cars	Navigation and diagnostic systems powered by Java programs
Keys	Java-powered rings and pass cards

Figure 3.7 ▸ Java-powered Net 'appliances'[61]

McNealy billed Java as the killer of Microsoft Windows. Sun claims Java is ideally suited for the 'network computer' (NC) — a low-cost machine that has no hard drive, relying instead on a network that would supply it with small Java programs. Plummeting personal computer prices have stalled the take-off of the NC, but McNealy and Sun remain committed to the idea. 'Every day, 27 000 people [at Sun] get up and do one thing: network computing', claims Ed Zander. 'That's a very, very powerful story.'[62]

Sun meets AOL/Netscape

In perhaps its greatest coup to date, on 24 November 1998, Sun signed an alliance agreement with America Online (AOL) in association with its US$4.2 billion purchase of Netscape Communications. Access to Netscape's e-commerce software allows Sun to hawk its servers and 'attract customers that want a more complete package'.[63] In addition, Sun has access to one of the three largest portals on the Web. In exchange for providing US$350 million in licensing, marketing and advertising fees for the deal, AOL agrees to buy US$500 million in Sun servers over the next three years. In addition, the companies cooperate on the iPlanet e-commerce enterprise.

Open system advocates were originally concerned about AOL's involvement in the deal. They felt that AOL might hinder the free distribution of Netscape's browser. However, Stephen Case, AOL founder, assures doubters that the partnership will continue to allow free access to Netscape's browser technology. He intends to depend on Sun Microsystems to develop systems to provide Internet access over next-generation devices.

As a partner with AOL and Netscape, Sun is now in a position to challenge IBM, Hewlett-Packard and others in developing the systems that will let corporations rebuild their businesses in cyberspace. 'The challenge for Sun CEO Scott McNealy will be to behave like the top-tier industry leader that this deal may finally make him. And he'll need to make sure that Sun not only talks like a good partner but behaves like one too.'[64]

A major factor in Sun's favour is a world in which companies will choose to outsource anything that's not a demonstrably clear competitive advantage. Things such as human resources, financials, e-mail and web hosting all will clearly follow in the steps of payroll and facility security — that is, they'll be outsourced. Sun's been saying that the network is the computer for at least a decade. Oracle has been talking the talk for about three years. SAP was founded on the principle of centralised control since the early 1970s. But so far, no vendor has been able to convince any company that it should put its technological assets into someone else's hands. This is starting to change.[65]

The firm most strategically positioned to take advantage of this shift is Sun or possibly IBM Global Services. Scott McNealy has stated several times that companies should never think about purchasing another server again. He means that companies should leave the costs of maintaining scalability and reliability of fundamental systems to someone that specialises in the technology.[66]

Even so, the Internet must continue to evolve in order for Sun to realise its vision. John McFarlane, head of Solaris software, puts it plainly:

> We depend upon extreme reliability, availability and scalability as a market differentiator …
> I know from my seventeen years as a Nortel employee how much it hurts when there's a
> service failure of any kind, and how great it feels when the network would take a licking and
> keep on ticking. The same ethic applies at Sun. We run our own company systems on Sun,
> and our average downtime is about 22 minutes per employee per year. Another way to put it is
> we experience about 99.96 per cent uptime for every company user. We won a contract with
> the New York Stock Exchange because of our ability to deliver their required 99.99 per cent
> uptime — and so far we're at 100 per cent. If the Internet is truly to succeed as the next great

communication medium for mainstream users, and the webtone is to truly represent the same level of connectivity as the dial tone, then that level of reliability must be our model for all users. We call it the utility model of computing.[67]

With all these changes going on, how does a company cope? McNealy sums up his strategy by arguing, 'If everybody thought that what we were doing was the right thing, everybody would do what we are doing. If you are controversial and you are wrong, you've got a big problem. You have to be very controversial and very right to make lots of money.'[68]

QUESTIONS

1. Sun contends that 'the network is the computer'. Do you agree?
2. Can Sun continue to be a leader in the server market with new competitors entering?
3. Is McNealy's vision of the Internet correct, or has something changed to alter it?
4. Who appears to be leading in the network appliance operating systems?

CONTEXT

PART 2

CHAPTER 4

Historical foundations of management

CHAPTER 4 STUDY QUESTIONS

▸ What can be learned from classical management thinking?

▸ What ideas were introduced by the human resource approaches?

▸ What is the role of quantitative analysis in management?

▸ What is unique about the systems view and contingency thinking?

▸ What are continuing management themes of the 21st century?

E-fulfilment innovations — what is the 'newest' old thing?

GETTING @ CONNECTED

Things don't just happen by magic when you go to a web site, decide you'd like to order a product such as a digital camera or the latest fashion clothing, and hit 'submit order' or 'buy now'. Did you ever wonder just what happens next to bring that new purchase to your doorstep, often in just one or two days time?

Welcome to the new world of one of business's oldest fundamentals — taking and fulfilling a customer's order. Advertising Distribution Services (ADS) is a progressive Australian company that offers a complete solution to warehousing, logistics and order fulfilment for businesses that sell their products over the Internet. Chief executive Bob Townsend is responsible for the strategic and day-to-day management of the business and has been a major player in the introduction and development of state-of-the-art information technology systems and processes to ADS. Clients get instant access to sales data, and their customers get a seamless shopping experience and rapid delivery of their purchases. Now when you hit the 'submit' button on Australian web sites, there is a good chance that ADS is behind the delivery.

A similar example of this type of e-fulfilment innovation in Australia is the e-partnership between retailer Myer Direct and CommercialWare. Myer Direct uses CommercialWare's retail.dot.commerce™ system as its end-to-end retail commerce infrastructure. According to managing director e.colesmyer, Jon Wood: 'Fulfilment is the make-or-break piece of the direct-to-consumer puzzle.'[1]

GET CONNECTED!

Visit www.adservices.com.au to find out how ADS works. Compare it to similar international sites like www.commercialware.com and www.ifulfillment.com. Consider the opportunities for new business ventures in the world of e-business.

GET CONNECTED!

www.ritzcarlton.com/
hotels/singapore/

The Ritz-Carlton Millenia, famous for being named best overall hotel in the Asia–Pacific region, is careful to employ talented staff. General manager Nicholas Clayton attributes the hotel's success to getting staff who complement the hotel's culture by getting the 'fine touches' right, such as great service and quality of workmanship.[6]

ADS is a good example of the many new opportunities that are emerging for fast, radical transformation of traditional businesses by technology-driven innovations. But even in the rush to an exciting future, one shouldn't sell history short. Knowledge gained through past experience can and should be used as a foundation for future success.

When Harvard University Press released *Mary Parker Follett — Prophet of Management: A Celebration of Writings from the 1920s*, it clearly reminded us of the wisdom of history.[2] Although writing in a different day and age, Follett's ideas are rich with foresight. She advocated cooperation and better horizontal relationships in organisations, taught respect for the experience and knowledge of workers, warned against the dangers of too much hierarchy, and called for visionary leadership. Today we pursue similar themes while using terms like empowerment, involvement, flexibility and self-management. Rather than naively believe that we are reinventing management practice, it may be better to recognise the historical roots of many modern ideas and admit that we are still trying to perfect them.[3]

In *The Evolution of Management Thought*, professor Daniel Wren traces management as far back as 5000 BC, when ancient Sumerians used written records to assist in governmental and commercial activities.[4] Management was important to the construction of the Egyptian pyramids, the rise of the Roman Empire and the commercial success of 14th-century Venice. By the time of the Industrial Revolution in the 1700s, great social changes helped prompt a great leap forward in the manufacture of basic staples and consumer goods. Industrial change was accelerated by Adam Smith's ideas of efficient production through specialised tasks and the division of labour. By the turn of the 20th century, Henry Ford and others were making mass production a mainstay of the modern economy. Since then, the science and practices of management have been on a rapid and continuing path of development.

The legacies of this rich history of management must be understood as we move rapidly into the new conditions and challenges of 21st-century management.[5] The historical context of management thinking can be understood in the following framework. The *classical management approaches* focus on developing universal principles for use in various management situations. The *behavioural management approaches* focus on human needs, the work group and the role of social factors in the workplace. The *quantitative management approaches* focus on applying mathematical techniques for management of problem solving. The *modern approaches* focus on the systems view of organisations and contingency thinking in a dynamic and complex environment. *Continuing themes* build from an emphasis on quality and performance excellence to embrace diversity and global awareness, and describe new leadership roles for a new era of management.

CLASSICAL APPROACHES TO MANAGEMENT

There are three major branches within the classical approach to management: scientific management, administrative principles and bureaucratic organisation. Figure 4.1 associates each with a prominent person in the history of management thought. These names are important to know since they are still widely used in management conversations today. Also, the figure shows that the branches all share a common assumption: people at work act in a rational manner that is primarily driven by economic concerns. Workers are expected to rationally consider opportunities made available to them and do whatever is necessary to achieve the greatest personal and monetary gain.[7]

Scientific management

In 1911 Frederick W. Taylor published *The Principles of Scientific Management*, in which he makes the following statement: 'The principal object of management should be to secure maximum prosperity for the employer, coupled with the maximum prosperity for the employee'.[8] Taylor, often called the 'father of scientific management', noticed that many workers did their jobs their own way and without clear and uniform specifications. He believed that this caused them to lose efficiency and perform below their true capacities. He also believed that this problem could be corrected if workers were taught and then helped by supervisors to always perform their jobs in the right way.

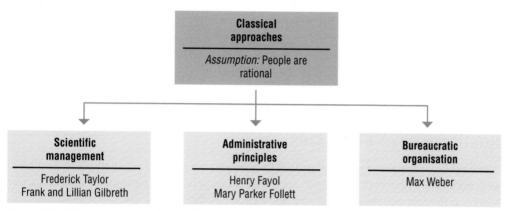

Figure 4.1 ▶ Major branches in the classical approach to management

Taylor used the concept of 'time study' to analyse the motions and tasks required in any job and to develop the most efficient ways to perform them.[9] He then linked these job requirements with both training for the worker and support from supervisors in the form of proper direction, work assistance and monetary incentives. This approach is known as **scientific management** and includes these four guiding action principles.

1. Develop for every job a 'science' that includes rules of motion, standardised work processes and proper working conditions.
2. Carefully select workers with the right abilities for the job.
3. Carefully train workers to do the job and give them the proper incentives to cooperate with the job 'science'.
4. Support workers by carefully planning their work and by smoothing the way as they go about their jobs.

Taylor tried to use scientific techniques to improve the productivity of people at work. The implications of his efforts, if not his exact scientific management principles, are found in many management settings today. A number of these are summarised in Manager's Notepad 4.1.

 Scientific management emphasises careful selection and training of workers, and supervisory support.

◀

Principles of scientific management

MANAGER'S NOTEPAD 4.1

Practical lessons from scientific management

- Make results-based compensation a performance incentive.
- Carefully design jobs with efficient work methods.
- Carefully select workers with the abilities to do these jobs.
- Train workers to perform jobs to the best of their abilities.
- Train supervisors to support workers so they can perform jobs to the best of their abilities.

Mentioned in Taylor's first principle, **motion study** is the science of reducing a job or task to its basic physical motions. As contemporaries of Taylor, Frank and Lillian Gilbreth pioneered motion studies as a management tool. In one famous study, they reduced the number of motions used by bricklayers and tripled their productivity.[10] The Gilbreths' work established the foundation for later advances in the areas of job simplification, work standards, and incentive wage plans — all techniques still used in the modern workplace.

The ideas of Taylor and the Gilbreths are evident in the growing call centre industry. It is an industry, however, with a big problem — an alarmingly high staff-attrition rate. For some companies, call centres are now their main point of contact with customers. But in many cases, the staff in those call centres are bored, disgruntled and inexperienced. Some say call centres are the new sweatshops. The cost of training new operators and the poor customer service that results from the high turnover have made staff recruitment and employee training programs a priority for call centre managers.[11]

Administrative principles

A second branch in the classical approach to management is based on attempts to document and understand the experiences of successful managers. Two prominent writers in this school of thought are Henri Fayol and Mary Parker Follett.

HENRI FAYOL

In 1916, after a career in French industry, Henri Fayol published *Administration Industrielle et Générale*.[12] The book outlines his views on the proper management of organisations and the people within them. It identifies the following five 'rules' or 'duties' of management, which closely resemble the four functions of management — planning, organising, leading and controlling — that we talk about today:

Fayol's rules of management

1. *Foresight* — to complete a plan of action for the future.
2. *Organisation* — to provide and mobilise resources to implement the plan.
3. *Command* — to lead, select and evaluate workers to get the best work toward the plan.
4. *Coordination* — to fit diverse efforts together and ensure information is shared and problems solved.
5. *Control* — to make sure things happen according to plan and to take necessary corrective action.

Most importantly, Fayol believed that management could be taught. He was very concerned about improving the quality of management and set forth a number of 'principles' to guide managerial action. A number of them are still part of the management vocabulary. They include Fayol's *scalar chain principle* (there should be a clear and unbroken line of communication from the top to the bottom in the organisation), the *unity of command principle* (each person should receive orders from only one boss), and the *unity of direction principle* (one person should be in charge of all activities that have the same performance objective).

MARY PARKER FOLLETT

Another contributor to the administrative principles school was Mary Parker Follett, who was eulogised at her death in 1933 as 'one of the most important women America has yet produced in the fields of civics and sociology'.[13] In her writings about businesses and other organisations, Follett displayed an understanding of groups and a deep commitment to human cooperation — ideas that are highly relevant today. For her, groups were mechanisms through which diverse individuals could combine their talents for a greater good. She viewed organisations as 'communities' in which managers and workers should labour in harmony, without one party dominating the other, and with the freedom to talk over and truly reconcile conflicts and differences. She believed it was the manager's job to help people in organisations cooperate with one another and achieve an integration of interests.

A review of *Dynamic Administration: The Collected Papers of Mary Parker Follett* helps to illustrate the modern applications of her management insights.[14] Follett believed that making every employee an owner in the business would create feelings of collective responsibility. *Today*, we address the same issues under such labels as 'employee ownership', 'profit sharing' and 'gain-sharing plans'. Follett believed that business problems involve a wide variety of factors that must be considered in relationship to one another. *Today*, we talk about 'systems' when describing the same phenomenon. Follett believed that businesses were services and that private profits should always be considered vis-à-vis the public good. *Today*, we pursue the same issues under the labels of 'managerial ethics' and 'corporate social responsibility'.

www.ozcallcentres.com

Call centre work can involve many problems associated with Taylor's notion of scientific management, such as stress and boredom. Visit the Oz Call Centres web site to learn more about the unique issues associated with call centres. One company tackling these problems is Corporate Express. Many of its staff have moved on to different roles in the company and are being trained to understand all areas of the business.[16]

COUNTER POINT ←

The downside of productivity

Organisations in Australia and New Zealand are increasingly pushing for greater productivity and greater profitability for their shareholders. Employees are working harder and longer hours, and work-related stress associated with this trend is increasingly being recognised as a legal issue because employers potentially face legal liability. For example, Bruce Moore, from law firm Mallesons Stephen Jaques, argues: 'Under common law principles, an employer has a duty to take reasonable care to avoid illness or injury to employees in connection with their employment. There is a similar, but usually stricter, duty imposed by the occupational health and safety legislation.'[15]

Bureaucratic organisation

Max Weber was a late 19th-century German intellectual whose insights have had a major impact on the field of management and the sociology of organisations. His ideas developed somewhat in reaction to what he considered to be performance deficiencies in the organisations of his day. Among other things, Weber was concerned that people were in positions of authority not because of their job-related capabilities, but because of their social standing or 'privileged' status in German society. For this and other reasons he believed that organisations largely failed to reach their performance potential.

At the heart of Weber's thinking was a specific form of organisation he believed could correct the problems just described — a **bureaucracy**.[17] This is an ideal, intentionally rational and very efficient form of organisation founded on principles of logic, order and legitimate authority. The defining characteristics of Weber's bureaucratic organisation are as follows:

- *Clear division of labour.* Jobs are well defined, and workers become highly skilled at performing them.
- *Clear hierarchy of authority.* Authority and responsibility are well defined for each position, and each position reports to a higher-level one.
- *Formal rules and procedures.* Written guidelines direct behaviour and decisions in jobs, and written files are kept for historical record.

A **bureaucracy** is a rational and efficient form of organisation founded on logic, order and legitimate authority.

Characteristics of Weber's bureaucracy

- *Impersonality.* Rules and procedures are impartially and uniformly applied with no one receiving preferential treatment.
- *Careers based on merit.* Workers are selected and promoted on ability and performance, and managers are career employees of the organisation.

Weber believed that organisations would perform well as bureaucracies. They would have the advantages of efficiency in utilising resources, and of fairness or equity in the treatment of employees and clients. In his words:

> The purely bureaucratic type of administrative organisation ... is, from a purely technical point of view, capable of attaining the highest degree of efficiency ... It is superior to any other form in precision, in stability, in the stringency of its discipline, and in its reliability. It thus makes possible a particularly high degree of calculability of results for the heads of the organisation and for those acting in relation to it. It is finally superior both in intensive efficiency and in the scope of its operations and is formally capable of application to all kinds of administrative tasks.[18]

This is the ideal side of bureaucracy. However, the terms *bureaucracy* and *bureaucrat* are now often used with negative connotations. The *possible disadvantages of bureaucracy* include excessive paperwork or 'red tape', slowness in handling problems, rigidity in the face of shifting customer or client needs, resistance to change and employee apathy. These disadvantages are most likely to cause problems for organisations that must be flexible and quick in adapting to changing circumstances — a characteristic of challenges in today's dynamic organisational environments. Researchers now try to determine when and under what conditions bureaucratic features work best. They also want to identify alternatives to the bureaucratic form. Indeed, current trends in management include many innovations that seek the same goals as Weber but with different approaches to how organisations can be structured.

BEHAVIOURAL APPROACHES TO MANAGEMENT

During the 1920s, an emphasis on the human side of the workplace began to establish its influence on management thinking. Major branches that emerged in this behavioural or human resource approach to management are shown in figure 4.2. They include the famous Hawthorne Studies and Maslow's theory of human needs, as well as theories generated from these foundations by Douglas McGregor, Chris Argyris and others. The behavioural approaches maintain that people are social and self-actualising. People at work are assumed to seek satisfying social relationships, respond to group pressures and search for personal fulfilment.

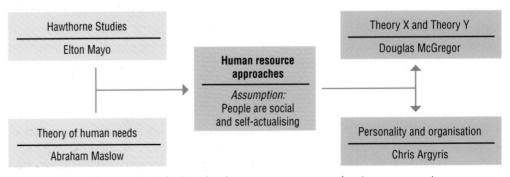

Figure 4.2 ▶ Foundations in the behavioural or human resource approaches to management

The Hawthorne Studies and human relations

In 1924, the Western Electric Company (predecessor to today's Lucent Technologies) commissioned a research program to study individual productivity at the Hawthorne Works of the firm's Chicago plant.[19] The initial 'Hawthorne Studies' had a scientific management perspective and sought to determine how economic incentives and the physical conditions of the workplace affected the output of workers. An initial focus was on the level of illumination in the manufacturing facilities — it seemed reasonable to expect that better lighting would improve performance. After failing to find this relationship, however, the researchers concluded that unforeseen 'psychological factors' somehow interfered with their illumination experiments. This finding and later Hawthorne Studies directed attention toward human interactions in the workplace and ultimately had a major influence on the field of management.

RELAY ASSEMBLY TEST-ROOM STUDIES

In 1927, a team led by Harvard's Elton Mayo began more research to examine the effect of worker fatigue on output. Care was taken to design a scientific test that would be free of the psychological effects thought to have confounded the earlier illumination studies. Six workers who assembled relays were isolated for intensive study in a special test room. They were given various rest pauses, and workdays and work weeks of various lengths, and production was regularly measured. Once again, researchers failed to find any direct relationship between changes in physical working conditions and output. Productivity increased regardless of the changes made.

Mayo and his colleagues concluded that the new 'social setting' created for workers in the test room accounted for the increased productivity. Two factors were singled out as having special importance. One was the *group atmosphere* — the workers shared pleasant social relations with one another and wanted to do a good job. The other was more *participative supervision*. Test-room workers were made to feel important, were given a lot of information and were frequently asked for their opinions. This was not the case in their, or in the other workers', regular jobs elsewhere in the plant.

EMPLOYEE ATTITUDES, INTERPERSONAL RELATIONS AND GROUP PROCESSES

Mayo's studies continued to examine these factors until the worsening economic conditions of the Depression forced their termination in 1932. Until then, interest focused on employee attitudes, interpersonal relations and group relations. In one study, over 21 000 employees were interviewed to learn what they liked and disliked about their work environment. 'Complex' and 'baffling' results led the researchers to conclude that the same things (e.g. work conditions or wages) could be sources of satisfaction for some workers and of dissatisfaction for others. The final Hawthorne study was conducted in the bank wiring room and centred on the role of the work group. A surprise finding here was that people would restrict their output in order to avoid the displeasure of the group, even if it meant sacrificing pay that could otherwise be earned by increasing output. Thus, it was recognised that groups can have strong negative, as well as positive, influences on individual productivity.

LESSONS OF THE HAWTHORNE STUDIES

As scholars now look back, the Hawthorne Studies are criticised for poor research design, weak empirical support for the conclusions drawn and the tendency of researchers to over-generalise their findings.[21] Yet the significance of these studies as a turning point in the evolution of management thought remains intact. The Hawthorne Studies helped shift the attention of managers and management researchers away from the technical and structural concerns of the classical approach, and toward social and human concerns as keys to productivity. They showed that people's feelings, attitudes and relationships with coworkers should be important to management, and they recognised the importance of the work group. They also identified the **Hawthorne effect** — the tendency of people who are singled out for special attention to perform as anticipated merely because of expectations created by the situation.

The Hawthorne Studies contributed to the emergence of the **human relations movement** as an important influence on management thought during the 1950s and 1960s. This movement was largely based on the viewpoint that managers who used good human relations in the workplace would achieve productivity. Furthermore, the insights of the human relations movement set the stage for what has now evolved as the field of **organisational behaviour**, the study of individuals and groups in organisations.

Maslow's theory of human needs

Among the insights of the human relations movement, the work of Abraham Maslow in the area of human 'needs' is a key foundation. **Needs** are physiological or psychological deficiencies a person feels the compulsion to satisfy. This is a significant concept for managers because needs create tensions that can influence a person's work attitudes and behaviours.

Maslow identified the five levels of human needs, shown in figure 4.3. From lowest to highest in order they are physiological, safety, social, esteem and self-actualisation needs. Maslow's theory is based on two underlying principles.[22] The first is the *deficit principle* — a satisfied need is not a motivator of behaviour. People act to satisfy 'deprived' needs, those for which a satisfaction 'deficit' exists. The second is the *progression principle* — the five needs exist in a hierarchy of 'prepotency'. A need at any level only becomes activated once the next-lower-level need has been satisfied.

According to Maslow, people try to satisfy the five needs in sequence. They progress step by step from the lowest level in the hierarchy to the highest. Along the way, a deprived need dominates individual attention and determines behaviour until it is satisfied. Then, the next-higher-level need is activated and progression up the hierarchy occurs. At the level of self-actualisation, the deficit and progression principles cease to operate. The more this need is satisfied, the stronger it grows.

Consistent with the human relations thinking, Maslow's theory implies that managers who can help people satisfy their important needs at work will achieve productivity. Although scholars now recognise that things are more complicated than this, discussed further in chapter 14 on motivation and rewards, Maslow's ideas are still relevant to everyday

The **Hawthorne effect** is the tendency of persons singled out for special attention to perform as expected.

The **human relations movement** suggests that managers using good human relations will achieve productivity.

Organisational behaviour is the study of individuals and groups in organisations.

Needs are unfulfilled physiological or psychological desires.

GET CONNECTED!

Visit the Productivity Commission's site www.pc.gov.au to discover the current trends in relation to productivity issues in Australia. Compare them with productivity trends in Singapore, available from SPRING Singapore (formerly the Singapore Productivity and Standards Board) www.spring.gov.sg/statistics/productivity.html.

GET CONNECTED!

management. Consider, for example, the case of dealing with volunteer workers who do not receive any monetary compensation. Managers in not-for-profit organisations have to create jobs and work environments that satisfy the needs of volunteers. If the work isn't fulfilling, the volunteers will redirect their energies and volunteer to work somewhere else.

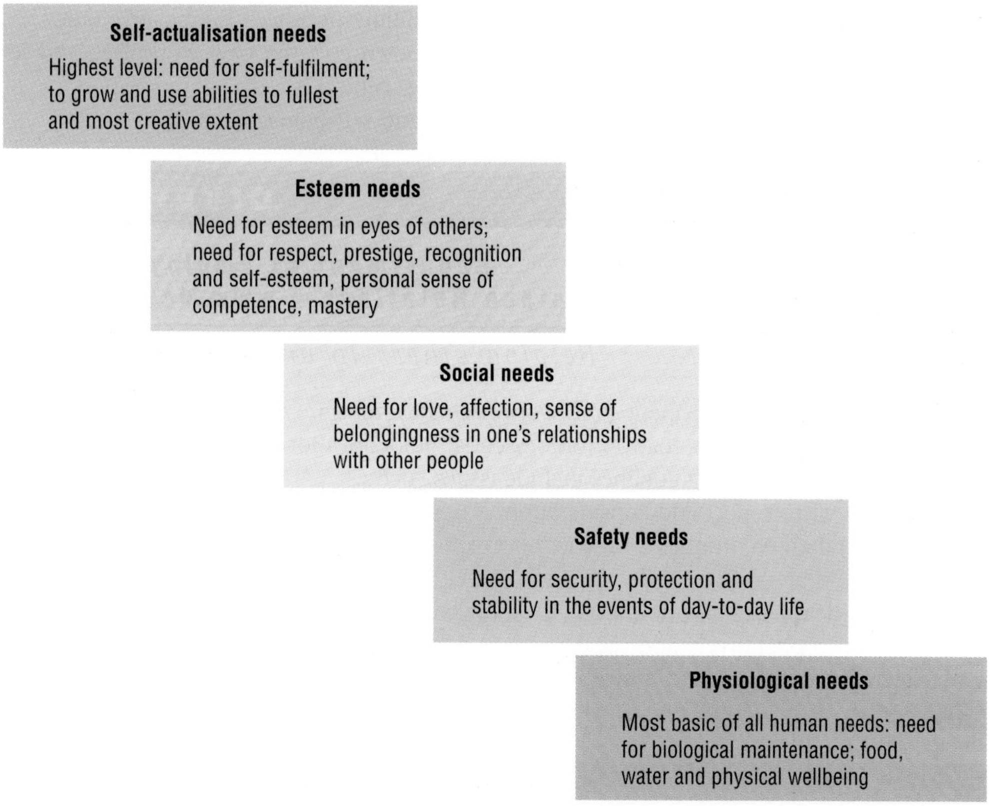

Self-actualisation needs
Highest level: need for self-fulfilment; to grow and use abilities to fullest and most creative extent

Esteem needs
Need for esteem in eyes of others; need for respect, prestige, recognition and self-esteem, personal sense of competence, mastery

Social needs
Need for love, affection, sense of belongingness in one's relationships with other people

Safety needs
Need for security, protection and stability in the events of day-to-day life

Physiological needs
Most basic of all human needs: need for biological maintenance; food, water and physical wellbeing

Figure 4.3 ▸ Maslow's hierarchy of human needs

McGregor's Theory X and Theory Y

Douglas McGregor was heavily influenced by both the Hawthorne Studies and Maslow. His classic book *The Human Side of Enterprise* advances the thesis that managers should give more attention to the social and self-actualising needs of people at work.[23] McGregor called upon managers to shift their view of human nature away from a set of assumptions he called 'Theory X' and toward ones he called 'Theory Y'.

According to McGregor, managers holding **Theory X** assumptions approach their jobs believing that those who work for them generally dislike work, lack ambition, are irresponsible, are resistant to change and prefer to be led rather than to lead. McGregor considers such thinking inappropriate. He argues instead for the value of **Theory Y** assumptions in which the manager believes people are willing to work, are capable of self-control, are willing to accept responsibility, are imaginative and creative, and are capable of self-direction.

An important aspect of McGregor's ideas is his belief that managers who hold either set of assumptions can create **self-fulfilling prophecies** — that is, through their behaviour they create situations where subordinates act in ways that confirm the original expectations. *Managers with Theory X assumptions* act in a very directive 'command-and-control' fashion that gives people little personal say over their work. These supervisory behaviours often

Theory X assumes people dislike work, lack ambition, are irresponsible and prefer to be led.

Theory Y assumes people are willing to work, accept responsibility, are self-directed and creative.

Self-fulfilling prophecies occur when people act in ways that confirm another's expectations.

create passive, dependent and reluctant subordinates who tend to do only what they are told to or required to do. This reinforces the original Theory X viewpoint. In contrast, *managers with Theory Y perspectives* behave in 'participative' ways that allow subordinates more job involvement, freedom and responsibility. This creates opportunities to satisfy esteem and self-actualisation needs, and causes workers to perform as expected with initiative and high performance. This time the self-fulfilling prophecy is a positive one.

Theory Y thinking is very consistent with developments in the new workplace and its emphasis on valuing workforce diversity. It is also central to the popular notions of employee participation, involvement, empowerment and self-management.[24]

DIVERSITY

Department of Employment and Workplace Relations • www.dewr.gov.au

Helping others to understand diversity

The Department of Employment and Workplace Relations in Australia has developed a workplace diversity strategy that outlines essential guidelines for managing diversity in the workplace. Some practical guidelines include issues such as:

- treat others with respect and consideration
- work to build an environment in which everyone can fully participate
- be open minded — listen and respond to the views of others
- contribute ideas and draw on our skills, knowledge and background
- identify and cooperatively address barriers to diversity and participation
- not tolerate harassment and discrimination
- consistently display in our work what we value in the department.[25]

Argyris's theory of adult personality

Ideas set forth by the well-regarded scholar and consultant Chris Argyris also reflect a belief in the higher order of human nature advanced by Maslow and McGregor. In his book *Personality and Organization*, Argyris contrasts the management practices found in traditional and hierarchical organisations with the needs and capabilities of mature adults.[26] He concludes that some practices, especially those influenced by the classical management approaches, are inconsistent with the mature adult personality.

Consider these examples. In scientific management, the principle of specialisation assumes that people will work more efficiently as tasks become better defined. Argyris believes that this may inhibit self-actualisation in the workplace. In Weber's bureaucracy, people work in a clear hierarchy of authority with top-level managers directing and controlling lower levels. Argyris worries that this creates dependent, passive workers who feel they have little control over their work environments. In Fayol's administrative principles, the concept of unity of direction assumes that efficiency will increase when a person's work is planned and directed by a supervisor. Argyris suggests that this may create conditions for psychological failure — psychological success occurs when people define their own goals.

Like McGregor, the belief that managers who treat people positively and as responsible adults will achieve productivity is central to Argyris's thinking. His advice is to expand job responsibilities, allow more task variety, and adjust supervisory styles to allow more participation and promote better human relations. He believes that the common problems of employee absenteeism, turnover, apathy, alienation and the like may be signs of a mismatch between workers' mature personalities and outdated management practices.

GET CONNECTED!

Learn more about the contemporary business leadership issues currently debated in Australasia by visiting these web sites: www.bca.com.au, www.nzsbc.com and www.nzbcsd.org.nz.

GET CONNECTED!

QUANTITATIVE APPROACHES TO MANAGEMENT

About the same time that some scholars were developing human resource approaches to management, others were investigating how quantitative techniques could improve managerial decision making. The foundation of the quantitative approaches to management is the assumption that mathematical techniques can be used to improve managerial decision making and problem solving. Today these applications are increasingly driven by computer technology and software programs.

Management science

The terms **management science** and *operations research* are often used interchangeably to describe the scientific applications of mathematical techniques to management problems. A typical approach proceeds as follows. A problem is encountered, it is systematically analysed, appropriate mathematical models and computations are applied, and an optimum solution is identified. In this process, a number of management science applications are commonly used. *Mathematical forecasting* helps make future projections that are useful in the planning process. *Inventory modelling* helps control inventories by mathematically establishing how much to order and when. *Linear programming* is used to calculate how best to allocate scarce resources among competing uses. *Queuing theory* helps allocate service personnel or workstations to minimise customer waiting time and service cost. *Network models* break large tasks into smaller components to allow for better analysis, planning and control of complex projects. And *simulation* makes models of problems so different solutions under various assumptions can be tested.

Management science uses mathematical techniques to analyse and solve management problems.

**www.spss.com.
australasia**

A popular and easy-to-use
software program for
statistical analysis is SPSS,
available from SPSS Inc.
From historical roots with
the software being a tool for
scholars and social science
researchers, the company has
grown into a major provider
of support-data-based
business problem solving,
with special applications to
customer relationship
management and business
intelligence.

Regardless of the specific technique used, the essence of the quantitative management approach includes these characteristics. There is a focus on decision making that has clear implications for management action. The techniques use 'economic' decision criteria, such as costs, revenues and return on investment. They also involve mathematical models that follow sophisticated rules and formulas.

Quantitative analysis today

University courses in management science, operations research and quantitative business analysis provide a good introduction to these quantitative management foundations. Courses in operations management apply them to the physical production of goods and services. Since many of the techniques are highly sophisticated, organisations often employ staff specialists to help managers take advantage of them effectively. But software developments are making these techniques more readily available through easy-to-use applications for desktop and even handheld personal computers. This availability greatly expands their use throughout the workplace and makes it even more important for managers to understand the value of each technique. In all cases, of course, mathematical solutions to problems must be supported by good managerial judgement and an appreciation of the human factor.

MODERN APPROACHES TO MANAGEMENT

The modern approaches to management grew directly from foundations established by the classical, human resource and quantitative schools of thought. Importantly, they also recognise that no one model or theory applies universally in all situations or to the exclusion of the others.

According to the modern management approaches, people are complex and variable. They have many varied needs that can change over time. They possess a range of talents and capabilities that can be developed. Organisations and managers, therefore, should respond to individual differences with a wide variety of managerial strategies and job opportunities. Key foundations of the modern management approaches include the systems view of organisations and contingency thinking.

Systems thinking

A **system** is a collection of interrelated parts working together for a purpose.

A **subsystem** is a smaller component of a larger system.

An **open system** transforms resource inputs from the environment into product outputs.

Formally defined, a **system** is a collection of interrelated parts that function together to achieve a common purpose.[27] A **subsystem** is a smaller component of a larger system.[27] One of the earliest management writers to adopt a systems perspective was Chester Barnard. His 1938 groundbreaking book *Functions of the Executive* was based on years of experience as a telephone company executive.[28] Barnard described organisations as cooperative systems in which the contributions of individuals are integrated for a common purpose. Importantly, Barnard considered this cooperation 'conscious, deliberate and purposeful'. It was the job of the executives, or managers, through communication to make this cooperation happen.

Systems thinking continues to influence management theory and practice today.[29] One application is described in figure 4.4. This figure first depicts the larger organisation as an **open system** that interacts with its environment in the continual process of transforming inputs from suppliers into outputs for customers. Within the organisation any number of critical subsystems can be described. In the figure, the operations and service management systems are a central point. They provide the integration among other subsystems — such

106   PART 2 | CONTEXT

as purchasing, accounting, sales and information — that are essential to the work of the organisation. Importantly, and as suggested by Barnard, high performance by the organisation as a whole occurs only when each subsystem both performs its tasks well and works well in cooperation with the other subsystems. It is the job of managers throughout the organisation to make this coordinated action possible.

Figure 4.4 ▸ Organisations as complex networks of interacting subsystems

Contingency thinking

Modern management is situational in orientation — that is, it attempts to identify management practices that are the best fit with the unique demands of a situation. It uses **contingency thinking** that tries to match managerial responses with the problems and opportunities specific to different settings, particularly those posed by individual and environmental differences. In the modern management approach, there is no expectation that one can or should find the 'one best way' to manage in all circumstances. Rather, the contingency perspective tries to help managers understand situational differences and respond to them in appropriate ways.[30]

Contingency thinking is an important theme in this book, and its implications extend to all of the management functions — from planning and controlling for diverse environmental conditions, to organising for different environments and strategies, to leading in different performance situations. For example, consider again the concept of bureaucracy — something Weber offered as an ideal form of organisation. From a contingency perspective the strict bureaucratic form is only one possible way of organising things. What turns out to be the 'best' structure in any given situation will depend on many factors, including environmental uncertainty, an organisation's primary technology and the strategy being pursued. Only when the environment is relatively stable and operations are predictable does the bureaucracy work best; in other situations, alternative structures may be needed. Contingency thinking recognises that what is a good structure for one organisation may not work well for another, and what works well at one time may not work as well in the future as circumstances change.[31] This contingency approach to organisation structure and design is examined further in chapters 10 and 11.

● **Contingency thinking** tries to match management practices with situational demands.

The clash of generations?

The future challenge for managers will be to manage effectively across generations.

What do you think are some of the issues in managing across generations?

CONTINUING MANAGEMENT THEMES

The many accumulating insights into management practice have set the foundation for important trends and directions in management thought that are well in evidence as we begin the 21st century. Among the most important is the recognition that we live and work in a dynamic and ever-changing environment that puts unique and never-ending competitive pressures on organisations. Key themes reflected in discussions throughout *Management: An Asia–Pacific Perspective* include continuing pressures for quality and performance excellence, an expanding global awareness, and the importance of new leadership in an age of information, knowledge workers and highly competitive business environments.

Quality and performance excellence

The quality theme was first introduced in chapter 1 and will continue throughout this book.[32] It remains a very important direction in management today. Managers and workers in truly progressive organisations are quality conscious. They understand the basic link between competitive advantage and the ability to always deliver quality goods and services to their customers. The best organisational cultures include quality as a core value and reinforce the quality commitment in all aspects of the work environment.

Every effort is made in total quality management (TQM) to build quality into all aspects of operations from initial acquisition of resources, through the transformation processes and work systems, all the way to ultimate product delivery to customers or clients. Figure 4.5 describes the systems context for TQM in respect to the **value chain** — a specific sequence of activities that transform raw materials into a finished good or service.[33] Quality must be maintained at each point in the value chain, whether it is performed directly by the organisation or is part of its network of relationships with suppliers and contractors.

> A **value chain** is the sequence of activities that transform materials into finished products.

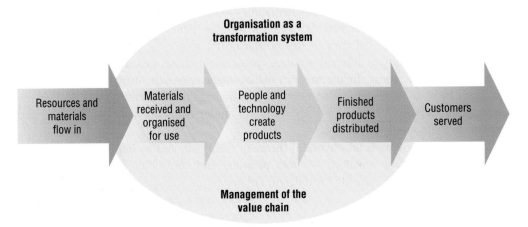

Figure 4.5 ▸ The organisational value chain

Closely aligned with the pursuit of quality is management commitment to performance excellence, a theme that became prominent when the book *In Search of Excellence: Lessons from America's Best-Run Companies* was published by Tom Peters and Robert Waterman.[34] Based on case investigations of successful companies, they identified the eight attributes of performance excellence shown in Manager's Notepad 4.2. These attributes are further representative of many themes and directions that are now common practice in organisations today.

Global awareness

We are just emerging from a decade in which the quality and performance excellence themes have been reflected in the rise of 'process reengineering', 'virtual organisations', 'agile factories', 'network firms' and other new concepts reviewed in this book. But while the best formulas for success continue to be tested and debated, an important fact remains — much of the pressure for quality and performance excellence is created by a highly competitive global economy. Nowhere is this challenge more evident than in the continuing efforts of businesses around the globe to transform themselves into truly world-class operations.

Like the lessons of performance excellence, current trends and directions in global awareness have ties back to the 1980s. That was a time when the success of Japanese industry caught worldwide attention and both scholars and consultants rushed to identify what could be learned from Japanese management practices. The books *Theory Z*, by William Ouchi, and *The Art of Japanese Management*, by Richard Tanner Pascale and Anthony G. Athos, were among the first that called attention to the possible link between unique Japanese practices and business success.[35] Ouchi used the term 'Theory Z' to describe a management framework that incorporates into Australasian and North American practices a variety of insights found in the Japanese models.[36] Prominent in the **Theory Z** management approach are such things as long-term employment, slower promotions and more lateral job movements, attention to career planning and development, use of consensus decision making, and emphasis on use of teamwork and employee involvement. And even though the Japanese economy and management systems face pressures of their own today, these early insights into the Japanese business experience helped to establish a global awareness that continues to enrich management thinking today. This international dimension of management is examined thoroughly in the next chapter, with special attention on understanding cultural influences on management practices.

Learning organisations

This remains the age of the **learning organisation**, described in chapter 3 as an organisation that operates with values and systems that result in 'continuous change and improvement based on the lessons of experience'.[37] Learning organisations require for their success a value-driven organisational culture that emphasises information, teamwork, empowerment, participation and leadership. Learning organisations also depend for their success on

GET CONNECTED!

A wired global world is not necessarily a connected one. The problem is not technology but managing within the technological context. Visit the Globalization Research Center www.cio.com/research/global to learn more about some contemporary globalisation issues.

GET CONNECTED!

Theory Z describes a management framework emphasising long-term employment and teamwork.

A **learning organisation** continuously changes and improves using the lessons of experience.

special leadership qualities. This topic is so important that part 5 of this book is entirely devoted to it, with special emphasis on motivation and rewards, communication, conflict and negotiation, teamwork and change leadership. And when it comes to leadership, perhaps no other management theme is more influenced by directions in the new economy. Once again, history sets the stage for the future. In his book, *No Easy Victories*, John Gardner speaks of leadership as a special challenge and his words are well worth considering today.

> Leaders have a significant role in creating the state of mind that is the society. They can serve as symbols of the moral unity of the society. They can express the values that hold the society together. Most important, they can conceive and articulate goals that lift people out of their petty preoccupations, carry them above the conflicts that tear a society apart, and unite them in the pursuit of objectives worthy of their best efforts.[38]

Leadership and the new directions of learning organisations will be singled out again and again in *Management: An Asia–Pacific Perspective* as important keys to personal and organisational performance. And performance by people and organisations, in turn, is the key to any society's economic development and growth. Managers of the 21st century will have to excel as never before to meet the expectations held of them and of the organisations they lead. Importantly, we must all recognise that new managerial outlooks and new managerial competencies appropriate to the new workplace are requirements for future leadership success. At the very least, the 21st-century manager must be a:

Characteristics of the 21st-century executive

- *global strategist* — understands interconnections among nations, cultures and economies; plans and acts with due consideration of them
- *master of technology* — comfortable with information technology; understands technological trends and their implications; able to use technology to best advantage
- *effective politician* — understands growing complexity of government regulations and the legal environment; able to relate them with the interests of the organisation
- *inspiring leader* — attracts highly motivated workers and inspires them with a high-performance culture where individuals and teams can do their best work.

In chapter 3 on information and decision making we discussed the special challenges of this age of information. It is an age in which Peter Drucker considers knowledge the principal resource of a competitive society. Drucker, you should recall, also cautions that knowledge constantly makes itself obsolete.[39] In a society where knowledge workers are increasingly important, new managers must be well educated . . . and they must continue that education throughout their careers. Success in turbulent times comes only through continuous improvement. The new economy requires everyone to be unrelenting in efforts to develop, refine and maintain job-relevant skills and competencies. It requires leaders with strong people skills, who are attuned to the nature of an information or service society, who understand the international dimensions, and who establish commitments to work-life balance. And, the new economy places a premium on personal leadership qualities. Consider, for example, this comment by former corporate CEO Ralph Sorenson: 'It is the *ability to make things happen* that most distinguishes the successful manager from the mediocre or unsuccessful one . . . The most cherished manager is the one who says "I can do it", and then does.'[40]

'Do it', advises Sorenson. 'Of course', you may quickly answer. But don't forget that the 21st-century manager must also do the 'right' things — the things that really count, the things that add value to the organisation's goods and/or services, the things that make a real difference in performance results and competitive advantage, and the ethical things. Those are challenging directions for leadership, learning organisations and career success in the new economy.

CHAPTER 4
Study guide

The chapter 4 study guide helps you review the chapter content, prepare for examinations, apply what you have learned and further build your career readiness. The summary briefly answers the study questions posed at the start of the chapter. The list of key terms allows you to double-check your familiarity with basic concepts and definitions. The applied activities help you test your comprehension of chapter content. Suggestions offered as career readiness activities direct your attention to relevant sections of the Career Readiness Workbook where you can test and develop your career skills and apply what you have learned. The list of electronic resources suggests activities from the *Management: An Asia–Pacific Perspective* web site and, finally, the case for critical thinking helps you apply your new management knowledge.

SUMMARY

What can be learned from classical management thinking?

- Frederick Taylor's four principles of scientific management focused on the need to carefully select, train and support workers for individual task performance.
- Henri Fayol suggested that managers should learn what are now known as the management functions of planning, organising, leading and controlling.
- Max Weber described bureaucracy with its clear hierarchy, formal rules and well-defined jobs as an ideal form of organisation.

What ideas were introduced by the human resource approaches?

- The human resource approaches shifted attention toward the human factor as a key element in organisational performance.
- The historic Hawthorne Studies suggested that work behaviour is influenced by social and psychological forces and that work performance may be improved by better 'human relations'.
- Abraham Maslow's hierarchy of human needs introduced the concept of self-actualisation and the potential for people to experience self-fulfilment in their work.
- Douglas McGregor urged managers to shift away from Theory X and toward Theory Y thinking, which views people as independent, responsible and capable of self-direction in their work.
- Chris Argyris pointed out that people in the workplace are adults and may react negatively when constrained by strict management practices and rigid organisational structures.

What is the role of quantitative analysis in management?

- The availability of high-power desktop computing provides new opportunities for mathematical methods to be used for problem solving.
- Many organisations employ staff specialists in quantitative management science and operations research to solve problems.
- Quantitative techniques in common use include various approaches to forecasting, linear programming and simulation, among others.

What is unique about the systems view and contingency thinking?

- Organisations are complex open systems that interact with their external environments to transform resource inputs into product outputs.
- Resource acquisition and customer satisfaction are important requirements in the organisation–environment relationship.
- Organisations are composed of many internal subsystems that must work together in a coordinated way to support the organisation's overall success.
- Contingency thinking avoids 'one best way' arguments, and recognises the need to understand situational differences and respond appropriately to them.

What are continuing management themes of the 21st century?

- The commitment to meet customer needs 100 per cent of the time guides organisations toward total quality management and continuous improvement of operations.
- The global economy is a dramatic influence on organisations today, and opportunities abound to learn new ways of managing from practices in other countries.
- This is the age of information in which knowledge and knowledge workers are major resources of modern society.
- New managers must accept and excel at leadership responsibilities to perform as global strategists, technology masters, consummate politicians and leader–motivators.

KEY TERMS

bureaucracy (p. 99)

contingency thinking (p. 107)

Hawthorne effect (p. 102)

human relations movement (p. 102)

learning organisation (p. 109)

management science (p. 105)

motion study (p. 98)

needs (p. 102)

open system (p. 106)

organisational behaviour (p. 102)

scientific management (p. 97)

self-fulfilling prophecies (p. 103)

subsystem (p. 106)

system (p. 106)

Theory X (p. 103)

Theory Y (p. 103)

Theory Z (p. 109)

value chain (p. 108)

APPLIED ACTIVITIES

Short-response questions

1. List three of McGregor's Theory Y assumptions that are consistent with the current emphasis on participation and involvement in the workplace.
2. How do the deficit and progression principles operate in Maslow's hierarchy-of-needs theory?
3. Define contingency thinking and give an example of how it might apply to management.
4. Explain why the external environment is so important in the open-systems view of organisations.

Application question

5. Greg Spencer has just been appointed the new manager of your local campus bookstore. Greg would like to make sure the store operates according to Weber's bureaucracy. Is this a good management approach for Greg to follow? Why or why not?

CAREER READINESS ACTIVITIES

Recommended individual and group learning activities from the end-of-text Career Readiness Workbook for this chapter include:

Career advancement portfolio   `WB`

Update your career advancement portfolio to reflect your new skills and experiences. Include skills and personal insights you gain from the following projects and exercises.

Research and presentation project   `WB`

• Project 2 — Changing corporate cultures

Cross-functional integrative case   `WB`

Read the integrative case on Sarina Russo and answer the following questions:

4.1   When considering Maslow's theory of human needs, what needs are fulfilled by the range of services by the businesses within the Sarina Russo Group?

4.2   What examples from the integrative case and associated research (e.g. Internet) can you identify would suggest that Sarina Russo is a 21st-century manager?

Exercises in teamwork   `WB`

• Exercise 5 — What would the classics say?
• Exercise 6 — The great management history debate
• Exercise 7 — What do you value in work?

Management skills assessment   `WB`

• Assessment 4 — A 21st-century manager

ELECTRONIC RESOURCES

Don't forget to take full advantage of the online support for *Management: An Asia–Pacific Perspective* at www.johnwiley.com.au/highered/management: chapter 4 practice tests, e-flashcards, crossword puzzles, interactive management skills assessments, interactive cases, the online career advancement portfolio and much more!

CASE FOR CRITICAL THINKING

Read the following case for critical thinking on Japan Airlines. While you are reading the case keep in mind what you have learned in this chapter, then answer the questions.

Japan Airlines (JAL) operates flights into 125 airports in 30 countries and territories. It 'maintains 112 offices of its own throughout the world in addition to using the services of numerous general sales agents'.[41] JAL is an example of a company that is only now coming to terms with the realities of the new workplace.

Corporate history

JAL 'was formed as a private company in 1951, but reorganised in 1953' to become 50 per cent government owned. In 1987, in accordance with Japanese government privatisation policies, JAL once again became a private company. JAL is Asia's largest airline, operating 135 passenger and cargo aircraft. It is the parent of JAL Group, a collection of 220 companies.[42] JAL re-entered the private sector encumbered with old-model organisational characteristics — clearly delineated and specialised positions and jobs, a formal hierarchy, formal rules and standard operating procedures, boundary limits for each department and standardised training and career paths.[43]

Clearly, JAL needed to change quickly as the company began making a loss in the early 1990s. Initiatives — such as separating group companies into independent entities, divesting unprofitable portfolios and reducing debt — began in 1991. In an effort to reduce costs and increase revenue, JAL expanded into subsidiary airlines to service low-yield segments of its route structure. From this decision, J-Air, JALways, JTA, JAA and JEX were established.[44] Coincidentally, JAL's employee base was downsized and employee remuneration cut.[45]

However, JAL's revenue continued to drop. The period 1990–97 saw JAL's yield in terms of revenue per passenger per kilometre (RPK) fall 30 per cent. In the same period, as a result of its belt-tightening strategy, JAL achieved a 50 per cent improvement in employee productivity and a reduction in labour costs of 40 per cent. Much of these savings resulted from hiring non-Japanese employees at lower wages. Losses were stemmed and JAL finally made a meagre profit in 1998.[46]

Diversity

In 1989, JAL began to hire non-Japanese (*gaijin*) pilots and flight engineers. These crew members are contracted to JAL via IASCO, a third-party crew leasing company. IASCO flight engineers make up about half of the total number of JAL flight engineers, while IASCO pilots make up approximately 10 per cent of all JAL pilots. Because IASCO crew members are not permanent employees of JAL and do not hold any supervisory positions, the structure of the flight operations department has become fragmented. JAL's management actions and perceived cultural differences have created a dysfunctional rift between Japanese and IASCO crew members. The large number of non-union IASCO crew members has diluted the Japanese crew members' union power. As a result, JAL has degraded working rules for *all* crew members.

For example, in 1993, JAL's management unilaterally decided that flight sector length requiring extra crew members would be extended. The Japanese union immediately filed a lawsuit in the Tokyo District Court claiming that increased basic-crew flight hours would erode safety and detrimentally affect crew members' health. In November 1999, the court decided in favour of the union and stated that JAL should return to its previous flight crew policy. However, JAL lodged an appeal at the Tokyo High Court and refused to abide by the lower court's ruling.[47] Although increased productivity has assisted JAL in its fight to remain competitive, management–employee relations had become severely strained by this dispute.

Cultural changes

The Japanese work ethic evolved from an overall culture based on Confucian principles of social ranking and hierarchical structure in the workplace.[48] Many Japanese workers, even today, anticipate lifetime employment and promotion based on seniority.[49] Because of a burdened economy, Japanese workers have become highly stressed from trying to improve their employer's bottom line.

IASCO crew members are contracted to JAL for a period of three years. These contracts are usually automatically renewed unless one or more parties wish otherwise. Japanese workers do not work on contract and consider those that do as mercenaries. Accordingly, JAL perceives IASCO crew members as owing allegiance to none but themselves and that they cannot be relied on to go the extra mile for the company.[50] IASCO crew members feel they are bound by an inequitable contract that virtually prevents them from seeking employment during the agreed term. For example, a crew member is required to give 90 days notice of intention to terminate his or her contract; whereas JAL, via IASCO, is only required to give an employee 30 days notice. Very few employers will hire someone who cannot start a job for 90 days. This could have a negative impact on crew members' stress levels and could lead to decreased job satisfaction, lower productivity, increased absenteeism and higher turnover.

JAL has continued hiring non-Japanese contract crew members and cabin-crew to offset the high cost of hiring Japanese employee equivalents.[51] A strong subculture of distrust and frustration in IASCO crew members has therefore developed. A chasm, or 'them and us' attitude, has developed between Japanese and IASCO crew members. Unless JAL's management make an effort to remedy this issue, its ability to adapt quickly to industry change may be impeded.[52] While debate continues over whether the lofty ideals of a learning organisation are achievable, there is little doubt that JAL needs to keep developing its cohesive ability to adapt to market changes. Forging better management and employee relations would be an integral component of this process.

QUESTIONS

1. What does JAL need to do to show that they really value workforce diversity?

2. How could JAL improve its crew members' socialisation into the organisation and what could be done to improve innovation?

3. The actions of top management — what they say and how they behave — have a major impact on an organisation's culture. What action could JAL's management take to show that they are putting people first for organisational success?

Global dimensions of management

CHAPTER 5 STUDY QUESTIONS

▸ What are international management challenges of globalisation?

▸ What are the forms and opportunities of international business?

▸ What are multinational corporations and what do they do?

▸ What is culture and how does it relate to global diversity?

▸ How do management practices and learning transfer across cultures?

GETTING @ CONNECTED

NTT DoCoMo — welcome to the 'wireless' world

Japan is leading the way, again. Of course, that's no surprise to those familiar with the world of international business. For years the major corporations of the Western world have studied Japanese management and organisational practices. Now they're studying again. The object of attention this time is NTT DoCoMo, an innovative and fast-growing powerhouse in the field of wireless communications.

The firm is guided by what it calls Vision 2010: 'There are three words that characterise the business of DoCoMo — mobile, wireless and personal. Our aim is to make the most of these features and pursue evolution of the mobile communications market'. NTT DoCoMo energised the wireless world with its i-mode service for mobile phones. With close to one million new subscribers each month, this allows users to access e-mail and the Internet including sites offering banking, weather and ticketing. Says President Dr Keiji Tachikawa: 'We knew that if we could get the vast amount of information already on the Internet into our phones, we would attract large numbers of users'. Succeed they did — the company now has over 30 million mobile phone customers and is rapidly expanding worldwide.

At the heart of NTT DoCoMo's operating success is a corporate culture that guides employees with what is called the DREAM. *D* is for *dynamics* — to change and grow continuously. *R* is for *relationship* — to accept and collaborate with each other. *E* is for *ecology* — to be aware of and to create a better natural environment. *A* is for *action* — to start and to accomplish things others haven't accomplished. *M* is for *multiview* — to keep a wide perspective and follow long-term thinking.

Is NTT DoCoMo coming your way? Most probably. The company has momentum. It has embarked on an ambitious plan for strategic partnerships around the globe. Already a player in Europe's wireless competition, DoCoMo is the biggest investor in AT&T Wireless. Says Dr Tachikawa: 'Our policy is to create alliances in regions around the world ... we want 'win–win' partnerships for everyone'.[1]

GET CONNECTED!

Look into the wireless industry, at home and around the world. Is NTT DoCoMo www.nttdocomo.com on the advantage? Someday soon the company's partnerships may even bring high-definition television (HDTV) to your mobile phone. In the meantime, there's no doubt the world is going wireless.

GET CONNECTED!

There is no doubt about it. We live and work in a global community, one that grows smaller and more immediately accessible by the day. Network television brings on-the-spot news from around the world into our homes, 24 hours a day. The world's newspapers from *The New York Times* to *The Australian* to *Le Monde* (France) to *The Japan Times* can be read from the Internet at the touch of a keyboard on your desktop PC; headlines may even be reached from your mobile phone. It is possible to board a plane in Sydney and fly nonstop to London; it is sometimes less expensive to fly from Brisbane, Australia, to New Zealand than to Melbourne. Universities and other tertiary institutions offer an increasing variety of study-abroad programs. E-mail and online chat rooms link us to friends and work partners around the world and at low cost.

This world of opportunities isn't just for tourists and travellers. It is time to recognise the emergence and implications of a global workplace. Multinationals are increasingly locating parts of their 'value chains' in different countries or time zones. For example, General Motors has spread its development and research activities across three countries — eight hours in Detroit, eight hours in Melbourne and eight hours in Frankfurt. Most of Nike's manufacturing is located in Indonesia, with its marketing and advertising located in the USA.[2] But these are just two examples of a business world in which national boundaries are increasingly blurred. The petrol station with the 'BP' logo in green, yellow and white is by British Petroleum, known as BP; the familiar 'Shell' station is brought to you courtesy of Royal-Dutch/Shell. And did you know that the majority of McDonald's sales are outside the USA, and that some of its most profitable restaurants are located in places like Moscow, Budapest and Beijing? Astute business investors know all this and more. They buy and sell only with awareness of the latest financial news from Hong Kong, London, Tokyo, New York, Johannesburg, Singapore, Sydney and other of the world's financial centres. In this time of high technology, furthermore, they don't even have to leave home to do it — the latest information is readily available on the Internet.

Yes, we live and work today in a truly global village. You, like the rest of us, must get connected with the world's opportunities.

INTERNATIONAL MANAGEMENT AND GLOBALISATION

In the **global economy**, resources, markets and competition are worldwide in scope.

Globalisation is the worldwide interdependence of resource flows, product markets and business competition.

This is the age of the **global economy** in which resource supplies, product markets and business competition are worldwide rather than purely local or national in scope.[3] It is also a time heavily influenced by the forces of **globalisation**, the process of growing interdependence among these components in the global economy. Harvard scholar and consultant Rosabeth Moss Kanter describes it as 'one of the most powerful and pervasive influences on nations, businesses, workplaces, communities and lives'.[4]

The global economy offers great opportunities of worldwide sourcing, production and sales capabilities.[5] But as businesses spread their reach around the world, the processes of globalisation also bring many adjustments to traditional patterns. Large multinational businesses are increasingly adopting transnational or 'global' identities, rather than being identified with a singular home. The growing strength and penetration of these businesses worldwide is viewed by some as a potential threat to national economies, and their local business systems, labour markets and cultures.[6] All this adds up to great uncertainty as executives move into new and uncharted competitive territories. AOL Time Warner's chairman Stephen M. Case describes the scene this way: 'I sometimes feel like I'm behind the wheel of a race car. One of the biggest challenges is there are no road signs to help navigate. And in fact … no one has yet determined which side of the road we're supposed to be on.'[7]

The term used to describe management in organisations with business interests in more than one country is **international management**. There is no denying its importance. Procter & Gamble, for example, pursues a global strategy with a presence in more than 70 countries. As the leaders of these companies press forward with global initiatives, the international management challenges and opportunities of working across borders — national and cultural — must be mastered. New tests of managerial skills and viewpoints are emerging. A new breed of manager, the **global manager**, is increasingly sought after. This is someone informed about international developments, transnational in outlook, competent in working with people from different cultures, and always aware of regional developments in a changing world.

What about you? Are you prepared for the challenges of international management? Are you informed about the world and the forces of globalisation?

Asia and the Pacific Rim

Asia has attained superpower status in the world economy. The Asian and Pacific Rim economies are soon expected to be larger than those of the current **European Union (EU)**. The Asia-Pacific Economic Cooperation (APEC) group has become the region's leading forum. APEC provides for 'Asia-Pacific economies to strengthen regional links and pursue common trade and economic goals'.[8] Australian and New Zealand businesses have access to over 2.5 billion consumers and around 60 per cent of global income in 21 APEC member economies. Three-quarters of Australia's merchandise exports are purchased by these economies. In the 1990s, APEC exports more than doubled to nearly $5 trillion, and APEC economies generated 195 million new jobs and 70 per cent of the increase in the world's economic growth. Member countries already represent one-third of the world's top market for cars and telecommunications equipment.

Another organisation of which Australia is a member is the Indian Ocean Rim Association for Regional Cooperation (IOR-ARC), whose aim it is to facilitate trade and investment in the region. This association consists of 19 Indian Ocean states. Australia and New Zealand pursue their trading interests bilaterally, regionally and in international forums. The Organisation for Economic Co-operation and Development (OECD www.oecd.org) 'will continue to play a critical role in analysing developments in the international trading system' as well as 'the impact of government policies on trade and performance'.[9] The OECD facilitates a developed-country economic forum in which Australia and New Zealand can meet with Japan, North America and Western Europe to discuss a full range of economic, trade and social policy concerns.

Australia's engagement with South-East Asia at a regional level remains an important priority. North Asia's economic importance to Australia is also on the increase. Strengthening its cooperation with these economies contributes to Australia's security and is integral to promoting international interests. The rise in trade with China and South Korea is particularly strong. This deepening economic relationship with China is evident from increased trade collaboration between the two countries. For example, BHP (Guangzhou) secured an additional steel import quota, and an Australian insurance company secured a Chinese insurance licence soon after China entered the World Trade Organization.[10]

The relationship between Australia and New Zealand remains strong as is evident from the progress on the continuing trans-Tasman trade and economic agenda. There is significant convergence between the two countries regarding their respective business law regimes

International management involves managing operations in more than one country.

A **global manager** is culturally aware and well informed on international affairs.

The **European Union (EU)** is a political and economic alliance of European countries.

GET CONNECTED!

Get fully informed. Learn about the case against globalisation and the WTO. Check Global Trade Watch at www.citizen.org/trade.

GET CONNECTED!

— in seeking to ensure that they reflect developing international norms and that there is a reduction in compliance costs for companies operating in both countries, for example. The report on the Trans-Tasman Mutual Recognition Arrangement and the formal 2003 review of the arrangement is another example of building relationships across borders. There is a drive to increase industry competitiveness by closer collaboration between industry sectors in both countries in the interests of maximising the global competitiveness of Australian and New Zealand companies.[11]

Europe

The new Europe is a place of dramatic political and economic developments.[12] The European Union (EU) is a grouping of 15 countries who agreed to support mutual economic growth by removing barriers that previously limited cross-border trade and business development. Expectations are that the EU will expand to include at least 25 members in the near future. At present only Switzerland and Norway from Western Europe remain outside the group. At least a dozen countries, including several new republics of the former Soviet Union, have applied to join or expressed interest in joining.

As an economic union, the EU is putting the rest of the world on notice that European business is a global force to be reckoned with. Members are linked through favourable trade and customs laws intended to facilitate the free flow of workers, goods and services, and investments across national boundaries. Businesses in each member country have access to a market of over 375 million consumers, compared to 220 million in the USA and 120 million in Japan. Among the important business and economic developments in the EU are agreements to eliminate frontier controls and trade barriers, create uniform minimum technical product standards, open government procurement to businesses from all member countries, unify financial regulations, lift competitive barriers in banking and insurance, and even offer a common currency — the **euro**. The emergence of the euro as a new common currency set the stage for what *Business Week* referred to as 'an unstoppable market process that will sweep away the structures Old Europe held so dear — national corporations and banks, rigid work rules, generous pension payments'.[13] The impact of the euro is being watched carefully as Europe marches into the 21st century. Although there is still political and economic risk, the expected benefits include higher productivity, lower inflation and steady growth.

The **euro** is the new common European currency.

All of this must also be considered in context with another dynamic element in the European scene — continuing legacies of the collapse of communism in the former Soviet Union and in nations formerly dominated by it. Changes in political systems and governments add to the risk for foreign investors. Yet, Western businesses are responding to opportunities not only in Russia but also in such diverse places as Belarus, Latvia and the Ukraine. The EU is among Australia and New Zealand's largest trading partners in terms of two-way trade, and is a large source of foreign direct investment. One of the primary objectives for Australia and New Zealand is the advancement of trade and investment in the EU economies.

The Americas

NAFTA is the North American Free Trade Agreement linking Canada, the USA and Mexico in a regional economic alliance.

Turning now to the Americas, the USA, Canada and Mexico have joined together in the North American Free Trade Agreement (**NAFTA**). This agreement largely frees the flow of goods and services, workers and investments within a region that has more potential consumers than its European rival, the EU. Getting approval of NAFTA from all three governments was not easy. Whereas Canadian firms worried about domination by US manufacturers, American politicians were concerned about the potential loss of jobs to

Mexico. Some calls were made for more government legislation and support to protect domestic industries from foreign competition. While Mexicans feared that free trade would bring a further intrusion of US culture and values into their country, Americans complained that Mexican businesses did not operate by the same social standards, particularly with respect to environmental protection and the use of child labour.

Often at issue in NAFTA controversies are the operations of *maquiladoras*, foreign manufacturing plants allowed to operate in Mexico with special privileges in return for employing Mexican labour.[14] The use of Mexican labour-force skills and the global reach of these operations are growing. At General Motors of Mexico, for example, Mexican engineers developed a right-hand-drive car for markets in Australia, New Zealand and South Africa.

Along with the EU, the USA is among Australia and New Zealand's largest trading partners and sources of foreign direct investment. Australia and New Zealand's interest in high quality US engagement in the Asia–Pacific region continues, especially the importance of good US relations with Japan, China, Indonesia and the Republic of Korea.[15] In 2000–01 Australia's merchandise exports to the USA grew by 21 per cent to $11.7 billion and New Zealand's exports rose by 18 per cent to NZ$4.85 billion.[16] Australia and new Zealand also maintain extensive bilateral cooperation with Canada, with exchanges on a range of government issues such as health and migration. An example of positive relations between Australia and Canada is 'Gateway Australia'. This public diplomacy program was organised by the High Commission in Ottawa in conjunction with the city's annual 'Winterlude' festival in February 2001. Australia was then selected as the 'showcase' country in a Canadian Technology in Government event in the second half of 2001.[17]

Optimism regarding business and economic potential extends throughout Central America and South America as well. Many countries of the region are cutting tariffs, updating their economic policies and welcoming foreign investors.

Australia and New Zealand are working towards greater opportunities for increased trade and investment with Latin America and improved market access. Examples of successful collaborations include a tariff exemption for wool, access for cereals and meat, and the supply of coal to Mexico's power industry. Other examples of collaborations include the opening of the Argentine markets to Australian producers, the exemption of Australian dairy products from Brazilian anti-dumping measures, the signing of the Cooperation on Education and Training Agreement, the initialling of a Nuclear Safeguards Agreement with Argentina, and the finalisation of the text of an Investment Promotion and Protection Agreement between Australia and Uruguay.[18] The significance of Latin America to world trade is increasingly being recognised by international businesses and government leaders.

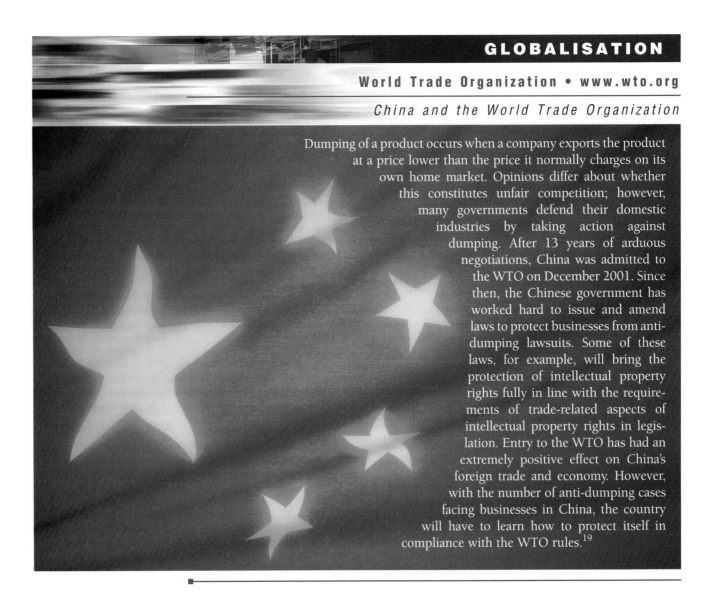

Dumping of a product occurs when a company exports the product at a price lower than the price it normally charges on its own home market. Opinions differ about whether this constitutes unfair competition; however, many governments defend their domestic industries by taking action against dumping. After 13 years of arduous negotiations, China was admitted to the WTO on December 2001. Since then, the Chinese government has worked hard to issue and amend laws to protect businesses from anti-dumping lawsuits. Some of these laws, for example, will bring the protection of intellectual property rights fully in line with the requirements of trade-related aspects of intellectual property rights in legislation. Entry to the WTO has had an extremely positive effect on China's foreign trade and economy. However, with the number of anti-dumping cases facing businesses in China, the country will have to learn how to protect itself in compliance with the WTO rules.[19]

Africa

To learn more about the advancement of open trade and economic cooperation in the Asia–Pacific region, visit the Asia-Pacific Economic Cooperation (APEC) web site www.apecsec.org.sg.
GET CONNECTED!

Africa is a continent increasingly featured in the news.[20] Although often the focus of reports on ethnic turmoil and civil strife in countries struggling along pathways to peace and development, Africa also stands as a region that beckons international business. Whereas foreign businesses tend to avoid the risk of trouble spots, they are giving increased attention to stable countries with growing economies. A *Wall Street Journal* analysis singles out Uganda, the Ivory Coast, Botswana, South Africa and Ghana for their positive business prospects.[21] The same report also notes that the Congo, Nigeria and Angola are especially rich in natural resources. On the discouraging side, the rates of economic growth in sub-Saharan Africa are among the lowest in the world. Many parts of the region suffer from terrible problems of poverty and the ravishment of a continuing AIDS epidemic. Africa's need for sustained assistance from the industrialised countries, including business investments and foreign aid, is well established.

The Southern Africa Development Community (SADC) links 14 countries of southern Africa in trade and economic development efforts. The objectives of SADC include harmonising and rationalising strategies for sustainable development among member countries.[22] More generally, a report by two Harvard professors recently analysed the foreign investment environment of Africa and concluded that the region's contextual problems are manageable.[23] 'In fact they should be viewed as opportunities', says James A. Austin, one of the co-authors. He adds: 'If a company has the managerial and organisational capabilities to deal with the region's unique business challenges, then it will be able to enter a promising market.'[24]

Post-apartheid South Africa, in particular, has benefited from political revival. A country of 44 million people and great natural resources, South Africa is experiencing economic recovery and attracting outside investors. It already accounts for half the continent's purchasing power.[25] Foreign investments in the country increased sharply after minority white rule ended and Nobel-prize winner Nelson Mandela became the nation's first black president. Since the end of apartheid (1993–94), Australia's exports to South Africa have more than doubled. At the beginning of the 21st century, exports to South Africa were almost $1.26 billion, which makes it Australia's 20th largest export market and 22nd largest trading partner overall.[26] New Zealand's exports to South Africa have more than trebled since 1990, and in 2002 were worth NZ$132 million.[27]

INTERNATIONAL BUSINESS CHALLENGES

John Chambers, CEO of Cisco Systems, Inc., a major networking technology firm with a worldwide reach, says: 'I will put my jobs anywhere in the world where the right infrastructure is, with the right educated workforce, with the right supportive government'.[28] Cisco and other firms like it are **international businesses**. They conduct for-profit transactions of goods and services across national boundaries. International businesses of all types and sizes are the foundations of world trade. They are the engines for moving raw materials, finished products and specialised services from one country to another in the global economy. The *reasons for international business*, the forces that drive companies to the marketplaces of the world, include the search for:

* *profits* — global operations offer profit potential
* *customers* — global operations offer new markets to sell products
* *suppliers* — global operations offer access to needed raw materials
* *capital* — global operations offer access to financial resources
* *labour* — global operations offer access to lower labour costs.

 International businesses conduct commercial transactions across national boundaries.

Reasons for engaging in international business

Competitive global business environment

The global environment of international business is complex and dynamic, and highly competitive. At the level of the task environment, global business executives must master the demands of operating with worldwide suppliers, distributors, customers and competitors. They must also understand and deal successfully with general environment conditions that present many differences in economic, legal–political and educational systems, among other aspects of business infrastructure.

Regional economic cooperation is increasing, but differences in *economic systems* around the world must still be recognised. Countries like Russia, Poland, Estonia and others of the former Soviet Union used to operate with *central-planning economies*. That is, the central government made basic economic decisions for an entire nation. Such decisions largely determined the allocations of raw materials, set product or service output quotas, regulated wages and prices, and even distributed qualified personnel among alternative employers. Now these countries are trying to establish viable *free-market economies* such as those common to Australia, New Zealand, Germany, Canada, the USA and other industrialised nations. Although they may vary in exact form, free-market economies operate under capitalism and the laws of market supply and demand. As economies transform from central planning to free markets, they often face controversies over rising prices, unemployment, business competition and the challenges of **privatisation** — the selling of state-owned enterprises into private ownership. Foreign investment is crucial to the success of these developments.[29]

Among the chief worldwide economic issues, the **World Trade Organization (WTO)** deserves special attention. The WTO is organised around an international accord setting up a mechanism for monitoring international trade and resolving disputes among countries. Member nations agree to ongoing negotiations and the reduction of tariffs and trade restrictions, but trading relationships are often complicated. **Protectionism**, in the form of political calls for tariffs and favourable treatments to help protect domestic businesses from foreign competition, is a common and complicating theme. For example, Australia has registered its concern over US assistance to agricultural exports and the impact of US food-aid allocations in commercial markets, especially of grains and dairy products, which disadvantaged Australian farmers.[30]

> **Privatisation** is the selling of state-owned enterprises into private ownership.
>
> In the **World Trade Organization (WTO)**, member nations agree to negotiate and resolve disputes about tariffs and trade restrictions.
>
> **Protectionism** is a call for tariffs and favourable treatments to protect domestic firms from foreign competition.

POINT ← COUNTER ↑

Acting global or acting local?

Going global does not mean acting global. According to one of the world's most influential thinkers on strategy, Michael Porter, the assumption that competition on a global scale has made geography irrelevant is being questioned by global companies that are working towards 'acting local'. Porter argues that global companies need a sound understanding of local issues and should be able to use local strengths.[31] For example, instead of outsourcing the production of goods and/or services to global companies, organisations should consider outsourcing these to local companies. The advantage of this is repeated relationship-building, a better information flow, frequent face-to-face interactions and the building of trust between local businesses.

Legal environments vary widely from place to place, and organisations are expected to abide by the laws of the host country in which they are operating. The more home and host-country laws differ, the more difficult and complex it is for international businesses to adapt to local ways. Common legal problems in international business involve incorporation practices and business ownership; negotiating and implementing contracts with foreign parties; protecting patents, trademarks and copyrights; and handling foreign exchange restrictions. In countries such as Australia, New Zealand and the USA, executives of foreign-owned companies must worry about antitrust (competition) issues that prevent competitors from regularly talking to one another. They also must deal with a variety of special laws regarding occupational health and safety, equal employment opportunity, sexual harassment and other matters — all constraints potentially different from those they find at home. For example, the global company Levi Strauss & Co responds to the needs of its global employees by incorporating detailed instruction on assessing compliance with discrimination standards into its training programs.[32]

People are essential resources of organisations, and as *educational systems* vary from one country to the next so too does the availability of labour. A survey of business leaders around the world reports that many are worried about actual or potential 'human resource deficits'.[33] They recognise that problems of illiteracy and the absence of appropriate skills in the available workforce can compromise operations. They also increasingly recognise the broader social challenge of becoming more actively involved in education and training to help build supplies of qualified labour in a host country.

Forms of international business

The common forms of international business are shown in figure 5.1. When a business is just getting started internationally, global sourcing, exporting/importing and licensing and franchising are the usual ways to begin. These are *market entry strategies* that involve the sale of goods or services to foreign markets but do not require expensive capital investments. Joint ventures and wholly owned subsidiaries are *direct investment strategies*. They require major capital commitments but create rights of ownership and control over operations in the foreign country.

Market entry strategies

| Global sourcing | Exporting and importing | Licensing and franchising |

Direct investment stategies

| Joint ventures | Wholly owned subsidiaries |

Increasing involvement in ownership and control of foreign operations

Figure 5.1 ▸ Common forms of international business — from market entry to direct investment strategies

MARKET ENTRY STRATEGIES

A common first step into international business, **global sourcing** is the process of purchasing on a contract basis manufacturing components and/or services from points around the world. It is an international division of labour in which activities are performed in countries where they can be done well at the lowest cost. In manufacturing, global sourcing for cars assembled in Australia may mean purchasing windshields, instrument panels, seats and fuel tanks from Asia as well as electronics for antilock braking systems from Germany. In services, global sourcing is rapidly expanding in a variety of white-collar fields ranging from accounting and customer support to science research and technology development, and more. In all cases the global sourcing opportunity is to take advantage of international wage gaps and the availability of skilled labour by dispersing more and more work to foreign locations.

A second form of international business involves **exporting**, selling locally made products in foreign markets, and/or **importing**, buying foreign-made products and selling them in domestic markets. Because the growth of export industries creates local jobs, governments often offer special advice and assistance to businesses that are trying to develop or expand their export markets. Austrade's Australian Export Awards and the Trade New Zealand Export Awards aim to showcase and promote leading exporters and to identify home-grown corporate role models.[34]

A foreign firm may pay a fee and enter into a **licensing agreement** giving it the rights to make or sell another company's products. This international business approach typically grants access to a unique manufacturing technology, special patent, or trademark rights held by the licensor. It is one way to transfer technology from one country to another. **Franchising** is a form of licensing in which the licensee buys the complete 'package' of

In **global sourcing**, materials or services are purchased around the world for local use.

In **exporting**, local products are sold abroad.

Importing is the process of acquiring products abroad and selling them in domestic markets.

A **licensing agreement** occurs when a firm pays a fee for the rights to make or sell another company's products.

Franchising provides the complete 'package' of support needed to open a particular business.

support needed to open a particular business. Firms like McDonald's, Subway and others sell facility designs, equipment, product ingredients and recipes, and management systems to foreign investors, while retaining certain product and operating controls.

DIRECT INVESTMENT STRATEGIES

⊘ **Joint ventures** establish operations in a foreign country through joint ownership with local partners.

To establish a direct investment presence in a foreign country, many organisations enter into **joint ventures** or co-ownership arrangements that pool resources and share risks and control for business operations. This form of international business may be established by equity purchases and/or direct investments by a foreign partner in a local operation; it may also involve the creation of an entirely new business by a foreign and local partner. International joint ventures are 'strategic alliances' that help participants to gain things through cooperation that otherwise would be difficult to achieve independently. This is a popular and expanding form of international business. In return for its investment in a local operation, for example, the outside or foreign partner often gains new markets and the assistance of a local partner who understands them. In return for its investment, the local partner often gains new technology as well as opportunities for its employees to learn new skills by working in joint operations. Manager's Notepad 5.1 offers a checklist for choosing joint venture partners.[35]

MANAGER'S NOTEPAD 5.1

Checklist for joint ventures

- Choose a partner familiar with your firm's major business.
- Choose a partner with a strong local workforce.
- Choose a partner with future expansion possibilities.
- Choose a partner with a strong local market for its own products.
- Choose a partner with shared interests in meeting customer needs.
- Choose a partner with good profit potential.
- Choose a partner in sound financial standing.

⊘ A **wholly owned subsidiary** is a local operation completely owned by a foreign firm.

A **wholly owned subsidiary** is a local operation completely owned and controlled by a foreign firm. Like joint ventures, foreign subsidiaries may be formed through direct investment in start-up operations or through equity purchases in existing ones. When making such investments, foreign firms are clearly taking a business risk. They must be confident that they possess the expertise needed to manage and conduct business affairs successfully in the new environment. This is where prior experience gained through joint ventures can prove very beneficial.

MULTINATIONAL CORPORATIONS

⊘ A **multinational corporation (MNC)** is a business with extensive operations in more than one foreign country.

Many companies participate in international business in one form or another. A true **multinational corporation (MNC)** is a business firm with extensive international operations in more than one foreign country. Premier MNCs found in annual listings such as *Fortune* magazine's Global 500 include such global giants as Telstra, News Corporation, AMP and National Australia Bank from Australia, Rio Tinto from the United Kingdom and

Australia, China Mobile and Hang Seng Bank from Hong Kong, Taiwan Semiconductor from Taiwan, Singapore Telecommunications from Singapore and General Electric and Wal-Mart from the USA. Also important on the world scene are *multinational organisations* (MNOs) — like the International Federation of Red Cross and Red Crescent Societies, the United Nations and the World Bank — whose not-for-profit missions and operations span the globe.

Types of multinational corporations

A typical MNC operates in many countries but has corporate headquarters in one home or host country. Microsoft, Rio Tinto and McDonald's are among the ready examples. Although deriving substantial sales and profits from international sources, they and others like them typically also have strong national identifications. Yet, as the global economy grows more competitive, many multinationals are acting more like **transnational corporations**. They increasingly operate worldwide without being identified with one national home.[36] Executives with transnationals view the entire world as the domain for acquiring resources, locating production facilities, marketing goods and services, and for brand image. They seek total integration of global operations, try to operate across borders without home-based prejudices, make major decisions from a global perspective, distribute work among worldwide points of excellence, and employ senior executives from many different countries.[37] BHP Billiton and PricewaterhouseCoopers are good examples of this.

Pros and cons of multinational corporations

Now that consumer demand, resource supplies, product flows and labour markets increasingly span national boundaries, the actions of MNCs are increasingly influential in the global economy. The United Nations has reported that MNCs hold one-third of the world's productive assets and control 70 per cent of world trade. Furthermore, more than 90 per cent of these MNCs are based in the Northern Hemisphere. While this may bring a sense of both accomplishment and future opportunity to some business leaders, it can also be very threatening to countries and their domestic industries.

HOST-COUNTRY ISSUES

Both the global corporations and the countries that 'host' their foreign operations should mutually benefit from any business relationship. Figure 5.2 shows how things can and do go both right and wrong in MNC–host country relationships. The *potential host-country benefits* include larger tax bases, increased employment opportunities, technology transfers, the introduction of new industries and the development of local resources. In respect to *potential host-country costs*, it has been claimed that MNCs extract excessive profits, dominate the local economy, interfere with the local government, do not respect local customs and laws, fail to help domestic firms develop, hire the most talented of local personnel and do not transfer their most advanced technologies.[38]

Of course executives of MNCs sometimes feel exploited as well in their relations with host countries. Consider China, for example, where major cultural, political and economic differences confront the outsider.[39] Profits have proved elusive for some foreign investors; some have faced government restrictions making it difficult to take profits out of the country; some have struggled to get needed raw materials, both domestically and from abroad.[40] The protection of intellectual property is an ongoing concern of foreign manufacturers, and managing relationships with government agencies can be very complicated.

Transnational corporations are MNCs that operate worldwide on a borderless basis.

www.riotinto.com

Multinational mining giant Rio Tinto grew out of the former Australian and United Kingdom mining conglomerates CRA Limited and RTZ Corporation respectively. After the merger of CRA and RTZ in 1995, management control of the newly formed Rio Tinto shifted to London. However, it is still listed on the Australian Stock Exchange, as well as on the London exchange. Rio Tinto has since acquired North and Ashton Mining, further expanding its Australian operations, but its Melbourne office is a shadow of its former size.

Although Motorola runs the largest foreign-owned operation inside China, for example, it must still negotiate business plans with the government. Says the firm's chief country representative K. P. To: 'Even if you're wholly owned, you still need strong support from the government'.[41]

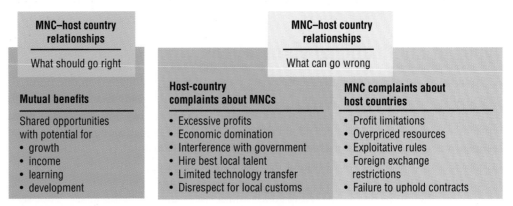

Figure 5.2 ▸ What should go right and what can go wrong in MNC–host country relationships

HOME-COUNTRY ISSUES

MNCs may also encounter difficulties in the country where their headquarters are located. Even as many MNCs try to operate more globally, home-country governments and citizens tend to identify them with local and national interests. When an MNC outsources, cuts back or closes a domestic operation to shift work to lower-cost international destinations, the loss of local jobs is controversial. Corporate decision makers are likely to be engaged by government and community leaders in critical debate about a firm's domestic social responsibilities. Home-country criticisms of MNCs include complaints about transferring jobs out of the country, shifting capital investments abroad and engaging in corrupt practices in foreign settings.

Ethical issues for multinational operations

The ethical aspects of international business deserve special attention, and will be discussed further in chapter 6 on managerial ethics and social responsibility. However, the issue of questionable practices must be raised in the international business context.

Corruption involves illegal practices to further one's business interests.

Corruption, engaging in illegal practices to further one's business interests, is a source of continuing controversy in various countries. In 1999, heads of government within the Commonwealth committed themselves to a policy of 'zero tolerance' of corruption. APEC has developed principles, albeit voluntary, that focus on issues such as transparency in the tender process and accountability; and the Council of Europe and the European Union have finalised comprehensive anti-corruption policies. However, critics believe these policies fail to recognise the 'reality' of business as practised in many foreign nations. They complain that companies adhering to these policies are at a competitive disadvantage because they can't offer the same 'deals' as competitors from other nations — deals that locals may regard as standard business practice.

Sweatshops employ workers at very low wages, for long hours, and in poor working conditions.

Sweatshops, business operations that employ workers at low wages for long hours and in poor working conditions, are another concern in the global business arena. Networks of outsourcing contracts are now common as manufacturers follow the world's low-cost labour supplies — countries like the Philippines, Sri Lanka and Vietnam are popular destinations. Yet Nike, Inc., has learned from problems in Asia that a global company will be held publicly accountable for the work standards and employment practices of its foreign subcontractors. Facing activist criticism, the company revised its labour practices with recommendations from a review by the consulting firm Goodworks International. Nike now offers a special web site, Transparency 101, offering reports and audit results on its international labour practices. Chairman and CEO Phil Knight has pledged to extend its monitoring efforts to more than 750 manufacturing sites and contractors in 50 countries.[42]

Child labour, the full-time employment of children for work otherwise done by adults, is another controversial issue. It has been made especially visible by activist concerns regarding the manufacture of handmade carpets in countries like Pakistan. Initiatives to eliminate child labour include an effort by the Rugmark Foundation to discourage purchases of carpets that do not carry its label. The 'Rugmark' label is earned by a certification process to guarantee that a carpet manufacturer does not use illegal child labour.[43]

Yet another ethical issue in international business relates to global concerns for environmental protection. Not only is the world's citizenry worried about disasters such as the pollution aftermath of wars, such as the Gulf War of 1990–91, but more generally it expects global corporations to always respect the natural environment and pursue safe industrial practices. Industrial pollution of cities, hazardous waste, depletion of natural resources and related concerns are now worldwide issues. The concept of **sustainable development** is a popular guideline advanced by activist groups. It is 'development that meets the needs of the present without compromising the ability of future generations to meet their own needs'.[44] As global corporate citizens, MNCs are increasingly expected to uphold high standards in dealing with sustainable development and protection of the natural evironment — whenever and wherever they operate. The available guidelines for responsible environmental policies include **ISO 14000**, a set of certification standards developed by the International Organization for Standardization and recognised worldwide.

CULTURE AND GLOBAL DIVERSITY

Culture is the shared set of beliefs, values and patterns of behaviour common to a group of people. Anyone who has visited another country knows that cultural differences exist. **Culture shock**, the confusion and discomfort a person experiences when in an unfamiliar culture, is a reminder that many of these differences must be mastered just to travel comfortably around the world. But the important business and managerial implications of sociocultural differences must also be understood. An American exporter, for example, once went to see a Saudi Arabian official. He sat in the office with crossed legs and the sole of his shoe exposed — an unintentional sign of disrespect in the local culture. He passed documents to the host using his left hand, which Muslims consider unclean, and he refused to accept coffee when it was offered, suggesting criticism of the Saudi's hospitality. What was the price for these cultural miscues? He lost a US$10 million contract to a Korean executive better versed in Arab ways.[45]

Ethnocentrism is the tendency to view one's culture as superior to others. It is surprisingly common in international business, but it must be avoided. Local customs vary in too many ways for most of us to become true experts in the many cultures of our diverse world. Yet there are things we can do to respect differences, successfully conduct business abroad and minimise culture shock. Self-awareness and reasonable sensitivity are the basic building blocks of cultural awareness, as suggested in Manager's Notepad 5.2.[46]

Child labour is the full-time employment of children for work otherwise done by adults.

Sustainable development meets the needs of the present without hurting future generations.

ISO 14000 offers a set of certification standards for responsible environmental policies.

Culture is a shared set of beliefs, values and patterns of behaviour common to a group of people.

Culture shock is the confusion and discomfort a person experiences when in an unfamiliar culture.

Ethnocentrism is the tendency to consider one's culture as superior to others.

MANAGER'S NOTEPAD 5.2

Stages in adjusting to a new culture

- *Confusion:* First contacts with the new culture leave you anxious, uncomfortable and in need of information and advice.

- *Small victories:* Continued interactions bring some 'successes', and your confidence grows in handling daily affairs.

- *The honeymoon:* A time of wonderment, cultural immersion and infatuation, with local things viewed most positively by you.

- *Irritation and anger:* A time when the 'negatives' overtake the 'positives', and the new culture becomes a target of your criticism.

- *Reality:* A time of rebalancing; you are able to enjoy the new culture while recognising its less desirable elements.

Popular dimensions of culture

The first impressions of a traveller often include recognition and even 'shock' over cultural differences. Among the popular dimensions of culture that should be understood are those relating to language, use of space, time orientation, religion and the role of contracts.[47] When executives at British Airways (BA) surveyed international customers, for example, a simple lesson emerged — don't assume people from different cultures will have the same dining habits and preferences. Japanese, for example, commented that BA's food was 'not bad for Westerners'. They also pointed out that the white china dishes were similar to those used in Japanese hospitals and prisons. 'The further away from our Western culture we go, the less satisfied our customers are', said one BA marketing manager. 'People from other cultures have felt looked down upon.' A major overhaul was undertaken to give the carrier a more truly global identity.[48]

LANGUAGE

Language is a medium of culture. It provides access to the type of cultural understanding needed to conduct business and develop relationships. Not only do languages vary around the world; the same language (such as English) can vary in usage from one country to the next (as it does from America to England to Australia to New Zealand). Although it isn't always possible to know a local language, such as Hungarian, it is increasingly usual in business dealings to find some common second language in which to communicate, such as English, French, German or Spanish. The importance of good foreign language training is critical for the truly global manager. When Larry Johnston arrived in Paris to head up GE's medical equipment operations in Europe, the Middle East and Africa, the first thing he did was study intensive French for a month. 'I went from 7 a.m. to 8 p.m. and learned enough to converse', he says.[49]

According to anthropologist Edward T. Hall, there are systematic and important differences in the way cultures use language in communication.[50] He describes **low-context cultures** as those in which most communication takes place via the written or spoken word. In places like the USA, Canada, Germany, New Zealand and Australia, for example, the message is delivered in very precise wording. You have to listen and read carefully to best understand what the message sender intends. Things are quite different in

> ☛ **Low-context cultures** emphasise communication via spoken or written words.

high-context cultures, where much communication takes place through non-verbal and situational cues, in addition to the written or spoken word. In such settings the words communicate only a (sometimes small) part of the message. The rest must be interpreted from the situational 'context' — body language, physical setting and even the past relationships among those involved. This process is often time consuming and very deliberate. In high-context Japan, for example, much emphasis is given to social settings in which potential partners develop a relationship and get to know one another; once this is accomplished, future business dealings can then be formed.

INTERPERSONAL SPACE

Hall considers the use of interpersonal space as one of the important 'silent languages' of culture.[51] Arabs and many Latin Americans, for example, prefer to communicate at much closer distances than is standard in Australian and New Zealand practice. Misunderstandings are possible if one businessperson moves back as another moves forward to close the interpersonal distance between them. Some cultures of the world also value space more highly than others. Americans tend to value large and private office space. The Japanese are highly efficient in using space; even executive offices are likely to be shared in major corporations.

TIME ORIENTATION

Time orientation is another dimension of the silent language of culture.[52] The way people approach and deal with time tends to vary widely. Mexicans, for example, may specify *hora Americana* on invitations if they want guests to appear at the appointed time; otherwise, it may be impolite to arrive punctually for a scheduled appointment. When working in Vietnam, by contrast, punctuality is important and communicates respect for one's host.[53] Hall describes **monochronic cultures** in which people tend to do one thing at a time, such as schedule a meeting and give the visitor one's undivided attention for the allotted time.[54] This is standard business practice in Australia and New Zealand. In **polychronic cultures**, by contrast, time is used to accomplish many different things at once. The New Zealander or Australian visitor to an Egyptian client may be frustrated by continued interruptions as people flow in and out of the office and various transactions are made.

RELIGION

Religion is also important as a cultural variable, and you should always be aware of religious traditions when visiting and working in other cultures. Religion is a major influence on many people's lives, and its impact may extend to practices regarding dress, food and interpersonal behaviour. It is a source of ethical and moral teaching, with associated personal and institutional implications. Islamic banks in the Middle East, for example, service their customers without any interest charges to remain consistent with teachings of the Koran. The traveller and businessperson should be sensitive to the rituals, holy days and other expectations associated with religions in foreign countries. When working with Muslims in Malaysia, for example, it is polite to schedule business dinners after 8 p.m. This allows them to complete the evening prayer before dining. Similarly, it should be remembered that the Islamic holy month of Ramadan is a dawn-to-dusk time of fasting.

Operating in 140 countries, Reebok is very sensitive to the traditions of other cultures and takes a non-religious approach. During the Christmas holidays, for example, the company steers clear of traditional green and red colours and sticks to the corporate colours of blue and silver.[55]

ROLE OF AGREEMENTS

Cultures vary in their use of contracts and agreements. In Australia and New Zealand, a contract is viewed as a final and binding statement of agreements. This tends to hold true in general with low-context cultures. In other parts of the world with high-context cultures, such as China, the written contract may be viewed as more of a starting point. Once in place, it will continue to emerge and be modified as the parties work together over time. McDonald's found this out when the Chinese government ignored the firm's lease on a restaurant site in downtown Beijing and tore down the building to make room for a development project. In Australia and New Zealand, contracts are expected to be in writing; however, requesting a written agreement from an Indonesian who has given his 'word' may be quite disrespectful.

Values and national cultures

As companies go global, their managers must become more global in viewpoints, experiences and cultural appreciation. An Australian project manager, for example, started work on a project in Bandung, Indonesia. She did not realise that religious holidays are so important in Indonesia, and that the office staff devoutly observed these. The importance staff placed on tending to the needs of their families — particularly their elderly relatives, and their children in the morning — was not known to her, as she only had to look after herself each morning. During the month of Ramadan, staff would often leave early and arrive late to meet the requirements of fasting and religious devotion. She felt quite frustrated until a colleague told her about the importance of these issues to Indonesians.[56]

It is helpful to have a framework for understanding how basic cultural differences can influence management and organisational practices. Geert Hofstede, a Dutch scholar and international management consultant, studied personnel from a US-based MNC operating in 40 countries. First published in his book *Culture's Consequences: International Differences in Work-Related Values*, his research offers one framework for understanding the management implications of broad differences in national cultures.[57] Figure 5.3 shows how selected countries rank on the five dimensions Hofstede now uses in his model.

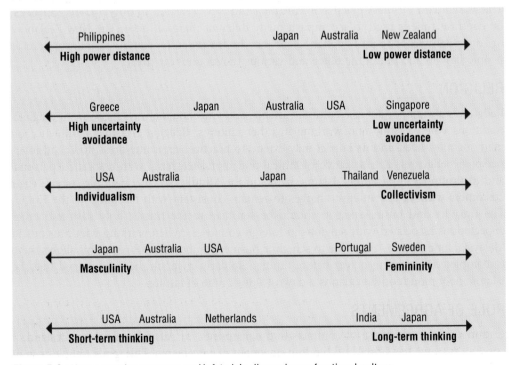

Figure 5.3 ▶ How countries compare on Hofstede's dimensions of national culture

1. *Power distance* — the degree to which a society accepts or rejects the unequal distribution of power in organisations and the institutions of society.
2. *Uncertainty avoidance* — the degree to which a society tolerates risk and situational uncertainties.
3. *Individualism–collectivism* — the degree to which a society emphasises individual accomplishment and self-interests, versus collective accomplishments and the good of groups.
4. *Masculinity–femininity* — the degree to which a society values assertiveness and material success, versus feelings and concern for relationships.
5. *Time orientation* — the degree to which a society emphasises short-term considerations versus greater concern for the future.[58]

Hofstede's dimensions of national cultures

Hofstede's framework helps identify useful managerial implications from these potential cultural differences. For example, workers from high power-distance cultures, such as Singapore, can be expected to show great respect to seniors and those in authority. In high uncertainty-avoidance cultures, employment practices that increase job security are likely to be favoured. In highly individualistic societies (the United States ranked as the most individualistic in Hofstede's sample), workers may be expected to emphasise self-interests more than group loyalty. Outsiders may find that the workplace in more masculine societies, such as Japan, displays more rigid gender stereotypes. Also, corporate strategies in more long-term cultures are likely to be just that — more long-term oriented.

Understanding cultural diversity

Consider this scene.[59] Interbrew SA of Belgium purchased 50 per cent ownership in Oriental Brewery of South Korea, bringing four Western senior managers into the Korean operation. 'It was a new experience', said Ms Park, one of Oriental's local staff. It was also a clash of two different business cultures. The newcomers wanted locals to express their ideas and work toward clear objectives; the locals were used to following orders and working through relationships. Some two years into the process of learning how to work together, Ms Park finally agreed that the Western and local staff were making progress toward building Oriental Brewery up to its performance potential.

Stepping into cross-cultural work and managerial situations of any sort is complicated; those associated with mergers and acquisitions are especially so. It takes all of one's understanding and skills to best deal with the challenges. In addition to the descriptions of popular and national cultures already discussed, the integrative framework of management scholar Fons Trompenaars can be helpful. In research with some 15 000 respondents from 47 countries, he identifies systematic cultural differences in the ways relationships are handled among people, attitudes toward time, and attitudes toward the environment.[60] By better understanding these patterns of difference, he suggests we can improve our cross-cultural work effectiveness.

RELATIONSHIPS WITH PEOPLE

According to Trompenaars's framework, there are five ways in which people differ culturally in how they handle relationships with one another. They include the individualism–collectivism notion just discussed, as well as additional considerations.
1. *Universalism vs particularism* — the degree to which a culture emphasises rules and consistency in relationships, or accepts flexibility and the bending of rules to fit circumstances.
2. *Individualism vs collectivism* — the degree to which a culture emphasises individual freedoms and responsibilities in relationships, or focuses more on group interests and consensus.

3. *Neutral vs affective* — the degree to which a culture emphasises objectivity and reserved detachment in relationships, or allows more emotionality and expressed feelings.
4. *Specific vs diffuse* — the degree to which a culture emphasises focused and in-depth relationships, or broader and more superficial ones.
5. *Achievement vs prescription* — the degree to which a culture emphasises an earned or performance-based status in relationships, or awards status based on social standing and non-performance factors.

ATTITUDES TOWARD TIME

Attitudes toward time in the Trompenaars framework differ in the relative emphasis given to the present versus the past and future. In cultures that take a *sequential view*, time is considered a continuous and passing series of events. This somewhat casual view of time may be represented by a circle and the notion that time is recycling, in the sense that a moment passed will return again. In cultures that take a *synchronic view*, by contrast, time takes on a greater sense of urgency. It is more linear, with an interrelated past, present and future. Pressures to resolve problems quickly so that time won't be 'lost' are more likely in synchronic than sequential cultures.

ATTITUDES TOWARD THE ENVIRONMENT

Trompenaars also recognises that cultures vary in their approach to the environment. In cultures that are *inner-directed*, people tend to view themselves as quite separate from nature. They are likely to consider the environment as something to be controlled or used for personal advantage. In cultures that are *outer-directed*, people tend to view themselves as part of nature. They are more likely to try and blend with or go along with the environment than to try to control it.

MANAGEMENT ACROSS CULTURES

The management process — planning, organising, leading and controlling — is as relevant to international operations as to domestic ones. Yet, as the preceding discussion of culture should suggest, these functions must be applied appropriately from one country and culture to the next. **Comparative management** is the study of how management systematically differs among countries and/or cultures. Today we recognise the importance of learning about how management is practised around the world. Competition and the global economy have given rise to *global managers*, defined earlier as managers comfortable with cultural diversity, quick to find opportunities in unfamiliar settings, and able to marshal economic, social, technological and other forces for the benefit of the organisation.[61] Says Robin Willett, Group Deputy Chairman of Willett Systems, Ltd of the United Kingdom: 'Our aim has always been to be a truly global company, not simply an exporter. We work very hard at developing and maintaining an international mindset that is shared by everyone — from senior management to staff.'[62] Global managers, simply put, apply the management functions successfully across national and cultural borders.

> **Comparative management** studies how management practices differ among countries and cultures.

Planning and controlling

The complexity of the international operating environment makes global planning and controlling especially challenging. Picture a home office somewhere in New Zealand, say Auckland. Foreign operations are scattered in Asia, Africa, South America and Europe. Planning must somehow link the home office and foreign affiliates, while taking into account different environments, cultures and needs. Increasingly, new technology facilitates the planning and control of global operations through vastly improved communications systems. Computer-based global networks allow home and field offices to share databases, electronically transfer documents, and even hold conferences and make group decisions through computer links and videoconferencing.

Organisations with investments in foreign countries must also factor into their planning the risks of doing business across political and economic borders. One risk is *currency* risk. Companies like McDonald's, for example, must eventually convert their foreign currency earnings into dollars. But, the value of the dollar against other currencies varies over time and is not always easy to predict. McDonald's earnings fell by 5 per cent in 2000, as the US dollar's value relative to the euro declined dramatically in just a few months. Another risk is **political risk**, the potential loss of one's investment in or managerial control over a foreign asset because of political changes in the host country. In general, the major threats of political risk come from social instabilities as a result of ethnic or other differences, armed conflicts and military disruptions, shifting government systems through elections or forced takeovers, and new laws and economic policies. Think about the political risks occurring in the world today. What ramifications can you see for organisations?

Political-risk analysis is a planning process that forecasts the probability of these and other political events that can threaten the security of a foreign investment. The stakes can be quite high. It is obvious, for example, that foreign investors suffer in the political turmoil of war and terrorism. It may be less obvious that an Australian company in a developing country could lose most of its foreign assets in a single day. This could happen if the host country decided to float its currency in the international money markets, resulting in the loss in value of the company's assets in that country in Australian dollars. Organisations that do political-risk analysis would be able to take protective measures against such a situation.

> **Political risk** is the possible loss of investment or control over a foreign asset because of political changes in the host country.

> **Political-risk analysis** forecasts how political events may impact foreign investments.

Organising and leading

The same factors that challenge the planning and controlling functions in the international arena also affect managerial efforts to organise and lead. The forces of globalisation are complex indeed. For Caltex, it has meant closing a corporate headquarters in Dallas, Texas, and moving to Singapore. It has meant setting up a web site development division in South Africa and an accounting division in the Philippines. The general manager of the firm's new Manila operation says: 'As technology and communication improve, we are scattering centres of excellence around the world'.[63]

A rule of thumb for staffing international operations can be stated this way: 'Hire competent locals, use competent locals and listen to competent locals'. But in addition, global success also frequently depends on the work of **expatriates**, employees who live and work in foreign countries on short-term or long-term assignments. For progressive firms, assigning home-office personnel to foreign operations is increasingly viewed as a strategic opportunity.[64] Not only does this offer the individuals challenging work experiences, it also helps bring into the executive suite culturally aware managers with truly global horizons and interpersonal networks of global contacts. Of course, not everyone performs well in an overseas assignment. Among the foundations for success are such personal attributes as a high degree of cultural awareness and sensitivity, a real desire to live and work abroad, family flexibility and support, as well as technical competence in one's job.

> **Expatriates** live and work in a foreign country.

A common organising approach for organisations just getting started in international business is to appoint a senior manager to oversee all foreign operations. This may be fine for limited international activity, but as global involvement expands it usually requires a more complex arrangement. The *global area structure* shown in figure 5.4 arranges production and sales functions into separate geographical units. This allows activities in major areas of the world to be given special executive attention. Another organising option is the *global product structure*, also shown in the figure. It gives worldwide responsibilities to product group managers, who are assisted by area specialists on the corporate staff. These specialists provide expert guidance on the unique needs of various countries or regions. When Carly Fiorina became CEO of Hewlett-Packard, for example, she found the firm losing touch with its international customers. Wanting to make it easier for them to buy HP products from anywhere in the world, she reorganised the firm into global sales and marketing groups to better match global services with local needs.[65]

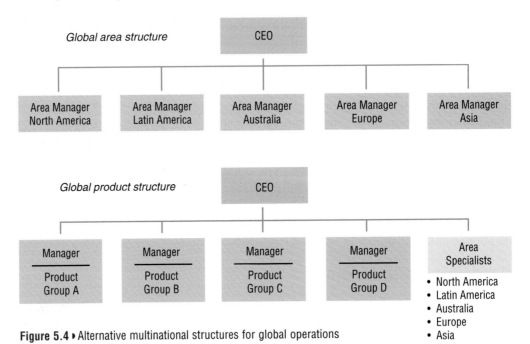

Figure 5.4 ▸ Alternative multinational structures for global operations

SingTel • www.singtel.com

SingTel plays its part in community

Multinationals are often accused of not doing enough in terms of their social responsibility in the local contexts in which they operate. SingTel, the giant integrated communications service provider in the Asia–Pacific, is an example of a multinational doing its part in supporting community and social development. For example, in Singapore, SingTel's festive charity campaign 'The Gift of Staying in Touch' raised S$500 000 for the Children's Cancer Foundation, Lions Befrienders, Movement for the Intellectually Disabled of Singapore (MINDS) and the Singapore Association of the Visually Handicapped. SingTel also made 1000 wishes of the beneficiaries come true, by giving items such as radios, cookers, watches, walking sticks and even a dinner date with actress Sharon Au.[66]

Are management theories universal?

Management practices in North America and Western Europe frequently have been used as models around the world. Increasingly, however, a significant question is asked: 'Are management theories universal?' Geert Hofstede, whose framework for understanding national cultures was introduced earlier, believes they should *not* be applied universally.[67] He worries that many of these theories are ethnocentric and fail to take into account cultural differences. For example, he argues that the American emphasis on participation in leadership reflects the culture's moderate stance on power distance. National cultures with lower scores, such as Sweden and Israel, are characterised by even more 'democratic' leadership initiatives. France and some Asian countries with higher power–distance scores seem less concerned with participative leadership.

Hofstede also points out that the motivation theories of American scholars are value laden, with an emphasis on individual performance. He considers this viewpoint consistent with the high individualism found in Anglo-American countries such as the USA, Canada, New Zealand and Australia. Elsewhere, where values are more collectivist, the theories may be less applicable. Even a common value, such as the desire for increased humanisation of work, may lead in different management directions. Until recently, practices in the USA largely emphasised designing jobs for individuals. Elsewhere in the world, such as in Sweden, the emphasis has been on designing jobs to be performed by groups of workers.

Consider as well the implications of transferring to the USA and other Western countries some of the Japanese management practices that have attracted great interest over the years.[68] These include lifetime employment, gradual career advancement, collective decision making and quality emphasis. All have been associated in one way or another with past successes in Japanese industry.[69] But as interesting as the practices may be, any transfers of practice must factor into account the distinctive Japanese cultural traditions in which they emerged, such as long-term orientation, collectivism and high power distance.[70] It should be noted also that management and organisational practices are changing in Japan, some argue toward the Western models, as its businesses adjust to the demands of a new economy and shifting trends in social values.[71]

Context also counts in evaluating management and organisational practices. In Japan, **keiretsu** have been part of the success stories. They are long-term industry alliances or business groups that link together various businesses — manufacturers, suppliers and finance companies — to attain common interests. The companies involved often own stock in one another, their boards of directors often overlap and they often do business with one another on a preferential basis. Not only must the influence of *keiretsu* on Japanese business success be recognised, it may be considered an unfair business practice in other countries such as the antitrust-conscious USA.

Global organisational learning

In the dynamic and ever-expanding global economy, cultural awareness is helping to facilitate more informed transfers of management and organisational practices. We live at a fortunate time when managers around the world are realising they have much to share with and learn from one another. Global organisational learning is a timely and relevant theme. This point is evident in the following words of Kenichi Ohmae, noted Japanese management consultant and author of *The Borderless World*:

> Companies can learn from one another, particularly from other excellent companies, both at home and abroad. The industrialized world is becoming increasingly homogeneous in terms of customer needs and social infrastructure, and only truly excellent companies can compete effectively in the global marketplace.[72]

REALITY CHECK

Minding your international manners

When meeting business associates in countries such as Japan and Singapore, present your business card using both hands to hold onto the corners as you pass it forward, stating your name and company as you do so. Upon receiving a business card, accept it with both hands and then study carefully what is written on it. In a formal situation, it is appropriate to place the card face up on the table in front of you and refer to it as necessary. In a less formal setting you may put it away after looking at it.

Do you follow this protocol when meeting Asian business associates?

A **keiretsu** is a group of Japanese manufacturers, suppliers and finance firms with common interests.

Yes, we do have a lot to learn from one another. Yet it must be learned with full appreciation of the constraints and opportunities of different cultures and country environments. Like the American management practices before them, Japanese approaches and those from other cultures must be studied and adapted for local use very carefully. This applies to the way management is practised in Singapore, Korea, Indonesia, New Zealand, or any other part of the world. As Hofstede states: 'Disregard of other cultures is a luxury only the strong can afford ... [The] consequent increase in cultural awareness represents an intellectual and spiritual gain. And as far as management theories go, cultural relativism is an idea whose time has come.'[73]

The best approach to comparative management and global management learning is an alert, open, inquiring and always cautious one. It is important to identify both the potential merits of management practices found in other countries *and* the ways cultural variables may affect their success or failure when applied elsewhere. We can and should be looking for new ideas to stimulate change and innovation. But we should hesitate to accept any practice, no matter how well it appears to work somewhere else, as a universal prescription to action. Indeed, the goal of comparative management studies is not to provide definitive answers but to help develop creative and critical thinking about the way managers around the world do things, and about whether they can and should be doing them better.

Go to the UN web site www.un.org/overview/rights.html and read the Universal Declaration of Human Rights adopted by the United Nations General Assembly on 10 December 1948.

GET CONNECTED!

CHAPTER 5
Study guide

The chapter 5 study guide helps you review the chapter content, prepare for examinations, apply what you have learned and further build your career readiness. The summary briefly answers the study questions posed at the start of the chapter. The list of key terms allows you to double-check your familiarity with basic concepts and definitions. The applied activities help you test your comprehension of chapter content. Suggestions offered as career readiness activities direct your attention to relevant sections of the Career Readiness Workbook where you can test and develop your career skills and apply what you have learned. The list of electronic resources suggests activities from the *Management: An Asia–Pacific Perspective* web site and, finally, the case for critical thinking helps you apply your new management knowledge.

SUMMARY

What are international management challenges of globalisation?

- International management is practised in organisations that conduct business in more than one country.
- Global managers are informed about international developments, transnational in outlook, competent in working with people from different cultures, and always aware of regional developments in a changing world.
- The global economy is making the diverse countries of the world increasingly interdependent regarding resource supplies, product markets and business competition.
- The global economy is now strongly influenced by regional developments that involve growing economic integration in Europe, the Americas, Asia and Australasia, and the economic emergence of Africa.

What are the forms and opportunities of international business?

- Five forms of international business are global sourcing, exporting and importing, licensing and franchising, joint ventures and wholly owned subsidiaries.
- The market entry strategies of global sourcing, exporting/importing and licensing are common for organisations wanting to get started internationally.
- Direct investment strategies to establish joint ventures or wholly owned subsidiaries in foreign countries represent substantial commitments to international operations.

What are multinational corporations and what do they do?

- Global operations are influenced by important environmental differences among the economic, legal–political and educational systems of countries.
- A multinational corporation (MNC) is a business with extensive operations in more than one foreign country.
- True MNCs are global firms with worldwide missions and strategies that earn a substantial part of their revenues abroad.
- MNCs offer potential benefits to host countries in broader tax bases, new technologies and employment opportunities. MNCs can also disadvantage host countries if they interfere in local government, extract excessive profits and dominate the local economy.

What is culture and how does it relate to global diversity?

- Management and global operations are affected by the dimensions of popular culture, including language, space perception, time perception, religion and the nature of contracts.
- Management and global operations are affected by differences in national cultures, including Hofstede's dimensions of power distance, uncertainty avoidance, individualism–collectivism, masculinity–femininity and time orientation.
- Differences among the world's cultures may be understood in respect to how people handle relationships with one another, their attitudes toward time and their attitudes toward the environment.

How do management practices and learning transfer across cultures?

- The management process must be used appropriately and applied with sensitivity to local cultures and situations.
- The field of comparative management studies how management is practised around the world and how management ideas are transferred from one country or culture to the next.
- Cultural values and management practices should be consistent with one another. Practices that are successful in one culture may work less well in others.
- The concept of global management learning has much to offer as the 'borderless' world begins to emerge and as the management practices of diverse countries and cultures become more visible.

KEY TERMS

child labour (p. 129)

comparative management (p. 134)

corruption (p. 128)

culture (p. 129)

culture shock (p. 129)

ethnocentrism (p. 129)

euro (p. 120)

European Union (EU) (p. 119)

expatriates (p. 135)

exporting (p. 125)

franchising (p. 125)

global economy (p. 118)

global manager (p. 119)

global sourcing (p. 125)

globalisation (p. 118)

high-context cultures (p. 131)

importing (p. 125)

international businesses (p. 123)

international management (p. 119)

ISO 14000 (p. 129)

joint ventures (p. 126)

keiretsu (p. 137)

licensing agreement (p. 125)

low-context cultures (p. 130)

monochronic cultures (p. 131)

multinational corporation (MNC) (p. 126)

NAFTA (p. 120)

political risk (p. 135)

political-risk analysis (p. 135)

polychronic cultures (p. 131)

privatisation (p. 124)

protectionism (p. 124)

sustainable development (p. 129)

sweatshops (p. 128)

transnational corporations (p. 127)

wholly owned subsidiary (p. 126)

World Trade Organization (WTO) (p. 124)

APPLIED ACTIVITIES

Short-response questions

1. Why is NAFTA important for American businesses?
2. Why do host countries sometimes complain about the operations of MNCs within their borders?
3. Why is the 'power–distance' dimension of national culture important in management?
4. Choose a region of the world (Europe, the Americas, Africa, Asia, Australasia) and describe its significance in the global economy.

Application question

5. Kim has just returned from her first business trip to Japan. While there, she was impressed with the use of quality circles and work teams. Now back in Brisbane, she would like to start the same practices in her book publishing company of 75 employees. Based on the discussion of culture and management in this chapter, what advice would you offer Kim?

CAREER READINESS ACTIVITIES

Recommended individual and group learning activities from the end-of-text Career Readiness Workbook for this chapter include:

Career advancement portfolio   **WB**

Update your career advancement portfolio to reflect your new skills and experiences. Include skills and personal insights you gain from the following projects and exercises.

Research and presentation project   **WB**

• Project 3 — Foreign investment in Australasia — 'what are the implications?'

Cross-functional integrative case   **WB**

Read the integrative case on Sarina Russo and answer the following question:

What form of international business is already being undertaken within the Sarina Russo Group?

Exercise in teamwork   **WB**

• Exercise 7 — What do you value in work?

Management skills assessment   **WB**

• Assessment 5 — Global awareness

ELECTRONIC RESOURCES

Don't forget to take full advantage of the online support for *Management: An Asia–Pacific Perspective* at www.johnwiley.com.au/highered/management: chapter 5 practice tests, e-flashcards, crossword puzzles, interactive management skills assessments, interactive cases, the online career advancement portfolio and much more!

CASE FOR CRITICAL THINKING

Read the following case for critical thinking on Cadbury Schweppes. While you are reading the case keep in mind what you have learned in this chapter, then answer the questions.

Cadbury Schweppes: obstacles and learning opportunities in Asia

In 1996, the global board of directors at Cadbury Schweppes plc decided to actively pursue development in the Asia region, which had traditionally been minimally serviced through small product exports from Ireland. To achieve this objective, responsibility for the Asia region was redeployed to the Australian board of directors for the following main reasons:

- possession of some knowledge of Asia through pre-existing beverage operations
- convenience in terms of time and distance
- relative proximity and therefore potential mobility of Australian workforce to be redeployed in Asia.

The journey that the Australian board embarked on presented many obstacles and learning opportunities in terms of the elements involved in international management.

The Cadbury Schweppes organisation

Cadbury Schweppes employs more than 40 000 people worldwide, and its brands are market leaders in many parts of the world. The business has confectionery and/or beverage operations in the United Kingdom, Europe, the Americas, the Asia–Pacific, Africa and other regions.[74]

Cadbury Schweppes is the world's third-largest beverage company and fourth-largest confectionery company. It is primarily a brand owner of beverages, franchising to independent or competitors' bottlers. The group owns confectionery operations in most developed countries. In developing beverage and confectionery markets, Cadbury Schweppes has joint ventures with commercial or financial partners. The core beverage market is the USA, where the Dr Pepper/Seven Up and Mott's businesses are based. Europe and Australia are core to the confectionery business. Major global brands include Cadbury Dairy Milk, Roses, Picnic, Time-Out, Dr Pepper, Schweppes, Canada Dry, A&W, Squirt and Oasis. The Cadbury Schweppes group also own food businesses such as Mott's in North America, Bromor Foods in South Africa and Cottee's Foods in Australia.

Cadbury Schweppes's governing objective is growth in shareholder value.[75] The main areas of strategy include:

- focus on core growth markets of confectionery and beverages
- development of robust and sustainable regional positions across the global business built on a platform of strong brands whose consumer licences are consistently and imaginatively supported
- growth through innovation in products, packaging and route to market
- strengthening of the business portfolio through value-enhancing acquisitions or disposals.[76]

Cadbury Asia

The Cadbury Asia operations have been in place since 1997, located in China. A joint venture was developed at the beginning, although Cadbury bought out its joint venture partner at the end of 1998 to assume full operational control. The main confectionery products in the Asia market include chocolate eclairs and mints. The Chinese palate is not accustomed to consuming straight chocolate; therefore, Cadbury entered with a sugar confectionery range first and will develop into full-cream chocolate once confectionery penetration increases.

Until 1997, the area of international cross-cultural management had been something that the Cadbury Australia board had been able to avoid. International operations had extended into New Zealand; however, there was relatively little cultural difference between the two countries. Entering the Asian market has proven to be a challenging task to Cadbury, owing to differences in economics, politics, religions and values.

Economy

The difference between the capitalist economy of Australia and the socialist-orientated economy of China represented the first significant issue for the business, as it was at the heart of many of the cultural differences between the two countries. Early issues involved the establishment of accurate factory outputs, labour rates, terms and conditions. The Cadbury Schweppes organisation learnt to be sensitive to employee-related issues from an earlier international expansion into Spain. In that case, Cadbury had failed to take into consideration the fact that there was no mandatory retirement age for their Spanish workforce, and that the culture was one of lifetime employment with one company. This left Cadbury with financial issues when they began closing the operation 15 years later — many employees had very sizeable redundancy packages that had not been anticipated.

Politics

The politics of China dictated the need for a joint venture operation. This provided a significant level of local assistance and knowledge that was considered an invaluable contributor to the set up and success of the plant. It also created a level of uncertainty for the Australian board, as they had little understanding of the political system of China.

Religion

The different beliefs of the Chinese people posed important concerns for the Australian board. Much of this resulted from the potential work ethic differences between the predominantly Protestant Australian workforce and the more fatalistic-orientated Chinese workforce. This made labour forecasting and output a difficult matter.

Value systems

A particular issue that faced Cadbury at the beginning of its operations in China was the way people from different cultures and countries preferred to relate to one another. The Chinese people did not often offer their personal opinion on matters and were more accepting of the mandates of their superiors. This was considerably different to the ways of the West and the culture that exists in Australia.

The first products introduced to the Chinese market were blocks of milk chocolate, similar in both taste and size to those you would find in Australia, New Zealand, Europe and the USA. Cadbury had conducted some research, using focus groups of Chinese consumers in different parts of the country, organised by their research centre in Australia. The results of this research were considered promising and indicated consumers would enjoy the product in a similar form.

Shortly after launch, and as a result of unexpectedly poor distribution, Cadbury reviewed this process and was able to draw some conclusions about Chinese consumers, such as how they should be researched and what their underlying purchase motivators were — all of which reflected their culture.

The review process found that, in a focus group environment, Chinese people would not wish to lose face by offering their own opinion. Moreover, they were reluctant to put themselves in a position where they would risk making the researcher lose face, as they considered that the researcher represented the manufacturer of the product. As a result, the research results had a positive bias.

One of the outcomes of this exercise was to alter the research approach by including a variety of products and asking respondents to sort them in order of preference. As there had to be a first and last, respondents felt more comfortable because they felt they were complimenting some of the range, which allowed them to feel better about rating other products badly.

The issue of product size was also dealt with in subsequent research. The large blocks offered in Western consumption-based cultures were considered too indulgent for the Chinese consumers, who preferred single-serve confectionery that was more conservative.

Cross-cultural economics

A significant economics-based cross-cultural issue that was pivotal in Cadbury's failure to gain distribution of chocolate and its ultimate success in sugar-based confectionery was the lack of cold storage in China. The Australian board had also failed to fully appreciate the economics and how that affected their route to market. The beverage experience had provided them with some idea of cold-storage distribution, but they had underestimated the demands on space in these fridges. Partially through the appreciation of this dynamic and product research, Cadbury launched Eclairs, which did not require cold storage and were in single-serve form.

Frame of reference

A further interesting dynamic for Cadbury related to the assumptions it had made about Chinese consumers and their frame of reference to the Cadbury product. This was evidenced by a television advertising campaign that was conducted for the launch of Cadbury chocolate, which showed a block of chocolate being passed from one child to another along a school bench. As each child received the block, he or she would break off one piece and pass it to the next child on the bench; but the audience could not see what was done with the chocolate after it had been broken off. This commercial was an adaptation of a successful English commercial and considered to be universal in its appeal. After research into the campaign awareness and attitudes to the commercial, Cadbury Australia realised that they had assumed that the Chinese consumer knew this product should be consumed and enjoyed. In fact, the research showed that people believed it was a bad product, because everyone kept passing it off to the next person and each child was simply doing their part in helping to dispose of it by breaking a piece off!

Summary

It is not difficult to see how quickly a brand or company can get into trouble by making too many assumptions about a country and culture. An interesting way to evaluate a country's culture is to consider the people's sense of humour. Is it self-effacing? Does it ridicule other cultures? Is it innocent? This can provide an insight into the approach that could be considered (or not considered) when tackling international cross-cultural management issues.

It is worth noting that the Cadbury Australia board, and other levels involved with the development into China, did receive a degree of outside training in cross-cultural management issues. However, this did not extend to cultural mapping exercises designed to specifically plot the key differences and potential areas of conflict between two different cultures, and cultural management theories were not considered. It is therefore critical that in any cross-cultural venture, an organisation and its international managers take time to learn about the economy, history, politics and value systems of the country where they are going to be working.[77]

QUESTIONS

1. Analyse the challenges faced by Cadbury when it entered the Asian market.
2. What recommendations do you have for an international manager starting work in a new country?

CHAPTER 6

CHAPTER 6

Ethical behaviour and social responsibility

CHAPTER 6 STUDY QUESTIONS

- What is ethical behaviour?

- How do ethical dilemmas complicate the workplace?

- How can high ethical standards be maintained?

- What is organisational social responsibility?

- How do organisations and government work together in society?

Goldman Environmental Prize — help make this world a better place

Each year six 'environmental heroes' from the world's continental regions receive prestigious awards from the Goldman Environmental Foundation www.goldmanprize.org for their outstanding work as grassroots environmentalists. The foundation annually contributes $750 000 to fund the Goldman Environmental Prize for these heroes. Recent recipients include:

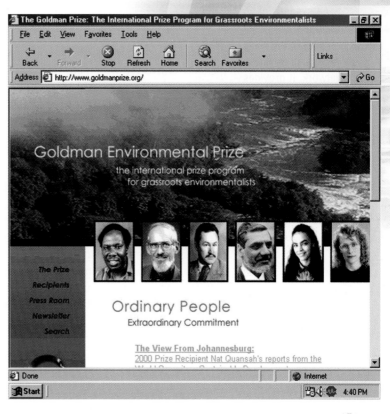

- Thailand's Pisit Charnsnoh, for his marine conservation efforts. He encouraged villages to protect the coastal fisheries and mangroves, and established nine community-managed forests.
- Australia's Jacqui Katona and Yvonne Margarula, for leading the Mirrar Aboriginal people in an opposition campaign against Jabiluka, one of the world's largest uranium mines. Their protest included legal action, education and gathering national and international support.
- New Zealand's Bill Ballantine, for his success in creating marine reserves for 'non-exploitative purposes'. His leadership led to the establishment of 14 reserves in New Zealand that offer a unique opportunity to enjoy and study the sea's natural processes. Many other proposals are currently being considered.

The list of past winners goes on — a Burmese exposing environmental and human rights abuses, a Cameroonian lawyer protecting regional rainforests. Each winner receives a 'no strings attached' award of US$125 000.

At a reunion, 42 recipients pledged to join forces in fighting what they called 'the destructive impacts of economic globalisation'. Goldman activists are concerned about harmful effects on health and living conditions, as well as the environment. They pledge to put more pressure on local governments and to continue campaigning publicly against multinational corporations to explain their activities.

Foundation president Richard Goldman says: 'During the past ten years, the recipients of the prize have opened our eyes to the obstacles and risks faced by individuals pursuing environmental interests worldwide. We believe that bringing attention to their issues raises the credibility of these individuals and offers them personal protection.'

Nominations for the Goldman Environmental Prize are submitted anonymously from a network of 21 environmental organisations spanning 50 nations. The awards are recognised by 113 heads of state worldwide.[1]

Shouldn't you know more about business in relationship with the natural environment? Explore sites such as earthsystems.org www.earthsystems.org, Environment Australia www.ea.gov.au and Envirolink www.envirolink.org. Find some other online resources regarding the link between business and the environment in other countries.

GET CONNECTED!

www.bf.rmit.edu.au/
Aben/

An example of an organisation that promotes ethical practices in business is the Australian Business Ethics Network. It provides a forum for discussing teaching and consulting ideas in the discipline of business ethics.

The good news is that some organisations employ 'environmental' managers to work on everything from a company's recycling program to long-term corporate environmental policies. Global warming, global sustainability and environmental protection are all on the agenda as organisations pursue what some call 'the greening of the bottom line'.[2] More and more companies are engaging in social outreach and including environmental issues and social concerns among top corporate goals.[3] Says the CEO of one large firm: 'A lot of the blue-chip multi-nationals have a long tradition of charitable and community programs that date back to their foundation. What is new is that corporate responsibility is being written into the business model.'[4] Lend Lease is a good example. The company is clear about its aim to develop sustained care for the community. It hopes to awaken in its employees, and the community at large, the spirit of contribution and commitment to others and the environment. Lend Lease believes that the impact of combined effort and concern outweighs that of straight cash donations, and therefore is involved with many projects where employees participate in community activities.[5]

The bad news is that not all stories from the corporate world are positive examples. Consider these actual reports from past news stories: 'Firm admits lowering phone contract bid after receiving confidential information from an insider that an initial bid "was not good enough to win"'; 'Company admits overcharging consumers and insurers more than $13 million for repairs to damaged rental cars'; 'Executives get prison terms for selling adulterated apple juice — the juice labelled "100% fruit juice" was actually a blend of synthetic ingredients'.

And that's not all. Consider these words from a commencement address delivered a few years ago at a well-known US business school: 'Greed is all right', the speaker said. 'Greed is healthy. You can be greedy and still feel good about yourself.' The students, it is reported, greeted these remarks with laughter and applause. The speaker was Ivan Boesky, once considered the 'king of the arbitragers'.[6] It wasn't long after his commencement speech that Boesky was arrested, tried, convicted and sentenced to prison for trading on inside information.

It is time to get serious about the moral aspects and social implications of decision making in organisations. In your career and in the work of any manager, the ultimate task must be considered to be more than simply meeting performance expectations. Performance goals must always be achieved through ethically and socially responsible action. The following reminder from Desmond Tutu, archbishop of Capetown, South Africa, and former winner of the Nobel Peace Prize, is applicable to managers everywhere:

> You are powerful people. You can make this world a better place where business decisions and methods take account of right and wrong as well as profitability ... You must take a stand on important issues: the environment and ecology, affirmative action, sexual harassment, racism and sexism, the arms race, poverty, the obligations of the affluent West to its less-well-off sisters and brothers elsewhere.[7]

WHAT IS ETHICAL BEHAVIOUR?

Ethics sets standards as to what is good or bad, or right or wrong in one's conduct.

Ethical behaviour is accepted as 'right' or 'good' in the context of a government moral code.

For our purposes, **ethics** can be defined as the code of moral principles that sets standards of good or bad, or right or wrong, in one's conduct and thereby guides the behaviour of a person or group.[8] Ethics provide principles to guide behaviour and help people make moral choices among alternative courses of action. In practice, **ethical behaviour** is that which is accepted to be 'good' and 'right' as opposed to 'bad' or 'wrong' in the context of the governing moral code.

Law, values and ethical behaviour

It makes sense that there should be a legal component to ethical behaviour; that is, one would expect that any legal behaviour should be considered ethical. Yet the White Australia Policy was once law in Australia.[9] That doesn't mean the policy was ethical; rather, we consider it unethical today. Furthermore, just because an action is not strictly illegal doesn't make it ethical. Living up to the 'letter of the law' is not sufficient to guarantee that one's actions will or should be considered ethical.[10] Is it truly ethical, for example, for an employee to take longer than necessary to do a job? To make personal telephone calls on company time? To call in sick to take a day off for leisure? To fail to report rule violations by a coworker? None of these acts are strictly illegal, but many people would consider any one or more of them to be unethical.

Most ethical problems in the workplace arise when people are asked to do, or find themselves about to do something that violates their personal conscience. For some, if the act is legal they proceed with confidence. For others, the ethical test goes beyond the legality of the act alone. The ethical question extends to personal **values** — the underlying beliefs and attitudes that help determine individual behaviour. To the extent that values vary among people, we can expect different interpretations of what behaviour is ethical or unethical in a given situation.

> **Values** are broad beliefs about what is or is not appropriate behaviour.

POINT⇐

COUNTER

Pressures affecting directors' judgement

Professional judgement and experience are two key ingredients when company directors exercise their right to make decisions. Recent cases like the demise of HIH and One.Tel in Australia have brought ethical decision making of directors into the spotlight. However, there are certain pressures that may impact on the ethical judgement of company directors. These pressures should not be seen as excuses, but they are part of the decision-making process that directors face every day. Time constraints and impossible deadlines may limit the ability to consult adequately, and all alternatives may not have been fully considered.

Consider what other issues may impact on the ethical decision making of managers.

Alternative views of ethical behaviour

There are many different interpretations of what constitutes ethical behaviour. Figure 6.1 shows four views of ethical behaviour that philosophers have discussed over the years.[11] The first is the **utilitarian view**. Behaviour that would be considered ethical from this perspective delivers the greatest good to the greatest number of people. Founded in the work of 19th-century philosopher John Stuart Mill, this is a results-oriented point of view that tries to assess the moral implications of decisions in terms of their consequences. Business decision makers, for example, are inclined to use profits, efficiency and other performance criteria to judge what is best for the most people. A manager may make a utilitarian decision to cut 30 per cent of a plant's workforce in order to keep the plant profitable and save jobs for the remaining 70 per cent.

The **individualism view** of ethical behaviour is based on the belief that one's primary commitment is to the advancement of long-term self-interests. When people pursue individual self-interests, they supposedly become self-regulating. For example, such things as lying and cheating for short-term gain should not be tolerated. If one person does it, everyone will do it, and no one's long-term interests will be served. The individualism view is supposed to promote honesty and integrity. But in business practice it may result in a pecuniary ethic, described by one business executive as the tendency to 'push the law to its outer limits' and 'run roughshod over other individuals to achieve one's objectives'.[12]

Ethical behaviour under a **moral-rights view** is that which respects and protects the fundamental rights of people. From the teachings of John Locke and Thomas Jefferson, for

> The **utilitarian view** considers ethical behaviour that which delivers greatest good to the most people.

> The **individualism view** considers ethical behaviour as that which advances long-term self-interests.

> The **moral-rights view** considers ethical behaviour as that which respects and protects fundamental rights.

example, the rights of all people in the USA to life, liberty and fair treatment under the law are considered inviolate. In US organisations today, this concept extends to ensuring that employees are always protected in their rights to privacy, due process, free speech, free consent, health and safety, and freedom of conscience. The issue of *human rights*, so characteristic of ethical concerns in the international business environment, is central to this perspective. The United Nations stands by the Universal Declaration of Human Rights passed by the General Assembly in 1948.

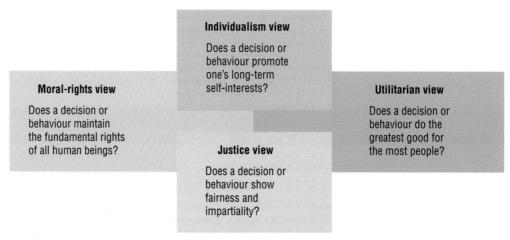

Figure 6.1 ▸ Four views of ethical behaviour

The **justice view** considers ethical behaviour as that which treats people impartially and fairly according to guiding rules and standards.

Procedural justice is concerned that policies and rules are fairly administered.

Distributive justice is concerned that people are treated the same regardless of individual characteristics.

Interactional justice is the degree to which others are treated with dignity and respect.

Finally, the **justice view** of moral behaviour is based on the belief that ethical decisions treat people impartially and fairly according to guiding rules and standards. This approach evaluates the ethical aspects of any decision on the basis of whether it is 'equitable' for everyone affected.[13] One justice issue in organisations is **procedural justice** — the degree to which policies and rules are fairly administered. For example, does a sexual harassment charge levied against a senior executive receive the same full hearing as one made against a first-level supervisor? A second issue is **distributive justice** — the degree to which outcomes are allocated without respect to individual characteristics based on ethnicity, race, gender, age or other particularistic criteria. For example, does a woman with the same qualifications and experience as a man receive the same consideration for hiring or promotion? A third issue is **interactional justice** — the degree to which others are treated with dignity and respect. For example, does a bank loan officer take the time to fully explain to an applicant why he or she was turned down for a loan?[14]

Cultural issues in ethical behaviour

The influence of culture on ethical behaviour is increasingly at issue as businesses and individuals travel the world. Corporate leaders must master difficult challenges when operating across borders that are cultural as well as national. Former Levi Strauss CEO Robert Haas once said that addressing ethical dilemmas as a corporate executive 'becomes even more difficult when you overlay the complexities of different cultures and values systems that exist throughout the world'.[15]

Cultural relativism suggests there is no one right way to behave; ethical behaviour is determined by its cultural context.

Those who believe that behaviour in foreign settings should be guided by the classic rule of 'when in Rome, do as the Romans do' reflect an ethical position of **cultural relativism**.[16] This is the notion that there is no one right way to behave and that ethical behaviour is always determined by its cultural context. When it comes to international business, for example, a

New Zealand executive guided by rules of cultural relativism would argue that the use of child labour is okay if it is consistent with local laws and customs. Figure 6.2, however, contrasts this position with the alternative of **universalism**. This ethical position suggests if a behaviour or practice is not okay in one's home environment, it shouldn't be acceptable practice anywhere else. In other words, ethical standards are universal and should apply absolutely across cultures and national boundaries. Critics of such a universal approach claim that it is a form of **ethical imperialism**, or the attempt to externally impose one's ethical standards on others.

Universalism suggests ethical standards apply across all cultures.

Ethical imperialism is an attempt to impose one's ethical standards on other cultures.

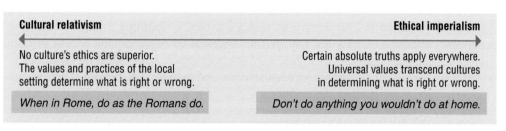

Cultural relativism	Ethical imperialism
No culture's ethics are superior. The values and practices of the local setting determine what is right or wrong.	Certain absolute truths apply everywhere. Universal values transcend cultures in determining what is right or wrong.
When in Rome, do as the Romans do.	*Don't do anything you wouldn't do at home.*

Figure 6.2 ▸ The extremes of cultural relativism and ethical imperialism

Source: Developed from Thomas Donaldson, 'Values in Tension: Ethics Away from Home', *Harvard Business Review*, vol. 74 (September–October 1996), pp. 48–62.

Business ethicist Thomas Donaldson discusses the debate between cultural relativism and ethical imperialism. Although there is no simple answer, he finds fault with both extremes. He argues instead that certain fundamental rights and ethical standards can be preserved while values and traditions of a given culture are respected.[17] The core values or 'hypernorms' that should transcend cultural boundaries focus on human dignity, basic rights and good citizenship. With a commitment to core values creating a transcultural ethical umbrella, Donaldson believes international business behaviours can be tailored to local and regional cultural contexts. In the case of child labour, for example, the New Zealand executive might ensure that any children working in a factory under contract to his or her business would be provided schooling as well as employment. See Manager's Notepad 6.1 for Donaldson's suggestions on how corporations can respect the core or universal values.[18]

MANAGER'S NOTEPAD 6.1

How multinationals can respect universal values

Respect for human dignity

- Create a culture valuing employees, customers and suppliers.
- Keep a safe workplace.
- Produce safe products and services.

Respect for basic rights

- Protect rights of employees, customers and communities.
- Avoid any threats to safety, health, education, living standards.

Be good citizens

- Support social institutions, economic and educational systems.
- Work with governments and institutions to protect environment.

ETHICS IN THE WORKPLACE

A classic quotation states: 'Ethical business is good business'. The same can be said for all persons and institutions throughout society. But the real test is when a manager or worker encounters a situation that challenges one's ethical beliefs and standards. Often ambiguous and unexpected, these 'ethical dilemmas' are part of the challenge of modern society.

What is an ethical dilemma?

An **ethical dilemma** is a situation that although offering potential benefit or gain is also unethical.

An **ethical dilemma** is a situation that requires a choice regarding a possible course of action that, although offering the potential for personal or organisational benefit or both, may be considered unethical. It is often a situation in which action must be taken but for which there is no clear consensus on what is 'right' and 'wrong'. The burden is on the individual to make good choices. An engineering manager, speaking from experience, sums it up this way: 'I define an unethical situation as one in which I have to do something I don't feel good about'.[19]

Ethical problems faced by managers

There are many potential sources of discomfort in managerial decision making, many of them with ethical overtones. Some of the problem areas where managers can get caught in ethical dilemmas, along with sample situations, include:[20]

Ethical problem areas for managers

- *discrimination* — where a manager denies promotion or appointment to a job candidate because of the candidate's race, religion, gender, age or other non-job-relevant criterion
- *sexual harassment* — where a manager makes a coworker feel uncomfortable because of inappropriate comments or actions regarding sexuality; or where a manager requests sexual favours in return for favourable job treatment
- *conflicts of interest* — where a manager takes a bribe or kickback or extraordinary gift in return for making a decision favourable to the gift giver
- *customer confidence* — where a manager has privileged information regarding the activities of a customer and shares that information with another party
- *organisational resources* — where a manager uses official stationery or a company e-mail account to communicate personal opinions or requests to community organisations.

In a survey of *Harvard Business Review* subscribers, many of the ethical dilemmas reported by managers involved conflicts with superiors, customers and subordinates.[21] The most frequent issues involved dishonesty in advertising and communications with top management, clients and government agencies. Problems in dealing with special gifts, entertainment and kickbacks were also reported. Significantly, the managers' bosses were singled out as sometimes pressuring their subordinates to engage in such unethical activities as supporting incorrect viewpoints, signing false documents, overlooking the boss's wrongdoings and doing business with the boss's friends.

Rationalisations for unethical behaviour

Why might otherwise reasonable people act unethically? Think back to the earlier examples and to those from your experiences. Consider the possibility of being asked to place a bid for a business contract using insider information, paying bribes to obtain foreign business, falsifying expense account bills and so on. 'Why', you should be asking, 'do people do things like this?' In fact, there are at least four common rationalisations that may be used to justify misconduct in these and other ethical dilemmas.[22]

1. Convince yourself that the behaviour is not really illegal.
2. Convince yourself that the behaviour is really in everyone's best interests.
3. Convince yourself that nobody will ever find out what you've done.
4. Convince yourself that the organisation will 'protect' you.

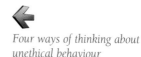

Four ways of thinking about unethical behaviour

After doing something that might be considered unethical, a rationaliser says, 'It's not really illegal'. This expresses a mistaken belief that one's behaviour is acceptable, especially in ambiguous situations. When dealing with shady or borderline situations in which you are having a hard time precisely defining right from wrong, the advice is quite simple: When in doubt about a decision to be made or an action to be taken, don't do it.

Another common statement by a rationaliser is: 'It's in everyone's best interests'. This response involves the mistaken belief that because someone can be found to benefit from the behaviour, the behaviour is also in the individual's or the organisation's best interests. Overcoming this rationalisation depends in part on the ability to look beyond short-run results to consider longer-term implications, and to look beyond results in general to the ways in which they are obtained. For example, in response to the question 'How far can I push matters to obtain this performance goal?', the recommended answer is often, 'Don't try to find out'.

Sometimes rationalisers tell themselves, 'No one will ever know about it'. They mistakenly believe that a questionable behaviour is really 'safe' and will never be found out or made public. Unless it is discovered, the argument implies, no crime was really committed. Lack of accountability, unrealistic pressures to perform and a boss who prefers 'not to know' can all reinforce such thinking. In this case, the best deterrent is to make sure that everyone knows that wrongdoing will be punished whenever it is discovered.

Finally, rationalisers may proceed with a questionable action because of a mistaken belief that 'the organisation will stand behind me'. This is misperceived loyalty. The individual believes that the organisation's best interests stand above all others. In return, the individual believes that top managers will condone the behaviour and protect the individual from harm. But loyalty to the organisation is not an acceptable excuse for misconduct; organisational loyalty should not stand above the law and social morality.

Can unethical behaviour be controlled?

In a survey by the accounting and consulting firm KPMG in the USA, some 75 per cent of respondents said they had witnessed unethical acts at work in the last 12 months.

Have you? Did you do anything about it?

Factors influencing ethical behaviour

It is almost too easy to confront ethical dilemmas from the safety of a textbook or a classroom. In practice, people are often challenged to choose ethical courses of action in situations where the pressures may be contradictory and great. Increased awareness of the factors influencing ethical behaviour can help you better deal with them in the future. Figure 6.3 shows these influences emanating from the person, the organisation, and the environment.

www.alcoa.com.au

Aluminium and alumina producer Alcoa gives ethics and environmental management a high priority. It also has a well-developed human rights policy. Generally, however, the mining sector is known for its poor on-the-ground environmental performance and this is something that needs to be turned around.

Figure 6.3 ▸ Factors influencing ethical managerial behaviour — the person, organisation and environment

THE PERSON

Family influences, religious values, personal standards and personal needs, financial and otherwise, will help determine a person's ethical conduct in any given circumstance. Managers who lack a strong and consistent set of personal ethics will find that their decisions vary from situation to situation as they strive to maximise self-interests. Those who operate with strong *ethical frameworks* (personal rules or strategies for ethical decision making) will be more consistent and confident since choices are made against a stable set of ethical standards.

THE ORGANISATION

The organisation is another important influence on ethics in the workplace. We noted earlier that a person's immediate supervisor can have an important effect on the employee's behaviour. Just exactly what a supervisor requests, and which actions are rewarded or punished, can certainly affect an individual's decisions and actions. The expectations and reinforcement provided by peers and group norms are likely to have a similar impact. Formal policy statements and written rules are also very important in establishing an ethical climate for the organisation as a whole. They support and reinforce the organisational culture, which can have a strong influence on members' ethical behaviour.

At The Body Shop, founder Anita Roddick created an 11-point charter to guide the company's employees: 'Honesty, integrity and caring form the foundations of the company and should flow through everything we do — we will demonstrate our care for the world in which we live by respecting fellow human beings, by not harming animals, by preserving our forests.' The fact that The Body Shop still has to respond to occasional criticisms about its operations demonstrates the inadequacy of formal policies alone to guarantee consistent ethical behaviour. A visit to The Body Shop web site, however, shows the firm's ongoing ethical commitments and provides answers to frequently asked questions regarding such controversial issues as animal testing in the cosmetics industry.[23]

THE ENVIRONMENT

Organisations operate in external environments composed of competitors, government laws and regulations, and social norms and values, among other influences. Laws interpret social values to define appropriate behaviours for organisations and their members; regulations help governments monitor these behaviours and keep them within acceptable standards. The policy of 'zero tolerance' for corruption adopted by Commonwealth countries in 1999 (discussed in chapter 5) is one example.

The climate of competition in an industry sets a standard of behaviour for those who hope to prosper within it. Sometimes the pressures of competition contribute further to the ethical dilemmas of managers. Former American Airlines president Robert Crandall once telephoned Howard Putnam, then president of now-defunct Braniff Airlines. Both companies were suffering from money-losing competition on routes from their home base of Dallas. A portion of their conversation follows:

Putnam: Do you have a suggestion for me?
Crandall: Yes ... Raise your fares 20 per cent. I'll raise mine the next morning.
Putnam: Robert, we —
Crandall: You'll make more money and I will, too.
Putnam: We can't talk about pricing.
Crandall: Oh, Howard. We can talk about anything we want to talk about.[24]

The US Justice Department disagreed. It alleged that Crandall's suggestion of a 20 per cent fare increase amounted to an illegal attempt to monopolise airline routes. The suit was later settled when Crandall agreed to curtail future discussions with competitors about fares.

SOCIAL RESPONSIBILITY

The Body Shop • www.thebodyshop.com.au

Growing by values

In its business transactions, The Body Shop always considers its high-profile role as an advocate of social and environmental causes. Its mission statement dedicates the company's business 'to the pursuit of social and environmental change', and its 'trading charter' tackles the three principal concerns of social responsibility, environmental sustainability and animal protection. The company believes it earns its right to campaign on public issues by demonstrating its 'commitment to reflection and self-improvement' on such concerns. The Body Shop's charter and mission are clearly different from those of a more traditional company — they commit the company to a wide range of stakeholders (not just customers, employees and stockholders) and make specific assertions as to its social responsibility. The Body Shop is committing *itself* to being a good corporate citizen. Without its social agenda, The Body Shop might have been just another cosmetics company and as such may not have attracted the tremendous exposure it currently receives.[25]

MAINTAINING HIGH ETHICAL STANDARDS

Progressive organisations support a variety of methods for maintaining high ethical standards in workplace affairs. Some of the most important efforts in this area involve ethics training, whistleblower protection, top management support, formal codes of ethics and strong ethical cultures.

Ethics training

Ethics training, in the form of structured programs to help participants understand the ethical aspects of decision making, is designed to help people incorporate high ethical standards into their daily behaviours. An increasing number of university curricula now include courses on ethics, and seminars on this topic are popular in the corporate world. But it is important to keep the purpose of ethics training in perspective. An executive once put it this way: 'We aren't teaching people right from wrong — we assume they know that. We aren't giving people moral courage to do what is right — they should be able to do that anyhow. We focus on dilemmas.'[26] Many ethical dilemmas arise as a result of the time pressures of decisions. Ethics training is designed to help people deal with ethical issues while under pressure.

Ethics training seeks to help people understand the ethical aspects of decision making and to incorporate high ethical standards into their daily behaviour.

Manager's Notepad 6.2 presents a seven-step checklist for making ethical decisions when confronting an ethical dilemma. It offers a convenient reminder that the decision-making process includes responsibility for double-checking a decision *before* taking action. The key issue in the checklist may well be step 6 — the risk of public disclosure of your action and your willingness to bear it. This is a strong way to test whether a decision is consistent with one's personal ethical standards.

GET CONNECTED!

Whistleblowers Australia has a goal to 'promote a society in which it is possible to speak out without reprisal about corruption, dangers to the public and other vital social issues, and to help those who speak out in this way to help themselves'.[27] Learn more about the organisation at www.uow.edu.au/arts/sts/bmartin/dissent/contacts/au_wba/.

GET CONNECTED!

MANAGER'S NOTEPAD 6.2

Checklist for making ethical decisions

Step 1. Recognise the ethical dilemma.

Step 2. Get the facts.

Step 3. Identify your options.

Step 4. Test each option: Is it legal? Is it right? Is it beneficial?

Step 5. Decide which option to follow.

Step 6. Double-check decision by asking follow-up questions:

  'How would I feel if my family found out about my decision?'

  'How would I feel about this if my decision were printed in the local newspaper?'

Step 7. Take action.

Whistleblower protection

Agnes Connolly pressed her employer to report two toxic chemical accidents, as she believed the law required. Dave Jones reported that his company was using unqualified suppliers in the construction of a nuclear power plant. Margaret Newsham revealed that her firm was allowing workers to do personal business while on government contracts. Barry Adams complained that his hospital followed unsafe practices.[28] They were **whistleblowers**, persons who expose the misdeeds of others in organisations in order to preserve ethical standards and protect against wasteful, harmful or illegal acts.[29] All were fired from their jobs. Indeed, whistleblowers face the risks of impaired career progress and other forms of organisational retaliation, up to and including termination.

Whistleblowers expose the misdeeds of others in organisations.

Today, federal and State laws in countries such as Australia and New Zealand increasingly offer whistleblowers some defence against 'retaliatory discharge'. But although signs indicate that the courts are growing supportive of whistleblowers, legal protection for whistleblowers can still be inadequate. Laws vary from State to State, and federal laws mainly protect government workers. Furthermore, even with legal protection, potential whistleblowers may find it hard to expose unethical behaviour in the workplace. Some organisational barriers to whistleblowing include a *strict chain of command* that makes it hard to bypass the boss, *strong work group identities* that encourage loyalty and self-censorship, and *ambiguous priorities* that make it hard to distinguish right from wrong.[30]

In the attempt to remove these and other blocks to the exposure of unethical behaviours, some organisations have formally appointed staff members to serve as 'ethics advisers'. Others have set up formal staff units to process reported infractions. One novel proposal goes so far as to suggest the convening of *moral quality circles* to help create shared commitments for everyone to work at their moral best.[31]

Ethical role models

Anita Roddick is founder, and currently an executive director, of The Body Shop International. She opened the first store in Brighton, England, in 1976, and there are now over 1900 stores worldwide. Undoubtedly one of the world's most outspoken business leaders, Roddick is also an activist. She has devoted most of her working life to finding new ways of doing business and looking for ways business can take the lead in making the world a better place.

Top managers, in large and small enterprises, have the power to shape an organisation's policies and set its moral tone. They also have a major responsibility to use this power well. They can and should serve as role models of appropriate ethical behaviour for the entire organisation. Not only must their day-to-day behaviour be the epitome of high ethical conduct, but top managers must also communicate similar expectations throughout the organisation ... and reinforce positive results. Unfortunately, communication from the top may subtly suggest that top management does not want to know about deceptive or illegal practices by employees, or simply doesn't care.

Even though top managers bear a special responsibility for setting the ethical tone of an organisation, every manager is also in a position to influence the ethical behaviour of the people who work for and with them. This means that all managers must act as ethical role models and set an ethical tone in their areas of responsibility. Care must be taken to do this in a positive and informed manner. The important supervisory act of setting goals and communicating performance expectations is a good case in point. A surprising 64 per cent of 238 executives in one study, for example, reported feeling under pressure to compromise personal standards to achieve company goals. A *Fortune* survey also reported that 34 per cent of its respondents felt a company president can create an ethical climate by setting *reasonable goals* 'so that subordinates are not pressured into unethical actions'.[32] Clearly, any manager, in his or her relationships with subordinates, may unknowingly encourage unethical practices by exerting *too* much pressure for them to accomplish goals that are *too* difficult. Part of the manager's ethical responsibility is to be realistic in setting performance goals for others.

www.hubbards.co.nz

In front of the offices of New Zealand cereal company Hubbards, you will find the following sign:

> **WARNING**
> This is a 'no nonsense' management zone. No management excesses, corporate ego trips, committee decisions, inter-company memos, buck passing, back stabbing, or any other dubious management decisions allowed on these premises.

Codes of ethics

Formal **codes of ethics** are official written guidelines on how to behave in situations susceptible to the creation of ethical dilemmas. They are found in organisations and in professions such as engineering, medicine, law and public accounting. In the professions such as accounting and engineering, ethical codes try to ensure that individual behaviour is consistent with the historical and shared norms of the professional group. Most codes of ethical conduct identify expected behaviours in terms of general organisational citizenship, the avoidance of illegal or improper acts in one's work, and good relationships with customers. In a related survey of companies with written codes, the items most frequently addressed included workforce diversity, bribes and kickbacks, political contributions, the honesty of books or records, customer–supplier relationships and the confidentiality of corporate information.[33]

In the increasingly complex world of international business, codes of conduct for manufacturers and contractors are becoming more prevalent. At Gap, Inc., global manufacturing is governed by a formal Code of Vendor Conduct.[34] Among the many areas covered, the document specifically deals with:

- *discrimination* — stating 'Factories shall employ workers on the basis of their ability to do the job, not on the basis of their personal characteristics or beliefs'

Codes of ethics are written guidelines that state values and ethical standards intended to guide the behaviour of employees.

- *forced labour* — stating 'Factories shall not use any prison, indentured or forced labour'
- *working conditions* — stating 'Factories must treat all workers with respect and dignity and provide them with a safe and healthy environment'
- *freeedom of association* — stating 'Factories must not interfere with workers who wish to lawfully and peacefully associate, organize or bargain collectively'.

Although interest in codes of ethical conduct is growing, it must be remembered that the codes have limits. They cannot cover all situations, and they are not automatic insurance for universal ethical conduct. But they do play important roles in setting the ethical tone and expectations in organisations. When fully integrated into the organisational culture, further-more, the moral fabric created has a strong influence on day-to-day behaviour. Ultimately, of course, the value of any formal code of ethics still rests on the underlying human resource foundations of the organisation — its managers and other employees. There is no replace-ment for effective hiring practices that staff organisations with honest and moral people. And there is no replacement for leadership by committed managers who are willing to set examples and act as positive ethical role models to ensure desired results.

SOCIAL RESPONSIBILITY

It is now time to shift our interest in ethical behaviour from the level of the individual to that of the organisation. To begin, it is important to remember that all organisations exist in com-plex relationships with elements in their external environment. In chapter 2, in fact, we described the environment of a business firm as composed of a network of other organisations and institutions with which it must interact. An important frame of reference is the field of **organisational stakeholders**, those persons, groups and other organisations directly affected by the behaviour of the organisation and holding a stake in its performance.[35] In this context, **corporate social responsibility** is defined as an obligation of the organisation to act in ways that serve both its own interests and the interests of its many external stakeholders.[36]

Stakeholder issues and practices

The positive examples are there. You just have to look for them. In the USA, ice-cream company Ben & Jerry's Homemade, Inc. has long been considered an example of a firm committed to 'linked prosperity' — sharing prosperity with its employees and the communities in which it operates. Each year 7.5 per cent of the company's pre-tax earnings go into a charitable foundation. Hewlett-Packard started the e-Inclusion program to help rural villagers around the world gain access to technology and its advantages. The online auctioneer eBay gave 100 000 of its pre-IPO shares to charity and another 100 000-plus after going public.[37] DuPont Singapore actively supports community causes through financial contributions and employee involvement. Support for the Boys' Brigade Sharity Gift Box is one of their recent initiatives.

The stakeholder pressures are there, too. Consumers, activist groups, not-for-profit organ-isations and governments are increasingly vocal and influential in directing organisations toward socially responsible practices. In today's information age, business activities are increas-ingly transparent. Irresponsible practices are difficult to hide, wherever in the world they take place. Not only do news organisations find and disseminate the information, well-known acti-vist organisations lobby, campaign and actively pressure organisations to respect and protect everything from human rights to the natural environment. Prominent among them are Amnesty International, Greenpeace International, World Wildlife Fund and Friends of the Earth. Increasingly important also are investor groups, such as the Interfaith Center on Corporate Responsibility, that publicise and lobby for social causes through share ownership.

⊘ Organisational stakeholders are directly affected by the behaviour of the organisation and hold a stake in its performance.

⊘ Corporate social responsibility is the obligation of an organisation to act in ways that serve the interests of its stakeholders.

GET CONNECTED!

@

Human Rights Watch is an organisation dedicated to protecting the human rights of people around the world. Check its web site www.hrw.org for current concerns and controversies.

GET CONNECTED!

The groups pool resources, buy shares in companies and then advance proxy resolutions and lobby corporate leadership to ensure the businesses perform in socially responsible ways.

Ultimately, organisational leadership is a critical influence on behaviour by organisations and their members. The leadership beliefs that guide socially responsible organisational practices have been described as follows:[38]

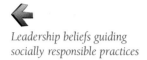

Leadership beliefs guiding
socially responsible practices

- *people* — belief that people do their best in healthy work environments with a balance of work and family life
- *communities* — belief that organisations perform best when located in healthy communities
- *natural environment* — belief that organisations gain by treating the natural environment with respect
- *long term* — belief that organisations must be managed and led for long-term success
- *reputation* — belief that one's reputation must be protected to ensure consumer and stakeholder support.

Perspectives on social responsibility

In academic and public-policy circles, two contrasting views of corporate social responsibility have stimulated debate, with one side arguing against it and the other arguing for it.[39] The *classical view* holds that management's only responsibility in running a business is to maximise profits. In other words — the business of business is business and the principal concern of management should always be to maximise shareholder value. This narrow 'shareholder' and 'profit-driven' model is supported by Milton Friedman, a respected freemarket economist and Nobel Laureate. He says: 'Few trends could so thoroughly undermine the very foundations of our free society as the acceptance by corporate officials of social responsibility other than to make as much money for their stockholders as possible'. The *arguments against corporate social responsibility* include fears that the pursuit of this goal will reduce business profits, raise business costs, dilute business purpose, give business too much social power, and do so without business accountability to the public.

By contrast, the *socioeconomic view* holds that management of any organisation must be concerned for the broader social welfare and not just for corporate profits. This broad-based and stakeholder model is supported by Paul Samuelson, another distinguished economist and Nobel Laureate. He states, 'A large corporation these days not only may engage in social responsibility, it had damn well better try to do so'.[40] Among the *arguments in favour of corporate social responsibility* are that it will add long-run profits for businesses, improve the public image of businesses and help them to avoid more government regulation. Businesses have the resources and ethical obligation to act responsibly.[41]

www.webmd.com

WebMD, a leading online company offering connectivity and a full suite of healthcare services, is also a global citzen. WebMD is using the Internet to spearhead a plan to deliver instant medical assistance to people in the world's least-developed nations.

Today, there is little doubt that the public at large wants businesses and other organisations to act with genuine social responsibility. Stakeholder expectations are increasingly well voiced and include demands that organisations integrate social responsibility into their core values and daily activities.

On the research side, there is increasing evidence that high performance in social responsibility can be associated with strong financial performance and, at worst, has no adverse financial impact. The argument that acting with a commitment to social responsibility will negatively affect the 'bottom line' is hard to defend. Indeed, recent evidence suggests the existence of a *virtuous circle* in which corporate social responsibility leads to improved financial performance for the firm, and this in turn leads to more socially responsible actions in the future.[43] There seems little reason to believe that businesses cannot serve the public good while advancing the financial interests of their shareholders. Even as the research and debate continues on this important concept, these historical comments by management theorist Keith Davis may still best sum up the corporate social responsibility debate.

Society wants business as well as all other major institutions to assume significant social responsibility. Social responsibility has become the hallmark of a mature, global organization … The business which vacillates or chooses not to enter the arena of social responsibility may find that it gradually will sink into customer and public disfavor.[44]

This has disturbing implications for many Australasian companies. The Australian Conservation Foundation participates in the 'Good Reputation Index' (conducted by the *Age* and *Sydney Morning Herald*), by analysing the environmental performance of the companies involved. In 2001, only 14 of Australia's top 100 companies managed to receive a respectable score of 15 or above out of a possible 30. The remainder of the companies obtained scores that were reflective of poor or very poor performance. The scenario is even worse for developing countries in the Asia–Pacific region that are under pressure to exploit their economic resources, and are particularly vulnerable to activities that can lead to environmental and social disasters. Ecologically sustainable development and management of natural resources within the context of social responsibility must begin with informed decision making by local communities.

Evaluating social performance

There are many action domains in which social responsibility can be pursued by business firms and other organisations. These include concerns for ecology and environmental quality, truth in lending and consumer protection and aid to education. They also include service to community needs, employment practices, diversity practices, progressive labour relations and employee assistance, and general corporate philanthropy, among other possibilities. At the organisational level, a **social audit** can be used at regular intervals to report on and systematically assess an organisation's resource commitments and action accomplishments in these and other areas. You might think of social audits as attempts to assess the social performance of organisations, much as accounting audits assess their financial performance.

A **social audit** is a systematic assessment of an organisation's accomplishments in areas of social responsibility.

A formal assessment of corporate social performance might include questions posed at these four levels:

- Is the organisation's *economic responsibility* met? Is it profitable?
- Is the organisation's *legal responsibility* met? Does it obey the law?
- Is the organisation's *ethical responsibility* met? Is it doing the 'right' things?
- Is the organisation's *discretionary responsibility* met? Does it contribute to the broader community?[45]

As you move up these levels, the assessment inquires into ever-greater demonstrations of social performance. An organisation is meeting its economic responsibility when it earns a profit through the provision of goods and services desired by customers. Legal responsibility is fulfilled when an organisation operates within the law and according to the requirements of various external regulations. An organisation meets its ethical responsibility when its actions voluntarily conform not only to legal expectations but also to the broader values and moral expectations of society. The highest level of social performance comes through the satisfaction of an organisation's discretionary responsibility. Here, the organisation voluntarily moves beyond basic economic, legal and ethical expectations to provide leadership in advancing the wellbeing of individuals, communities and society as a whole.

Social responsibility strategies

Figure 6.4 describes four strategies of corporate social responsibility. The continuum shows a desirable shift in emphasis from acting obstructionist, at the lowest level, to displaying progressive citizenship, at the highest.[46] An **obstructionist strategy** ('fight the social demands') reflects mainly economic priorities — social demands lying outside the organisation's perceived self-interests are resisted. If the organisation is criticised for wrongdoing, it can be expected to deny the claims. A **defensive strategy** ('do the minimum legally required') seeks to protect the organisation by doing the minimum legally necessary to satisfy expectations. Corporate behaviour at this level conforms only to legal requirements, competitive market pressure and perhaps activist voices. If criticised, intentional wrongdoing is likely to be denied.

An **obstructionist strategy** avoids social responsibility and reflects mainly economic priorities.

A **defensive strategy** seeks to protect the organisation by doing the minimum legally required to satisfy social expectations.

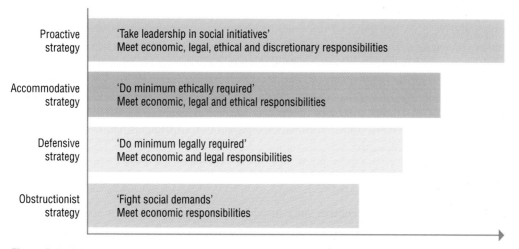

Figure 6.4 ▸ Four strategies of corporate social responsibility, from 'obstructionist' to 'proactive' behaviour

Organisations pursuing an **accommodative strategy** ('do the minimum ethically required') accept their social responsibilities. They try to satisfy economic, legal and ethical criteria. Corporate behaviour at this level is congruent with society's prevailing norms, values and expectations, but at times it may be so only because of outside pressures. An oil firm, for example, may be willing to 'accommodate' with cleanup activities when a spill occurs, but remain quite slow in taking actions to prevent them in the first place. Finally, the **proactive strategy** ('take leadership in social initiatives') is designed to meet all the criteria of social performance, including discretionary performance. Corporate behaviour at this level takes preventive action to avoid adverse social impacts from company activities, and it even anticipates or takes the lead in identifying and responding to emerging social issues.

An **accommodative strategy** accepts social responsibility and tries to satisfy prevailing economic, legal and ethical performance criteria.

A **proactive strategy** meets all the criteria of social responsibility, including discretionary performance.

ORGANISATIONS AND SOCIETY

The fact remains, not all managers and not all organisations accept the challenge of committing to a proactive social responsibility strategy. Some may accept it, but have difficulty meeting the challenge. In this action, arena government, as the voice or instrument of the people, is often called upon to act in the public behalf.

How government influences organisations

Governments often pass laws and establish regulating agencies to control and direct the behaviour of organisations. It may not be too far-fetched to say that behind every piece of legislation — national, State or local — is a government agency charged with the responsibility of monitoring and ensuring compliance with its mandates.

Many themes already discussed as being key areas of social responsibility are backed by major laws. Business executives often complain many laws and regulations are overly burdensome.[47] Public outcries to 'dismantle the bureaucracy' and/or 'deregulate business' reflect concerns that specific agencies and their supportive legislation are not functional. But, the reality is that the legal environment is both complex and constantly changing. Managers must stay informed about new and pending laws as well as existing ones.

Like most other developed countries, Australia and New Zealand have many pieces of legislation specifically developed to enforce social responsibility on businesses. These laws and regulations are usually in the form of minimum standards which must be met in terms of occupational health and safety (OHS), fair labour practices, environmental protection and the like. Regarding OHS, for example, the National Occupational Health & Safety Commission (NOHSC) has led much of the push to improve the health and safety record of Australian businesses. This organisation sets national standards, provides OHS statistics, and advises on research, consulting and training matters. New Zealand's Occupational Safety and Health Service of the Department of Labour provides similar services.[48]

Another example of legislation that could profoundly affect businesses concerns antidiscrimination in labour practices (discussed further in chapter 12 on human resource management). The federal antidiscrimination legislation in Australia is handled by the *Racial Discrimination Act 1975*, the *Sex Discrimination Act 1984*, the *Disability Discrimination Act 1992* and the *Equal Opportunity for Women in the Workplace Act 1999*.[49] In New Zealand, antidiscrimination legislation is covered by the *Human Rights Act 1993* and the *Employment Relations Act 2000*.

Consumer protection is another area in which the government takes an active role in regulating business affairs. In Australia, the *Trade Practices Act 1974* aims to promote competition and protect consumer interests. It gives the government the authority to force a business to withdraw from sale any product that it feels is hazardous to the consumer — for example, children's toys and flammable fabrics. In New Zealand, consumers are protected by the *Consumer Guarantee Act 1993*, the *Fair Trading Act 1986*, the *Lay of Sales Act 1971* and the *Hire Purchase Act 1971*.[50]

How organisations influence government

The line of influence between government and organisations is not one way, with the government simply passing legislation and acting as a regulator. Just as governments take a variety of actions to influence organisations, so do the leaders and representatives of organisations take action to influence government. There are a number of ways in which businesses in particular attempt to influence government to adopt and pursue policies favourable to them.

Through *personal contacts and networks* executives get to know important people in government. These contacts can be used for persuasion. Through *public relations campaigns* executives can communicate positive images of their organisations to the public at large, with the potential for them to speak positively on the business's behalf. Through **lobbying**, often with the assistance of professional lobbying consultants, executives can have their positions and preferences communicated directly to government officials. Finally, it must also be admitted that *illegal acts* sometimes occur. Executives can unfortunately resort to use of bribes or illegal financial campaign contributions in the attempt to gain influence over public officials.

✅ **Lobbying** expresses opinions and preferences to government officials.

Why managers make the difference

Trends in the evolution of social values point to ever-increasing demands from governments and other organisational stakeholders that managerial decisions reflect ethical as well as high-performance standards. Today's workers and managers, as well as tomorrow's, must accept personal responsibility for doing the 'right' things. Broad social and moral criteria must be used to examine the interests of multiple stakeholders in a dynamic and complex environment. Decisions must always be made and problems solved with ethical considerations standing side by side with high-performance objectives, be they individual, group or organisational. Indeed, the point that profits and social responsibility can go hand in hand is being confirmed in new and creative ways.

As public demands grow for organisations to be accountable for ethical and social performance as well as economic performance, the manager stands once again in the middle. It is the manager whose decisions affect 'quality-of-life' outcomes in the critical boundaries between people and organisations and between organisations and their environments. Everyone must be more willing to increase the weight given to ethical and social responsibility considerations when making these decisions. *Management: An Asia–Pacific Perspective* focuses your attention throughout on the demands depicted in figure 6.5. It presents the manager's or team leader's challenge this way: to fulfil an accountability for achieving performance objectives, while always doing so in an ethical and socially responsible manner. The full weight of this responsibility holds in every organisational setting — small to large, and private or not-for-profit — and at every managerial level, from bottom to top. There is no escaping the ultimate reality — being a manager is a very socially responsible job!

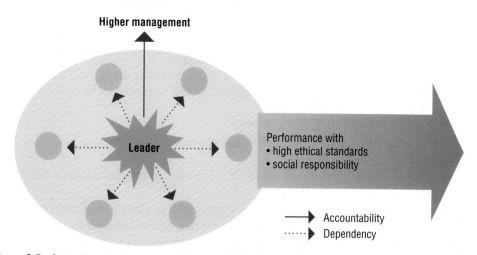

Figure 6.5 ▸ Centrality of ethics and social responsibility in leadership and the managerial role

Study guide

The chapter 6 study guide helps you review the chapter content, prepare for examinations, apply what you have learned and further build your career readiness. The summary briefly answers the study questions posed at the start of the chapter. The list of key terms allows you to double-check your familiarity with basic concepts and definitions. The applied activities help you test your comprehension of chapter content. Suggestions offered as career readiness activities direct your attention to relevant sections of the Career Readiness Workbook where you can test and develop your career skills and apply what you have learned. The list of electronic resources suggests activities from the *Management: An Asia–Pacific Perspective* web site and, finally, the case for critical thinking helps you apply your new management knowledge.

SUMMARY

What is ethical behaviour?

- Ethical behaviour is that which is accepted as 'good' or 'right' as opposed to 'bad' or 'wrong'.
- Simply because an action is not illegal does not necessarily make it ethical in a given situation.
- Because values vary, the question of 'What is ethical behaviour?' may be answered differently by different people.
- Four ways of thinking about ethical behaviour are the utilitarian, individualism, moral-rights and justice views.
- Cultural relativism argues that no culture is ethically superior to any other.

How do ethical dilemmas complicate the workplace?

- When managers act ethically they have a positive impact on other people in the workplace and on the social good performed by organisations.
- An ethical dilemma occurs when someone must decide whether to pursue a course of action that, although offering the potential for personal or organisational benefit or both, may be considered potentially unethical.
- Managers report that their ethical dilemmas often involve conflicts with superiors, customers and subordinates over such matters as dishonesty in advertising and communications as well as pressure from their bosses to do unethical things.
- Common rationalisations for unethical behaviour include believing the behaviour is not illegal, is in everyone's best interests, will never be noticed, or will be supported by the organisation.

How can high ethical standards be maintained?

- Ethics training in the form of courses and training programs helps people better deal with ethical dilemmas in the workplace.
- Whistleblowers expose the unethical acts of others in organisations, even while facing career risks for doing so.
- Top management sets an ethical tone for the organisation as a whole, and all managers are responsible for acting as positive models of appropriate ethical behaviour.
- Written codes of ethical conduct formally state what an organisation expects of its employees regarding ethical conduct at work.

What is organisational social responsibility?

- Corporate social responsibility is an obligation of the organisation to act in ways that serve both its own interests and the interests of its many external publics, often called stakeholders.
- Criteria for evaluating corporate social performance include economic, legal, ethical and discretionary responsibilities.
- Corporate responses to social demands include obstructionist, defensive, accommodative, and proactive, with more progressive organisations taking proactive stances.

How do organisations and government work together in society?

- Government agencies are charged with monitoring and ensuring compliance with the mandates of law.
- Managers must be well informed about existing and pending legislation in a variety of social responsibility areas, including environmental protection and other quality-of-life concerns.
- Organisations exert their influence on government in many ways, including interpersonal contacts of executives and use of lobbyists.
- All managerial decisions and actions in every workplace should fulfil performance accountability with commitments to high ethical standards and socially responsible means.

KEY TERMS

accommodative strategy (p. 161)

codes of ethics (p. 157)

corporate social responsibility (p. 158)

cultural relativism (p. 150)

defensive strategy (p. 161)

distributive justice (p. 150)

ethical behaviour (p. 148)

ethical dilemma (p. 152)

ethical imperialism (p. 151)

ethics (p. 148)

ethics training (p. 155)

individualism view (p. 149)

interactional justice (p. 150)

justice view (p. 150)

lobbying (p. 163)

moral-rights view (p. 149)

obstructionist strategy (p. 161)

organisational stakeholders (p. 158)

proactive strategy (p. 161)

procedural justice (p. 150)

social audit (p. 160)

universalism (p. 151)

utilitarian view (p. 149)

values (p. 149)

whistleblowers (p. 156)

APPLIED ACTIVITIES

Short-response questions

1. Explain the difference between the individualism and justice views of ethical behaviour.
2. List four common rationalisations for unethical managerial behaviour.
3. What are the major elements in the socioeconomic view of corporate social responsibility?
4. What role do government agencies play in regulating the socially responsible behaviour of businesses?

Application question

5. A small outdoor clothing company has just received an attractive offer from a business in Bangladesh to manufacture its work gloves. The offer would allow for substantial cost savings over the current supplier. The company manager, however, has read reports that some Bangladesh businesses break their own laws and operate with child labour. How would differences in the following corporate responsibility strategies affect the manager's decision regarding whether to accept the offer: obstructionist, defensive, accommodative and proactive?

CAREER READINESS ACTIVITIES

Recommended individual and group learning activities from the end-of-text Career Readiness Workbook for this chapter include:

Career advancement portfolio   WB

Update your career advancement portfolio to reflect your new skills and experiences. Include skills and personal insights you gain from the following projects and exercises.

Research and presentation projects   WB

- Project 4 — Corporate social responsibility — 'what's the status?'
- Project 5 — Affirmative action directions — 'where do we go from here?'

Cross-functional integrative case   WB

Read the integrative case on Sarina Russo and answer the following questions:

6.1 If you were called upon by the Russo Institute of Technology to develop a code of ethics, what would you include? What would you not include and why?

6.2 How might teachings on ethical sensitivity be included in the diploma courses taught by the Russo Institute of Technology?

6.3 In what ways could the Russo Institute of Technology and Sarina Russo Job Access demonstrate their commitment to corporate social responsibility?

Exercises in teamwork   WB

- Exercise 8 — Confronting ethical dilemmas
- Exercise 15 — Interviewing job candidates

Management skills assessment   WB

- Assessment 6 — The ethical reasoning inventory

ELECTRONIC RESOURCES

Don't forget to take full advantage of the online support for *Management: An Asia–Pacific Perspective* at www.johnwiley.com.au/highered/management: chapter 6 practice tests, e-flashcards, crossword puzzles, interactive management skills assessments, interactive cases, the online career advancement portfolio and much more!

CASE FOR CRITICAL THINKING

Read the following case for critical thinking on HIH. While you are reading the case keep in mind what you have learned in this chapter, then answer the questions.

Ethical behaviour, or rather the lack thereof, could be demonstrated in the HIH collapse. The repercussions of the case will cast a shadow over many issues that could impact on the Australian economy.[51]

During 2000, at the Institute of Actuaries of Australia's annual seminar on general insurance, two senior actuaries, Peter McCarthy and Geoff Trahair, presented a paper that rang alarm bells for HIH Insurance. Even though HIH was not mentioned in the paper (entitled 'Lack of industry profitability and other stories'), the insurance industry was accused of under-pricing policies, pressuring actuaries to reduce the projected level of outstanding claims liabilities, and of having poor quality staff and senior management. This was a forewarning of what seems to have gone wrong at Australia's second-largest general insurance company.[52]

According to McCarthy and Trahair, the main problem was bad management. They outlined 'poorly trained and low-skilled staff, with inadequate or non-existent pricing models, combined with poor underwriting controls'. They also suggested that poor claims management, careless data collection and imprecise monitoring led to incomplete analyses of portfolio performance, if done at all. Senior-management level did not escape criticism either. 'The management progression path seems to be dominated by those who have risen through the ranks, starting out as either underwriters or case officers. While this gives a good grasp of the micro-picture, it fails to deliver the broader macro-picture that is required to make the transition from managing individual policies and claims to managing whole portfolios or companies.'[53]

Former HIH director Rodney Adler confirmed these views when he wrote to the managing director of HIH, Ray Williams, in September 1999. He claimed the long-serving management team 'had fallen into a rut'. Another HIH insider described the culture of the organisation as macho, in which senior managers knew about their own area only and nothing about the rest of the business.

In their paper, McCarthy and Trahair recommended greater actuarial influence on the pricing of policies, and argued that any actuarial 'suggestions' need to have some authority. Their paper included a light-hearted supplement — the top ten tips for running a general insurer. The ninth tip was: 'When the actuary says the rates need to go up by 50 per cent, ignore them. After all, those actuaries are so uncommercial, they just don't live in the real world!'[54]

Insolvency specialist David Lombe prepared a report showing HIH continued to lose millions even though a revival package showed they were making a profit. They failed to take into account future insurance claims and they also declared they had net assets of $939 million which was not a true picture.

The collapse of HIH forced a New South Wales judge to freeze the assets of the three key figures — Ray Williams (CEO), Domenic Fodera (CFO) and Rodney Adler (former director).[55] The mismanagement of investments and acquisitions by these management executives had a downward-spiral effect on many people's lives. The Australian Securities and Investments Commission (ASIC) claimed that the three men 'breached their duties by showing a lack of good faith, care and diligence for HIH's assets'.[56]

ASIC cited that an HIH payment of $10 million was made to a company wholly owned by Adler, without following policies and procedures of the company. Adler's lawyer stated this transaction was not a matter of public interest: 'This is a discrete little dispute about a particular investment that involved a modest sum of money'. Evidence given in court also showed Williams owned real estate worth $6.5 million in addition to 'a lot of boats'.[57]

The lack of understanding of company policies and procedures added to the downfall of HIH Insurance. ASIC believes that the three men had breached the Corporations Law, and 'asked the court to order them to pay compensation, fines of $200 000, and that they be banned from management positions'.[58] The impact of these monetary decisions at director level forced the federal government to announce a royal commission into the downfall of HIH.[59]

The influence of the HIH collapse casts a shadow over other issues, such as the recovery of the housing industry. This in turn can affect the Australian economy. Katie Lahey, chief executive of the Business Council of Australia, has said: 'A leader today has to be well read and to know what's going on in the environment as a whole. You can't imagine a leader of any significant company not knowing the fundamentals of the economy, or what's happening to the economies of our trading partners. Big issues for the whole country. A leader has to be tuned in to those.'[60]

The collapse of such a large insurance organisation also had a major impact on the existence of smaller companies, as well as individuals in terms of their ability to absorb levies for future insurance services. In an article on balancing technology, management and leadership, US management consultant Jim Clemmer said: 'An organisation can be using the latest technologies and be highly people-focused, but if the methods and approaches used to structure and organise work are weak, performance will suffer badly'.[61] This seems to sum up what happened at HIH Insurance and at other corporations that have recently suffered similar collapses.

QUESTIONS

1. Critically evaluate the ethical dilemma in the HIH case.
2. What were the factors influencing the ethical behaviour of management at HIH?
3. Discuss social responsibility in the context of the HIH case.

MISSION

PART 3

Planning and controlling

CHAPTER 7 STUDY QUESTIONS

- How do managers plan?

- What types of plans do managers use?

- What are the useful planning tools, techniques and processes?

- What is the control process?

- What control systems are used in organisations?

Australian Art Resources — expanding in an uncertain market

Australian Art Resources (AAR) is Australia's leading modern art gallery, with major corporate and individual clients. It is planning further expansion to consolidate its position as the leading supplier of modern Australian art and sculpture. Its corporate headquarters are in Melbourne, and in 2002 it opened a new gallery in Sydney to rival its very successful Melbourne operation (the galleries trade as Axia Modern Art). It has long-term plans to open galleries in other States and overseas.

The art market in Australia is volatile, but even given global uncertainty and the recent high level of domestic corporate bankruptcies, AAR is experiencing record sales levels and is remaining buoyant while some other private Australian art galleries and suppliers have either closed or are on the verge of bankruptcy. Its success is based on systematic organisational planning and tight financial control, which includes a carefully executed e-business model.

What is AAR's competitive strength? AAR credits its success to three major factors. First, it has established strong relationships with Australia's major contemporary artists. This relationship has been cultivated over a 20-year period, with the company providing both financial and pastoral support to its artists when necessary. Second, it is located in the two major Australian art markets — Melbourne and Sydney. Third, it has high quality marketing and publicity. Kerri Keiwan, a high-profile marketing and public relations professional from the Sydney Opera House, has transformed AAR's marketing and publicity. The company's visibility on national television and in the national press has risen dramatically. AAR's new web site and its provision for online purchasing has enhanced its market position and strengthened its customer service focus.

To see how a business can use the Internet to increase sales and improve its customer service, take a tour of the Australian Art Resources web site at www.axiamodernart.com.au. Create an idea for an online business using insights from an e-business model such as AAR's or the Art Bank at www.artbank.gov.au.

GET CONNECTED!

Strategic management consultant Gary Hamel believes many of today's companies aren't going to make it for the long run. Why? 'Organisations that succeed in this new century will be as different from industrial-era organisations as those companies themselves were different from craft-based industries,' he says. 'Companies are going to have to re-invent themselves much more frequently than before.'[1] Quite fittingly, the title of his latest book is *Leading the Revolution*.[2]

The chapter opening example of Australian Art Resources shows an 'old economy' company stepping forward to implement plans designed to meet the challenges of the emerging 'new economy'. Rather than bask in past successes, Australian Art Resources management is acting today in order to best prepare the firm for future opportunities.

In management, an organisation needs the ability to look ahead, make good plans, and then help others work effectively to best meet the challenges of the future. With the future uncertain, however, the likelihood is that even the best of plans made today may have to be changed tomorrow. Thus, managers also need the courage to be flexible in response to new circumstances, and the discipline to maintain control even as situations become hectic and the performance pressures are unrelenting.

HOW AND WHY MANAGERS PLAN

In chapter 1 the management process was described as planning, organising, leading and controlling the use of resources to achieve performance objectives. The first of these functions, **planning**, sets the stage for the others. It is a process of setting objectives and determining how to best accomplish them. Said a bit differently, planning involves deciding exactly what you want to accomplish and how to best go about it.

Planning is the process of setting objectives and determining how to accomplish them.

IMPORTANCE OF PLANNING

Although many management gurus and senior managers consider setting **objectives** and planning to be an old-fashioned practice, there is still considerable support for long-term planning in many large and small organisations. What has changed is that planning no longer means a complex and rigid series of five- or ten-year plans produced by corporate bureaucrats. It is a process that generates a series of 'what if' scenarios. This **scenario planning** process is used to get general managers at all levels of the organisation to think about the environment in which they operate so that they can be better prepared for 'shocks' to their industry. These may be caused by the introduction of revolutionary new technology, a sudden global economic downturn or even a major terrorist event such as the attack on the World Trade Center in 2001.

Objectives are specific results that one wishes to achieve.

Scenario planning identifies alternative future scenarios and makes plans to deal with each.

When scenario planning is used properly it produces a solid base from which further managerial actions can emanate. These include: *organising* — allocating and arranging organisational resources to achieve key tasks; *leading* — guiding the efforts of the organisation's staff to ensure high levels of task accomplishment; and *controlling* — monitoring and assessing task accomplishment and taking necessary corrective action.

The importance of planning in the management process is illustrated in figure 7.1 — it provides the guiding direction for the other important management functions of organising, controlling and leading. Planning may involve strategies for obtaining and maintaining an organisation's competitive edge over other organisations in its industry, but it may equally involve joint ventures and cooperative arrangements with competitors. For example, a German multinational, Siemens, entered into an agreement with a US electronics company,

Motorola, to share mobile communication infrastructure and technology patents to stem the competition from other European and Japanese companies. Defending or improving an organisation's market position is likely to involve a combination of competitive strategies that mean that the organisation must become more effective at its core tasks and must cooperate with other organisations to share costs. Planning should identify these possibilities, based upon likely future environmental conditions, and inform the necessary decisions to allow the organisation to fully exploit any opportunities.

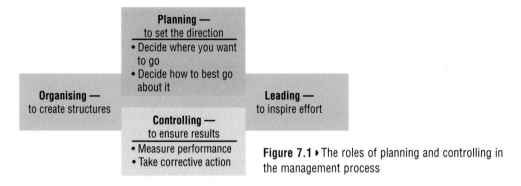

Figure 7.1 ▸ The roles of planning and controlling in the management process

There are several ways managers in progressive organisations attempt to gain a competitive advantage over other organisations. First, they can survey customers about their product or service requirements. For example, in Australia and New Zealand, Freedom Furniture uses a web-based questionnaire to ask customers about the company's products and services and ways in which they could be improved. Second, they can scan the environment searching for technologies, techniques or methods from their own industry or from other sectors that they can modify or apply. For example, a boat building firm in Melbourne, ARF Marine, adopted computer-aided design and testing software developed for the aerospace industry to design faster and more stable yachts. Third, managers can search for joint-venture partners to strengthen their current market position or to diversify into other markets. For example, the merger between Australia's BHP and the United Kingdom's Billiton to form BHP Billiton, the world's largest resource company, was designed to create a stronger company with a greater resource and knowledge base. Through the planning process, both companies had identified merger as the most effective way to secure their long-term future.

The planning process

The planning process begins with an organisation identifying specific outcomes that it wishes to achieve. It may set different targets depending on the environment it encounters, especially where the environment is uncertain or changing rapidly. This 'what if' or scenario planning is practised by an increasing number of organisations. Organisations may also include in their plans actions to help shape or stabilise the environment. These actions could include lobbying governments locally and overseas, creating industry networks or philanthropy. The organisation's **plan** is a statement of the actual steps required to achieve its objectives. There are five sequential action steps in the systematic planning process:

1. *Define your objectives.* Identify desired outcomes or results in very specific ways. Know where you want to go; be specific enough that you will know you have arrived when you get there or know how far off the mark you are at various points along the way.

A **plan** is a statement of intended means for accomplishing objectives.

Five steps in the planning process

Where do you think the job market is heading? An important issue in career planning is to prepare yourself for the future job market. It could be very different from the current one, given the rapid rate of change in the global economy.

The Australian Bureau of Statistics and Statistics New Zealand provide comprehensive data on employment growth, unemployment, the consumer price index, productivity and earnings. They also provide profiles on the major industries, including primary industries such as mining and agriculture, secondary industries such as manufacturing, construction and food processing, and tertiary industries such as financial services, multimedia, tourism, hospitality, health care, security services and education. The tertiary sector has witnessed the strongest job growth in the past decade, with much of this in the new technology industries. Consequently, there has been a strong demand for computer engineers, computer programmers, systems analysts, database administrators and desktop/multimedia specialists.

Government statisticians use sophisticated forecasting models to predict trends in employment and occupations, but there are limits to their accuracy. Such predictions should be viewed as a guide and be considered together with other information about the economy and labour market.

Questions

Are you aware of which jobs are in demand and which are in decline in Australia or New Zealand?

Have you set your sights on a high-demand or low-demand occupation?

Does your career planning recognise the need to acquire both knowledge and technology-based skills and to update them regularly?

2. *Determine where you stand vis-à-vis objectives.* Evaluate current accomplishments relative to the desired results. Know where you stand in reaching the objectives; know what strengths work in your favour and what weaknesses may hold you back.

3. *Develop premises regarding future conditions.* Try to anticipate future events. Generate alternative 'scenarios' for what may happen; identify for each scenario things that may help or hinder progress toward your objectives.

4. *Analyse and choose among action alternatives.* List and carefully evaluate the possible actions that may be taken. Choose the alternative(s) most likely to accomplish your objectives; describe step by step what must be done to follow the chosen course of action.

5. *Implement the plan and evaluate results.* Take action and carefully measure your progress toward objectives. Do what the plan requires; evaluate results; take corrective action, and revise plans as needed.

The planning process just described is an application of the decision-making process introduced in chapter 3. It is a systematic way to approach two important tasks: setting performance objectives, and deciding how to best achieve them. Importantly, in the complex setting of the modern workplace this is not a process that managers do while working alone in quiet rooms, free from distractions, and at scheduled times. Rather, planning should be part of a manager's everyday work routine. It should be an ongoing activity that is continuously done even while dealing with an otherwise hectic and demanding work setting.[3] Importantly, the best planning is always done with the active participation and involvement of those people whose work efforts will eventually determine whether the objectives are accomplished.

Benefits of scenario planning

In today's uncertain and dynamic global economy, organisations are facing pressures from many sources. External pressures include regulations imposed by governments (such as the goods and services tax (GST) that was introduced in New Zealand in 1986 and in Australia in 2000), increasingly complex or changing technologies, economic uncertainty, and the costs of investment in capital, labour and other supporting resources. Internal pressures include the need for operating efficiencies through work practice reforms, new management structures and technologies, increased workplace diversity, heightened job expectations from an increasingly educated workforce, and related managerial challenges. Given the growing uncertainty and complexity of the environment, scenario planning offers a number of benefits. It allows organisations to plan for the most likely course of events, but also allows for other situations. Many organisations now include multiple scenarios in their planning.

SCENARIO PLANNING IMPROVES FOCUS AND FLEXIBILITY

Thorough scenario planning improves organisational focus and flexibility, both of which are essential for successful individual and group performance in highly competitive and dynamic environments. An *organisation with focus* knows what it does best, knows the needs of its customers and knows how to serve them well. An *individual with focus* knows where he or she wants to go in a career or situation and is able to retain that objective even when difficulties arise. An *organisation with flexibility* is willing and able to change and adapt to shifting circumstances, and operates with an orientation toward the future rather than the past or present. An *individual with flexibility* factors into career plans the problems and opportunities posed by new and developing situations — personal and organisational.

SCENARIO PLANNING IMPROVES ACTION ORIENTATION

Scenario planning helps individuals and organisations weather difficult circumstances and stay ahead of the competition. It places organisations in a state of readiness for a variety of situations and counters tendencies toward complacency, both in individuals and in the organisation. It also keeps the future visible as a performance target and reminds us that the best decisions are often made before events force them upon us. Management consultant Stephen R. Covey points out that the most successful executives 'zero in on what they do that "adds value" to an organisation'. Instead of working on too many things, Covey advises us to step back and identify the most important things to be doing.[4] Indeed, planning helps us to stay proactive rather than reactive in our approach to things. It does so because it makes us more:

- *results oriented* — creating a performance-oriented sense of direction
- *priority oriented* — making sure the most important things get first attention
- *advantage oriented* — ensuring that all resources are used to best advantage
- *change oriented* — anticipating problems and opportunities so they can be best dealt with.[5]

SCENARIO PLANNING IMPROVES COORDINATION

Scenario planning improves coordination. The many different individuals, groups and sub-systems in organisations are each doing many different things at the same time. But even as they pursue their specific tasks and objectives, their accomplishments must add up to meaningful contributions toward the needs of the organisation as a whole. Good planning throughout an organisation creates a *hierarchy of objectives* in which objectives at each level of work are linked together in means–ends fashion. Higher-level objectives as ends are directly tied to lower-level objectives as the *means* for their accomplishment.

Figure 7.2 uses the example of quality management to show how a hierarchy of objectives can guide and integrate efforts within a large manufacturing firm. The corporate-level quality objective is 'Deliver error-free products that meet customer requirements 100 per cent of the time'. This translates down the hierarchy in means–ends fashion as a series of supporting objectives at each level. For one of the team leaders, it finally becomes a formal commitment to 'assess capabilities of machine operators and provide/arrange appropriate training'. Good planning helps ensure that the team leader's hard work in this example will make a positive contribution to the corporate-level quality objective.

www.dyson.com

The UK-based Dyson Limited produced the world's first bagless vacuum cleaner using Dual Cyclone™ technology. Dyson systematically collects information from its customers and employees on how to improve its products. This continuous improvement program has resulted in new designs and new manufacturing processes.[6]

Corporate quality objectives	Manufacturing division quality objectives	Plant quality objectives	Shift supervisor quality objectives
Deliver error-free products that meet customer requirements 100% of the time	Become a preferred supplier by achieving 100% on-time delivery of all products	Increase percentage accepted by 16% to meet customer's delivery requirements	Assess capabilities of machine operators and provide/arrange appropriate training

Figure 7.2 ▸ A sample hierarchy of objectives for total quality management

SCENARIO PLANNING IMPROVES TIME MANAGEMENT

One of the side benefits that planning offers is better time management. Lewis Platt, former chairman of Hewlett-Packard, says: 'Basically, the whole day is a series of choices.'[7] These choices have to be made in ways that allocate your time to the most important priorities. Platt says that he is 'ruthless about priorities' and that you 'have to continually work to optimise your time'.

Most of us have experienced the difficulties of balancing available time with the many commitments and opportunities we would like to fulfil. Each day, we are bombarded by a multitude of tasks and demands in a setting of frequent interruptions, crises and unexpected events — the manager's job is especially subject to such complications. It is easy to lose track of time and fall prey to what consultants identify as 'time wasters'. In the process, too many of us allow our time to be dominated by other people and/or by what can be considered non-essential activities.[8] 'To do' lists can help, but it is important to determine which 'to dos' are the priorities, and then deal with them.[9] Some additional tips on how to manage your time are included in Manager's Notepad 7.1.

MANAGER'S NOTEPAD 7.1

Tips on how to manage your time

- *Do* say 'No' to requests that divert you from work you should be doing.
- *Don't* get bogged down in details that should be left to others.
- *Do* establish a system for screening telephone calls and e-mail.
- *Don't* let 'drop-in' visitors use too much of your time.
- *Do* prioritise work tasks in order of importance and urgency.
- *Don't* become 'calendar bound' by losing control of your schedule.
- *Do* work tasks in priority order.

SCENARIO PLANNING IMPROVES CONTROL

When planning is done well, it is easier to exercise control by measuring performance results and taking action to improve things as necessary. Planning helps make this possible by defining the objectives along with the specific actions through which they are to be pursued. If results are less than expected, either the objectives or the action being taken, or both, can be evaluated and then adjusted in the control process. In this way planning and controlling work together closely in the management process. Without planning, control lacks a framework for measuring how well things are going and what could be done to make them go better. Without control, planning lacks the follow-through needed to ensure that things work out as intended.

TYPES OF PLANS USED BY MANAGERS

Managers face different planning challenges in the flow of activity in organisations. In some cases the planning environment is stable and quite predictable; in others it is more dynamic and uncertain. In all cases managers must understand the different types of plans and be able to use them effectively.

Short-range and long-range plans

Organistions require plans that cover different time horizons. A rule of thumb is that *short-range plans* cover one year or less, *intermediate-range plans* cover one to two years and *long-range plans* look three or more years into the future. Top management is most likely to be involved in setting long-range plans and directions for the organisation as a whole, while lower management levels focus more on intermediate and short-range plans that serve the long-term objectives. Importantly, all levels should understand the organisation's long-range plans. In the absence of an integrated hierarchy of objectives and a long-range plan, there is always risk that the pressures of daily events may create confusion and divert attention from important tasks. In other words, we may be working hard but without achieving sustainable and clear long-term results.

ENTREPRENEURSHIP

Ocean Spirit Cruises •
www.oceanspirit.com.au

Five-star dining on the Great Barrier Reef

In the mid 1990s Ocean Spirit Cruises had one ship sailing daily from Cairns in Far North Queensland out to the Great Barrier Reef. The trip was aimed at customers seeking a three- to four-star service. In 1996 the company recruited Craig Pocock from the Mayne Nickless Group — a major health, logistics and transportation company. He identified the need for a five-star cruising experience that would be attractive to international travellers. By 1997 he had introduced a second ship, refurbished the existing one, and established Ocean Spirit as the premier cruising experience from Cairns to the Great Barrier Reef. Revenues and return on investment increased dramatically. He capitalised on this investment by introducing evening cruises around the Cairns harbour. He also marketed the company's products through its own shop and through the upmarket hotels in the region, such as the prestigious Cairns Hilton and Sheraton Mirage Port Douglas. His successful management and expansion of the company won him the Australian Institute of Management's Queensland Manager of the Year award in 1999.[10]

Management researcher Elliot Jaques suggested that people vary in their capability to think out, organise and work through events of different time horizons.[11] In fact, he believed that most people work comfortably with only three-month time spans; a smaller group works well with a one-year span; and only about one person in several million can handle a 20-year time frame. These are provocative ideas. Although a team leader's planning challenges may rest mainly in the weekly or monthly range, a chief executive is expected to have a vision extending five or more years into the future. Career progress to higher management levels requires the conceptual skills to work well with longer-range time frames.[12]

Complexities and uncertainties in today's environments are putting pressure on these planning horizons. In an increasingly global economy, planning opportunities and challenges are often worldwide in scope, not just local. And, of course, the information age is ever present in its planning implications. We now talk about planning in Internet time, where businesses are continually changing and updating plans. Even top managers must now face the reality that Internet time keeps making the 'long' range of planning shorter and shorter.

Strategic and operational plans

Plans differ not only in time horizons but also in scope. **Strategic plans** define long-term needs and set comprehensive action directions for an organisation or subunit. Top management planning of this scope involves determining objectives for the entire organisation and then deciding on the actions and resource allocations to achieve them. There was a time, for example, when many large businesses sought to diversify into unrelated areas. A successful oil firm might have acquired an office products company, or a successful cereal manufacturer might have acquired an apparel company. These decisions represent strategic choices regarding future directions for these companies and their use of scarce resources. Instead of reinvesting in areas of core competency, they were spending available monies on unrelated and probably unfamiliar areas of business activity. In the next chapter on strategic management we will examine the process through which such strategic choices are made and how they can be analysed. For now, it is enough to say that diversification strategies haven't always proved successful. Many companies following them have since reversed course and followed the alternative strategy of divesting of unrelated businesses to focus on their core areas of expertise.

Operational plans define what needs to be done in specific areas to implement strategic plans and achieve strategic objectives. Typical operational plans in an organisation include:

- *production plans* — dealing with the methods and technology needed by people in their work
- *financial plans* — dealing with the money required to support various operations
- *facilities plans* — dealing with the facilities and work layouts required to support task activities
- *marketing plans* — dealing with the requirements of selling and distributing goods or services
- *human resource plans* — dealing with the recruitment, selection and placement of people into various jobs.

Policies and procedures

Among the many plans in organisations, *standing plans* in the form of organisational policies and procedures are designed for use over and over again. They set guidelines that direct behaviour in uniform directions for certain types of situations regardless of where or when they occur in an organisation. A **policy** communicates broad guidelines for making decisions and taking action in specific circumstances. In matters relating to the workforce, for example, typical human resource policies deal with such matters as employee hiring, termination, performance appraisals, pay increases and discipline.

Policies should focus attention on matters of particular importance to the organisation and then direct people in how they are supposed to deal with them. Consider the issue of 'blowing the whistle' on unethical or unlawful activities within an organisation. In recent years many public sector organisations have established procedures to protect staff who disclose information about wrongdoing within the workplace. State laws in Australia have also assisted. For example, in Queensland there is a Whistleblowers Act that clearly outlines procedures on how information should be disclosed and the protection afforded to those disclosing it. This legislation, together with initiatives taken by individual organisations, has helped to expose corruption and unethical practices in the public and private sectors. Legislation of this kind is particularly important in the current era of high-level corporate corruption, as illustrated by the Enron, Arthur Andersen and Xerox examples in the USA.

Procedures or **rules** are plans that describe exactly what actions are to be taken in specific situations. They are often found stated in employee handbooks or manuals as 'SOPs' — standard operating procedures.

Budgets and project schedules

In contrast to standing plans, which remain in place for extended periods of time, *single-use plans* are each used once to meet the needs of well-defined situations in a timely manner. **Budgets** are single-use plans that commit resources to activities, projects or programs. They are powerful tools that allocate scarce resources among multiple and often competing uses. Good managers are able to bargain for and obtain adequate budgets to support the needs of their work units or teams. They are also able to achieve performance objectives while keeping resource expenditures within the allocated budget.

A *fixed budget* allocates resources on the basis of a single estimate of costs. The estimate establishes a fixed pool of resources that can be used, but not exceeded, in support of the specified purpose. For example, a manager may have a $25 000 budget for equipment purchases in a given year. A *flexible budget*, by contrast, allows the allocation of resources to vary in proportion with various levels of activity. Managers operating under flexible budgets can expect additional resource allocations when activity increases from one estimated level to the next. For example, a manager may have a budget allowance for hiring temporary workers if production orders exceed a certain volume.

In a **zero-based budget**, a project or activity is budgeted as if it were brand new. There is no assumption that resources previously allocated to a project or activity will simply be continued in the future. Instead, all projects compete anew for available funds. The intent is to totally reconsider priorities, objectives and activities at the start of each new budget cycle. Australasian organisations including the Mayne Nickless Group, Fisher & Paykel, Optus and ANZ have used zero-based budgets since the early 1990s. Businesses, government agencies and other types of organisations use zero-based budgeting to make sure that only the most desirable and timely programs receive funding.

Project schedules are single-use plans that identify the activities required to accomplish a specific major project — for example, the completion of a new student activities building on a campus, the development of a new computer software program, or the implementation of a new advertising campaign for a sports team. In each case, the project schedule would

A **policy** is a standing plan that communicates broad guidelines for decisions and action.

Procedures or **rules** precisely describe actions that are to be taken in specific situations.

Budgets are plans that commit resources to projects or activities.

A **zero-based budget** allocates resources to a project or activity as if it were brand new.

Project schedules are single-use plans for accomplishing a specific major project.

define specific task objectives, activities to be accomplished, due dates and timetables for the activities, and resource requirements. Importantly, a good project schedule sets priorities so that everyone involved knows not only what needs to be done but also in what order so that the entire project gets finished on time.

PLANNING TOOLS, TECHNIQUES AND PROCESSES

Planning is essential for successful management in any organisation. Planning works best when it is comprehensive, systematic and based on well-established foundations. Today's planners utilise a broad array of planning tools, techniques and processes. These include forecasting, specific contingency planning, benchmarking, participative or team-based planning, and the use of staff planners.

Forecasting

A **forecast** is an attempt to predict future outcomes.

A **forecast** is a vision of the future. Forecasting is the process of making assumptions about what will happen in the future.[13] All good plans involve forecasts, either implicit or explicit. Business journals such as the *Bulletin*, *Business Review Weekly* or the *Economist* regularly report a variety of business and economic forecasts for their readers. These include forecasts of consumer spending, business investment, interest rates, unemployment, balance of payments and inflation. For companies operating on a global scale it is essential to access forecasts for economies outside their immediate region. Journals and financial newspapers such as the *Financial Times*, *Guardian*, *Wall Street Journal*, *Fortune* and *Business Week* cover much of North America and Europe, whereas the *Singapore Business Times*, *China Daily*, *Straits Times* and *Asian Wall Street Journal* provide forecasts for the Asia–Pacific region.

Some forecasts are based on *qualitative forecasting*, which uses expert opinions to predict the future. In this case, a single person of special expertise or reputation or a panel of experts may be consulted. Others involve *quantitative forecasting* that uses mathematical and statistical analysis of data banks to predict future events. Time-series analysis makes predictions by using statistical routines such as regression analysis to project past trends into the future. General economic trends are often forecast by econometric models that simulate events and make predictions based on relationships discovered among variables in the models. Statistical analysis of opinion polls and attitude surveys, such as those reported in newspapers and on television, are typically used to predict future consumer tastes, employee preferences, and political choices, among other issues.

In the final analysis forecasting always relies on human judgement. Even the results of highly sophisticated quantitative approaches still require interpretation. Forecasts should always be viewed as subject to error and therefore treated cautiously. Managers should remember that forecasting is not planning; planning is a more comprehensive activity that involves deciding what to do about the implications of forecasts once they are made. Large multinational corporations such as Sony, Pfizer, AEG, Ford, BHP Billiton and News Corporation analyse economic and business forecasts for each region and country. They must ascertain the correct mix of products and services and the correct marketing strategies before committing to an investment plan. While some requirements may be generic in an increasingly standardised global economy, there are still substantial regional or country-specific differences that need to be considered. Many US-based multinational corporations

Visit the *Business Review Weekly* www.brw.com.au, the National Business Review www.nbr.co.nz or the economist's corner at Austrade www.austrade.gov.au to find a current business or economic forecast.

GET CONNECTED!

have assumed that what works in the USA will be successful elsewhere. They have not taken into account important social, cultural, historical and religious differences between nations.

Contingency planning

Planning, by definition, involves thinking ahead. But the more uncertain the planning environment, the more likely that the original assumptions, predictions and intentions may prove to be in error. Even the most carefully prepared projections may prove inadequate as experience develops. Unexpected problems and events frequently occur. When they do, plans may have to be changed. It is best to anticipate during the planning process that things might not go as expected. Alternatives to the existing plan can then be developed and readied for use when and if circumstances make them appropriate. The attacks on New York city and Washington on 11 September 2001 are extreme examples of the type of events to be taken into account when planning for the unexpected.

This is the process of **contingency planning**, identifying alternative courses of action that can be implemented if and when an original plan proves inadequate because of changing circumstances. Of course, changes in the planning environment must be detected as early as possible. 'Trigger points' that indicate that an existing plan is no longer desirable must be preselected and then monitored. Sometimes this is accomplished simply by good forward thinking on the part of managers and staff planners. At other times, it can be assisted by a 'devil's advocate' method, in which planners are formally assigned to develop worst-case forecasts of future events.

Contingency planning identifies alternative courses of action for use if and when circumstances change with time.

Scenario planning

Scenario planning is the long-term version of contingency planning. As we have seen earlier in this chapter, a recognition of the need to identify and plan for a variety of possible future scenarios or situations should be at the heart of all planning. Identifying a range of different possible future scenarios helps organisations operate more flexibly and respond more rapidly in uncertain and changing environments. In Asia, the Taiwanese information technology manufacturer Acer has adopted a flexible and dynamic approach to corporate planning because of the uncertainty of the markets for personal computers and other IT-based products, such as mobile telephones, coupled with concerns about Taiwan's long-term relationship with mainland China. Whereas the mainland China market is critical for Acer to become a global company, it also injects 'uncertainty' into the equation because of the political tensions between the two nations.

Although recognising that planning scenarios can never be inclusive of all future possibilities, a planning coordinator once said that scenarios help 'condition the organisation to think' and remain better prepared than its competitors for 'future shocks'. Among the issues and concerns for scenario planning today are geopolitical change, terrorism, climate change, sustainable development, human rights and biodiversity.

Benchmarking

Another important influence on the success or failure of planning involves the frame of reference used as a starting point. All too often planners have only a limited awareness of what is happening outside the immediate work setting. Successful planning must challenge the status quo; it cannot simply accept things the way they are. One way to do this is through **benchmarking**, a technique that makes use of external comparisons to better evaluate an

Benchmarking uses external comparisons to gain insights for planning.

organisation's current performance and identify possible actions for the future.[14] The purpose of benchmarking is to find out what other people and organisations are doing very well and to then plan how to incorporate these ideas into your organisation's operations. This powerful planning technique is increasingly popular in today's competitive business world. It is a way for progressive companies to learn from other 'excellent' companies, not just competitors. It allows them to analyse and thoroughly compare all systems and processes for efficiencies and opportunities for innovation.

Use of staff planners

As the planning needs of organisations grow, there is a corresponding need to increase the sophistication of the overall planning system itself. In some cases, staff planners are employed to help coordinate planning for the organisation as a whole or for one of its major components. These planners should be skilled in all steps of the formal planning process, including the benchmarking and scenario-planning approaches just discussed. They should also understand the staff, or advisory, nature of their roles. Given clear responsibilities and their special planning expertise, staff planners can bring focus to efforts to accomplish important, often strategic, planning tasks. But one risk is a tendency for a communication 'gap' to develop between staff planners and line managers. This can cause a great deal of difficulty. Resulting plans may lack relevance, and line personnel may lack commitment to implement them even if they are relevant. One trend in organisations today is to de-emphasise the role of large staff planning groups and to place much greater emphasis on the participation and involvement of line managers in the planning process.

Participation and involvement

⊘ Participatory planning includes the people who will be affected by plans and/or whose help is needed to implement them.

Participation is a key word in the planning process. The concept of **participatory planning** requires that the process include people who will be affected by the resulting plans and/or will be asked to help implement them. This brings to the organisation many benefits. Participation can increase the creativity and information available for planning. It can also increase the understanding, acceptance and commitment of people to final plans. Indeed, planning should be organised and accomplished in a participatory manner that includes the contributions of many people representing diverse responsibilities and vantage points. This includes the level of strategic planning, once considered only the province of top management. The more aware all levels are of strategic plans and the more they are involved in helping to establish them, the greater the commitment throughout the organisation to their accomplishment.

The centrality of participation in the planning process is highlighted in figure 7.3. To create and implement the best plans, proper attention must always be given to genuinely involving others during all planning steps. Even though this process may mean that planning takes more time, it can improve results by improving implementation. When 7-Eleven executives planned for a dramatic overhaul of the organisation — including a new information system and the introduction of new 'upscale' products and services such as selling fancy meals-to-go — they learned a hard lesson on the value of participation in planning. Although their ideas sounded good at the top, franchisees baulked at the level of operations. The executives found that they needed to take time to sell their ideas to the franchise owners before the advantages of their new corporate strategies could be realised. Now 'University 7-Eleven' acts as a training hub to prepare workers for the new economy. The firm is planning a V.com service that allows videos and books to be ordered online and delivered to the local 7-Eleven store.[15]

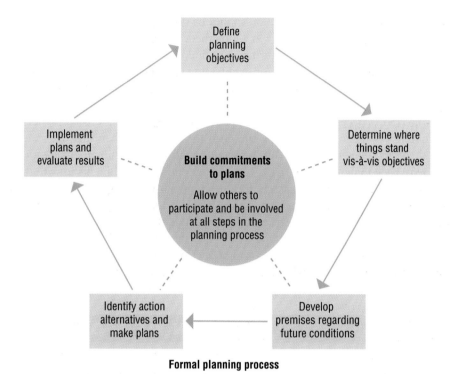

Formal planning process

Figure 7.3 ▸ How participation and involvement help build commitments to plans

ORGANISATIONAL CONTROL PROCESSES

All organisations require some form of control to ensure that their planning objectives are met. If there is agreement inside and outside the organisation about its aims and objectives, and the means to secure them, then control is less likely to be a contentious issue. If there is dissension surrounding these objectives then individuals or groups of stakeholders may disrupt the planned objectives through resisting or boycotting the control mechanisms that are designed to ensure goal compliance. This is why the word 'control' often has negative connotations. Also, if the actual control mechanisms are draconian and alienate staff then there is likely to be collective resistance. The *scientific management* approach to organisational control, pioneered by Frederick Taylor[16] in the USA, is widely viewed in such a negative light for its dehumanising attitude toward work control. This approach caused a great deal of industrial conflict between management and labour in companies such as Ford, General Motors, Alcoa and BHP from the 1930s to the 1980s. It has since been largely replaced by more humanistic concepts of control. Control can therefore take a variety of different forms and is likely to change form as societal values shift. Broadly speaking, **controlling** is the process of measuring performance and taking action to ensure the planned outcomes are achieved.

Controlling is the process of measuring performance and taking action to ensure desired results.

Rationale for controlling

Control is aimed at ensuring that plans are fulfilled and that performance targets are met. Control can be important not only for guaranteeing that the performance level is met but also for ensuring that performance is contained. For instance, Stan Shih, the founder and chairman of Acer, Taiwan's highest-profile computer company, wants his organisation to be in the top three in the mainland China personal computer market, but he does not want it to be number one. He believes that the premier position should be occupied by China's own PC producer, Legend. If Acer were the market leader in China there would be resistance from the Chinese government which could, potentially, further sour diplomatic relations between the two countries. The art of diplomacy is essential for maintaining workable Taiwanese–Chinese business relations.[17] Carefully controlling the performance levels of an organisation requires accurate and timely flows of information on the key operational variables and outcomes. Enron and Xerox in the USA — recent examples of companies reporting profit levels far higher than the actual amounts — demonstrate vividly the need for control mechanisms that can quickly detect and correct unlawful and corrupt behaviour at all levels within an organisation.

If you refer back to figure 7.1 on page 175, it shows how controlling fits in with the rest of the management process. Planning sets the directions and allocates resources. Organising brings people and material resources together in working combinations. Leading inspires people to best utilise these resources. Controlling sees to it that the right things happen, in the right way, and at the right time. It helps ensure that the performance contributions of individuals and groups are consistent with organisational plans. It helps ensure that performance accomplishments throughout an organisation are consistent with one another in means–ends fashion. And it helps ensure that people comply with organisational policies and procedures.

HIGH PERFORMANCE

The United Kingdom's Special Air Service (SAS)

The paradox of control

Issues of global security are uppermost in the minds of many politicians and senior managers. The increased use of special forces units, such as Australia's and the UK's Special Air Service (SAS) and the US Green Berets, highlights a paradox of control. Special forces teams are meant to be self-controlling, able to take the initiative. However, as their role has developed, so the need for generals and political leaders to control their behaviour and actions has become critical. A good early example of the control issues facing governments that deploy these teams is the six-day siege of the Iranian embassy in London in 1980. Gunmen held 26 hostages until the UK SAS stormed the embassy.

The public saw the response to the siege as a rapid and dramatic mix of automatic weapons and stun grenades. But the SAS only began the assault on the embassy after lengthy communications and official clearance involving the prime minister, senior members of the Cabinet, the SAS commander and the heads of police. The key decision makers were close by. Would the operation have been as successful if the decision makers were further removed? When bureaucratic approval is required before every action taken on the ground thousands of kilometres away can commence, such as in Afghanistan in 2002, then special forces lose their defining qualities — speed and surprise. Communications technology advancements and the streamlining of decision-making processes provide opportunities to overcome this problem.[18]

Steps in the control process

The classic example of the control process operating in its purest form is a home thermostat. We set the thermostat to a desired temperature. When the room gets too cold or hot, the thermostat senses the deviation and takes corrective action by turning on the heater or air conditioner. Once the desired temperature is achieved, the heating system or air conditioner is automatically turned off. This illustrates a **cybernetic control system** — one that is self-contained in its performance-monitoring and correction capabilities. The control process as practised in organisations is not cybernetic, but it does follow similar principles.

As shown in figure 7.4, the management control process involves four steps: establish objectives and standards; measure actual performance; compare results with objectives and standards; and take corrective action as needed. While essential to management, the process and its implications apply equally well to personal career planning. Think about it. Without career objectives, how do you know where you really want to go? How can you allocate your time and other resources to take best advantage of available opportunities? Without measurement standards, how can you assess any progress being made? How can you adjust current behaviour to improve the prospects for future results?

A **cybernetic control system** is self-contained in its performance-monitoring and correction capabilities.

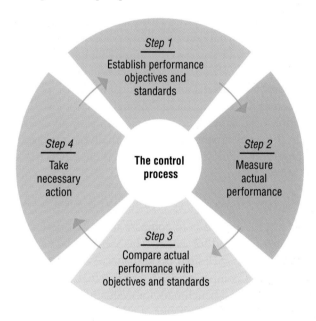

Figure 7.4 ▸ Four steps in management control

STEP 1: ESTABLISH OBJECTIVES AND STANDARDS

The control process starts with planning, when performance objectives and standards for measuring them are set. It can't begin without them. Performance objectives, furthermore, should represent key results to be achieved. The word 'key' in the prior sentence is important. The focus in planning should be on describing 'critical' or 'essential' results that will make a substantial difference in the success of the organisation. The standards are important, too, and they must also be considered right from the beginning. As key results are identified, the standards or specific measures that will be taken to indicate success or failure in their accompliment must also be specified. At Skyrail Rainforest Cableway in Far North Queensland, for example, customers rate the staff on various aspects of their cableway experience. Every month the feedback is analysed and compared with customer satisfaction targets. The results are discussed with employees and managers in each of the eight departments of the company. The 'customer satisfaction index' score is compared with that of previous months to identify the causes of any changes. The customer satisfaction index scores are used to determine the performance-related pay segment of staff salaries.[19]

Two types of standards are common to the organisational control process. **Output standards** measure performance results in terms of outcomes like quantity, quality, cost or time of accomplished work. Examples of output standards include percentage error rate, dollar deviation from budgeted expenditures, and the number of units produced or customers serviced in a time period. **Input standards**, by contrast, measure effort in terms of the amount of work expended in task performance. They are used in situations where outputs are difficult or expensive to measure. Examples of input standards include conformance to rules and procedures, efficiency in the use of resources, and work attendance or punctuality.

⚙ **Output standards**
measure performance
results in terms of quantity,
quality, cost or time.

⚙ **Input standards**
measure work efforts that go
into a performance task.

STEP 2: MEASURE ACTUAL PERFORMANCE

The second step of the control process is to measure actual performance. The goal here is to accurately measure the performance results (output standards) and/or the performance efforts (input standards). In both cases, the measurement must be accurate enough to spot significant differences between what is really taking place and what was originally planned. A common management failure in this regard is an unwillingness or inability to measure the performance of people at work. Yet without measurement, effective control is not possible.

Increasingly, managers are required to assess organisational performance. This means measuring actual outcomes. It can be achieved through analysing statistical/quantitative data collected either by employees, supervisors or managers, or by an external organisation, and typically presented in the form of spreadsheets. Alternatively, managers can use qualitative techniques such as observing employees at work. This is often referred to as management by wandering around (MBWA).[20]

www.shrm.org

Are you familiar with the Society for Human Resource Management in the USA? SHRM reports that up to 25 per cent of job applications and résumés contain errors. It is always important to check the references of job applicants to make sure that you fit the right person to the right job.

STEP 3: COMPARE RESULTS WITH OBJECTIVES AND STANDARDS

The third step in the control process is to compare measured performance with objectives and standards to establish the need for action. This step can be expressed as the following *control equation*: Need for action = Desired performance − Actual performance.

There are different ways of comparing desired and actual performance. A *historical comparison* uses past performance as a benchmark for evaluating current performance. A *relative comparison* uses the performance achievements of other persons, work units or organisations as the evaluation standard. An *engineering comparison* uses engineered standards set scientifically through such methods as time and motion studies. For instance, the delivery routines of drivers for TNT and Mayne Nickless are carefully measured in terms of the expected time taken to make a delivery on various routes.

Earlier, the concept of benchmarking was formally introduced as a planning approach. Its importance to the control process is also clear. Benchmarking is rapidly gaining popularity as a means of identifying best practices, with the emphasis always on the question: What can I or we do better? Without rigorous and regular measurement comparisons — be they historical, relative or engineering driven — answers to this question are difficult to get. In an Ernst & Young survey of fast-growing small businesses, for example, more than 80 per cent were found to be using benchmarking to improve their performances. The comparisons were most likely to involve industry norms, a primary competitor, the industry leader and similar world-class organisations.[21]

STEP 4: TAKE CORRECTIVE ACTION

The control equation indicates that the greater the measured difference between desired and actual performance, the greater the need for action. The final step in the control process, accordingly, is taking any action necessary to correct or improve things. This allows for a judicious use of **management by exception** — the practice of giving priority attention to situations that show the greatest need for action. This approach can save valuable time, energy and other resources, while allowing all efforts to be concentrated on the areas of greatest need.

Two types of exceptions may be encountered. The first is a *problem situation* in which actual performance is below the standard. The reasons for this performance deficiency must be understood. Corrective action is required to restore performance to the desired level. The second exception is an *opportunity situation* in which actual performance is above the standard. The reasons for this extraordinary performance must also be understood. Action should then be taken to continue this higher level of accomplishment in the future. The original plan, objectives and standards can also be reviewed to determine whether they should be updated.

Measurement is certainly an important key to the control process. But so too is the willingness to confront the implications of the measurements, to learn from experience, and to actively plan to improve future performance. For instance, the Victorian-based art company, Australian Art Resources, and the Queensland-based Skyrail Rainforest Cableway both use **after-action review** processes. These are structured reviews of problems encountered, lessons learned and actual outcomes achieved on completed projects or special events. Staff members are asked to respond to questions about the stated objectives of the project, the actual outcomes, the lessons learned and how future projects might best be tackled. Both organisations use a team-based structure and so much of the review concentrates on how the team can be more effective. However, improving team performance may require upgrading the knowledge base and job skills of individuals. The after-action review is an integral part of an organisation's continuous improvement process because it makes review a part of the organisational culture and it encourages the people involved to take responsibility for their performance and accomplishments.

Management by exception focuses managerial attention on substantial differences between actual and desired performance.

An **after-action review** formally examines results to identify lessons learned in a completed project or special operation.

Types of controls

There are three major types of managerial controls — feedforward, concurrent and feedback controls, as shown in figure 7.5.[22] Each is relevant to a different phase of the organisation's input-throughput-output cycle of activities. Each offers significant opportunities for actions to be taken that advance organisational productivity and high performance. And importantly, each offers the opportunity for performance-oriented organisational and personal learning through systematic assessment of actions and results.

Work inputs	**Work throughputs**	**Work outputs**
Feedforward controls	**Concurrent controls**	**Feedback controls**
Ensure the right directions are set and the right resource inputs are available	Ensure the right things are being done as part of work-flow operations	Ensure that final results are up to desired standards

Figure 7.5 ▶ Feedforward, concurrent and feedback controls in the management process

FEEDFORWARD CONTROLS

Feedforward controls ensure that directions and resources are right before the work begins.

Feedforward controls, also called *preliminary controls*, are accomplished before a work activity begins. They ensure that objectives are clear, that proper directions are established, and that the right resources are available to accomplish them. By making sure that the stage is properly set for high performance, feedforward controls are preventive in nature. They are designed to eliminate the potential for problems later on in the process by asking an important but often-neglected question: What needs to be done before we begin? This is a forward-thinking and proactive approach to control rather than a reactive and defensive one.

The quality of resources is a key concern of feedback controls. At McDonald's, for example, preliminary control of food ingredients plays an important role in the organisation's quality program. The company requires that suppliers of its hamburger buns produce them to exact specifications, covering everything from texture to uniformity of colour. Internationally, the organisation works hard to develop local suppliers that can offer dependable quality.[23]

CONCURRENT CONTROLS

Concurrent controls focus on what happens during the work process.

Concurrent controls focus on what happens during the work process. Sometimes called *steering controls*, they monitor ongoing operations and activities to make sure things are being done according to plan. Ideally, concurrent controls allow corrective actions to be taken before a task is completed. The key question is: What can we do to improve things before we finish? Here, the focus is on quality of task activities during the work process. This approach to control can reduce waste in the form of unacceptable finished products or services.

Taking McDonald's again as an example, ever-present shift leaders provide concurrent control through direct supervision. They constantly observe what is taking place even while helping out with the work. They are trained to intervene immediately when something is not done right and to correct things on the spot. Detailed instruction manuals also 'steer' workers in the right directions as their jobs are performed.

POINT ⬅ / COUNTER ⬆

Controlling for maximum profit

Since the Industrial Revolution managers have been obsessed by the need to control the workforce. More recently management ideas have stressed the need for control mechanisms that emphasise staff recognition and accountability, but these employee empowerment approaches still have the same aim — to ensure that workers accept and embrace the goals of the company. The Human Relations School has strongly influenced this type of approach, but this does not mask the fact that it is still a control mechanism. In fact, these human relations approaches were largely a response to the failure of the authoritarian control regime of scientific management. Poor relations between managers and workers, high levels of industrial unrest and declining profits forced companies to re-evaluate how they controlled employees at work. Many large companies used psychologists to devise systems of control to empower staff. Quality circles, team working, autonomous work groups and self-assessment resulted from this approach. These are the politically correct control methods of the modern, profit-maximising company.

FEEDBACK CONTROLS

Feedback controls, also called *postaction controls*, take place after work is completed. They focus on the quality of end results rather than on inputs and activities. They ask the question: Now that we are finished, how well did we do? Restaurants, for example, ask how you liked a meal — after it is eaten; a final exam grade tells you how well you performed — after the course is over; a budget summary informs managers of any cost overruns — after a project is completed. In these and other circumstances the feedback provided by the control process is useful information for improving things in the future. It also provides formal documentation of accomplishments that may be used for allocating performance-based rewards.

Employees at a McDonald's restaurant never know when a corporate evaluator may stop in to sample the food and the service. When this happens, however, the evaluator provides feedback with the goal of improving future operations.

⊘ Feedback controls take place after an action is completed.

Internal and external control

Managers have two broad options with respect to control. They can rely on people to exercise self-control over their own behaviour. This strategy of **internal control** allows motivated individuals and groups to exercise self-discipline in fulfilling job expectations. Alternatively, managers can take direct action to control the behaviour of others. This is a strategy of **external control** that occurs through personal supervision and the use of formal administrative systems. Organisations with effective control typically use both strategies to good advantage. However, the trend today is to increase the emphasis on internal or self-control. This is consistent with the renewed emphasis on participation, empowerment and involvement in the workplace.

Internal control is exercised by people who are motivated to take charge of their own behaviour on the job, and who are given the chance to do so. Douglas McGregor's Theory Y perspective, introduced in chapter 4, recognises the willingness of people to exercise self-control in their work.[24] Of course, McGregor also recognised that people are most likely to do this when they participate in setting performance objectives and standards. Reliance on an internal control strategy also requires a high degree of trust. When people are expected to work on their own and exercise self-control, managers must give them a chance to meet performance expectations.

The potential for self-control is increased when capable people have a clear sense of organisational mission, know their performance objectives, and have the resources necessary to do their jobs well. It is also enhanced by participative organisational cultures in which people are expected to treat each other with respect and consideration, are allowed to exercise personal initiative, and are given ample opportunities to experience satisfaction through job performance.

⊘ Internal control occurs through self-discipline and self-control.

⊘ External control occurs through direct supervision or administrative systems such as rules and procedures.

ORGANISATIONAL CONTROL SYSTEMS

Each component in an organisation's control systems should contribute to maintaining predictably high levels of performance. Internal control should be encouraged and supported; external control should be appropriate and rigorous. The management process provides for a certain amount of control when planning, organising and leading are well done. Additional and comprehensive control is provided by appropriate systems such as those dealing with remuneration and benefits, employee discipline, financial information and operations management.

Female senior executives in Australia

The International Labour Organization reports that Australia has the lowest proportion of female managers of all industrialised countries — women hold just 1.3 per cent of senior executive positions. A Boardroom Partners report found women hold only 4.89 per cent of available board seats in Australia.[25]

Why is this the case?

Compensation and benefits

Base compensation plays an important role in attracting a highly qualified workforce to the organisation. If compensation is attractive and competitive in the prevailing labour markets, it can make the organisation highly desirable as a place of employment. And if you get the right people into jobs, you can reduce costs and boost productivity over the long run. After all, the more capable a person is, the more self-control you can expect that person to exercise. When the wage and salary structure of an organisation is unattractive and uncompetitive, however, it will be difficult to attract and retain a staff of highly competent workers. The less capable the workforce, the greater the burden on external controls to ensure that desired levels of performance are achieved and maintained.

The use of incentive compensation systems, discussed in chapter 14 on motivation and rewards, also helps. When properly implemented, 'pay-for-performance', 'performance-related pay' and 'merit pay' plans serve as control systems. They can be strong influences on individual and group behaviour. The logic is quite straightforward, as described this way by a corporate executive: 'Pay very poorly for poor performance; pay poorly for average performance; pay well for above-average performance; pay obscenely well for outstanding performance.'[26]

Because of the growing importance of a worker's total compensation package, fringe benefits also have control implications. Their attractiveness can also affect an organisation's ability to recruit and retain a qualified workforce. In today's environment of rising costs and workforce diversity, fringe benefits — from increased superannuation contributions to company cars — can be very expensive. Many employers are now trying to provide individuals with more choice in selecting benefits that suit their diverse needs. At the same time, employers are seeking ways to reduce expenditures by asking employees to pay more of the fringe benefits' cost — an unpopular move with employees and trade unions alike.

Do you know what you are worth? Check out where you're at and where you could be at http://salary.monster.com.au or http://salary.monster.co.nz.

GET CONNECTED!

Discipline is the act of influencing behaviour through reprimand.

Progressive discipline is the process of tying reprimands to the severity and frequency of misbehaviour.

Employee discipline systems

Absenteeism, tardiness, sloppy work — the list of undesirable conduct can go on to even more extreme actions: falsifying records, sexual harassment, embezzlement. All are examples of behaviours that can and should be formally addressed in employee discipline systems. **Discipline** is the act of influencing behaviour through reprimand. Ideally, this form of managerial control is handled in a fair, consistent and systematic way.

Progressive discipline ties reprimands to the severity and frequency of the employee's infractions. Under such a system, penalties vary according to how significant a disruptive behaviour is and how often it occurs. For example, the progressive discipline guidelines of one university state: 'The level of disciplinary action shall increase with the level of severity of behaviour engaged in and based on whether the conduct is of a repetitive nature.' In this particular case, the ultimate penalty of 'discharge' is reserved for the most severe behaviours (for example, any criminal act) or for continual infractions of a less severe nature (for example, being continually late for work and failing to respond to a series of written reprimands and/or suspensions).

The goal of a progressive discipline system is to achieve compliance with organisational expectations through the least extreme reprimand possible. But even this type of control can have unpleasant consequences. Sometimes the relationships between managers and disciplined workers take on an adversarial character. Sometimes managers wait too long and fail to take disciplinary action until a problem is very severe. And sometimes, poor attitudes form among persons who can't seem to change and so keep receiving ever-harsher punishments.[27]

One way to develop a consistent personal approach to disciplinary situations is to remember the analogy of the 'hot stove rules' of discipline. They begin with a simple rule: 'When a stove is hot, don't touch it.' We also know that when this rule is violated, you get burned — immediately, consistently, but usually not beyond the possibility of repair. Six 'hot stove rules' for using reprimands in disciplinary action are described in Manager's Notepad 7.2.[28]

MANAGER'S NOTEPAD 7.2

'Hot stove rules' of employee discipline

- A reprimand should be immediate; a hot stove burns the first time you touch it.
- A reprimand should be directed toward someone's actions, not the individual's personality; a hot stove doesn't hold grudges, doesn't try to humiliate people and doesn't accept excuses.
- A reprimand should be consistently applied; a hot stove burns anyone who touches it, and it does so every time.
- A reprimand should be informative; a hot stove lets a person know what to do to avoid getting burned in the future — 'Don't touch'.
- A reprimand should occur in a supportive setting; a hot stove conveys warmth but with an inflexible rule — 'Don't touch'.
- A reprimand should support realistic rules; the don't-touch-a-hot-stove rule isn't a power play, a whim or an emotion of the moment; it is a necessary rule of reason.

Information and financial controls

The pressure is ever present today for all organisations to use their resources well and to perform with maximum efficiency. The use of information in financial analysis of organisational performance is critical in managerial control. At a minimum, managers should be able to understand and assess for control purposes the following important financial aspects of organisational performance: *liquidity* — ability to generate cash to pay bills; *leverage* — ability to earn more in returns than the cost of debt; *asset management* — ability to use resources efficiently and operate at minimum cost; and *profitability* — ability to earn revenues greater than costs.

These financial performance indicators can be assessed using a variety of financial ratios, including those shown in Manager's Notepad 7.3. Such ratios provide a framework for historical comparisons within the organisation and external benchmarking relative to industry performance. They can also be used to set financial targets or goals to be shared with employees and tracked to indicate success or failure in their accomplishment. For example, New Zealand-based whitegoods manufacturer Fisher & Paykel and the Pizza Hut restaurant chain regularly share quarterly and annual key financial, performance and technological information with their employees. These companies, with operations in Australia, New Zealand and overseas, believe that providing a financial scorecard to staff has numerous benefits. It informs them of the current position of the company, helps them focus on how they can work more effectively and strengthens personal commitments to improving corporate profitability. This sharing of information is coupled with profit sharing and performance-related pay systems.[29]

Operations management and control

Control is integral to operations management, where the emphasis is always on utilising people, resources and technology to best advantage. The areas of purchasing control, inventory control and statistical quality control are all receiving current managerial attention.

PURCHASING CONTROL

Rising costs of materials are a fact of life in today's economy. Controlling these costs through efficient purchasing management is an important productivity tool. Like an individual, a thrifty organisation must be concerned about how much it pays for what it buys. To leverage buying power, more organisations are centralising purchasing to allow buying in volume. They are committing to a small number of suppliers with whom they can negotiate special contracts, gain quality assurances and get preferred service. They are also finding ways to work together in supplier–purchaser partnerships so they can operate in ways that allow each partner to better contain its costs. It is now more common, for example, that parts suppliers keep warehouses in their customer's facilities. The supplier maintains inventory and stocks it in accordance with forecast demand. The customer provides the space; the supplier does the rest. The benefits to the customer are lower purchasing costs and preferred service; the supplier gains an exclusive customer contract and more sales volume.

INVENTORY CONTROL

Inventory is the amount of materials or products kept in storage. Organisations maintain inventories of raw materials, work in process and/or finished goods. The goal of inventory control is to make sure that an inventory is just the right size to meet performance needs, thus minimising the cost. The **economic order quantity** (EOQ) method of inventory control involves ordering a fixed number of items every time an inventory level falls to a predetermined point. When this point is reached, a decision is automatically made (typically by computer) to place a standard order to replenish the stock. Standard order

Inventory control by **economic order quantity** *orders replacements whenever inventory level falls to a predetermined point.*

sizes are mathematically calculated to minimise costs of inventory. The best example is the local supermarket, where hundreds of daily orders are routinely made on this basis.

Another approach to inventory control is **just-in-time (JIT) scheduling**. Made popular by the productivity of Japanese industry, JIT systems try to reduce costs and improve work-flow by scheduling materials to arrive at a workstation or facility 'just in time' to be used. This minimises carrying costs since almost no inventories are maintained — materials are ordered or components produced only as needed. The just-in-time approach is an impor-tant productivity-enhancing management innovation. The system allows production and purchasing to be done in small quantities and no earlier than necessary for use.

Just-in-time (JIT) scheduling minimises inventory by routing materials to work stations 'just in time' to be used.

STATISTICAL QUALITY CONTROL

Consistent with the total quality management theme in today's workplace, the practice of **quality control** involves checking processes, materials, products and services to ensure that they meet high standards. This responsibility applies to all aspects of operations, from the selection of raw materials and supplies right down to the last task performed to deliver the finished good or service. In *statistical quality control*, the process is supported by rigorous statistical analysis. Typically this means taking samples of work, measuring quality in the samples, and then determining the acceptability of results. Unacceptable results in a sample call attention to the need for investigation and corrective action to bring operations back up to standard. The power of statistics allows the sampling to be efficiently used as the basis for decision making. At General Electric, for example, a Six Sigma program drives the quest for competitive advantage. This means that statistically the firm's quality performance will tolerate no more than 3.4 defects per million — a perfection rate of 99.9997 per cent! As tough as it sounds, 'Six Sigma' is a common quality standard for the new workplace.

Quality control checks processes, materials, products and services to ensure that they meet high standards.

MBO: integrated planning and controlling

As shown throughout this chapter, planning and controlling must work together. A useful technique for integrating them in day-to-day practice is **management by objectives (MBO)**. This is a structured process of regular communication in which a supervisor or team leader and subordinate or team member jointly set performance objectives and review results accomplished.[30] In its simplest terms, MBO requires a formal agreement between the supervisor and subordinate concerning the subordinate's performance objectives for a given time period; the plans through which they will be accomplished; standards for measuring whether they have been accomplished; and procedures for reviewing performance results.

Management by objectives (MBO) is a process of joint objective setting between a superior and subordinate.

MBO PROCESS

The MBO process is illustrated in figure 7.6. Note that the supervisor and subordinate *jointly* establish plans and *jointly* control results in any good MBO action framework. They agree on the high-priority performance objectives for the subordinate along with a timetable for their accomplishment and the criteria to be used in evaluating results.

Performance objectives are essential parts of MBO. The way objectives are specified and how they are established will influence the success of the MBO process. Three types of objectives may be specified in an MBO contract. *Improvement objectives* document intentions for improving performance in a specific way and with respect to a specific factor. An example is 'to reduce quality rejects by 10 per cent'. *Personal development objectives* pertain to personal growth activities, often those resulting in expanded job knowledge or skills. An example is 'to learn the latest version of a computer spreadsheet package'. Some MBO contracts also include *maintenance objectives*, which formally express intentions to maintain performance at an existing level. In all cases, performance objectives are written and formally agreed to by both the superior and subordinate. They also meet the following four *criteria of a good performance objective*:

Criteria of a good performance objective

1. *specific* — targets a key result to be accomplished
2. *time defined* — identifies a date for achieving results
3. *challenging* — offers a realistic and attainable challenge
4. *measurable* — is as specific and quantitative as possible.

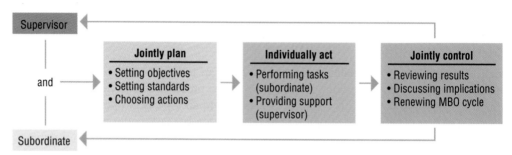

Figure 7.6 ▸ Management by objectives — an integrated planning and control framework

One of the more difficult aspects of MBO relates to the last criterion — the need to state performance objectives as specifically and quantitatively as possible. Ideally, this occurs as agreement on a *measurable end product* — for example, 'to reduce housekeeping supply costs by 5 per cent by the end of the fiscal year'. But some jobs, particularly managerial ones, involve performance areas that are hard to quantify. Rather than abandon MBO in such cases, it is often possible to agree on performance objectives that are stated as *verifiable work activities*. The accomplishment of the activities can then serve as an indicator of progress under the performance objective. An example is 'to improve communications with my subordinates in the next three months by holding weekly group meetings'. Whereas it can be difficult to measure 'improved communications,' it is easy to document whether the 'weekly group meetings' have been held.

MBO PROS AND CONS

MBO is one of the most talked about and debated management concepts of the past 25 years, and it has many advocates and critics.[31] As a result, good advice is available on what to do and what not to do if MBO is to be used to maximum advantage. Things to avoid doing in MBO include tying it to pay, focusing too much attention on easy objectives, requiring excessive paperwork, and having supervisors simply *tell* subordinates their objectives.

A major advantage of MBO is that it clearly focuses the subordinate's work efforts on the most important tasks and objectives; another is that it focuses the supervisor's work efforts on areas of support that can truly help the subordinate meet the agreed-upon objectives. Because the process involves direct face-to-face communication between supervisor and subordinate, MBO contributes to relationship building. It also gives the subordinate a structured opportunity to participate in decisions that affect his or her work. This encourages self-management rather than external control.[32] The motivational value of goal setting, discussed in chapter 14, further suggests that participation in the MBO process can create a powerful enthusiasm to fulfil one's performance obligations.[33]

None of this potential is lost on many of today's best managers. Although they may describe what they are doing by different names, it has a common thread that is consistent with the MBO concept: if you want high performance from individual contributors, you must hire the best people, work with them to set challenging performance objectives, give them the best possible support and hold them accountable for results.

Many of Australasia's large and medium-sized corporations use some form of MBO system. However, like a number of European and Asian companies, they have increasingly used the concept for teams rather than individuals. As more companies set group- or team-based tasks they have fine-tuned the control system to reflect a collective responsibility for outcomes. And countries and cultures that take a collective rather than an individualistic approach to decision making and accountability, such as the Asian, Scandinavian and Germanic countries, have extensively modified MBO systems to reflect a group or team perspective.

Study guide

The chapter 7 study guide helps you review the chapter content, prepare for examinations, apply what you have learned and further build your career readiness. The summary briefly answers the study questions posed at the start of the chapter. The list of key terms allows you to double-check your familiarity with basic concepts and definitions. The applied activities help you test your comprehension of chapter content. Suggestions offered as career readiness activities direct your attention to relevant sections of the Career Readiness Workbook, where you can test and develop your career skills and apply what you have learned. The list of electronic resources suggests activities from the *Management: An Asia-Pacific Perspective* web site and, finally, the case for critical thinking helps you apply your new management knowledge.

SUMMARY

How do managers plan?

- Planning is the process of setting performance objectives and determining what should be done to accomplish them.
- A plan is a set of intended actions for accomplishing important objectives.
- Scenario planning sets the stage for the other management functions — organising, leading and controlling.
- The steps in the planning process are: define your objectives, determine where you stand vis-á-vis objectives, develop your premises regarding future conditions, identify and choose among alternative ways of accomplishing objectives, and implement action plans and evaluate results.
- The benefits of scenario planning include better focus and flexibility, action orientation, coordination, control and time management.

What types of plans do managers use?

- Short-range plans tend to cover a year or less, while long-range plans extend up to five years or more.
- Strategic plans set critical long-range directions; operational plans are designed to implement strategic plans.
- Organisational policies, such as a sexual harassment policy, are plans that set guidelines for the behaviour of an organisation's members.
- Organisational procedures and rules are plans that describe actions to be taken in specific situations, such as the steps to be taken when someone believes they have been sexually harassed or victimised, or have witnessed unethical or corrupt practices.
- Organisational budgets are plans that allocate resources to activities, projects or programs.

What are the useful planning tools, techniques and processes?

- Forecasting, which attempts to predict what might happen in the future, is a planning aid but not a planning substitute.

- Contingency planning identifies alternative courses of action that can be implemented if and when circumstances change in certain ways over time.
- Scenario planning, through the use of alternative versions of the future, is a useful form of contingency planning.
- Planning through benchmarking utilises external comparisons to identify desirable action directions.
- Participation and involvement open the planning process to valuable inputs from people whose efforts are essential to the effective implementation of plans.

What is the control process?

- Controlling is the process of monitoring performance and taking corrective action as needed.
- The four steps in the control process are: establish performance objectives, measure actual performance, compare results with objectives, and take necessary action to resolve problems or explore opportunities.
- Feedforward controls are accomplished before a work activity begins; they ensure that directions are clear and that the right resources are available to accomplish them.
- Concurrent controls monitor ongoing operations and activities to make sure that things are being done correctly; they allow corrective actions to be taken while the work is being done.
- Feedback controls take place after an action is completed and focus on end results; they address the question 'Now that we are finished, how well did we do and what did we learn for the future?'
- External control is accomplished through personal supervision and the use of formal administrative systems.
- Internal control is self-control and occurs as people exercise self-management and take personal responsibility for their work.

What control systems are used in organisations?

- An appropriate compensation and benefits system assists in organisational control by helping to attract and retain a high-quality workforce.
- Discipline, the process of influencing behaviour through reprimand, must be handled in a fair and systematic way.
- Use of financial information and the analysis of financial ratios, such as those dealing with liquidity, assets and profitability, are important aspects of organisational control systems.
- Operations management contributes to the control process with a focus on efficiencies in such areas as purchasing and inventory control, as well as in the use of statistical approaches to quality control.
- Management by objectives is a process through which supervisors work with their subordinates to 'jointly' set performance objectives and review performance results.
- The MBO process is highly participatory and should clarify performance objectives for a subordinate while identifying support that should be provided by a supervisor. In many companies it has been adapted to embrace groups or teams of workers.

KEY TERMS

after-action review (p. 189)

benchmarking (p. 183)

budgets (p. 181)

concurrent controls (p. 190)

contingency planning (p. 183)

controlling (p. 185)

cybernetic control system (p. 187)

discipline (p. 192)

economic order quantity (p. 194)

external control (p. 191)

feedback controls (p. 191)

feedforward controls (p. 190)

forecast (p. 182)

input standards (p. 188)

internal control (p. 191)

just-in-time (JIT) scheduling (p. 195)

management by exception (p. 189)

management by objectives (MBO) (p. 195)

objectives (p. 174)

operational plans (p. 180)

output standards (p. 188)

participatory planning (p. 184)

plan (p. 175)

planning (p. 174)

policy (p. 181)

procedures or rules (p. 181)

progressive discipline (p. 192)

project schedules (p. 181)

quality control (p. 195)

scenario planning (p. 174)

strategic plans (p. 180)

zero-based budget (p. 181)

APPLIED ACTIVITIES

Short-response questions

1. List the five steps in the planning process.
2. How might planning through benchmarking be used by the owner or manager of a local bookstore?
3. How does Douglas McGregor's Theory Y relate to the concept of internal control?
4. How does a progressive discipline system work?

Application question

5. Put yourself in the position of a management trainer. You are asked to make a short presentation to the local Chamber of Commerce at their biweekly breakfast meeting. The topic you are to speak on is 'How each of you can use management by objectives for better planning and control'. What will you tell them and why?

CAREER READINESS ACTIVITIES

Recommended individual and group learning activities from the end-of-text Career Readiness Workbook for this chapter include:

Career advancement portfolio   *WB*

Update your career advancement portfolio to reflect your new skills and experiences. Include skills and personal insights you gain from the following projects and exercises.

Research and presentation projects   *WB*

- Project 5 — Affirmative action directions — 'where do we go from here?'
- Project 6 — Controversies in CEO pay — 'is it too high?'

Cross-functional integrative case WB

Read the integrative case on Sarina Russo and answer the following questions:

7.1 The case notes that a star rating system was introduced in 2001 to assess the performance of Job Network providers. In the first round of performance assessments, Sarina Russo Job Access scored one of the highest ratings — 4.5 out of a possible 5 stars — based in part on its performance in making job-match placements. How else might the performance of Job Network providers be assessed?

7.2 How might planning through benchmarking be used by Sarina Russo for the Russo Institute of Technology?

Exercises in teamwork WB

- Exercise 7 — What do you value in work?
- Exercise 9 — Beating the time wasters
- Exercise 10 — Personal career planning
- Exercise 12 — The MBO contract
- Exercise 25 — Force-field analysis

Management skills assessment WB

- Assessment 7 — Time management profile

ELECTRONIC RESOURCES

Don't forget to take full advantage of the online support for *Management: An Asia–Pacific Perspective* at www.johnwiley.com.au/highered/management: chapter 7 practice tests, e-flashcards, crossword puzzles, interactive management skills assessments, interactive cases, the online career advancement portfolio and much more!

CASE FOR CRITICAL THINKING

Read the following case for critical thinking on Skyrail ITM. While you are reading the case keep in mind what you have learned in this chapter, then answer the questions.

CASE FOR CRITICAL THINKING
Skyrail ITM:
swinging high with the best

Skyrail International Tourism Management (Skyrail ITM) is an innovative, evolving organisation that operates cableway tourist experiences in Australia — at Cairns and Taronga Zoo, Sydney — and has two new operations planned for Hong Kong and China, with a third likely in the USA. The company prides itself on the quality of its product and professional delivery of its tourist experience.

The Cairns operation, which was established in 1995, consists of a 7.5 kilometre gondola cableway journey from the coastal plain up through World Heritage tropical rainforest to Kuranda, on the Atherton Tablelands. It is the longest journey of its kind in the world. Visitors can stop off at two rainforest boardwalks and an interpretive centre during their journey up or down the range.

Skyrail ITM has won numerous domestic and international tourism awards. In 2000, it won a prestigious British Airways 'Tourism for Tomorrow' award for its ecotourism operation.[34] In 2002 it received Green Globe 21 Certification — the first cableway attraction in the world to receive this certification, which recognises the company's commitment to operating at the world's highest environmental standard. Skyrail ITM's managing director, Ken Chapman, received the coveted certification from the Australian Federal Minister for Tourism.[35]

The success of the Cairns operation led this 100 per cent locally owned, sixth-generation North Queensland family business to form the shelf company, Skyrail ITM, to actively pursue new business opportunities as a tourism-focused organisation. Skyrail ITM's strength is in its knowledge of the tourism industry, particularly in operating cableways and the professional customer service that accompanies it. This requires efficient strategic human resources planning and control. The human resource strategies used to support Skyrail ITM have been developed through the experience of its parent company, Skyrail, which has over 100 employees. Indeed, Skyrail is viewed as the nursery for developing human resource strategies and practices and is an important source of staff for its Skyrail ITM operations. The human resource strategy is to develop best-practice management processes and controls to ensure the highest quality staff and performance outcomes. Underpinning this is an annual planning process, with six-monthly reviews, to identify the ongoing and future skills requirements and the quantity of staff necessary for Skyrail ITM.

From this planning process, Skyrail ITM either identifies specific individuals for progression within the organisation or looks to the external labour market to meet its human resource requirements. With external recruitment, the company makes a conscious decision on where such staff should be recruited and how. Senior positions are often filled through this means, particularly where a certain skill set is required (such as information technology and engineering specialists) that does not exist within the company.

Remuneration planning is undertaken at the same time as recruitment and selection planning. Skyrail ITM sets remuneration levels for most of its middle to senior level positions using the local industry standard and Brisbane, the closest metropolitan centre, as benchmarks. Line staff positions are paid at the local market rates. While remuneration levels are competitive, Skyrail ITM motivates its staff through its participative, team-working culture and internal recognition of staff performance, which includes performance-related bonuses.

In addition, each staff member, on completion of a three-month probationary period, has his or her own career path development plan formulated in consultation with senior management and reviewed quarterly. These plans demonstrate management's long-term commitment to their staff, which is repaid by employees through their loyalty to the company. This is reflected in very low staff turnover rates, national recognition for its high standard of customer service and high scores on staff morale surveys.

The promotion of individual staff development through Skyrail ITM's organisational culture is important for controlling staff behaviour and organisational outcomes. Much of this is contained in staff manuals, policies and procedures regarding issues such as training and development, performance bonuses, team working and flexible working practices. In addition, every manager is assessed on a 'balanced scorecard basis', which means that they must undertake a broad range of management actions and meet a diversity of objectives. This management system has been accredited as ISO 9001:2000 certified, making Skyrail ITM the only cableway in the world to have this certification and one of the first businesses in the world to have been accredited under the new 9001:2000 series. The general manager for Skyrail ITM in Cairns notes that the company 'now has a fully documented plan which ensures that a review and improve process is continued on a regular basis so that Skyrail ITM operates to a world class standard'. The quality management system, ISO 9001:2000, ensures that Skyrail ITM's visitors receive a consistently high-quality experience that exceeds customer expectations.

This accredited management system requires that the following tasks be undertaken:
- Six-monthly staff surveys must be conducted to measure the effectiveness of the organisational culture and staff morale.
- Annual performance appraisals must be conducted requiring the completion of an individual development sheet and strategy that is reviewed on a quarterly basis.
- Formal scheduled monthly meetings must be held to communicate and reinforce the corporate vision to staff.
- Non-arbitrary performance-based pay reviews must be undertaken.
- Intra- and inter-departmental training programs must be arranged in order to expand staff skill sets and knowledge.
- Succession planning must be undertaken for all staff positions.

Skyrail ITM traineeships form an important part of overall organisational and human resource planning, allowing staff to advance through the company in a structured way. The Skyrail ITM board of directors continually monitors and assesses the outcomes of the traineeships. For more senior staff, postgraduate management degrees, such as MBAs, and specialised management development programs are sourced from outside the organisation.

Skyrail ITM's success is based around the selection of a good product, a strong business structure and planning process, and a carefully selected and nurtured staff. This produces the organisational commitment that consistently delivers world-class service levels to the thousands of domestic and international tourists that visit Skyrail ITM attractions every year.[36]

QUESTIONS

1. Who would be Skyrail ITM's major competitors and what threat would they pose to the company?
2. Why is human resource planning considered to be so critical to Skyrail's success?
3. What types of organisational control methods have Skyrail ITM used to ensure high performance, and should they change them as the geographical scope of the business expands?
4. What benefits does a quality management system, such as ISO 9001:2000, give a company such as Skyrail ITM? How would you use this expertise to financially benefit the company?

CHAPTER 8

CHAPTER 8

Strategic management

CHAPTER 8 STUDY QUESTIONS

▸ What are the foundations of strategic competitiveness?

▸ What is strategic management?

▸ What types of strategies are used by organisations?

▸ How are strategies formulated?

▸ What are current issues in strategy implementation?

Virgin Blue — think global but act local

The success of Virgin Blue, Australia's new low-fare passenger airline, can be attributed to its global approach to business — represented by its worldwide Virgin insignia — combined with its ability to act, operate and brand itself locally. The 'Blue' component to its company name represents this localised response and cleverly exploits Australians' strong association of the word with patriotism and integrity. Of course, 'Virgin' is one of the most valuable global brands and is used worldwide to sell a broad range of products and services — mobile phones, CDs, videos, airline travel and vacations, passenger railway services, television and radio broadcasting, and even cola. The Virgin brand is strongly associated with being dynamic, young, 'cool', easy to use and value for money.

Virgin entered the Australian domestic passenger market in 2000. Operating with just a handful of leased aircraft and flying only the major routes — Melbourne to Sydney and Melbourne to Brisbane — it represented a small presence in a deregulated airline industry in which there were three other major competitors — Qantas, Ansett and Impulse. However, a dramatic change in the domestic aviation market presented Virgin Blue with an opportunity to rapidly accelerate its expansion strategy in Australia. In 2001, within the space of six months, both Impulse and the 60-year-old Ansett Airlines ceased operation. Impulse was absorbed into the large Qantas operation and Ansett was declared bankrupt after a failed attempt to re-launch the airline in 2002. Virgin Blue's strategy is to gain a 30 per cent share of the domestic airline market by 2005 and to establish an international service that will supply increased passenger numbers for its domestic operation.[1]

Will Virgin Blue be able to succeed in the face of competition from Qantas? Learn as much as you can about Virgin Blue www.virginblue.com.au and competitors such as Qantas www.qantas.com.au. What are the risks of an aggressive growth strategy? Enter the world of the corporate strategist.

GET CONNECTED!

The no-frills strategy used by Virgin Blue has applications in a wide range of industries. Australia's Seven Television Network established a no-frills pay television sports service, C7. Subscriber growth was driven through lower rates, helped by programming costs that were substantially less than those charged by its rival, Foxtel. Even though there was an abundance of program content available locally and internationally, Seven's strategy was held up for a number of years through a legal dispute with the Foxtel shareholders — Rupert Murdoch's News Corporation, Kerry Packer's Publishing and Broadcasting Limited (PBL) and Telstra — to gain access to Foxtel's cable after commercial negotiations had failed. The Australian Competition and Consumer Commission ruled that cable operators had to open up their networks to third parties. This decision paved the way for competition in the pay television market.

Although C7 was granted access to Telstra's broadband cable in 2002, it clashed with Telstra over a technical matter; then in March 2002, Optus and Austar ceased to carry C7's sports channels. Consequently, C7 was forced to discontinue operation, and its future remains uncertain.

Seven's goal of becoming a multimedia company with free-to-air broadcasting, pay television services, interactive broadcasting, home shopping and T-mail (television mail using interactive television) was opposed by its competitors, but its chief executive, Kerry Stokes, was determined to pursue this technology-led strategy. Stokes had to compete against large, powerful corporations in much the same way that Virgin has in the airline, mobile phone and music retail industries. The C7 example demonstrates the competitive nature of TV broadcasting and the influence that other companies can have on the success of your business, particularly if you are reliant on their technology and services to deliver your product to the consumer.[2]

The stories at Virgin Blue and the Seven Network can be told and retold for most organisations operating in any industry. Similar forces and challenges confront managers in all settings. As an increasing number of industries are being deregulated and government companies, such as gas and electricity utilities, are privatised, more organisations are being exposed to market forces. Consequently, more than ever, today's environment places a great premium on effective 'strategy' and 'strategic management' as prerequisites for organisational success. Strategy formulation must become an important part of all senior managers' work.

SUSTAINABLE STRATEGIC COMPETITIVENESS

A **competitive advantage** allows an organisation to deal with market and environment forces better than its competitors.

Competitive advantage arises when an organisation acquires or develops an attribute or combination of attributes that allows it to outperform its competitors. These attributes can include access to natural resources, such as high-grade ores or inexpensive power, or access to highly trained and skilled personnel — human resources. New technologies such as robotics and information technology — either to be included as part of the product, or to assist in making it — are often important sources of competitive advantage. For example, Dyson Limited's dual cyclone vacuum cleaner technology has allowed it to make substantial inroads into the vacuum cleaner market, while many companies are attempting to copy the technology. In Australia and New Zealand considerable advances in agricultural technologies have given the livestock, sugar cane and wine industries a competitive advantage over their international rivals. This has also been the case for the nickel, copper and strategic metals and energy resources industries, where companies like Comalco have patented numerous techniques for improving efficiency and quality. The aim for any organisation, however, is not just to achieve competitive advantage but to make it sustainable in spite of competitors' attempts to copy or duplicate a success story.

Sustainable competitive advantage is the hallmark of successful companies such as Sony, Volkswagen, Dyson and Fisher & Paykel. In all these companies, technological leadership has been central to the strategy of sustainable competitive advantage and has been driven by senior management with almost crusading zeal and passion. Sustainable competitive advantage can also be achieved through applying technologies developed by other industries. For example, in Australia and New Zealand the supermarket chain Woolworths has used continuous IT improvement and a strong customer focus as a centrepiece of its corporate strategies.

Achieving and sustaining competitive advantage is a challenging task for even the largest organisations, all of which are very aware that new technologies, changes in the global economy or world geopolitics, and sudden shifts in consumer demand could lead to their demise. Even the chief executive of Microsoft, Bill Gates, has publicly admitted that he constantly fears that new computer software from competitors could fatally harm his company. Indeed, the history of capitalism is littered with examples of corporate extinction. For example, in 1950 there were more than 100 car manufacturers in the USA and more than 60 in the United Kingdom. Today, there are fewer than ten major car manufacturers worldwide. Many ceased operation, while others such as Australian-owned Holden were taken over by companies such as General Motors, which expanded globally through acquisition.

ENTREPRENEURSHIP

Gippsland Aeronautics •
www.gippsaero.com

Finding a niche in the aircraft industry

Pursuing the goals of low price, low maintenance costs and high customer service has been a highly successful strategy for Australia's only commercial aircraft manufacturer, Gippsland Aeronautics. The company has more than 100 staff and produces about 55 aircraft a year at its factory in Victoria. Marketing director, Michael Hall, reveals that the Victorian-designed GA-8 Airvan fills tourist operators' desire for low-cost, easy-to-run and affordable-to-maintain aircraft to replace their ageing fleets. The Australian dollar also makes the aircraft attractive to overseas buyers. The USA and Canada are particularly important markets for the company. The company has also supplied several defence forces in the Asia–Pacific region.

The challenge for Gippsland Aeronautics is to maintain its success in the future. The external challenges will relate to exchange rates (the current value of the Australian dollar favours exporters) and the robustness of the global economy. The internal challenge will be to continue its success in designing and manufacturing affordable, low-maintenance aircraft that have technology appropriate for the end users. The company's continued success will rest on clearly identifying its niche market, exploiting future niche opportunities and establishing a clear vision about future tactics and actions.

Competition tends to destroy competition, leading to a concentration of ownership and control in many industries. The telecommunications, insurance, airline, retailing and multi-media industries will have fewer players as the process of competition 'weeds out' the weaker organisations. How many of today's big corporate names will be tomorrow's dino-saurs? Which ones will cease to operate or be swallowed up by their competitors? In other words, which organisations have the right strategy to survive and have a sustainable future? This process is not unlike what the 19th century UK scientist Charles Darwin described for the biological world in his seminal book *The Origin of Species by Means of Natural Selection*. Hannan and Freeman have developed a very similar argument for the organisational world, which they call the 'population ecology of organisations'.[3]

What is sustainability?

The buzzword in many organisations today is 'sustainability', but what does it really mean? In Australia, New Zealand, North America and many European nations sustainability is a focus for a new value debate about the shape of the future. While there is agreement about the need for sustainability there is great debate about the best path to take organisations forward.

Sustainability results from activities that:

- extend the productive life of organisations and maintain high levels of corporate performance
- maintain decent levels of welfare for present and future generations of humanity
- enhance society's ability to maintain itself to solve its major problems
- enhance the planet's ability to maintain and renew the viability of the biosphere and protect all living species.

While many organisations remain preoccupied with extending their productive life and maintaining high profitability, an increasing number of organisations are proactive in dealing with the other three activities. Many Scandinavian, German and New Zealand com-panies, such as Ikea, Siemens, Daimler Chrysler and Fisher & Paykel, are at the forefront of this trend. Von Weizsacker and others in their book, *Factor 4: Doubling Wealth, Halving Resource Use*, provide many examples of businesses that have quadrupled their productivity while halving their resource use. Rather than reducing productivity and profits, an increasing number of organisations are discovering that embracing sustainability actually enhances these outcomes.[4] Developing a strategy is an important part of achieving such goals.

Some organisations have vigorously pursued a goal of zero emissions, or in other words eliminating all waste or recycling it. The Japanese brewing company Kirin has reached zero emissions at its Nagoya brewery. Beer spillage is used as livestock feed, yeast is recycled for pharmaceuticals, and other by-products that used to be discarded are now sold to other organisations.[5]

Through eliminating waste, recycling and developing environmentally friendly pro-duction processes, products and services it is possible to 'reduce the footprint' of our activi-ties on the planet. Recycling has been the most frequently used method in Australasia, with Australian companies such as R-recycle Australia using US technology to process worn vehicle tyres. The outcome is a highly versatile product that offers better performance in items such as retreads, shoes and conveyor belts, while cutting material costs by up to 30 per cent. With 18 million tyres thrown away in Australia each year, the waste represents a valuable new resource.[6]

There are enormous differences in the readiness of organisations to develop and implement sustainable competitive practices. Some organisations are highly advanced in investment in their human capital through educating, training and developing their staff, but have devoted meagre or no resources to ecological sustainability. In other organisations the reverse applies. So far, very few have vigorously pursued both. Pressure to pursue greater ecological sustainability has come from political parties, such as the Greens, and from government-funded institutions. For example, a Victorian government-supported initiative called Experimenta's Waste program explores and highlights the excesses of contemporary culture — environmental waste, technical obsolescence and historical residue. It argues that the products and ideas that a society discards reveal a great deal about its priorities. Visit them at www.experimenta.org.

The simultaneous processes of industrialisation and urbanisation have created the large cities in which much of the population lives. Even in a large country such as Australia with a population of less than 20 million, 85 per cent of the population lives in cities, and 60 per cent lives in the five largest capital cities. In the last 200 years an extraordinary global process of urbanisation has occurred, driven by the rapid expansion and development of the Western market economy. Business growth and urban growth have gone hand in hand. In 1800, there were only two cities in the world with a population of more than one million people — London and Beijing — and the world's 100 largest cities had a total population of 20 million. In 2000, the world's 100 largest cities accommodated 600 million people.[7] Today we do not live in a civilisation, we live in a 'globalisation' — globalisation of resources, globalisation of business activity, globalisation of humanity. And developing nations such as China, Korea, Malaysia, Indonesia and Thailand want to be part of this globalisation.

Cities in the developing world now look like New York or Sydney and the industries, buildings and transportation systems depend on fossil fuels such as oil, gas and coal. Do businesses need to dig deeper into the Earth's crust to provide the resources? Is it acceptable for companies to fill containers with consumable goods and transport them halfway around the world to be used for a couple of weeks and end up as landfill? Sustainability is about calculating human impact on the future, based on current activities. We have to look at the metabolism of our urban areas, viewing the cities as super-organisms in terms of resource use. Currently our cities and industries have an essentially linear metabolism — goods, water, fuel and food go in and then come out as waste materials at the other end. This is not sustainable in the long term. The key concept for the future is how to convert this linear metabolism into a loop or cyclical metabolism that minimises resource consumption and reduces waste. The difficulty is that on the one hand governments and businesses are increasingly supporting sustainable development, but on the other they are signed-up to economic growth.[8]

In the USA and Europe major achievements have been made in the field of recycling. For example, pulp mills are no longer built next to forests but next to cities because the raw material for new paper, such as disused clothing and old newspapers, accumulates there. Authorities in the modern Chinese city of Shanghai have a policy of ensuring that the vegetables eaten in the city come from the city. The authorities have ensured that half of the city area is set aside for the purpose of growing vegetables.

How can cities and industries, which are primarily the product of the availability of fossil fuels, develop energy systems to make them sustainable in the future? There are hybrid sustainable business solutions that use fossil fuels and passive and active solar energy to dramatically reduce energy consumption. However, the future lies with totally renewable energy. There are many prototype building and factory designs that demonstrate that it is possible to operate on solar, wind and recycled energy sources. For example, Denmark supplies 20 per cent of its entire electricity from wind power.[9]

Companies such as BP Solar www.bpsolar.com are also trying to encourage the adoption of renewable energy sources.

As the benefits of a sustainable approach for cities and industries are increasingly promoted, organisations are finding that renewing natural resources rather than wasting or degrading them, and investing in people rather than divesting them, also makes good business sense. These corporate strategies are the secret to creating the high-performance organisations of the future and will inevitably contribute to the sustainability of society and our general way of life.

Environmental concerns are crucial to global sustainability. Business, governments and individuals must consider the metabolism of industries and cities, turning this metabolism from a linear process — consuming resources and generating waste — to something cyclical — renewable resources and recycling waste. The abundance of sunshine in Australia and New Zealand gives them an opportunity to become world leaders in the development of solar-powered industries and cities in the 21st century. Governments can play an important role in encouraging this through subsidies, tax incentives and education.

SOCIAL RESPONSIBILITY

IKEA • www.ikea.co

Social responsibility through environmental goal setting

Swedish-based multinational IKEA has major retail outlets in Europe, North America, Asia and Australia. Since the 1990s, IKEA has established a systematic approach to environmental issues as part of its corporate social responsibility strategy. The company follows a

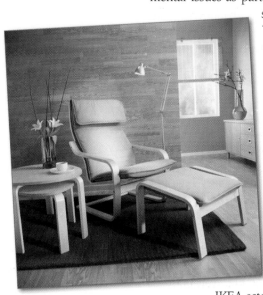

step-by-step approach to improving its environmental performance. The Natural Step program includes three-year plans that set out clear objectives against which the company's performance can be measured and managed. The current three-year plan, covering 2000–03, has identified the following areas for improvement:

- resource use reduction and increased use of recycled and reusable materials
- acquisition of forest products from the Forestry Stewardship Council's certified timber plantations
- adherence by all IKEA suppliers to the company's four-point supplier environmental accreditation scheme that was developed in Sweden
- measurement of the environmental impact of transporting IKEA products, including greenhouse gas emissions and fossil fuel depletion
- waste reduction and improved energy efficiency targets for retail outlets.

IKEA established cross-functional project teams to identify environmental issues and assist in integrating environmental policies and practices across the company. The Natural Step program adopts a cascading model for the diffusion of these practices in the organisation. Managers undertake the program, followed by employees, so that everyone in the company develops a shared understanding of emerging strategies.[10]

What is organisational strategy?

Canadian management researcher Henry Mintzberg describes organisational **strategy** as 'a pattern in a stream of decisions'.[11] This decision-based concept of strategy has two important implications. First, strategy is not necessarily apparent from the analysis of just one decision, because it must be viewed in the context of several decisions and the consistency among the decisions. Second, the organisation must be aware of decision alternatives in all of its decisions. A deliberate strategy can be contained in a formal document that identifies long-term goals and outlines resource use to accomplish them. These are useful in focusing attention on the competitive environment and indicating how corporate objectives can be secured even as conditions alter.

Importantly, a strategy provides the plan for allocating and using resources with consistent **strategic intent** — that is, with all organisational energies directed toward a unifying and compelling target or goal.[12] At Coca-Cola, for example, strategic intent has been described as: 'to put a Coke within "arm's reach" of every consumer in the world'. Given the focus provided by this strategic intent, we would not expect Coca-Cola to be diversifying by investing in snack foods, as does its arch-rival PepsiCo.

In our fast-paced world of globalisation and changing technologies, the 'long-term' aspect of strategy is becoming ever shorter. As it does so, the challenges to the strategist become even greater. It used to be that companies could count on traditional 'build-and-sell' business models that put them in control. In the early days of the automobile industry, for example, Henry Ford once said: 'The customer can have any color he wants as long as it's black'. His firm, quite literally, was in the driver's seat. Today things have changed and strategy is increasingly driven by customers and flexibility. Says John M. Jordan, director of e-commerce research for Ernst & Young: 'Customers are calling the shots, telling companies what they want, and companies have to respond to those desires or lose out'. Stephen Haeckel, director of strategic studies at IBM's Advanced Business Institute, describes the shift in approach this way: 'It's a difference between a bus, which follows a set route, and a taxi, which goes where customers tell it to go'.[13]

> A **strategy** is a pattern in a stream of organisational decisions.

> **Strategic intent** focuses and applies organisational energies on a unifying and compelling goal.

Strategic management

For companies such as BHP Billiton, Coles Myer, Harvey Norman, Fisher & Paykel, Hyundai, Sony and even Gippsland Aeronautics, devising strategy may seem a deceptively simple task. Find out what customers want, then develop or use the appropriate production or product technologies to deliver it to them at an affordable price and with the best service. In practice this task is made risky because of the uncertainties and unpredictability of global markets. Every strategist must remember that at the same time they are trying to create competitive advantage for an organisation, competitors are always attempting to do the same. This gives rise to demands for strategies that can be called 'bold', 'aggressive', 'fast-moving' and 'innovative'. But call them what you will, strategies don't just happen. They must be created. And strategies alone don't automatically bring success. They must be both well chosen and well implemented.

Strategic management is the process of formulating and implementing strategies to accomplish long-term goals and sustain competitive advantage. The essence of strategic management is looking ahead, understanding the environment and the organisation, and effectively positioning the organisation for competitive advantage in changing times. Chief executives must think strategically as they try to position their organisations for new 21st-century markets. They must think strategically in deciding how to use new technologies to maximum advantage. They must think strategically in deciding how to take advantage of the global economy. And, they must think strategically where it really counts — in respect to what customers and clients really want.

> **Strategic management** is the process of formulating and implementing strategies.

Strategic management goals

Michael Porter, Harvard scholar and strategy consultant, says that 'sound strategy starts with having the right goal'.[14] He argues that the ultimate goal for any business should be superior profitability. This creates value for investors in the form of **above-average returns**, returns that exceed what an investor could earn by investing in alternative opportunities of equivalent risk.[15] At PepsiCo, this goal is stated as: 'To increase the value of our shareholder's investment'.

⚙ **Above-average returns**
exceed what could be
earned from alternative
investments of equivalent
risk.

The nature of the competition within an organisation's environment largely determines whether above-average returns are achievable. An understanding of the organisation's markets is crucial for setting strategic management goals. Good economic analysis is therefore essential. Indeed, Michael Porter has long recognised that the roots of the structural and market analysis within strategic management lie within economics.[16]

Organisations compete in environments that vary according to their market structures. Where a *monopoly environment* exists there is only one organisation and no competition. This creates absolute competitive advantage, delivering sustainable and probably excessive business profits. This absolute competitive advantage may not be in the public interest — lack of consumer choice and high prices are the likely outcomes. Consequently, most Western governments have passed legislation preventing or limiting monopolies. For example, the Australian Competition and Consumer Commission investigates market dominance and competitive activity that is contrary to the Australian public interest.

Until recently, most monopolies in Australia and New Zealand were government-owned organisations accountable to the people through the democratic process. With the privatisation of many of these organisations, in industries such as telecommunications, transportation and energy retailing, private monopolies have been created that have little or no accountability. To provide accountability their market structures must be changed to be more competitive, but in many cases this has been difficult to achieve. Some economists have called for the re-nationalisation of these companies to better serve the public interest, rather than making monopoly profits for their shareholders.

An *oligopoly environment* or oligopolistic competition is a market where a small number of competitors feel themselves constrained more by the actions of their rivals than by those of their customers. Organisations within an oligopoly sustain long-term competitive advantages within defined market segments. In the absence of competition within these segments, they can reap excessive business profits. Aircraft manufacturers, major machine tool producers, defence manufacturers, national newspapers, photographic film manufacturers, natural resource extraction operations and segments of the food manufacturing industry are in an oligopolistic environment. Aircraft manufacture is a particularly good example, where the European consortium Airbus Industrie and the US-based Boeing need to keep a close eye on each other's actions if they are to prosper. This often leads to industrial espionage, with Airbus Industrie claiming that the US government uses its intelligence-gathering organisations, such as the CIA, to obtain confidential information about its operations for its competitor.

An effective understanding of the principles of game theory therefore becomes a critical skill of the strategist under oligopoly. They need to guess correctly what a rival's response to a price change will be; to understand when a new entrant to the industry should be accommodated rather than driven out; and to know when to collude with a rival, either explicitly or implicitly, rather than fighting a cut-throat action. The domestic airline industry in Australia, with its rivalry between Qantas and Virgin Blue, constitutes a duopoly — a form of oligopolistic competition.

The global economy has helped to create for many businesses today an *environment of hypercompetition*.[17] This is an environment in which there are at least several players who

REALITY CHECK

**B2B changes the world
of outsourcing**

It is reported that
businesses purchasing
supplies in online
auctions save as much
as 20 per cent. To date
the biggest users are
found in the computer
and electronics industry.

*What are the downsides
of outsourcing?*

directly compete with one another. An example is the fast-food industry where McDonald's, KFC, Pizza Hut and many other restaurant chains all compete for largely the same customers. Because the competition is direct and intense, any competitive advantage that is realised is temporary. Successful strategies are often copied and organisations must continue to find new strategies that deliver new sources of competitive advantage, even while trying to defend existing ones. In hypercompetition, there are always some winners and losers. Business profits can be attractive but intermittent. The customer generally gains in this environment through lower prices and more product/service innovation.

In the Internet search engine market, Google www.google.com has emerged as the world's most popular choice, handling more than 2000 queries every second. Since its 1998 debut, Google — nimble, streamlined and reliable in returning relevant results — has set a benchmark in search technology. Its strategy was to design a search engine that directly serves the interest of the consumer first, and the advertiser second. Currently, Google's market leadership is unchallenged, but inevitably there will be a technological challenge to its position in the competitive search engine market.

THE STRATEGIC MANAGEMENT PROCESS

Strategic management is successful when organisations, even those operating in environments of hypercompetition, achieve sustainable competitive advantage and earn above-average returns. Successful strategies are crafted from insightful understandings of the competitive environment as well as intimate knowledge of the organisation. And they are implemented with commitment and resolution. Figure 8.1 describes a series of steps involved in fulfilling the two major responsibilities of the strategic management process — strategy formulation and strategy implementation.

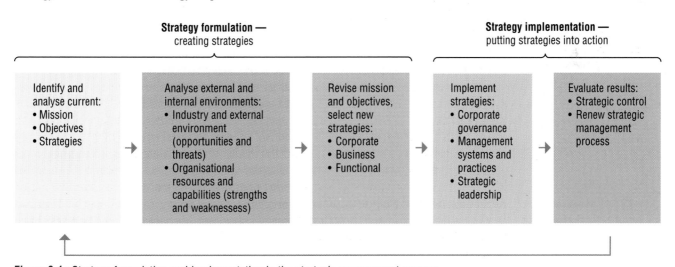

Figure 8.1 ▸ Strategy formulation and implementation in the strategic management process

The first strategic management responsibility is **strategy formulation**, the process of creating strategy. This involves assessing existing strategies, the organisation and your environment to develop new strategies and strategic plans capable of delivering future competitive advantage. Peter Drucker associates this process with a set of five strategic questions: *What is our business mission? Who are our customers? What do our customers consider value? What have been our results? What is our plan?*[18]

Strategy formulation is the process of creating strategies.

Strategy implementation is the process of putting strategies into action.

The second strategic management responsibility is **strategy implementation**, the process of allocating resources and putting strategies into action. Once strategies are created, they must be successfully acted upon to achieve the desired results. As Drucker says, 'The future will not just happen if one wishes hard enough. It requires decision — now. It imposes risk — now. It requires action — now. It demands allocation of resources, and above all, of human resources — now. It requires work — now.'[19] This is the responsibility for putting strategies and strategic plans into action. Every organisational and management system must be mobilised to support and reinforce the accomplishment of strategies. Scarce resources must be used for maximum impact on performance. All of this, in turn, requires a commitment to mastering the full range of strategic management tasks posed in Manager's Notepad 8.1.[20]

MANAGER'S NOTEPAD 8.1

Five strategic management tasks

1. Identify organisational mission and objectives.
   Ask: 'What business are we in? Where do we want to go?'

2. Assess current performance in relation to mission and objectives.
   Ask: 'How well are we currently doing?'

3. Create strategic plans to accomplish purpose and objectives.
   Ask: 'How can we get where we really want to be?'

4. Implement the strategic plans.
   Ask: 'Has everything been done that needs to be done?'

5. Evaluate results; change strategic plans and/or implementation processes as necessary.
   Ask: 'Are things working out as planned? What can be improved?'

Analysis of mission, values and objectives

The strategic management process begins with a careful assessment and clarification of organisational mission, values and objectives.[21] A clear sense of mission and objectives sets the stage for critically assessing the organisation's resources and capabilities as well as competitive opportunities and threats in the external environment.

MISSION

The **mission** is the organisation's reason for existence in society.

As first discussed in chapter 1, the **mission** or purpose of an organisation may be described as its reason for existence in society. Strategy consultant Michael Hammer believes that a mission should represent what the strategy or underlying business model is trying to accomplish. He suggests asking: 'What are we moving to?' 'What is our dream?' 'What kind of a difference do we want to make in the world?'[22]

Successful organisations have a clear sense of vision and mission and they use their resources with a clear strategic purpose. For example, Foster's has a vision of 'inspiring global enjoyment', 'whether through beer, wine, spirits, leisure or property'. The company's corporate mission is: 'To work together, respecting each other, our heritage, diversity, skills and knowledge to: build premium quality, first-choice brands; deliver service excellence to customers and consumers; generate superior returns for shareholders; create an inspiring workplace; and be welcomed in the communities in which we operate'.[23]

The Special Broadcasting Service (SBS), Australia's very successful multicultural and multi-lingual public broadcaster, was established with the mission to give voice and exposure to multicultural Australia. Specifically, the broadcaster was established by the federal government to define, facilitate and promote Australia's cultural heterogeneity in accordance with their charter obligation. Fisher & Paykel's mission is 'to seek profitable growth by designing, manufacturing and marketing a range of appliances that care for the needs of our customers'.[24]

The Australian natural resources firm, Comalco, which is owned by the global resource giant RTZ, strives to achieve world-class capability in its three core business areas: bauxite mining, alumina refining and aluminium smelting. It has pursued a strategy to be the best performer in health, safety and environment, cost and productivity in its industry. The ways in which staff work together and assets are used well are vital for Comalco's success. However, strategic initiatives can often create conflict with stakeholders and, in Comalco's case, its employment strategy of direct communication with staff, effectively bypassing the trade unions, has led to a series of industrial disputes over the past ten years. Its strident union avoidance strategy has locked it into conflict with the CFMEU (Construction, Forestry, Mining and Energy Union), which represents workers in the mining industry.[25]

A good *mission statement* identifies the *domain* in which the organisation intends to operate — including the customers it intends to serve, the *products* and/or *services* it intends to provide, and the *location* in which it intends to operate. The mission statement should also communicate the underlying philosophy that will guide employees in these operations. Consider the mission statement for Merck, one of the world's leading pharmaceutical companies: 'To provide society with superior products and services — innovations and solutions that improve the quality of life and satisfy customer needs; to provide employees with meaningful work and advancement opportunities, and investors with a superior rate of return'.[26]

An important test of corporate purpose and mission is how well it serves the organisation's **stakeholders**. You should recall that these are individuals and groups — including customers, shareholders, suppliers, creditors, community groups and others, who are directly affected by the organisation and its strategic accomplishments. In the strategic management process, the stakeholder test can be done as a strategic constituencies analysis. Here, the specific interests of each stakeholder are assessed along with the organisation's record in responding to them. Figure 8.2 gives an example of how stakeholder interests can be reflected in a mission statement.

Stakeholders are individuals, groups and institutions directly affected by an organisation's performance.

Figure 8.2 ▸ External stakeholders and the mission statement

CORE VALUES

Behaviour in and by organisations will always be affected in part by *values*, which are broad beliefs about what is or is not appropriate. **Organisational culture** was first defined in chapter 2 as the predominant value system of the organisation as a whole.[27] Through organisational cultures, the values of managers and other members are shaped and pointed in common directions. In strategic management, the presence of strong core values for an organisation helps build institutional identity. It gives character to an organisation in the eyes of its employees and external stakeholders, and it backs up the mission statement. Shared values also help guide the behaviour of organisation members in meaningful and consistent ways. For example, Merck backs up its mission with a public commitment to core values that include preservation and improvement of human life, scientific excellence, ethics and integrity, and profits from work that benefits humanity. Intel backs up its mission by stating values such as customer orientation, results orientation, risk taking, great place to work, quality and discipline.

OBJECTIVES

Whereas a mission statement sets forth an official purpose for the organisation and the core values describe appropriate standards of behaviour for its accomplishment, **operating objectives** direct activities toward key and specific performance results. These objectives are shorter-term targets against which actual performance results can be measured as indicators of progress and continuous improvement. Any and all operating objectives should have clear means–end linkages to the mission and purpose. Any and all strategies should, in turn, offer clear and demonstrable opportunities to accomplish operating objectives. According to Peter Drucker, the *operating objectives of a business* might include the following:[28]

- *profitability* — producing at a net profit in business
- *market share* — gaining and holding a specific market share
- *human talent* — recruiting and maintaining a high-quality workforce
- *financial health* — acquiring capital; earning positive returns
- *cost efficiency* — using resources well to operate at low cost
- *product quality* — producing high-quality goods or services
- *innovation* — developing new products and/or processes
- *social responsibility* — making a positive contribution to society.

Analysis of organisational resources and capabilities

Two critical steps in the strategic management process are analysis of the organisation and analysis of its environment. They may be approached by a technique known as **SWOT analysis** — the internal analysis of organisational **S**trengths and **W**eaknesses as well as the external analysis of environmental **O**pportunities and **T**hreats.

As shown in figure 8.3, a SWOT analysis begins with a systematic evaluation of the organisation's resources and capabilities. A major goal is to identify **core competencies** in the form of special strengths that the organisation has or where it does exceptionally well in comparison with competitors. They are capabilities that by virtue of being rare, costly to imitate, and non-substitutable become viable sources of competitive advantage.[29] Core competencies may be found in special knowledge or expertise, superior technologies, efficient manufacturing technologies or unique product distribution systems, among many other possibilities. But always, and as with the notion of strategy itself, they must be viewed relative to the competition. Simply put, organisations need more competencies that do important things better than the competition and that are very difficult for competitors to duplicate.

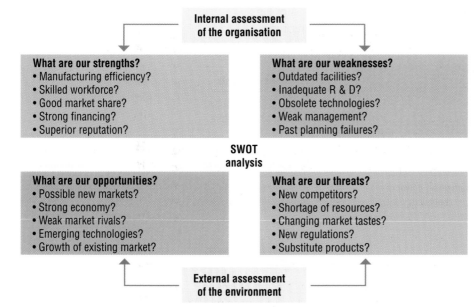

Figure 8.3 ▸ SWOT analysis of strengths, weaknesses, opportunities and threats

Figure 8.3 highlights several reference points for the internal analysis of organisational strengths. Organisational weaknesses, of course, are the other side of the picture. They can also be found in the same or related areas and must be identified to gain a realistic perspective on the formulation of strategies. The goal in strategy formulation is to create strategies that leverage core competencies for competitive advantage by building upon organisational strengths and minimising the impact of weaknesses.

Analysis of industry and environment

A SWOT analysis is not complete until opportunities and threats in the external environment are also analysed. They can be found among *macroenvironment* factors such as technology, government, social structures and population demographics, the global economy, and the natural environment. They can also include developments in the *industry environment* of resource suppliers, competitors and customers. As shown in figure 8.3, opportunities may exist as possible new markets, a strong economy, weaknesses in competitors and emerging technologies. Weaknesses may be identified in such things as the emergence of new competitors, resource scarcities, changing customer tastes and new government regulations, among other possibilities.

In respect to the external environment as a whole, the more stable and predictable it is, the more likely that a good strategy can be implemented with success for a longer period of time. But when the environment is composed of many dynamic elements that create uncertainties, more flexible strategies that change with time are needed. Given the nature of competitive environments today, strategic management must be considered an ongoing process in which strategies are formulated, implemented, revised and implemented again in a continuous manner.

Michael Porter offers the five forces model shown in figure 8.4 as a way of adding sophistication to this analysis of the environment.[30] His framework for competitive industry analysis directs attention toward understanding the following forces:

1. *industry competitors* — intensity of rivalry among firms in the industry
2. *new entrants* — threats of new competitors entering the market

Porter's five competitive forces

3. *suppliers* — bargaining power of suppliers
4. *customers* — bargaining power of buyers
5. *substitutes* — threats of substitute products or services.

Figure 8.4 ▸ Porter's model of five strategic forces affecting industry competition

Source: Developed from Michael E. Porter, *Competitive Strategy* (New York: Free Press, 1980).

From Porter's perspective, the foundations for any successful strategy rest with a clear understanding of these competitive environmental forces. He calls this the 'industry structure'. The strategic management challenge is to position an organisation strategically within its industry, taking into account the implications of forces that make it more or less attractive. In general, an *unattractive industry* is one in which rivalry among competitors is intense, substantial threats exist in the form of possible new entrants and substitute products, and suppliers and buyers are very powerful in bargaining over such things as prices and quality. An *attractive industry*, by contrast, has less existing competition, few threats from new entrants or substitutes, and low bargaining power among suppliers and buyers.[31] By systematically analysing industry attractiveness in respect to the five forces, Porter believes that strategies can be chosen to give the organisation a competitive advantage relative to its rivals.

STRATEGIES USED BY ORGANISATIONS

The strategic management process encompasses the three levels of strategy shown in figure 8.5. Strategies are formulated and implemented at the organisational or corporate level, business level and functional level. All should be integrated in means–ends fashion to accomplish objectives and create sustainable competitive advantage.

Levels of strategy

⚙ A **corporate strategy** sets long-term direction for the total enterprise.

The level of **corporate strategy** directs the organisation as a whole toward sustainable competitive advantage. For a business it describes the scope of operations by answering the following *strategic question*: In what industries and markets should we compete? The purpose of corporate strategy is to set direction and guide resource allocations for the entire enterprise. In large, complex organisations like General Electric, corporate strategy identifies the different areas of business in which a company intends to compete. The organisation presently pursues business interests in aircraft engines, appliances, capital services, lighting, medical systems, broadcasting, plastics and power systems, for example. Typical strategic decisions at the corporate level relate to the allocation of resources for acquisitions, new business development, divestitures and the like across this business portfolio. Increasingly, corporate strategies for many businesses include an important role for global operations such as international joint ventures and strategic alliances.

Business strategy is the strategy for a single business unit or product line. It describes strategic intent to compete within a specific industry or market. Large conglomerates like General Electric, the biggest company in the world, are composed of many businesses, with many differences among them in product lines and even industries. The term **strategic business unit (SBU)** is often used to describe a single business or a component that operates with a separate mission within a larger enterprise. The selection of strategy at the business level involves answering the *strategic question*: How are we going to compete for customers in this industry and market? Typical business strategy decisions include choices about product/service mix, facilities locations, new technologies, and the like. In single-business enterprises, business strategy is the corporate strategy.

Functional strategy guides the use of organisational resources to implement business strategy. This level of strategy focuses on activities within a specific functional area of operations. Looking again at figure 8.5, the standard business functions of marketing, manufacturing, finance and research and development illustrate this level of strategy. The *strategic question* to be answered in selecting functional strategies becomes: How can we best utilise resources to implement our business strategy? Answers to this question typically involve the choice of progressive management and organisational practices that improve operating efficiency, product or service quality, customer service or innovativeness.

> ⌗ A **business strategy** identifies how a division or strategic business unit will compete in its product or service domain.
>
> ⌗ A **strategic business unit (SBU)** is a major business area that operates with some autonomy.
>
> ⌗ A **functional strategy** guides activities within one specific area of operations.

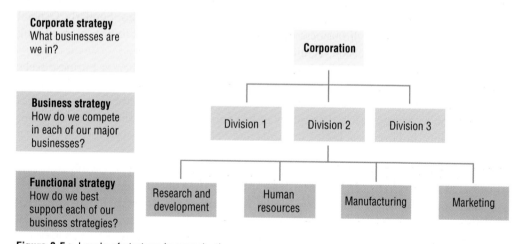

Corporate strategy
What businesses are we in?

Business strategy
How do we compete in each of our major businesses?

Functional strategy
How do we best support each of our business strategies?

Corporation

Division 1 · Division 2 · Division 3

Research and development · Human resources · Manufacturing · Marketing

Figure 8.5 ▸ Levels of strategy in organisations

Growth and diversification strategies

Traditionally one of the most common and popular of the grand or master strategies pursued by organisations at the corporate or business levels is growth.[32] **Growth strategies** pursue an increase in size and the expansion of current operations. They are popular in part because growth is viewed as necessary for long-run survival in some industries. One approach to growth is through **concentration**, where expansion is within the same business area. Bank of Queensland, for example, is pursuing an aggressive market share growth

> ⌗ **Growth strategies** involve expansion of the organisation's current operations.
>
> ⌗ Growth through **concentration** is within the same business area.

strategy to ensure long-term survival. It plans to grow by increasing activity among existing customers and by attracting new customers, particularly in regional Queensland. Currently, most of the bank's business is in home loans, but it sees potential to move into financing small- and medium-sized companies. The bank's traditional emphasis on personal service is central to its strategy. The four major Australian banks — the Commonwealth, National, Westpac and ANZ — are closing branches and rationalising and relocating many of their customer services to capital cities, but the Bank of Queensland is opening new branches in both urban and regional locations and providing a full range of services at these locations.

Another approach to growth is through **diversification**, where expansion takes place through the acquisition of or investment in new and sometimes different business areas. A strategy of *related diversification* involves growth by acquiring new businesses or entering business areas that are related to what the organisation already does. This strategy seeks the advantages of growth in areas that utilise core competencies and existing skills. For example, the Coles Myer retailing group has established a network of Officeworks superstores throughout Australia, including regional locations. Although Officeworks specialises in office stationery and equipment and photocopying services, the business is related to Coles Myer's expertise in the retail industry. A corporate strategy of *unrelated diversification* involves growth by acquiring businesses or entering business areas that are different to what the organisation already does. For example, before the creation of St.George Bank, the organisation was a building society providing mortgages for home buyers. It acquired banking status in order to offer a full range of financial services to consumers and commercial customers. Optus, a telecommunications company, has formed OptusTV in partnership with News Corporation's Foxtel, dominating the pay television industry. Occasionally, a company will invest in a market that is completely unrelated to its current operations. For example, the US-based conglomerate ITT, which designs and manufactures telecommunication equipment, purchased the Sheraton Hotels chain and several banks and insurance companies. Similarly, General Electric has a large number of business units across a diverse range of industries, including heavy engineering, jet propulsion, lighting, finance and transportation.

Diversification can also take the form of **vertical integration**, where a business seeks added value creation by acquiring suppliers (*backward vertical integration*) or distributors (*forward vertical integration*). In the automobile industry, backward vertical integration has been common as firms purchased suppliers of key parts to ensure quality and control over their availability. In beverages, both Coca-Cola and PepsiCo have pursued forward vertical integration by purchasing some of their major bottlers.

There is a tendency to equate growth with effectiveness, but that is not necessarily true. Any growth strategy, whether by concentration or some form of diversification, must be well planned and well managed to achieve the desired results. Increased size of operation in any form adds challenge to the management process. Diversification, in particular, brings the difficulties of complexity and the need to manage and integrate very dissimilar operations. Research indicates that business performance may decline with too much unrelated diversification.[33]

Restructuring and divestiture strategies

When organisations experience performance problems, perhaps due to unsuccessful diversification, retrenchment of some sort often takes place. The most extreme **retrenchment strategy** is *liquidation*, when operations cease due to the complete sale of assets or the declaration of bankruptcy. Less extreme but still of potential dramatic performance impact is **restructuring**. This changes the scale and/or mix of operations in order to gain efficiency and improve performance. The decision to restructure can be difficult for managers to make

Growth through **diversification** is by acquisition of or investment in new and different business areas.

Growth through **vertical integration** is by acquiring suppliers or distributors.

A **retrenchment strategy** involves reducing the scale of current operations.

Restructuring changes the scale and/or mix of operations to gain efficiency and improve performance.

because, at least on the surface, it seems to be an admission of failure. But in today's era of challenging economic conditions and environmental uncertainty, restructuring is used frequently and with new respect.

Restructuring is sometimes accomplished by **downsizing**, which decreases the size of operations with the intent to become more streamlined.[34] The expected benefits are reduced costs and improved operating efficiency. A common way to downsize is cutting the size of the workforce. Research has shown that such downsizing is most successful when the workforce is reduced strategically, or in a way that allows for better focusing of resources on key performance objectives.[35] Downsizing with a strategic focus is sometimes referred to as *rightsizing*. This contrasts with the less-well-regarded approach of simply cutting staff 'across the board'.

Restructuring by **divestiture** involves selling off parts of the organisation to refocus on core competencies, cut costs and improve operating efficiency. This is a common strategy for organisations that find they have become overdiversified and are encountering problems managing the complexity of diverse operations. It is also a way for organisations to take advantage of the value of internal assets by 'spinning off' or selling to shareholders a component that can stand on its own as an independent business. The Anglo-Australian company BHP Billiton has sold off its steel-making operation, now known as OneSteel, in order to concentrate on the core revenue earner and strategic direction of the company — resource extraction. Steel making used to be of strategic importance to the former BHP but became increasingly less important as global steel-making capacity outstripped demand and the world price fell. Low-cost competition from Japan, Korea, China and Taiwan further reduced the strategic importance of BHP's steel-making operations.

> **Downsizing** decreases the size of operations with the intent to become more streamlined.

> **Divestiture** sells off parts of the organisation to focus attention and resources on core business areas.

Cooperation in business strategies

In recent years increasing globalisation and regionalisation of markets has led to the dramatic growth of cross-border cooperation between companies. The steady reduction of trade barriers has been accompanied by considerable economic turbulence and uncertainty in world markets, and the spread of a high degree of trade liberalisation in most countries of the world. A major response to this has been the growth of **strategic alliances** and other forms of cooperative strategy between companies, particularly in technology and marketing. For Porter and Fuller, the basic motivation for an alliance is that: 'Coalitions that arise when performing a value chain activity with a partner are superior to any other way ... Coalitions can be a valuable tool in many aspects of global strategy, and the ability to exploit them will be an important source of international advantage.'[36]

> In **strategic alliances** organisations join together in partnership to pursue an area of mutual interest.

In chapter 5 on global dimensions of management, *international joint ventures* were discussed as a common form of international business and constitute one among many forms of strategic alliance. For example, in the airline industry most companies have entered into some form of strategic marketing alliance. Qantas, British Airways and American Airlines established Oneworld to give customers seamless access to global routes covering much of the Western world. A further five companies — Aer Lingus, Cathay Pacific, Finnair, Iberia and LanChile — joined the alliance, working together to give customers the best service possible. Check out Oneworld's marketing strategy at www.oneworld.com. In the television broadcasting industry, the British Broadcasting Corporation (BBC) and USA's Public Broadcasting Service (PBS) jointly produce numerous documentaries and dramas in order to share production costs and gain access to larger audiences. Similar alliances have been formed between the BBC and Discovery Channel. The Australian Broadcasting Corporation (ABC) and the BBC have jointly produced programming for use in their home markets and overseas, such as a special series of *The Bill*, which was filmed in Australia.

Another way to cooperate strategically is through outsourcing alliances — contracting to purchase important services from another organisation. Many organisations are outsourcing their payroll, recruitment, information technology and security functions to specialised companies. This is often driven by a combination of motives — the desire to reduce costs and to gain access to expertise that does not exist within the company. Supplier alliances, in which preferred supplier relationships ensure a smooth and timely flow of supplies among alliance partners, stem from cooperation in the supply chain. For example, car manufacturers such as General Motors and Ford relied on multisourcing during much of the 20th century, but in the 1980s began to develop supplier alliances which were necessary for their just-in-time (JIT) production system and to guarantee improved component quality.[37]

Distribution alliances are another cooperative approach. These involve organisations joining together to accomplish product or service sales and distribution. For example, Telstra and the USA's Cisco Systems have an alliance to jointly market Internet services to business customers. In Europe, the French electronics manufacturer, Thomson, and Japan's Matsushita established an alliance in the 1990s whereby Thomson would use their European marketing and sales network to sell the Japanese company's electrical products. While Thomson possessed expert knowledge of the European market, Matsushita had considerable expertise in efficient production of televisions, video recorders and music systems for a mass market.

POINT ←

COUNTER ↑

The ancient art of strategic thinking

Many strategic management authors argue that strategic thinking is a new phenomenon. But businesses have always adopted strategies to increase market share, increase profits or simply ensure long-term survival. The colonial trading companies of the 17th and 18th centuries, such as the Dutch East India Company, the Hudson Bay Company and the South Pacific Trading Company, devised and implemented strategies — often with the assistance of their home governments — to protect their access to suppliers and markets. In many cases, such as in India, China and Indonesia, colonial governments were willing to declare war to further the strategies of these companies. Successful companies throughout the history of mercantilism and capitalism have acted strategically to protect and further their interests. Today, the difference is that many organisations approach this in a more formal and structured way, with the agreed strategy contained in a lengthy written document and displayed on the organisation's web site. Strategic thinking is as ancient as humankind and has been evident in the actions and writings of army generals, rulers and businessmen for thousands of years. The most famous example is *The Art of War* by the Chinese author Sun Tzu, written over 2000 years ago.[38]

E-business strategies

⊘ An **e-business strategy** strategically uses the Internet to gain competitive advantage.

Without a doubt, one of the most frequently asked questions these days for the business executive is: 'What is your **e-business strategy**?' This is the strategic use of the Internet to gain competitive advantage.

Popular e-business strategies involve B2B (business-to-business) and B2C (business-to-customer) applications. *B2B business strategies* involve the use of IT and the Internet to vertically link organisations with members of their supply chains. One of the interesting developments in this area involves the use of online auctions as a replacement for preferred supplier relationships and outsourcing alliances. Organisations can now go to the Internet to participate in auction bidding for supplies of many types. Whether small or large in size they immediately have access to potential suppliers competing for their attention from around the world. One of the largest of the online auctioneers is Freemarkets.com. Participants in its auctions save an average of 20 per cent over their normal purchase prices.

B2C business strategies use IT and the Internet to link organisations with their customers. A common B2C strategy has already been illustrated several times in this chapter — *e-tailing* or the sale of goods directly to customers via the Internet. For some organisations, e-tailing is all that they do; these are 'new economy' organisations and the business strategy is focused entirely on Internet sales — examples include Amazon.com, priceline.com and Dell.com. For others, part of the traditional or 'old economy', e-tailing has been added as a component in their business strategy mix — including David Jones, Coles, Woolworths, ANZ and BNZ. By way of further introduction, Manager's Notepad 8.2 lists some of the web-based business models now being tried.[39]

MANAGER'S NOTEPAD 8.2

Web-based business models

- *Brokerage* — bringing buyers and sellers together to make transactions (e.g. eBay)
- *Advertising* — providing information or services while generating revenue from advertising (e.g. Yahoo!)
- *Merchant model* — selling products wholesale and retail through the Web, e-tailing (e.g. Shopfast.com)
- *Subscription model* — selling access to the site through subscription (e.g. *Australian Financial Review*)
- *Infomediary model* — collecting information on users and selling to other businesses (e.g. ePinions.com)
- *Community model* — supporting site by donations from a community of users (e.g. community arts and volunteer groups).

STRATEGY FORMULATION

Michael Porter says: 'The company without a strategy is willing to try anything'.[40] With a good strategy in place, by contrast, the resources of the entire organisation can be focused on the overall goal — superior profitability or above-average returns. Whether one is talking about building e-business strategies for the new economy or crafting strategies for more traditional operations, it is always important to remember this goal and the need for sustainable competitive advantage. The major *opportunities for competitive advantage* are found in the following areas, which should always be considered in the strategy formulation process:[41]

- *cost and quality* — where strategy drives an emphasis on operating efficiency and/or product or service quality
- *knowledge and speed* — where strategy drives an emphasis on innovation and speed of delivery to market for new ideas

Opportunities for sustainable competitive advantage

Dendy Cinemas and Dendy Distribution specialises in independent films that mainstream cinemas will not screen. Companies that offer a niche product to a small but distinct market segment are a common feature of an era in which consumers demand distinctive and differentiated products.

- *barriers to entry* — where strategy drives an emphasis on creating a market stronghold that is protected from entry by others
- *financial resources* — where strategy drives an emphasis on investments and/or loss sustainment that competitors can't match.

Importantly, any advantage gained in today's global and information-age economy of intense competition must always be considered temporary, at best. Things change too fast. Any advantage of the moment will sooner or later be eroded as new market demands, copy-cat strategies and innovations by rivals take their competitive toll over time.[42] The challenge of achieving sustainable competitive advantage is thus a dynamic one. Strategies must be continually revisited, modified and changed if the organisation is to keep pace with changing circumstances. Formulating strategy to provide overall direction for the organisation thus becomes an ongoing leadership responsibility.[43]

Fortunately, a number of strategic planning models or approaches are available to help executives in the strategy formulation process. At the business level, one should understand Porter's generic strategies model and product life cycle planning. At the corporate level, it is helpful to understand portfolio planning, adaptive strategies and incrementalism and emergent strategies.

Porter's generic strategies

Michael Porter's five forces model for industry analysis was introduced earlier. Use of the model helps answer the question: Is this an attractive industry for us to compete in? Within an industry, however, the initial strategic challenge becomes positioning one's organisation and products relative to competitors. The strategy question becomes: How can we best compete for customers in this industry?[44] Porter advises managers to answer this question by using his generic strategies framework shown in figure 8.6.

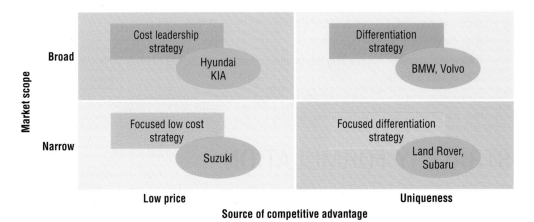

Figure 8.6 ▸ Porter's generic strategies framework: motor vehicle industry examples

According to Porter, business-level strategic decisions are driven by two basic factors: *market scope* — ask: 'How broad or narrow is your market target?'; and *source of competitive advantage* — ask: 'How will you compete for competitive advantage, by lower price or product uniqueness?' As shown in the figure, these factors combine to create the following four generic strategies that organisations can pursue. The examples in the figure and shown here are of competitive positions within the motor vehicle industry.

224   PART 3 | MISSION

1. *Differentiation* — where the organisation's resources and attention are directed toward distinguishing its products from those of the competition (for example, BMW, Volvo).
2. *Cost leadership* — where the organisation's resources and attention are directed toward minimising costs to operate more efficiently than the competition (for example, Hyundai, KIA).
3. *Focused differentiation* — where the organisation concentrates on one special market segment and tries to offer customers in that segment a unique product (for example, Land Rover, Subaru).
4. *Focused cost leadership* — where the organisation concentrates on one special market segment and tries in that segment to be the provider with lowest costs (for example, Suzuki).

Organisations pursuing a **differentiation strategy** seek competitive advantage through uniqueness. They try to develop goods and services that are clearly different from those made available by the competition. The objective is to attract customers who become loyal to the organisation's products and lose interest in those of competitors. This strategy requires organisational strengths in marketing, research and development, technological leadership and creativity. It is highly dependent for its success on continuing customer perceptions of product quality and uniqueness. An example in the apparel industry is Polo Ralph Lauren, retailer of upscale classic fashions and accessories. In Ralph Lauren's words, Polo 'redefined how American style and quality is perceived. Polo has always been about selling quality products by creating worlds and inviting our customers to be part of our dream.'[45] Australia's Mariana Hardwick is an example, albeit in haute couture.

Organisations pursuing a **cost leadership strategy** try to continuously improve the operating efficiencies of production, distribution and other organisational systems. The objective is to have lower costs than competitors and therefore achieve higher profits. This requires tight cost and managerial controls as well as products that are easy to manufacture and distribute. Of course, quality must not be sacrificed in the process. In fast food, McDonald's remains the most cost-effective operation of its type through preferential bulk-purchasing agreements with suppliers, de-skilled and often automated in-house operations, and large customer volume providing economies of scale. It also uses one of the youngest, largely female and least expensive labour forces. It pays the minimum wage and keeps most staff on part-time or casual employment, thereby escaping government requirements to pay superannuation and other statutory full-time entitlements.[46] In spite of its cost-effective operation, the recent global financial performance of McDonald's has been disappointing, due to consumer perception that the product range is unhealthy and does not meet new consumer tastes.

Since its inception in 1992, Aussie Home Loans has captured a small but significant share of the Australian mortgage market from the traditional lenders — banks and building societies — through keeping its costs low and passing these savings on to the consumer. Its low overheads and younger staff profile have been key ingredients of its low-cost strategy.

Organisations pursuing a **focused differentiation strategy** or a **focused cost leadership strategy** concentrate attention on a special market segment with the objective of serving its needs better than anyone else. The strategies focus organisational resources and expertise on a particular customer group, geographical region or product or service line. They seek to gain competitive advantage in product differentiation or cost leadership. Importantly, focus strategies require willingness to concentrate and the ability to use resources to special advantage in a single area. Cathay Pacific Airlines, based in Hong Kong and long one of Asia's leading airlines, refocused on the tourist trade to bolster lagging revenues during the region's economic crisis. The organisation offers dramatic discounts and special travel packages in attempting to lure customers from its rivals.

A **differentiation strategy** offers products that are unique and different from the competition.

A **cost leadership strategy** seeks to operate with lower costs than competitors.

A **focused differentiation strategy** offers a unique product to a special market segment.

A **focused cost leadership strategy** seeks the lowest costs of operations within a special market segment.

Mariana Hardwick

Creating and selling haute couture

Mariana Hardwick's haute couture clothing company is the winner of five awards in the Fashion Industries of Australia National Annual Awards. The company's avant garde and experimental strategic approach to female fashion has rapidly created a successful and expanding business. The company was established in 1994, with design and production facilities in Brunswick Street, Fitzroy — one of Australia's 'coolest' and most bohemian streets. The building, which was previously a warehouse, comprises the retail emporium, workroom and factory clearance. The products are created and manufactured by joint design and production teams, with the founder providing much of the design inspiration and strategy for the company. However, junior designers are given the opportunity to create products and develop their professional skills as part of the company's commitment to ongoing staff development. Each garment is produced to standards comparable to that of the best Paris, London and Milan fashion houses, using highly skilled dressmakers and artisans in the Fitzroy workroom.

Product life cycle planning

Product life cycle is the series of stages a product or service goes through in the 'life' of its marketability.

Another way to consider the dynamic nature of business strategy formulation is in terms of **product life cycle**. This is a series of stages a product or service goes through in the 'life' of its marketability. In terms of planning, different business stratgies are needed to support products in the life cycle stages of *introduction*, *growth*, *maturity* and *decline*.[47] Products in the introduction and growth stages lend themselves to differentiation strategies. They require investments in advertising and market research to establish a market presence and build a customer base. In the maturity stage, the strategic emphasis shifts toward keeping customers and gaining production efficiencies. This may involve focus and an attempt at cost leadership. These strategies may hold initially as the product moves into decline. But at some point, strategic planners must seek new ways to extend product life.

Understanding product life cycles and adjusting strategy accordingly is an important business skill. Especially in dynamic times, managers need to recognise when a product life cycle is maturing. They should have contingency plans for dealing with potential decline, and they should be developing alternative products with growth potential. Consider what happened at IBM, an organisation that dominated the market for large mainframe computers for years. As customers began to use ever-more-powerful PCs, the mainframe became less important to their operating systems. When the mobile phone industry was starting to use new digital technologies, Motorola continued to emphasise its successful, but older, analogue products. Both IBM's and Motorola's top managers failed to properly consider industry trends. Their companies lost momentum to very aggressive competitors, such as Hewlett-Packard, Compaq and Dell in the computer industry and Nokia, Ericsson and Alcatel in the mobile phone industry.

Portfolio planning

In a single-product or single-business organisation the strategic context is one industry. Corporate strategy and business strategy are the same, and resources are allocated on that basis. When organisations move into different industries, resulting in multiple product or service offerings, they become internally more complex and often larger in size. This makes resource allocation a more challenging strategic management task, since the mix of businesses must be well managed. The strategy problem is similar to that faced by an individual with limited money who must choose among alternative stocks, bonds and real estate in a personal investment portfolio. In multibusiness situations, strategy formulation also involves **portfolio planning** to allocate scarce resources among competing uses.[48]

BCG MATRIX

Figure 8.7 summarises an approach to business portfolio planning developed by the Boston Consulting Group and known as the **BCG matrix**. This framework ties strategy formulation to an analysis of business opportunities according to industry or market growth rate and market share.[49] As shown in the figure, this comparison results in the following four possible business conditions, with each being associated with a strategic implication: *stars* — high market share, high-growth businesses; *cash cows* — high market share, low-growth businesses; *question marks* — low market share, high-growth businesses; and *dogs* — low market share, low-growth businesses.

A **portfolio planning** approach seeks the best mix of investments among alternative business opportunities.

The **BCG matrix** analyses business opportunities according to market growth rate and market share.

SBU = strategic business unit

Figure 8.7 ▸ The BCG matrix approach to corporate strategy formulation

Stars are high market share businesses in high-growth markets. They produce large profits through substantial penetration of expanding markets. The preferred strategy for stars is growth, and further resource investments in them are recommended. *Question marks* are low market share businesses in high-growth markets. They do not produce much profit but compete in rapidly growing markets. They are the source of difficult strategic decisions. The preferred strategy is growth, but the risk exists that further investments will not result in improved market share. Only the most promising question marks should be targeted for growth; others are restructuring or divestiture candidates.

Cash cows are high market share businesses in low-growth markets. They produce large profits and a strong cash flow. Because the markets offer little growth opportunity, the preferred strategy is stability or modest growth. 'Cows' should be 'milked' to generate cash that can be used to support needed investments in stars and question marks. *Dogs* are low market share businesses in low-growth markets. They do not produce much profit, and they show little potential for future improvement. The preferred strategy for dogs is retrenchment by divestiture.

GE BUSINESS SCREEN

The appeal of portfolio planning is its ability to help managers focus attention on the comparative strengths and weaknesses of multiple businesses and/or products. Although the BCG matrix is easy to understand and use, it is criticised for limiting attention to only market share and business growth. Business situations are more complex than that. At General Electric (GE), for example, corporate strategy must achieve the best allocation of resources among the mix of some 150-plus businesses owned by the conglomerate at any point in time. The businesses operate in very different environments, use different business models, and have different competitive advantages. What is known as the *GE Business Screen*, shown in figure 8.8, was developed as an alternative portfolio planning framework. In fact, GE became famous under the leadership of CEO Jack Welch for following a rigorous decision rule in strategic planning — either a business is or has the potential to be number 1 or number 2 in its industry, or it is removed from the GE portfolio.

The **GE Business Screen** analyses business strength and industry attractiveness for strategy formulation.

www.simonjohnson.com

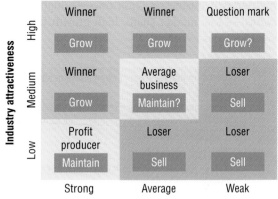

By selecting a specific market niche — high quality imported foods — Simon Johnson does not have to compete directly with large general retailers of food, such as Woolworths and Coles.

Figure 8.8 ▸ The GE Business Screen as a portfolio planning framework

In the **GE Business Screen**, the key planning dimensions are business strength and industry attractiveness.[50] Each is analysed on multiple factors similar to a SWOT analysis. Industry attractiveness is considered in terms of market size and growth, capital requirements and competitive intensity. Business strength or competitive position is assessed not only on market share but also on things like technological advantage, product quality, operating costs and price competitiveness. The resulting nine-cell matrix allows for a finer classification of business units as 'winners', 'question marks', 'average businesses', 'profit producers' or 'losers'. The recommended strategic directions are to invest for growth in winners and question marks, maintain or stabilise average businesses and profit producers, and retrench or sell losers.

Adaptive strategies

The Miles and Snow adaptive model of strategy formulation suggests that organisations should pursue product/market strategies congruent with their external environments.[51] A well-chosen strategy, in this sense, allows an organisation to successfully adapt to environmental challenges. The *prospector strategy* involves pursuing innovation and new opportunities in the face of risk and with prospects for growth. This is best suited to a dynamic and high-potential environment. A prospector 'leads' an industry by using existing technology to new advantage and creating new products to which competitors must respond. Fred Smith's original idea for Federal Express, the company he founded, was based on this strategic approach. This contrasts with a *defender strategy*, in which an organisation avoids change by emphasising existing products and current market share without seeking growth. Defence as a strategy is suited only for a stable environment and perhaps declining industries. Defenders, as do many small local retailers, try to maintain their operating domains with only slight changes over time. As a result, many suffer long-term decline in the face of competition.

The *analyser strategy* seeks to maintain the stability of a core business while exploring selective opportunities for innovation and change. This strategy lies between the prospector and reactor strategies. It is a 'follow-the-leader-when-things-look-good' approach. Many of the 'clone' makers in the personal computer industry are analysers; that is, they wait to see what the industry leaders do and how well it works out before modifying their own operations. Organisations pursuing a *reactor strategy* are primarily responding to competitive pressures in order to survive. This is a 'follow-as-last-resort' approach. Reactors do not have long-term and coherent strategies. Some public utilities and other organisations operating under government regulation may use this strategy to some extent.

Incrementalism and emergent strategy

Not all strategies are clearly formulated at one point in time and then implemented step by step. Not all strategies are created in systematic and deliberate fashion and then implemented as dramatic changes in direction. Instead, strategies sometimes take shape, change and develop over time as modest adjustments to past patterns. James Brian Quinn calls this a process of *incrementalism*, whereby modest and incremental changes in strategy occur as managers learn from experience and make adjustments.[53] This approach has much in common with Henry Mintzberg's and John Kotter's descriptions of managerial behaviour, as described in chapter 1.[54] They view managers as planning and acting in complex interpersonal networks and in hectic, fast-paced work settings. Given these challenges, effective managers must have the capacity to stay focused on long-term objectives while still remaining flexible enough to master short-run problems and opportunities as they occur.

Emergent strategies develop over time as managers learn from and respond to experience.

Such reasoning has led Mintzberg to identify what he calls **emergent strategies**.[55] These are strategies that develop progressively over time as 'streams' of decisions made by managers as they learn from and respond to work situations. There is an important element of 'craftsmanship' here that Mintzberg worries may be overlooked by managers who choose and discard strategies in rapid succession while using the formal planning models. He also believes that incremental or emergent strategic planning allows managers and organisations to become really good at implementing strategies, not just formulating them.

STRATEGY IMPLEMENTATION

No strategy, no matter how well formulated, can achieve longer-term success if it is not properly implemented. This includes the willingness to exercise control and make modifications as required to meet the needs of changing conditions. More specifically, current issues in strategy implementation include re-emphasis on excellence in all management systems and practices, the responsibilities of corporate governance, and the importance of strategic leadership.

Management practices and systems

www.ebay.com.au
www.ebay.co.nz

eBay Australia and eBay New Zealand are part of the global eBay electronic commerce company. Auctions are conducted on the company's web site with buyers and sellers able to bid and watch the auction's progress from their personal computers.

(*Source:* These materials have been reproduced with the permission of eBay Inc. Copyright © eBay Inc. All rights reserved.)

The rest of *Management: An Asia–Pacific Perspective* is all about strategy implementation. In order to successfully put strategies into action the entire organisation and all of its resources must be mobilised in support of them. This, in effect, involves the complete management process from planning and controlling through organising and leading. No matter how well or elegantly selected, a strategy requires supporting structures, the right technology, a good allocation of tasks and workflow designs, and the right people to staff all aspects of operations. The strategy needs to be enthusiastically supported by leaders who are capable of motivating everyone, building individual performance commitments, and utilising teams and teamwork to best advantage. And, the strategy needs to be well and continually communicated to all relevant persons and parties. Only with such total systems support can strategies succeed through implementation in today's environments of change and innovation.

Common strategic planning pitfalls that can hinder implementation include both failures of substance and failures of process. *Failures of substance* reflect inadequate attention to the major strategic planning elements — analysis of mission and purpose, core values and corporate culture, organisational strengths and weaknesses, and environmental opportunities and threats. *Failures of process* reflect poor handling of the ways in which the various aspects of strategic planning were accomplished. An important process failure is the *lack of participation error*. This is failure to include key persons in the strategic planning effort.[56] As a result, their lack of commitment to all-important action follow-through may severely hurt strategy implementation. Process failure also occurs with too much centralisation of planning in top management or too much delegation of planning activities to staff planners or separate planning departments. Another process failure is the tendency to get so bogged down in details that the planning process becomes an end in itself instead of a means to an end. This is sometimes called 'goal displacement'.

Corporate governance

Corporate governance is the system of control and performance monitoring of top management.

Organisations today are experiencing new pressures at the level of **corporate governance**. This is the system of control and performance monitoring of top management that is maintained by boards of directors and other major stakeholder representatives. In businesses, for example, corporate governance is enacted by boards, institutional investors in a company's assets, and other ownership interests. Each in its own way is a point of accountability for top management.[57] The trend toward strategic alliances within and between industries raises new issues for corporate governance.[58]

Boards of directors are formally charged with ensuring that an organisation operates in the best interests of its owners and/or the representative public in the case of not-for-profit organisations. Controversies often arise over the role of *inside directors*, who are chosen from the senior management of the organisation, and *outside directors*, who are chosen from other organisations and positions external to the organisation. In the past, corporate boards may have been viewed as largely endorsing or confirming the strategic initiatives of top management. Today they are increasingly expected to exercise control and take active roles in ensuring that the strategic management of an enterprise is successful.

If anything, the current trend is toward greater emphasis on the responsibilities of corporate governance. Top managers probably feel more accountability for performance than ever before to boards of directors and other stakeholder interest groups. Furthermore, this accountability relates not only to financial performance but also to broader social responsibility concerns. As discussed in chapter 6 on ethics and social responsibility, for example, institutional investors such as the US organisation Interfaith Center for Corporate Social Responsibility purposely buy stock in a company to gain a voice in shareholder meetings. They do this to bring pressure on organisations to behave in socially responsible ways. Such pressure has been felt by PepsiCo and Texaco for their controversial involvements in Burma, a country whose totalitarian rulers were accused of human rights abuses. Under pressure, both PepsiCo and Texaco terminated their business interests in that country.

Strategic leadership

Strategic management is a leadership responsibility. Effective strategy implementation and control depends on the full commitment of all managers to supporting and leading strategic initiatives within their areas of supervisory responsibility. To successfully put strategies into action the entire organisation and all of its resources must be mobilised in support of them. In our dynamic and often-uncertain environment, the premium is on **strategic leadership** — the capability to enthuse people to successfully engage in a process of continuous change, performance enhancement and implementation of organisational strategies.[59] The broad issues associated with strategic leadership are so important that part 5 of *Management: An Asia–Pacific Perspective* is devoted in its entirety to leadership and issues related to leadership development — including leadership models, motivation, communication, interpersonal dynamics and teamwork.

Porter argues that the managing director or CEO of an organisation has to be the chief strategist, someone who provides strategic leadership.[60] He describes the task in the following way. A strategic leader has to be the *guardian of trade-offs*. It is the leader's job to make sure that the organisation's resources are allocated in ways consistent with the strategy. This requires the discipline to sort through many competing ideas and alternatives to stay on course and not get sidetracked. A strategic leader also needs to *create a sense of urgency*, not allowing the organisation and its members to grow slow and complacent. Even when doing well, the leader keeps the focus on getting better and being alert to conditions that require adjustments to the strategy. A strategic leader needs to *make sure that everyone understands the strategy*. Unless strategies are understood, the daily tasks and contributions of people lose context and purpose. Everyone might work very hard, but without alignment to strategy the impact is dispersed rather than advancing in a common direction to accomplish

Strategic leadership enthuses people to continuously change, refine and improve strategies and their implementation.

Importance of leadership qualities

Anecdotal evidence in Australasia suggests that students believe that a high degree of technological competency is crucial for good strategic leadership.

How would you rank it among the other important leadership qualities?

the goals. Importantly, a strategic leader must *be a teacher*. It is the leader's job to teach the strategy and make it a 'cause', says Porter. In order for strategy to work it must become an ever-present commitment throughout the organisation. Everyone must understand the strategy that makes their organisation different from others. This means that a strategic leader must *be a great communicator.*

Finally, it is important to note that the challenges faced by organisations today are so complex that it is often difficult for one individual to fulfil all strategic leadership needs. Strategic management in large firms is increasingly viewed as a team leadership responsibility. When Michael Dell founded Dell Computer in the USA, he did it in his dormitory room at college. Now the firm operates globally with $30 billion in sales. Dell is still chairman and CEO, but he has two vice-chairmen to help with top management tasks. He observes: 'I don't think you could do it with one person ... there's way too much to be done.'[61] As discussed in chapter 17 on teams and teamwork, it takes hard work and special circumstances to create a real team — at the top or anywhere else in the organisation.[62] Top management teams must work up to their full potential in order to bring the full advantages of teamwork to strategic leadership. Dell believes that his top management team has mastered the challenge. 'We bounce ideas off each other,' he says, 'and at the end of the day if we say who did this, the only right answer is that we all did. Three heads are better than one.'[63]

CHAPTER 8

Study guide

The chapter 8 study guide helps you review the chapter content, prepare for examinations, apply what you have learned and further build your career readiness. The summary briefly answers the study questions posed at the start of the chapter. The list of key terms allows you to double-check your familiarity with basic concepts and definitions. The applied activities help you test your comprehension of chapter content. Suggestions offered as career readiness activities direct your attention to relevant sections of the Career Readiness Workbook where you can test and develop your career skills and apply what you have learned. The list of electronic resources suggests activities from the *Management: An Asia-Pacific Perspective* web site and, finally, the case for critical thinking helps you apply your new management knowledge.

SUMMARY

What are the foundations of strategic competitiveness?

- Competitive advantage is achieved by operating in ways that are difficult for competitors to imitate.
- A strategy is a comprehensive plan that sets long-term direction and guides resource allocation to achieve sustainable competitive advantage.
- The strategic goals of a business should include superior profitability and the generation of above-average returns for investors.
- Strategic thinking involves the ability to understand the different challenges of monopoly, oligopoly and hypercompetition environments.

What is strategic management?

- Strategic management is the process of formulating and implementing strategies that achieve organisational goals in a competitive environment.
- The strategic management process begins with analysis of mission, clarification of core values and identification of objectives.
- A SWOT analysis systematically assesses organisational resources and capabilities and industry/environmental opportunities and threats.
- Porter's five-forces model analyses industry attractiveness in terms of competitors, new entrants, substitute products and the bargaining power of suppliers and buyers.

What types of strategies are used by organisations?

- Corporate strategy sets direction for an entire organisation; business strategy sets direction for a business division or product/service line; functional strategy sets direction for the operational support of business and corporate strategies.
- The grand or master strategies used by organisations include growth — pursuing expansion; retrenchment — pursuing ways to scale back operations; stability — pursuing ways to maintain the status quo; and combination — pursuing the strategies in combination.

How are strategies formulated?

- The three options in Porter's model of competitive strategy are: differentiation — distinguishing one's products from the competition; cost leadership — minimising costs relative to the competition; and focus — concentrating on a special market segment.
- The product life cycle model focuses on different strategic needs at the introduction, growth, maturity and decline stages of a product's life.
- The BCG matrix is a portfolio planning approach that classifies businesses or product lines as 'stars', 'cash cows', 'question marks' or 'dogs'.
- The adaptive model focuses on the congruence of prospector, defender, analyser or reactor strategies with demands of the external environment.
- The incremental or emergent model recognises that many strategies are formulated and implemented incrementally over time.

What are current issues in strategy implementation?

- Management practices and systems — including the functions of planning, organising, leading and controlling — must be mobilised to support strategy implementation.
- Among the pitfalls that inhibit strategy implementation are failures of substance, such as poor analysis of the environment, and failures of process, such as lack of participation in the planning process.
- Corporate governance, involving the role of boards of directors in the performance monitoring of organisations, is being addressed as an important element in strategic management today.
- Strategic leadership involves the ability to manage trade-offs in resource allocations, maintain a sense of urgency in strategy implementation, and effectively communicate the strategy to key constituencies.
- Increasingly, organisations use top management teams to energise and direct the strategic management process.

KEY TERMS

above-average returns (p. 212)

BCG matrix (p. 227)

business strategy (p. 219)

competitive advantage (p. 206)

concentration (p. 219)

core competencies (p. 216)

corporate governance (p. 230)

corporate strategy (p. 218)

cost leadership strategy (p. 225)

differentiation strategy (p. 225)

diversification (p. 220)

divestiture (p. 221)

downsizing (p. 221)

e-business strategy (p. 222)

emergent strategies (p. 230)

focused cost leadership strategy (p. 225)

focused differentiation strategy (p. 225)

functional strategy (p. 219)

GE Business Screen (p. 228)

growth strategies (p. 219)

mission (p. 214)

operating objectives (p. 216)

organisational culture (p. 216)

portfolio planning (p. 227)

product life cycle (p. 226)

restructuring (p. 220)

retrenchment strategy (p. 220)

stakeholders (p. 215)

strategic alliances (p. 221)

strategic business unit (SBU) (p. 219)

strategic intent (p. 211)

strategic leadership (p. 231)

strategic management (p. 211)

strategy (p. 211)

strategy formulation (p. 213)

strategy implementation (p. 214)

SWOT analysis (p. 216)

vertical integration (p. 220)

Short-response questions

1.   What is the difference between corporate strategy and functional strategy?
2.   How would a manager perform a SWOT analysis?
3.   What is the difference between the BCG matrix and GE Business Screen as portfolio planning approaches?
4.   What is strategic leadership?

Application question

5.   William Wong is the owner of an independent bookshop close to Singapore's two major universities. His shop serves the local university market and a nearby trendy inner-city area with an increasing number of young professionals. He stocks a wide range of books to service this diverse market. A large, international discount bookshop has just opened across the street from his store. It is offering lower prices on university textbooks. It is a no-frills operation and its lower prices are attracting business away from William Wong's shop. Assume you are part of a student team assigned to do a management class project for William. His question for the team is: 'How can I apply Porter's generic business strategies to better deal with my strategic planning challenges in this situation?' How will you reply?

Recommended individual and group learning activities from the end-of-text Career Readiness Workbook for this chapter include:

Career advancement portfolio   *WB*

Update your career advancement portfolio to reflect your new skills and experiences. Include skills and personal insights you gain from the following projects and exercises.

Research and presentation project   *WB*

• Project 2 — Changing corporate cultures

Cross-functional integrative case   *WB*

Read the integrative case on Sarina Russo and answer the following questions:

8.1   Prepare a mission statement for either Sarina Russo Job Access or the Russo Institute of Technology. You may wish to review the corporate information presented on the web site www.sarinarusso.com.au as a starting point.

8.2   Based on information provided in the integrative case and on your research of the Sarina Russo Group web site www.sarinarusso.com.au, prepare a SWOT analysis for either Sarina Russo Job Access or the Russo Institute of Technology.

8.3   Sarina Russo appears to have been pursuing a growth strategy for the Sarina Russo Group. What approach is she using?

Exercises in teamwork WB

- Exercise 2 — What managers do
- Exercise 13 — The future workplace

Management skills assessment WB

- Assessment 8 — Are you a strategic manager?

ELECTRONIC RESOURCES

Don't forget to take full advantage of the online support for *Management: An Asia–Pacific Perspective* at www.johnwiley.com.au/highered/management: chapter 8 practice tests, e-flashcards, crossword puzzles, interactive management skills assessments, interactive cases, the online career advancement portfolio and much more!

CASE FOR CRITICAL THINKING

Read the following case for critical thinking on Procter & Gamble. While you are reading the case keep in mind what you have learned in this chapter, then answer the questions.

Procter & Gamble: a web-based turnaround?

Introduction

Procter & Gamble, one of the world's largest consumer products companies, markets more than 300 products to more than five billion consumers in 140 countries.[64] It began in 1837 as a small soap- and candle-making firm in Ohio, USA, and is widely recognised as a leading 'old economy' organisation. The question becomes: Can P&G learn to live with the new economy Internet?'

The P&G story

Its impressive list of consumer products include Tide, Crest, Pantene, Tampax, Pringles, Pampers, Oil of Olay, Jif, Cover Girl, Downy, Dawn, Bounty, Charmin and IAMS pet foods — and P&G has worldwide sales of over US$40 billion.

From the beginning, P&G has pioneered new ways of doing business, from new

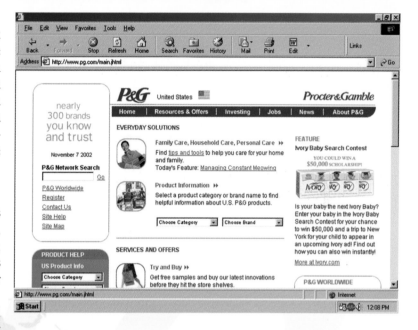

product innovations to new ways of reaching out to its consumers. It pioneered the use of radio and television advertising as new media to reach the mass market. It remains one of the largest advertisers in the world, spending US$3.5 billion in advertising. It was one of the first organisations to use profit sharing, a company research laboratory and mass advertising.

P&G has entered into a host of new product markets, including:

- health care, through the acquisition of Norwich Eaton Pharmaceuticals in 1982 and Richardson-Vicks in 1985
- beauty care with Noxell, Max Factor and Ellen Betrix in the late 1980s and early 1990s
- the $25 billion pet food industry with its purchase of Iams Pet Foods.

The company that began as a small partnership has grown into one of the USA's largest multinational corporations.[65]

P&G has a history of strong leaders, including John Smale, Edwin L. Artzt, John Pepper and Durk Jager. P&G suffered from a 1990s phenomenon of weakening brand identification among consumers, with the resulting effect of sluggish sales growth. Artzt, known during his tenure as the 'prince of darkness', had kept profits moving upwards by slashing 30 production plants and cutting 13 000 jobs. Pepper, with Jager as his chief operating officer, set the ambitious goal of doubling sales to US$70 billion by 2006 through rapid product innovation and the exploitation of markets outside the USA.[66] Pepper eventually stepped aside in 1998 to allow his more aggressive subordinate to take over.

Jager took over a company that had become overly paternalistic, formula-driven, risk-averse and inbred. The smallest decisions had to be referred to senior management and employees' adherence to strict rules and policies earned them the name of 'Proctoids' from outside analysts.[67] Events in the 1990s, including lower-priced copycat products and store brands offered by the large chain stores put even more pressure on P&G's margins. Jager brought in a new approach, represented by his motto: 'If it ain't broke, break it'.[68] He announced a reorganisation that removed another 15 000 jobs and moved the company away from a country-based approach to that of product categories. It turned out to be too much in too short of a time. Failed takeover targets, including Gillette, Warner-Lambert and American Home Products, along with disappointing sales and profit figures, doomed Jager's attempt at changing the corporate culture.

After only 18 months at the helm, Jager was replaced by Pepper's return as chairman and Alan Lafley, known as a consensus builder, as chief executive. Lafley immediately made it clear that P&G intended to slow down the change process and restore sagging employee morale by returning to the organisation's core values. Its stock price, after dropping to US$53.63 from US$117.75, has recovered somewhat.[69] The question arises: Where does P&G go from here?

P&G and the Internet

Lafley has made it clear that: 'We are making the Web a part of everything we do. We believe it multiplies the value of all of our strengths.' He claims that P&G is 'quietly transforming into a new-economy company' and that the 'the biggest opportunity to leverage scale may be the Internet'.[70]

Evidence of this transformation exists in a bevy of web initiatives, including Reflect.com, Yet2.com, InnovationNet and Transora. These sites support one-to-one marketing initiatives and Internet-enabled personalisation of products. Lafley intends to use the Internet to remake the consumer products industry in the same way that P&G used radio and television.[71] From its main web site www.pg.com, the organisation wants to deepen the consumer's relationship with everything P&G. Early success is represented by 7 million hits a month on Pampers.com and 1.2 million per month on the MrClean.com location.

P&G is moving away from its reliance on 'big bang' advertising campaigns in favour of gradually 'diffusing' a new brand into the culture. Its new US hair care product, Physique, was publicised heavily from its www.physique.com site. The result: 5 million hits on Club Physique, allowing the organisation to gather huge amounts of customer data in exchange for free samples.

P&G's prime web site acts as a portal to its other subordinate sites and is packed with information and suggestions for a variety of uses for its long product list. The site is 'transaction enabled', so P&G can both offer samples and sell products. This has some of P&G's retailers nervous about the organisation reaching out to consumers directly. However, P&G's chief information officer, Steve David, states that: 'We are not going to be in the distribution business. First and foremost this is about trial. And it's good for our mainline retailers because it helps them create demand for new products.'[72]

Individuals are invited to 'help create new products' at the firm's home site. 'The whole Internet is enabling us to cut our marketing research costs by anywhere from half to 70 per cent', claims Wade Miquelon, co-director of P&G's venture capital fund. Focus groups cannot match the speed of the Web. 'Concept testing is going from weeks to days', states Miquelon.[73]

At Reflect.com, the firm targets 'upscale' women by designing unique cosmetic formulations for each woman and branding them with the name of her choice.[74] The increased cost of making 'one-offs' is offset by the huge gross margins inherent to cosmetics. In addition, the firm learns first hand about the preferences of its users, thereby providing invaluable feedback to its brand managers.

Yet2.com attempts to license the valuable patent rights from P&G's research and development practices. If the organisation can license just 100 patents per year 'you're starting to talk real money', claims Conrad Langenhagen, director of strategic planning at Yet2.com. 'And most of this is just pure profit — 97 per cent to 99 per cent.'[75]

InnovationNet and Transora are two internal intranet initiatives. InnovationNet supports discussions from a database searchable by 18 000 employees from R&D, engineering, licensing and purchasing. It provides a 'virtual global lunchroom' to encourage product and process innovations. Transora is an online commodity auction site that supports B2B exchanges. Steve David argues that P&G has the potential to save 10–15 per cent on the cost of non-strategic raw materials.

P&G's most ambitious foray involves MIT and technology known as 'smart packaging' or 'auto-ID'. The process involves embedding ultra-cheap microchips into packages, creating the ultimate in seamless, integrated supply-chain management through the supermarket checkout.[76] When a shopper pulls a bottle of Tide off the shelf it would, via the Internet, charge the shopper's credit card and instantaneously inform the factory to produce more Tide.

Not everyone is as excited as Lafley about the potential impact of the Web on P&G. Merrill Lynch's Heather Murren worries more about employee morale and long-term earnings than the Internet. 'It's hard to envision it being important to a company like Procter & Gamble,' she says.[77] Others are more supportive. 'If not everything they're trying today works, that's OK', argues securities analyst Daniel Peris. 'Enough of these ventures will work that it's going to benefit them. They don't have to win on all fronts, they just have to win a little bit.'[78]

QUESTIONS

1. Can Lafley turn P&G's bureaucratic structure around in order to become more responsive to consumers?
2. Can P&G really become a new economy company?
3. What might the 'new' P&G look like because of the Internet?

CHAPTER 9

CHAPTER 9

Entrepreneurship and new ventures

CHAPTER 9 STUDY QUESTIONS

- What is entrepreneurship?

- What is special about small businesses?

- How do you start a new venture?

- What resources support entrepreneurship and business development?

Wizard — the new kid on the home loan block

Wizard hit the highly competitive home loans market with a strategy that would differentiate it from the banks and building societies. While the banks were closing branches, Wizard opened branches; and while the competitors communicated only in English, Wizard employed managers who could speak languages such as Cantonese and Lebanese, common in Sydney neighbourhoods. Wizard also offers its branch principals a financial stake in the business as part of an ongoing business partnership. This strategy of providing more personalised service through local branches, targeting significant ethnic communities and empowering local managers was complemented by an aggressive pricing strategy. The company also has many branches in New Zealand.

Within six years, Wizard became Australia's sixth-largest provider of new loans. The brightly-orange-coloured branches are visible not only in the suburbs of Australasia's largest cities but also in the CBD, often located close to the major banks. Wizard and competitor, Aussie Home Loans, have established themselves as crusaders for working families who want to realise the 'dream' of home ownership. Although they are competitors, there are substantial differences in their strategies. Aussie Home Loans focuses its strategy around a low-cost network of mobile lenders and direct selling, whereas Wizard relies on the relatively well-established and more costly concept of branches, but with aggressive promotion and friendly neighbourhood service.[1]

GET CONNECTED!

Why does the approach of Wizard www.wizard.com.au appear to be successful? How does it differ from the strategy of Aussie Home Loans www.aussiehomeloans.com.au? Can you think of other industries where a low-cost, high-volume business model could be very successful? What business-level strategies would need to be adopted to ensure that costs remained low and that business volume stayed high?

GET CONNECTED!

Wizard is an entrepreneurial organisation led by its managing director and founder, Mark Bouris. It has identified a market niche for a low-price home loan product that caters for working people and for ethnic groups — people who have not been a strong focus for banks and non-bank lenders. Even its name is innovative and creative in an industry that is generally seen as conservative and staid. With more than 100 branches it is clear that the organisation has been able to work some 'magic' through its focused target-market strategy and expertise in managing and controlling its operating costs. Wizard has the strategy, organisation and leadership that could bring it long-term success. It is an interesting example of what is possible using creativity, initiative and experience in the world of work today. In fact this is a chapter of examples. Its goal is not only to inform you — make you more familiar with the nature of entrepreneurship and new venture creation — it is also to enthuse and stimulate you to consider starting your own business, become self-employed and make your own contribution to society.

Consider Wizard again. It is an interesting example of how new and creative approaches to a business can be brought to life through energy, enthusiasm and creativity. This should be motivating to you, suggesting that there should be no excuses for not trying ... for not giving your ideas a chance. What about it? You may be the next 'wizard' in business.

THE NATURE OF ENTREPRENEURSHIP

Today's dynamic environment demands that organisations and their managers adapt and renew themselves continually to succeed over time. People and organisations must change frequently and at a rapidly accelerating pace. Success in the highly competitive business environments, in particular, depends on **entrepreneurship**. This term is used to describe strategic thinking and risk-taking behaviour that results in the creation of new opportunities for individuals and/or organisations.

Entrepreneurship is dynamic, risk-taking, creative and growth-oriented behaviour.

Who are the entrepreneurs?

An **entrepreneur** is willing to pursue opportunities in situations others view as problems or threats.

An **entrepreneur** is a risk-taking individual who takes action to pursue opportunities others may fail to recognise or may even view as problems or threats. In the business context, an entrepreneur starts new ventures that bring to life new product or service ideas.

Entrepreneurs such as Steve Jobs (who co-founded Apple Computers), Richard Branson (who established the Virgin Group) and all the entrepreneurs who set up small businesses worldwide provide many of the new products, processes and marketing technologies that allow the global economy to evolve, innovate and prosper. In recent years, the importance of these entrepreneurs has been recognised through awards, which not only raise the profiles of their businesses locally but also enhance their profiles worldwide. Their value is also evident by their inclusion in government think tanks. Entrepreneurs often participate in programs encouraging other budding entrepreneurs, where they can share success stories, advice on business plans, networking opportunities and possibly identify new markets.

Researchers are interested in the characteristics of entrepreneurs. They want to know whether and how entrepreneurs are different, and what it takes to achieve entrepreneurial success. Before examining the findings, though, let's meet some real, high-profile entrepreneurs. Their stories are rich with ideas for all of us to consider. Although the people and what was accomplished are all different, they share something in common. These entrepreneurs built successful long-term businesses from good ideas and hard work.[2]

Dick Smith

Born in Sydney in 1944, Dick Smith established his own electronics business in Australia and New Zealand. He had become so successful by the age of 38 that he was able to retire and channel his energy into other projects. He sold his electronics interests to Woolworths in 1982. His love of adventure and the great outdoors has driven much of his entrepreneurial strategy in recent years. This has included starting *Australian Geographic* magazine in 1986, organising adventure trips to remote areas (including being the first person to fly around the world via the poles in 1989) and making the first helicopter flight to the North Pole in 1987. He has also shared his business skills with Australia's indigenous community through his position as Ambassador for the Council for Aboriginal Reconciliation, and in 1986 he was made Australian of the Year. In 1999 he founded Dick Smith Foods, which he believes is important for Australia because it employs Australians and is locally owned, so the profits remain in the country to create wealth.[3]

Poppy King

At only 18 years of age, Poppy King founded Poppy Industries Pty Ltd to take advantage of a gap in the market for matte lipstick. The company began merchandising its products in 1992 and quickly developed a strong brand awareness. It recovered the $40 000 set-up costs and returned profits three months after trading commenced. At one stage sales were increasing at 1200 per cent per month. Poppy King quickly became one of Australia's most celebrated entrepreneurs and was named Young Australian of the Year in 1995. Her commitment to ethical business practices and creative product development were guiding philosophies.[4] In December 2002, Poppy King sold the Poppy trademark to the US-based Estée Lauder Group, and production ceased at Poppy Industries. Even though Poppy King no longer owns her own business, her entrepreneurial spirit lives on.

Richard Branson

Want to start an airline? Richard Branson did, but he started first in his native England with a student literary magazine and small mail-order record business. Since then, he's built Virgin into one of the world's most recognised brand names. The business conglomerate now employs some 25 000 people around the globe in over 200 companies, including Virgin Airlines, Virgin Records and even Virgin Cola. It's all very creative and ambitious. But that's Branson. 'I love to learn things I know little about', he says. Branson's Australian airline venture, Virgin Blue, is profiled at the start of chapter 8.

Anita Roddick

In 1973 Anita Roddick was a 33-year-old housewife looking for a way to support herself and her two children. She spotted a niche for natural-based skin and health care products, and started mixing and selling her own from a small shop in Brighton, England. The Body Shop PLC has grown to some 1500 outlets in 47 countries with 24 languages, selling a product every half-second to one of its 86+ million customers. Known for building the firm with a commitment to human rights, the environment and economic development, Roddick believes in business social responsibility. She says: 'If you think you're too small to have an impact, try going to bed with a mosquito.'

Gerry Harvey

Gerry Harvey is one of Australia's most prominent retailers. Retail is his consuming passion. Harvey started his career as a vacuum cleaner salesman and real estate sales agent, and in 1961 he and Ian Norman opened a store to sell electrical goods. A year later another store was added and the Norman Ross chain was born. In 1982 they sold the original business and established the Harvey Norman retail chain. The company, which consists of a collection of franchisees running departments in each store, is establishing new stores around Australia and expanding into Asia and Europe. Gerry Harvey is convinced that he can successfully export the Harvey Norman brand and style of retailing. In 1999, he bought 50.6 per cent of Singapore electronics retailer Pertama, rebranding its stores as Harvey Norman in January 2001.[5]

Characteristics of entrepreneurs

Do you sense any common patterns in the prior examples? A common image of an entrepreneur is as the founder of a new business enterprise that achieves large-scale success, like the ones just mentioned. But, entrepreneurs also operate on a smaller and less-public scale. Those who take the risk of buying a local McDonald's franchise, opening a small retail shop or going into a self-employed service business are also entrepreneurs. Similarly, anyone who assumes responsibility for introducing a new product or service or change in operations within an organisation is also demonstrating the qualities of entrepreneurship.

Obviously there's a lot to learn about entrepreneurs and entrepreneurship. Starting with the individual, however, indications are that entrepreneurs tend to share certain attitudes and behavioural tendencies. The general profile is of an individual who is very self-confident, determined, resilient, adaptable and driven to excel.[6] You should be able to identify these attributes in the prior examples. In addition, the following typical *characteristics of entrepreneurs* will also be evident.[7]

- *Internal locus of control.* Entrepreneurs believe that they are in control of their own destiny; they are self-directing and like autonomy.
- *High energy level.* Entrepreneurs are persistent, hard working and willing to exert extraordinary efforts to succeed.
- *High need for achievement.* Entrepreneurs are motivated to accomplish challenging goals; they thrive on performance feedback.
- *Tolerance for ambiguity.* Entrepreneurs are risk takers; they tolerate situations with high degrees of uncertainty.
- *Self-confidence.* Entrepreneurs feel competent, believe in themselves and are willing to make decisions.
- *Action oriented.* Entrepreneurs try to act ahead of problems; they want to get things done quickly and do not want to waste valuable time.
- *Desire for independence.* Entrepreneurs want independence; they are self-reliant and want to be their own boss, not work for others.

Characteristics of entrepreneurs

Entrepreneurs are sometimes distinguishable in terms of background and experiences, not just the prior personal characteristics.[8] *Childhood experiences and family environment* seem to make a difference. Evidence links entrepreneurs with parents who were entrepreneurial and self-employed. Similarly, entrepreneurs tend to be raised in families that encourage responsibility, initiative and independence. Another issue is *career or work history*. Entrepreneurs who try one venture often go on to others. Prior career or personal experience in the business area or industry is also helpful. It also appears that entrepreneurs tend to emerge during certain *windows of career opportunity*. Most entrepreneurs start their businesses between the ages of 22 and 45. This appears to be an age spread that allows for risk taking.

Finally, a report in the internationally renowned *Harvard Business Review* suggests that, in general, entrepreneurs may have unique and *deeply embedded life interests*. The article describes entrepreneurs as having strong interests in creative production — enjoying project initiation, working with the unknown and creating unconventional solutions. They also have strong interests in enterprise control — described as finding enjoyment from running things. The combination of creative production and enterprise control is characteristic of people who want to start things and move things toward a goal.[9] See Manager's Notepad 9.1 for some additional thoughts on the nature of entrepreneurs and entrepreneurship.[10]

Do you think you can learn the characteristics of an entrepreneur or do you have to be born with them? See the Australian Institute of Management www.aim.com.au and the Australian and New Zealand Academy of Management www.gsm.mq.edu.au/anzam/ web sites for the latest stories on entrepreneurs.

GET CONNECTED!

MANAGER'S NOTEPAD 9.1

Challenging the myths about entrepreneurs

- *Entrepreneurs are born, not made.* Not true! Talent gained and enhanced by experience is a foundation for entrepreneurial success.
- *Entrepreneurs are gamblers.* Not true! Entrepreneurs are risk takers, but the risks are informed and calculated.
- *Money is the key to entrepreneurial success.* Not true! Just having money is no guarantee of success — there's a lot more to it than that; many entrepreneurs start with very little.
- *You have to be young to be an entrepreneur.* Not true! Age alone is no barrier to entrepreneurship; with age often comes experience, contacts and other useful resources.
- *You have to have a degree in business to be an entrepreneur.* Not true! You may not need a degree at all; you don't need a business degree in preference to other majors; you can benefit from learning about business fundamentals.

High quality

SBS Independent

Taking risks on innovative film and television productions

Australian film producers are noted for their emphasis on quality and innovation, even though this has often been achieved on modest budgets (in contrast to higher budget US productions). These high production values are firmly entrenched in SBS Independent (SBSi), which is the Special Broadcasting Service's documentary and drama production company. It has commissioned programs that have won more than 250 national and international awards and have been sold to numerous overseas customers. Unlike the three commercial channels (7, 9 and 10) and the ABC, which largely imitate overseas products, SBSi directs its resources into productions that are often risky and challenging. Consequently, SBSi has developed a much-respected reputation for innovation in program production and is recognised as Australia's premier film and television producer. It is a powerhouse of originality and has some of the highest production standards in Australia.

Questions

Do you see an entrepreneurial dimension to your career plans?

What types of entrepreneurial activity interest you, if any?

What motivates someone to work for a public broadcaster such as SBS, ABC or the world-renowned BBC?

Diversity and entrepreneurship

Increasingly women, minority ethnic groups and indigenous people are establishing their own businesses. Several factors appear to account for this, including frustration over direct and indirect discrimination, a growing need for self-fulfilment and control over their destinies, and the increased support by governments for small businesses. The existence in many Australian organisations of the so-called glass ceiling — a form of sexual discrimination that prevents many female managers rising to the senior ranks — has led a number of businesswomen to start their own companies. Many women claim that they have not been recognised or valued by their former employers, they have not been taken seriously, and male employees have been promoted ahead of them. In addition, the structural shift in the Australian and New Zealand economies to more casual and part-time positions and fewer secure, full-time jobs has forced many individuals to create their own full-time employment through self-employment. Increased levels of education and training have also given confidence to many individuals to strike out on their own and become entrepreneurs.

The role of governments in entrepreneurship

While some critics claim that governments obstruct or stifle entrepreneurship, an objective analysis reveals that governments divert substantial resources into encouraging and supporting entrepreneurs. In fact, many entrepreneurs would never have succeeded without government help. Even well established businesses often owe their continued existence to government financial and technical support. A wide range of training programs, technical support and targeted subsidies is available at both the federal and State levels. And both federal and State governments provide export assistance through their trade and industry ministries and departments. Successful new businesses create jobs and, importantly, tax revenue for governments. So for governments, their support is an investment in future potential revenue as well as an application of general policies on economic, regional and employment growth. For example, in Australia, the federal government supports indigenous businesses through the Aboriginal and Torres Strait Islander Commission's Business Development Program (BDP) that offers an alternative to mainstream financial institutions by providing a variety of business development facilities. The aim is to promote indigenous economic development by enabling indigenous people and communities to acquire or develop commercially successful enterprises. Currently an estimated 1.3 per cent of indigenous people are self-employed, compared to 4.8 per cent of the general population. The BDP tailors assistance to the needs of individual businesses and provides two basic types of services: business finance and business support.

Tjapukai • www.tjapukai.com.au

Aboriginal tourism experience

Tjapukai is a 'cultural tourism experience' operated by the Tjapukai tribe in conjunction with a non-indigenous management group. It is situated north of Cairns in Queensland. Visitors can explore the history, customs and rituals of the local people through dance, re-creations of their history and practical displays of spear and boomerang throwing. Bush tucker tastings and displays of Aboriginal art are also featured.

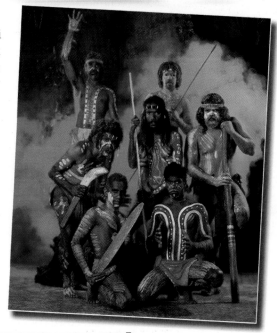

Tjapukai has won numerous tourism awards for its realistic and confrontational depiction of European colonisation, showing the full extent of the genocide against the local indigenous people.

The company's success is not confined to Far North Queensland. In 2003, the Tjapukai creative team, which includes indigenous and non-indigenous Australians, won a multimillion-dollar contract to design a Buddhist theme park on Lantau Island in Hong Kong. Using their substantial expertise they triumphed over competitors, such as the Walt Disney Company, to win the project, which will see the creation of the largest Buddhist cultural tourism experience in the world.[11]

ENTREPRENEURSHIP AND SMALL BUSINESS

A **small business** is often defined as one that has sales of less than $2 million and fewer than 100 employees. Over 90 per cent of all businesses in Australia and New Zealand are small businesses. Small employers have provided 90 per cent of all new jobs in Australia in the last decade.[12] Most small businesses are run by one owner who oversees virtually all aspects of the business, from marketing and hiring staff to budgeting and operations. A growing number of women are joining the small business ranks, with almost 50 per cent of all small businesses owned by women. Almost one-half of small businesses are in the service sector; the next largest group is retail businesses, and manufacturing operations are the third-largest group. Only 50 per cent of all new businesses survive the critical first three years of operation. This high failure rate does not stem from the owners' lack of technical expertise in their field, but rather from weak managerial and business skills.

Most Australians (80 per cent) view small businesses as a positive influence on national life. Small businesses account for more than 40 per cent of the offline economy, create three of every four new jobs, and generate a majority of Australian innovations. Small businesses and home offices account for 40 per cent of all technology investment in Australia and New Zealand.[13]

The entrepreneurial spirit embodies inventiveness, an ability to think laterally, enthusiasm, energy and a willingness to take risks — and is independent of race, ethnicity, gender and class. Most small business success stories have a common theme. Small business entrepreneurs take advantage of opportunities they have identified in niche markets through their specialised skills

A **small business** has fewer than 100 employees, is independently owned and operated and is normally one of many competitors in its industry. Small businesses are common in the restaurant, building, retailing and personal services sectors.

and expertise. They make intelligent or appropriate use of technology and develop close working relationships with their clients, which gives them a distinct edge over their competitors.

The future of small business entrepreneurship is vital for the future of all communities in the Asia–Pacific region and there has never been a time when managing a small business has been more challenging. The impact of new technology, increasing competition and new taxation regimes such as the GST, and the accessibility of new markets through e-commerce and the Internet have been the catalyst for new and smarter ways of doing business.

The most common ways for an entrepreneur to get involved in a small business are to start one, buy an existing one or buy and run a **franchise** — where a business owner sells to another the right to operate the same business in another location. A franchise runs under the original owner's business name and guidance. In return the franchise parent receives a share of income or a flat fee from the franchisee.

> ⚙ A **franchise** is when one business owner sells to another the right to operate the same business in another location.

ENTREPRENEURSHIP

Adacel Technologies Limited •
www.adacel.com

Australian corporate minnow succeeds in global aerospace market

Software development company Adacel Technologies secured a $40 million contract to supply software for a landmark air traffic control system being rolled out in the USA in 2004. The Victorian-based company signed an agreement with the US global aircraft manufacturer and air traffic systems provider Lockheed Martin, which has a US$217 million contract with the US Federal Aviation Administration (FAA) to provide a system for monitoring aircraft when they are not covered by radar. Air traffic controllers now display the location of such aircraft using radio communication with pilots coupled with the flight path logged before departure. Adacel managing director Silvio Salom believes it will be the first of many agreements as Lockheed Martin has established an office in Moscow and Adacel has established links in Asia, particularly in the expanding Chinese market.[14]

Internet entrepreneurship

The growth of Internet entrepreneurship in Australia and New Zealand has been less rapid than in North America. In some respects, purchasing over the Internet is an extension of catalogue purchasing, which has always been more popular in North America — retailers such as Sears generated a large proportion of their income from catalogue sales. Also, North America has the highest percentage of households in the world connected to the Internet, which increases the potential for e-businesses. Whereas many Australasian businesses have a web site, not all will necessarily offer Internet purchasing. Even when they do, companies such as Harvey Norman have reported relatively modest sales over the Internet compared to total revenue.

While Australasian entrepreneurs are embracing the Internet, the region's unique cultural and geographic characteristics are likely to produce slightly different outcomes from those in North America and Europe. The smaller, more fragmented markets in Australasia may not warrant the costs of establishing a sophisticated e-business for all entrepreneurs. It is important to determine the appropriate business model for the market that the product or service is targeting.

Organisations intent on using the Internet to enter new markets, expand in current markets or transform their relationships with current suppliers, customers and employees often find that the key to success is not the technology. E-business is not about technology any more than it is about finding ways of using new tools, and there is as much opportunity for small business to use the new e-business tools as there is for large organisations. Using the Internet to establish a new organisation, to revolutionise business practices or to change the way an existing organisation does business requires information technology (IT) governance. That is, senior management must develop the processes for making decisions about IT and monitoring IT performance. And rather than using a single e-business strategy, it is better to adopt a portfolio approach.

Some guiding principles for e-business success for small to large organisations were identified by two directors from the Boston Consulting Group, David C. Michael and Greg Sutherland.[15] The six organisational principles followed by the most successful companies were:

1. Create a sense of urgency.
2. Carefully balance the need to leverage the core business with the reality that e-business often disrupts that business.
3. Adopt a small but powerful central function to make e-business decisions.
4. Bring in outside people and ideas and incorporate them effectively.
5. Design management processes that are ready for e-business.
6. Use partnerships to leverage the core and accelerate the online business.

Another area for Internet entrepreneurship is B2B, specialised business-to-business web sites that link buyers and sellers. But as with all entrepreneurship, B2B in the small business sector is considered risky. Analysts are cautious on its future, questioning whether they can garner enough users to withstand early start-up costs, whether enough small businesses are sufficiently automated to take advantage of the services, and whether smaller businesses are willing to give up their traditional distributor relationships for the online exchange.[16]

REALITY CHECK

How entrepreneurs get started

In a survey of 448 business owners in the USA, some 18 per cent indicated they began while working for a larger company.

What is your path to being an entrepreneur?

International business entrepreneurship

In chapter 5 on the global dimensions of management the reasons why businesses go international were discussed. The same ones apply to the strategic opportunities for smaller businesses. They also often find that international business brings opportunities for expanded markets, additional financing, access to quality and possibly lower-cost resources, access to labour and technical expertise, and onsite locations for low-cost manufacturing or outsourcing. The Internet now makes selling overseas relatively easy; today's advanced distribution organisations also make product delivery quick and easy. Additionally, smaller businesses can find alliance opportunities in strategic ventures with foreign partners.

As the economies of the world's countries improve and the overall standards of living rise, consumer demand for goods and services grows as well. With this comes greater international business opportunities for exporting and importing in particular. Governments, federal and State, encourage exporting and try to support the growth of small businesses through exporting. Like most states, the Victorian State government, for example, offers export development assistance to entrepreneurs through its Department of State and Regional Development.

The federal government's export and investment facilitation agency Austrade — the Australian Trade Commission — assists Australian organisations to win export business and generate inward and outward investment. Austrade helps organisations determine their readiness to export and provides initial advice and market statistics to guide them on how best to proceed. It provides suggestions to organisations of all sizes on which overseas markets have the highest sales potential for their product, how they can develop a presence in these markets, and the kinds of business assistance that are available. Austrade operates an international network of offices located in 108 cities in 63 countries and is able to identify potential buyers or agents and to pass on specific business opportunities as they arise. It works closely with Australian organisations to link Australian suppliers with interested local contacts and to provide access to local business and government networks.

The New Zealand Trade Development Board (Trade New Zealand) undertakes similar functions for its country's organisations. It also links investors with competitive New Zealand companies and creates international business alliances, with a strong emphasis on supporting entrepreneurs and small business. New Zealand has a stronger central government structure, unlike Australia's federal system, so the New Zealand government is the main provider of export assistance to industry. In Australia, all the State governments have their own departments to encourage expansion of their State's businesses overseas and to attract foreign investors to their region.

Family businesses

Family businesses — ones owned and financially controlled by family members — represent the largest percentage of businesses operating worldwide. In Australia, family businesses provide 50 per cent of the nation's employment and account for more than 65 per cent of new jobs created. On average, an Australian family business is approximately 50 years old, and nearly 90 per cent of family-owned businesses are managed by second- and third-generation family members. Fifty per cent of family-owned businesses generate sales in the $5 million to $20 million region and have more than 100 employees. It has been estimated that family businesses contribute more than 50 per cent of Australia's gross domestic product, and that 75 per cent of Australia's businesses are family owned and controlled.[17]

Family businesses must solve the same problems as other small or large businesses — meeting the challenges of strategy, competitive advantage and operational excellence. When everything goes right, the family business is almost an ideal situation — everyone working together, sharing values and a common goal, and knowing that what they do benefits the family. But it doesn't always work out this way or stay this way over time and successive generations. Family businesses face problems that are quite unique to their situation.

'Okay, Dad, so he's your brother. But does that mean we have to put up with inferior work and an erratic schedule that we would never tolerate from anyone else in the business?'[18]

GET CONNECTED!

How would a budding entrepreneur find out what assistance is available? The Business Entry Point www.bep.gov.au and the Foundation for Research, Science and Technology www.frst.govt.nz are the business gateways to government.
GET CONNECTED!

Family businesses are owned and controlled by family members.

This line introduces a problem that can all too often set the stage for failure in a family business — the *family business feud*. Simply put, members of the controlling family get into disagreements about work responsibilities, business strategy, operating approaches, finances or other matters. The example is indicative of an intergenerational problem, but the feud can be between spouses, among siblings, between parents and children; it really doesn't matter. The key point is that unless the disagreements are resolved satisfactorily among the members and to the benefit of the business itself, the business will have difficulty surviving, especially in a highly competitive environment.

Another significant problem faced by family businesses is the **succession problem** — transferring leadership from one generation to the next. A survey of small and medium-sized family businesses by Arthur Andersen indicated that 66 per cent planned on keeping the business within the family.[19] The management question is: How will the assets be distributed and who will run the business when the current head leaves? Although this problem is not specific to the small business, it is especially significant in the family business context, and particularly in those cases where the current head of the business is the founder — the entrepreneur who started the business and built it into what it is today. The statistics on succession are eye-opening. About 30 per cent of family businesses survive to the second generation; only 12 per cent survive to the third; only 3 per cent are expected to survive beyond that.[20]

A family business that has been in operation for some time is a source of both business momentum and financial wealth. Both must be maintained in the process of succession. Business advisers recommend that this problem be addressed ahead of time through a **succession plan** — a formal statement that describes how the leadership transition and related financial matters will be handled when the time for changeover arrives. Operational considerations of the plan should include, among other possibilities, procedures for choosing or designating the business's new leadership, legal aspects of any ownership transfer, and any financial and estate plans relating to the transfer. Ideally, the foundations for effective implementation of a succession plan are set up well ahead of the need to use it. The plan should be shared and understood among all affected by it. Ideally, the leadership successor is identified ahead of time, and then well prepared through experience and training to perform the new role when needed.

In recent years organisations have been established to assist family businesses to tackle short- and longer-term organisational and strategic issues. One important organisation in Australia is Family Business Australia (FBA). It is a national member-based, not-for-profit organisation existing 'to improve the effectiveness of Australian families in business through the sharing of practical experience and knowledge, to promote the value and contribution that family businesses make to our society, and to represent Australian family businesses as a strong and united voice'.[21] FBA was established in 1998 following the merger of the Family Business Council and the Foundation for Family and Private Business. It deals with a very real need to understand the demands of family businesses and their social and economic significance to Australia. It attempts to increase the performance of family-based businesses and provides advice to member businesses.

Why small businesses fail

Small businesses have a high failure rate; one high enough to be scary. As many as 60 to 80 per cent of new businesses fail in their first five years of operation. Succession problems account for part of the failures. But a large part comes from management mistakes. Business failures are largely due to poor decision making by the original entrepreneurs and owners

The **succession problem** is the issue of who will run the business when the current head leaves.

A **succession plan** describes how the leadership transition and related financial matters will be handled.

www.fambiz.com.au

Family Business Australia provides information and inspiration for family businesses. It helps member businesses gain the knowledge and skills necessary to develop strategies, overcome problems and achieve success.

on matters of consequence. Often, the entrepreneur is unable to successfully make the transition from entrepreneur to strategic leader and manager. Among the *reasons for new business failures* are:[22]

Reasons for new business failures

- *lack of experience* — not having sufficient know-how to run a business in the chosen market or area
- *lack of expertise* — not having expertise in the essentials of business operations, including finance, purchasing, selling and production
- *lack of strategy and strategic leadership* — not taking the time to craft a vision and mission, and formulate and properly implement strategy
- *poor financial control* — not keeping track of the numbers and failure to control business finances
- *growing too fast* — not taking the time to consolidate a position, fine tune the organisation, and systematically meet the challenges of growth
- *lack of commitment* — not devoting enough time to the requirements of running a competitive business
- *ethical failure* — falling prey to the temptations of fraud, deception and embezzlement.

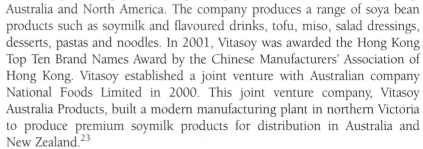

GLOBALISATION

Vitasoy • www.vitasoy.com

Vitasoy expands its products and markets

In 1940 Dr K. S. Lo founded Vitasoy, a company dedicated to manufacturing and selling soya bean milk in Asia. In the 1950s the company built new factories in Hong Kong and by the mid 1970s Vitasoy was Hong Kong's leading supplier of soymilk products. During the 1980s the company looked overseas, with an expansion program that has resulted in the product being sold in 30 countries and processing plants being set up in mainland China, Hong Kong, Australia and North America. The company produces a range of soya bean products such as soymilk and flavoured drinks, tofu, miso, salad dressings, desserts, pastas and noodles. In 2001, Vitasoy was awarded the Hong Kong Top Ten Brand Names Award by the Chinese Manufacturers' Association of Hong Kong. Vitasoy established a joint venture with Australian company National Foods Limited in 2000. This joint venture company, Vitasoy Australia Products, built a modern manufacturing plant in northern Victoria to produce premium soymilk products for distribution in Australia and New Zealand.[23]

NEW VENTURE CREATION

Now that the reasons for business failure have been described, let's talk about doing it right. Whether your interest is low-tech or high-tech, online or offline, opportunities for new ventures are always there for the true entrepreneur.[24] To pursue the entrepreneurship process and start a new venture, you just need good ideas and the courage to give them a chance. You must also be prepared to meet and master the test of strategy and competitive advantage. Can you identify a market niche that is being missed by other established businesses? Can you identify a new market that has not yet been discovered by existing businesses? Can you generate **first-mover advantage** by exploiting a niche or entering a market before competitors? These are the questions that entrepreneurs ask and answer in the process of beginning a new venture. A focus on the customer is critical, as suggested by the guidelines in Manager's Notepad 9.2.[25]

⊘ A **first-mover advantage** comes from being first to exploit a niche or enter a market.

MANAGER'S NOTEPAD 9.2

Questions that keep a new venture customer focused

- Who is your customer?
- How will you reach key customer market segments?
- What determines customer choices to buy your product/service?
- Why is your product/service a compelling choice for the customer?
- How will you price your product/service for the customer?
- How much does it cost to make and deliver your product/service?
- How much does it cost to attract a customer?
- How much does it cost to support and retain a customer?

Life cycles of entrepreneurial organisations

Figure 9.1 describes the stages common to the life cycles of entrepreneurial organisations. It shows the relatively predictable progression of the small business.[26] The organisation begins with the *birth stage* — where the entrepreneur struggles to get the new venture established and survive long enough to test the viability of the underlying business model in the marketplace. The organisation then passes into the *breakthough stage* — where the business model begins to work well, growth is experienced, and the complexity of managing the business operation expands significantly. Next comes the *maturity stage* — where the entrepreneur experiences the advantages of market success and financial stability, while also facing continuing challenges of meeting the needs for professional management skills.

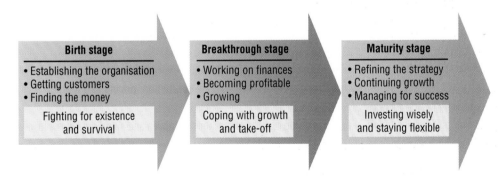

Figure 9.1 ▸ Stages in the life cycle of an entrepreneurial organisation

Entrepreneurs often face control and management dilemmas when their businesses experience growth, including possible diversification or global expansion. These are very challenging in terms of the management and strategic leadership skills required to maintain success. It is here that entrepreneurs encounter a variation of the succession problem described earlier for family businesses. This time the problem is succession from entrepreneurial leadership to professional strategic leadership. The former brings the venture into being and sees it through the early stages of life; the latter manages and leads the venture into maturity as an ever-evolving and perhaps still-growing corporate enterprise. If the entrepreneur is incapable or unwilling to meet the organisation's needs in later life-cycle stages, continued business survival and success may well depend on the business being sold or management control being passed to professionals.

Writing the business plan

When people start new businesses, either independent ones or as new components of larger organisations, they can greatly benefit from having a good **business plan**. This is a plan that describes the details needed to obtain start-up financing and operate a new business. When well done, a business plan offers clear direction to an enterprise.[27] Banks and other financiers want to see a business plan before they loan money or invest in a new venture; senior managers want to see a business plan before they allocate scarce organisational resources to a new project. Importantly, the detailed thinking required to prepare a business plan can contribute to the success of the new initiative.[28]

Although there is no single template for a successful business plan, there is general agreement that a plan should have an executive summary, cover certain business fundamentals, be well organised with headings, be easy to read, and be no more than about 20 pages in length. Basic items that should be included in a business plan are summarised in Manager's Notepad 9.3.[29] One of the great advantages of such a plan, of course, is forcing the entrepreneur to think through all of these issues and challenges before starting out.

MANAGER'S NOTEPAD 9.3

What to include in a business plan

- *Executive summary* — overview of business purpose and highlight of key elements of the plan.
- *Industry analysis* — nature of the industry, including economic trends, important legal or regulatory issues and potential risks.
- *Company description* — mission, owners and legal form.
- *Products and services description* — major goods or services, with special focus on uniqueness in relation to competition.
- *Market description* — size of market, competitor strengths and weaknesses, five-year sales goals.
- *Marketing strategy* — product characteristics, distribution, promotion, pricing and market research.
- *Operations description* — manufacturing or service methods, supplies and suppliers, and control procedures.
- *Staffing description* — management and staffing skills needed and available, compensation, human resource systems.
- *Financial projection* — cash flow projections for 1–5 years, break-even points, and phased investment capital.
- *Capital needs* — amount of funds needed to run the business, amount available, amount requested from new sources.

In addition to what you will find in books and magazines, there are many online resources now available to assist in the development of a business plan. Among the alternatives are the Center for Family-Owned Business www.cfob.com and BizPlanIt www.bizplanit.com. Many examples of successful business plans are published on the Internet by the Moot Corp www.mootcorp.org. The examples include plans from annual competitions in which MBA students from around the world present business plans to panels of potential investors in quest of actual financing for their start-up ideas.

Choosing the form of ownership

One of the important choices that must be made in starting a new venture is the legal form of ownership. There are a number of alternatives, and the choice among them involves careful consideration of their respective advantages and disadvantages. Briefly, the ownership forms include the following.

A **sole proprietorship** is simply an individual or a married couple pursuing business for a profit. This does not involve incorporation; it is simple to start, run and terminate. However, the business owner is personally liable for business debts and claims. This is the most common form of small business ownership in Australia and New Zealand.

A **partnership** is formed when two or more people agree to contribute resources to start and operate a business together. Most typically it is backed by a legal and written partnership agreement. Business partners agree on the contribution of resources and skills to the new venture, and on the sharing of profits, losses and management responsibilities. The *general partnership* just described is the simplest and most common form. A *limited partnership* consists of a general partner and one or more 'limited' partners who do not participate in day-to-day business management. They share in profits, but their losses are limited to the amount of their investment.

A **company**, commonly identified by the 'Ltd' designation in a name, is a legal entity that exists separately from its owners. The company can be for profit, such as Coles Myer Ltd, or not for profit, such as Melbourne University Private Ltd. The company form grants the organisation certain legal rights (for example, to engage in contracts), and it is also responsible for its own liabilities. This separates the owners from personal liability and gives the company a life of its own that can extend beyond that of its owners. Both are important advantages. However, if an organisation continues to trade when it is insolvent, its senior managers would be personally liable for corporate losses. Insolvency law is designed to protect creditors and has grown in importance over the last 20 years following a series of dramatic bankruptcies in Australia in the 1980s and 1990s.

Financing the new venture

Starting a new venture takes money, and that money often must be raised. Most likely, the cost of start up will exceed the amount available from personal sources. In these instances, there are two major sources from which the entrepreneur can obtain outside financing for the new venture. **Debt financing** involves going into debt by borrowing money from another person, a bank or financial institution. This loan must be paid back over time with interest. A loan also requires collateral that pledges assets of the business or personal assets such as a home to secure the loan in case of default. **Equity financing** involves exchanging ownership shares in the business in return for outside investment monies. This money does not need to be paid back. It is an investment on the part of the provider, who assumes the risk for the outcomes of that investment. In return for taking that risk, the equity investor assumes some proportionate ownership control.

A **sole proprietorship** is an individual pursuing business for a profit.

A **partnership** is when two or more people agree to contribute resources to start and operate a business together.

A **company** is a legal entity that exists separately from its owners.

Debt financing involves borrowing money that must be repaid over time with interest.

Equity financing involves exchanging ownership shares for outside investment monies.

Venture capitalists make large investments in new ventures in return for an equity stake in the business.

An **initial public offering (IPO)** is an initial selling of shares of stock to the public and for trading on a stock exchange.

An **angel investor** is a wealthy individual willing to invest in return for equity in a new venture.

Equity financing is usually obtained from **venture capitalists**, companies that pool capital and make investments in new ventures in return for an equity stake in the business. Typically, venture capitalists finance only a very small proportion of new ventures. They tend to focus on relatively large investments, such as $1 million or more, and they usually take a management role in order to grow the business and add value as soon as possible. Sometimes that value is returned in a fast-growing business that gains a solid market base and becomes a candidate for an **initial public offering**, commonly known as an **IPO**. This is when shares of stock in the business are sold to the public and begin trading on a major stock exchange. When an IPO is successful and the share prices are bid up by the market, the original investments of the venture capitalist and entrepreneur rise in value. The anticipation of such return on investment is a large part of the venture capitalist's motivation; indeed, it is the nature of the venture capital business.

When venture capital isn't available to the entrepreneur, male or female, another important financing option is the **angel investor**. This is a wealthy individual who is willing to invest a portion of this wealth in return for equity in a new venture. Angel investors are especially common and helpful in the very early start-up stage. The presence of angel investment can help raise the confidence of venture capitalists and attract additional venture funding that would otherwise not be available.

POINT ← COUNTER ↑

The real barriers to entrepreneurism

The idea that almost anyone can become an entrepreneur is widely held in developed countries, where it is claimed that all individuals have the freedom to operate their own businesses and accumulate wealth. Nowhere is this idea stronger than in countries like Australia, the United Kingdom, the USA and New Zealand. Here individualism and the freedom of the individual to determine their own economic destiny is enshrined in constitutions and the law. However, the reality for most people living in the global economy is that such freedom is often difficult to achieve. There are very high failure rates associated with new businesses. This, and the domination of most sectors of the economy by large global companies such as McDonald's, GE, BHP Billiton, Microsoft, Ford, Siemens and News Corporation, presents serious obstacles to many aspiring entrepreneurs. Large companies often use highly competitive pricing policies to prevent the entrance of new organisations into their industry. While there are some notable examples of successful new entrepreneurs, such as Anita Roddick and Dick Smith, there are also many failures, evidenced by the recent demise of numerous dot-com enterprises.

ENTREPRENEURSHIP AND BUSINESS DEVELOPMENT

Entrepreneurship and the creative spark to launch new ventures is indispensable to the economy at large. It drives the formation of small businesses and new ventures that are so important to job creation and economic development. Larger enterprises need the same spark. Even as they operate more flexibly, in networks and with the advantages of IT, they too depend on entrepreneurship within the system to drive innovation for sustained competitive advantage.

Intrapreneurship and large enterprises

Just like their smaller counterparts, large organisations depend on the entrepreneurial spirit. High performance is increasingly based on the contributions of workers who are willing to assume risk and encourage the creativity and innovation so important to continued success in dynamic and competitive environments. Yet this task is especially challenging in very large and complex systems whose natural tendencies may be toward stability, rigidity and avoidance of risk. The concept of **intrapreneurship** — described as entrepreneurial behaviour on the part of people and subunits operating within large organisations — brings deserved attention to this situation.[30] Through the efforts of *intrapreneurs* large organisations are able to turn new ideas into profitable new products, services and business ventures. Many large organisations are also making greater use of the knowledge in their various subsidiaries and far-flung business units.[31]

To enhance their competitive edge through intrapreneurship, however, managers often find that success depends on the ability of large organisations to act like small ones. To do this, some large organisations create small subunits, often called **skunkworks** in the USA and **innovation groups** in Australia, in which teams are allowed to work together in a unique setting that is highly creative and free of operating restrictions in the larger parent organisation. A classic example occurred at Apple Computer, Inc., where a small group of enthusiastic employees was once sent off to a separate facility in Cupertino, California. Their mandate was straightforward: to create a state-of-the-art, user-friendly personal computer. The group operated free of the organisation's normal product development bureaucracy, set its own norms, and worked together without outside interference. The 'Jolly Roger' was even raised over their building as a symbol of independence. It worked. This is the team that brought the now-famous Macintosh computer into being.

> **Intrapreneurship** is entrepreneurial behaviour displayed by people or subunits within large organisations.

> **Innovation groups** or **skunkworks** are teams allowed to work creatively together, free of constraints from the larger organisation.

Business incubation

One of the advantages of intrapreneurship is that it takes place in a larger organisational environment that can be highly supportive in terms of money and other start-up resources. Individual entrepreneurs who must start on their own face quite a different set of challenges. Even though entrepreneurship and new venture creation are exciting prospects, they are also potentially daunting in complexity and required resources. One way that the motivation toward entrepreneurship can be maintained without suffering the discouragement of start-up requirements is through the support of a **business incubator**. This is a special facility that offers space, a variety of shared administrative services, and management advice to help small businesses get started. Some ideas are focused on specific areas such as technology, manufacturing or services; some are in more rural areas, others are city based. But regardless of focus and location, incubators share the common goal of helping to build successful new businesses that create jobs and improve economic development. They pursue this goal by nurturing start-up businesses in the incubators to improve the chances for them to grow more quickly and become healthy enough to survive on their own. And, of course, with survival the economic benefits of job creation and new members joining the local business community are expected.

> A **business incubator** offers space, shared services and advice to help small businesses get started.

The first successful example of a business incubator was created by the University of Cambridge, Europe's leading research university. It established the Cambridge Science Park in the 1960s to commercialise many of the technologies developed by its scientists. The emerging companies created new, high-paying employment for the region. Australia's Technology Park in Sydney and the planned Bio-industries Technology Centre at James Cook University in Cairns use this business incubator model.

Enterprising Top End architects redefining our response to the environment and social behaviour

The vast majority of Australian buildings are designed using concepts and technologies that are outdated and that do not contribute to sustainability and quality of living. Since the early 1980s Troppo Architects have attempted to redefine Australian architecture by developing concepts and technologies that improve our response to the environment and reflect our social behaviour. In doing so they have developed a unique and regionally specific architectural enterprise in northern Australia, with offices in Darwin and Townsville. However, their design concepts, technology and models have much wider application for Australia and the Asia–Pacific Rim region. The company has won numerous architecture awards and its recent projects include the Kakadu National Park Interpretative Centre, the Top End Hotel, the Pukatja Aged Care Facility and the redevelopment of the Australian Defence Force's Lavarack Barracks in Townsville.

When Troppo was established by Adrian Welke and Phil Harris in 1981, they developed a set of general concepts and guidelines based on scientific models and pragmatic responses to the environment and changing social behaviour. Troppo's approach to architectural design and technology is embodied in the following themes. Buildings are organisms of adaptation with *adjustable skin* like that of human beings, allowing an infinitely receptive tissue. This translates into the use of louvres, translucent polycarbonate shading products, high technology glasses with ultraviolet filters, slatted buildings and the inventive use of high-tech shade cloths and roller blinds. Troppo is an outstanding example of a thriving and innovative regional business.[32]

Source: © Patrick Bingham-Hall

CHAPTER 9
Study guide

The chapter 9 study guide helps you review the chapter content, prepare for examinations, apply what you have learned and further build your career readiness. The summary briefly answers the study questions posed at the start of the chapter. The list of key terms allows you to double-check your familiarity with basic concepts and definitions. The applied activities help you test your comprehension of chapter content. Suggestions offered as career readiness activities direct your attention to relevant sections of the Career Readiness Workbook where you can test and develop your career skills and apply what you have learned. The list of electronic resources suggests activities from the *Management: An Asia–Pacific Perspective* web site and, finally, the case for critical thinking helps you apply your new management knowledge.

SUMMARY

What is entrepreneurship?

- Entrepreneurship is risk-taking behaviour that results in the creation of new opportunities for individuals and/or organisations.
- An entrepreneur is someone who takes strategic risks to pursue opportunities in situations others may view as problems or threats.
- There are many examples of entrepreneurs worldwide like Dick Smith, Poppy King, Richard Branson, Gerry Harvey and Anita Roddick whose experiences can be a source of learning and inspiration for others.
- Entrepreneurs tend to be creative people who are very self-confident, determined, resilient, adaptable and driven to excel; they like to be masters of their own destinies.
- Entrepreneurship is rich with diversity, with women and minority-owned business start ups increasing in numbers.

What is special about small businesses?

- Entrepreneurship results in the founding of many small business enterprises that offer job creation and other benefits to economies.
- The Internet has opened a whole new array of entrepreneurial possibilities, including online buying and selling and the more formal pursuit of new 'dot-com' businesses.
- Smaller businesses are pursuing more global opportunities in the quest for expanded markets, access to labour and technical expertise, and locations for low-cost manufacturing or outsourcing.
- Family businesses that are owned and financially controlled by family members represent the largest percentage of businesses operating worldwide.
- A significant problem faced by family businesses is the succession problem of transferring leadership from one generation to the next.
- Small businesses have a high failure rate; as many as 50 per cent of new businesses fail in their first three years of operation.
- Small business failures are largely due to poor management, when owners make bad decisions on matters of major business consequence.

How do you start a new venture?

- Entrepreneurial organisations tend to follow the life cycle stages of acceptance, breakthrough and maturity, with each stage offering different management challenges to the entrepreneur.
- New start ups should be guided by a good business plan that describes the intended nature of the business, how it will operate, and how financing will be obtained to operate it.
- An important issue is choice of the form of business ownership, with the proprietorship and company forms offering different advantages and disadvantages.
- Two basic ways of financing a new venture are through debt financing, by taking loans, and equity financing, which involves exchanging ownership shares in return for outside investment.
- Venture capitalists are companies that pool capital and make investments in new ventures in return for an equity stake in the business.
- The angel investor is a wealthy individual who is willing to invest a portion of his of her wealth in return for equity in a new venture.

What resources support entrepreneurship and business development?

- Intrapreneurship, or entrepreneurial behaviour within larger organisations, is important in today's competitive environments.
- Business incubators offer space, shared services and advice to small businesses in the start-up stages.

KEY TERMS

angel investor (p. 256)

business incubator (p. 257)

business plan (p. 254)

company (p. 255)

debt financing (p. 255)

entrepreneur (p. 242)

entrepreneurship (p. 242)

equity financing (p. 255)

family businesses (p. 250)

first-mover advantage (p. 253)

franchise (p. 248)

initial public offering (IPO) (p. 256)

innovation groups (p. 257)

intrapreneurship (p. 257)

partnership (p. 255)

skunkworks (p. 257)

small business (p. 247)

sole proprietorship (p. 255)

succession plan (p. 251)

succession problem (p. 251)

venture capitalists (p. 256)

APPLIED ACTIVITIES

Short-response questions

1. What is the relationship between diversity and entrepreneurship?
2. In what ways can the Internet be a driving force for entrepreneurship?
3. What are the advantages of choosing a limited partnership form of small business ownership?
4. How can a large organisation stimulate entrepreneurship within itself?

Application question

5. Assume for the moment that you have a great idea for a potential Internet-based start-up business. In discussing the idea with a friend, she advises you to ensure you tie your business idea to potential customers and then describe it well in a business plan. 'After

all,' she says, 'you won't succeed without customers and you'll never get a chance to succeed if you can't attract financial backers through a good business plan.' With these words to the wise, you proceed. What questions will you ask and answer to ensure that you are customer-focused in this business? What are the major areas that you would address in writing your initial business plan?

CAREER READINESS ACTIVITIES

Recommended individual and group learning activities from the end-of-text Career Readiness Workbook for this chapter include:

Career advancement portfolio *WB*

Update your career advancement portfolio to reflect your new skills and experiences. Include skills and personal insights you gain from the following projects and exercises.

Research and presentation project *WB*

• Project 1 — Diversity lessons — 'what have we learned?'

Cross-functional integrative case *WB*

Read the integrative case on Sarina Russo and answer the following questions:

9.1 Would you classify Sarina Russo as an entrepreneur? What enterpreneurial characteristics does she appear to demonstrate?

9.2 Comment on Sarina Russo's background and early experiences in terms of their influence on her becoming an entrepreneur.

Exercises in teamwork *WB*

• Exercise 4 — What is your propensity for taking risks?
• Exercise 24 — Creative solutions

Management skills assessment *WB*

• Assessment 9 — An entrepreneurial quiz

ELECTRONIC RESOURCES

Don't forget to take full advantage of the online support for *Management: An Asia–Pacific Perspective* at www.johnwiley.com.au/highered/management: chapter 9 practice tests, e-flashcards, crossword puzzles, interactive management skills assessments, interactive cases, the online career advancement portfolio and much more!

CASE FOR CRITICAL THINKING

Read the following case for critical thinking on Masport. While you are reading the case keep in mind what you have learned in this chapter, then answer the questions.

Masport: designing, manufacturing and marketing innovative products

Harold Mason and Reuben Porter began manufacturing mechanical milking machines, vacuum pumps and a range of farm equipment engines in Auckland, New Zealand, in 1910. Initially, their products serviced New Zealand's largely rural economy, but then they began producing petrol engines for a wider range of uses, including agricultural and marine. The two entrepreneurs developed a reputation for innovative engineering and manufacturing excellence.

Growth, innovation and technology

They introduced their hand and power lawnmowers in the 1930s and also began manufacturing components for the newly established business, Fisher & Paykel, which was producing GE washing machines under licence. The rapid growth of Masport's finished products and components business led to the construction of a new factory at Mount Wellington in 1940. During World War II, the company manufactured military supplies and ammunition.[33]

In the post-war period there was substantial growth in the scope of Masport's activities, with strong emphasis placed on production process innovation in order to further improve cost efficiencies and product quality. This strategy was designed to launch Masport into the lucrative North American and UK markets for vacuum pumps. Since the 1960s the company has become a leading international producer of Rotary Vane and Liquid Ring vacuum pumps, which have wide application in the dairy and liquid waste extraction industries. Masport's exports account for over 40 per cent of the company's sales.[34]

Consumer products expansion

While much of its output is for industrial use, Masport also produces a very successful range of consumer products, such as lawnmowers and wood and gas flame effect fires, which are exported to over 35 countries. The company produces a range of innovative lawnmowers, including the world's first mower to have a separate mulching function for branches. This new concept allows a lawnmower to do more than simply cut grass. Masport is often referred to as the Fisher & Paykel of the lawnmower and home heating industries due to its product innovation. Its lawnmowers use high-tech materials, new blade design, ergonomic principles and a wide selection of user functions to give consumers effortless mowing and assistance with other gardening tasks. The mowers use a key for quick starting, are self-propelled, and include extra wide cut blades for covering a much larger area than a conventional machine. Masport also pioneered a double blade system for chipping, catching and mulching and an ergonomically designed mower handle (the Ergo Handle) that allows the user to set the handle height that is most suitable for them. Their Comfort Start technology also avoids users having to bend all the way down to the engine to pull the start cord. Today, their lawnmower range includes over 35 different models.[35]

The company has adopted the same innovative approach with its wood and gas flame effect fires, making the Masport name synonymous with home heating throughout Australasia. The company constantly modifies the technology in its heaters to improve fuel efficiency and heat dispersion. It has the most modern and technologically advanced foundry in New Zealand.[36]

Training, research and development

Masport's reputation for innovation comes from employing young engineers and designers, utilising group-based product development teams, and remaining close to the customer through in-depth market research. Masport also invests heavily in training staff and encourages superior output through a performance-related pay system. It also offers a limited number of scholarships for students wishing to study engineering, marketing and management. Consequently, the company attracts many of New Zealand's brightest engineers and designers and has received numerous design and export awards. It has also avoided the temptation to diversify into non-related products where it lacks expertise.

The original entrepreneurs, Mason and Porter, have died; however, the company's entrepreneurial spirit lives on through the maintenance of its organisational culture. A number of relatives of the original founders also hold key positions at Masport. The careful selection of senior managers has been critical in ensuring continuity and growth. The company also ensures ongoing innovation through nominating entrepreneurs to the board of directors. The board has a central role in determining new product and marketing directions for the company.[37]

QUESTIONS

1. What allowed Harold Mason and Reuben Porter to develop Masport into one of New Zealand's most successful and sustainable businesses with major export markets?

2. What has Masport done to differentiate its products?

3. Do you have what it takes to be entrepreneurial in today's business environment?

4. Are all entrepreneurs born with business skills or can they be acquired through training and experience?

ORGANISATION

PART 4

Organising

▸ What is organising as a
management function?

▸ What are the major types of
organisation structures?

▸ What are the new developments in
organisation structures?

▸ What organising trends are changing
the workplace?

GETTING @ CONNECTED

BP — an organisation structure for innovation, change and cost control

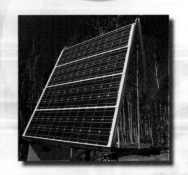

Ten years ago, the global multinational British Petroleum (BP), which has extensive operations in Australia and the Asia–Pacific region, had eight layers of management. Now, the 150 business units (BUs) are separated from the company's executive management by one layer. It has one of the flattest structures of any global multinational. This means that BP's BU leaders are able to operate as if they are running their own separate businesses — subject to compliance with group policies, and accountable for the fulfilment of a performance contract which they negotiate with the executive committees of their business stream.

Performance contracts cover all the essential elements of each business, including key financial and operational data. They also embrace important non-financial targets such as safety and environmental performance. The contracts exist at various levels, including one between the group chief executive and the board. They are subject to regular monitoring and assessment to ensure that what has been agreed upon is delivered. These reviews are the quid pro quo for the freedom which BU leaders enjoy in every other way. Performance contracts are designed to challenge and to produce results and are one of the main ways in which improvements in one business are captured for the group as a whole.

GET CONNECTED!

@

BP's flat structure and accompanying management processes support the company's corporate strategies, but would this structure be appropriate for all organisations? Familiarise yourself with options available to different companies. For example, visit ITT www.itt.com and Woolworths www.woolworths.com.au to examine some of the differences between company structures.

GET CONNECTED!

The Canadian management scholar and consultant Henry Mintzberg is well known internationally for his work in the area of strategy and structure. Writing with a colleague in the *Harvard Business Review*, he points out both that organisations are changing very fast in today's world and that people within them are struggling to find their place.[1] The point is, people need to understand how their organisations work if they are to work well within them. Mintzberg notes some common questions: What parts connect to one another? How should processes and people come together? Whose ideas have to flow where? These and related questions raise critical issues about organisation structures and how well they meet an organisation's performance needs.

The Australian management scholar John Campling is well known for his work on organisation structures in trade unions, which have performance needs like any other organisation. His work suggests that structures are often driven by environmental requirements or dependencies and that organisations need to adjust their structures regularly in line with such external changes.[2] His later work on organisation structures in the Australian hospitality, telecommunications and construction industries draws similar conclusions.[3]

The organising approach of BP — management through a strong corporate executive with autonomous business units — is one entrepreneurial benchmark. By building a strategically focused yet market-responsive organisation structure, the company has grown in the highly competitive energy industry. While this management structure has been successful for BP, it is not the only way to structure for success. There are many options open to organisations that wish to be successful in their industry and there are examples in many industries of new organisational forms through which businesses seek to gain competitive advantage. Some businesses use designs that can be described as team-centred, networks, or even 'boundaryless' and 'virtual'. Others restructure, which may involve workforce reductions (downsizing) and organisational delayering — reducing the number of management levels, such as occurred in BP.

Among the vanguard organisations, those that consistently deliver above-average returns and outperform their competitors, consistent themes are found. Regardless of the specific approaches taken, they all emphasise empowerment, support for employees, responsiveness to client or customer needs, flexibility in dealing with a dynamic environment, and continual attention to quality improvements. They also strive for positive cultures and high-quality-of-work-life experiences for members and employees. Importantly, nothing is constant; at least not for long. Change is always a possibility. Managers in progressive organisations are always seeking new ways to better organise the workplace to support strategies and achieve high-performance goals. In the Internet industry, Google has developed into a strong, high-performing technological company by attending to the performance factors noted above.

ORGANISING AS A MANAGEMENT FUNCTION

Organising is the process of assigning tasks, allocating resources and arranging activities to implement plans.

Formally defined, **organising** is the process of arranging people and other resources to work together to accomplish a goal. As one of the basic functions of management it involves both creating a division of labour for tasks to be performed and then coordinating results to achieve a common purpose. Figure 10.1 shows the central role organising plays in the management process. Once plans are created, the manager's task is to see to it that they are carried out. Given a clear mission, core values, objectives and strategy, organising begins the process of implementation by clarifying jobs and working relationships. It identifies who is to do what, who is in charge of whom, and how different people and parts of the organisation relate to and work with one another. All of this, of course, can be done in different ways. This is where an understanding of situational contingencies becomes important. The strategic leadership challenge is to choose the best organisational form to fit the strategy and other situational demands.

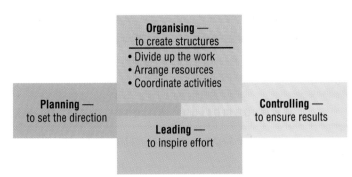

Figure 10.1 ▶ Organising viewed in relationship with the other management functions

What is organisation structure?

The way in which the various parts of an organisation are formally arranged is usually referred to as the **organisation structure**. It is the system of tasks, workflows, reporting relationships and communication channels that link together the work of diverse individuals and groups. Any structure should both allocate task assignments through a division of labour and provide for the coordination of performance results. A good structure that does both of these things well can be an important asset to an organisation.[4] Unfortunately, it is easier to talk about good structures than it is to actually create them. This is why you often read and hear about organisations *restructuring*, or changing their structures in an attempt to improve performance. There is no one best structure that meets the needs of all circumstances. Structure must be handled in a contingency fashion; as environments and situations change, structures must often be changed too. To make good choices, a manager must know the alternatives and be familiar with current trends and developments.

> **Organisation structure** is a system of tasks, workflows, reporting relationships and communication linkages.

Formal structure

You may know the concept of structure best in the form of an **organisation chart**. This is a diagram that shows reporting relationships and the formal arrangement of work positions within an organisation.[5] A typical organisation chart identifies various positions and job titles as well as the lines of authority and communication between them. This is the **formal structure**, or the structure of the organisation in its official state. It represents the way the organisation is intended to function. Manager's Notepad 10.1 identifies some of the things that you can learn by reviewing an organisation chart.

> An **organisation chart** describes the arrangement of work positions within an organisation.
>
> **Formal structure** is the official structure of the organisation.

MANAGER'S NOTEPAD 10.1

What you can learn from an organisation chart

- *Division of work.* Positions and titles show work responsibilities.
- *Supervisory relationships.* Lines show who reports to whom.
- *Communication channels.* Lines show formal communication flows.
- *Major subunits.* Positions reporting to a common manager are shown.
- *Levels of management.* Vertical layers of management are shown.

**Siemens • www.siemens.com
and
Cambridge Science Park •
www.cambridge-science-park.co.uk**

Designing for informal learning

At the German engineering and electronics multinational, Siemens, informal learning occurs during lunch and tea breaks as staff share ideas, problems and solutions with one another in the company cafeterias. The high quality cafeterias are appreciated by the employees, and their provision has positive outcomes for the company through this discussion and sharing of ideas. A win–win outcome for staff and management.

The creation of communal areas, such as cafeterias and bars, has long been recognised for its positive contribution to organisational learning. Cambridge University's pioneering Science Park integrated these types of facilities into its building design in order to stimulate greater cross-fertilisation of ideas and solutions — 'hot beds' of idea generation. The Cambridge Science Park is a world leader in the development of computer and biogenetic technology. Australia's Technology Park, located close to Sydney's CBD, is modelled on the Cambridge approach.

Informal structure

> The **informal structure** is the set of unofficial relationships among an organisation's members.

Behind every formal structure typically lies an **informal structure**. This is a 'shadow' organisation made up of the unofficial, but often critical, working relationships between organisational members. If the informal structure could be drawn, it would show who talks to and interacts regularly with whom regardless of their formal titles and relationships. The lines of the informal structure would cut across levels and move from side to side. They would show people meeting for coffee, in exercise groups and in friendship cliques, among other possibilities. Importantly, no organisation can be fully understood without gaining insight into the informal structure as well as the formal one.[6]

Informal structures can be very helpful in getting needed work accomplished in any organisation. Indeed, they may be considered essential in many ways to organisational success. This is especially true during times of change when out-of-date formal structures may simply not provide the support people need to deal with new or unusual situations. Because it takes time to change or modify formal structures, this is a common occurrence. Through the emergent and spontaneous relationships of informal structures, people benefit by gaining access to interpersonal networks of emotional support and friendship that satisfy important social needs. They also benefit in task performance by being in personal contact with others who can help them get things done when necessary. In fact, what is known as *informal learning* is increasingly recognised as an important resource for organisational development. This is learning that takes place as people interact informally throughout the work day and in a wide variety of unstructured situations.

Of course, informal structures also have potential disadvantages. Because they exist outside the formal authority system, the activities of informal structures can sometimes work against the best interests of the organisation as a whole. They can also be susceptible to rumour, carry inaccurate information, breed resistance to change and even divert work efforts from important objectives. Also, 'outsiders' or people who are left out of informal groupings may feel less a part of daily activities and suffer a loss of satisfaction. Some expatriate managers of Japanese firms, for example, at times complain about being excluded from the 'shadow cabinet'. This is an informal group of Japanese executives who hold the real power to get things done in the organisation and sometimes do so without the participation of others.[7]

TRADITIONAL ORGANISATION STRUCTURES

A traditional principle of organising is that performance gains are possible when people are allowed to specialise and become expert in specific jobs or tasks. Given this division of labour, however, decisions must then be made on how to group work positions into formal teams or departments and then link them together in a coordinated fashion within the larger organisation. These decisions involve a process called **departmentalisation** and it has traditionally resulted in three major types of organisation structures — the functional, divisional and matrix structures.[8]

Functional structures

In **functional structures**, people with similar skills and performing similar tasks are formally grouped together into work units. Members of functional departments share technical expertise, interests and responsibilities. The first example in figure 10.2 shows a common functional structure in a business. In this case senior management is arranged by the functions of marketing, finance, production and human resources. In this functional structure, manufacturing problems are the responsibility of the production director, marketing problems are the province of the marketing director and so on. The key point is that members of each function work within their areas of expertise. If each function does its jobs properly, the expectation is that the business will operate successfully.

Functional structures are not limited to businesses. The figure also shows how this form of departmentalisation can be used in other types of organisations such as banks and hospitals. These types of structures typically work well for small organisations that produce only one or a few products or services. They also tend to work best in relatively stable environments where problems are predictable and the demands for change and innovation are limited. The major *advantages of functional structures* include the following:
- economies of scale with efficient use of resources
- task assignments consistent with expertise and training
- high-quality technical problem solving
- in-depth training and skill development within functions
- clear career paths within functions.

There are also potential *disadvantages of functional structures*. Common problems with functional structures involve difficulties in pinpointing responsibilities for things like cost containment, product or service quality, timeliness and innovation in response to environmental changes. Such problems with functional structures become magnified as organisations grow in size and environments begin to change.

Restructuring, outsourcing and efficiency

Surveys reveal that large organisations are restructuring to place greater emphasis on their core business areas. This involves selling off non-core businesses and contracting out tasks that outside organisations can more effectively perform, such as security, human resources and cleaning.

What are the consequences for informal structures in the organisations?

 Departmentalisation is the process of grouping together people and jobs into work units.

 Functional structures group together people with similar skills who perform similar tasks.

Advantages of functional structures

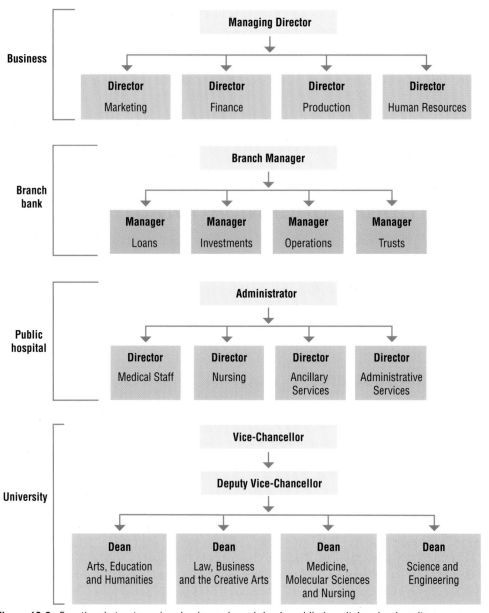

Figure 10.2 ▸ Functional structures in a business, branch bank, public hospital and university

💡 The **functional chimneys problem** is a lack of communication and coordination across functions.

Another significant concern is often called the **functional chimneys problem**. This refers to the lack of communication, coordination and problem solving across functions. Because the functions become formalised not only on an organisation chart but also in the mindsets of people, the sense of cooperation and common purpose breaks down. When functional units develop self-centred and narrow viewpoints they lose the total system perspective. When problems occur with another unit, they are too often referred up to higher levels for resolution rather than being addressed by people at the same level. This slows decision making and problem solving and can result in a loss of advantage in competitive situations. For example, when Ford took over as the new owner of Jaguar, it had to resolve many quality problems. The quality turnaround took longer than anticipated, in part because of what Jaguar's chairman called 'excessive compartmentalisation'. In building cars, the different departments did very little talking and working with one another. Ford's response was to push for more interdepartmental coordination, consensus decision making and cost controls — an approach that is now paying off.[9]

Divisional structures

A second organisational alternative is the **divisional structure**. It groups together people who work on the same product or process, serve similar customers, and/or are located in the same area or geographical region. As illustrated in figure 10.3, divisional structures are common in complex organisations that have multiple and differentiated products and services, serve diverse customers, pursue diversified strategies, and/or operate in various and different competitive environments. The three major types of divisional approaches are the product, geographical and process structures.

Divisional structures attempt to avoid problems common to functional structures. They are especially popular among organisations with diverse operations that extend across many products, territories, customers and work processes.[10] The potential *advantages of divisional structures* include the following:

- more flexibility in responding to environmental changes
- improved coordination across functional departments
- clear points of responsibility for product or service delivery
- expertise focused on specific customers, products and regions
- greater ease in changing size by adding or deleting divisions.

 A **divisional structure** groups together people working on the same product, in the same area, with similar customers, or on the same processes.

Advantages of divisional structures

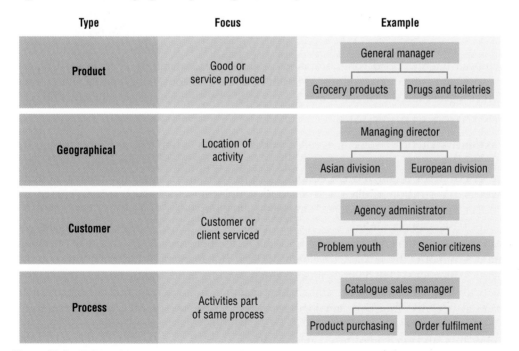

Figure 10.3 ▸ Divisional structures based on product, geography, customer and process

As with other alternatives, there are potential *disadvantages of divisional structures*. They can reduce economies of scale and increase costs through the duplication of resources and efforts across divisions. They can also create unhealthy rivalries as divisions compete for resources and attention; and they emphasise division needs and goals to the detriment of the goals of the organisation as a whole.

PRODUCT STRUCTURES

Product structures group together people and jobs working on a single product or service.

Product structures, sometimes called *market structures*, group together jobs and activities working on a single product or service. They clearly identify costs, profits, problems and successes in a market area with a central point of accountability. Consequently, managers are encouraged to be responsive to changing market demands and customer tastes. Common in large organisations, product structures may even extend into global operations. The global food processing company H. J. Heinz restructured its organisation from one based on countries and regions — a geographical structure — to one based on product divisions. The senior management believed that a product structure would bring the best brand management to all countries and enhance cooperation around the world within product businesses. This change in structure has improved the company's financial performance in recent years.

GEOGRAPHICAL STRUCTURES

Geographical structures group together people and jobs performed in the same location.

Geographical structures, sometimes called *area structures*, group together jobs and activities being performed in the same location or geographical region. They are typically used when there is a need to differentiate products or services in various locations, such as in different regions of a country. They are also quite common in international operations, where they help to focus attention on the unique cultures and requirements of particular regions. For example, the French-based global resort and tourism operator Club Med groups its operations into four areas: Europe, North America, Asia and Oceania. The latter region also includes its two cruising yachts, which operate in the Pacific and Atlantic oceans and the Mediterranean Sea. Similarly, General Motors structures its global operations into four areas: North America, Asia–Pacific, Europe, and Latin America, Africa and the Middle East.[11] With increasing market pressure for corporate 'globalisation' a number of companies have restructured into either product- or customer-based divisions. The introduction of improved Internet-based communications systems, the dismantling of trade barriers, and the weakening of national cultures in favour of a homogeneous global culture will promote further organisational changes from a geographical to a product or customer structure.

CUSTOMER STRUCTURES

Customer structures group together people and jobs that serve the same customers or clients.

Customer structures, sometimes called *market structures*, group together jobs and activities that are serving the same customers or clients. The major appeal is the ability to best serve the special needs of the different customer groups. With increasing differentiation of global markets, this structure is often well suited to complex businesses such as BHP Billiton and 3M. The Anglo-Australian resource company BHP Billiton is designed around customer sector groups (CSGs) for aluminium, base metals, carbon steel materials, energy coal, stainless steel materials, petroleum and steel. These CSGs are focused on customers rather than operations and are supported by finance, development, legal and marketing (including transport and logistics) functions. BHP Billiton's finance group provides value-adding financial solutions in line with BHP Billiton's strategy and charter, ensuring the preservation of the organisation's financial integrity. Transport and logistics is responsible for coordinating and managing logistics and freight tasks across the CSGs, with a dedicated logistics team under each customer group. It is structured into three core competency service groups: Chartering and Freight Trading for freight optimisation; Logistics Solutions for logistics optimisation; and Marine Services for management of marine operations and risk. These core groups are comprised of highly skilled people specialising in individual or long-chain logistics solutions, e-technology, freight and sector trading, chartering, project management and support, industry representation, and customer service and support.[12] At 3M the company is organised to focus attention around the world on the following markets: consumer and office, specialty materials, industrial, health care, electronics and communications, transportation, graphics and safety.[13]

PROCESS STRUCTURES

A *work process* is a group of tasks related to one another that collectively create something of value to a customer.[14] An example is order fulfilment — when you telephone a catalogue retailer and request a particular item. The process of order fulfilment takes the order from point of initiation by the customer to point of fulfilment by a delivered order. A **process structure** groups together jobs and activities that are part of the same processes. In the example of figure 10.3 (page 273), this might take the form of product-purchasing teams, order-fulfilment teams and systems-support teams for the mail-order catalogue business. The importance of understanding work processes and designing process-driven organisations has been popularised by management consultant and author Michael Hammer.[15] The essentials of Hammer's ideas on work process design are discussed in the next chapter.

A **process structure** groups jobs and activities that are part of the same processes.

Matrix structures

The **matrix structure**, often called the *matrix organisation*, combines the functional and divisional structures just described. In effect, it is an attempt to gain the advantages and minimise the disadvantages of each. This is accomplished in the matrix by using permanent cross-functional teams to integrate functional expertise in support of a clear divisional focus on a product, project or program.[16] As shown in figure 10.4, workers in a matrix structure belong to at least two formal groups at the same time — a functional group and a product, program or project team. They also report to two bosses — one within the function and the other within the team.

A **matrix structure** combines functional and divisional approaches to emphasise project or program teams.

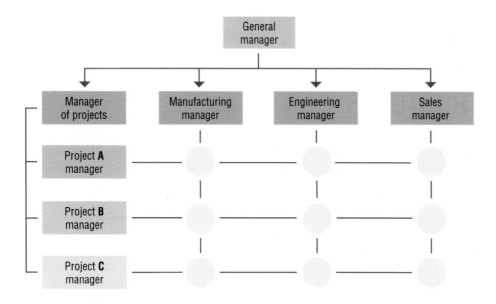

Functional personnel assigned to both projects and functional departments

Figure 10.4 ▸ Matrix structure in a small multiproject business

The matrix organisation has gained a strong foothold in the workplace, with applications in such diverse settings as manufacturing (for example, aerospace, electronics, pharmaceuticals), service industries (for example, banking, brokerage, retailing), professional fields (for example, accounting, advertising, law), and the not-for-profit sector (for example, city,

State, and federal agencies, hospitals, universities). Matrix structures are also found in multinational organisations, where they offer the flexibility to deal with regional differences as well as multiple product, program or project needs. Matrix structures are common in organisations pursuing growth strategies in dynamic and complex environments.

The main contribution of matrix structures to organisational performance lies in the use of permanent cross-functional teams. Team members work closely together to share expertise and information in a timely manner to solve problems. The potential *advantages of matrix structures* include the following:

Advantages of matrix structures

- better interfunctional cooperation in operations and problem solving
- increased flexibility in adding, removing and/or changing operations to meet changing demands
- better customer service, since there is always a program, product or project manager informed and available to answer questions
- better performance accountability through the program, product or project managers
- improved decision making as problem solving takes place at the team level, where the best information is available
- improved strategic management, since top managers are freed from unnecessary problem solving to focus time on strategic issues.

Predictably, there are also potential *disadvantages of matrix structures*. The two-boss system is susceptible to power struggles, as functional supervisors and team leaders vie with one another to exercise authority. The two-boss system can also be frustrating for matrix members if it creates task confusion and conflicts in work priorities. Team meetings in the matrix are also time consuming. Teams may develop 'groupitis', or strong team loyalties that cause a loss of focus on larger organisational goals. And the requirements of adding the team leaders to a matrix structure can result in increased costs.[17]

DEVELOPMENTS IN ORGANISATION STRUCTURES

The realities of a global economy and the demands of strategies driven by hypercompetition are putting increasing pressures on organisation structures. The performance demands are for more speed to market, greater customer orientation, constant productivity improvements, better technology use and more. The environment is unrelenting in such demands. As a result, managers are continually searching for new ways to better structure their organisations to meet the demands of situations rife with complexity and constant pressure.

Structural innovation is always important in the search for productivity improvement and competitive advantage. The right structure becomes a performance asset; the wrong one becomes a liability — one that inhibits rather than facilitates people as they try to work with technologies and processes, and work well together.[18] Today, the vertical and control-oriented structures of the past are proving less and less sufficient to master the tasks at hand. The matrix structure is a first step toward improving flexibility and problem solving through better cross-functional integration. It is now part of a broader movement toward more horizontal structures that decrease hierarchy, increase empowerment, and more fully mobilise the talents of people to drive organisational performance. When combined with the ever-increasing power of information technologies, the new horizontal structures become much more responsive to environmental demands and much better aligned with organisational strategies. Manager's Notepad 10.2 offers guidelines for mobilising the opportunities of horizontal structures.[19]

Team structures

Organisations are being restructured for greater internal integration. As the traditional vertical structures give way to more horizontal ones, teams are serving as the basic building blocks.[20] Organisations using **team structures** mobilise both permanent and temporary teams extensively to solve problems, complete special projects and accomplish day-to-day tasks.[21]

As illustrated in figure 10.5, a team structure involves teams of various types working together as needed to solve problems and explore opportunities, either on a full-time or part-time basis. These are often **cross-functional teams** composed of members from different areas of work responsibility.[22] The intention is to break down the functional chimneys or barriers inside the organisation and create more effective lateral relations for ongoing problem solving and work performance. They are also often **project teams** that are convened for a particular task or project and disband once it is completed. The intention here is to quickly convene people with the needed talents and focus their efforts intensely to solve a problem or take advantage of a special opportunity.

Team structures use permanent and temporary cross-functional teams to improve lateral relations.

Cross-functional teams bring together members from different functional departments.

Project teams are convened for a particular task or project and disband once it is completed.

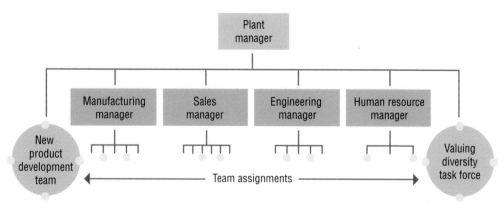

Figure 10.5 ▸ How a team structure uses cross-functional teams for improved lateral relations

There are many potential *advantages of team structures*. They are frequently tried when an organisation experiences difficulties with communication and decision making due to the functional chimneys problem described earlier. At the same time that team assignments help

www.kpmgcampus.com

The multinational accounting and consulting giant KPMG abandoned a functional organisation for an integrated team approach. Within industry-focused lines of business, regional areas have their own teams that draw upon local, national and international information technology resources to serve customer needs.

to break down barriers between operating departments, they can also boost morale as people from different parts of an organisation get to know more about one another. Because the teams focus shared knowledge and expertise on specific problems, they can also improve the speed and quality of decisions in many situations. People working in teams can experience a greater sense of involvement and identification, increasing their enthusiasm for the job.

All organisational structures should harness the full talents of the workforce. However, in team structures this goal is pursued relentlessly and with full recognition of the value of group as well as individual contributions. Within teams and under the guidance of formal and informal leaders, individuals are expected to work together through cooperation, shared commitments to a common purpose, and consensus.[23] After a research team at Polaroid Corporation developed a new medical imaging system in three years, when most had predicted it would take six, a senior executive said: 'Our researchers are not any smarter, but by working together they get the value of each other's intelligence almost instantaneously'.[24]

The complexities of teams and teamwork are discussed in chapter 17. They contribute to the potential *disadvantages of team structures*. These include conflicting loyalties among members to both team and functional assignments. They also include issues of time management and group process. By their very nature, teams spend a lot of time in meetings. Not all of this time is productive. How well team members spend their time together often depends on the quality of interpersonal relations, group dynamics and team management. All of these concerns, as described in chapter 17, are manageable. There is no doubt about it — teams and teamwork are hard work. But with good leadership and a committed membership, they are also invaluable organisational resources.

HIGH PERFORMANCE

Goodman Fielder •
www.goodmanfielder.com

Rationalising and divesting for profitability

Goodman Fielder is the largest Australian-owned food-product company. It produces many of Australia's and New Zealand's most popular and well-known brands, such as Uncle Tobys and Meadow Lea, as well as products and ingredients for the food service, commercial and industrial sectors. Goodman Fielder has manufacturing, marketing and distribution systems in more than 40 countries and has more than 16 000 employees. Chief executive, Tom Park, is restructuring the food giant. The company's strategic action plan is to simplify the business and focus on its retail brand products. Park said it was the group's intention to identify a strategic partner for its milling and commercial mixing businesses and then 'enter into an appropriate input supply agreement for our baked goods businesses in Australia'. The company's milling business consists of ten flour mills and two mixing sites in various parts of Australia. In 2000, the group revealed its strategic action plan — an initiative aimed at streamlining the group's operations and cutting about $60 million from its cost base over three years. In the restructure, food-related businesses in Australia and New Zealand were merged and a few underperforming assets sold. In Australia, the Uncle Tobys and Meadow Lea assets were merged into a $1 billion business; whereas in New Zealand, GF Milling & Baking, Bluebird and Meadow Lea were amalgamated.[25]

Network structures

Organisations using variations of the **network structure** operate with a central core that is linked through 'networks' of relationships with outside contractors and suppliers of essential services. With the great advantages offered by communications and information technology today, new emphasis is being given to strategically employing them to simplify and streamline organisational structures. Network structures accomplish this by engaging in a shifting variety of strategic alliances and business contracts that sustain operations. The old model was for organisations to own everything. The new model is to network and operate without the costs of owning all supporting functions or directly employing persons with all needed expertise. Network organisations own only the most essential or 'core' components. They are able to do this by employing information technology now available to support aggressive outsourcing strategies.[26]

A **network structure** uses IT to link with networks of outside suppliers and service contractors.

Figure 10.6 illustrates a network structure as it might work for a mail-order company selling outdoor furniture through a catalogue. The company itself is very small, consisting of relatively few full-time employees working from a central headquarters. Beyond that, it is structured as a series of business relationships, maintained operationally using the latest in information technology.

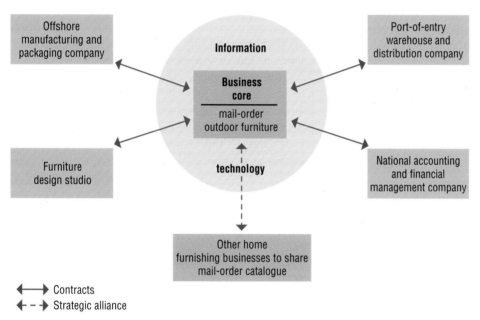

Figure 10.6 ▸ A network structure for a catalogue-based retail business

Merchandise is designed on contract with a furniture design firm — which responds quickly as designs are shared and customised via computer networking. The furniture is manufactured and packaged by subcontractors located around the world — wherever materials, quality and cost are found at best advantage. Stock is maintained and shipped from a contract warehouse — ensuring quality storage and on-time expert shipping.

All of the accounting and financial details are managed on contract with an outside company — providing better technical expertise than the furniture company could afford to employ on a full-time basis. The quarterly catalogue is designed, printed and mailed cooperatively as a strategic alliance with two other businesses that sell different home

CAREER

Social responsibility

ACEnet

Harnessing the power of networks for economic development
www.acenetworks.org

June Holley, president of the Appalachian Center for Economic Networks (ACEnet), uses network organisation concepts to support economic development in rural USA. The Athens, Ohio, centre serves as a *networking hub for small businesses* — microenterprises that come together to share expertise and connections in order to develop new business initiatives.

ACEnet offers information and business incubator support, including the facilities of a large community kitchen. More than 100 area farmers and entrepreneurs have so far rented kitchen space to test new products. As they cook, they rub elbows with one another. When Chris Chmiel started experimenting with a wild local fruit, pawpaw, he ended up talking with someone from the local Casa Nueva restaurant. Now the restaurant serves 'pawpaw coladas'.

Holley began ACEnet with the goal of tapping local ingenuity and resources for economic development. The pathway to progress was connection — bringing people into contact with one another. By finding one another and combining skills and products, Holley believed an engine for economic growth could be unlocked. ACEnet was to become the networking hub that fuelled the engine.

Networking performs for ACEnet. Holley says that 'poverty is due to isolation'. By breaking the isolation ACEnet provides a valuable community service. 'Put two people together in a room', Holley says, 'and they'll figure out how to come out ahead together.'

Why can't we have more organisations like this?

Questions

What's the status of economic development in your community or region?

Are there any organisations like ACEnet tackling rural and/or urban development needs in Australia and New Zealand?

Is there a role for you in harnessing the power of networks for social good?

furnishings with a related price appeal. All of this, of course, is supported by a company web site maintained also by an outside contractor.

The creative use of information technology adds to the potential *advantages of network structures*. With the technological edge, the mail-order company in the prior example can operate with fewer full-time employees and less complex internal systems. Network structures are very lean and streamlined. They help organisations stay cost competitive through reduced overhead and increased operating efficiency. Network concepts allow organisations to internally employ outsourcing strategies and contract out specialised business functions rather than maintain full-time staff to do them. A bank may contract with local firms to provide mailroom, cafeteria and legal services; an airline might contract out customer service jobs at various airports. Information technology also allows the business relationships of networks to operate across great distances rather than face to face. Such arrangements are increasingly common in the international arena, where the Internet, e-mail, net meetings and other computer networks bring the advantages of global operations into easy reach at minimum cost.

Within the operating core of a network structure, a variety of interesting jobs are created for those who must coordinate the entire system of relationships. In fact, the potential *disadvantages of network structures* largely lie with the demands of this responsibility. The more complex the business or mission of the organisation, the more complicated the network of contracts and relationships that must be maintained. It may be difficult to control and coordinate among them. If one part of the network breaks down or fails to deliver, the entire system suffers the consequences. Also, there is the potential for loss of control over activities contracted out, and for a lack of loyalty to develop among contractors who are used infrequently rather than on a long-term basis.

As information technology continues to develop and as the concept of network structures becomes better understood, there is no doubt that they will grow in number and range of applications in the future. They are great for smaller businesses and organisations, including entrepreneurial ones. They are also valuable for larger organisations, where the network approach offers great advantages of efficiency of operations, speed to market and customer orientation. Project management organisations, such as Airbus Industries in Europe and Hannaford's (a leading special events company) in Australia, use web-based network computing to communicate with their geographically dispersed suppliers.

Boundaryless organisations

It is increasingly popular today to speak about creating a **boundaryless organisation** that eliminates internal boundaries linking component parts and external boundaries linking with the external environment.[27] The boundaryless organisation can be viewed as a combination of the team and network structures just described, with the addition of 'temporariness'. In the internal context, teamwork and communication — spontaneous, as needed, and intense — replace formal lines of authority. There is an absence of boundaries that traditionally and structurally separate organisational members from one another. In the external context, organisational needs are met by a shifting mix of outsourcing contracts and operating alliances that form and disband with changing circumstances. A 'photograph' that documents an organisation's configuration of external relationships today will look different from one taken tomorrow, as the form naturally adjusts to new pressures and circumstances. Figure 10.7 shows how the absence of internal and external barriers helps people work in ways that bring speed and flexibility to the boundaryless firm.

A **boundaryless organisation** eliminates internal boundaries among parts and external boundaries with the external environment.

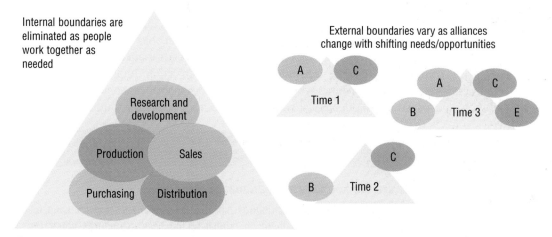

Figure 10.7 ▸ The boundaryless organisation eliminates internal and external barriers.

Key requirements of boundaryless organisations are the absence of hierarchy, empowerment of team members, technology use and acceptance of impermanence. Work is accomplished by empowered people who come together voluntarily and temporarily to apply their expertise to a task, gather additional expertise from whatever sources may be required to perform it successfully, and stay together only as long as the task is a work in process. The focus in the boundaryless form is on talent for task. The assumption is that empowered people working together without bureaucratic restrictions can accomplish great things. Such a work setting is supposed to encourage creativity, quality, timeliness and flexibility, while reducing inefficiencies and increasing speed. At General Electric, for example, the drive toward boundaryless operations is supported in part by aggressive 'digitisation'. The organisation is moving more and more administrative work onto the Web — where it can be done faster and among persons directly involved. Intermediaries in the form of support personnel are not needed.[28]

Knowledge sharing is an essential component of the boundaryless organisation. One way to think of this is in the context of a very small organisation, perhaps a start up. In the small firm, everyone pitches in to help out as needed and when appropriate to get things done. There are no formal assignments and there are no job titles or job descriptions standing in the way. People with talent work together as needed to get the job done. The boundaryless organisation, in its pure form, is just like that. Even in the larger organisational context, meetings and spontaneous sharing are happening continuously, perhaps involving thousands of people working together in hundreds of teams that form and disband as needed. Again, the great opportunities of information technology help make all of this possible. At consulting giant PricewaterhouseCoopers (PwC), for example, knowledge sharing brings together 160 000 partners spread across 150 countries in a vast virtual learning and problem-solving network. PwC partners collaborate electronically through online databases where information is stored, problems posted, and questions asked and answered in real time by those with experience and knowledge relevant to the problem at hand. Technology makes collaboration instantaneously and always possible, breaking down boundaries that might otherwise slow or impede the organisation's performance.[29]

A **virtual organisation** is a shifting network of strategic alliances that are engaged as needed.

In the organisation–environment interface, boundaryless operations emerge in a special form that is sometimes called the **virtual organisation**.[30] This is an organisation that operates in a shifting network of external alliances that are engaged as needed, and with the support of extensive technology use. The boundaries that traditionally separate a business from its suppliers, customers and even competitors are largely eliminated, temporarily and in respect to a given transaction or business purpose. Virtual organisations come into being as needed when alliances are called into action to meet specific operating needs and objectives. When mobilised, alliance members contribute for mutual benefit their special expertise and competencies. When the work is complete, the alliance rests until next called into action. Importantly, the virtual organisation operates in this manner with the mix of mobilised alliances continuously shifting and with an expansive pool of potential alliances always ready to be called upon as needed.

POINT ← COUNTER ↑

Individuals are the key to organisational success

A preoccupation with organisation structures can distract managers from focusing on the other organisational issues that are so critical for success. Structures count for nothing unless managers properly attend to the micro-level issues of leadership, employee motivation, learning and rewards. Strong leadership can inspire all employees, from senior managers down to the first-line staff, to achieve the organisation's goals. And if leadership, motivation and staff rewards are given centre stage then the organisation is likely to flourish regardless of the structure it adopts. Indeed, organisations with quite different structures can be equally successful within the same industry if these micro-level issues are consistently well managed.

An organisation is defined by both its people and its structure. Managers who focus on issues of bureaucracy and the scientific principles of management should redistribute their energies to attend to the human factors that are critical for organisational success. It is individuals that make organisations successful.

ORGANISING TRENDS

The **upside-down pyramid** puts customers at the top, served by workers whose managers support them.

Change is part of organisational life. Even as traditional structures are modified, refined and abandoned in the search for new ones, the organising practices that create and implement them must change too. In chapter 1 the concept of the **upside-down pyramid** was introduced as an example of the new directions in management. By putting customers on top, served by workers in the middle, who are in turn supported by managers at the bottom, this notion tries to refocus attention on the marketplace and customer needs. Although more of a concept than a depiction of an actual structure, such thinking is representative of forces shaping new directions in how the modern workplace is organised. Among the organising trends to be discussed next, a common theme runs throughout — making the adjustments needed to streamline operations for cost efficiency, higher performance and increased participation by workers.

Shorter chains of command

A typical organisation chart shows the **chain of command**, or the line of authority that vertically links each position with successively higher levels of management. The classical school of management suggested that the chain of command should operate according to the *scalar principle*: There should be a clear and unbroken chain of command linking every person in the organisation with successively higher levels of authority up to and including the top manager.

When organisations grow in size they tend to get taller, as more and more levels of management are added to the chain of command. This increases overhead costs; it tends to decrease communication and access between top and bottom levels; it can greatly slow decision making; and it can lead to a loss of contact with the client or customer. These are all reasons why 'tall' organisations with many levels of management are often criticised for inefficiencies and poor productivity. The current trend in organising seeks to address this problem directly.

Trend. Organisations are being 'streamlined' by cutting unnecessary levels of management; flatter and more horizontal structures are viewed as a competitive advantage.

> The **chain of command** links all persons with successively higher levels of authority.

Less unity of command

Another classical management principle describes how the chain of command should operate in daily practice. The *unity-of-command principle* states that each person in an organisation should report to one and only one supervisor. This notion of 'one person–one boss' is a foundation of the traditional pyramid form of organisation. It is intended to avoid the confusion potentially created when a person gets work directions from more than one source. Unity of command is supposed to ensure that everyone clearly understands assignments and does not get conflicting instructions. It is violated, for example, when a senior manager bypasses someone's immediate supervisor to give him or her orders. This can create confusion for the subordinate and also undermine the supervisor's authority.

The 'two-boss' system of matrix structure is a clear violation of unity of command. Whereas the classical advice is to avoid creating multiple reporting relationships, the matrix concept creates them by design. It does so in an attempt to improve lateral relations and teamwork in special programs or projects. Unity of command is also less predominant in the team structure and in other arrangements that emphasise the use of cross-functional teams or task forces. Clearly, the current trend is for less, not more, unity of command in organisations.

British Petroleum (BP) provides a good example of how cross-functional teams can strengthen an organisation's performance. These teams, known as *peer groups*, form a linking network of related BUs within a specific business stream — particularly those facing similar technological, operational or relationship issues. In structure, they resemble a federation. In practice, they are a vehicle for sharing knowledge. Peer groups are also the forums in which BUs must 'fight for their corner', justify their promises to their closest colleagues and prove they deserve the resources they seek in competition with other BUs. One of the keys to this process is transparency based on reliable and credible data that can form a platform for assessing every part of BP in a consistent fashion.

www.intel.com

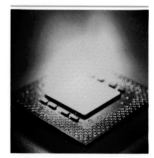

Intel is a major player in the dynamic computer chip industry. It is a fast-moving company, and it operates in a fast-moving environment. To stay ahead of its competitors, such as Motorola, Intel relies heavily on a team organisation. Hierarchy takes a back seat to teamwork. Says one team member: 'We report to each other'.

The greatest attribute of this management structure is its ability to facilitate rapid and innovative responses to new situations without the incursion of red tape and without the need for constant referrals upwards — but within a context that allows for scrutiny and performance challenge. Essentially, the organisation structure supports BP's corporate strategies.

Trend. Organisations are using more cross-functional teams, task forces and horizontal structures, and they are becoming more customer conscious. As they do so, employees often find themselves working for more than one 'boss'.

Wider spans of control

Span of control refers to the number of subordinates directly reporting to a manager.

The **span of control** relates to the number of persons directly reporting to a manager. When span of control is 'narrow', only a few people are under a manager's immediate supervision; a 'wide' span of control indicates that the manager supervises many people. There was a time in the history of management thought when people searched for the ideal span of control. Although the magic number was never found, this *span-of-control principle* evolved: there is a limit to the number of people one manager can effectively supervise; care should be exercised to keep the span of control within manageable limits.

Figure 10.8 shows the relationship between span of control and the number of levels in the hierarchy of authority. *Flat structures* have wider spans of control — they have few levels of management; *tall structures* have narrow spans of control — they have many levels of management. Because tall organisations have more managers, they are more costly. They are also generally viewed as less efficient, less flexible and less customer sensitive than flat organisations. Before making spans of control smaller, therefore, serious thought should always be given to both the cost of the added management overhead and the potential disadvantages of a taller chain of command. When spans of control are increased, by contrast, overhead costs are reduced, and workers with less direct supervision in the flatter structure may benefit from more independence.[31]

Trend. Many organisations are shifting to wider spans of control as levels of management are eliminated and empowerment gains prominence; individual managers are taking responsibility for larger numbers of subordinates who operate with less direct supervision.

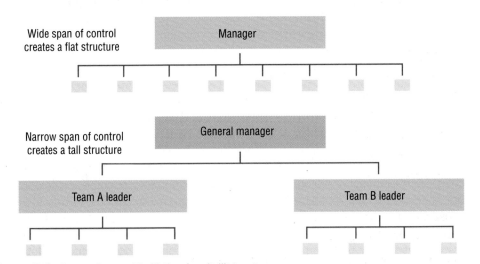

Figure 10.8 ▸ Spans of control in 'flat' versus 'tall' structures

More delegation and empowerment

All managers must decide what work they should do themselves and what should be left for others. At issue here is **delegation** — the process of entrusting work to others by giving them the right to make decisions and take action. There are three steps to delegation. In step 1, *the manager assigns responsibility* by carefully explaining the work or duties someone else is expected to do. This *responsibility* is an expectation for the other person to perform assigned tasks. In step 2, *the manager grants authority to act.* Along with the assigned task, the right to take necessary actions (for example, to spend money, direct the work of others, use resources) is given to the other person. *Authority* is a right to act in ways needed to carry out the assigned tasks. In step 3, *the manager creates accountability.* By accepting an assignment, the person takes on a direct obligation to the manager to complete the job as agreed upon. *Accountability*, originally defined in chapter 1, is the requirement to answer to a supervisor for performance results.

> **Delegation** is the process of distributing and entrusting work to other persons.

A classical principle of organisation warns managers not to delegate without giving the subordinate sufficient authority to perform. When insufficient authority is delegated, it will be very hard for someone to live up to performance expectations. They simply don't have the authority needed to get the job done. The *authority-and-responsibility principle* states: authority should equal responsibility when work is delegated from a supervisor to a subordinate. Useful guidelines for delegating are offered in Manager's Notepad 10.3.[32]

A common management failure is unwillingness to delegate. Whether due to a lack of trust in others or to a manager's inflexibility in the way things get done, failure to delegate can be damaging. It overloads the manager with work that could be done by others; it also denies others many opportunities to fully utilise their talents on the job. When well done, by contrast, delegation leads to empowerment, in that people have the freedom to contribute ideas and do their jobs in the best possible ways. This involvement can increase job satisfaction for the individual and frequently results in better job performance.

Trend. Managers in progressive organisations are delegating more; they are finding more ways to empower people at all levels to make more decisions affecting themselves and their work.

MANAGER'S NOTEPAD 10.3

Ground rules for effective delegation

- Carefully choose the person to whom you delegate.
- Define the responsibility; make the assignment clear.
- Agree on performance objectives and standards.
- Agree on a performance timetable.
- Give authority; allow the other person to act independently.
- Show trust in the other person.
- Provide performance support.
- Give performance feedback.
- Recognise and reinforce progress.
- Help when things go wrong.
- Don't forget *your* accountability for performance results.

Decentralisation with centralisation

Centralisation is the concentration of authority for most decisions at the top level of an organisation.

Decentralisation is the dispersion of authority to make decisions throughout all levels of the organisation.

A question frequently asked by managers is: 'Should most decisions be made at the top levels of an organisation, or should they be dispersed by extensive delegation throughout all levels of management?' The former approach is referred to as **centralisation**; the latter is called **decentralisation**. There is no classical principle on centralisation and decentralisation. The traditional pyramid form of organisation may give the impression of being a highly centralised structure, whereas decentralisation is characteristic of newer structures and many recent organising trends. But the issue doesn't have to be framed as an either/or choice. Today's organisations can operate with greater decentralisation without giving up centralised control. This is facilitated by developments in information technology.

With computer networks and advanced information systems, managers at higher levels can more easily stay informed about a wide range of day-to-day performance matters. Because they have information on results readily available, they can allow more decentralisation in decision making.[33] If something goes wrong, presumably the information systems will sound an alarm and allow corrective action to be taken quickly. At BancOne, Inc. in the USA and Wizard Home Loans in Australia and New Zealand, for example, the demands of growth and an expanding geographical base have not blurred the lines of authority and accountability. Individual branches in geographically dispersed locations are closely monitored for performance results. With the guiding theme of centralising administration and decentralising people, BancOne and Wizard Home Loans have decentralised branch operations while retaining central control.

Trend. Whereas empowerment and related forces are contributing to more decentralisation in organisations, advances in information technology simultaneously allow for the retention of centralised control.

Reduced use of staff

Specialised staff provide technical expertise for other parts of the organisation.

When it comes to coordination and control in organisations, the issue of line–staff relationships is important. Chapter 1 described the role of staff as providing expert advice and guidance to line personnel. This can help ensure that performance standards are maintained in areas of staff expertise. **Specialised staff** perform a technical service or provide special problem-solving expertise for other parts of the organisation. This could be a single person, such as a corporate safety director, or a complete unit, such as a corporate safety department. Many organisations rely on staff specialists to maintain coordination and control over a variety of matters. In a large retail chain, line managers in each store typically make daily operating decisions regarding direct sales of merchandise. But staff specialists at the corporate or regional levels provide direction and support so that all the stores operate with the same credit, purchasing, employment and advertising procedures.

Personal staff are 'assistant-to' positions that support senior managers.

Organisations may also employ **personal staff**, individuals appointed in 'assistant-to' positions with the purpose of providing special support to higher-level managers. Such assistants help by following up on administrative details and performing other duties as assigned. They can benefit also in terms of career development through the mentoring relationships that such assignments offer. An organisation, for example, might select promising junior managers as temporary administrative assistants to senior managers. This helps them gain valuable experience at the same time that they are facilitating the work of executives.

Problems in line–staff distinctions can and do arise. In too many cases, organisations find that the staff grows to the point where it costs more in administrative overheads than it is worth. This is why staff cutbacks are common in retrenchment and other turnaround efforts. There are also cases where conflicts in line–staff relationships cause difficulties. This often occurs when line and staff managers disagree over the extent of staff authority. At the one extreme, staff has purely *advisory authority* and can 'suggest' but not 'dictate'. At the other extreme, it has *functional authority* to actually 'require' that others do as requested within the boundaries of staff expertise. For example, a human resource department may advise line managers on the desired qualifications of new workers being hired (advisory authority); the department will likely require the managers to follow equal employment opportunity guidelines in the hiring process (functional authority).

There is no one best solution to the problem of how to divide work between line and staff responsibilities. What is best for any organisation will be a cost-effective staff component that satisfies, but doesn't overreact to, needs for specialised technical assistance to line operations. The current trend is to reduce staff as organisations are being restructured to increase productivity and lower costs.

Trend. Organisations are reducing the number of staff; they are seeking increased operating efficiency by employing fewer staff personnel and using smaller staff units.

Study guide

The chapter 10 study guide helps you review the chapter content, prepare for examinations, apply what you have learned and further build your career readiness. The summary briefly answers the study questions posed at the start of the chapter. The list of key terms allows you to double-check your familiarity with basic concepts and definitions. The applied activities help you test your comprehension of chapter content. Suggestions offered as career readiness activities direct your attention to relevant sections of the Career Readiness Workbook where you can test and develop your career skills and apply what you have learned. The list of electronic resources suggests activities from the *Management: An Asia–Pacific Perspective* web site and, finally, the case for critical thinking helps you apply your new management knowledge.

SUMMARY

What is organising as a management function?

- Organising is the process of creating work arrangements of people and resources, be it for a small unit, a large division or an entire enterprise.
- To organise a work setting, decisions must be made about how to divide up the work that needs to be done, allocate people and resources to do it, and coordinate results to achieve productivity.
- Structure is the system of tasks, reporting relationships and communication that links together the people and positions within an organisation.
- Formal structure, such as shown on an organisation chart, describes how an organisation is supposed to work.
- The informal structure of organisation consists of the unofficial working relationships among members.

What are the major types of organisation structures?

- Departmentalisation is the process of creating structure by grouping people together in formal work units or teams.
- In functional structures, people with similar skills who perform similar activities work together under a common manager.
- In divisional structures, people who work on a similar product, work in the same geographical region, serve the same customers or participate in the same work process are grouped together under common managers.
- A matrix structure combines the functional and divisional approaches to create permanent cross-functional project teams.

What are the new developments in organisation structures?

- Increasing complexity and greater rates of change in the environment are challenging the performance capabilities of traditional organisation structures.
- New developments include the growing use of team structures that create horizontal organisations using cross-functional teams and task forces to improve lateral relations and improve problem solving at all levels.

- New developments are also underway in respect to network structures that cluster systems of contracted services and strategic alliances around a core business or organisational centre.
- Boundaryless organisations eliminate internal and external organisational boundaries to utilise a shifting mix of internal teams and teamwork to accomplish temporary tasks and projects.
- Virtual organisations eliminate external organisational boundaries and mobilise a shifting mix of strategic alliances to accomplish specific tasks and projects.

What organising trends are changing the workplace?

- Traditional vertical command-and-control structures are giving way to more horizontal structures strong on employee involvement and flexibility.
- Many organisations today are operating with shorter chains of command and less unity of command.
- Many organisations today are operating with wider spans of control and fewer levels of management.
- The emphasis in more organisations today is on effective delegation and empowerment.
- Advances in information technology are making it possible to operate with decentralisation while still maintaining centralised control.
- Reduction in the size of staff is a trend in organisations seeking greater efficiency and productivity.

KEY TERMS

boundaryless organisation (p. 281)

centralisation (p. 286)

chain of command (p. 283)

cross-functional teams (p. 277)

customer structures (p. 274)

decentralisation (p. 286)

delegation (p. 285)

departmentalisation (p. 271)

divisional structure (p. 273)

formal structure (p. 269)

functional chimneys problem (p. 272)

functional structures (p. 271)

geographical structures (p. 274)

informal structure (p. 270)

matrix structure (p. 275)

network structure (p. 279)

organisation chart (p. 269)

organisation structure (p. 269)

organising (p. 268)

personal staff (p. 286)

process structure (p. 275)

product structures (p. 274)

project teams (p. 277)

span of control (p. 284)

specialised staff (p. 286)

team structures (p. 277)

upside-down pyramid (p. 282)

virtual organisation (p. 282)

APPLIED ACTIVITIES

Short-response questions

1. What is the difference between a product divisional structure and a geographical or area divisional structure?
2. What are some of the symptoms that might indicate a functional structure is causing problems for the organisation?
3. Explain by example the concept of a network organisation structure.
4. What positive results might be expected when levels of management are reduced and the chain of command shortened in an organisation?

Application question

5. Jeff McGarry supervises a group of seven project engineers. His unit is experiencing a heavy workload as the demand for different versions of one of his company's computer components is growing. Jeff finds that he doesn't have time to follow up on all design details for each version. Up until now he has tried to do this all by himself. Two of the engineers have shown interest in helping him coordinate work on the various designs. As a consultant, what would you advise Jeff in terms of delegating work to them?

CAREER READINESS ACTIVITIES

Recommended individual and group learning activities from the end-of-text Career Readiness Workbook for this chapter include:

Career advancement portfolio · WB

Update your career advancement portfolio to reflect your new skills and experiences. Include skills and personal insights you gain from the following projects and exercises.

Research and presentation project · WB

- Project 2 — Changing corporate cultures

Cross-functional integrative case · WB

Read the integrative case on Sarina Russo and answer the following question:

Have a look at the Sarina Russo Group web site www.sarinarusso.com.au. Now prepare a possible organisation structure for the business that takes into account the decentralised nature of its many offices and further expansion potential.

Exercise in teamwork · WB

- Exercise 13 — The future workplace

Management skills assessment · WB

- Assessment 10 — Managerial assumptions

ELECTRONIC RESOURCES

Don't forget to take full advantage of the online support for *Management: An Asia–Pacific Perspective* at www.johnwiley.com.au/highered/management: chapter 10 practice tests, e-flashcards, crossword puzzles, interactive management skills assessments, interactive cases, the online career advancement portfolio and much more!

CASE FOR CRITICAL THINKING

Read the following case for critical thinking on Australian Airlines. While you are reading the case keep in mind what you have learned in this chapter, then answer the questions.

Qantas launched its new, low-cost, wholly-owned subsidiary — Australian Airlines — in October 2002 with an inaugural flight from Cairns to Japan. The airline has its operational base in Cairns and its head office in Sydney. It flies daily return trips to Nagoya, Osaka, Fukuoka, Singapore, Tapei, Hong Kong, Kuala Lumpur, Sarawak and Phuket. A second Australian operating base in either Sydney or Melbourne is planned for early 2005, and there are longer-term plans to include flights to India, Greece and Turkey. The all-economy service largely targets leisure destinations where the majority of travellers are seeking economy airfares and a no-frills in-flight service. The airline has over ten aircraft in its fleet, mostly Boeing 767-300s. There has always been strong demand for a leisure-focused airline in Asia and outbound Australia, but its long-term sustainability rests on establishing a low cost base, which would have been difficult using the structure and processes traditionally used by three-class fleets such as Qantas and the now defunct Ansett. The key for Australian Airlines is to achieve a high yield through volume and low-cost operation, much like Price-line and Target have achieved in the discount retail industry. To ensure maximum volume, Australian Airlines will not compete directly with Qantas on routes.

Operational independence

Much of the projected long-term success of the new business unit derives from its organisation structure and internal operating procedures. Its success depends upon operating on a cost base that is 25 to 30 per cent less than its parent company, Qantas. Australian Airlines operates as a strategic business unit (SBU) and is viewed as a profit centre for the Qantas Group. There is no cross-subsidisation of the airline. Its chief executive, Denis Adams, has repeatedly stated that it must be able to operate independently of its parent company and that any financial subsidies would only create a false sense of success. The airline is a new stand-alone business or division within Qantas and this is reflected in its separate financial status. Adams has carefully studied the structure and operating practices of Virgin Blue, and has imitated them in designing Australian Airlines.[34]

In addition to its independent company status, Australian Airlines is clearly a separate entity from Qantas in a number of other important aspects. Its head office has approximately 20 staff, which is very small by traditional industry standards. While some of the staff are from Qantas, the majority are new employees with non-airline backgrounds in finance, marketing and human resources. Australian Airlines deliberately chose to employ these staff in order to bring new ideas and outside practices to the company. The staff is predominantly aged between the mid 20s and the early 40s.

Cost efficiencies

The Cairns operating base keeps costs to a minimum through a variety of strategies:

- It outsources its maintenance to Qantas on commercial terms, but has the freedom to switch if a lower cost provider bids for the contract. It currently has the lowest cost maintenance contract in Australasia.
- Its cabin crews are largely recruited from outside the Qantas Group and are selected for their friendly customer predisposition, 'youthful attitude' and willingness to be multi-skilled and to engage in flexible, multitasking work practices. For example, flight attendants check in passengers, complete all the necessary civil aviation departure documentation, provide in-flight attendant services and complete all arrival documentation. They are also required to be fluent in at least one designated Asian language and to participate in occasional marketing and promotional campaigns and events. Their salaries are 20 per cent less than their counterparts at Qantas.
- The check-in counter processes have been simplified by eliminating paper tickets in favour of electronic ones, and by reducing the number of data entry steps to allow a 30–40 per cent efficiency increase in passenger processing. This means that checking in is faster and requires fewer staff.
- Catering costs have been reduced through competitive contracting-out of food preparation and by reducing the number of service items, such as plates and cups, used in flight.
- An all-economy service allows the airline to add another 40 seats to an international Boeing 767 flight, thereby boosting revenue with only a small increase in costs.[35]

By 2005, the airline's board of directors expects profits to be above the industry average; whereas more modest profit levels are deemed acceptable in the first two years following the airline's start up. Again, they have used the fledging Virgin Blue as their benchmark for profitability targets. While the organisation structure and management practices have been designed to drive down operational cost, the air fares are comparable to those of other Asian airlines operating in the leisure-focused aviation market and to what Qantas quotes for its economy-class tour group passengers. In other words, Australian Airlines is low cost but not low fare.[36]

QUESTIONS

1. Should Australian Airlines stay with its all-economy fare structure or, as it expands, add business and first-class services?

2. Evaluate Australian Airlines' business strategy using Porter's competitive strategy framework.

3. Evaluate Qantas's decision to establish Australian Airlines using Miles and Snow's adaptive model.

4. To what extent are the Australian Airlines staffing arrangements in line with international employment trends?

CHAPTER 11

Organisational design and work processes

CHAPTER 11 STUDY QUESTIONS

▸ What are the essentials of organisational design?

▸ How do contingency factors influence organisational design?

▸ What are the major issues in subsystems design?

▸ How can work processes be reengineered?

LG — designed for autonomy, innovation and value creation

LG, perhaps best known in Australia and New Zealand for high-tech whitegoods and consumer electronics, is Korea's third-largest company, with annual revenues of over $160 billion and 130 000 employees worldwide.

It started in chemicals in the 1940s, operating under the name GoldStar, and LG has evolved into a truly global company with regional headquarters in key locations around the world and a home office in Seoul, Korea. LG comprises 50 affiliated companies with some 300 offices and subsidiaries. It now operates in four areas — chemicals and energy, electronics and telecommunications, finance and service.

LG recently embarked on a restructuring program to improve its global competitiveness. The program was driven by a 'select' and 'focus' strategy — the company exited businesses that were considered to have limited growth potential. LG also made changes to its organisation structure. Previously structured as a union of interdependent firms, LG adopted a holding company system to create an alliance of autonomous firms, all of which share the LG brand and business philosophy. This organisational redesign of LG is supported by several strategies. First, there is an emphasis on the principle of 'Management of Substance'. By implementing profit-led management practices it has generated strong financial results for many of the LG companies. Second, LG has developed an extensive range of innovative products and services. Third, LG has changed its attitude to business by quickly adopting new best practices in core businesses and setting more challenging targets than its competitors.[1]

GET CONNECTED!

Learn more about LG's structure by visiting the company's web site at www.lge.com. Can you think of a local company that produces innovative products and services? What factors have contributed to this? Can you think of potential new products and services and the type of management structures and practices that would foster them? Search the Internet for innovative local companies.

GET CONNECTED!

Different organisations will adopt different organisational structures to help achieve their goals. The type of structure they adopt will be determined by a range of factors, such as the country and industry environment, the organisation's history and size, and technology. Whereas LG consists of an alliance of autonomous companies that share the LG brand and business philosophy, the Swiss food multinational company, Nestlé, emphasises integration of its different business units to obtain **organisational synergy**. Nestlé's union of interdependent business units is achieved through transferring managers between regions and continuously sharing among them new ideas for improved operations. The company is strongly growth-orientated while recognising the need to adapt its strategies to fit regional conditions, where appropriate. LG's structure is very similar to many Korean and East Asian companies — that is, a **conglomerate** with relatively independent business units. Because conglomerates operate across a wide range of often quite different industries, there may be less potential to realise organisational synergies. Nestlé developed its more integrated structure over its long period of operation as a multinational company, whereas LG is a relatively new player only beginning to develop greater coordination among its business units.

Organisations everywhere are changing and adapting their structures to best meet competitive demands in the new economy. Traditional structures are being flattened, networks are being developed, IT is being utilised, and decision making is decentralised to the point where knowledge exists. The goals are clear: improved teamwork, more creativity, shorter product development cycles, better customer service and higher productivity overall. Changing times require more flexible and well-integrated organisations that can deliver high-quality products and services while still innovating for sustained future performance. We already know that team structures and network organisations are gaining in popularity.[2] Yet organisations face widely varying problems and opportunities, and there is no one best way to structure and manage them. The key to success is finding the best design to master the unique situational needs and challenges for each organisation.[3]

ORGANISATIONAL DESIGN ESSENTIALS

A variety of organisational structures were examined in the preceding chapter. The point was made that managers must be ever alert to prospects for improving performance through adjustments in structure. Change is the ever-present fact of life in organisations today. The various trends in organisation and management practices that were described in chapter 10 are resulting in fundamental changes in the way people work and organisations operate. Today, there is more sharing of tasks, reduced emphasis on hierarchy, greater emphasis on lateral communication, more teamwork, and more decentralisation of decision making and empowerment.

What is organisational design?

Organisational design is the process of choosing and implementing structures that best arrange resources to serve the organisation's mission and objectives.[4] The ultimate purpose of organisational design is to create an alignment between supporting structures and situational challenges. As shown in figure 11.1, this includes taking into consideration the implications of environment, strategies, people, technology and size.[5] Importantly, the process of organisational design is a problem-solving activity that should be approached in a contingency fashion that takes all of these factors into account. There is no universal design that applies in all circumstances. The goal is to achieve a best fit among structure and the unique situation faced by each organisation.

Organisational synergy is obtained when a combination of ideas and knowledge from different parts of an organisation creates improvements in the productive processes and outputs throughout the organisation.

A conglomerate is an organisation with a diverse range of business units spanning a wide variety of industries.

GET CONNECTED!

Want to learn more about a company? Check the company research tools at the web sites of the Australian Stock Exchange www.asx.com.au, the New Zealand Stock Exchange www.nzse.co.nz, the Australian Securities and Investments Commission www.asic.gov.au and the Securities Commission of New Zealand www.sec-com.govt.nz.

GET CONNECTED!

Organisational design is the process of creating structures that best serve mission and objectives.

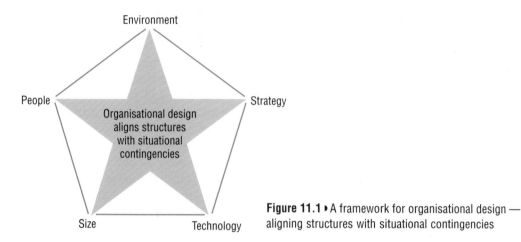

Figure 11.1 ▸ A framework for organisational design — aligning structures with situational contingencies

Key directions for changes in organisations today involve a basic shift in attention away from a traditional emphasis on more vertical or authority-driven structures to ones that are more horizontal and task-driven. In management theory, these developments are framed by an important distinction between bureaucratic designs that are mechanistic and vertical in nature, and adaptive designs that are more organic and horizontal in nature. This distinction itself is viewed from the *contingency position* that there is no one best way to organise, and that the choice of organisational design should always be made to achieve the best fit with situational needs.

HIGH PERFORMANCE

PricewaterhouseCoopers •
www.pwcglobal.com

Restructuring for client services

The global professional services organisation PricewaterhouseCoopers was created in 1998 from the merger of two giants in the industry — Price Waterhouse and Coopers & Lybrand. With offices worldwide, including a strong presence in Australia, New Zealand and South-East Asia, the merged organisation inevitably reflected former cultures, goals, people and structures. Under the new structure, corporate was minimised with more decision making decentralised to regional managers. PricewaterhouseCoopers's medium-term objective was to retain the audit, business advisory and tax services, and separate the organisation's management consulting, business process outsourcing, and corporate and human resource consulting services. The separation of accounting and auditing functions from the business consulting services finally took place in 2002, in line with the changing regulatory and capital markets environment associated with the Enron and other corporate scandals in the USA. The consulting business was sold to IBM.

Bureaucratic designs

As first introduced in the discussion on historical foundations of management in chapter 4, a *bureaucracy* can be described as a form of organisation based on logic, order and the legitimate use of formal authority. Its distinguishing features include a clear-cut division of labour, strict hierarchy of authority, formal rules and procedures, and promotion based on competency. According to sociologist Max Weber, bureaucracies were supposed to be orderly, fair and highly efficient.[6] In short, they were a model form of organisation. Yet if you use the term 'bureaucracy' today, it may well be interpreted with a negative connotation. If you call someone a 'bureaucrat', it may well be considered an insult. Instead of operating efficiency, the bureaucracies that we know are often associated with 'red tape'; instead of being orderly and fair, they are often seen as cumbersome and impersonal to the point of insensitivity to customer or client needs. And the bureaucrats? Don't we assume that they work only according to rules, diligently following procedures and avoiding any opportunities to take initiative or demonstrate creativity?

Management researchers recognise that there are limits to bureaucracies, particularly in their tendencies to become unwieldy and rigid.[7] Instead of viewing all bureaucratic structures as inevitably flawed, however, management theory takes a contingency perspective. The critical contingency questions to be asked and answered are: When is a bureaucratic form a good choice for an organisation? What alternatives exist when it is not a good choice?

A basis for answering these questions lies in pioneering research conducted in England during the early 1960s by Tom Burns and George Stalker.[8] After investigating 20 manufacturing companies, Burns and Stalker concluded that two quite different organisational forms could be successful, with the choice among them depending upon the nature of an organisation's external environment. A more bureaucratic form, which Burns and Stalker called a *mechanistic approach*, thrived when the environment was stable. But it experienced difficulty when the environment was rapidly changing and uncertain. In these dynamic situations, a much less bureaucratic form, called an *organic approach*, performed best. Figure 11.2 portrays these two approaches as opposite extremes on a continuum of organisational design alternatives.

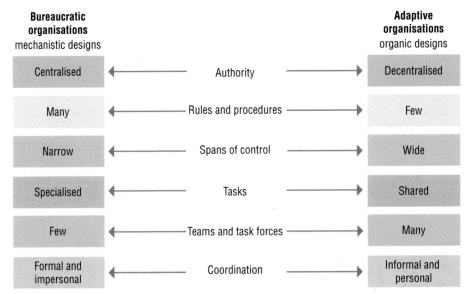

Figure 11.2 ▸ A continuum of organisational design alternatives — from bureaucratic to adaptive organisations

Organisations that operate with more **mechanistic designs** are highly bureaucratic in nature. As shown in the figure, they typically operate with more centralised authority, many rules and procedures, a precise division of labour, narrow spans of control and formal means of coordination. Mechanistic designs are described as 'tight' structures of the traditional vertical or pyramid form.[9] An example is your local KFC or McDonald's. A relatively small operation, each store operates quite like others in the franchise chain and according to rules established by the corporate management. You will notice that service personnel work in orderly and disciplined ways, guided by training, rules and procedures, and close supervision by crew leaders who work alongside them. Even their appearances are carefully regulated, with everyone working in a standardised uniform. These restaurants perform well as they repetitively deliver items that are part of their standard menus. You quickly encounter the limits, however, if you try to order something not on the menu. The servers aren't allowed to prepare anything out of the ordinary. The chains also encounter difficulty when consumer tastes change or take on regional preferences that are different from what the corporate menu provides. Adjustments to the system are typically a long time coming.

Mechanistic designs are centralised with many rules and procedures, a clear-cut division of labour, narrow spans of control and formal coordination.

Adaptive designs

The limits of bureaucracy are especially apparent in organisations that must operate in the highly competitive environments created by the forces of globalisation and ever-changing technologies. It's hard, for example, to find a technology company, consumer products firm, financial services business or dot-com retailer these days that isn't making continual adjustments in operations and organisational design. Things keep changing on them, and many of the changes are very difficult to predict.

'It's a millennial change', says Dee Hock, the founder of Visa International. 'We can't run 21st-century society with 17th-century notions of organization.'[10] Enlightened managers are helping organisations reconfigure into new forms that emphasise flexibility and speed without losing sight of important performance objectives. Harvard scholar and consultant Rosabeth Moss Kanter notes that the ability to respond quickly to shifting environmental challenges often distinguishes successful organisations from less successful ones. Specifically, Kanter states:

> The organizations now emerging as successful will be, above all, flexible; they will need to be able to bring particular resources together quickly, on the basis of short-term recognition of new requirements and the necessary capacities to deal with them . . . The balance between static plans — which appear to reduce the need for effective reaction — and structural flexibility needs to shift toward the latter.[11]

The organisational design trend is now toward more **adaptive organisations** that operate with a minimum of bureaucratic features and with cultures that encourage worker empowerment and participation. They display features of the **organic designs** portrayed in figure 11.2, including more decentralised authority, fewer rules and procedures, less precise division of labour, wider spans of control and more personal means of coordination. They are described as relatively loose systems in which a lot of work gets done through informal structures and networks of interpersonal contacts.[12] Organic designs recognise and legitimise these linkages and give them the resources they need to operate best. This works well for organisations facing dynamic environments that demand flexibility in dealing with changing conditions. They are also increasingly popular in the new workplace, where the demands of total quality management and competitive advantage place more emphasis on internal teamwork and responsiveness to customers.

Adaptive organisations operate with a minimum of bureaucratic features and encourage worker empowerment and teamwork.

Organic designs are decentralised with fewer rules and procedures, open divisions of labour, wide spans of control and more personal coordination.

Above all, adaptive organisations are built upon trusting that people will do the right things on their own initiative. They move organisational design in the direction of what some might call *self-organisation*, where the focus is on freeing otherwise capable people from unnecessarily centralised control and restrictions. Moving toward the adaptive form means letting workers take over production scheduling and problem solving; it means letting workers set up their own control techniques; it means letting workers use their ideas to improve customer service. In the ultimately adaptive organisations, it means that members are given the freedom to do what they can do best — get the job done. This creates what has been described in earlier chapters as a **learning organisation**, one designed for continuous adaptation through problem solving, innovation and learning.[13]

CONTINGENCIES IN ORGANISATIONAL DESIGN

Good organisational design decisions should result in supportive structures that satisfy situational demands and allow all resources to be used to best advantage. This is true contingency thinking. Among the contingency factors in the organisational design checklist featured in Manager's Notepad 11.1 are the environment, strategy, technology, size and life cycle, and human resources.

MANAGER'S NOTEPAD 11.1

Organisational design checklist

- *Check 1:* Does the design fit well with the major problems and opportunities of the external environment?
- *Check 2:* Does the design support the implementation of strategies and the accomplishment of key operating objectives?
- *Check 3:* Does the design support core technologies and allow them to be used to best advantage?
- *Check 4:* Can the design handle changes in organisational size and different stages in the organisational life cycle?
- *Check 5:* Does the design support and empower workers and allow their talents to be used to best advantage?

Environment

The organisation's external environment and the degree of uncertainty it offers are of undeniable importance in organisational design.[14] A *certain environment* is composed of relatively stable and predictable elements. As a result, an organisation can succeed with relatively few changes in the goods or services produced or in the manner of production over time. Bureaucratic organisations and mechanistic designs are quite adequate under such conditions. An *uncertain environment* will have more dynamic and less predictable elements. Changes occur frequently and may catch decision makers by surprise. As a result, organisations must be flexible and responsive over relatively short time horizons. This requires more adaptive organisations and organic designs. Figure 11.3 summarises these relationships, showing how increasing uncertainty in organisational environments calls for more horizontal and adaptive designs.

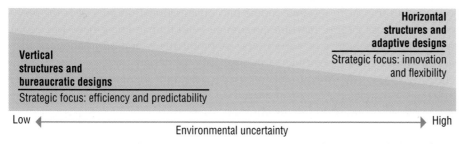

Figure 11.3 ▸ Environmental uncertainty and the performance of vertical and horizontal designs

POINT ⇐
COUNTER ⬆

Organisational restructuring and design — bandaid solutions for capitalist companies?

The attempt to discover the optimum organisation structure and design for companies in a capitalist economy is considered a fruitless task by some economists and business researchers. According to these critical management theorists, the very nature of market or capitalist economies, with their owners and managers on the one hand and workers on the other, creates conflict and crisis. The economic recessions of the 19th and 20th centuries reveal capitalism's tendency towards cyclical crisis and disruption. Though organisational restructuring may help alleviate the short-term problems facing companies, it cannot resolve the underlying tendency towards crisis and struggle within the capitalist organisation. It may help manage the problem in the short term but does not provide a sustainable, long-term solution.

Strategy

The nature of organisational strategies and objectives should influence the choice of structure. Research on these contingency relationships is often traced to the pioneering work of Alfred Chandler.[15] Chandler concluded that 'structure follows strategy'. An organisation's structure must support its strategy if the desired results are to be achieved.[16]

When strategy is stability oriented, the choice of organisational design should be based on the premise that little significant change will be occurring in the external environment. This means that plans can be set and operations programmed to be routinely implemented. To best support this strategic approach, the organisation should be structured to operate in well-defined and predictable ways. This is most characteristic of bureaucratic organisations that use more mechanistic design alternatives.

When strategy is growth oriented and when strategy is likely to change frequently, the situation as a whole becomes more complex, fluid and uncertain. Operating objectives are likely to include the need for innovation and flexible responses to changing competition in the environment. Operations and plans are likely to have short life spans, and require frequent and even continuous modification over time. The most appropriate structure is one that allows for internal flexibility and freedom to create new ways of doing things. This is most characteristic of the empowerment found in adaptive organisations using more organic design alternatives.

Technology

Technology is the combination of knowledge, skills, equipment, computers and work methods used to transform resource inputs into organisational outputs. It is the way tasks are accomplished using tools, machines, techniques and human know-how. The availability of appropriate technology is a cornerstone of productivity, and the nature of the core technologies in use must be considered in organisational design.

In the early 1960s, Joan Woodward conducted a study of technology and structure in more than 100 English manufacturing organisations. She classified core *manufacturing technology* into three categories.[17] In **small-batch production**, such as a racing bicycle shop, a variety of custom products are tailor-made to order. Each item or batch of items is made somewhat differently to fit customer specifications. The equipment used may not be elaborate, but a high level of worker skill often is needed. In **mass production**, the organisation produces a large number of uniform products in an assembly-line system. Workers are highly dependent on one another, as the product passes from stage to stage until completion. Equipment may be sophisticated, and workers often follow detailed instructions while performing simplified jobs. Organisations using **continuous-process production** are highly automated. They produce a few products by continuously feeding raw materials — such as liquids, solids and gases — through a highly automated production system with largely computerised controls. Such systems are equipment intensive but can often be operated by a relatively small labour force. Classic examples are automated chemical plants, steel mills, oil refineries and power plants.

Woodward found that the right combination of structure and technology was critical to organisational success. The best small-batch and continuous-process plants in her study had more flexible organic structures; the best mass-production operations had more rigid mechanistic structures. The implications of this research became known as the **technological imperative**: technology is a major influence on organisation structure.

The importance of technology for organisational design applies in services as well as manufacturing, although the core *service technologies* are slightly different.[18] In health care, education and related services, an **intensive technology** focuses the efforts of many people with special expertise on the needs of patients or clients. In banks, real estate firms, insurance companies, employment agencies and others like them, a **mediating technology** links together parties seeking a mutually beneficial exchange of values — typically a buyer and seller. Finally, a **long-linked technology** can function like mass production, where a client is passed from point to point for various aspects of service delivery.

Size and life cycle

Typically measured by number of employees, *organisational size* is another contingency factor in organisational design.[19] Although research indicates that larger organisations tend to have more mechanistic structures than smaller ones, it is clear that this is not always best for them.[20] In fact, a perplexing managerial concern is that organisations tend to become more bureaucratic as they grow in size and consequently have more difficulty adapting to changing environments.

It is especially important to understand the design implications of the **organisational life cycle**, or the evolution of an organisation over time through different stages of growth. The *stages in the organisational life cycle* can be described as:[21]

1. *birth stage* — when the organisation is founded by an entrepreneur
2. *youth stage* — when the organisation starts to grow rapidly
3. *midlife stage* — when the organisation has grown large with success
4. *maturity stage* — when the organisation stabilises at a large size.

In its *birth stage* the founder usually runs the organisation. It stays relatively small, and the structure is quite simple. The organisation starts to grow rapidly during the *youth stage* and management responsibilities extend among more people. Here, the simple structure begins to exhibit the stresses of change. An organisation in the *midlife stage* is even larger, with a more complex and increasingly formal structure. More levels appear in the chain of command, and the founder may have difficulty remaining in control. In the *maturity stage*, the organisation stabilises in size, typically with a mechanistic structure. It runs the risk of becoming complacent and slow in competitive markets. Bureaucratic tendencies toward stability may lead an organisation at this stage toward decline. Steps must be taken to counteract these tendencies and allow for needed creativity and innovation.

One way of coping with the disadvantages of large size is *downsizing*, that is, taking actions to reduce the scope of operations and number of employees. This response is often used when top management is challenged to reduce costs quickly and increase productivity.[22] But, perhaps more significantly, good managers in many organisations find unique ways to overcome the disadvantages of large size before the crisis of downsizing hits. They are creative in fostering **intrapreneurship**, described in chapter 9 as the pursuit of entrepreneurial behaviour by individuals and subunits within large organisations.[23] They also find ways for smaller entrepreneurial units to operate with freedom and autonomy within the larger organisational framework. **Simultaneous systems**, for example, are organisations that utilise both mechanistic and organic designs to meet the need for production efficiency and continued innovation. This 'loose-tight' concept in organisational design is depicted in figure 11.4.

Intrapreneurship is entrepreneurial behaviour displayed by people or subunits within large organisations.

Simultaneous systems operate when mechanistic and organic designs operate together in an organisation.

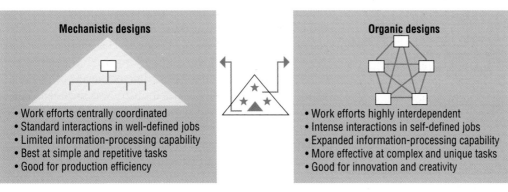

Figure 11.4 ▸ Simultaneous 'loose-tight' properties of team structures support efficiency and innovation.

Human resources

Another contingency factor in organisational design is people — the human resources that staff the organisation for action. A good organisational design provides people with the supporting structures they need to achieve both high performance and satisfaction in their work. Modern management theory views people-structure relationships in a contingency fashion. The prevailing argument is that there should be a good 'fit' between organisation structures and the human resources.[24]

An important human resource issue in organisational design is skill. Any design should allow the expertise and talents of organisational members to be unlocked and utilised to the fullest. Especially in the age of information and knowledge workers, high-involvement organic designs with their emphasis on empowerment are crucial. When IBM purchased

Increased workforce diversity

Recent census data in Australia and New Zealand reveal that racial and ethnic diversity is increasing. There are far greater numbers of Asians and Pacific Islanders in mainstream businesses in Sydney, Melbourne and Auckland compared with the early 1990s.

What might be behind this trend?

Subsystems are smaller components of a larger system.

the software firm Lotus, for example, the intention was to turn it into a building block for the organisation's networking business. But Lotus was small and IBM was huge. The whole thing had to be carefully handled or IBM might lose many of the talented people who created the popular Lotus Notes and related products. The solution was to adapt the design to fit the people. IBM gave Lotus the space it needed to retain the characteristics of a creative software house. Said the organisation's head of software at the time: 'You have to keep the people, so you have to ask yourself why it is they like working there'.[25]

SUBSYSTEMS DESIGN AND INTEGRATION

Organisations are composed of **subsystems**, such as a department or work unit headed by a manager, that operate as smaller parts of a larger and total organisational system. Ideally, the work of subsystems serves the needs of the larger organisation. Ideally, too, the work of each subsystem supports the work of others. Things don't always work out this way, however. Another challenge of organisational design is to create subsystems and coordinate relationships so that the entire organisation's interests are best met.

Important research in this area was reported in 1967 by Paul Lawrence and Jay Lorsch of Harvard University.[26] They studied ten companies in three different industries — plastics, consumer goods and containers. The companies were chosen because they differed in performance. The industries were chosen because they faced different levels of environmental uncertainty. The plastics industry was uncertain; containers was more certain; consumer goods was moderately uncertain. The results of the Lawrence and Lorsch study can be summarised as follows.

First, the total system structures of successful companies in each industry matched their respective environmental challenges. Successful plastics companies in uncertain environments had more organic designs; successful container companies in certain environments had more mechanistic designs. This result was consistent with the earlier research by Burns and Stalker already discussed in this chapter.[27] Second, Lawrence and Lorsch found that subsystem structures in the successful companies matched the challenges of their respective subenvironments. Subsystems within the successful companies assumed different structures to accommodate the special problems and opportunities of their operating situations. Third, the researchers found that subsystems in the successful companies worked well with one another, even though they were very different from one another.

Subsystem differences

Figure 11.5 depicts operating differences between three divisions in one of the companies studied by Lawrence and Lorsch. The illustration shows how research and development, manufacturing and sales subunits may operate differently in response to unique needs. This illustrates **differentiation**, which is the degree of difference that exists between the internal components of the organisation.

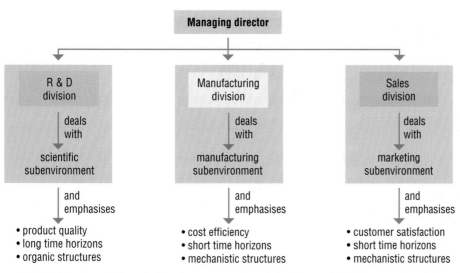

Differentiation is the degree of difference between subsystems in an organisation.

Figure 11.5 › Subsystems differentiation among research and development (R&D), manufacturing and sales divisions

There are four common *sources of subsystems differentiation*. First, the planning and action horizons of managers vary from short term to long term. Sometimes *differences in time orientation* become characteristic of work units themselves. In a business, for example, the manufacturing subsystem may have a shorter-term outlook than does the research and development group. These differences can make it difficult for personnel from the two units to work well together. Second, the different tasks assigned to work units may also result in *differences in objectives*. For example, cost-conscious production managers and volume-conscious marketing managers may have difficulty agreeing on solutions to common problems. Third, *differences in interpersonal orientation* can affect subsystem relations. To the extent that patterns of communication, decision making and social interaction vary, it may be harder for personnel from different subsystems to work together. And fourth, *differences in formal structure* can also affect subsystem behaviours. Someone who is used to flexible problem solving in an organic setting may find it very frustrating to work with a manager from a mechanistic setting who is used to strict rules.

How to achieve integration

The term **integration** in organisation theory refers to the level of coordination achieved among an organisation's internal components. Organisational design involves the creation of both differentiated structures and appropriate integrating mechanisms. A basic *organisational design* paradox, however, makes this a particularly challenging managerial task. Increased differentiation among organisational subsystems creates the need for greater integration; however, integration becomes harder to achieve as differentiation increases.

Integration is the level of coordination achieved among subsystems in an organisation.

Manager's Notepad 11.2 identifies several mechanisms for achieving subsystem integration.[28] The first integrating mechanisms listed in the notepad rely more on vertical coordination and the use of authority relationships in the chain of command. The use of rules and procedures, hierarchical referral and planning work best when differentiation is low. Integrating mechanisms that emphasise horizontal coordination and improved lateral relations work better when differentiation is high.[29] They include the use of direct contact between managers, liaison roles, task forces, teams and matrix structures.

MANAGER'S NOTEPAD 11.2

How to improve subsystem integration

- *Rules and procedures.* Clearly specify required activities.
- *Hierarchical referral.* Refer problems upward to a common superior.
- *Planning.* Set targets that keep everyone headed in the same direction.
- *Direct contact.* Have subunit managers coordinate directly.
- *Liaison roles.* Assign formal coordinators to link subunits together.
- *Task forces.* Form temporary task forces to coordinate activities and solve problems on a timetable.
- *Teams.* Form permanent teams with the authority to coordinate and solve problems over time.
- *Matrix organisations.* Create a matrix structure to improve coordination on specific programs.

WORK PROCESS DESIGN

Process reengineering systematically analyses work processes to design new and better ones.

From the emphasis on subsystems integration and more cross-functional collaboration in organisational design has come a popular development known as business **process reengineering**.[30] This is defined by consultant Michael Hammer as the systematic and complete analysis of work processes and the design of new and better ones.[31] The goal of a reengineering effort is to focus attention on the future, on customers and on improved ways of doing things. It tries to break people and mindsets away from habits, preoccupation with past accomplishments and tendencies to continue implementing old and outmoded ways of doing things. Simply put, reengineering is a radical and disciplined approach to changing the way work is carried out in organisations.

What is a work process?

A work process is a related group of tasks that together create a value for the customer.

In his book *Beyond Reengineering*, Michael Hammer defines a **work process** as 'a related group of tasks that together create a result of value for the customer'.[32] They are the things people do to turn resource inputs into goods or services for customers. Hammer goes further to highlight the following key words in this definition and their implications:

- *group* — tasks are viewed as part of a group rather than in isolation
- *together* — everyone must share a common goal
- *result* — the focus is on what is accomplished, not on activities
- *customer* — processes serve customers and their perspectives are the ones that really count.

The concept of **workflow**, or the movement of work from one point to another in the manufacturing or service delivery processes, is central to the understanding of processes.[33] The various aspects of a work process must all be completed to achieve the desired results, and they must typically be completed in a given order. An important starting point for a reengineering effort is to diagram or map these workflows as they actually take place. Then each step can be systematically analysed to determine whether it is adding value and to consider ways of streamlining to improve efficiency. Since some form of computer support is typically integral to organisational workflows today, special attention should be given to maximising the contribution of new technology to the reengineering of processes.

 Workflow is the movement of work from one point to another in a system.

How to reengineer core processes

Given the mission, objectives and strategies of an organisation, business process reengineering can be used to regularly assess and fine-tune work processes to ensure that they directly add value to operations. Each process is viewed as a 'black box' with inputs and outputs. The process is what turns the inputs into outputs, and the outputs should have greater value coming out than did the inputs as they went in. Through a technique called **process value analysis**, core processes are identified and carefully evaluated for their performance contributions. Each step in a workflow is examined. Unless a step is found to be important, useful and contributing to the value added, it is eliminated. Process value analysis typically involves the following steps.[34]

1. Identify the core processes.
2. Map the core processes in respect to workflows.
3. Evaluate all tasks for the core processes.
4. Search for ways to eliminate unnecessary tasks or work.
5. Search for ways to eliminate delays, errors and misunderstandings.
6. Search for efficiencies in how work is shared and transferred among people and departments.

Process value analysis identifies and evaluates core processes for their performance contributions.

Steps in process value analysis

Figure 11.6 shows an example of how reengineering and better use of computer technology can streamline a purchasing operation. A purchase order should result in at least three value-added outcomes: order fulfilment, a paid bill and a satisfied supplier. Work to be successfully accomplished includes such things as ordering, shipping, receiving, billing and payment. A traditional business system might have purchasing, receiving and accounts payable as separate functions, with each communicating with the others and the supplier. Alternatively, reengineering might design a new purchasing support team whose members handle the same work more efficiently and with the support of the latest computer technology.[35]

Process-driven organisations

Customers, teamwork and efficiency are central to Hammer's notion of process reengineering. He describes the case of Aetna Life & Casualty Company where a complex system of tasks and processes once took as much as 28 days to accomplish.[36] Customer service requests were handled in step-by-step fashion by many different people. After an analysis of workflows, the process was redesigned into a 'one and done' format, where a single customer service provider handled each request from start to finish. One of Aetna's customer account managers said after the change was made: 'Now we can see the customers as individual people. It's no longer "us" and "them" '.[37]

www.shopfast.com.au

E-tailer Shopfast supplies more than 120 000 customers in Sydney, Wollongong and the central coast of NSW. It keeps costs low by buying locally at wholesale prices. It uses all in-house staff and work groups in its dispatch centre, and maintains customer contact through deliverers, e-mail, a toll-free phone line and SMS messages.[38]

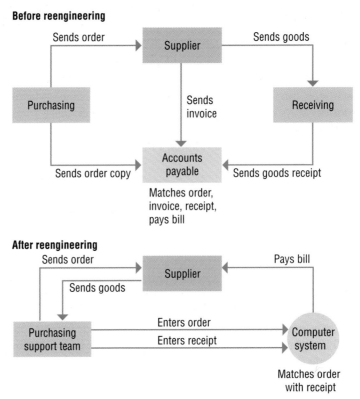

Before reengineering

Sends order → Supplier → Sends goods

Purchasing

Sends order copy → Accounts payable ← Sends goods receipt

Supplier → Sends invoice → Accounts payable

Receiving

Accounts payable: Matches order, invoice, receipt, pays bill

After reengineering

Sends order → Supplier ← Pays bill

Sends goods

Purchasing support team → Enters order → Computer system

Purchasing support team → Enters receipt → Computer system

Computer system: Matches order with receipt

Figure 11.6 ▸ How reengineering can streamline core business processes

Hammer also describes reengineering at GTE, now a unit of the new Verizon Communications. Before reengineering, customer enquiries for telephone service and repairs required extensive consultation between technicians and their supervisors. After process value analysis, technicians were formed into geographical teams that handled their own scheduling, service delivery and reporting. They were given mobile telephones and laptop computers to assist in managing their work, resulting in the elimination of a number of costly supervisory jobs. The technicians enthusiastically responded to the changes and opportunities. 'The fact that you've got four or five people zoned in a certain geographical area,' said one, 'means that we get personally familiar with our customers' equipment and problems.'[39]

The prior examples describe the essence of process reengineering. The approach tries to redesign processes to centre control for them with an identifiable group of people, and to focus each person and the entire system on meeting customer needs and expectations. It tries to eliminate duplication of work and systems bottlenecks, and in so doing tries to reduce costs and increase efficiency while creating an ever-present capacity for change. As Hammer says in describing the ultimate *process-driven organisation*:

> Traditional organizations were designed for execution, not for change; they lacked the mechanisms for recognizing and responding to change, and their rigid structures made accommodating change a traumatic event. Not so with a process enterprise. Its intrinsic customer focus and its commitment to outcome measurement make it vigilant and proactive in perceiving the need for change; the process owner, freed from other responsibilities and wielding the power of process design, is an institutionalized agent of change; and employees who have an appreciation for customers and who are measured on outcomes are flexible and adaptable.[40]

PHYSICAL FACTORS IN THE WORKPLACE

While process reengineering has captured the attention of many companies there is now also renewed interest in how physical factors in the workplace affect employee productivity and wellbeing. Attention to physical factors in the workplace can increase gains made from the other management methods discussed in this chapter — they are an important dimension of workplace design and it is important for managers to recognise their contribution to organisational performance.

Physical factors in the workplace were the original inspiration for much early management research, such as the Hawthorne Studies in the 1920s. While much contemporary management research emphasises the importance of social and psychological factors, the importance of physical factors must not be overlooked. Some of the key physical factors affecting workplace productivity and wellbeing are discussed in the following sections.

Lighting the workplace

Of all the machinery and systems used in industry, most dependence is placed on the human eye. Relevant information about materials and tools being used must be clearly visible, as must the tools and materials themselves. This is particularly important in industries such as electronics, biotechnology, medical and personal care services, and advanced manufacturing. Workers must be able to pay attention to the task object, surface texture and colours, shape of machines and tools, size of details to be resolved, duration of task, degree of physical activity, and stroboscopic effects.

Ergonomic workstations

Injuries to staff resulting from poorly designed workplace equipment and furniture reduce productivity substantially. Many European companies, such as Volvo in Sweden and Siemens in Germany, have pioneered the development of ergonomic workstations and equipment to reduce common problems such as back injuries, joint and muscle stress disorders resulting from repetitive movements, and premature fatigue.

Climate control

Optimum temperature and humidity levels maximise the physical and mental performance of people, thereby increasing productivity and reducing possible workplace accidents. US, Japanese and European companies have pioneered developments in this area, including air-conditioning systems that produce the correct electromagnetic balance to maximise human alertness, and computer-controlled feedback systems to ensure continually optimal climate control in the workplace. The Japanese company, Daiken, is a world leader in workplace climate control systems, supplying global organisations such as Toyota, Nissan, Ford and P&O.

CHAPTER 11
Study guide

The chapter 11 study guide helps you review the chapter content, prepare for examinations, apply what you have learned and further build your career readiness. The summary briefly answers the study questions posed at the start of the chapter. The list of key terms allows you to double-check your familiarity with basic concepts and definitions. The applied activities help you test your comprehension of chapter content. Suggestions offered as career readiness activities direct your attention to relevant sections of the Career Readiness Workbook where you can test and develop your career skills and apply what you have learned. The list of electronic resources suggests activities from the *Management: An Asia–Pacific Perspective* web site and, finally, the case for critical thinking helps you apply your new management knowledge.

SUMMARY

What are the essentials of organisational design?

- Organisational design is the process of choosing and implementing structures that best arrange resources to serve mission and purpose.
- Bureaucratic or mechanistic organisational designs are vertical in nature and perform best for routine and predictable tasks.
- Adaptive or organic organisational designs are horizontal in nature and perform best in conditions requiring change and flexibility.

How do contingency factors influence organisational design?

- Environment, strategy, technology, size and people are all contingency factors influencing organisational design.
- Certain environments lend themselves to more vertical and mechanistic organisational designs. Uncertain environments require more horizontal and adaptive organisational designs.
- Technology — including the use of knowledge, equipment and work methods in the transformation process — is an important consideration in organisational design.
- Although organisations tend to become more mechanistic as they grow in size, designs must be used to allow for innovation and creativity in changing environments.

What are the major issues in subsystems design?

- Organisations are composed of subsystems that must work well together.
- Differentiation is the degree of difference that exists between various subsystems; integration is the level of coordination achieved among them.
- As organisations become more highly differentiated they have a greater need for integration, but as differentiation increases integration is harder to accomplish.
- Low levels of differentiation can be handled through authority relationships and more vertical organisational designs.
- Greater differentiation requires more intense coordination through horizontal organisational designs, with an emphasis on cross-functional teams and lateral relations.

How can work processes be reengineered?

- A work process is a related group of tasks that together create value for a customer.
- Business process engineering is the systematic and complete analysis of work processes and the design of new and better ones.
- In reengineering, the workflows of an organisation are diagrammed to identify how work moves from one point to another throughout a system.
- In process value analysis, all elements of a process and its workflows are examined to identify their exact contributions to key performance results.

KEY TERMS

adaptive organisations (p. 299)

conglomerate (p. 296)

continuous-process production (p. 302)

differentiation (p. 305)

integration (p. 305)

intensive technology (p. 302)

intrapreneurship (p. 303)

learning organisation (p. 300)

long-linked technology (p. 302)

mass production (p. 302)

mechanistic designs (p. 299)

mediating technology (p. 302)

organic designs (p. 299)

organisational design (p. 296)

organisational life cycle (p. 302)

organisational synergy (p. 296)

process reengineering (p. 306)

process value analysis (p. 307)

simultaneous systems (p. 303)

small-batch production (p. 302)

subsystems (p. 304)

technological imperative (p. 302)

technology (p. 302)

work process (p. 306)

workflow (p. 307)

APPLIED ACTIVITIES

Short-response questions

1. 'Organisational design should always be addressed in contingency fashion.' Explain this statement.
2. What difference does environment make in organisational design?
3. Describe the relationship between differentiation and integration as issues in subsystems design.
4. If you were a reengineering consultant, how would you describe the steps in a typical approach to process value analysis?

Application question

5. Two businesswomen, former university friends, are discussing their jobs and careers over lunch. You overhear one saying to the other: 'I work for a large corporation. It is bureaucratic and very authority driven. However, I have to say that it is also very successful. I like working there.' Her friend commented somewhat differently. She said: 'I wouldn't like working there at all. In my organisation things are very flexible and the structures are loose. We have a lot of freedom and the focus on operations is much more horizontal than vertical. And, we too are very successful.' After listening to the conversation and using insights from management theory, how can these two very different 'success stories' be explained?

CAREER READINESS ACTIVITIES

Recommended individual and group learning activities from the end-of-text Career Readiness Workbook for this chapter include:

Career advancement portfolio `WB`

Update your career advancement portfolio to reflect your new skills and experiences. Include skills and personal insights you gain from the following projects and exercises.

Research and presentation project `WB`

• Project 4 — Corporate social responsibility — 'what's the status?'

Cross-functional integrative case `WB`

Read the integrative case on Sarina Russo and answer the following questions:

11.1 How might each of the contingency factors — environment, people, strategy, size and technology — affect the organisational design of the Russo Institute of Technology?

11.2 In what stage of the organisational life cycle is the Sarina Russo Group? What challenges might this stage bring to the organisation? Be specific with reference to the organisation.

Exercises in teamwork `WB`

• Exercise 3 — Defining quality
• Exercise 5 — What would the classics say?

Management skills assessment `WB`

• Assessment 11 — Organisational design preferences

ELECTRONIC RESOURCES

Don't forget to take full advantage of the online support for *Management: An Asia–Pacific Perspective* at www.johnwiley.com.au/highered/management: chapter 11 practice tests, e-flashcards, crossword puzzles, interactive management skills assessments, interactive cases, the online career advancement portfolio and much more!

CASE FOR CRITICAL THINKING

Read the following case for critical thinking on PricewaterhouseCoopers. While you are reading the case keep in mind what you have learned in this chapter, then answer the questions.

CASE FOR CRITICAL THINKING
PricewaterhouseCoopers:
changing economy, mission, design

Introduction

From the late 1980s, the US accounting–consulting industry was dominated by the Big Six — Arthur Andersen & Co., Coopers & Lybrand LLP, Deloitte and Touche, Ernst & Young, KPMG and Price Waterhouse. In September 1997, Price Waterhouse and Coopers & Lybrand announced plans to merge their operations to create the second-largest organisation behind Arthur Andersen. What were the outcomes for both these organisations and the industry in general?

From six to five

Mergers are not new to the US accounting industry. Once there was the Big Eight, but in the late 1980s the mergers of Deloitte Haskins & Sells with Touche Ross & Company to form Deloitte & Touche, and of Ernst & Whinney with Arthur Young & Company to form Ernst & Young, shrank the industry to the Big Six.[41] Price Waterhouse attempted to merge with Deloitte in 1984, but talks were cancelled. In 1989, Price Waterhouse once again was set to merge, this time with Arthur Andersen, but the deal fell apart after quarrels over a new name.[42] However, Price Waterhouse remained under pressure to combine with a larger player. In September 1997, it announced that it intended to merge with Coopers & Lybrand in a deal that would create an organisation with combined worldwide revenues of $12 billion, over 130 000 employees, and more than 8500 partners. As the fifth- (Coopers) and sixth- (Price) largest players in the accounting/consulting market, their combination may have been inevitable. 'Had Price Waterhouse not done this deal, they were in danger of fast becoming a niche player as the smallest of the Big Six,' claimed Arthur Bowman, editor of *Bowman's Accounting Reports*.[43]

In addition to its US operation, Price was active in Asia, Australasia and South America, representing such industries as chemicals, entertainment and media, and energy. Coopers had a strong presence in Europe and specialised in consumer products, manufacturing and communications on an international scale. The need to develop a larger presence in consulting appears to have been one of the main motivations for the merger.[44] In 1996, for the first time, the 100 biggest accountancy firms in the USA earned more from consulting ($8.3 billion) than they did from either auditing ($7.9 billion) or tax ($5 billion).[45]

While previous mergers in the industry were motivated by the need to reduce the size of the organisation and reduce overheads, the Price–Coopers union was motivated by the need for global support and seamless business consulting. Shortly after the Price–Coopers announcement, KPMG and Ernst & Young announced that they too would be merging. However, in early March of 1998, they announced they had abandoned their proposed $18 billion merger after four tumultuous months of negotiations.

The need for economies of scale is starkly evident when revenues per partner are compared across the organisations in the industry. On average, Price Waterhouse's 3300 partners generated $1.5 million apiece in 1996, with Coopers's 5200 partners averaging $1.3 million. By comparison, Arthur Andersen's 2611 partners generated an average of $3.6 million each.

A number of forces in the rapidly changing accounting–consulting industry both support and aggravate the combinations arising from such mergers. The market for professional business services is growing more rapidly elsewhere than it is in the USA.[46] Globalisation of the industry is expected to become increasingly prevalent. The *U.S. Industry and Trade Outlook* forecasts that demand for US management, consulting and public relations services overseas will continue to grow at 14 to 15 per cent annually, compared to a domestic growth rate averaging about 5 per cent annually.[47]

Another cause for concern is legal liability. All Big Five accounting organisations became limited liability partnerships in an effort to protect their partners from litigation. Especially as the organisations strengthen their global presence, partners in Australia, for example, do not wish to be sued for alleged errors of their colleagues in the USA. For example, in 2002 Arthur Andersen was indicted by the US Government for obstruction of justice for its role in the collapse of energy company, Enron. Andersen Australia had attracted criticism over its auditing of failed insurance group HIH. Following the Enron collapse, in a bid to minimise the fallout for the company (including Enron shareholder lawsuits, a US criminal charge related to the alleged shredding of documents and an exodus of blue-chip clients), Arthur Andersen began merger talks with global accounting giant KPMG, but the talks were abandoned. Talks then began with Ernst & Young and, by October 2002, Ernst & Young had combined with Arthur Andersen in 57 countries, seeing Ernst & Young move to second in size behind PricewaterhouseCoopers.[48]

Even more pervasive is the conflict between accountants and consultants, which tends to pull the two major revenue sources in opposite directions. Indeed, many clients have problems with the one-stop organisations, as conflicts of interest arise when they are independently audited by the same company that provides professional business advice. In October 2002, PricewaterhouseCoopers completed the sale of its global management consulting and technology services unit, PwC Consulting, to IBM.

The future

One of the biggest problems with any merger as large as that of Price Waterhouse and Coopers & Lybrand is the potential for clashing cultures. A former Coopers & Lybrand partner likens Price Waterhouse to a Roman legion — pristine, well-equipped and efficiently drilled. Alternatively, Coopers 'are the Visigoths of the industry, throwing stones from the tops of trees'.[49] Price has a strong team culture; new business at Coopers is fought over 'tooth and nail' internally.[50] Howard Schilit, an accounting professor who is president of the Center for Financial Research and Analysis, worried that 'each of the firms has a very special culture and it will be difficult to merge the two together'.[51]

QUESTIONS

1. Compare the cultures of Price Waterhouse and Coopers & Lybrand. Are there differences? Investigate changes that have occurred at PricewaterhouseCoopers over the past few years. Can any of these be traced to the differing cultural influences of Price and Coopers?

2. What pressure did the merger put on the rest of the industry?

3. Would you classify the accounting–consulting work design as small batch, mass production or continuous process according to Joan Woodward's classification?

Human resource management

CHAPTER 12 STUDY QUESTIONS

- Why do people make the difference?

- What is strategic human resource management?

- How do organisations attract a quality workforce?

- How do organisations develop a quality workforce?

- How do organisations maintain a quality workforce?

AstraZeneca — making people its top priority

Imagine working at an organisation which is widely recognised as a leader in supporting, rewarding and developing its people, a company which truly 'regards its employees as its most valuable resource'. Sydney-based pharmaceutical company AstraZeneca Australia (a subsidiary of its Swedish–British parent, AstraZeneca) is one such company.

During 2002, AstraZeneca Australia was named by the Australian Human Resources Institute as a finalist in its Excellence in People Management Awards, alongside McDonald's Australia, the Queensland Treasury, St.George Bank and the University of Queensland.

AstraZeneca has a worldwide workforce of over 47 000 and employs around 900 people in Australia, including 400 at its $68 million North Ryde manufacturing facility. It is the world leader in gastrointestinal medicines and anaesthesia and in the world's top five in anti-cancer, respiratory and cardiovascular medicines.

Through a number of human resource strategies, the company 'expects that through teamwork, open communication, flexibility and respect for the individual we will have a work environment that enables people to fulfil their potential and make a positive impact on the company's success'. For instance, its learning and career development strategy uses methods such as self-paced learning, videos, on-the-job training, project team participation, coaching, internal and external courses, lateral moves, promotions, mentoring and job swaps and rotations to provide development opportunities for AstraZeneca employees.[1]

At AstraZeneca's web site www.astrazeneca.com.au you can view further information on the company's human resources strategies. You can also view the company's history and explore the job opportunities on offer, both in Australia and internationally.

GET CONNECTED!

Today, perhaps more than ever before, the pressures of global competition and social change are influencing not just the organisations in which we work, but the very nature of employment itself. Almost a decade ago, *Fortune* magazine hailed the onset of a human resources 'revolution'.[2] Well, the revolution continues in full swing and its developments are affecting organisations of all types and sizes. The watchwords and buzzwords of changing times are all around — reengineering, rightsizing, digitising, outsourcing, networking, empowering and the like. You should be reading and thinking seriously about them. They have important implications for those of us who seek satisfying and successful careers in the new economy. In his book, *The Future of Success*, Robert Reich calls this 'the age of the terrific deal' and describes it as follows:

> Combine the Internet, wireless satellites, and fiber optics, great leaps in computing power ... a quantum expansion of broadband connection ... a map of the human genome and tools to select and combine genes and even molecules — and you've got a giant, real-time, global bazaar of almost infinite choice and possibility.[3]

The choices and possibilities in the new economy are already bringing about fundamental changes in the employer–employee relationship. Reich, for example, points to a shift away from a system in which people work loyally as traditional 'employees' for 'employers' who provide them career-long job and employment security. He sees the shift toward a system where we become sellers of our services (talents) to those buyers (employers) who are willing to pay for them. Those who do 'buy' are looking for the very best people, whose capabilities and motivations match the demands of high-performance organisations. At Cisco Systems, CEO John Chambers says: 'We realized early on that a world-class engineer with 5 peers can outproduce 200 regular engineers ... So your success is dependent on your ability to attract the very best talent and then get out of the way and empower them.'[4]

A study of the best companies to work for in Australia found that they shared four characteristics. First, they were strong on 'people leadership'. They contained leaders who could effectively and enthusiastically communicate with their people. Next, they provided a 'compelling employment offer'. They were competitive in terms of remuneration, benefits and the promise of rewards for high achievement. Third, they provided accelerated career development and training. Finally, the companies possessed an appropriate culture, balancing the need for high performance with the need for celebration, recognition and fun.[5] Clearly, all four characteristics indicate that people management is a critical management skill. Recruiting, developing and retaining the best people is also crucial for the success of organisations in every sector. This chapter aims to give you an overview of these crucial tasks, and to demonstrate just how important human resource management can be to the knowledge-driven organisations of the 21st century.

DIVERSITY AND THE PRIMACY OF PEOPLE

We know that organisations are changing rapidly.[6] Structures are moving from the vertical to the more horizontal; teams and teamwork are increasingly essential to strategic advantage; working across functions, in networks, in virtual links and in real time are part and parcel of today's high-performance work settings. Developments in information technology are making communication increasingly intense while information itself becomes more rich, abundant and timely than ever before. Everywhere, people are expected to work with emphasis on serving customers and performing core processes as needed, in the best ways, and with freedom to make the necessary choices while doing so. But what also stands out in this new workplace with all of its technological advantages and structural changes is one undeniable fact. People still drive the system.

Why people make the difference

Human resource development has to be a top priority in any organisation with high performance aspirations. Testimonials like these say it all: 'People are our most important asset'; 'It's people who make the difference'; 'It's the people who work for us who ... determine whether our company thrives or languishes'.[7] Found on web sites, in annual reports and in executive speeches, they communicate a very specific understanding. Even with the guidance of the best strategies and supported by the best designs, an organisation must be well staffed with capable and committed people if it is to fully achieve its objectives.

There is ample research available to support this viewpoint. In an *Academy of Management Executive* article entitled 'Putting People First for Organizational Success', Jeffrey Pfeffer and John F. Veiga state: 'There is a substantial and rapidly expanding body of evidence ... that speaks to the strong connection between how firms manage their people and the economic results achieved.'[8] They forcefully argue that organisations perform better when they treat their members better. The management practices associated with successful organisations are employment security, decentralisation, use of teams, good compensation, extensive training and information sharing. However, Pfeffer also points out that too many organisations fail to operate in this manner, and calls them 'toxic workplaces' that treat their employees poorly.[9]

Additional backup for the primacy of people is offered by James Baron and David Kreps in their book, *Strategic Human Resources: Frameworks for General Managers*.[10] Stating that 'human resources are key to organizational success or failure', they summarise empirical research showing a positive relationship between human resource policies and organisational performance.[11] A study of 170 organisations in the high-technology sector shows that the founders' initial decisions on human resource policies and practices had long-term impact on company performance. Those start ups whose founders showed strong and early commitments to a positive human resource philosophy were able to operate in the future with fewer managers and with greater reliance on self-management by their employees.

Australian companies increasingly seem to be accepting the view that a focus on people is good for business. Organisational policies that link employee compensation with individual and organisational performance are on the rise, as are policies that provide flexibility in working hours and the design of jobs. There is also greater use of performance appraisals, with 66 per cent of manual staff, 86 per cent of clerical employees, and more than 93 per cent of professionals and managers undertaking regular appraisals. Of these, 95 per cent of their companies use the appraisals to determine individual training needs, 70 per cent use them for career development, and 65 per cent to determine employee promotion potential.[12]

McKinsey's Michael Rennie says of a new people-focused management style implemented at Australia's Woodside Petroleum: 'We get up to an 800 per cent difference between the highest performing group and the average'.[13] According to DDI-Asia Pacific chief executive David Tessman-Keys, human resource management is taking on higher significance because of the effects of the ageing population, the shrinking executive talent pool, and the steady fall in the retirement age for many in the workforce. Companies are increasingly looking for the best staff while the pool of top-quality people shrinks due to these kinds of factors.[14]

The diversity advantage

Throughout this book diversity has been linked with competitive advantage. It brings to problem solving and strategy formulation an array of talents, perspectives, experiences and world views that broaden any organisation's repertoire of skills and capabilities.

Changing work patterns in Australia

A recent study found that almost 40 per cent of Australian employees are able to work extra hours in return for time off at other times, and around one-third have variable start and finish times.[15]

How does this compare to your experience and the experience of people you know?

www.mcdonalds.com.au
www.mcdonalds.co.nz

In Australia and New Zealand, McDonald's has long been recognised for its human resource management competencies, particularly in training. McDonald's employees can complete programs to gain nationally recognised qualifications, from certificates to diplomas, run in conjunction with tertiary institutions.[19]

That's one side of the diversity story — finding the best talent available. The other side of the story is tapping it — finding ways to allow diversity to work its advantages to help create high-performing organisations. To do this, the diversity advantage not only must be recognised, it must be fully unlocked. Diversity consultant and author R. Roosevelt Thomas Jr puts the challenge this way: 'Managers must find ways to get the highest level of contribution from their workers. And they will not be able to do that unless they are aware of the many ways that their understanding of diversity relates to how well, or how poorly, people contribute.'[16] Thomas goes further to identify what he calls the *diversity rationale* that must drive organisations today:

> To thrive in an increasingly unfriendly marketplace, companies must make it a priority to create the kind of environment that will attract the best new talent and will make it possible for employees to make their fullest contribution.[17]

Many companies are doing just this. AstraZeneca Australia, featured at the beginning of this chapter, states that:

> AstraZeneca is committed to a policy of equal employment opportunity and a workplace that is free from discrimination and harassment. We base all employment decisions on merit and actively promote working relationships based upon mutual respect and valuing diversity.[18]

Job-relevant talent is not restricted because of anyone's race, gender, religion, marital or parental status, sexual orientation, ethnicity or other diversity characteristics. If an organisation lets these characteristics interfere with finding, hiring and developing the best job talents available, the loss will be someone else's gain. The best employers and the best managers know that. They know that to succeed in building high-performing organisations with sustainable competitive advantage in today's challenging times, they must place a primacy on people. This includes all people with the talent and desire to do good work.

GLOBALISATION

Drake Beam Morin • www.dbm.com

Changing jobs in the Asia–Pacific

Human resource management consultancy Drake Beam Morin (DBM) recently undertook a survey of 3956 retrenched executives in Korea, Japan, Hong Kong, Malaysia, Vietnam, Thailand and Singapore. The vast majority (89 per cent) had been retrenched because of the changes resulting from company acquisitions, mergers, restructures and downsizings. A switch of industry and/or job role was a common response of executives, with 69 per cent of Hong Kong executives reporting that they had moved to a new industry. Some 41 per cent of the executives found a new job through networking. This figure is similar to that found by DBM in other parts of the world. It is curious that the proportion obtaining jobs via networks was not higher given the importance of networks, connections and relationships (known as guanxi) to Chinese businesses, which generally rely on comprehensive networks of personal contacts to support and develop business relationships.[20]

HUMAN RESOURCE MANAGEMENT

The process of **human resource management** (HRM) involves attracting, developing and maintaining a talented and energetic workforce to support organisational mission, objectives and strategies. In order for strategies to be well implemented, workers with relevant skills and enthusiasm are needed. The task of human resource management is to make them available. For example, Fred Harrison, chief executive officer of the Ritchies supermarket chain in Victoria says: 'Leadership is about being able to get the very best out of your people. And this means treating each person individually. To do that you have to almost be a psychologist. It's the role of a coach.'[21]

⊘ Human resource management is the process of attracting, developing and maintaining a quality workforce.

POINT ⇐

COUNTER

Do good looks pay?

When research indicates that good-looking people earn more than those viewed as less attractive, the extent to which organisations practise diversity compared to what they preach remains open to question. Studies by Donald Hamermesh of the University of Texas found that men viewed as handsome receive 5 per cent more than the average salary, whereas those viewed as unattractive earned 9 per cent less than the average. In research undertaken by Monster www.monster.com.au, 95 per cent of the 2040 Australian employees surveyed thought that attractive workers received more favourable treatment. Interestingly, a 1995 study of Dutch advertising agencies found that better-looking executives produced an average of 10 per cent higher revenue than those of average looks. Hamermesh argues that the ability of attractive people to earn more creates incentives for companies to employ more attractive people.[22]

Should we be worried about these findings? Should looks be added to the list of personal characteristics covered by anti-discrimination legislation? If so, how could this be policed?

Employment discrimination

Discrimination involves 'making a distinction between individuals or groups so as to advantage some and disadvantage others'.[23] Employers specifically and managers generally must take care in their human resource management practices not to discriminate between people on the basis of characteristics such as age, disability, marital status, ethnicity, family responsibilities or social origin. In sum, they must provide **equal employment opportunity** (EEO), wherever this is reasonable, for all. Further, as shown in table 12.1, both direct and more subtle, indirect forms of discrimination must be avoided.[24]

Anti-discrimination measures are incorporated into a number of Commonwealth laws, including the *Human Rights and Equal Opportunity Commission Act 1986*, the *Racial Discrimination Act 1975*, the *Disability Discrimination Act 1992*, and the *Sex Discrimination Act 1984*. In New Zealand, the *Human Rights Act 1993* replaced the *Race Relations Act 1971*, and **sexual harassment** is included in the *Employment Relations Act 2000*.[25]

Discrimination may occur in any part of the human resource management process, from recruitment and selection to promotion and appraisal. For instance, in one New Zealand case, a service station owner advertised for a 'keen Christian person aged 16–18 who is not

⊘ Discrimination occurs when someone is denied a job or a job assignment for reasons not job relevant.

⊘ Equal employment opportunity is the right to employment and advancement without regard to race, sex, religion, colour or national origin.

⊘ Sexual harassment occurs as behaviour of a sexual nature that affects a person's employment situation.

Australian and New Zealand laws protecting against job discrimination

afraid of work'. The Equal Opportunity Tribunal found that it was unlawful for the employer to discriminate for this position on the basis of religious beliefs.[26]

Table 12.1 ▶ Direct discrimination versus indirect discrimination

	Direct discrimination	**Indirect discrimination**
Definition	Treating a person or group less favourably than another person or group in similar circumstances.	A practice that appears inoffensive but that results in a person or group being disadvantaged.
Example	An employer dismisses a female purely on the basis of her gender.	A company makes promotion dependent upon five years continuous service. This disadvantages women who often take time off to have children.
Remedy	Damages — pecuniary loss, hurt and humiliation.	Damages — pecuniary loss, hurt, loss of career prospects, stress, humiliation.

Source: © Raymond J. Stone, *Human Resource Management*, 4th edn (Brisbane: John Wiley & Sons, 2002), p. 99.

Discrimination is permitted, however, where it can be demonstrated that certain characteristics are essential in the performance of a job. For instance, ministers of religion and teachers at religious schools can be selected for their observance of particular religious beliefs, whereas jobs demanding bilingual or multilingual capabilities can discriminate among applicants on the presence or absence of such skills.[27]

Employers must also consider other relevant discrimination-related legislation, such as **affirmative action** (AA) legislation. The *Equal Opportunity for Women in the Workplace Act 1999* (EOWW Act) applies to all organisations employing 100 or more workers and demands that employers develop policies and practices that respond to the existence of historic and structural workplace discrimination. The Act requires that employers report annually to the federal government on their progress on AA. It aims to encourage employers to consider whether any of their current or historic practices diminish the likelihood of women taking on roles long dominated by men. For instance, an employer may see that requesting five years continuous employment in order to be considered for promotion can work against women who may take time off for family responsibilities and then return to the workplace. A positive response to this inequity may involve adjusting promotion criteria to reflect the different, but not necessarily less valuable, career decisions taken by women.[28]

Women continue to dominate some types of occupations, such as secretarial, nursing and personal services, and still encounter barriers to gaining highly paid positions in business and management. Women comprise just 24 per cent of Australia's managers and administrators and hold only 10.7 per cent of the 2345 directorships in Australia's top 300 companies.[29] Of the 33 biggest companies in Hong Kong, none has a woman chief executive and 17 have no women directors. Those women who are directors are the wife, sister or mother of the male founder. According to politician Tse Wing-ling, 'it boils down to Chinese culture. Women are indoctrinated to have low expectations of themselves.'[30]

⚙ Affirmative action commits the organisation to hiring and advancing minority groups and women.

Organisations can realise significant benefits through incorporating EEO and AA principles in their human resource management practices. For example, Rank Xerox cites savings of more than $2 million from better staff retention encouraged through its EEO program; and the insurance company NRMA successfully implemented a range of EEO and AA strategies to reduce the recruitment and selection costs flowing from the need to replace the 35 per cent of NRMA staff who were resigning each year.[31]

Diversity management represents a more proactive approach to these issues. Moving beyond the requirements of the law, diversity management involves 'identifying and managing those employee characteristics likely to have a significant impact on the organisation's ability to achieve its strategic objectives'.[32] This may include literacy and numeracy skills, career and life-stage issues, decision or problem-solving styles, and individual approaches to risk taking. The aim is to integrate and develop individual competencies in ways that maximise workplace participation and effectiveness for non-traditional groups.[33]

According to Lynne Bennington and Ruth Wein of La Trobe University, few employers take a diversity management approach. In fact, they suggest that the majority of employers 'do not really understand the ramifications of the legislation and simply continue to discriminate', concluding that anti-discrimination legislation has had a limited effect to date.[34] In addition, their analysis of the contents of 47 secretarial and 59 managerial job applications found that most applicants continue to reveal much unnecessary information about themselves, inviting employers to discriminate on this basis.[35]

Occupational health and safety

It has been estimated that there are around 2900 work-related deaths and 650 000 workplace injuries in Australia each year.[37] The annual losses to the economy from poor workplace safety are said to be more than $27 billion. The major causes of work-related deaths include mechanical failure, being hit by a moving object, contamination by chemicals and other substances, and falls, trips and slips.[38] According to Stone:

> Poor occupational health and safety (OHS) performance equates with poor human resource management, and poor ethical, legal and social responsibility. It represents a management failure to realise that safe organisations are more effective organisations.[39]

The benefits of sound OHS are obvious. Organisations can enjoy lower workers compensation costs and absenteeism, while employees can be more productive knowing that they can operate productively in a safe working environment. Companies like Wesfarmers and Orica demonstrate that good safety management is good business. Wesfarmers ties executive incentive rewards to safety performance. Orica

Diversity management involves identifying and managing those employee characteristics likely to have a significant impact on the organisation's ability to achieve its strategic objectives.

CONNECTION

Human resources

Are you comfortable with diversity?

One of the critical skills of management is being able to work with colleagues, customers and suppliers from other ethnic backgrounds. With 35 per cent of Sydney's population and 33 per cent of Auckland's population born overseas, the reality is that you will need to manage or be managed by others of diverse backgrounds.

Fujitsu Australia CEO Neville Roach claims that few organisations take real advantage of the opportunities that come from a diverse workforce, whereas Clarence da Gama Pinto of the Mount Eliza Business School argues that the development of diversity management skills is hampered by the lack of discussion on these issues in most workplaces. Da Gama Pinto argues that the first step in learning to manage diversity is to develop a greater self-awareness of your personal biases and prejudices. Next, you should develop knowledge of your culture and its inherent biases. The third step is to teach migrants the 'rules of engagement' for participating fully in the culture of their new nation.[36]

Questions

What steps can you take during the years ahead to improve your diversity management competency? What can you do now so that you can demonstrate this competency to potential employers?

Australia reduced injuries by more than 50 per cent within five years — from 20 per million working hours to less than 9 per million working hours — for a total saving of around $3 million.[40]

The federal government sets national workplace occupational health and safety standards through Worksafe Australia. State governments have generally set State-wide occupational health and safety laws consistent with the standards established by Worksafe Australia. In Victoria, for instance, the *Occupational Health and Safety Act 1985* establishes the responsibilities of employers and employees for the maintenance of safe workplaces. Employer responsibilities include providing and maintaining safe plant and systems of work, and providing adequate welfare facilities such as change rooms, dining areas and lockers. The Act encourages employers and employees to work together in the pursuit of workplace safety via the establishment of health and safety representatives and committees.[41]

Safety standards vary around the Asia–Pacific region. Australia's coalmining industry has one of the world's worst safety records, but in China, where government regulations have yet to take effect and mining practices remain poorly controlled, the death rate from accidents is some 500 to 1000 times that experienced in Australian mines. In Hong Kong, at least one worker is killed on a building site every week, and in Shenzen, China, one to two workers die every week in industrial accidents and more than 200 lose arms or legs.[42]

Industrial relations in the Asia–Pacific region

The International Labour Organization is part of the United Nations and aims to assist nations in ratifying common rules and protocols and implementing international labour standards in areas such as child labour and work safety. Learn more about its work at www.ilo.org.

Australia and New Zealand have broadly similar industrial relations systems. **Industrial relations** (sometimes called workplace relations) is the process of negotiation and bargaining between employers and employees. Even though there are several players in the Australian industrial relations system, recent changes to industrial relations laws have meant that individual employers and employees have the most significant roles. The proportion of employees who are members of **unions** has declined. Union membership was around 60 per cent in the 1950s, but today unions directly represent only about 26 per cent of the workforce. Unions remain particularly influential in the manufacturing, mining and government sectors. **Business associations**, such as the Metal Trades Industry Association, representing a number of employers in the same industry remain common, but are also considerably less influential than in the days when employers were required to band together to negotiate with unions under the system of compulsory arbitration.[43]

Industrial relations is the process of negotiation and bargaining between employers and employees.

Unions represent the interests of employees in an industry, occupation or organisation.

Business associations represent the interests of organisations in an industry or region.

The Howard Liberal–National Government extended the reform process of the Labor Government of the 1980s and early 1990s by enacting the *Workplace Relations Act 1996*. The provisions of this Act encourage direct negotiations between employers and employees without the involvement of third parties, such as industrial courts and tribunals or, in some cases, unions. Individuals can negotiate Australian workplace agreements (AWAs) directly with their employer. The agreements are subject to a number of minimum requirements and conditions. For instance, the AWA must be no less favourable to the individual than the relevant award (which describes the minimum wage, conditions of work and benefits such as long service leave) and any relevant laws. This is known as the 'no disadvantage test'. Employers must also explain the effect of the AWA to the employee and the employee must grant his or her genuine consent to the agreement. When employees join together to negotiate with their employer, with or without the assistance of their union, certified agreements (CAs) can be established. Again, these must meet the no disadvantage test.[44]

It should be noted that many employees in Australia are covered by State-based industrial relations laws. This includes employees in professions such as nursing, teaching and policing, as well as State government employees in areas such as transport and housing.[45]

Similar industrial relations processes occur in New Zealand, with the *Employment Contracts Act 1991* legislating many of the changes which subsequently took place in Australia, particularly in relation to the encouragement of individual contracts between employers and employees and reduction in the power of third parties such as unions.[46] This Act was replaced with the *Employment Relations Act 2000* following the election of the Labor Government, but the new Act makes only minimal changes to the previous regime. One change made was that 'employers, employees and unions will all be required to deal with one another in good faith'. The Act sets out some basic requirements for good faith bargaining.[47] In summary, employers and unions involved in collective bargaining (the traditional style of industrial relations negotiation involving workers represented by a union and employers potentially using an employer association to represent their interests) must:

- use their best endeavours to agree to an effective bargaining process
- meet and consider and respond to proposals made by each other
- respect the role of the other's representative by not seeking to bargain directly with those for whom the representative acts
- not do anything to undermine the bargaining process or the authority of the other's representative.

Industrial relations and human resource management processes are quite different in some countries of the Asia–Pacific region, such as China. According to Stone, specific challenges facing the industrial relations or human resource manager in China include the fact that nothing is ever black and white — everything is negotiable. He cites the popular saying that 'nothing is illegal in China, but at the same time, nothing is legal either'.[48] In addition, politics impacts on all human resource management activities, so that independent unions, for example, are not permitted. Labour laws often differ substantially between Chinese provinces, and remuneration usually involves complex legal arrangements and an array of benefits unique to the country. In contrast, company-based unions are very common in Japan and the objectives of the unions will usually be similar to those of management. The emphasis of the Japanese industrial relations and human resource management systems is upon maintaining harmonious relations within the organisation, so that individually based pay-for-performance systems are less common than having base pay, a twice-yearly company bonus, and allowances based on position, merit, housing requirements and special skills. It is primarily through the allowance system that individuals receive greater or lesser rewards than others.[49]

International human resource management

Human resource management practices generally need to become more sophisticated and culturally sensitive when an organisation operates in the international context. For instance, when supporting staff who leave their home country to work in an international office, the human resource manager's responsibilities must be expanded to ensure the employee is appropriately relocated, oriented to the new context, satisfied in the work and retained following the assignment.[50]

When relocating staff, issues such as immigration and travel details, housing, shopping, medical care, recreation, and schooling for children must be considered. The expatriate will no doubt be subject to a different taxation regime, so salaries and benefits must be adjusted to ensure that the employee is no worse off by taking an international assignment. The costs associated with inconvenience and the selling or renting of the employee's home should also be considered. A number of other issues also arise, particularly if the language and culture of the new country differ from that of the employee's home country. Translation options, cross-cultural awareness and communication training, and ethical differences need to be investigated, discussed and resolved.[51] It is estimated that Australian expatriates are heavily concentrated in the countries of south-east and east Asia, including Hong Kong (20 per cent), Singapore (18 per cent), China and Indonesia (15 per cent each), Malaysia (12 per cent) and Japan (8 per cent), so these issues are clearly crucial to many Australian managers taking international assignments.[52]

Human resource managers involved in supporting international employees need to take a broader perspective than do human resource personnel looking after local employees. They must incorporate national and regional differences into the development of equitable and attractive international human resource policies. They will generally assume a greater degree of involvement in the lives of international employees, frequently being called on to assist employees in managing the detail of their lives, from banking to visits home. International human resource managers should be familiar with the government structures and business systems of the countries in which international staff are located, and contingency plans should be developed in case unrest, terrorism or natural disasters affect the security of the international employees in their care.

Some interesting research has been undertaken by Nick Forster of the University of Western Australia on the experiences of UK-based women managers who had taken international assignments. While the rate of expatriate failure (around 3 per cent) was significantly lower than that for men (8 per cent), many of the companies tended to send women for more junior management positions than would occur in their local operations. Not surprisingly, a number of the women reported that adaptation was quite difficult in east Asian cultures such as China and Japan. This was as a result of differences in culture between Asia and the United Kingdom in relation to the general acceptance of women managers.[53]

The human resource management process

Visit the web sites of the Australian Human Resources Institute www.ahri.com.au or the Human Resources Institute of New Zealand www.hrinz.org.nz for access to a wealth of useful information about human resource management.

GET CONNECTED!

The human resource management (HRM) process involves attracting, developing and maintaining a quality workforce. The first responsibility of *attracting a quality workforce* includes human resource planning, recruitment and selection. The second responsibility of *developing a quality workforce* includes employee orientation, training and development, and career planning and development. The third responsibility of *maintaining a quality workforce* includes management of employee retention and turnover, performance appraisal and compensation and benefits.

Human resource specialists often assist line managers in fulfilling these three responsibilities. A human resource department appears on many organisation charts and is often headed by a senior executive reporting directly to the chief executive officer. It is also increasingly common to find organisations outsourcing various technical aspects of the human resource management process. There are a growing number of career opportunities with consulting firms that provide such specialised services as recruiting, compensation planning, outplacement and the like. In a dynamic environment complicated by legal issues, labour shortages, economic turmoil, changing corporate strategies, new organisation and job designs, high technology, and changing personal values and expectations, human resource specialists become ever-more important. Many belong to the Australian Human Resources Institute (AHRI), a professional organisation dedicated to keeping its membership up to date in all aspects of HRM and its complex legal environment.

Strategic human resource management

Any organisation should at all times have the right people available to do the work required to achieve and sustain competitive advantage. **Strategic human resource management** applies the HRM process to ensure the effective accomplishment of organisational mission.[54] Strategic HRM mobilises human resources to implement strategies and sustain competitive advantage. This requires a top-level commitment to **human resource planning**, a process of analysing staffing needs and planning how to satisfy these needs in a way that best serves organisational mission, objectives and strategies.[55]

The major elements in strategic human resource planning are shown in figure 12.1. The process begins with a review of organisational mission, objectives and strategies. This establishes a frame of reference for forecasting human resource needs and labour supplies, both within and outside the organisation. Ultimately, the planning process should help managers identify staffing requirements, assess the existing workforce, and determine what additions and/or replacements are required to meet future needs. It is no secret, for example, that high-tech workers are in great demand today and many organisations are experiencing or are anticipating difficulty in meeting their staffing needs. At GE Medical Systems, a multi-generational staffing plan is used to help resolve the problem. Every new product plan has a human resource plan associated with it — one that covers all generations of the product's anticipated life.[56]

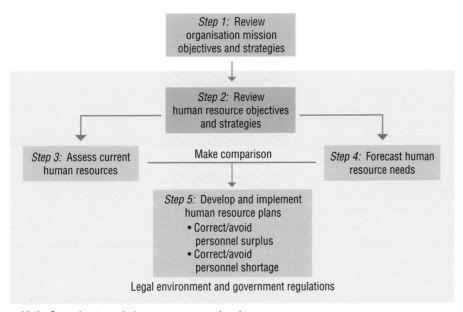

Figure 12.1 ▸ Steps in strategic human resource planning

To plan successfully to meet strategic human resource requirements, managers must not only understand the mission and strategies, they must also understand the jobs that need to be done. The foundations for human resource planning are set by **job analysis** — the orderly study of job facts to determine just what is done, when, where, how, why, and by whom in existing or potential new jobs.[57] The job analysis provides useful information that can then be used to write and/or update a **job description**. This is a written statement of job duties and responsibilities. The information in a job analysis can also be used to create a **job specification** that lists the qualifications — such as education, prior experience and skill requirements — needed by any person hired for or placed in a given job.

⌖ Strategic human resource management involves attracting, developing and maintaining a quality workforce to implement organisational strategies.

⌖ Human resource planning analyses staffing needs and identifies actions to fill those needs.

⌖ Job analysis studies job requirements and facts that can influence performance.

⌖ A job description details the duties and responsibilities of a job holder.

⌖ A job specification lists the qualifications required of a job holder.

ATTRACTING A QUALITY WORKFORCE

With a human resource plan prepared, the process of attracting a quality workforce begins. An advertisement once run by the Motorola Corporation identified the goal this way: 'Productivity is learning how to hire the person who is *right* for the job'. To attract the right people to its workforce, an organisation must first know exactly what it is looking for — it must have a clear understanding of the jobs to be done and the talents required to do them well. Then it must have the systems in place to excel at employee recruitment and selection.

The recruiting process

Recruitment is a set of activities designed to attract a *qualified* pool of job applicants to an organisation. Emphasis on the word 'qualified' is important. Effective recruiting should bring employment opportunities to the attention of people whose abilities and skills meet job specifications. The three steps in a typical recruitment process are advertisement of a job vacancy, preliminary contact with potential job candidates and initial screening to create a pool of qualified applicants.

In university recruiting, for example, advertising is done by the company posting short job descriptions in print or on line through the campus placement centre and/or in the campus newspaper. Preliminary contact is made after candidates register for interviews with company recruiters on campus. This typically involves a short 20- to 30-minute interview, during which the candidate presents a written résumé and briefly explains his or her job qualifications. As part of the initial screening, the recruiter shares interview results and résumés from the campus visits with appropriate line managers. Decisions will then be made about who to include in the final pool of candidates to be invited for further interviews during a formal visit to the organisation.

Given that both the shortage of skilled people in some sectors and an ageing workforce are creating greater competition for the best people, recruiting has become a critical human resource management process for organisations seeking to retain or build their competitive advantage. In Australia, for instance, significant skill shortages have recently existed in a number of industries. In business services there is a shortage of IT staff, sales managers and accountants; the finance sector has experienced shortages of tax specialists and financial planners; the telecommunications sector has shortages of design engineers and technical sales staff; and in the retail sector, sales and trades personnel have been in short supply.[58]

Skill shortages may occur at both senior levels and at relatively more junior levels of an organisation. For instance, during 2001 the retail giant Coles Myer replaced a number of senior managers — including the chief executives of Target, Myer Grace Brothers and Kmart, as well as its general managers of human resources and corporate affairs. In every case, the company recruited from outside the industry — an indicator of a lack of well-developed talent within the Coles Myer organisation. In contrast, companies like David Jones, Colorado and McDonald's work hard to train and develop staff so that the best people can be promoted from within the organisation, bringing with them an intimate knowledge of customers and the company culture. For example, Peter Breckenridge has, at 24, taken on the role of operations consultant at McDonald's, responsible for the quality, service, profitability and cleanliness of five McDonald's outlets in suburban Melbourne. During his studies for a double degree in electrical engineering and computer science, Breckenridge worked his way from trainee to store manager. McDonald's gave him the opportunity to use his studies as a development manager in its construction department, but his love for working with people led him to seek a position combining his people skills, qualifications and experience. He is pleased with his progress. 'When I made the move, my fellow university students thought I was silly and my parents said "you spent all that money on your education", but I don't regret my move for a day.' McDonald's is putting Breckenridge through its in-house advanced diploma of management, and his next move will be to become a franchise consultant with responsibility for 15–20 McDonald's restaurants.[59]

EXTERNAL AND INTERNAL RECRUITMENT

The university recruiting already mentioned is an example of *external recruitment*, in which job candidates are sought from outside the hiring organisation. Specialist web sites like www.mycareer.com.au, www.nzjobs.com and the Monster and Seek sites, and newspapers, employment agencies, universities, personal contacts, walk-ins, employee referrals and even persons in competing organisations are all sources of external recruits. Competition is especially tough in the very tight labour markets characteristic of the new economy. When Nokia, the Finnish mobile-phone maker, needed high-tech talent it went global with its recruiting process. Nokia posted all job openings on a web site and received thousands of résumés from all over the world. In just two years, the percentage of non-Finns in the company workforce rose some 10 per cent. The head of Nokia's recruiting strategy says: 'There are no geographical boundaries anymore'.[60]

Internal recruitment seeks applicants from inside the organisation. Most organisations have a procedure for announcing vacancies through newsletters, electronic bulletin boards and the like. They also rely on managers to recommend subordinates as candidates for advancement. Internal recruitment creates opportunities for long-term career paths. Consider the story of Robert Goizueta. As CEO of Coca-Cola when he died, Goizueta owned over $1 billion of the company's stock. He made his way to the top over a 43-year career in the company, an example of how loyalty and hard work can pay off.[61]

Both recruitment strategies offer potential advantages and disadvantages. External recruiting brings in outsiders with fresh perspectives. It also provides access to specialised expertise or work experience not otherwise available from insiders. Internal recruitment is usually less expensive. It also deals with persons whose performance records are well established. A history of serious internal recruitment can also be encouraging to employees. It builds loyalty and motivation, showing that you can advance in the organisation by working hard and achieving high performance at each point of responsibility.

Using its company Internet site and intranet, SingTel Optus spends 90 per cent less on recruitment companies and classified advertising than it did before it launched its electronic recruitment strategy.[62] Existing employees are being increasingly encouraged to recommend their friends or associates for jobs. Cisco Australia has a staff referral program where current employees can receive a $1500 bonus if they recommend someone who is subsequently hired. The company now hires 55 per cent of new staff in this way. According to group human resource manager Alec Bashinsky, 'once someone has been at Cisco for a while, they know the type of person we would be after'.[63] For NRMA's human resource manager, David Smith, it is a question of getting the mix right. He says 'attraction and retention are the key to successful people management, but so is developing and growing internal talent. It comes down to a question of striking the appropriate balance.'[64]

www.
workplaceinfo.com.au

In Australia organisations can subscribe to Workplace Info, an electronic provider of key resource information for human resource professionals, including remuneration trends and forecasts, sample workplace policies for EEO and OHS, and HRM cases and legislation.

REALISTIC JOB PREVIEWS

There is another important recruitment issue that must be considered — honesty and full information. In what may be called *traditional recruitment*, the emphasis is on selling the organisation to job applicants. In this case, only the most positive features of the job and organisation are communicated to potential candidates. Bias may even be introduced as these features are exaggerated while negative features are concealed. This form of recruitment is designed to attract as many candidates as possible. The problem is that it may create unrealistic expectations that result in costly turnover when new employees leave prematurely. The individual suffers a career disruption; the employer suffers lost productivity and the additional recruiting costs of finding another candidate.

The alternative is to provide **realistic job previews** that give the candidate *all* pertinent information about the job and organisation without distortion and *before* the job is accepted.[65] Instead of 'selling' only positive features of a job, this approach tries to be realistic and balanced in the information provided. It tries to be fair in depicting actual job and organisational features, both favourable and unfavourable. The interviewer providing a realistic job preview to a job candidate, for example, might be overheard to use phrases such as these: 'Of course, there are some downsides . . .' 'Things don't always go the way we hope . . .' 'Something that you will want to be prepared for is . . .' 'We have found that some new employees had difficulty with . . .'

When engaged in this type of conversation about the job and organisation, the candidate gets a more complete and balanced view of the future employment possibility. This helps to establish more 'realistic' job expectations when starting work as a new employee. With expectations more realistic, the individual is better prepared to handle the 'ups and downs' of a new job. A better perspective on the employment relationship, higher levels of early job satisfaction, and less inclination to quit prematurely are among the benefits of this interview approach.

In a competitive job market like that for the best accounting graduates, providing realistic job previews can be a key means of attracting the best people and minimising any concerns they may have before starting a job. According to Caroline Barry, human resource manager at Brisbane accounting firm BDO Kendalls, which hires 20 new graduates a year, the best graduates may receive offers from six large accounting firms. For this reason, BDO Kendalls works hard to become the employer of choice. She says accounting firms should 'let them (new graduates) meet your team at the office. In the year's lead time before they join, stay in close touch and invite them to all your socials . . . Flag the cultural things that matter . . . Let students know you are a dynamic firm winning good jobs, and with a training and technology backup.' While the salary offered is only one part of the package, Barry argues that 'you must still get the pay right'.[66]

Realistic job previews provide job candidates with all pertinent information about a job and the organisation.

Making selection decisions

Selection is choosing from a pool of the best-qualified job applicants.

The process of **selection** involves choosing from a pool of applicants the person or persons who offer the greatest performance potential. Steps in a typical selection process are shown in figure 12.2. They are completion of a formal application form, interviewing, testing, reference checks, physical examination and final analysis and decision to hire or reject. As with all aspects of the human resource management process the best employers exercise extreme care in making selection decisions. At Federal Express, for example, psychological testing is used to identify what the firm calls 'risk taking and courage of conviction'.[67]

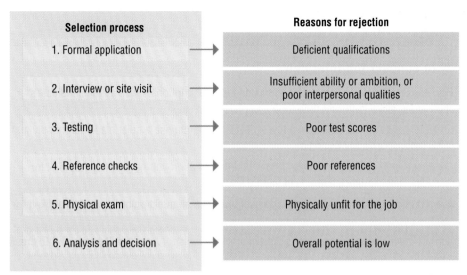

Figure 12.2 ▸ Steps in the selection process: the case of a rejected job applicant

In using any selection devices, including such testing, it is important to know that they meet the important criteria of reliability and validity. **Reliability** means that the device is consistent in measurement; it returns the same results time after time. **Validity** means that there is a demonstrable relationship between a person's score or rating on a selection device and their eventual job performance. In simple terms, validity means that a good score really does predict good performance. Many university students, for example, question the validity of employers using their grades as predictors of future job performance when screening job applicants. Are they just making excuses for not using their time well in university, or do they have a legitimate point?

🔵 **Reliability** means a selection device measures consistently over repeated uses.

🔵 **Validity** means a selection device has a demonstrated link with future job performance.

APPLICATION FORMS

The application form declares the individual to be a formal candidate for a job. It documents the applicant's personal history and qualifications. The personal résumé is often included with the job application. This important document should accurately summarise an applicant's special qualifications. As a job applicant, you should exercise great care in preparing your résumés for job searches. (See the Career Advancement Portfolio® section in the end-of-text Career Readiness Workbook for advice on résumé preparation.) As a recruiter, you should also learn how to screen applications and résumés for insights that can help you make good selection decisions. Importantly, the application should request only information that is directly relevant to the job and the applicant's potential job success.

INTERVIEWS

Interviews are extremely important in the selection process because of the information exchange they allow.[68] It is a time when both the job applicant and potential employer can learn a lot about one another. However, interviews are also recognised as potential stumbling blocks in the selection process. Sometimes interviewers ask the wrong things, sometimes they talk too much, sometimes the wrong people do the interviewing. Other times, the interviewer falls prey to personal biases and makes a judgement that fails to fully consider the applicant's capabilities. Among the recommendations for how to interview a job applicant are those shown in Manager's Notepad 12.1.

How to conduct job interviews

- *Plan ahead.* Review the job specifications and job description as well as the candidate's application; allow sufficient time for a complete interview.

- *Create a good interview climate.* Allow sufficient time; choose a quiet place; be friendly and show interest; give the candidate your full attention.

- *Conduct a goal-oriented interview.* Know what information you need and get it; look for creativity, independence and a high energy level.

- *Avoid questions that may imply discrimination.* Focus all questioning on the job applied for and the candidate's true qualifications for it.

- *Answer the questions asked of you, and others that may not be asked.* Do your part to create a realistic job preview.

- *Take notes.* Document details and impressions for later deliberation and decision making.

- *Keep your notes and records.* In case of future litigation, keep your records in a safe location.

www.scjohnson.com.au
www.scjohnson.co.nz

Recognised as one of the best employers to work for in Australia and New Zealand, SC Johnson aims to encourage its people to achieve a balance between work and home through programs such as sabbatical leave, telecommuting, paid parental leave and flexible working hours. It provides an onsite gym and arranges the pick-up and delivery of drycleaning for its staff!

An **assessment centre** examines how job candidates handle simulated work situations.

Vaughn and McLean have found that Australian managers have a very strong preference for unstructured or minimally structured interviews, allowing interviewers considerable freedom to conduct interviews as they wish. More structured interviews are favoured in countries such as the United Kingdom, Scandinavia, Germany, Austria and Spain.[69]

EMPLOYMENT TESTS

Testing is often used in the screening of job applicants. Some common employment tests are designed to identify intelligence, aptitudes, personality and interests; others ask the applicant to indicate how he or she would respond to a series of job-relevant situations. Australian corporations using psychological tests include ANZ, Lion Nathan, Qantas, Macquarie Bank and Boral.[70] Whenever tests are used and in whatever forms, however, the goal should be to gather information that will help predict the applicant's eventual performance success. Like any selection device, an employment test should meet the criteria of *reliability* and *validity* described earlier. Any employment test, furthermore, should be legally defensible on the grounds that it actually measures an ability required to perform the job.

New developments in testing extend the process into actual demonstrations of job-relevant skills and personal characteristics. An **assessment centre** evaluates a person's potential by observing his or her performance in experiential activities designed to simulate daily work. Activities undertaken at assessment centres may include interviews, group discussions, in-basket exercises, psychological tests and business games. While popular in the USA and the United Kingdom, assessment centres have proven less popular in the Asia–Pacific region. Organisations that use assessment centres for internal selection (promotion) and employee development include BHP Billiton, Cathay Pacific, Coles Myer, Hong Kong Shanghai Bank and the New South Wales Government.[71]

REFERENCE AND BACKGROUND CHECKS

Reference checks are inquiries to previous employers, academic advisers, coworkers and/or acquaintances regarding the qualifications, experience and past work records of a job applicant. Although they may be biased if friends are prearranged 'to say the right things if called', reference checks can be helpful in revealing important information not discovered elsewhere in the selection process. It is estimated that up to 25 per cent of job applications and résumés contain errors.[72] The references given by a job applicant can also add credibility to an application if they include a legitimate and even prestigious list of persons. An organisation that does not disclose negative information about ex-employees may be held responsible for economic losses suffered by another organisation that relied on this information when employing a new staff member.[73]

PHYSICAL EXAMINATIONS

Many organisations ask job applicants to take a physical examination. This health check helps ensure that the person is physically capable of fulfilling job requirements. It may also be used as a basis for enrolling the applicant in health-related fringe benefits such as life, health and disability insurance programs. A recent and controversial development in this area is the emerging use of drug testing. This has become part of pre-employment health screening and a basis for continued employment at some organisations. At a minimum, care must be exercised that any required test is job relevant and does not discriminate in any way against the applicant.

FINAL DECISIONS TO HIRE OR REJECT

The best selection decisions are most likely to be those involving extensive consultation among the manager or team leader, potential coworkers and human resource staff. Importantly, the emphasis in selection must always be comprehensive and focus on all aspects of the person's capacity to perform in a given job. After all, the selection decision poses major consequences for organisational performance and for the internal environment or work climate. Just as a 'good fit' can produce long-term advantage, a 'bad fit' can be the source of many and perhaps long-term problems. Sometimes the people who know this lesson best are those who run small businesses. Says one store owner who knew the importance of customer service in retail sales: 'If applicants have a good attitude, we can do the rest … but if they have a bad attitude to start with, everything we do seems to fail'.[74]

DEVELOPING A QUALITY WORKFORCE

When people join an organisation, they must 'learn the ropes' and become familiar with the way things are done. It is important that newcomers be helped to fit into the work environment in a way that furthers their development and performance potential. **Socialisation** is the process of influencing the expectations, behaviour and attitudes of a new employee in a way considered desirable by the organisation.[75] The intent of socialisation in human resource management is to help achieve the best possible fit between the individual, the job and the organisation.

Socialisation systematically changes the expectations, behaviour and attitudes of new employees.

Employee orientation

Socialisation of newcomers begins with **orientation** — a set of activities designed to familiarise new employees with their jobs, coworkers and key aspects of the organisation as a whole. This includes clarifying mission and culture, explaining operating objectives and job expectations, communicating policies and procedures, and identifying key personnel.

The first six months of employment are often crucial in determining how well someone is going to perform over the long run. It is a time when the original expectations are tested, and patterns are set for future relationships between an individual and employer. Unfortunately, orientation is sometimes neglected and newcomers are often left to fend for themselves. They may learn job and organisational routines on their own or through casual

Orientation familiarises new employees with jobs, coworkers and organisational policies and services.

interactions with coworkers, and they may acquire job attitudes the same way.[76] The result is that otherwise well-intentioned and capable persons may learn inappropriate attitudes and/or behaviours. Good orientation, by contrast, enhances a person's understanding of the organisation and adds purpose to his or her daily job activities. Increased performance, greater job satisfaction and greater work commitment are the desired results.

Orientation is particularly important for employees being sent on international assignments. About 90 per cent of Australian organisations undertake international orientation. The failure to do so can result in tragedy, as happened in a case cited in *The Economist*. An oil company's expatriate (international) employees placed young local workers in supervisory positions. Within a week, all of the young supervisors had had their throats cut. No-one had told the expatriates that age was equated with superior status.[77]

Training and development

Training is a set of activities that provides the opportunity to acquire and improve job-related skills. This applies both to the initial training of an employee and to upgrading or improving someone's skills to meet changing job requirements. A major concern of US employers is the lack of educational preparation of some workers for jobs, often high-technology jobs, in the new workplace. These concerns even extend to the basic skills of reading, writing and arithmetic, as well as to computer skills. Progressive organisations offer extensive training programs to ensure that their workers always have the skills and computer literacy needed to perform well.

A recent survey of the training practices of the Western Australian hospitality sector found that over 90 per cent of companies offered their employees internal and external training programs. The majority identified improved employee productivity and commitment and almost 90 per cent reported reduced staff turnover as a result of training their people.[79] Similarly, a study of training programs in the healthcare fields in the USA and New Zealand found that employees who feel that they have appropriate access to training are more likely to have a greater degree of commitment towards their organisations.[80]

ON-THE-JOB TRAINING

On-the-job training takes place in the work setting while someone is doing a job. A common approach is job rotation that allows people to spend time working in different jobs to expand the range of their job capabilities. Another is **coaching**, in which an experienced person provides performance advice to someone else. One form of coaching is **mentoring**, in which early-career employees are formally assigned as protégés to senior persons. The mentoring relationship gives them regular access to advice on developing skills and getting a good start in their careers. An informal type of coaching involves **modelling**. This occurs when someone demonstrates through day-to-day personal behaviour that which is expected of others. One way to learn managerial skills, for example, is to observe and practise the techniques displayed by good managers. Modelling is a very important influence on behaviour in organisations. A good example is how the behaviours of senior managers help set the ethical culture and standards for other employees.

OFF-THE-JOB TRAINING

Off-the-job training is accomplished outside the work setting. It may be done within the organisation at a separate training room or facility or at an offsite location. Examples of the latter include attendance at special training programs sponsored by universities, trade or professional associations, or consultants. The willingness of organisations to invest in training is

Gilding the lily

According to Joanne Gorman, general manager of Recruitment Solutions, almost everyone exaggerates or adds untruthful information to their job applications. 'I think there's poetic licence on just about every résumé we would see … Some of it is harmless, some of it is extreme.'[78]

How do you best promote your abilities without being misleading?

✔ **Training** provides learning opportunities to acquire and improve job-related skills.

✔ **Coaching** involves an experienced person offering performance advice to a less-experienced person.

✔ **Mentoring** assigns early-career employees as protégés to more senior ones.

✔ **Modelling** demonstrates through personal behaviour the job performance expected of others.

a good indicator of their commitment to the people they hire. Intel, for example, allocates a percentage of its annual payroll to spend on training through its in-house university.[81]

An important form of off-the-job training involves **management development**, designed to improve a person's knowledge and skill in the fundamentals of management. For example, *beginning managers* often benefit from training that emphasises delegating duties; *middle managers* may benefit from training to better understand multifunctional viewpoints; *top managers* may benefit from advanced management training to sharpen their decision-making and negotiating skills and to expand their awareness of corporate strategy and direction. Moves to blend different types of training are becoming increasingly popular. Because individuals have different learning styles and approaches, it makes sense to provide employees with a range of training options to meet their needs. E-learning, for instance, uses the Internet and CD-ROMs to encourage less pressured, more reflective, self-paced learning. It can be used to supplement other methods such as outdoor experiences or face-to-face discussions.[82]

Management development is training to improve knowledge and skills in the management process.

Performance management systems

Performance has to be measured. The rule holds whether you are talking about a hospital's contribution to the community, a business's quarterly financial results, a work team's project accomplishment or an individual's job performance. With measurement comes the opportunity to not only document results but to also take steps toward their future improvement. Part of the human resource management responsibility is design and implementation of a successful **performance management system**. This is a system that ensures that performance standards and objectives are set, that performance is regularly assessed for accomplishments, and that actions are taken to improve performance potential in the future.

A **performance management system** sets standards, assesses results and plans for performance improvements.

PURPOSE OF PERFORMANCE APPRAISAL

The process of formally assessing someone's work accomplishments and providing feedback is **performance appraisal**. It serves two basic purposes in the maintenance of a quality workforce: evaluation and development. The *evaluation purpose* is intended to let people know where they stand relative to performance objectives and standards. The *development purpose* is intended to assist in their training and continued personal development.[83]

Performance appraisal is the process of formally evaluating performance and providing feedback to a job holder.

The evaluation purpose of performance appraisal focuses on past performance and measures results against standards. Performance is documented for the record and to establish a basis for allocating rewards. The manager acts in a *judgemental role* in which he or she gives a direct evaluation of another person's accomplishments. The development purpose of performance appraisal, by contrast, focuses on future performance and the clarification of success standards. It is a way of discovering performance obstacles and identifying training and development opportunities. Here the manager acts in a *counselling role*, focusing on a subordinate's developmental needs.

Like employment tests, any performance appraisal method can fulfil these purposes only when the criteria of *reliability* and *validity* are met. To be reliable, the method should consistently yield the same result over time and/or for different raters; to be valid, it should be unbiased and measure only factors directly relevant to job performance. Both these criteria are especially important in today's complex legal environment. A manager who hires, fires or promotes someone is increasingly called upon to defend such actions — sometimes in specific response to lawsuits alleging that the actions were discriminatory. At a minimum, written documentation of performance appraisals and a record of consistent past actions will be required to back up any contested evaluations.

PERFORMANCE APPRAISAL METHODS

Organisations use a variety of performance appraisal methods. One of the simplest is a **graphic rating scale**, such as the example in figure 12.3. Such scales offer the appraisers checklists of traits or characteristics thought to be related to high performance outcomes in a given job. A manager rates the individual on each trait using a numerical score. The primary appeal of graphic rating scales is that they are relatively quick and easy to complete. Their reliability and validity are questionable, however, because the categories and scores are subject to varying interpretations.

> 🔘 A **graphic rating scale** uses a checklist of traits or characteristics to evaluate performance.

Name _Leslie Whiteson_

Job title _Financial Analyst_

Supervisor _H. Simpson_

Date _1 July_

Rating factors	Rating
Quantity of work: amount of work normally accomplished..........................	3
Quality of work: accuracy and quality of work normally accomplished..................	2
Job knowledge: understanding of job requirements and task demands..............	3
Cooperation: willingness to accept assignments and work with others...........	1
Dependability: conscientiousness in attendance and in completion of work........	2
Enthusiasm: initiative in offering ideas and seeking increased responsibilites........	2

Ratings:
    3 = Outstanding
    2 = Satisfactory
    1 = Unsatisfactory

Figure 12.3 ▸ Sample graphic rating scale for performance appraisal

> 🔘 A **behaviourally anchored rating scale** uses specific descriptions of actual behaviours to rate various levels of performance.

A more advanced approach is the **behaviourally anchored rating scale** (BARS), which offers an appraiser rating scales for actual behaviours that exemplify various levels of performance achievement in a job. Look at the case of a customer service representative illustrated in figure 12.4. 'Extremely poor' performance is clearly defined as rude or disrespectful treatment of a customer. Because performance assessments are anchored to specific descriptions of work behaviour, a BARS is more reliable and valid than the graphic rating scale. The behavioural anchors can also be helpful in training people to master job skills of demonstrated performance importance.

> 🔘 The **critical-incident technique** keeps a log of someone's effective and ineffective job behaviours.

The **critical-incident technique** involves keeping a running log or inventory of effective and ineffective job behaviours. By creating a written record of positive and negative performance examples, this method documents success or failure patterns that can be specifically discussed with the individual. Using the case of the customer service representative again, a critical-incidents log might contain the following types of entries: *Positive example* — 'Took extraordinary care of a customer who had purchased a defective item from a company store in another city'; *negative example* — 'Acted rudely in dismissing the complaint of a customer who felt that a sale item was erroneously advertised'.

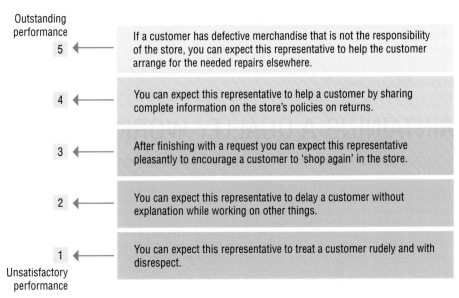

Outstanding performance

5 — If a customer has defective merchandise that is not the responsibility of the store, you can expect this representative to help the customer arrange for the needed repairs elsewhere.

4 — You can expect this representative to help a customer by sharing complete information on the store's policies on returns.

3 — After finishing with a request you can expect this representative pleasantly to encourage a customer to 'shop again' in the store.

2 — You can expect this representative to delay a customer without explanation while working on other things.

1 — You can expect this representative to treat a customer rudely and with disrespect.

Unsatisfactory performance

Figure 12.4 ▸ Sample behaviourally anchored rating scale for performance appraisal

Some performance management systems use **multiperson comparisons**, which formally compare one person's performance with that of one or more others. Such comparisons can be used on their own or in combination with some other method. They can also be done in different ways. In *rank ordering*, all persons being rated are arranged in order of performance achievement. The best performer goes at the top of the list, the worst performer at the bottom; no ties are allowed. In *paired comparisons*, each person is formally compared with every other person and rated as either the superior or the weaker member of the pair. After all paired comparisons are made, each person is assigned a summary ranking based on the number of superior scores achieved. In *forced distribution*, each person is placed into a frequency distribution that requires that a certain percentage fall into specific performance classifications, such as top 10 per cent, next 40 per cent, next 40 per cent, and bottom 10 per cent.

Not all performance appraisals are completed only by an employee's immediate boss. It is increasingly popular today to expand the role of a job's stakeholders in the appraisal process. The new workplace often involves use of *peer appraisal*, including in the process others who work regularly and directly with a job holder, and *upward appraisal*, including in the process subordinates reporting to the job holder. An even broader stakeholder approach is known as **360° feedback,** where superiors, subordinates, peers and even internal and external customers are involved in the appraisal of a job holder's performance.[84]

It is estimated that around 20 per cent of Australian companies use some kind of ratings system. Whereas the head of human resources at St.George Bank, Brett Wright, views ratings systems as a way of promoting communication and understanding between employers and employees, Griffith University lecturer Campbell Fraser argues that an

Multiperson comparisons compare one person's performance with that of others.

360° feedback includes in the appraisal process superiors, subordinates, peers and even customers.

employee's ratings are often a reflection of their 'likeability' and personality rather than an objective measure of performance — 'it becomes a popularity vote'.[85]

Research suggests that performance appraisals are often undertaken poorly or inappropriately, and that many appraisals are actually a waste of an organisation's time and resources. An Australian study by Bradley and Ashkanasy found that the effectiveness of performance appraisals related directly to the effectiveness of employee support and supervision at other times of the year. That is, when supervisors did not provide appropriate support and feedback at other times, the appraisals were not seen as particularly useful. Interestingly, when consistent and regular feedback and support were provided throughout the year, appraisals were viewed as somewhat of a 'waste of time' since the appraisal was occurring in other ways on an ongoing basis.[86]

MAINTAINING A QUALITY WORKFORCE

An important goal of human resource management is to maintain a qualified workforce, even in a dynamic environment with constantly shifting work demands and labour markets. It is not enough to attract and develop workers with the talents to achieve high-performance results for the short term only. They must be successfully retained, nurtured and managed for long-term effectiveness. When adverse turnover occurs and talented workers leave to pursue other opportunities, the resulting costs for the employer can be staggering. The best employers commit themselves to progressive human resource systems that support the retention of those workers who count most — the talented ones.

Career development

In his book *The Age of Unreason*, British scholar and consultant Charles Handy discusses dramatic new developments in the world of work and careers. Specifically, Handy says: 'The times are changing and we must change with them'.[87] Each of us should take this advice and take charge of our careers. The Career Advancement Portfolio® in the end-of-text Career Readiness Workbook is a useful resource in helping you meet this challenge.

It should be said, however, that the best companies do not leave career development just to individual employees. A study of Australian companies found that the best employers emphasised the career development of their people in an effort to keep employees satisfied with their jobs and their own personal development. The best employers were more likely to implement one-on-one mentoring and leadership development programs than other organisations. They were committed to building a tripartite commitment to career development, involving the organisation as well as each individual's manager or supervisor; and in addition employees were involved in their own development plans.[88]

A **career** is a sequence of jobs that constitute what a person does for a living.

Formally defined, a **career** is a sequence of jobs and work pursuits that constitute what a person does for a living. For many of us, a career begins on an anticipatory basis with our formal education. From there it progresses into an initial job choice and any number of subsequent choices that may involve changes in task assignments, employing organisations and even occupations. A *career path* is a sequence of jobs held over time during a career. Career paths vary between those that are pursued internally with the same employers and those pursued externally among various employers. Whereas many organisations place great emphasis on making long-term career opportunities available to their employees, Handy's view of the future is that external career paths will be increasingly important.

Career planning is the process of systematically matching career goals and individual capabilities with opportunities for their fulfilment. It involves answering such questions as 'Who am I?', 'Where do I want to go?', 'How do I get there?' While some suggest that a career should be allowed to progress in a somewhat random but always opportunistic way, others view a career as something to be rationally planned and pursued in a logical step-by-step fashion. In fact, a well-managed career will probably include elements of each. The carefully thought-out plan can point you in a general career direction; an eye for opportunity can fill in the details along the way.

When you think about adult life stages or transitions, you should note that sooner or later most people's careers level off. A **career plateau** is a position from which someone is unlikely to move to a higher level of work responsibility.[89] Three common reasons for career plateaus are personal choice, limited abilities and limited opportunities. For some, the plateau may occur at a point in life when it suits their individual needs; for others, the plateau may be unwanted and frustrating. Perhaps it is because of career plateaus that older employees are far more likely than younger employees to move into self-employment, consulting, community service, retirement or some combination of these choices.[90]

Work-life balance

'Hiring good people is tough', starts an article in the *Harvard Business Review*. The sentence finishes with 'keeping them can be even tougher'.[91] A very important issue in maintaining a quality workforce relates to today's fast-paced and complicated life styles that bring with them inevitable pressures on the balance between work and personal time. This issue of **work-life balance** deals with how people balance the demands of careers with their personal and family needs. 'Family' in this context includes not just children, but also elderly parents and other relatives in need of care. Among progressive employers, human resource policies and practices that support a healthy work-life balance are increasingly viewed as positive investments. Benchmarks are available and they are growing in number. At Hewlett-Packard Australia, for instance, specific attention is paid to helping employees achieve a balance between their work and personal lives. Many employees are free to choose their own working hours as long as company objectives are being met. Hewlett-Packard Australia supports this policy by providing laptops, mobile phones and home Internet connections.[92]

Included among work-life balance concerns are the unique needs of *single parents*, who must balance complete parenting responsibilities with a job, and *dual-career couples*, who must balance the career needs and opportunities of each partner. The special needs of both working mothers and working fathers are also being recognised. A recent Australian study of nine male and 11 female managers from dual-career couples found that pursuing a balance between the demands of work and family requires deliberate attention to managing time and priorities so that individual, work and family needs can be met. Imbalances are more likely when employees do not give serious attention to these issues but instead allow external events and factors to control their time and priorities.[93]

Compensation and benefits

Chapter 7 pointed out that good compensation and benefit systems improve control by attracting qualified people to the organisation, and helping to retain them. **Base compensation** in the form of salary or hourly wages can make the organisation a desirable place of employment. It can help get the right people into jobs to begin with; by making

Career planning is the process of systematically matching careers goals and individual capabilities with opportunities for their fulfilment.

A **career plateau** is a position from which someone is unlikely to move to a higher level of work responsibility.

Work-life balance involves balancing career demands with personal and family needs.

Base compensation is a salary or hourly wage paid to an individual.

outside opportunities less attractive it can also help keep them there. Unless an organisation's prevailing wage and salary structure is competitive in the relevant labour markets, it will be difficult to attract and retain a staff of highly competent workers. A basic rule of thumb is to carefully study the labour market and pay at least as much as, and perhaps a bit more than, what competitors are offering. The additional area of *incentive pay* is discussed in detail in chapter 14 on motivation and rewards. In Australia, for instance, the average compensation for a national sales manager is between \$130 000 and \$150 000, plus an additional \$10 000 to \$15 000 in bonus and incentive pay. A company financial controller can expect around \$175 000 to \$200 000 in base pay and another \$15 000 to \$25 000 in annual incentives, whereas a product development manager in the manufacturing sector earns around \$80 000 to \$110 000 in base pay and another \$5000 to \$10 000 in incentive pay.[94] The typical Australian manager's package comprises 52 per cent salary, 17 per cent short-term incentives such as bonuses, and 31 per cent long-term incentives such as share options. In the three years to 2001, the average chief executive officer of one of Australia's 150 largest companies experienced a 73 per cent pay rise, with the average package being \$1.3 million per annum.[95] Within the top 500 companies, the average package is closer to \$700 000.[96]

Fringe benefits are non-monetary compensation in the form of health insurance, retirement plans, etc.

The organisation's employee-benefit program also plays a role in attracting and retaining capable workers. **Fringe benefits** are the additional non-wage or non-salary forms of compensation provided to an organisation's workforce. Among senior executives in Australia, the most popular fringe benefits offered are salary-sacrificed superannuation (offered by 80 per cent of companies); company cars (79 per cent); additional employer-paid superannuation (71 per cent); performance rewards (39 per cent); laptop computers (39 per cent); a second company car (32 per cent); mobile phones (30 per cent); and membership of professional associations (28 per cent). Interestingly, Mercer Human Resource Consulting has found that there is a gap between the benefits that executives would like to receive and those that are offered by their companies. For instance, 67 per cent of executives would like home loans provided by or through their employer, but only 15 per cent of employers offer such loans. While 56 per cent of managers would like holidays or entertainment to be provided within their package, only 11 per cent of companies offer these. And 57 per cent of executives wish that their employers could assist with health insurance, but just 21 per cent of companies provide health insurance to their executives.[97]

Flexible benefits programs allow employees to choose from a range of benefit options.

An increasingly common approach overall is **flexible benefits**, sometimes known as cafeteria benefits, which let the employee choose a set of benefits within a certain dollar amount. The employee gains when such plans are better able to meet individual needs; the employer gains from being more responsive to a wider range of needs in a diverse workforce. It is crucial that organisations design their reward systems to take account of their employees' individual preferences for different rewards. It is also critical that organisations ensure that they reward performance toward key objectives and goals so that employee behaviour is consistently channelled in this direction. According to Jarek Czechowicz, many reward systems fail, whether they are designed for executives or other employees of the organisation. He states that:

> The main flaw with present reward systems is that their use is often distorted so that a few people feel successful for their exceptional performance and the rest are left to feel inadequate. This has a flow-on effect. Customers and others can tell when someone is unhappy or being friendly only because they want a bonus, a commission or a promotion. The intended result of reward systems is to improve behavior; but the real result for many employees is just more stress.[98]

Retention and turnover

The several steps in the human resource management process both conclude and recycle with *replacement* decisions — that is, with the management of promotions, transfers, terminations, layoffs and retirements. Any replacement situation should be approached as an opportunity to review human resource plans, update job analyses, rewrite job descriptions and job specifications, and ensure that the best people are selected to perform the required tasks.

Some replacement decisions shift people between positions within the organisation. *Promotion* is movement to a higher-level position; *transfer* is movement to a different job at a similar level of responsibility. Another set of replacement decisions relates to *retirement*, something most people look forward to ... until it is close at hand. Then the prospect of being retired often raises fears and apprehensions. Many organisations offer special counselling and other forms of support for retiring employees, including advice on company benefits, money management, estate planning and use of leisure time. Downsizing is sometimes accompanied by special offers of early retirement — that is, retirement before formal retirement age but with special financial incentives. Where this is not possible, organisations may provide outplacement services to help terminated employees find other jobs.

The most extreme replacement decisions involve *termination*, the involuntary and permanent dismissal of an employee. In some cases the termination is based on performance problems. The person involved is not meeting the requirements of the job or has violated key organisational policy. In other cases the termination may be due to financial conditions of the employer, such as those requiring downsizing or restructuring. The people involved may be performing well, but are being terminated as part of a workforce reduction. In any case, it may be hard for the person being dismissed to accept the decision. Especially in the case of workforce reduction, the termination notice may come by surprise and without the benefit of advance preparation for either the personal or the financial shock. The experts' advice to the employee is to ask at least three tough questions of the ex-boss: Why am I being released? What are my termination benefits? Can I have a good reference? Advice for the manager who must handle a termination is offered in Manager's Notepad 12.2.

Employee turnover in places such as Australia and Hong Kong has historically been high, and is viewed as a significant factor hampering the growth of workforce productivity. The costs of turnover can be quite high, with one US study estimating that labour turnover costs a $30 billion company almost $150 million a year in lost productivity and in the costs associated with recruiting, selecting and orientating new employees.[99]

MANAGER'S NOTEPAD 12.2

Things to remember when handling a dismissal

- Dismissal can be as personally devastating as a divorce or the death of a loved one.
- Dismissal should always be legally defensible and done in complete compliance with organisational policies.
- Dismissal should not be delayed unnecessarily; it is best done as soon as the inevitability of the dismissal is known.
- Dismissal of good performers should include offers of assistance to help them re-enter the labour market.
- All records associated with dismissal should be kept.

Study guide

The chapter 12 study guide helps you review the chapter content, prepare for examinations, apply what you have learned and further build your career readiness. The summary briefly answers the study questions posed at the start of the chapter. The list of key terms allows you to double-check your familiarity with basic concepts and definitions. The applied activities help you test your comprehension of chapter content. Suggestions offered as career readiness activities direct your attention to relevant sections of the Career Readiness Workbook where you can test and develop your career skills and apply what you have learned. The list of electronic resources suggests activities from the *Management: An Asia–Pacific Perspective* web site and, finally, the case for critical thinking helps you apply your new management knowledge.

SUMMARY

Why do people make the difference?

- Even in this age of information, high technology and globalisation, people still drive the system; they make organisations work.
- Organisations with positive human resource policies and practices are gaining significant performance advantages in such areas as lower turnover, more sales, higher profits and increased shareholder wealth.
- The commitment to human resources made by founders of start ups has long-term consequences for organisational performance.
- The challenges of complexity and uncertainty in highly competitive environments are best met by a diverse and talented workforce.
- The diversity advantage is gained only when the talents of all persons, regardless of personal characteristics, are unlocked and they are given the opportunity to perform.

What is strategic human resource management?

- The human resource management process is the process of attracting, developing and maintaining a quality workforce.
- A complex legal environment influences human resource management, giving special attention to equal employment opportunity.
- Human resource planning is the process of analysing staffing needs and identifying actions to satisfy these needs over time.
- The purpose of human resource planning is to make sure the organisation always has people with the right abilities available to do the required work.

How do organisations attract a quality workforce?

- Recruitment is the process of attracting qualified job candidates to fill vacant positions.
- Recruitment can be both external and internal to the organisation.
- Recruitment should involve realistic job previews that provide job candidates with accurate information on the job and organisation.
- Managers typically use interviews, employment tests and references to help make selection decisions; the use of assessment centres and work sampling is becoming more common.

How do organisations develop a quality workforce?

- Orientation is the process of formally introducing new employees to their jobs, performance requirements and the organisation.
- On-the-job training may include job rotation, coaching, apprenticeship, modelling and mentoring.
- Off-the-job training may include a range of formal courses and programs, as well as simulations and other training specifically tailored to job needs.
- Performance management systems focus on the establishment of work standards and the assessment of results through performance appraisal.
- Common performance appraisal methods are graphic rating scales, narratives, behaviourally anchored rating scales and multiperson comparisons.

How do organisations maintain a quality workforce?

- Career planning systematically matches individual career goals and capabilities with opportunities for their fulfilment.
- Programs that address work-life balance and the complex demands of job and family responsibilities are increasingly important in human resource management.
- Compensation and benefits packages must be continually updated so the organisation maintains a competitive position in external labour markets.
- Whenever workers must be replaced over time because of promotions, transfers, retirements and terminations, the goal should be to treat everyone fairly while ensuring that jobs are filled with the best personnel available.

KEY TERMS

affirmative action (p. 322)

assessment centre (p. 332)

base compensation (p. 339)

behaviourally anchored rating scale (p. 336)

business associations (p. 324)

career (p. 338)

career planning (p. 339)

career plateau (p. 339)

coaching (p. 334)

critical-incident technique (p. 336)

discrimination (p. 321)

diversity management (p. 323)

equal employment opportunity (p. 321)

flexible benefits (p. 340)

fringe benefits (p. 340)

graphic rating scale (p. 336)

human resource management (p. 321)

human resource planning (p. 327)

industrial relations (p. 324)

job analysis (p. 327)

job description (p. 327)

job specification (p. 327)

management development (p. 335)

mentoring (p. 334)

modelling (p. 334)

multiperson comparisons (p. 337)

orientation (p. 333)

performance appraisal (p. 335)

performance management system (p. 335)

realistic job previews (p. 330)

recruitment (p. 328)

reliability (p. 331)

selection (p. 330)

sexual harassment (p. 321)

socialisation (p. 333)

strategic human resource management (p. 327)

360° feedback (p. 337)

training (p. 334)

unions (p. 324)

validity (p. 331)

work-life balance (p. 339)

APPLIED ACTIVITIES

Short-response questions

1. How do internal recruitment and external recruitment compare in terms of advantages and disadvantages for the employer?
2. Why is orientation an important part of the staffing process?
3. What is the difference between the graphic rating scale and the BARS as performance appraisal methods?
4. How does mentoring work as a form of on-the-job training?

Application question

5. Simon Smith is not doing well in his job. The problems began to appear shortly after Simon's job was changed from a manual to a computer-based operation. He has tried but is just not doing well in terms of learning to use the computer and meet the performance expectations. As a 55-year-old employee with over 30 years with the company, Simon is both popular and influential among his work peers. Along with his performance problems you have also noticed the appearance of some negative attitudes — a tendency for Simon to 'badmouth' the company. As Simon's manager, what options would you consider in terms of dealing with the issue of his retention in the job and in the company? What would you do and why?

CAREER READINESS ACTIVITIES

Recommended individual and group learning activities from the end-of-text Career Readiness Workbook for this chapter include:

Career advancement portfolio   **WB**

Update your career advancement portfolio to reflect your new skills and experiences. Include skills and personal insights you gain from the following projects and exercises.

Research and presentation project   **WB**

• Project 5 — Affirmative action directions — 'where do we go from here?'

Cross-functional integrative case   **WB**

Read the integrative case on Sarina Russo and answer the following questions:

12.1 Arguably Sarina Russo experienced discrimination in her early career before establishing The Office Business Academy. Could this happen today? What protection does the law provide for employees today that might have been of benefit to Sarina Russo had it been available in the 1970s?

12.2 If you were seeking a job with the Russo Institute of Technology, what information about the organisation would you like to see presented in a realistic job preview?

Exercises in teamwork WB

- Exercise 3 — Defining quality
- Exercise 7 — What do you value in work?
- Exercise 13 — The future workplace

Management skills assessment WB

- Assessment 12 — Performance appraisal assumptions

ELECTRONIC RESOURCES

Don't forget to take full advantage of the online support for *Management: An Asia–Pacific Perspective* at www.johnwiley.com.au/highered/management: chapter 12 practice tests, e-flashcards, crossword puzzles, interactive management skills assessments, interactive cases, the online career advancement portfolio and much more!

CASE FOR CRITICAL THINKING

Read the following case for critical thinking on Outback Steakhouse. While you are reading the case keep in mind what you have learned in this chapter, then answer the questions.

Outback Steakhouse: an unconventional approach with an Australian flavour

In 1988, three friends — Chris Sullivan, Bob Basham and Tim Gannon — established the Outback Steakhouse company with the opening of two restaurants in Florida in the USA. Each of the three had started early in their careers in the restaurant industry — Chris as a busboy, Bob as a dishwasher and Tim as a chef's assistant. Chris and Bob funded the venture with the proceeds of the sale of their interests in another restaurant franchise. Tim brought to the venture his 25 years of experience as a chef. Between them they had more than 60 years of restaurant experience.

The partners saw an untapped opportunity between high-priced and budget steakhouses to serve quality steaks at an affordable price. They wanted a casual theme for their restaurants, but felt that the western theme had been overused. Ultimately, they focused on an Australian theme, including 'Bonzer Salads', 'Rockhampton Rib-Eye' steaks, a 'Chocolate Thunder From Down Under' dessert and other 'Aussie-flavoured' menu items. At the time, Australia had a high profile in the USA: a few years earlier Australia had won the America's Cup; Australia was preparing to celebrate its bicentennial; and the hit movie *Crocodile Dundee* had just been released. The partners planned to build five casual dining restaurants to provide enough income to allow them more leisure time and more time with their families.

A high-growth success story

In its first year of operation the company had sales of US$2.7 million from its two restaurants. By the end of 1994 the chain had exceeded all of the founders' expectations, with over 200 restaurants and US$549 million in system-wide sales. The company was being hailed by the business press as one of the biggest success stories in corporate USA in recent years.[100]

By 2001 there were 645 Outback Steakhouses in 13 countries. Outback's approach to human resources (it doesn't have a human resources department!), management and ownership is a big part of its success.[101]

A fun place to work

Outback has achieved a staff turnover rate less than half that of other casual dining operators with its unconventional approach to human resource management.

The conventional approach in the restaurant industry is to open for as many hours as possible. However, Outback restaurants take a dinner-only approach, opening daily for seven hours from 4.30 to 11.30 p.m. This has been highly successful and has led to the effective use of systems, staff and management. Aspiring restaurant owners often underestimate the effort required to make a restaurant successful. Running a restaurant is hard work and could easily involve 80 to 100 hours of work each week. A manager and part-owner of one Outback restaurant said:

> The other organization [I worked for] had long hours when you were open from 11:30 in the morning until 1 or 2 in the evening. Those hours have a tendency to burn people out ... At Outback, from the [supplier] level all the way down to the dishwasher level we all work as a team. That is another difference between Outback and the organization I used to work for ... Here at Outback we don't have those rules and regulations ... Chris always claims he plays a lot of golf in the daytime and has a lot of fun ... He will come up to you and ask, 'Are you having fun?' [We say] 'Oh, we're having a great time.'

Furthermore, the dinner-only theme minimises the strain on staff. Outback employees who wait on customers typically handle only three tables at a time. This allows closer customer attention than in many competitors' restaurants and helps avoid staff burnout that commonly occurs among busy waiting staff. One manager put it this way:

> I've heard so many times, 'I love coming to your restaurant because your staff is so upbeat, they are so happy'. They are always great people to have work for you. People just love the people here ... I see us as a McDonald's of the future, but a step up. I don't think anybody can come close to our efficiency because it is so simplistic and everyone is so laid back about it from the owners on down. And we are having such fun, making so much money. No one wants to go anywhere. I will never work for another company as long as I live ... You have that feeling mixed with the great food.

The company takes steps to ensure that Outback is a fun place to work and keeps stress to a minimum. The founders of Outback were convinced that any enduring concept must place a heavy emphasis upon fun, family, quality food and community. Bob Basham explained:

> I don't care what business you are in, if you aren't having fun, you shouldn't be in that business ... Chris, Tim and I have a lot of fun doing what we are doing, and we want our people to have a lot of fun doing what they are doing. We try to set it up so they can do that.

Facility design is also a crucial component. Generally, about 45 per cent of Outback's restaurant unit is dedicated to the kitchen. While industry observers had pointed out that Outback could enlarge the dining area, the Outback owners considered it logical to retain its original design:

> Restaurants get busy on a Friday night or a Saturday night when most people go out to eat. That's when you are trying to make the best impression on people. [But] physically, the kitchen cannot handle the demand. So if you have standards in your operation of a 12-minute cook time ... [it's] impossible to execute that way. We all decided we would not have it happening in our restaurant. So we underdesigned the front of the house and overdesigned the back of the house. That has worked very, very well for us. To this day we limit the number [of tables]. Even in our busiest restaurants where people tell us we could be twice as big and do twice the sales, we still discipline ourselves to build our restaurants one size.

Management at each restaurant is responsible for all recruitment, training and other personnel matters for their outlet. Founder Chris Sullivan said the lack of a centralised human resources department meant it was more likely managers would work with staff to resolve any problems rather than passing on the problem or just firing the staff member.[102]

Staff development

Founder Tim Gannon focuses on continual training of restaurant staff throughout the Outback system. He holds about ten meetings a year in various parts of the country with staff members from various regional restaurants. Typically, about 50 kitchen managers and other kitchen staff attend these meetings. Half of the group attend a presentation from a special guest in the front of the restaurant, while the other half work on 'the basics' in the kitchen. Then the two groups exchange places. Tim feels that these meetings are crucial for generating new ideas, sometimes from very new kitchen staff employees. For example, one new employee had urged attention to the dessert sauces. Discussion of this issue ultimately resulted in a reformulation of the sauces so that they did not crystallise so easily, as well as the installation of warmers that held the sauces at a constant temperature. This innovation allowed the restaurants to serve desserts more quickly.

Community involvement

Along with its successful human resources approach, Outback's strategy included a high degree of visibility and involvement in the community. Community involvement includes not only top management but everyone at Outback. Each new store opening involves community participation and community service to charities. For many charity events Outback provided the food while staff donated their time. As Basham explains: 'We are really involved in the community ... That goes throughout our company.'

Every worker an owner

The founders keenly remembered their early desires to own their own restaurant. Consequently, Outback provided ownership opportunities at three levels in the organisation: at the individual restaurant level; through multiple store arrangements (joint venture and franchise opportunities); and through an employee share ownership plan. Senior management selected the joint venture partners and franchisees. Franchisees and joint venture partners in turn hired the general managers at each restaurant. All of the operating partners and general managers were required to complete a comprehensive 12-week training course that emphasised the company's operating strategy, procedures and standards.

From the beginning, the founders wanted ownership opportunities for each restaurant general manager and formed a limited partner arrangement.[103] Each manager's name appeared over the restaurant door with the designation 'Proprietor'. After the company went public in 1991, it began to give restaurant managers non-qualified share options at the time they became managing partners. The options vested at the end of five years. Outback's attractive arrangements for restaurant general managers resulted in a 1994 management turnover of 5 per cent, compared to 30 per cent to 40 per cent industry-wide.

In 1993 the company instituted a share ownership plan for employees at the restaurant level. At the time the plan was established, all employees received shares proportional to their time in service. Each employee received a yearly statement. The share ownership program required no investment from the employees and vested after five years.

Source: Adapted from Marilyn L. Taylor, Krishnan Ramaya and George Puia, 'Outback Steakhouse, Inc.: Fueling the Fast-Growth Company', *Case Research Journal* (1998). © Marilyn L. Taylor, George Puia.

QUESTIONS

1. Describe the HR practices that contribute to Outback's success.
2. The case states that Outback does not have an HR department. Why not?
3. It appears easier to establish high-performance people-management practices in a new organisation (such as Outback Steakhouse) than at existing companies. What could older companies learn from Outback's approach? How could new ideas be implemented?

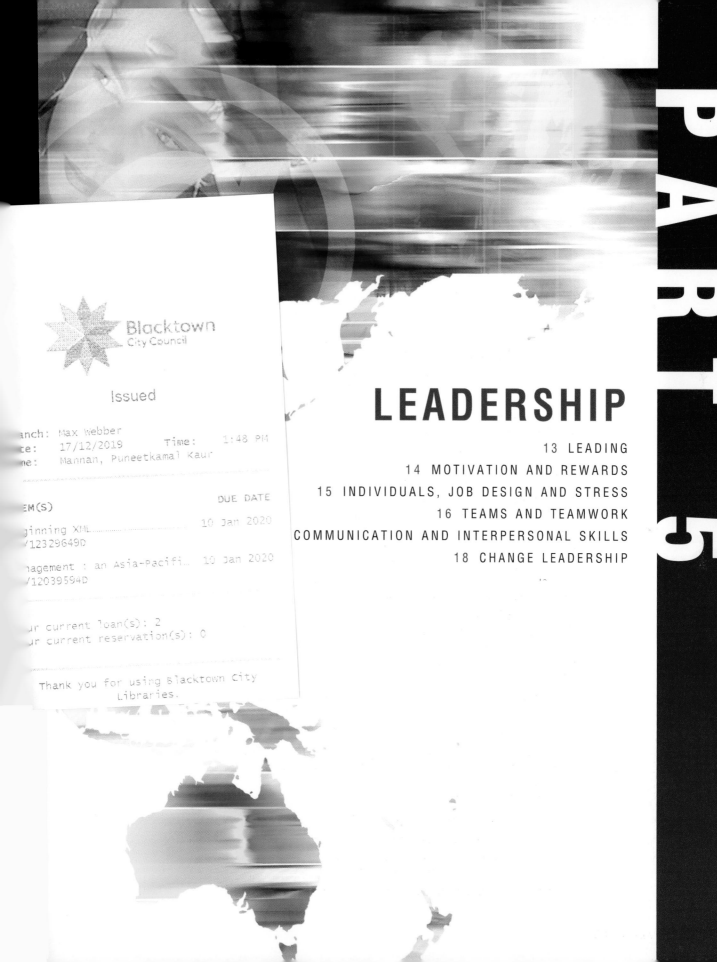

LEADERSHIP

P A R T 5

CHAPTER 13

CHAPTER 13

Leading

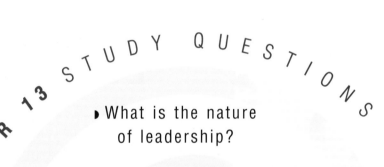

Michael Chaney — Australia's most admired business leader

Wesfarmers CEO Michael Chaney's exceptional business leadership skills have won him the admiration of Australia's top executives. Chaney is a science graduate of the University of Western Australia and holds an MBA from Harvard. He spent several years as a petroleum geologist in Australia and the USA and was regional manager of the Australian Industry Development Corporation before joining Wesfarmers in 1983. He became the company's CEO in 1992.

With interests in chemicals, hardware retailing, freight, transport and agricultural supplies, Wesfarmers maintains a conglomerate structure at a time when conglomerates are unfashionable. The company has often faced criticism for operating in too many sectors, but it has achieved extraordinary results in sometimes difficult circumstances. Under Chaney's leadership, Wesfarmers's revenues grew from $2.4 billion in 1995–96 to $4.4 billion in 2000–2001 and its net profit rose from $93 to $251 million.

Australian CEOs voted Chaney the most admired Australian business leader for 2001 and 2002 and chose Wesfarmers as Australia's most admired company.

According to Chaney: 'Being able to choose the right people is the fundamental skill for management success'.[1] Staff are hired for their ability to combine academic, business and commercial abilities, as well as their potential for getting along with others.

Chaney's analytical, conceptual and people skills have helped make Wesfarmers financially disciplined, adaptive and undeniably successful.[2]

A trip to the Wesfarmers web site www.wesfarmers.com.au provides access to the company's annual report, profiles of its key managers, and information about employment opportunities at the company. Check out what Wesfarmers is looking for in the graduates it employs. Do you fit the profile? If not, what can you do to improve your chances of landing a job at an excellent employer like Wesfarmers?

GET CONNECTED!

The success of Wesfarmers suggests that Michael Chaney's leadership style works well, but there is often more than a little luck influencing a company's financial results. In addition, what works well in one organisation may not work well in another; senior managers often find that they cannot match earlier leadership successes when they switch organisations. Why? Because other elements are at play, including the culture of the organisation, the actions of its competitors and the general economic environment. Yet there is little doubt that leaders *do* make a difference and many leave a lasting imprint on the organisations they lead.

Leadership can be viewed in different ways. It can be seen as the expression of individual characteristics that leaders bring to their jobs. For example, naturally outgoing people may display an open and friendly approach in the way they seek to lead others. It can be viewed as a flexible, situation-specific response to the particular events confronting leaders at particular times, so that the leader appears more or less outgoing depending on the situation. Leadership can be seen as most useful when it is simply creating an environment in which others can perform.

This chapter encourages a complex and realistic understanding of leadership, where individual characteristics are important but not entirely fixed. You can work to develop your leadership strengths and respond to your leadership weaknesses. Situations are important, but not fully determinant on your effectiveness as a leader. You *choose your response* to situations. In reading this chapter, we hope that you will begin to understand how organisations identify, develop and evaluate leadership, and that you will reflect on your own potential to lead.

THE NATURE OF LEADERSHIP

Leading is the process of arousing enthusiasm and directing efforts toward organisational goals.

A glance at the shelves in your local bookstore will quickly confirm that leadership or **leading** — the process of inspiring others to work hard to accomplish important tasks — is one of the most popular management topics. As shown in figure 13.1, it is also one of the four functions that constitute the management process. Planning sets the direction and objectives; organising brings the resources together to turn plans into action; leading builds the commitments and enthusiasm needed for people to apply their talents fully to help accomplish plans; and controlling makes sure things turn out right.

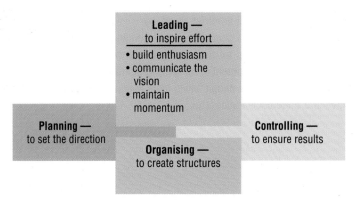

Figure 13.1 ▸ Leading viewed in relationship to the other management functions

Today's leaders are being challenged in new and demanding ways. The time frames for getting things accomplished are becoming shorter; leaders are expected to get things right the first time, with second chances few and far between; the problems to be resolved through leadership are complex, ambiguous and multidimensional; leaders are expected to be long-term oriented even while meeting demands for short-term performance results.[3]

Anyone aspiring to career success in leadership must rise to these challenges, and more.[4] To succeed as a leader in our new workplace, one must be good at dealing with all aspects of communication, interpersonal relations, motivation, job design, teamwork and change — all topics covered in this final part of *Management: An Asia–Pacific Perspective*.

Leadership and vision

'Great leaders', it is said, 'get extraordinary things done in organisations by inspiring and motivating others toward a common purpose.'[5] Frequently today, leadership is associated with **vision** — a future that one hopes to create or achieve in order to improve upon the present state of affairs. The term **visionary leadership** describes a leader who brings to the situation a clear and compelling sense of the future as well as understanding of the actions needed to get there successfully.[6] But there is more to it than that — simply having the vision of a desirable future is not enough. Truly great leaders are extraordinarily good at turning their visions into concrete results. Importantly, this involves the essential ability to communicate one's vision in such a way that others commit their hard work to its fulfilment. Visionary leaders, simply put, inspire others to take the actions necessary to turn vision into reality. At General Electric, for example, an 'A' leader is considered to be someone '. . . with vision and the ability to articulate that vision to the team, so vividly and powerfully that it also becomes their vision'.[7]

The accompanying Manager's Notepad 13.1 offers five principles for meeting the challenges of visionary leadership.[8] Recognise that the suggestions go beyond a manager's responsibilities for making long-term plans and drafting budgets. They go beyond putting structures in place and assigning people to jobs. And they go beyond making sure that results are consistent with the original plan. Leadership with vision means doing all these things and more. It means beginning with a clear vision; it means communicating that vision to all concerned; and it means getting people motivated and inspired to pursue the vision in their daily work. It means bringing meaning to the work that people do — making what they do worthy and valuable. Visionary leadership is a cornerstone of managerial success in dynamic leadership settings around the world.

Vision is a term used to describe a clear sense of the future.

Visionary leadership brings to the situation a clear sense of the future and an understanding of how to get there.

MANAGER'S NOTEPAD 13.1

Five principles of visionary leadership

- *Challenge the process.* Be a pioneer; encourage innovation and support people who have ideas.
- *Show enthusiasm.* Inspire others through personal enthusiasm to share in a common vision.
- *Help others to act.* Be a team player and support the efforts and talents of others.
- *Set the example.* Provide a consistent role model of how others can and should act.
- *Celebrate achievements.* Bring emotion into the workplace and rally 'hearts' as well as 'minds'.

Power and influence

The foundations of effective leadership lie in the way a manager uses power to influence the behaviour of other people. **Power** is the ability to get someone else to do something you want done. It is the ability to make things happen the way you want them to.[9] Research

Power is the ability to get someone else to do something you want done or to make things happen the way you want.

recognises that a need for power is essential to executive success.[10] But this need for power is not a desire to control for the sake of personal satisfaction; it is a desire to influence and control others for the good of the group or organisation as a whole. This 'positive' face of power is the foundation of effective leadership. Figure 13.2 shows one set of power sources that is based in the position a person holds and a second set that is based in one's personal qualities.[11]

Position power Based on things managers can offer to others.	**Personal power** Based on the ways managers are viewed by others.
Reward — 'If you do what I ask, I'll give you a reward.'	**Expert** — as a source of special knowledge and information.
Coercion — 'If you don't do what I ask, I'll punish you.'	**Referent** — as a person with whom others like to identify.
Legitimacy — 'Because I am the boss; you *must* do as I ask.'	

Figure 13.2 ▸ Sources of position power and personal power used by managers

SOURCES OF POSITION POWER

One important source of power is a manager's official status, or position, in the organisation's hierarchy of authority. Whereas anyone holding a managerial position theoretically has this power, how well it is used will vary from one person to the next. Consequently, leadership success will vary as well. The three bases of *position power* are reward power, coercive power and legitimate power.

Reward power is the ability to influence through rewards. It is the capability to offer something of value — a positive outcome — as a means of influencing the behaviour of other people. This involves the control of rewards or resources such as pay rises, bonuses, promotions, special assignments and verbal or written compliments. To mobilise reward power, a manager says, in effect, 'If you do what I ask, I'll give you a reward'.

Coercive power is the ability to influence through punishment. It is the capacity to punish or withhold positive outcomes as a way to influence the behaviour of other people. A manager may attempt to coerce someone by threatening him or her with verbal reprimands, pay penalties and even termination. To mobilise coercive power, a manager says, in effect, 'If you don't do what I want, I'll punish you'.

Legitimate power is the ability to influence through authority — the right by virtue of one's organisational position or status to exercise control over persons in subordinate positions. It is the capacity to influence the behaviour of other people by virtue of the rights of office. To mobilise legitimate power, a manager says, in effect, 'I am the boss and therefore you are supposed to do as I ask'.

SOURCES OF PERSONAL POWER

Another source of power lies in the individual manager and the unique personal qualities she or he brings to a leadership situation. This is a very important source of power that a truly successful leader cannot do without. Two bases of *personal power* are expert power and referent power.

Expert power is the ability to influence through special expertise. It is the capacity to influence the behaviour of other people because they recognise your knowledge, understanding and skills. Expertise derives from the possession of technical know-how or information pertinent to the issue at hand. This is developed by acquiring relevant skills or competencies or by gaining a central position in relevant information networks. It is

⚙ Reward power is the capacity to offer something of value as a means of influencing other people.

⚙ Coercive power is the capacity to punish or withhold positive outcomes as a means of influencing other people.

⚙ Legitimate power is the capacity to influence other people by virtue of formal authority, or the rights of office.

⚙ Expert power is the capacity to influence other people because of specialised knowledge.

maintained by protecting your credibility and not overstepping the boundaries of true understanding. When a manager uses expert power, the implied message is, 'You should do what I want because of my special expertise or information'.

Referent power is the ability to influence through identification. It is the capacity to influence the behaviour of other people because they admire you and want to identify positively with you. Reference is a power derived from charisma or interpersonal attractiveness. It is developed and maintained through good interpersonal relations that encourage the admiration and respect of others. When a manager uses referent power, the implied message is, 'You should do what I want in order to maintain a positive self-defined relationship with me'.

> **Referent power** is the capacity to influence other people because of their desire to identify personally with you.

GLOBALISATION

Jac Nasser

Australian crashes through . . . then crashes

When Melbourne-raised Jac Nasser was appointed CEO of Ford Motor Company, his 'can do' approach seemed just the tonic for the struggling motor vehicle company. In his previous job as Ford's new product development chief, Nasser had introduced new models, radically altered Ford designs, committed Ford to buying out its dealers, and had purchased Volvo for US$6.5 billion. In 2000, he was paid more than $24 million for his work at Ford.

By 2001, however, several models had failed, the company was selling off its dealerships, market share had declined from 24.9 per cent to 23.3 per cent, and it faced lawsuits over the deaths of 203 people allegedly linked to the failure of tyres on the Ford Explorer/ Mountaineer. In Australia, some Ford employees blamed Nasser for the poor sales performance of the AU Falcon, arguing that his forceful style led to poor design decisions. In October 2001, Nasser was fired. Analysts noted that the Ford family was unhappy with Nasser's dictatorial control of the company and had long viewed with concern Nasser's centralisation of power in which 14 top executives reported only to him. In early 2002, new CEO Nick Scheele listed insufficient spending on new programs, high marketing costs and employee lawsuits among Ford's greatest problems, whereas analysts added factors such as declining market share, poor product quality and a weak balance sheet to the list. Why would Jac Nasser's 'can do' approach fail after so many years of success within the Ford organisation?[12]

TURNING POWER INTO INFLUENCE

To succeed at leadership, you must be able to acquire all types of power and appropriately use them to achieve goals and pursue a shared vision.[13] To begin, the best leaders and managers understand that different outcomes are associated with use of the various power bases. When a leader relies on rewards and legitimacy to influence others, the likely outcome

is temporary compliance. The follower will do what the leader requests, but only so long as the reward continues and/or the legitimacy persists. Inability to continue the reward or attempting to influence outside the range of legitimacy will result in a loss of compliance. When a leader relies on coercion to gain influence, compliance is also dependent on the continued threat of punishment. In this case, however, the compliance is very temporary and often accompanied by resistance. Use of expert and referent power creates the most enduring influence; they create commitment. Followers respond positively because of internalised understanding or beliefs that create their own long-lasting effects on behaviour.

Position power alone is often insufficient to achieve and sustain needed influence. Personal power and the bases of expert and referent power often make the difference between leadership success and mediocrity. This is particularly true in the ability to influence the behaviour of peers and superiors in the organisation. Four points to keep in mind are: there is no substitute for expertise; likeable personal qualities are very important; effort and hard work breed respect; and personal behaviour must support expressed values.[14]

In organisations, power and influence are also linked to where one fits and how one acts in the structures and networks of the workplace. *Centrality* is important. Managers, for example, must establish a broad network of interpersonal contacts and get involved in the important information flows within them. They must avoid becoming isolated. *Criticality* is important. To gain power, managers must take good care of others who are dependent on them. They should take care to support them exceptionally well by doing things that add value to the work setting. *Visibility* is also important. It helps to become known as an influential person in the organisation. Good managers don't hesitate to make formal presentations, participate in key task forces or committees, and pursue special assignments that can display their leadership talents and capabilities.

Ethics and the limits to power

On the issue of ethics and the limits to power, it is always helpful to remember Chester Barnard's *acceptance theory of authority*. He identified four conditions that determine whether a leader's directives will be followed and true influence achieved.[16]

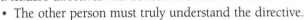

Barnard's acceptance theory of authority

- The other person must truly understand the directive.
- The other person must feel capable of carrying out the directive.
- The other person must believe that the directive is in the organisation's best interests.
- The other person must believe that the directive is consistent with personal values.

When the complexities of ethical dilemmas were discussed in chapter 6, it was noted that many such dilemmas begin when leaders and managers pressure followers to do questionable things. Using the acceptance theory of authority as a starting point, the ethical question a follower must always be prepared to ask is: Where do I (or will I) draw the line; at what point do I (or will I) refuse to comply with requests? Some day you may face a situation in which you are asked by someone in authority to do something that violates personal ethics and/or even the law. Can you … will you … when will you say 'no'? After all, as Barnard said, it is 'acceptance' that establishes the limits of managerial power.

Leadership and empowerment

Empowerment distributes decision-making power throughout an organisation.

At many points in this book we have talked about **empowerment**, the process through which managers enable and help others to gain power and achieve influence within the organisation. Effective leaders empower others by providing them with the information, responsibility, authority and trust to make decisions and act independently within their areas of expertise. They know that when people feel empowered to act, they tend to follow through with commitment and high-quality work. They also realise that power in organisations is not a 'zero-sum' quantity. That is, in order for someone to gain power, it isn't necessary for someone else to give it up. Indeed, today's high-performance organisations are masters at mobilising power and commitment to the vision throughout all ranks of employees.

Trust is undeniably a crucial part of effective empowerment. Prominent Australian company director Meredith Hellicar, for example, notes: 'As a junior and middle level employee, my own happiest times have been when energy and trust abound'.[17] Management consultant Peter Stephenson argues that empowerment can provide people with a sense of responsibility and accountability which can improve service across the organisation. In the case of a hotel chain, for example, he provides a scenario where 'staff with heavy customer interface are given five-figure budgets to rectify customers' problems with no need to seek authorisation first. Thus, we have the CEO housekeeper, the CEO doorman and so forth!' The employees become, in effect, business leaders.[18]

Manager's Notepad 13.2 offers tips on how leaders can empower others.[19] There are many benefits for managers who are successful at doing so. On the one hand, empowerment allows people to act independently and feel more 'adult' in their work activities. On the other hand, a manager who empowers others tends to gain power too. Having a high-performing work unit certainly helps establish the criticality, centrality and visibility of a manager's position. The very act of empowering others may create a positive relationship and build referent power.[20] And, what better way to demonstrate expertise than to show that your team does a great job?

MANAGER'S NOTEPAD 13.2

How to empower others

- Get others involved in selecting their work assignments and the methods for accomplishing tasks.
- Create an environment of cooperation, information sharing, discussion and shared ownership of goals.
- Encourage others to take initiative, make decisions and use their knowledge.
- When problems arise, find out what others think and let them help design the solutions.
- Stay out of the way; give others the freedom to put their ideas and solutions into practice.
- Maintain high morale and confidence by recognising successes and encouraging high performance.

LEADERSHIP TRAITS AND BEHAVIOURS

For centuries, people have recognised that some persons perform very well as leaders, whereas others do not. The question still debated is 'Why?' Historically, the issue of leadership success has been studied from the perspective of the trait, behavioural and contingency approaches to be discussed here. Each takes a slightly different tack in attempting to explain both leadership effectiveness and identify the pathways to leadership development.

Search for leadership traits

An early direction in leadership research involved the search for universal traits or distinguishing personal characteristics that would separate effective and ineffective leaders.[21] Sometimes called the *great person theory*, the notion was to identify successful leaders and then determine what made them great. If a listing of definitive universal leadership traits could be made, it would then be easy to select for leadership positions only those people with the requisite characteristics. Those wanting to become leaders or those seeking to improve their leadership success could set personal development goals for aquiring them.

Historically, researchers struggled with their inability to find consistent patterns of leadership traits. More recent research indicates that certain personal traits may be important, but that they must be considered along with other situational factors. Briefly, the results of many years of research in this direction can be summarised as follows. Physical characteristics such as a person's height, weight and physique make no difference in determining leadership success. On the other hand, certain personal traits do seem to differentiate leaders. A study of more than 3400 managers, for example, found that followers rather consistently admired certain things about leaders.[22] The most respected leaders were described by their followers as honest, competent, forward-looking, inspiring and credible. Such positive feelings may enhance a leader's effectiveness, particularly with respect to creating vision and a sense of empowerment. In a comprehensive review of research to date, Shelley Kirkpatrick and Edwin Locke further identify these personal traits as being common among successful leaders:[23]

Personal traits of successful leaders

- *Drive.* Successful leaders have high energy, display initiative and are tenacious.
- *Self-confidence.* Successful leaders trust themselves and have confidence in their abilities.
- *Creativity.* Successful leaders are creative and original in their thinking.
- *Cognitive ability.* Successful leaders have the intelligence to integrate and interpret information.
- *Business knowledge.* Successful leaders know their industry and its technical foundations.
- *Motivation.* Successful leaders enjoy influencing others to achieve shared goals.
- *Flexibility.* Successful leaders adapt to fit the needs of followers and demands of situations.
- *Honesty and integrity.* Successful leaders are trustworthy; they are honest, predictable and dependable.

A recent Australian study of senior executives from a range of industries found that these traits continue to be identified as important in determining whether managers progress to senior leadership positions. According to those surveyed, leaders differentiate themselves from their colleagues by possessing a strong need to achieve results; the ability to see the big picture; the ability to exercise initiative; the ability to persuade and influence others; high internal work standards; and sound overall business sense. Clearly, interpersonal qualities such as the ability to work both alone and with others and to think strategically are viewed as crucial if leadership roles are to be assumed.[24]

Focus on leadership behaviours

Leadership style is the recurring pattern of behaviours exhibited by a leader.

Recognising that the possession of certain traits alone is not a guarantee of leadership success, researchers next turned their attention to examine how leaders behave when working with followers. In effect this shifted attention from a focus on *who* leaders are toward concern for *what* leaders do. Generally known as *behavioural theories of leadership*, work in this tradition sought to determine which **leadership style** — the recurring pattern of behaviours exhibited by a leader — worked best.[25] If the preferred style could be identified, the implications were straightforward and practical: train leaders to become skilled at using the ideal style to best advantage.

Most research in the leader behaviour tradition focused on two dimensions of leadership style: concern for the task to be accomplished and concern for the people doing the work. The terminology used to describe these dimensions varies among many studies. Concern for task is sometimes called *initiating structure*, *job-centredness* and *task orientation*; concern for people is sometimes called *consideration*, *employee-centredness* and *relationship orientation*. But regardless of the terminology, the behaviours characteristic of each dimension are quite clear. A *leader high in concern for task* plans and defines work to be done, assigns task responsibilities, sets clear work standards, urges task completion and monitors performance results. By contrast, a *leader high in concern for people* acts warm and supportive towards followers, maintains good social relations with them, respects their feelings, is sensitive to their needs and shows trust in them.

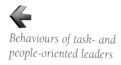

Behaviours of task- and people-oriented leaders

The results of leader behaviour research at first suggested that followers of people-oriented leaders would be more productive and satisfied than those working for more task-oriented leaders.[26] Later results, however, suggested that truly effective leaders were high in both concern for people and concern for task. Figure 13.3 describes one of the popular versions of this conclusion — the Leadership Grid® of Robert Blake and Jane Mouton.[27] This grid is designed not only to describe alternative leadership styles and identify a preferred one, but also to assist in the process of leadership development. The approach uses assessments to first determine where someone falls with respect to people and task concerns. Then a training program is designed to help shift the person's style in the preferred direction of becoming strong on both dimensions. Blake and Mouton called this preferred style *team management*. This leader shares decisions with subordinates, encourages participation and supports the teamwork needed for high levels of task accomplishment. In today's terminology, this could also be a manager who 'empowers' others.

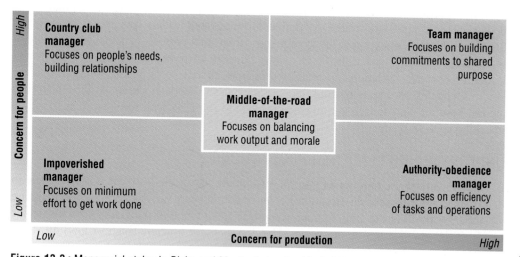

Figure 13.3 ▸ Managerial styles in Blake and Mouton's Leadership Grid®

Visit the Australian Indigenous Leadership Centre web site www.aiatsis.gov.au/ailc to learn how the centre provides leadership training for Aboriginal and Torres Strait Islander community leaders. Classes include 'Working with Government' and 'Indigenous Leaders in the Corporate Sector'. GET CONNECTED!

An important personal question in leadership development is, of course: Which type of leader are you? Is your style most typically perceived by others as one of team management? Or, is it one of the following styles that are considered by Blake and Mouton to be much less effective? *Impoverished management* displays low concern for both people and tasks. Leaders with this style turn most decisions over to the work group and show little interest in the work process or its results. *Authority-obedience management* shows high concern for the task and low concern for people. Leaders with this style make most of the decisions for the work group, give directions and expect their orders to be followed. *Country club management* shows high concern for people and low concern for tasks. Leaders with this style are warm in interpersonal relationships, avoid conflict and seek harmony in decision making. *Middle-of-the-road management* is noncommital in emphasising both task and people concerns. This leader puts forth minimum required effort in balancing the task and people needs of the group to maintain adequate but not exemplary performance.

CONTINGENCY APPROACHES TO LEADERSHIP

As leadership research continued to develop, scholars recognised the need to probe still further beyond leader behaviours alone and examine them in relationship to situational attributes. Interest thus turned to yet another question: When and under what circumstances is a particular leadership style preferable to others? This is the essence of the following *contingency approaches*, which share the goal of understanding the conditions for leadership success in widely varying situations.

Fiedler's contingency model

An early contingency leadership model developed by Fred Fiedler was based on the premise that good leadership depends on a match between leadership style and situational demands.[28] Leadership style is measured on what Fiedler calls the *least-preferred coworker scale*. Known as the LPC scale, it is available as assessment 13 in the end-of-text Career Readiness Workbook. According to Fiedler, a person's LPC score describes tendencies to behave either as a task-motivated or relationship-motivated leader. This either/or concept is important. Fiedler believes that leadership style is part of a person's personality; therefore, it is relatively enduring and difficult to change. Instead of trying to train a task-motivated leader to behave in a relationship-motivated manner, or vice versa, Fiedler suggests that the key to leadership success is putting the existing styles to work in situations for which they are the best 'fit'. This is true contingency leadership thinking with the goal of successfully matching style with situational demands.

UNDERSTANDING LEADERSHIP SITUATIONS

In Fiedler's theory, the amount of control a situation allows the leader is a critical issue in determining the correct style–situation fit. Three contingency variables are used to diagnose situational control. The *quality of leader–member relations* (good or poor) measures the degree to which the group supports the leader. The *degree of task structure* (high or low) measures the extent to which task goals, procedures and guidelines are clearly spelt out. The *amount of position power* (strong or weak) measures the degree to which the position gives the leader power to reward and punish subordinates. Figure 13.4 shows eight leadership situations that result from different combinations of these variables. They range from the most favourable situation of high control (good leader–member relations, high task structure, strong position power), to the least favourable situation of low control (poor leader–member relations, low task structure, weak position power).

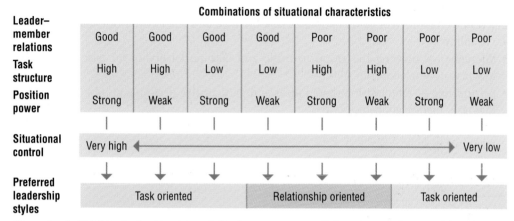

Combinations of situational characteristics

Leader–member relations	Good	Good	Good	Good	Poor	Poor	Poor	Poor
Task structure	High	High	Low	Low	High	High	Low	Low
Position power	Strong	Weak	Strong	Weak	Strong	Weak	Strong	Weak

Situational control — Very high ← ——————————————— → Very low

Preferred leadership styles	Task oriented			Relationship oriented			Task oriented	

Figure 13.4 ▸ Matching leadership style and situation: summary predictions from Fiedler's contingency theory

MATCHING LEADERSHIP STYLE AND SITUATION

Figure 13.4 also summarises Fiedler's extensive research on the contingency relationships between situation control, leadership style and leader effectiveness. Neither the task-oriented nor the relationship-oriented leadership style is effective all the time. Instead, each style appears to work best when used in the right situation. The results can be stated as two propositions. *Proposition 1* is that a task-oriented leader will be most successful in either very favourable (high-control) or very unfavourable (low-control) situations. *Proposition 2* is that a relationship-oriented leader will be most successful in situations of moderate control.

Fiedler believes that leadership success depends on a good leader–situation match. This means that prospective leaders should actively seek situations for which their predominant style is most appropriate. Assume, for example, that you are the leader of a team of bank tellers. The tellers seem highly supportive of you, and their job is clearly defined regarding what needs to be done. You have the authority to evaluate their performance and to make pay and promotion recommendations. This is a high-control situation consisting of good leader–member relations, high task structure and high position power. Figure 13.4 shows that a task-motivated leader would be most effective in this situation.

Now take another example. Suppose that you are chairperson of a committee asked to improve labour–management relations in a manufacturing plant. Although the goal is clear, no one can say for sure how to accomplish it. Task structure is low. Because committee members are free to quit any time they want, the chairperson has little position power. Because not all members believe the committee is necessary, poor leader–member relations are apparent. According to figure 13.4, this low-control situation also calls for a task-motivated leader.

Finally, assume that you are the new head of a retail section in a large department store. Because you were selected over one of the popular sales clerks you now supervise, leader–member relations are poor. Task structure is high since the clerk's job is well defined. Your position power is low because the clerks work under a seniority system and fixed wage schedule. Figure 13.4 shows that this moderate-control situation requires a relationship-motivated leader.

Hersey–Blanchard situational leadership model

The Hersey–Blanchard situational leadership model suggests that successful leaders adjust their styles depending on the *maturity* of followers, indicated by their readiness to perform in a given situation.[30] 'Readiness', in this sense, is based on how able and willing or confident

www.ezypay.com.au

Empowerment is in at Ezypay, an automated billing company that is among Australia's fastest growing companies. Founder George Holman says his smartest move has been to delegate authority. 'Surround yourself with competent people so you can remain focused on the strategic picture', he says.[29]

followers are to perform required tasks. As shown in figure 13.5, the possible leadership styles that result from different combinations of task-oriented and relationship-oriented behaviours are as follows:

Leadership styles in the situational model

- *delegating* — allowing the group to make and take responsibility for task decisions; a low-task, low-relationship style
- *participating* — emphasising shared ideas and participative decisions on task directions; a low-task, high-relationship style
- *selling* — explaining task directions in a supportive and persuasive way; a high-task, high-relationship style
- *telling* — giving specific task directions and closely supervising work; a high-task, low-relationship style.

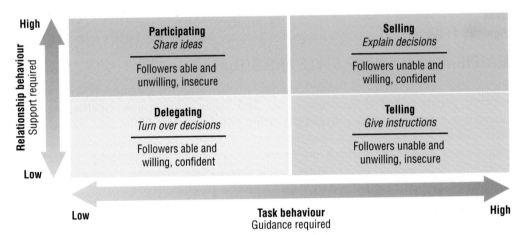

Figure 13.5 ▸ Leadership implications of the Hersey–Blanchard situational leadership model

Managers using this model must be able to implement the alternative leadership styles as needed. The *delegating style* works best in high-readiness situations of able and willing or confident followers; the *telling style* works best at the other extreme of low readiness, where followers are unable and unwilling or insecure. The *participating style* is recommended for low-to-moderate readiness (followers able but unwilling or insecure) and the *selling style* for moderate-to-high readiness (followers unable but willing or confident). Hersey and Blanchard further believe that leadership styles should be adjusted as followers change over time. The model also implies that if the correct styles are used in lower-readiness situations, followers will 'mature' and grow in ability, willingness and confidence. This allows the leader to become less directive as followers mature.[31]

A significant Australian study was recently undertaken on this model. Gayle Avery of the Macquarie Graduate School of Management found that senior and middle managers preferred using the participating style over the other styles, whereas supervisors and junior managers preferred using the participating and selling styles. Avery argues that this may reflect the traditional Australian value of 'mateship' influencing leadership styles, general trends toward more empowered and democratic workplaces, and leadership 'success' in Australian workplaces relying more strongly on managers relating individually with their subordinates compared to their counterparts in other countries.

The study also found that subordinates did not perceive their managers' preferred leadership styles as particularly effective, indicating that Australian managers may actually be oversupportive in their leadership approach.[32]

House's path–goal leadership theory

A third contingency leadership approach is the *path–goal theory* advanced by Robert House.[33] This theory suggests that an effective leader is one who clarifies paths through which followers can achieve both task-related and personal goals. The best leaders help people progress along these paths, remove any barriers that stand in their way, and provide appropriate rewards for task accomplishment. House identifies four leadership styles that may be used in this 'path–goal' sense:

- *directive leadership* — letting subordinates know what is expected; giving directions on what to do and how; scheduling work to be done; maintaining definite standards of performance; clarifying the leader's role in the group
- *supportive leadership* — doing things to make work more pleasant; treating group members as equals; being friendly and approachable; showing concern for the wellbeing of subordinates
- *achievement-oriented leadership* — setting challenging goals; expecting the highest levels of performance; emphasising continuous improvement in performance; displaying confidence in meeting high standards
- *participative leadership* — involving subordinates in decision making; consulting with subordinates; asking for suggestions from subordinates; using these suggestions when making a decision.

Leadership styles in the path–goal theory

PATH–GOAL PREDICTIONS AND MANAGERIAL IMPLICATIONS

The path–goal leadership theory is summarised in figure 13.6. It advises a manager to always use leadership styles that complement situational needs. This means that the leader adds value by contributing things that are missing from the situation or that need strengthening; she or he specifically avoids redundant behaviours. For example, when team members are expert and competent at their tasks it is unnecessary and not functional for the leader to tell them how to do things. The important contingencies for making good path–goal leadership choices include subordinate personal characteristics (ability, experience and locus of control) and the work environment characteristics (task structure, authority system and work group).

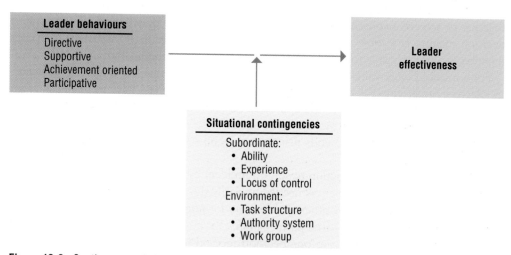

Figure 13.6 ▸ Contingency relationships in the path–goal leadership theory

In path–goal theory, for example, the match of leader behaviours and situation might take the following forms.[34] When *job assignments* are unclear, directive leadership is appropriate to clarify task objectives and expected rewards. When *worker self-confidence* is low, supportive leadership is appropriate to increase confidence by emphasising individual abilities and offering needed assistance. When *performance incentives* are poor, participative leadership is appropriate to clarify individual needs and identify appropriate rewards. When *task challenge* is insufficient in a job, achievement-oriented leadership is appropriate to set goals and raise performance aspirations. In all these examples, the value added by the choice of leadership style is expected to lead to greater effort by the subordinate and improve satisfaction and performance.

SUBSTITUTES FOR LEADERSHIP

Path–goal theory has also contributed to the recognition of what some theorists call **substitutes for leadership**.[35] These are aspects of the work setting and the people involved that can reduce the need for a leader's personal involvement. In effect, they make leadership from the 'outside' unnecessary because leadership is already built into the situation. Possible substitutes for leadership include *subordinate characteristics* such as ability, experience and independence; *task characteristics* such as routineness and availability of feedback; and *organisational characteristics* such as clarity of plans and formalisation of rules and procedures. When substitutes are present, managers should avoid redundant leadership behaviours and concentrate on things that truly require outside attention.

> **Substitutes for leadership** are factors in the work setting that direct work efforts without the involvement of a leader.

Vroom–Jago leader-participation model

The Vroom–Jago leader-participation model is designed to help a leader choose the method of decision making that best fits the nature of the problem being faced. In this approach, an effective leader is someone able to consistently choose and implement from the following alternatives the most appropriate decision methods.[36]

An **authority decision** is one made by the leader and then communicated to the group. Participation is minimised. No input is asked of group members other than to provide specific information on request. A **consultative decision** is made by the leader after asking group members for information, advice or opinions. In some cases, group members are consulted individually; in others, the consultation occurs during a meeting of the group as a whole. In a **group decision**, all members participate in making a decision and work together to achieve a consensus regarding the preferred course of action. This approach to decision making is a form of empowerment, and it is successful to the extent that each member is ultimately able to accept the logic and feasibility of the final group decision.[37]

> An **authority decision** is a decision made by the leader and then communicated to the group.
>
> A **consultative decision** is a decision made by a leader after receiving information, advice or opinions from group members.
>
> A **group decision** is a decision made with the full participation of all group members.

When participation works best

For a manager who wants to be successful at leading through participation, the challenge in effectively managing the decision process is twofold. First, the leader must know when each decision method is the preferred approach. Second, the leader must be able to properly implement each when needed. As shown in figure 13.7, Vroom–Jago's normative model of leadership effectiveness recommends using more group-oriented and participative decision methods when:

- leaders lack sufficient information to solve a problem by themselves
- the problem is unclear and help is needed to clarify the situation
- acceptance of the decision by others is necessary for implementation
- adequate time is available for true participation.

In true contingency fashion, no one decision method is considered by the Vroom–Jago model as universally superior to any others. Rather, leadership success results when the decision method used correctly matches the characteristics of the problem to be solved. Each of the three decision methods is appropriate in certain situations, and each has its advantages and disadvantages. The key rules guiding the choice relate to: *decision quality* —

based on the location of information needed for problem solving; and *decision acceptance* — based on the importance of subordinate acceptance to eventual solution implementation. You may think of these in the context of an equation: Decision effectiveness = Decision quality × Decision acceptance.

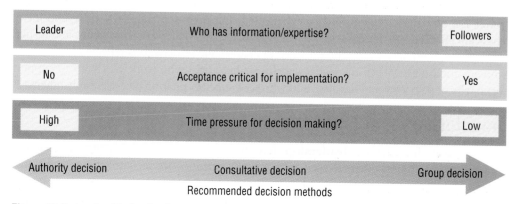

Figure 13.7 ▸ Leadership implications of the Vroom–Jago leader-participation model

Use of participative decision methods offers important benefits to the leader.[38] They help improve decision quality by bringing more information to bear on the problem. They help improve decision acceptance as participants gain understanding and become committed to the process. And, they also contribute to the development of leadership potential in others through the experience of active participation in the problem-solving process. However, there is also a cost to be considered. The greater the participation, the more time required for the decision process. Leaders do not always have sufficient time available; some problems must be resolved immediately. In such cases, the authority decision may be the only option. As shown in figure 13.7, the more authority-oriented decisions work best when leaders personally have the expertise needed to solve the problem, they are confident and capable of acting alone, others are likely to accept the decision they make, and little or no time is available for discussion.

POINT ⇐

COUNTER ⇑

How realistic is our view of leadership?

Is it possible that leadership makes much less difference than we often think? Some leadership writers are beginning to think so. James Meindl argues that we often take a 'romantic' view of leadership. He says that we like to attribute a business's success or failure to the actions of its leaders, but organisations may be so large and complex that the influence of their leaders may be little more than symbolic. Further, the success or failure of organisations may be as much the result of external factors such as the general economic environment, the decisions of competitors, and industry fashions, as of deliberate decisions made by an organisation's CEO. As is the case when sporting teams sack their coach for the team's poor performances, we like to see the CEOs of poorly performing organisations given their marching orders. In both cases, we should ask whether the coach or CEO is really to blame for poor performance, but we rarely take the time to think through such issues.[39]

Do we really have a 'romantic' view of leadership? If so, how should we change?

ISSUES IN LEADERSHIP DEVELOPMENT

Current trends in leadership thinking seek to integrate and extend the insights discussed so far in this chapter.[40] This is the era of 'superleaders' who, through vision and strength of personality, have a truly inspirational impact on others.[41] Their leadership efforts result in followers not only meeting performance expectations but performing above and beyond them. These are **charismatic leaders** who develop special leader–follower relationships and inspire others in extraordinary ways. The presence of charismatic leadership is reflected in followers who are enthusiastic about the leader and his or her ideas, who work very hard to support them, who remain loyal and devoted, and who seek superior performance accomplishments.[42]

 Charismatic leaders develop special leader–follower relationships and inspire followers in extraordinary ways.

Transformational leadership

 Transformational leadership is inspirational leadership that gets people to do more in achieving high performance.

 Transactional leadership is leadership that directs the efforts of others through tasks, rewards and structures.

The term **transformational leadership** describes someone who is truly inspirational as a leader and who arouses others to seek extraordinary performance accomplishments. A transformational leader uses charisma and related qualities to raise aspirations and shift people and organisational systems into new high-performance patterns. Scholars differentiate this from **transactional leadership**, which describes someone who is more methodical in keeping others focused on progress toward goal accomplishment. A transactional leader adjusts tasks, rewards and structures to move followers toward accomplishing organisational objectives.[43]

Importantly, these are not mutually exclusive leadership approaches. Transactional leadership is a foundation or building block that helps support transformational leadership. On its own, however, transactional leadership is acknowledged to be insufficient to meet the leadership challenges and demands of today's dynamic work environments. In settings where continuous and often large-scale change is a high priority, the additional inspirational impact of transformational leadership is essential to achieve sustainable high-performance results.

The notion of transformational leadership offers a distinct management challenge, with important personal development implications. It is not enough to possess leadership traits, know the leadership behaviours and understand leadership contingencies to act effectively from a transactional perspective. Any manager must also be prepared to lead in an inspirational way and with a compelling personality. The transformational leader provides a strong aura of vision and contagious enthusiasm that substantially raises the confidence, aspirations and commitments of followers to meet high-performance demands. The special qualities that are often characteristic of such transformational leaders include the following:[44]

Attributes of transformational leaders

- *vision* — having ideas and a clear sense of direction; communicating them to others; developing excitement about accomplishing shared 'dreams'
- *charisma* — arousing others' enthusiasm, faith, loyalty, pride and trust in themselves through the power of personal reference and appeals to emotion
- *symbolism* — identifying 'heroes', offering special rewards and holding spontaneous and planned ceremonies to celebrate excellence and high achievement
- *empowerment* — helping others develop, removing performance obstacles, sharing responsibilities and delegating truly challenging work
- *intellectual stimulation* — gaining the involvement of others by creating awareness of problems and stirring their imagination to create high-quality solutions
- *integrity* — being honest and credible, acting consistently out of personal conviction and following through commitments.

The former CEO of BHP Billiton, Paul Anderson, was a leader who typified transformational leadership values in the Asia–Pacific region. Anderson joined BHP in 1998, the year that the company announced an annual loss of $1.47 billion. An American, Anderson came to BHP with substantial experience in the US energy sector. The 1998 loss was a far cry from BHP's earlier decades of success which had culminated in its 1986 net profit of $1 billion, the first Australian company to reach this mark. He inherited an inwardly focused organisation with a complex organisational structure of eight divisions and a bloated executive leadership group of 95 members. How could Anderson turn BHP around? His effectiveness provides a case study in transformational leadership. Anderson pursued a three-phase approach. First, he sought to have the company face up to and resolve its immediate problems. This included the sale of some $3.7 billion in non-core and non-performing assets between 1999 and 2001, the creation of a new management team with improved financial and commercial skills, and the development and promotion of the 'BHP Charter', incorporating values such as integrity, high performance, the pursuit of win–win relationships and the courage to lead change. Anderson also refocused BHP on its strengths in natural resources. Second, BHP sought to build a new relationship between the company and its staff, using new performance-dependent incentive programs and 360° feedback programs as ways to help align employee effort with company goals. Third, BHP sought to pursue its goals of becoming a major player in the minerals sector and a niche operator in the petroleum industry through a $58 billion merger with resources company Billiton. A number of transformational leadership qualities are evident in Anderson's role in returning BHP to profitability. Like Wesfarmers CEO Michael Chaney (profiled at the start of this chapter), Paul Anderson won recognition as one of Australia's most admired business leaders, and the speed with which BHP has been transformed is one of the most notable business success stories of the 21st century.[45]

Another transformational manager is New Zealand's most admired business leader, Keith McLaughlin. By continually expanding his vision, McLaughlin made Baycorp Holdings the market leader in credit reporting and debt collection. Baycorp then announced that it would merge with Data Advantage of Australia to create a $2 billion business intelligence and credit services giant. McLaughlin worked hard to build a company culture which encourages positive change and he was not daunted by the challenge of combining Data Advantage's 400 staff with Baycorp's 350 employees. He said, 'We have an attitude that we wake up each day and come in to change the business. When you come in with that approach, change doesn't become something you fear, but something you embrace.'[46] McLaughlin's approach seems to be working, with Baycorp achieving seven straight years of profit growth in excess of 20 per cent. In addition, more than 40 of McLaughlin's staff have been with the company for more than ten years, indicating that his positive approach to change has not discouraged key staff from staying with the organisation for the long haul.

Emotional intelligence

An area of leadership development that is currently very popular is **emotional intelligence**, first discussed in chapter 1 as an element of the essential human skills of managers. As popularised by the work of Daniel Goleman, emotional intelligence is defined as 'the ability to manage ourselves and our relationships effectively'.[47] According to his research, a leader's emotional intelligence is an important influence on his or her effectiveness, especially in more senior management positions. In Goleman's words, 'the higher the rank of the person considered to be a star performer, the more emotional intelligence capabilities showed up as the reason for his or her effectiveness'.[48] This is a strong endorsement, indeed, for consideration of one's emotional intelligence in a developing portfolio of comprehensive leadership capabilities. Important too is Goleman's belief that emotional intelligence skills can be learned at any age — it's never too late.

⊘ Emotional intelligence is the ability to manage ourselves and our relationships effectively.

For purposes of research and training, Goleman breaks emotional intelligence down into five critical components.[49] He argues that each of us should strive to build competencies in each component and thereby maximise our ability to utilise emotional intelligence and build better relationships with others. The critical components of emotional intelligence are the following:

→

Dimensions of emotional intelligence

- *Self-awareness* is an ability to understand our own moods and emotions, and understand their impact on our work and on others.
- *Self-regulation* is the ability to think before we act and to control otherwise disruptive impulses.
- *Motivation* is the ability to work hard with persistence and for reasons other than money and status.
- *Empathy* is the ability to understand the emotions of others and to use this understanding to better relate to them.
- *Social skill* is the ability to establish rapport with others and to build good relationships and networks.

According to Goleman, these skills in emotional intelligence are necessary for leadership success. A person lacking in emotional intelligence, for example, might fail to recognise how excessive stress is contributing to bad attitudes and negative behaviour among team members. As a team leader, he or she might push too hard for performance results and further complicate the situation. A leader high in emotional intelligence would be quicker to notice that emotions were running high due to stress and thus take action to help the team members better deal with the stressful conditions. Team performance would likely improve as a result of this more 'emotionally intelligent' leadership response to a problem situation.

CONNECTION

Globalisation
Managing across cultures

Managing in a global environment is considered the most significant challenge for organisational leaders in the decade ahead. Managing across cultures is never easy and undertaking global leadership roles can be particularly difficult. Global supply chains, marketing strategies and human resource management approaches require constant coordination and finetuning. Whether you wish to lead a global corporation, as Australians Douglas Daft at Coca-Cola and Geoff Bible at Phillip Morris are doing, or simply hope to develop international leadership skills, an overseas job assignment can provide an array of new skills and experiences.

A survey of 300 Australian general managers found that the traditional highly individualistic, consultative Australian leadership style is inappropriate when transferred to the hierarchical, group-oriented cultures of many Asian countries. A global mindset is required in which managers adapt their style to the cultures in which they operate. This mindset can be developed through regular exposure to the business cultures of the Asia–Pacific, and an international assignment is one obvious way to achieve this. Undertaking international management and cross-cultural subjects at university is also highly recommended.[53]

Questions

Have you considered the need to develop competencies in international management? What experience do you have of global business? In what ways can you develop these competencies?

Gender and leadership

Female executives interviewed for a recent Australian study noted that they faced the difficult balancing act of needing to appear strong and effective in order to be taken seriously while also needing to appear feminine so that they would not be perceived as a threat by 'blokey' Australian males. They saw themselves as being less autocratic and directive and more adaptable and flexible than their male counterparts while still being just as results focused. This approach is typified in the comments of Gillian Franklin, owner of the cosmetics company The Heat Group which distributes Max Factor, Cover Girl and Caboodles cosmetics in Australia as well as its own brand, Goss. Franklin describes her management style as 'visionary, educational and motivational; tough, but appreciative of the talents of others', noting 'I expect a lot, but I give a lot'.[50]

The evidence clearly supports that both women and men can be effective leaders.[51] As suggested by the prior example, however, they may tend toward somewhat different styles.[52]

Victor Vroom and his colleagues have investigated gender differences in respect to the leader-participation model discussed earlier.[54] They find women managers to be significantly more participative than their male counterparts. Although followers in their studies value participation by all leaders, they tend to value participation by female leaders more highly than by male leaders. Women may tend toward a style sometimes referred to as *interactive leadership*.[55] This style focuses on the building of consensus and good interpersonal relations through communication and involvement. Leaders of this style display behaviours typically considered democratic and participative — such as showing respect for others, caring for others, and sharing power and information with others. This interactive style also has qualities in common with the transformational leadership just discussed.[56] Men, by contrast, may tend toward more of a transactional approach to leadership — relying more on directive and assertive behaviours, and using authority in a traditional 'command and control' sense.

Given the emphasis on shared power, communication, cooperation and participation in the new-form organisations of today, these results are provocative. Gender issues aside, the interactive leadership style seems to be an excellent fit with the demands of a diverse workforce and the new workplace. As Harvard Professor and consultant Rosabeth Moss Kanter says: 'Women get high ratings on exactly those skills required to succeed in the Global Information Age, where teamwork and partnering are so important'.[57] Regardless of whether the relevant behaviours are displayed by women or men, it seems clear that future leadership success will rest more often on capacity to lead through positive relationships and empowerment than through aloofness and formal authority. The chapters that follow on leading through motivation, communication, interpersonal relations, group dynamics and teamwork, and change leadership are highly relevant to this issue.

Drucker's 'old-fashioned' leadership

Peter Drucker offers another very pragmatic approach to leadership in the new workplace. It is based on what he refers to as a 'good old-fashioned' view of the plain hard work it takes to be a successful leader. Consider, for example, Drucker's description of a telephone conversation with a potential consulting client who was the human resources vice-president of a big bank: 'We'd want you to run a seminar for us on how one acquires charisma', she said. Drucker's response was not what she expected. He advised her that there's more to leadership than the popular emphasis on personal qualities that offer a sense of personal 'dash' or charisma. In fact, he said that 'leadership ... is work'.[58]

Drucker's observations on leadership offer a useful complement to the transformational leadership ideas just discussed. He identifies the following three essentials of leadership. First, Drucker believes that the foundation of effective leadership is *defining and establishing a sense of mission*. A good leader sets the goals, priorities and standards. A good leader keeps them all clear and visible, and maintains them. In Drucker's words, 'The leader's first task is to be the trumpet that sounds a clear sound'. Second, he believes in *accepting leadership as a responsibility rather than a rank*. Good leaders surround themselves with talented people. They are not afraid to develop strong and capable subordinates. And they do not blame others when things go wrong. As Drucker says, 'The buck stops here' is still a good adage to remember. Third, Drucker stresses the importance of *earning and keeping the trust of others*. The key here is the leader's personal integrity. The followers of good leaders trust them. This means that they believe the leader means what he or she says and that his or her actions will be consistent with what is said. In Drucker's words again, 'Effective leadership ... is not based on being clever; it is based primarily on being consistent'.

Leading for success

Consultants Booz Allen Hamilton identified three rules for CEOs pursuing success in the 21st century. They must produce consistent and acceptable shareholder returns; avoid mistakes and have realistic expectations; and rapidly develop and implement change initiatives. [59]

Why do you think these requirements are so important?

Ethical aspects of leadership

Firmly embedded in the concept of transformational leadership and good old-fashioned leadership is **integrity** — the leader's honesty, credibility and consistency in putting values into action. Leaders have an undeniable responsibility to set high ethical standards to guide the behaviour of followers. For managers, the ethical aspects of leadership are important and everyday concerns. At General Electric, for example, the 'A' leader is described as someone with 'the instinct and courage to make the tough calls'. This leader also does so 'decisively, but with fairness and absolute integrity'.[60]

Concerned about what he perceives as a lack of momentum in organisational life, John W. Gardner talks about the 'moral aspects' of leadership.[61] 'Most people in most organizations most of the time', he writes, 'are more stale than they know, more bored than they care to admit.' Leaders, according to Gardner, have a moral obligation to supply the necessary spark to awaken the potential of each individual — to urge each person 'to take the initiative in performing leader-like acts'. He points out that high expectations tend to generate high performance. It is the leader's job to remove 'obstacles to our effective functioning — to help individuals see and pursue shared purposes'.

Gardner's premise is that people with a sense of ownership of their jobs will naturally outperform those who feel they are outsiders. Moral leaders instil ownership by truly respecting others and helping them to do their best. By doing so they build organisations that consistently perform to society's expectations.[62] Moral leadership, therefore, must be clearly and strongly anchored in a true commitment to people.

This wisdom is evident in the following leadership advice from Lyn Odland, the CEO of Deloitte Touche Tohmatsu (Australia):

> The notion of empowering and trusting people is contagious. As young people come into the organisation, you give them some training and coaching and then you say, 'We would like you to take on this responsibility and we would like you to do it your way; so don't go to page 42 in the manual; do it the way you think it should be done'.[63]

Integrity in leadership is honesty, credibility and consistency in putting values into action.

CHAPTER 13
Study guide

The chapter 13 study guide helps you review the chapter content, prepare for examinations, apply what you have learned and further build your career readiness. The summary briefly answers the study questions posed at the start of the chapter. The list of key terms allows you to double-check your familiarity with basic concepts and definitions. The applied activities help you test your comprehension of chapter content. Suggestions offered as career readiness activities direct your attention to relevant sections of the Career Readiness Workbook where you can test and develop your career skills and apply what you have learned. The list of electronic resources suggests activities from the *Management: An Asia–Pacific Perspective* web site and, finally, the case for critical thinking helps you apply your new management knowledge.

SUMMARY

What is the nature of leadership?

- Leadership is the process of inspiring others to work hard to accomplish important tasks.
- Vision, or a clear sense of the future, is increasingly considered to be an essential ingredient of effective leadership.
- Visionary leaders are able to communicate their vision to others and build the commitments needed to perform the required work.
- Power, the ability to get others to do what you want them to do, is an essential ingredient of effective leadership.
- Managerial power may be gained through the formal position in the organisation and/or through personal sources of influence.
- Sources of position power include rewards, coercion and legitimacy or formal authority; sources of personal power include expertise and reference.
- Effective leaders empower others — that is, they help and allow others to take action and make job-related decisions on their own.

What are the important leadership traits and behaviours?

- Early leadership studies searched unsuccessfully for a definitive set of personal traits that differentiated successful and unsuccessful leaders.
- Traits that seem to have a positive impact on leadership include drive, integrity and self-confidence, among others.
- Research on leader behaviours focused on alternative leadership styles that involved concerns for task and concerns for people.
- One suggestion of leader-behaviour researchers is that effective leaders will be good at team-based or participative leadership that is high in both task and people concerns.

What are the contingency theories of leadership?

- Contingency leadership approaches point out that no one leadership style always works best; rather, the best style is one that properly matches the demands of each unique situation.
- Fiedler's contingency theory describes how situational differences in task structure, position power and leader–member relations may influence which leadership style works best.

- House's path–goal theory suggests leaders add value to situations by responding with supportive, directive, achievement-oriented and/or participative styles as needed.
- The Hersey–Blanchard situational model recommends using task-oriented and people-oriented behaviours, depending on the 'maturity' of the group.
- The Vroom–Jago leader-participation theory advises leaders to choose decision-making methods (individual, consultative, group) that best fit the problems they are trying to resolve.

What are current issues in leadership development?

- Transactional leadership focuses on tasks, rewards and structures to influence follower behaviour.
- Charismatic leadership creates a truly inspirational relationship between leader and followers.
- Transformational leaders use charisma and related qualities to inspire extraordinary efforts in support of innovation and large-scale change.
- Emotional intelligence, the ability to manage our relationships and ourselves effectively, is an important dimension of leadership capability.
- The interactive leadership style seems consistent with the demands of the new workplace and the emphasis on communication, involvement and interpersonal respect.
- All leadership is 'hard work' that always requires a personal commitment to meeting the highest ethical and moral standards.

KEY TERMS

authority decision (p. 364)

charismatic leaders (p. 366)

coercive power (p. 354)

consultative decision (p. 364)

emotional intelligence (p. 367)

empowerment (p. 356)

expert power (p. 354)

group decision (p. 364)

integrity (p. 370)

leadership style (p. 358)

leading (p. 352)

legitimate power (p. 354)

power (p. 353)

referent power (p. 355)

reward power (p. 354)

substitutes for leadership (p. 364)

transactional leadership (p. 366)

transformational leadership (p. 366)

vision (p. 353)

visionary leadership (p. 353)

APPLIED ACTIVITIES

Short-response questions

1. Why does a person need both position power and personal power to achieve long-term managerial effectiveness?
2. What is the major insight offered by the Vroom–Jago leader-participation model?
3. What are the three variables that Fiedler's contingency theory uses to diagnose the favourability of leadership situations, and what does each mean?
4. How does Peter Drucker's view of 'good old-fashioned leadership' differ from the popular concept of transformational leadership?

Application question

5. When Jason Mitchell took over as leader of a new product development team, he was both excited and apprehensive. 'I wonder', he said to himself on the first day in his new

assignment, 'if I can meet the challenges of leadership.' Later that day, Jason shares this concern with you during a coffee break. Based on the insights of this chapter, how would you describe to him the essential implications for his personal leadership development of the current thinking on charismatic or transformational leadership?

CAREER READINESS ACTIVITIES

Recommended individual and group learning activities from the end-of-text Career Readiness Workbook for this chapter include:

Career advancement portfolio **WB**

Update your career advancement portfolio to reflect your new skills and experiences. Include skills and personal insights you gain from the following projects and exercises.

Research and presentation projects **WB**

- Project 1 — Diversity lessons — 'what have we learned?'
- Project 2 — Changing corporate cultures

Cross-functional integrative case **WB**

Read the integrative case on Sarina Russo and answer the following questions:

13.1 What would you say is Sarina Russo's vision? What might have been her vision back in 1978 when establishing The Office Business Academy?

13.2 Describe Sarina Russo's power in terms of the position that she holds and in terms of her personal qualities.

Exercises in teamwork **WB**

- Exercise 2 — What managers do
- Exercise 18 — Sources and uses of power
- Exercise 20 — Gender differences in management

Management skills assessment **WB**

- Assessment 13 — Least-preferred coworker scale

ELECTRONIC RESOURCES

Don't forget to take full advantage of the online support for *Management: An Asia–Pacific Perspective* at www.johnwiley.com.au/highered/management: chapter 13 practice tests, e-flashcards, crossword puzzles, interactive management skills assessments, interactive cases, the online career advancement portfolio and much more!

CASE FOR CRITICAL THINKING

Read the following case for critical thinking on John Symond and Aussie Home Loans. While you are reading the case keep in mind what you have learned in this chapter, then answer the questions.

John Symond and Aussie Home Loans: how long can charisma last?

John Symond is the charismatic and dynamic CEO and owner (Symond owns 90 per cent) of Aussie Home Loans. His is the original and still best-known face of the non-bank home loan market. By 1998, however, Symond faced the questions that confront many business founders as they watch their enterprise grow: how can you move your business to the next phase of growth and improve operations while still taking a hands-on approach to managing every important aspect of the business? Is it possible to continue as chief strategist, promoter and operations manager of a company as it grows in size and expands into new locations and products?

Business history

Symond never had it easy in his quest for business success. During the 1980s, he lost $10 million in commercial land dealings that soured with the economic recession of the late 1980s and early 1990s. After selling all of his assets, including his family home, Symond fell $3 million short of paying off his debts. For some time he refused to take the easy option of bankruptcy and instead looked for other ways to escape his financial mess. The stress cost Symond his marriage. This period was significant, however, in giving Symond the determination to overcome his problems and pursue future success. He said, 'I had to go broke, I had to be emotionally shattered, and go through humiliation and end up on the mat to really understand the way society is and understand people who are disadvantaged. All this gave me the knowledge and the strength to get where I am today.'[64]

Discovering that Australian banks had the highest profit margin in the world on home loans, Symond sought backing to establish a low-overhead, no-frills mortgage provider that could beat the banks at their own game. With the financial backing of several small regional banks looking to establish a presence in the east coast market without facing significant costs, Symond moved to establish Aussie Home Loans. The cost of shopfronts was saved by using mobile lenders and potential customers were attracted to the idea of having lenders meet with them at convenient times in their own homes.

Without a substantial advertising budget, Symond aggressively used television advertisements and publicity to paint himself as the 'battler's friend' ready to help the mums and dads of suburban Sydney in their quest for a good-value home loan. The response was so strong that Aussie Home Loans could hardly keep pace with demand. By 1996, non-bank lenders held 16 per cent of the home loan market. Aussie was the segment leader with 5 per cent of the total market.

A need for change

During 1998, however, Aussie Home Loans faced a significant problem. Despite a 40 per cent increase in business in comparison with 1997, Aussie's profits dropped from $8 million to $4.5 million. Its internal systems were not coping with the volume of business, and the company seemed to lack the internal expertise to ensure that it retained its competitive edge at a time when banks were beginning to hit back with home loan products directly targeted at Aussie's market.

Until that time, Symond's leadership style could be characterised as energetic, hands-on and charismatic. He was in constant contact with staff members throughout the organisation, involved in all aspects of managing the business, and would give motivational talks based on his life experiences to salespeople so that they would perform with the kind of energy which characterised Symond's own work. Symond based many of his decisions on 'gut feel' and experience.

Symond realised that Aussie needed greater coordination and expertise. With offices around Australia, new products, 400 employees and possible international expansion looming, Symond sought the assistance of management consultants to suggest ways of restructuring and revitalising the company. The Morgan and Banks consultancy provided suggestions to improve Aussie's human resource management, while Pricewaterhouse-Coopers provided accounting expertise. In response, Symond hired a number of experienced specialist managers, devolved authority for many operational decisions to lower levels, and introduced regular strategic planning conferences. Since Symond could no longer meet regularly with all staff, Aussie Home Loans introduced regular employee surveys to monitor employee views and opinions. With 'gut feel' no longer appropriate for many decisions, new processes were introduced to ensure that all new proposals were considered through appropriate business measures.

Inevitably, the changes were not perfect. Existing employees found the changes were a significant threat to their traditional ways of working and to their organisational relationships. Many staff members found it difficult to withdraw from their close personal relationships with Symond.

The future for Aussie

Symond remains the public face of Aussie Home Loans, and retains a strong grip on the direction and management of the company. His comments indicate that he continues to view his role as central and critical in guiding Aussie's fortunes. He said, 'I represent it [Aussie Home Loans] and I am it … There is no way I would put John Symond in the position of not being able to make the decisions in control of the company.'[65]

Only time will tell whether Aussie continues to grow and whether it can restore its historic levels of profitability. For John Symond, there is no shortage of confidence in the company's future.[66]

QUESTIONS

1. How has John Symond's leadership style changed over the years?
2. What potential problems can you see arising from the changes made at AHL? What are the potential benefits?
3. Can you identify other examples of charismatic business leaders who have struggled with the transition as they sought to become large businesses?
4. Do you think that these changes will ensure the long-term success of John Symond and Aussie Home Loans? Why or why not?

CHAPTER 14

Motivation and rewards

CHAPTER 14 STUDY QUESTIONS

- What is motivation?

- What are the different types of individual needs?

- What are the process theories of motivation?

- What role does reinforcement play in motivation?

- What are the trends in motivation and compensation?

The Body Shop — keeping staff motivated in a high-turnover sector

The Body Shop, a retailer of natural cosmetics and toiletries, is attracting and keeping a stable, committed and highly motivated workforce in the dynamic retail sector.

It has achieved an employee turnover rate far lower than many of its competitors, with the average employee staying with The Body Shop for 5.4 years. How?

Staff at The Body Shop respond positively to the company's willingness to flex around their lifestyles. Many staff find that the company's image and philosophy complement their own attitudes to the environment and social justice.

Kam Vurlow of The Body Shop's Bourke Street store in Melbourne is a good example of how the company's approach succeeds. He has worked on and off for the company for eight years at stores in Geelong, Melbourne and Perth. He has also spent time working in Romania with The Body Shop's 'Children on the Edge' program.

Vurlow continues to work at The Body Shop while building a career in the film industry. 'I have so much passion, so much loyalty, towards this company. My mates work in other companies and, when we talk about work, I know just how unique this company is. Because of how The Body Shop treats me, I put in for them', he says.[1]

What do you want from work? Companies like The Body Shop offer staff the opportunity to combine their views on social issues with their job responsibilities. Visit www.thebodyshop.com.au to discover more information about The Body Shop and its approach to motivating and rewarding its staff.

GET CONNECTED!

Why do some people work enthusiastically, often doing more than required to turn out extraordinary performance? Why do others hold back and do the minimum needed to avoid reprimand or termination? How can a team leader or manager build a high-performance work setting? What can be done to ensure that the highest possible performance is achieved by every person in every job on every workday? These questions are, or should be, asked by managers in all work settings. Good answers begin with a true respect for people, with all of their talents and diversity, as the human capital of organisations. The best managers aleady know this. Like in the opening example of The Body Shop, the work cultures they create invariably reflect an awareness that 'productivity through people' is an essential ingredient of long-term organisational success. Consider these comments by those who know what it means to lead a high-performance organisation.

> If people connect with their meaning, an enormous energy and productivity can be released.[2]
>
> Michael Rennie, director of McKinsey & Co.

> Creating that kind of atmosphere, where people are gaining confidence in themselves, where they believe that by working here — whether it is one year or ten years — they are gaining something themselves; that they are better prepared, more marketable, have more things to offer to the world and to the marketplace then that is the hallmark of a really successful company in our business, and that is what separates us from the mediocre.[3]
>
> Bob Joss, Dean of the Graduate School of Business at Stanford University, and former CEO of Westpac Bank

> My number one customer is my team around me. I can't carry out the function and deliver the message myself. If you can inspire their confidence, their enthusiasm will roll out to your paying customers.[4]
>
> John Symond, CEO of Aussie Home Loans

It is easy to say as a leader or in a mission statement that 'people are our most important asset'. But the proof comes with backing such a statement up with actions that support it. This means consistently demonstrating that the organisation is committed to people and that it offers a truly 'motivational' work environment. In this sense, however, human nature is always both fascinating and challenging. The human side of the workplace becomes complicated as the intricacies of human psychology come into play with daily events and situations. At a packaging plant, for example, senior executive Kevin Kelley learned that a supervisor was starting to retire on the job. The man had worked his 20 years and felt it was time to slow down. He was unresponsive to gentle 'nudging' from coworkers and managers. But when Kelley politely confronted him with the facts, saying, 'We need your talent, your knowledge of those machines', the supervisor responded with new vigour in his work and earned the praise of his peers. For his part, Kelley believes in employee involvement and claims that one of the best motivators is information on the company's competitive environment. With information, so to speak, comes the motivation to work hard and keep the company competitive.[5]

WHAT IS MOTIVATION?

Motivation accounts for the level, direction and persistence of effort expended at work.

This chapter contains many ideas on how managers exercise leadership in ways that encourage other people to work hard in their jobs. The concept of **motivation** is central to this goal. The term is used in management theory to describe forces within the individual that account for the level, direction and persistence of effort expended at work. Simply put, a highly motivated person works hard at a job; an unmotivated person does not. A manager who leads through motivation does so by creating conditions under which other people feel consistently inspired to work hard. Obviously, a highly motivated workforce is indispensable to the achievement of sustained high-performance results.

Motivation and rewards

A *reward* is a work outcome of positive value to the individual. A motivational work setting is rich in rewards for people whose performance accomplishments help meet organisational objectives. In management, it is useful to distinguish between two types of rewards, extrinsic and intrinsic. **Extrinsic rewards** are externally administered. They are valued outcomes given to someone by another person, typically a supervisor or higher-level manager. Common workplace examples are pay bonuses, promotions, time off, special assignments, office fixtures, awards and verbal praise. In all cases, the motivational stimulus of extrinsic rewards originates outside of the individual; the rewards are made available by another person or by the organisational system.[6]

Intrinsic rewards, by contrast, are self-administered. They occur 'naturally' as a person performs a task and are, in this sense, built directly into the job itself. The major sources of intrinsic rewards are the feelings of competency, personal development and self-control people experience in their work.[7] In contrast to extrinsic rewards, the motivational stimulus of intrinsic rewards is internal and does not depend on the actions of some other person. Being self-administered, they offer the great advantage and power of 'motivating from within'. An air traffic controller, for example, says, 'I don't know of anything I'd rather be doing. I love working the airplanes.'[8]

Extrinsic rewards are provided by someone else.

Intrinsic rewards occur naturally during job performance.

Rewards and performance

Starbucks, the popular coffee house chain, seems to have the recipe right — not just for coffee, but also for rewards and performance. The company offers a store option plan to all its US employees. Called 'bean stock', the incentive plan offers employees share options linked to their base pay. This means they can buy the company's shares at a fixed price in the future; if the market value is higher than the price of their option, they gain. CEO Howard Schulz says the plan had an immediate impact on attitudes and performance. The phrase 'bean-stocking it' came to be used by employees when they found ways to reduce costs or increase sales. Schulz is committed to the motivational value of the innovative reward plan.[9]

There are many possible ways to creatively link rewards and performance in the new workplace — that is, to establish performance-contingent rewards. To take full advantage of the possibilities, however, managers must respect diversity and individual differences, clearly understand what people want from work and allocate rewards to satisfy the interests of both individuals and the organisation. Among the insights into this complex process that are available, the *content theories of motivation* help us to understand human needs and how people with different needs may respond to different work situations. The *process theories of motivation* offer additional insights into how people give meaning to rewards and then respond with various work-related behaviours. The *reinforcement theory of motivation* focuses attention on the environment as a major source of rewards and influence on human behaviour.

CONTENT THEORIES OF MOTIVATION

Most discussions of motivation begin with the concept of individual **needs** — the unfulfilled physiological or psychological desires of an individual. Content theories of motivation use individual needs to explain the behaviours and attitudes of people at work. The basic

Needs are unfulfilled physiological or psychological desires.

logic is straightforward. People have needs. They engage in behaviours to obtain extrinsic and intrinsic rewards to satisfy these needs. Although each of the following theories discusses a slightly different set of needs, all agree that needs cause tensions that influence attitudes and behaviours. Good managers and leaders establish conditions in which people are able to satisfy important needs through their work. They also take action to eliminate work obstacles that interfere with the satisfaction of important needs.

ENTREPRENEURSHIP

IBM • www.ibm.com

Investing in people

For organisations dedicated to innovation and customer service, there's no substitute for human capital in the form of knowledge, skills and experience. For IBM in Australia and New Zealand, getting and keeping the best talent is essential for success in the highly competitive information technology industry. Newly employed graduates complete an orientation course, are assigned to a 'buddy mentor' and regularly complete individual development plans. A range of benefits are available, from employee share ownership plans to health insurance discounts, and work-life balance is encouraged through individualised work schedules, flexible work weeks and telecommuting options.[10]

Hierarchy of needs theory

> **Lower-order needs** are physiological, safety and social needs in Maslow's hierarchy.

> **Higher-order needs** are esteem and self-actualisation needs in Maslow's hierarchy.

The theory of human needs developed by Abraham Maslow was introduced in chapter 4 as an important foundation of the history of management thought. Recall that according to his hierarchy of human needs, **lower-order needs** include physiological, safety and social concerns, and **higher-order needs** include esteem and self-actualisation concerns.[11] Whereas lower-order needs are desires for social and physical wellbeing, the higher-order needs represent a person's desires for psychological development and growth.

Maslow offers two principles to describe how these needs affect human behaviour. The *deficit principle* states that a satisfied need is not a motivator of behaviour. People are expected to act in ways that satisfy deprived needs — that is, needs for which a 'deficit' exists. The *progression principle* states that a need at one level does not become activated until the next-lower-level need is already satisfied. People are expected to advance step by step up the hierarchy in their search for need satisfactions. At the level of self-actualisation, the more these needs are satisfied, the stronger they are supposed to grow. According to Maslow, a person should continue to be motivated by opportunities for self-fulfilment as long as the other needs remain satisfied.

Although research has not verified the strict deficit and progression principles just presented, Maslow's ideas are very helpful for understanding the needs of people at work and for determining what can be done to satisfy them. His theory advises managers to recognise that deprived needs may negatively influence attitudes and behaviours. By the same token, providing opportunities for need satisfaction may have positive motivational consequences.

Figure 14.1 illustrates how managers can use Maslow's ideas to better meet the needs of the people with whom they work. Notice that the higher-order self-actualisation needs are served entirely by intrinsic rewards. The esteem needs are served by both intrinsic and extrinsic rewards. Lower-order needs are served solely by extrinsic rewards.

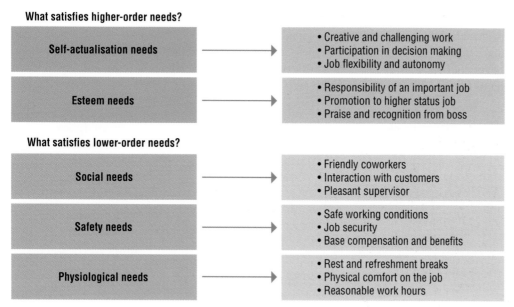

Figure 14.1 ▸ Opportunities for satisfaction in Maslow's hierarchy of human needs

ERG theory

One of the most promising efforts to build on Maslow's work is the ERG theory proposed by Clayton Alderfer.[13] This theory collapses Maslow's five needs categories into three. *Existence needs* are desires for physiological and material wellbeing. *Relatedness needs* are desires for satisfying interpersonal relationships. *Growth needs* are desires for continued psychological growth and development. Alderfer's ERG theory also differs from Maslow's theory in other respects. This theory does not assume that lower-level needs must be satisfied before higher-level needs become activated. According to ERG theory, any or all of these three types of needs can influence individual behaviour at a given time. Alderfer also does not assume that satisfied needs lose their motivational impact. ERG theory thus contains a unique *frustration–regression principle*, according to which an already-satisfied lower-level need can become reactivated and influence behaviour when a higher-level need cannot be satisfied. Alderfer's approach offers an additional means for understanding human needs and their influence on people at work.

Two-factor theory

Another framework for understanding the motivational implications of work environments is the two-factor theory of Frederick Herzberg.[14] The theory was developed from a pattern identified in the responses of almost 4000 people to questions about their work. When questioned about what 'turned them on', they tended to identify things relating to the nature of the job itself. Herzberg calls these **satisfier factors**. When questioned about what 'turned them off', they tended to identify things relating more to the work setting. Herzberg calls these **hygiene factors**.

Satisfier factors are found in job content, such as a sense of achievement, recognition, responsibility, advancement and personal growth.

Hygiene factors are found in the job context, such as working conditions, interpersonal relations, organisational policies and salary.

As shown in figure 14.2, the two-factor theory associates hygiene factors, or sources of job dissatisfaction, with aspects of *job context*. That is, 'dissatisfiers' are considered more likely to be a part of the work setting than of the nature of the work itself. The *hygiene factors* include such things as working conditions, interpersonal relations, organisational policies and administration, technical quality of supervision and base wage or salary. It is important to remember that Herzberg's two-factor theory would argue that improving the hygiene factors, such as by adding piped music or implementing a no-smoking policy, can make people less dissatisfied with these aspects of their work. But they would not in themselves contribute to increases in satisfaction. That requires attention to an entirely different set of factors and managerial initiatives.

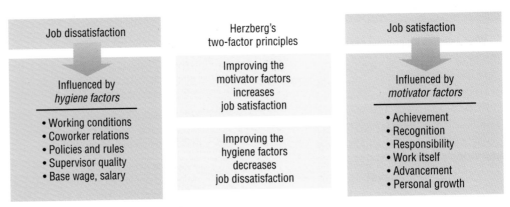

Figure 14.2 ▸ Herzberg's two-factor theory

To really improve motivation, Herzberg advises managers to give proper attention to the satisfier factors. As part of *job content* the satisfier factors deal with what people actually do in their work. By making improvements in what people are asked to do in their jobs, Herzberg suggests that job satisfaction and performance can be raised. The important *satisfier factors* include such things as a sense of achievement, feelings of recognition, a sense of responsibility, the opportunity for advancement and feelings of personal growth.

Scholars have criticised Herzberg's theory as being method-bound and difficult to replicate.[15] For his part, Herzberg reports confirming studies in countries located in Europe, Africa, the Middle East and Asia.[16] Other studies indicate that there is, at best, limited support for the theory. One study undertaken in New Zealand, for instance, found that the quality of supervision and interpersonal relationships were significant causes of satisfaction and motivation, but these are hygiene factors (associated with dissatisfaction) in the Herzberg model. Nonetheless, the model remains popular around the world, perhaps due to its simplicity and to the intuitive appeal of its concepts.[17] At the very least, the two-factor theory remains a useful reminder that there are two important aspects of all jobs: *job content* — what people do in terms of job tasks; and *job context* — the work setting in which they do it. Herzberg's advice to managers is still timely: always correct poor context to eliminate actual or potential sources of job dissatisfaction; and be sure to build satisfier factors into job content to maximise opportunities for job satisfaction. The two-factor theory also cautions managers not to expect too much by way of motivational improvements from investments in such things as special office fixtures, attractive lounges for breaks, and even high base salaries. Instead, it focuses on the nature of the job itself and directs attention toward such things as responsibility and opportunity for personal growth and development. These directions are very consistent with themes in the new workplace.

Acquired needs theory

In the late 1940s, David McClelland and his colleagues began experimenting with the Thematic Apperception Test (TAT) as a way of examining human needs. The TAT asks people to view pictures and write stories about what they see. The stories are then content analysed for themes that display individual needs.[18] From this research, McClelland identified three needs that are central to his approach to motivation. **Need for achievement (nAch)** is the desire to do something better or more efficiently, to solve problems, or to master complex tasks. **Need for power (nPower)** is the desire to control other people, to influence their behaviour, or to be responsible for them. **Need for affiliation (nAff)** is the desire to establish and maintain friendly and warm relations with other people.

According to McClelland, people acquire or develop these needs over time as a result of individual life experiences. In addition, he associates each need with a distinct set of work preferences. Managers are encouraged to recognise the strength of each need in themselves and in other people. Attempts can then be made to create work environments responsive to them. People high in the need for achievement, for example, like to put their competencies to work, they take moderate risks in competitive situations and they are willing to work alone. As a result, the work preferences of high-need achievers include individual responsibility for results, achievable but challenging goals and feedback on performance.

Through his research McClelland concludes that success in top management is not based on a concern for individual achievement alone. It requires broader interests that also relate to the needs for power and affiliation. People high in the need for power are motivated to behave in ways that have a clear impact on other people and events. They enjoy being in control of a situation and being recognised for this responsibility. A person with high need for power prefers work that involves control over other persons, has an impact on people and events and brings public recognition and attention.

Importantly, McClelland distinguishes between two forms of the power need. The *need for 'personal' power* is exploitative and involves manipulation for the pure sake of personal gratification. This type of power need is not successful in management. By contrast, the *need for 'social' power* is the positive face of power. It involves the use of power in a socially responsible way, one that is directed toward group or organisational objectives rather than personal ones. This need for social power is essential to managerial leadership.

People high in the need for affiliation seek companionship, social approval and satisfying interpersonal relationships. They take a special interest in work that involves interpersonal relationships, work that provides for companionship and work that brings social approval. McClelland believes that people very high in the need for affiliation alone may not make the best managers. For these managers, the desire for social approval and friendship may complicate managerial decision making. There are times when managers and leaders must decide and act in ways that other persons may disagree with. To the extent that the need for affiliation interferes with someone's ability to make these decisions, managerial effectiveness will be sacrificed. Thus, the successful executive, in McClelland's view, is likely to possess a high need for social power that is greater than an otherwise strong need for affiliation.

Questions and answers on content theories

Figure 14.3 shows how the human needs identified by Maslow, Alderfer, Herzberg and McClelland compare with one another. Although the terminology varies, there is a lot of common ground. The insights of the theories can and should be used together to add to our understanding of human needs in the workplace. By way of summary, the following questions and answers further clarify the content theories and their managerial implications.[20]

⊘ **Need for achievement (nAch)** is the desire to do something better, to solve problems, or to master complex tasks.

⊘ **Need for power (nPower)** is the desire to control, influence, or be responsible for other people.

⊘ **Need for affiliation (nAff)** is the desire to establish and maintain good relations with people.

www.paulhanna.com

Paul Hanna is one of Australia's most popular motivational speakers and writers. More than 8000 McDonald's staff and 5000 Toyota staff have attended his seminars. Telstra, Optus, NRMA and Qantas are among other corporate clients. Charlie Bell, former CEO of McDonald's Australia, says that Hanna 'causes us all to challenge ourselves, to do better, to try harder, and to enjoy what we do'.[19]

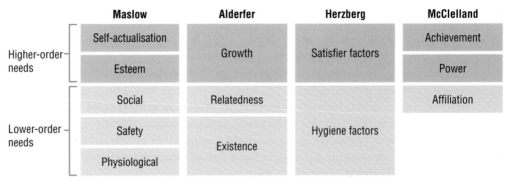

Maslow	Alderfer	Herzberg	McClelland

Higher-order needs

| Self-actualisation | Growth | Satisfier factors | Achievement |
| Esteem | | | Power |

Lower-order needs

Social	Relatedness		Affiliation
Safety	Existence	Hygiene factors	
Physiological			

Figure 14.3 ▸ Comparison of Maslow's, Alderfer's, Herzberg's and McClelland's motivation theories

How many different individual needs are there? Research has not yet identified a perfect list of individual needs at work. But, as a manager, you can use the ideas of Maslow, Alderfer, Herzberg and McClelland to better understand the various needs that people may bring with them to the work setting.

Can a work outcome or reward satisfy more than one need? Yes, work outcomes or rewards can satisfy more than one need. Pay is a good example. It is a source of performance feedback for the high need achiever. It can be a source of personal security for someone with strong existence needs. It can also be used indirectly to obtain things that satisfy social and ego needs.

Is there a hierarchy of needs? Research does not support the precise five-step hierarchy of needs postulated by Maslow. It seems more legitimate to view human needs as operating in a flexible hierarchy, such as the one in Alderfer's ERG theory. However, it is useful to distinguish between the motivational properties of lower-order and higher-order needs.

How important are the various needs? Research is inconclusive as to the importance of different needs. Individuals vary widely in this regard. For example, money may be an important reward, but studies show that it may not be the primary motivator for many employees. A recent New Zealand study of more than 600 people found that being able to contribute to organisational decisions, learn new things and confront exciting challenges, and having appropriate freedom and autonomy, top the list of workplace motivators.[21] People may also value needs differently at different times and at different ages or career stages. A number of writers have argued that the needs of baby boomer employees (those born in the years following the Second World War) are significantly different to those of generation X and generation Y employees. Baby boomers tend to be loyal and ambitious, value job status and security, and believe in process over outcomes. Generation Xers tend to be resourceful, individualistic, irreverent and difficult to retain given their preference for new career challenges and disdain for organisational hierarchies. In a recent survey, they listed job satisfaction, recognition and diversity of work/special projects as the three most important elements they desired in a job. Generation Yers are characterised by their information technology savvy and even greater idealism than generation Xers. Their focus on individuality will make traditional 'one size fits all' approaches to motivation even more outdated than they are today.[22] This is another reason that managers should use the insights of all the content theories to understand the differing needs of people at work.

PROCESS THEORIES OF MOTIVATION

Although the details vary, each of the content theories described in the last section can help managers better understand individual differences and deal positively with workforce diversity. Another set of theories, the process theories, add to this understanding. The equity, expectancy and goal-setting theories each offer advice and insight on how people actually make choices to work hard or not, based on their individual preferences, the available rewards and possible work outcomes.

Equity theory

The equity theory of motivation is best known through the work of J. Stacy Adams.[23] It is based on the logic of social comparisons and the notion that perceived inequity is a motivating state. That is, when people believe that they have been unfairly treated in comparison to others, they will be motivated to eliminate the discomfort and restore a perceived sense of equity to the situation. The classic example is pay. The equity question is: In comparison with others, how fairly am I being compensated for the work that I do? According to Adams's equity theory, an individual who perceives that she or he is being treated unfairly in comparison to others will be motivated to act in ways that reduce the perceived inequity.

Figure 14.4 shows how the equity dynamic works in the form of input-to-outcome comparisons. Equity comparisons are especially common whenever managers allocate extrinsic rewards like compensation, benefits, preferred job assignments and work privileges. The comparison points may be coworkers in the group, workers elsewhere in the organisation and even persons employed by other organisations. Perceived inequities occur whenever people feel that the rewards received for their work efforts are unfair given the rewards others appear to be getting for their work efforts. Adams predicts that people will try to deal with perceived negative inequity, the case where the individual feels disadvantaged in comparison with others, by:

- changing their work inputs by putting less effort into their jobs
- changing the rewards received by asking for better treatment
- changing the comparison points to make things seem better
- changing the situation by leaving the job.

Possible responses to perceived inequity

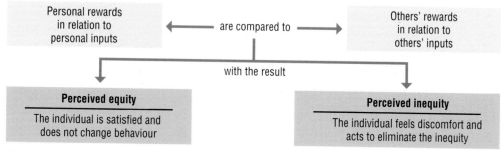

Figure 14.4 ▸ Equity theory and the role of social comparison

The research on equity theory has largely been accomplished in the laboratory. It is most conclusive with respect to perceived negative inequity. People who feel underpaid, for example, experience a sense of anger. This causes them to try to restore perceived equity to the situation by pursuing one or more of the actions described in the prior list, such as reducing current work efforts to compensate for the missing rewards or even quitting the job.[24] By the same token there is evidence that the equity dynamic occurs among people who feel overpaid. This time the perceived inequity is associated with a sense of guilt. The attempt to restore perceived equity may involve, for example, increasing the quantity or quality of work, taking on more difficult assignments, or working overtime.

Equity theory is another good reminder of a key point discussed in chapter 17 — people behave according to their perceptions. Here, the issue is the way rewards are perceived by their recipients. What influences individual behaviour is not the reward's absolute value or the manager's intentions. The recipient's perceptions of the reward in its social context determines the motivational outcomes. Rewards perceived as equitable should have a positive result on satisfaction and performance; those perceived as inequitable may create dissatisfaction and cause performance problems.

It is every manager's responsibility to ensure that any negative consequences of the equity comparison are avoided, or at least minimised, when rewards are allocated. Informed managers anticipate perceived negative inequities whenever especially visible rewards such as pay or promotions are allocated. Instead of letting equity concerns get out of hand, they carefully communicate the intended value of rewards being given, clarify the performance appraisals upon which they are based and suggest appropriate comparison points.

As mentioned earlier, pay is a common source of equity controversies in the workplace and its significance should never be underestimated. In addition to the general equity issues involved, two additional equity situations deserve special consideration. First is the issue of *gender equity*. Research undertaken by the Australian Council of Trade Unions reveals that the average taxable income for males is around 46 per cent higher than for females, reflecting differences in pay for men and women both within occupations as well as between occupations.[25] This difference is most evident in occupations traditionally dominated by men, such as the legal professions, but it also includes ones where females have traditionally held most jobs, such as teaching. Second is the issue of *comparable worth*. This is the concept that people doing jobs of similar value based on required education, training and skills (such as nursing and accounting) should receive similar pay. Advocates of comparable worth claim that it corrects historical pay inequities and is a natural extension of the 'equal-pay-for-equal-work' concept. Critics claim that 'similar value' is too difficult to define and that the dramatic restructuring of wage scales would have a negative economic impact on society as a whole.

A growing issue of workplace equity concerns the massive salaries paid to company CEOs and other senior managers. Some employees feel it is simply unfair that their own wage or salary seems so small compared to that of their organisation's leader. Some senior managers aim to lower this concern by actively demonstrating that they contribute to the organisation in a variety of ways. For example, Woolworths CEO Roger Corbett regularly visits his company's supermarkets. While there, he speaks to every staff member, shakes hands and makes eye contact with staff and customers, and encourages Woolworths employees to call him by his first name. He has also made sure that the remuneration of senior managers is closely linked to the performance of their department and to the overall performance of the company. By demonstrating his commitment to relating with all staff, listening to customers and walking the shop floor, Corbett aims to build confidence in the company and convince his staff that the rewards given to senior employees are deserved.[26]

Expectancy theory

Victor Vroom introduced to the management literature another process theory of work motivation that has made an important contribution.[28] The expectancy theory of motivation asks a central question: What determines the willingness of an individual to work hard at tasks important to the organisation? In response to this question, expectancy theory suggests that 'people will do what they can do when they want to do it'. More specifically,

REALITY CHECK

How much do bosses earn?

The average salary and benefits package of CEOs among 500 Australian companies surveyed was $700 000 in the 2000–01 financial year. Reflecting uncertain market conditions, the average had fallen 8 per cent from 1999–2000 levels after having risen 22 per cent in 1998–99.[27]

Do you think CEO pay is reasonable?

Vroom suggests that the motivation to work depends on the relationships between the *three expectancy factors*, depicted in figure 14.5 and described here.

- **Expectancy** is a person's belief that working hard will result in a desired level of task performance being achieved (this is sometimes called effort-performance expectancy).
- **Instrumentality** is a person's belief that successful performance will be followed by rewards and other potential outcomes (this is sometimes called performance-outcome expectancy).
- **Valence** is the value a person assigns to the possible rewards and other work-related outcomes.

Three expectancy factors

Expectancy is a person's belief that working hard will result in high task performance.

Instrumentality is a person's belief that various outcomes will occur as a result of task performance.

Valence is the value a person assigns to work-related outcomes.

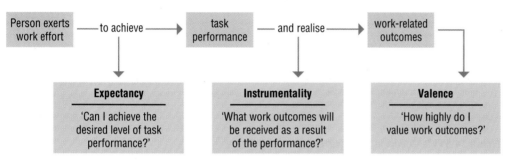

Figure 14.5 ▸ Elements in the expectancy theory of motivation

Expectancy theory posits that motivation (*M*), expectancy (*E*), instrumentality (*I*) and valence (*V*) are related to one another in a multiplicative fashion: $M = E \times I \times V$. In other words, motivation is determined by expectancy times instrumentality times valence. This multiplier effect among the expectancy factors has important managerial implications. Mathematically speaking, a zero at any location on the right side of the equation (that is, for *E*, *I* or *V*) will result in zero motivation. Managers are thus advised to act in ways that maximise all three components of the equation — expectancy (people must believe that if they try they can perform), instrumentality (people must perceive that high performance will be followed by certain outcomes) and valence (people must value the outcomes). Not one of these factors can be left unattended.

Suppose, for example, that a manager is wondering whether the prospect of earning a promotion will be motivational to a subordinate. A typical assumption is that people will be motivated to work hard to earn a promotion. But is this necessarily true? Expectancy theory predicts that a person's motivation to work hard for a promotion will be low if any one or more of the following three conditions apply. First, *if expectancy is low motivation will suffer*. The person may feel that he or she cannot achieve the performance level necessary to get promoted. So why try? Second, *if instrumentality is low motivation will suffer*. The person may lack confidence that a high level of task performance will result in being promoted. So why try? Third, *if valence is low motivation will suffer*. The person may place little value on receiving a promotion. It simply isn't much of a reward. So, once again, why try?

Expectancy theory makes managers aware of such issues. It can help them better understand and respond to different points of view in the workplace. As shown in figure 14.6, the management implications include being willing to work with each individual to maximise his or her expectancies, instrumentalities and valences in ways that support organisational objectives. Stated a bit differently, a manager should work with others to clearly link effort and performance, confirm performance-outcome relationships and reward performance with valued work outcomes.

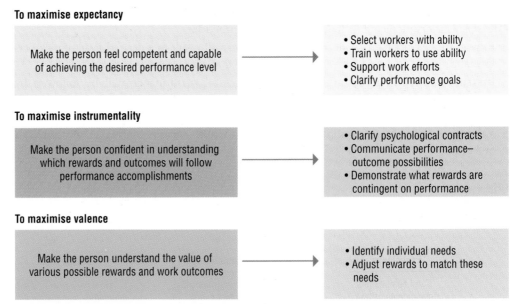

To maximise expectancy

Make the person feel competent and capable of achieving the desired performance level

- Select workers with ability
- Train workers to use ability
- Support work efforts
- Clarify performance goals

To maximise instrumentality

Make the person confident in understanding which rewards and outcomes will follow performance accomplishments

- Clarify psychological contracts
- Communicate performance–outcome possibilities
- Demonstrate what rewards are contingent on performance

To maximise valence

Make the person understand the value of various possible rewards and work outcomes

- Identify individual needs
- Adjust rewards to match these needs

Figure 14.6 ▸ Managerial implications of expectancy theory

Goal-setting theory

Another process theory, as described by Edwin Locke, focuses on the motivational properties of task goals.[29] The basic premise of this goal-setting theory is that task goals can be highly motivating — *if* they are properly set and *if* they are well managed. Goals give direction to people in their work. Goals clarify the performance expectations between a supervisor and subordinate, between coworkers, and across subunits in an organisation. Goals establish a frame of reference for task feedback. Goals also provide a foundation for behavioral self-management.[30] In these and related ways, Locke believes goal setting can enhance individual work performance and job satisfaction.

To achieve the motivational benefits of goal setting, research by Locke and his associates indicates that managers and team leaders must work with others to set the right goals in the right ways. The key issues and principles in managing this goal-setting process are described in Manager's Notepad 14.1, and 'participation' is an important element. The degree to which the person expected to do the work is involved in setting the performance goals can influence his or her satisfaction and performance. Research indicates that a positive impact is most likely to occur when the participation allows for increased understanding of specific and difficult goals and provides for greater acceptance and commitment to them. Along with participation, the opportunity to receive feedback on goal accomplishment is also essential to motivation.

The concept of *management by objectives* (MBO), first introduced in chapter 7 on planning and controlling, is a good illustration of a participative approach to joint goal setting by supervisors and subordinates. The MBO process helps to unlock and apply the motivational power of goal-setting theory. In addition to MBO, managers should be aware of the participation options. It may not always be possible to allow participation when selecting exactly which goals need to be pursued, but it may be possible to allow participation in the decisions about how to best pursue them. Furthermore, the constraints of time and other factors operating in some situations may not allow for participation. In these settings, research suggests that workers will respond positively to externally imposed goals if the supervisors assigning them are trusted and if the workers believe they will be adequately supported in their attempts to achieve them.

How to make goal setting work for you

* *Set specific goals.* They lead to higher performance than more generally stated ones, such as 'Do your best'.

* *Set challenging goals.* When viewed as realistic and attainable, more difficult goals lead to higher performance than do easier goals.

* *Build goal acceptance and commitment.* People work harder for goals they accept and believe in; they resist goals forced on them.

* *Clarify goal priorities.* Make sure that expectations are clear as to which goals should be accomplished first and why.

* *Provide feedback on goal accomplishment.* Make sure that people know how well they are doing in respect to goal accomplishment.

* *Reward goal accomplishment.* Don't let positive accomplishments pass unnoticed; reward people for doing what they set out to do.

At an Adelaide accounting firm, Perks Chartered Accountants, staff are encouraged to set goals that take them out of their comfort zones. For some, it might mean enrolling in an MBA program. For founder Greg Perks and manager Justin Hogan, the goal was to reach Base Camp 3, 6500 metres up Mount Everest. Perks said he hoped that setting 'stretch goals' would help take the company to 'new heights'.[31]

REINFORCEMENT THEORY OF MOTIVATION

The content and process theories described so far use cognitive explanations of behaviour. They are concerned with explaining 'why' people do things in terms of satisfying needs, resolving felt inequities, and/or pursuing positive expectancies and task goals. Reinforcement theory, by contrast, views human behaviour as determined by its environmental consequences. Instead of looking within the individual to explain motivation and behaviour, it focuses on the external environment and the consequences it holds for the individual. The basic premises of the theory are based on what E. L. Thorndike called the **law of effect** — behaviour that results in a pleasant outcome is likely to be repeated; behaviour that results in an unpleasant outcome is not likely to be repeated.[32]

Reinforcement strategies

Psychologist B. F. Skinner popularised the concept of **operant conditioning** as the process of applying the law of effect to control behaviour by manipulating its consequences.[33] You may think of operant conditioning as learning by reinforcement. In management the term is often discussed in respect to **organisational behaviour modification (OB Mod)**, the application of operant conditioning techniques to influence human behaviour in the workplace.[34] The goal of OB Mod is to use reinforcement principles to systematically reinforce desirable work behaviour and discourage undesirable work behaviour.

Four strategies of reinforcement are used in operant conditioning. **Positive reinforcement** strengthens or increases the frequency of desirable behaviour by making a pleasant consequence contingent on its occurrence. For example, a manager nods to express approval to

The **law of effect** states that behaviour followed by pleasant consequences is likely to be repeated; behaviour followed by unpleasant consequences is not.

Operant conditioning is the control of behaviour by manipulating its consequences.

Organisational behaviour modification (OB Mod) is the application of operant conditioning to influence human behaviour at work.

Positive reinforcement strengthens a behaviour by making a desirable consequence contingent on its occurrence.

Negative reinforcement strengthens a behaviour by making the avoidance of an undesirable consequence contingent on its occurrence.

Punishment discourages a behaviour by making an unpleasant consequence contingent on its occurrence.

Extinction discourages a behaviour by making the removal of a desirable consequence contingent on its occurrence.

someone who makes a useful comment during a staff meeting. **Negative reinforcement** increases the frequency of or strengthens desirable behaviour by making the avoidance of an unpleasant consequence contingent on its occurrence. For example, a manager who has been nagging a worker every day about tardiness does not nag when the worker comes to work on time one day. **Punishment** decreases the frequency of or eliminates an undesirable behaviour by making an unpleasant consequence contingent on its occurrence. For example, a manager issues a written reprimand to an employee who reports late for work one day. **Extinction** decreases the frequency of or eliminates an undesirable behaviour by making the removal of a pleasant consequence contingent on its occurrence. For example, a manager observes that a disruptive employee is receiving social approval from coworkers; the manager counsels coworkers to stop giving this approval.

An example of how these four reinforcement strategies can be applied in management is shown in figure 14.7. The supervisor's goal in the example is to improve work quality as part of a total quality management program. Note how the supervisor can use each of the strategies to influence continuous improvement practices among employees. Note, too, that the strategies of both positive and negative reinforcement strengthen desirable behaviour when it occurs. The punishment and extinction strategies weaken or eliminate undesirable behaviours.

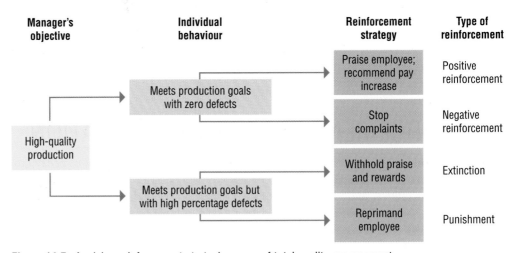

Figure 14.7 ▸ Applying reinforcement strategies: case of total quality management

Positive reinforcement

Among the reinforcement strategies, positive reinforcement deserves special attention. It should be a central part of any manager's motivational strategy. The multilevel marketing sector is one of the best examples of the successful use of this approach. Amway has long provided recognition pins for its distributors as they reach new levels of success, and companies such as Nutrimetics and Tupperware provide company cars to their best performers.

All managers would do well to understand two important laws of positive reinforcement. First, the *law of contingent reinforcement* states: For a reward to have maximum reinforcing value, it must be delivered only if the desired behaviour is exhibited. Second, the *law of immediate reinforcement* states: The more immediate the delivery of a reward after the occurrence of a desirable behaviour, the greater the reinforcing value of the reward. Managers should use these laws to full advantage in the everyday pursuit of the benefits of positive reinforcement. Several useful guidelines are presented in Manager's Notepad 14.2.

Guidelines for positive reinforcement . . . and punishment

Positive reinforcement

- Clearly identify desired work behaviours.
- Maintain a diverse inventory of rewards.
- Inform everyone what must be done to get rewards.
- Recognise individual differences when allocating rewards.
- Follow the laws of immediate and contingent reinforcement.

Punishment

- Tell the person what is being done wrong.
- Tell the person what is being done right.
- Make sure the punishment matches the behaviour.
- Administer the punishment in private.
- Follow the laws of immediate and contingent reinforcement.

> **Shaping** is positive reinforcement of successive approximations to the desired behaviour.

www.tupperware.com.au
www.tupperware.co.nz

At plastic and giftware company Tupperware, distributors who reach 'manager' level receive a station wagon, whereas those who become 'executive directors' may choose from a range of prestige vehicles. To reach this level, the team of distributors recruited by the Tupperware distributor must be selling more than $750 000 in Tupperware products each year.[35]

The power of positive reinforcement can be mobilised through a process known as **shaping**. This is the creation of a new behaviour by the positive reinforcement of successive approximations to it. The timing of positive reinforcement can also make a difference in its impact. A *continuous reinforcement schedule* administers a reward each time a desired behaviour occurs. An *intermittent reinforcement schedule* rewards behaviour only periodically. In general, a manager can expect that continuous reinforcement will elicit a desired behaviour more quickly than will intermittent reinforcement. Also, behaviour acquired under an intermittent schedule will be more permanent than will behaviour acquired under a continuous schedule. One way to succeed with a shaping strategy, for example, is to give reinforcement on a continuous basis until the desired behaviour is achieved. Then an intermittent schedule can be used to maintain the behaviour at the new level.

Punishment

As a reinforcement strategy, punishment attempts to eliminate undesirable behaviour by making an unpleasant consequence contingent with its occurrence. To punish an employee, for example, a manager may deny the individual a valued reward, such as verbal praise or merit pay, or the manager may administer an unpleasant outcome, such as a verbal reprimand or pay reduction. Like positive reinforcement, punishment can be done poorly or it can be done well. Unfortunately, it may often be done poorly. If you look back to Manager's Notepad 14.2, it offers guidance on how to best handle punishment as a reinforcement strategy. Remember, too, that punishment can be combined with positive reinforcement.

Ethical issues in reinforcement

The use of OB Mod and reinforcement techniques in work settings has produced many success stories of improved safety, decreased absenteeism and tardiness, and increased productivity.[36] But there are also debates over both the results and the ethics of controlling human behaviour. Opponents are concerned that use of operant conditioning principles ignores the individuality of people, restricts their freedom of choice and ignores the fact that people can be motivated by things other than externally administered rewards. Advocates attack the criticisms straight on. They agree that reinforcement involves the control of behaviour, but they argue that control is part of every manager's job. The real question may be not whether it is ethical to control behaviour but whether it is ethical not to control behaviour well enough so that the goals of both the organisation and the individual are well served. Even as research continues, the value of reinforcement techniques seems confirmed. This is especially true when they are combined with the insights of the other motivation theories discussed in this chapter.[37]

MOTIVATION AND COMPENSATION

By way of summary, figure 14.8 offers an integrative view of motivation that takes advantage of insights from each of the theoretical perspectives discussed so far. It shows how they can be combined into one model of motivational dynamics in the workplace. In this figure motivation leads to effort that, when combined with appropriate individual abilities and organisational support, leads to performance. The motivational impact of any rewards received for this performance depends on equity and reinforcement considerations. Ultimately, satisfaction with rewards should lead to increased motivation to work hard in the future.

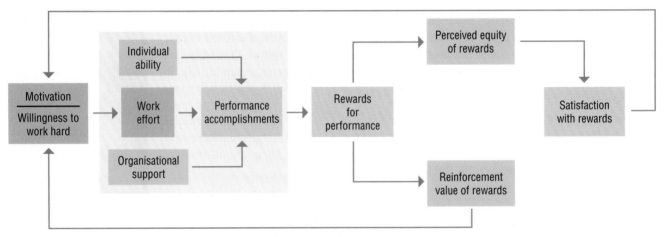

Figure 14.8 ▸ An integrated approach to motivational dynamics

Of the motivation issues that can be addressed within this framework, perhaps none receives as much attention as the special case of compensation.[38] There are many advantages, both individual and organisational, to be gained from a truly motivational compensation scheme. In general, the success of any such system lies in its ability to apply the alternative motivation theories in positive and credible ways. In practice, however, the link between motivation and compensation is usually very complicated.

Pay for performance

Merit pay awards pay increases in proportion to performance contributions.

The notion of paying people for their performance is consistent with the equity, expectancy and reinforcement theories.[39] Formally defined, **merit pay** is a compensation system that awards pay increases in proportion to individual performance contributions. By allocating pay increases in this way, managers are attempting to recognise and positively reinforce high performers and to encourage them to work hard for similar accomplishments in the future. They are also attempting to remind low performers of their lack of achievement and send a signal that they must do better in the future.

The concept of merit pay is a logical extension of the motivation theories. In principle at least, it makes sense to reward people in proportion to their work contributions. Because of the difficulty of actually linking pay with performance in a truly contingent and equitable manner, however, merit pay does not always achieve the desired results. A successful merit pay system must have a solid foundation in agreed-upon and well-defined 'performance measures'. Any weakness in the performance appraisal methods can undermine a merit pay system, and lack of consistency in applying merit pay at all levels of the organisation can jeopardise its credibility. There is concern today, for example, that CEO pay isn't adequately linked to performance. Magazines like *BRW* and *Fortune* regularly report on the issues. The impression of some is that CEOs are well rewarded no matter how well the company performs. For example, after recording a $291 million annual loss, failed telecommunications company One.Tel paid directors Jodee Rich and Brad Keeling a $6.9 million bonus on top of their $500 000 salaries. The bonus was based on the company's sharemarket value at the time, rather than on profits. One.Tel appears to have been struggling during the period in which the bonuses were paid and the company collapsed just months later. When One.Tel's investors, customers and the general public claimed mismanagement, Rich and Keeling offered to return their bonuses. Their pain may not have been too great, however, since they had earlier shared more than $50 million when James Packer and Lachlan Murdoch bought into the company.[40]

For these and related reasons, not everyone believes in merit pay. John Whitney, author of *The Trust Factor*, suggests that pay for performance may not work very well. While pointing out that market forces should determine base pay, Whitney believes that organisations can benefit by making the annual merit increase an equal percentage of base. This communicates a universal sense of importance and helps to avoid frustrations and complaints when merit increases are tied to performance differences. Says Whitney: 'Quibbling over whether someone should get a 4.7% raise or 5.1% is a colossal waste of time'.[41]

POINT ←

COUNTER ↑

Do US motivational methods work in Australia and New Zealand?

Can motivational methods developed within the culture of the USA be used effectively in Australian and New Zealander organisations? Don Meij, a Queensland Domino's Pizza franchisee, has found that they can. Meij was convinced some of the enthusiasm and excitement seen among Australian sport crowds could be created in the workplace. Meij uses US-style motivational techniques such as football-style chants and pep talks to keep his 200, mostly young, staff motivated. He also uses hatpins to recognise skill advancement and gives small prizes for quality and speed. It seems to work. Domino's recognised Meij as its best franchisee outside the USA in 1996, and store profitability and productivity is so high that Meij can pay off each store in less than two-and-a-half years.[42]

Do you think these motivational methods could be successfully transferred to other sectors and to people in other age groups, or has Meij discovered the only niche in which they could succeed?

Incentive compensation systems

Today, employees at all levels in more and more organisations are benefiting from special incentive compensation systems of many forms. Examples include pay for knowledge, bonus pay plans, profit-sharing plans, gain-sharing plans and employee share ownership plans.[43] As you consider the descriptions that follow, however, remember that any incentive compensation system will work only as well as its implementation. The well-known compensation scholar and consultant Edward Lawler, for example, tells of this experience.[44] While consulting with a furniture manufacturing plant, he became convinced that a 'gain sharing' incentive plan would be helpful and thus advised the plant manager on starting one. The manager proceeded only reluctantly, claiming, 'These guys are already paid enough … they should be happy to have a job'. Says Lawler: 'Although the program was somewhat successful, the plant manager's continuing tendency to call it an "employee bribe program" definitely limited its success'.

Skills-based pay is a system of paying workers according to the number of job-relevant skills they master.

PAY FOR KNOWLEDGE

In addition to paying for performance, some organisations now emphasise paying for knowledge. A concept called **skills-based pay**, for example, pays workers according to the number of job-relevant skills they master. Many government departments and agencies reward their people in this way. The government of the Australian Capital Territory, for instance, has developed a framework which incorporates more than 200 individual competency units, 21 qualifications and an overall assessment regime which seeks to link rewards to the skills, competencies and qualifications of its employees.[45] Skills-based pay systems are common in self-managing teams where part of the 'self-management' includes responsibilities for the training and certification of coworkers in job skills.

BONUS PAY

Bonus pay plans provide one-off or lump-sum payments to employees based on the accomplishment of specific performance targets or some other extraordinary contribution, such as an idea for a work improvement. They typically do not increase base salary or wages. Bonuses have been most common at the executive level, but they are now being used more extensively. Bonuses are not always inevitable, and are raised or cut in line with company performance. For example, the chief executive of publishing company John Fairfax Holdings, Fred Hilmer, had more than $216 000 sliced from his performance bonus in 2001 after the company's performance slipped.[46]

PROFIT SHARING

Profit-sharing plans distribute to some or all employees a proportion of net profits earned by the organisation during a stated performance period. The exact amount typically varies according to the level of profits and each person's base compensation. Profit-sharing schemes have long been common in professions such as accounting and law and are becoming increasingly common elsewhere. At accounting firm PricewaterhouseCoopers, profit splits are determined by each partner's level of responsibilities and by a performance appraisal conducted by their immediate supervisors. At Ernst & Young an internal committee allocates points for performance on the basis of recommendations from the managing partner.[48]

GAIN SHARING

Gain-sharing plans extend the profit-sharing concept by allowing groups of employees to share in any savings or 'gains' realised through their efforts to reduce costs and increase productivity. Specific formulas are used to calculate both the performance contributions and gain-sharing awards. The classic example is the Scanlon plan, which usually results in 75 per cent of gains being distributed to workers and 25 per cent being kept by the company. Recognising that each work situation is different, there is a general move away from pre-defined formulas to custom-designed approaches that reinforce the link between pay and performance for specific work groups.[49]

EMPLOYEE SHARE OWNERSHIP

Employee share ownership plans (ESOPs) involve employees in ownership through the purchase of shares in the companies that employ them. Whereas formal ESOPs are often used as financing schemes to save jobs and prevent business closings, share ownership by employees is an important performance incentive. It can be motivating to have an ownership share in one's place of employment. An approach to employee ownership through share options gives the option holder the right to buy shares at a future date at a fixed price. This links ownership directly with a performance incentive, since employees holding share options presumably are motivated to work hard to raise the price of the company's shares. When the price has risen they can exercise their option and buy the shares at a discount, thus realising a financial gain. Share options are most common in senior executive compensation, but their use is spreading to include lower-level employees.

Many of the most admired companies in the Asia–Pacific region offer share options to their workforces. At Flight Centre, more than 50 per cent of all employees bought shares in the company when they were initially offered during 1995. By 2000, the share price had risen from the listing price of 75 cents to more than $20. A survey by KPMG found that only a small number of Australian companies offered share ownership schemes, but a significant number of companies planned to introduce ESOPs in the near future. Of companies using ESOPs, 63 per cent said the scheme was a contributing factor to improved business performance.[50] One of the issues to be considered with share options, however, relates to their risk. If a company's shares perform poorly, the options it is offering as a performance incentive are worth less; their motivational value is largely eliminated. When the technology companies experienced a downturn in the stock market, for example, many employees were disappointed with incentive pay that was tied to share options. Many firms experienced turnover problems as talented employees resigned to pursue other and more promising opportunities. As a result, there was a resurgence of interest in adding cash bonuses to the incentive compensation packages. In an industry where human capital is paramount to success, the most progressive employers responded. How would you like to someday receive a letter like this one sent to two top executives by Amazon.com's chairman Jeff Bezos? 'In recognition and appreciation of your contributions', his letter read, 'Amazon.com will pay you a special bonus in the amount of $1 000 000 (one million dollars).'[51] Not bad for a performance incentive!

GET CONNECTED!

View the results of the Hewitt Associates 'Best Employers to Work For in Australia' survey at www.bestemployers australia.com.

GET CONNECTED!

Study guide

The chapter 14 study guide helps you review the chapter content, prepare for examinations, apply what you have learned and further build your career readiness. The summary briefly answers the study questions posed at the start of the chapter. The list of key terms allows you to double-check your familiarity with basic concepts and definitions. The applied activities help you test your comprehension of chapter content. Suggestions offered as career readiness activities direct your attention to relevant sections of the Career Readiness Workbook where you can test and develop your career skills and apply what you have learned. The list of electronic resources suggests activities from the *Management: An Asia–Pacific Perspective* web site and, finally, the case for critical thinking helps you apply your new management knowledge.

SUMMARY

What is motivation?

- Motivation involves the level, direction and persistence of effort expended at work; simply put, a highly motivated person works hard.
- Extrinsic rewards are given by another person; intrinsic rewards derive naturally from the work itself.
- To maximise the motivational impact of rewards, they should be allocated in ways that respond to both individual and organisational needs.
- The three major types of motivation theories are the content, process and reinforcement theories.

What are the different types of individual needs?

- Maslow's hierarchy of human needs suggests a progression from lower-order physiological, safety and social needs to higher-order ego and self-actualisation needs.
- Alderfer's ERG theory identifies existence, relatedness and growth needs.
- Herzberg's two-factor theory points out the importance of both job content and job context factors in satisfying human needs.
- McClelland's acquired needs theory identifies the needs for achievement, affiliation and power, all of which may influence what a person desires from work.
- Managers should respect individual differences and diversity to create motivating work environments.

What are the process theories of motivation?

- Adams's equity theory recognises that social comparisons take place when rewards are distributed in the workplace.
- People who feel inequitably treated are motivated to act in ways that reduce the sense of inequity; perceived negative inequity may result in someone working less hard in the future.
- Vroom's expectancy theory states that Motivation = Expectancy × Instrumentality × Valence.
- Expectancy theory encourages managers to make sure that any rewards offered for motivational purposes are both achievable and individually valued.

- Locke's goal-setting theory emphasises the motivational power of goals; people tend to be highly motivated when task goals are specific rather than ambiguous, difficult but achievable and set through participatory means.

What role does reinforcement play in motivation?

- Reinforcement theory recognises that human behaviour is influenced by its environmental consequences.
- The law of effect states that behaviour followed by a pleasant consequence is likely to be repeated; behaviour followed by an unpleasant consequence is unlikely to be repeated.
- Reinforcement strategies used by managers include positive reinforcement, negative reinforcement, punishment and extinction.
- Positive reinforcement works best when applied according to the laws of contingent and immediate reinforcement.

What are the trends in motivation and compensation?

- The area of compensation provides a good test of a manager's ability to integrate and apply the insights of all motivation theories.
- Pay for performance in the form of merit pay plans ties pay increases to performance increases.
- Various incentive compensation programs, such as bonuses, gain sharing and profit sharing, allow workers to benefit materially from improvements in profits and productivity.
- Pay-for-knowledge systems typically link pay to the mastery of job-relevant skills.

KEY TERMS

expectancy (p. 387)

extinction (p. 390)

extrinsic rewards (p. 379)

higher-order needs (p. 380)

hygiene factors (p. 381)

instrumentality (p. 387)

intrinsic rewards (p. 379)

law of effect (p. 389)

lower-order needs (p. 380)

merit pay (p. 392)

motivation (p. 378)

need for achievement (nAch) (p. 383)

need for affiliation (nAff) (p. 383)

need for power (nPower) (p. 383)

needs (p. 379)

negative reinforcement (p. 390)

operant conditioning (p. 389)

organisational behaviour modification (OB Mod) (p. 389)

positive reinforcement (p. 389)

punishment (p. 390)

satisfier factors (p. 381)

shaping (p. 391)

skills-based pay (p. 394)

valence (p. 387)

APPLIED ACTIVITIES

Short-response questions

1. What types of preferences does a person high in the need for achievement bring with him or her to the workplace?
2. Why is participation important to goal-setting theory?
3. What is motivation to work?
4. What is the managerial significance of Herzberg's distinction between factors in the job content and job context?

Application question

5. How can a manager combine the powers of goal setting and positive reinforcement to create a highly motivational environment for workers with high needs for achievement?

CAREER READINESS ACTIVITIES

Recommended individual and group learning activities from the end-of-text Career Readiness Workbook for this chapter include:

Career advancement portfolio   **WB**

Update your career advancement portfolio to reflect your new skills and experiences. Include skills and personal insights you gain from the following projects and exercises.

Research and presentation project   **WB**

• Project 6 — Controversies in CEO pay — 'is it too high?'

Cross-functional integrative case   **WB**

Read the integrative case on Sarina Russo and answer the following questions:

14.1 Identify examples of extrinsic and intrinsic rewards with reference to Sarina Russo.

14.2 Discuss the three needs identified by David McClelland with reference to Sarina Russo. Which do you think might dominate in her case?

14.3 McClelland distinguishes between two forms of the power need: personal power and social power. Which is most applicable to Sarina Russo? Who might represent examples of the other form of power thought less applicable to Sarina Russo?

Exercises in teamwork   **WB**

• Exercise 7 — What do you value in work?
• Exercise 11 — Essentials of motivation
• Exercise 17 — Compensation and benefits debate

Management skills assessment   **WB**

• Assessment 14 — Two-factor profile

ELECTRONIC RESOURCES

Don't forget to take full advantage of the online support for *Management: An Asia–Pacific Perspective* at www.johnwiley.com.au/highered/management: chapter 14 practice tests, e-flashcards, crossword puzzles, interactive management skills assessments, interactive cases, the online career advancement portfolio and much more!

CASE FOR CRITICAL THINKING

Read the following case for critical thinking on the Saturn Corporation. While you are reading the case keep in mind what you have learned in this chapter, then answer the questions.

CASE FOR CRITICAL THINKING
Saturn Corporation: making pay for performance pay off

As one of the world's best known brands, Saturn, the General Motors car division that brought new production and marketing concepts to American car manufacturers, faces tough questions in an increasingly competitive global market. Its reliance on a limited offering of compact models hurts its performance in the face of declining sales. Can it continue to set the standards for customer satisfaction and reliability and depend on an innovative employee pay-for-performance package?

The Saturn story

Jack Smith Jr, appointed CEO and president of General Motors Corporation in 1992 after a revolt of the outside members of the board of directors, noted that the firm had turned around its losing ways by focusing on its customers. In a speech to car dealers, he cited the success of the Saturn Division of GM for setting the standard for 'hassle-free purchasing and services, and . . . exceeding customer expectations'. Smith further noted that this success had led to the addition of a third shift at the Tennessee complex that produced Saturns. Moreover, Saturn dealers continued to lead all dealer organisations in the USA in unit sales per outlet.[52]

The original plan, developed in 1982, was given to Richard LeFauve, who was named President of Saturn Corporation after its first president died shortly after the company was set up. The plan called for a US$5 billion investment in a series of plants that would produce up to 350 000 cars per year. By 1988, when the plant was just about completed, the investment had been trimmed to approximately US$3 billion.

The Saturn complex was comprised of a series of six interconnected buildings. Four of the six buildings were manufacturing and assembly plants. The other two were a maintenance and utilities facility and a training and administration building. The complex had a rated production capacity of 240 000 cars per year. This was to be expanded to 310 000 with the addition of a third shift in 1993.

The Saturn Corporation was the first new automotive division of General Motors since 1918. The purpose of developing a new division was to meet the competition of Japanese manufacturers, particularly at the lower end of the product line.[53] GM had seen its share of the US market fall throughout the 1970s. This was especially true for lower-priced cars. US car consumers no longer had confidence in the ability of GM to be able to produce a low-priced, high-quality car. Roger Smith, then CEO of GM, felt that the only way to overcome this perception was to launch an entirely new line of cars. The technology, labour policies, work rules and marketing of this new product were to be developed from scratch; there would be no preconceived notions concerning any of these areas brought in from the existing organisation structure or culture.[54]

The initial phase of planning for the Saturn Corporation was carried out by bringing together managers and workers from 55 plants in 17 GM divisions. The 'Group of 99' — so named because it consisted of 99 United Auto Workers (UAW) members, GM managers and staff personnel — started meeting in 1984.[55] The group quickly split into separate research teams to study all aspects of the new operation. One of the teams realised that labour relations would be a critical factor in the development and implementation of a successful new offering. GM entered into separate negotiations with the UAW to develop a new contract strictly for the Saturn Corporation.

The rest of GM was covered by a master contract with the UAW, which covered not only wages, benefits and hours of work, but also a complex series of work rules that restricted

GM's ability to transfer workers from one task to another on the production line. GM felt that the effectiveness of the new Saturn Corporation would be dependent on more flexible work rules. Management wanted the ability to develop the kind of work flexibility found in most Swedish and Japanese car plants. The UAW finally agreed to a system of self-governing work teams on the production line at the Saturn assembly plant. These teams would be designed to follow the construction of a car unit throughout the entire assembly line. Under the terms of the contract, workers would be cross-trained so that the members of each team could switch between the various tasks required to complete the assembly of each individual unit.

Saturn uses a 'risk and reward compensation system' that puts 12 per cent of a worker's pay at risk, contingent on performance as follows:

1. 5 per cent risk on quality — a threshold, measured in reduction of sample defects per vehicle, that must be met before the reward portion, which also contains a quality goal, can kick in
2. 5 per cent risk on training
3. 2 per cent risk on team skills.

All Saturn workers are paid at a rate equal to 88 per cent of average GM compensation. The 12 per cent at risk brings pay 'up to a line' roughly equal with industry averages, with the reward portion providing possibilities 'above the line'.[56] The basis for the reward portion contains provisions regarding schedules, productivity and quality. Saturn uses the Uniform Vehicle Evaluation system, an international standard in which auditors enter the plant and select 20 to 25 cars at random and evaluate these for sample defects.[57] With the US public's loss of appetite for small cars, the system may need to be revamped for cost reduction rather than output. In early 1998, the Saturn union voted to retain the innovative system — 4052 in favour with 2120 opposed.[58]

In many ways, this was similar to the assembly process employed by Volvo at some of its car plants which had led to increased quality, decreased boredom and increased job satisfaction on the part of its workers. Each member of the Saturn work team was put through an extensive training program before joining the assembly line. The 350 hours of training were designed to cover both technical and team-building aspects of the job.

Richard LeFauve was selected as the new president of Saturn Corporation because of his experience within GM. He had spent two years in charge of GM's Adam Opel unit in Germany, where he had supervised the development of a sporty new Kadett model. Moreover, LeFauve had gained experience with the German labour-management system. Under German co-determination laws, labour is required to have a say in decision making and management is required to grant labour a position on the board of directors. This, it was felt, would give LeFauve better insight into the problems that might develop as the new labour contract was implemented.

GM management sought and developed new technology and machinery consistent with the new labour agreement. A great many robots and other forms of automation were incorporated into the production line to help reduce employee boredom and fatigue and to help ensure high quality standards. Furthermore, company engineers developed a platform that was designed to move along with the car. In this manner, workers no longer needed to walk at a steady pace beside the car to be able to complete their tasks; instead, workers and the car moved together on the new platform.

The new organisation was built around several key factors. They included:

- quality as a top priority
- ownership by all
- equality of all
- total trust
- people orientation
- union–management partnership
- authority commensurate with responsibility.

These factors were put to the test in 1991. Unfortunately, the results of the first year of operation indicated that the Saturn plant would not meet its goals. Under the terms of the Saturn–UAW contract, workers could suffer penalties that would mean their salary would equal approximately 80 per cent of the average GM worker's annual wages. There was concern that the workers would find this unacceptable since some of the failure was not their fault. Furthermore, there had been quality lapses in the initial products. Even though many had been caught and corrected before the cars left the plant, other cars had to be recalled. All of these factors led to lower production, productivity and quality standards than had originally been planned for the first year.

Management decided to share the responsibility for falling short of the first-year goals. It relaxed the terms of the contact and essentially granted bonuses that brought Saturn salaries to approximately 95 per cent of an hourly worker's average annual wage. Management hoped this would convince the workers that the company planned to live up to the seven key points outlined earlier.

It was still unclear, however, whether the Saturn cars being sold were replacing Japanese sales or cars that would have been sold by other GM units. Moreover, GM management realised that sales of Saturn cars could not possibly recoup the original US$3 billion investment in the new unit. They would have to be able to transfer the ideas, technology, concepts and labour relations developed for the Saturn plants to other parts of the GM organisation to make the investment worthwhile.

To compound problems, the new workers that were being added to the Saturn workforce were being recruited from closed GM plants, under an agreement with the UAW. These new workers were being rushed onto the production line with only one-third the training time of the original Saturn workers. Many managers and original members of the Saturn union felt that these two factors might reduce morale at the Saturn complex and could lead to a decline in the quality standards that had contributed to the success of this unit. Both Smith and LeFauve knew that the continued growth and quality of the Saturn projects and service would be key factors in the success of GM as a whole.

Saturn's future

The Saturn story has been one of alternating success and failure in the 1990s. IntelliChoice ranked the 1997 SL1, SL2, SC1 and SC2 models as the 'Best Overall Values' in their respective classes. J. D. Power put Saturn in first place for sales satisfaction and seventh in customer satisfaction. (The top six were all luxury cars — Lexus, Infiniti, Acura, Mercedes-Benz, Cadillac and Jaguar.)

At the same time, the competition in the small-car market is increasing dramatically. Experts claim that Saturn's limited line-up is holding back sales, with the car company only offering a coupe, sedan and wagon — all small cars based on the same architecture and looking much the same. Saturn brought a new midsize car on line in 1999, and added a sport-utility vehicle in 2001.[59] Saturn desperately needs to broaden its product line in order to stay competitive.[60]

New initiatives include an attempt to open foreign markets, with Japan targeted with 80 dealerships. In addition, GM wants Saturn to market its electric vehicle, the EV-1.[61] Mike Bennett, head of the UAW Local 1853 at Saturn, states: 'We're going to be a 100-year car company, right? Well, if we're going to be a 100-year car company, we need to be a learning organization.'[62]

QUESTIONS

1. Describe the changes that GM is trying to implement at Saturn.
2. What are the critical factors in developing the management of the Saturn plants?
3. What problems might GM management face in trying to transplant the Saturn concept to other GM units?
4. Evaluate the pluses and minuses of Saturn's new risk and reward compensation system.

Individuals, job design and stress

BridgeClimb — excited staff in exciting jobs

GETTING @ CONNECTED

Imagine climbing to the top of the Sydney Harbour Bridge on a sunny Sydney day and enjoying one of the best views in the world. Sound fantastic? It is, and more than one million climbers have enjoyed the experience.

Established by Paul Cave in 1998, the climb has become one of Australia's premier tourist attractions.

One of the key reasons for BridgeClimb's success is undoubtedly its people and the jobs they perform. Each climbing group is skilfully led by a climb leader who takes each group through the steps required to prepare for the climb, from dressing in the right gear to taking a practice climb. The highly trained leaders discuss safety issues, and work to encourage a sense of fun and friendship among a group of people who will often be from different nations and age groups and who in all probability will never meet again. That this is carried out rigorously and to a very strict schedule is not lost on climbers who universally provide positive feedback after completing their climb.

Climbers acknowledge the professionalism of the BridgeClimb operation and express their admiration for the positive, friendly approach of its staff. Looking at BridgeClimb's success, it is clear that these outcomes are no accident.

GET CONNECTED!

BridgeClimb's web site www.bridgeclimb.com.au includes a careers section where you can check out the key selection criteria for new staff. Would this kind of job suit you? Make sure that any employer you choose has the job design, culture and learning environment that is the best fit for you.

GET CONNECTED!

For managers in organisations of all types and sizes, both for-profit and not-for-profit, a critical pathway toward performance improvement is better mobilising and better unlocking the great potential of human talent.[1] The ideal situation is a loyal and talented workforce that is committed to organisational goals and highly motivated to work hard on their behalf. But saying this is one thing; achieving it is quite another. Even in the best of circumstances the management of human resources is a challenging task. It becomes even more complicated when organisations aggressively seek operating efficiencies by outsourcing more work, restructuring operations, downsizing payrolls and the like.[2]

No one doubts that every employer must attract, develop and maintain a talented pool of human resources. This is, however, just the starting point. In order for the talent to have an impact on organisational performance, it must be supported, nurtured and allowed to work to its best advantage. All too often it is not, observe scholars Jeffrey Pfeffer and Charles O'Reilly. They believe that too many organisations underperform because they operate with great untapped 'hidden value' in human resources — they fail to take full advantage of the talent they already have available.[3] O'Reilly and Pfeffer criticise organisations 'with smart, motivated, hard-working, decent people who nevertheless don't perform very well because the company doesn't let them shine and doesn't really capitalize on their talent and motivation'. They also praise true high-performance organisations as ones able to 'produce extraordinary results from almost everybody'.

This praise frames our inquiry into the topics of this chapter and the next — to learn how to design jobs and build work settings so that almost everybody can produce extraordinary work results. The present chapter considers this challenge in terms of individuals, job design and work stress; the next one focuses on teams and teamwork. A central premise of both chapters, consistent with all of *Management: An Asia–Pacific Perspective*, is that when the work experience is well designed, people — the essential and irreplaceable human resources of organisations — can both achieve high-performance results and experience a high-quality work life.

ENTREPRENEURSHIP

Audrey Y. Que

Bringing fun to work

Filipino businesswoman Audrey Y. Que has found a novel and lucrative way to link her sense of humour to her job. After a successful stint owning a T-shirt and hair accessories business, Que established a comic book importing and distribution company. She then began the Humor Post chain of retail outlets to sell humour-related gifts. Que personally finds and purchases the items her stores stock. 'I really wanted to get into something I would enjoy and look forward to doing every day', says Que. And the success of the business speaks volumes for this strategy.[4]

THE MEANING OF WORK

What do you think about when you see or hear the word *work*? Is it a 'turn-on' or a 'turn-off'? When Dolly Parton sang 'Working 9 to 5; what a way to make a living', she reminded us of an unfortunate reality — that work is not a positive experience for everyone. Dolly's song continued: 'Barely getting by; it's all taking and no giving. They just use your mind, and they never give you credit. It's enough to drive you crazy if you let it.'[5] Isn't it a shame when this is what work really means to someone?

Unfortunately, some people, too many people, work under conditions that fail to provide them with respect and satisfaction. It does not have to be this way. More and more employers are coming to the same conclusion — people, individuals like you and me, are the foundation for high performance in the workplace. When managers value people and create jobs and work environments that respect people's needs and potential, everyone gains.

Psychological contracts

Work should involve a positive give and take, or exchange of values, between the individual and the organisation. This sense of mutual benefit is expressed in the concept of a **psychological contract**, which is defined as an informal understanding about what an individual gives to and receives from an organisation as part of the employment relationship.[6] The ideal work situation is one in which the exchange of values in the psychological contract is considered fair. When the psychological contract is broken, however, morale problems easily develop. This problem surfaced in Japan where workers historically enjoyed high job security and, in return, put in long work hours at great personal sacrifice. But when the Japanese economy experienced difficulty and companies cut back on job protections, worker morale declined. The psychological contract shared between worker and employer had been damaged.[7]

As shown in figure 15.1, a healthy psychological contract offers a balance between contributions made to the organisation and inducements received in return. A person offers *contributions*, or valued work activities, such as effort, time, creativity and loyalty. These are among the things that make the individual a desirable resource. *Inducements* are things of value that the organisation gives to the individual in exchange for these contributions. Typical inducements include pay, fringe benefits, training and opportunities for personal growth and advancement. Such inducements should be valued by employees and should make it worthwhile for them to work hard for the organisation.

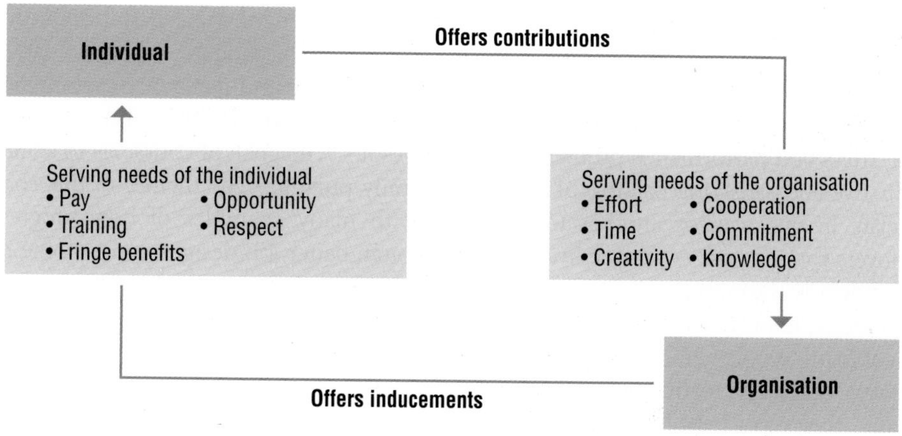

GET CONNECTED!

Visit the web site of Women At Work Australia www.womenatwork australia.com and see how this organisation assists women to re-enter the workforce after leaving it for any reason.

GET CONNECTED!

A **psychological contract** is the set of expectations held by an individual about working relationships with the organisation.

Figure 15.1 ▸ Components in the psychological contract

An Australian management consultant, Tim Baker, argues that our view of the psychological contract should be updated to reflect the modern decline in job security confronting individuals in most industries, as well as the challenges facing organisations in managing employees who are more independent and ambitious than ever before. In response to today's realities, where employees expect to work in a range of organisations and receive progressively greater responsibilities and challenges, organisations should provide greater flexibility in employment, focus on rewarding performance rather than long-term loyalty, and provide work that is stimulating and which offers meaning.[8]

Work and the quality of life

www.nohsc.gov.au
www.osh.dol.govt.nz

Dr Niki Ellis, an Australian medical consultant focusing on occupational health, says that job redesign is required in many call centres, where office automation has increased the number of repetitive strain injuries (RSIs). The National Occupational Health and Safety Commission provides resources on RSI and its treatment and prevention.[11]

The term *quality of work life* (QWL) was first used in chapter 1 to describe the overall quality of human experiences in the workplace. Most people spend many hours a week, and many years of their lives, at work. What happens to them at work, how they are treated and what their work is like can all have an influence on their overall lives. Simply put, the quality of work is an important component in the quality of life for most of us.[9] Anyone who serves as a manager, therefore, must accept that this job carries a high level of social responsibility. The way managers treat people at work may have consequences extending far beyond the confines of the actual work setting. Our experiences at work can and often do spill over to affect our non-work activities and lives, just as our non-work experiences sometimes affect our attitudes and performance at work.

Poor management practices can diminish a person's overall quality of life, not just the quality of work life. Good management, by contrast, has the potential to enhance both. And if you think the preceding comments are an overstatement, consider the implications of this steelworker's compelling words, once shared with the noted American author Studs Terkel:

> When I come home, know what I do for the first twenty minutes? Fake it. I put on a smile. I got a kid three years old. Sometimes she says, 'Daddy, where've you been?' I say, 'Work'. I could have told her I'd been in Disneyland. What's work to a three-year-old kid? If I feel bad, I can't take it out on the kid. Kids are born innocent of everything but birth. You can't take it out on your wife either. That is why you go to a tavern. You want to release it there rather than do it at home. What does an actor do when he's got a bad movie? I got a bad movie every day.[10]

Today's managers are increasingly expected to focus their attention on creating work environments within which people can have positive experiences while performing to high levels of expectation. A term relevant in this respect is *work-life balance*, described earlier in this book as the fit between one's job or work responsibilities and personal or family needs. When job demands get to the point of interfering with personal responsibilities and vice versa, stress and performance problems are likely results. The goal, of course, is to achieve a productive and satisfying balance of career and family pursuits. The themes of this chapter all relate in one way or another to this goal, with many examples of how progressive employers can increase employee involvement through better job designs and become more family friendly through alternative work schedules and stress management assistance. Recognition for the importance of people, for example, is a core value at Deloitte Touche Tohmatsu. The company stands behind this value with a commitment to work-life balance described in this way: 'Talented, creative people need control over where, how and when they work and, at times, they need help managing and coping with the responsibilities, opportunities and challenges life can present'.[12]

SATISFACTION, PERFORMANCE AND JOB DESIGN

A **job** is a collection of tasks performed in support of organisational objectives. The process of **job design** is one of creating or defining jobs by assigning specific work tasks to individuals and groups. Job design uses the insights of motivation theories discussed in the last chapter to help accomplish two major goals — high levels of both job satisfaction and job performance. Jobs can and should be designed so that satisfaction and performance go hand in hand. One without the other is simply insufficient to meet the high standards expected of today's workplace. There is no reason why you or anyone else cannot experience personal satisfaction while making high-performance work contributions.

> A **job** is the collection of tasks a person performs in support of organisational objectives.

> **Job design** is the allocation of specific work tasks to individuals and groups.

Job satisfaction

One measure of quality of work life is **job satisfaction**.[13] This is the degree to which an individual feels positively or negatively about various aspects of the job. We have all heard someone criticised for having a 'bad attitude'. In the present context, job satisfaction is an important attitude that can and does influence behaviour at work. The question becomes: How can we develop job satisfaction and positive work attitudes? In answering this question, satisfaction with such things as pay, tasks, supervision, coworkers, work setting and advancement opportunities must be considered. These are all facets of job satisfaction that can be handled through job design in the attempt to improve attitudes and raise the quality of work life.

> **Job satisfaction** is the degree to which an individual feels positively or negatively about a job.

Researchers know that there is a strong relationship between job satisfaction and *absenteeism*. Workers who are more satisfied with their jobs attend more regularly; they are absent less often than those who are dissatisfied. There is also a relationship between job satisfaction and *turnover*. Satisfied workers are more likely to stay and dissatisfied workers are more likely to quit their jobs. Both of these findings are important since absenteeism and turnover are costly in terms of the additional recruitment and training that are needed to replace workers, as well as in the productivity lost while new workers are learning how to perform up to expectations.

Closely related to job satisfaction are two other concepts with quality of work life implications. **Job involvement** is defined as the extent to which an individual is dedicated to a job. Someone with high job involvement, for example, would be expected to work beyond expectations to complete a special project. **Organisational commitment** is defined as the loyalty of an individual to the organisation itself. Someone with a high organisational commitment would identify strongly with the organisation and take pride in considering himself or herself a member.

> **Job involvement** is defined as the extent to which an individual is dedicated to a job.

> **Organisational commitment** is defined as the loyalty of an individual to the organisation.

There appears to be a link between organisational commitment and job satisfaction. Professor Amanda Sinclair of the Melbourne Business School argues that many jobs in areas such as retail, banking and call centres have been stripped of their ability to provide intrinsic satisfaction to employees, limiting the potential of these jobs to foster organisational commitment. 'Unachievable targets, queues that get longer, coworkers who hardly know one another because there is rarely time to chat. Jobs like these inevitably prompt even the most enthusiastic employee to withdraw that potential reservoir of productivity — commitment.'[14]

A recent survey of 1000 Australian workers found that while 70 per cent had a positive attitude to at least some aspects of their work lives, 22 per cent found their work uninteresting and 20 per cent worried about their career prospects. Interestingly, levels of workplace dissatisfaction as recorded in the survey tended to increase with the age of workers.[15]

In an effort to provide job satisfaction, managers should always seek to find the real reasons for job dissatisfaction rather than relying too superficially on the comments of workers. Managers and students of management regularly indicate that higher pay and rewards will maximise job satisfaction, but, as indicated in chapter 14, monetary rewards may not be the answer.[16] A survey of Australia's best employers undertaken by Hewitt Associates found that while their levels of remuneration and benefits were competitive, the companies were seen as attractive by employees because of their ability to provide 'engagement' with employees through challenging work assignments, flexibility in work arrangements and regular training. It is argued by some that material comforts can never fully satisfy people in the workplace or elsewhere since people are 'human beings' with the need for relationships rather than merely 'human resources'.[17]

JOB SATISFACTION IN THE ASIA–PACIFIC

Levels of job satisfaction in other parts of the Asia–Pacific are not dissimilar to those indicated by research findings in Australia and New Zealand. A study of more than 94 000 employees from Singapore, Malaysia, China, Hong Kong, Taiwan, Japan and the Philippines found that around 62 per cent of employees across the region were satisfied with their jobs. Specifically, around 65 per cent were satisfied with workplace relationships and between 50 and 60 per cent were satisfied with elements such as employment security, training, supervision and the organising of their work. On the downside, only 45 per cent were satisfied with workplace communication and only 35 per cent were satisfied with their pay.[18]

Two aspects of this study are particularly interesting. First, satisfaction levels have been relatively stable over time, even in the wake of the economic downturn experienced in Asia after the financial turmoil of the late 1990s. Second, significant differences exist between nations, with employees in Japan and Hong Kong, for instance, being more likely to express dissatisfaction with staffing issues and with managers changing work objectives and priorities too frequently. In contrast, employees in the Philippines were generally more positive across the range of satisfaction indicators. The study's author notes that cultural differences should be considered in interpreting the results: 'It is not the case that employees are always more satisfied with their employer in the Philippines and Malaysia, nor that working conditions and morale are always worse in Japan and Hong Kong. Rather, these scores are what could be considered "normal" levels of satisfaction in these countries for these topics related to work life.'[19]

Individual performance

Somewhere in Michigan near a Ford Motor Company plant, the following sign once hung in a tavern: 'I spend forty hours a week here — am I supposed to work too?' The message in these words is an important one in management: it is one thing for people to come to work; it is quite another for them to perform at high levels while they are on the job. Formally defined, **job performance** is the quantity and quality of tasks accomplished by an individual or group at work. Performance, as is commonly said, is the 'bottom line' for people at work. It is a cornerstone of productivity, and it should contribute to the accomplishment of organisational objectives. As earlier examples have suggested, however, some workers achieve a sense of personal satisfaction from their jobs and others do not; some perform at high levels of accomplishment, while others do not. The test of a manager's skill is to discover what work means to other people and then to create job designs that help them to achieve satisfaction along with high performance.

Job performance is the quantity and quality of task accomplishment by an individual or group.

Consider the insights of the individual performance equation: Performance = Ability × Support × Effort. The logic of this equation is straightforward and very practical. If high performance is to be achieved in any work setting, the individual contributor must possess the right abilities (creating the *capacity* to perform), work hard at the task (showing the *willingness* to perform) and have the necessary support (creating the *opportunity* to perform).[20] All three factors are important and necessary; failure to provide for any one or more is likely to cause performance losses and establish limited performance ceilings.

Individual performance equation

PERFORMANCE BEGINS WITH ABILITY

Ability counts. As the basic foundation of aptitudes and skills it establishes an individual's capacity to perform at a high level of accomplishment. This is the central issue in human resource management, as discussed in chapter 12. Proper employee selection brings people with the right abilities to a job; poor selection does not. Good training and development keep people's skills up to date and their jobs relevant; poor or insufficient training does not.

The goal of maintaining and increasing the ability of workers in every job should be central to all human resource development initiatives and policies. The best managers never let a job vacancy or training opportunity pass without giving it serious attention. The best managers make sure every day that all jobs under their supervision are staffed up to the moment with talented people. By renewing and redoubling their commitments to the ability factor and best practices in human resource management, managers can make substantial contributions to performance development.

PERFORMANCE REQUIRES SUPPORT

The support factor in the individual performance equation can be easily neglected in day-to-day management practice. But such oversight comes at a high cost. Even the most capable and hard-working individual will not achieve the highest performance levels unless proper support is available. Support creates a work environment rich in opportunities to apply one's talents to maximum advantage. To fully utilise their abilities, workers need sufficient resources, clear goals and directions, freedom from unnecessary rules and job constraints, appropriate technologies and performance feedback. Providing these and other forms of direct work support is a basic managerial responsibility. Doing it right, however, requires a willingness to get to know the jobs to be done and the people doing them. The best information on the need for support, of course, comes from the workers themselves. Wouldn't it be nice to hear more managers speak the following words in everyday conversations with their subordinates: How can I help you today?

PERFORMANCE INVOLVES EFFORT

Without any doubt, effort — the willingness to work hard at a task — is an irreplaceable component of the high-performance workplace. Even the most capable workers won't achieve consistent high performance unless they are willing to try hard enough. But the decision by anyone to work hard or not rests squarely on the shoulders of the individual alone. This is the ultimate test of the motivation theories discussed in chapter 14.

All any manager (or teacher, or parent) can do is attempt to create the conditions under which the answer to the all-important question — 'Should I work hard today?' — is more often 'Yes!' than 'No!' And quite frankly, the most powerful and enduring 'Yes' is the one driven by forces within the individual — intrinsic motivation — rather than by outside initiatives such as supervisory appeals, offers of monetary reward or threats of punishment. Good managers understand this reality as they design jobs for people in organisations.

Job design alternatives

Job design is in many ways an exercise in 'fit'. A good job design provides a good fit between the individual worker and the task requirements. To explore this notion further, consider a short case.[21] Datapoint Corporation manufactures a line of personal computers. Jackson White has just been employed by Datapoint. He is a competent person who enjoys interpersonal relationships. He also likes to feel helpful or stimulating to others. How do you think he will react to each of the following job designs?

In *Job 1*, Jackson reports to a workstation on the computer assembly line. A partially assembled circuit board passes in front of him on a conveyor belt every 90 seconds. He adds two pieces to each board and lets the conveyor take the unit to the next workstation. Quality control is handled at a separate station at the end of the line. Everyone gets a 10-minute break in the morning and afternoon and a 30-minute lunch period. Jackson works by himself in a quiet setting.

In *Job 2*, Jackson works on the same assembly line. Now, however, a circuit board comes to his station every 12 minutes, and he performs a greater number of tasks. He adds several pieces to the board, adds a frame and installs several electric switches. Periodically, Jackson changes stations with one of the other workers and does a different set of tasks on earlier or later stages of the same circuit board. In all other respects, the work setting is the same as in the first job described.

In *Job 3*, Jackson is part of a team responsible for completely assembling circuit boards for the computers. The team has a weekly production quota but makes its own plans for the speed and arrangement of the required assembly processes. The team is also responsible for inspecting the quality of the finished boards and for correcting any defective units. These duties are shared among the members and are discussed at team meetings. Jackson has been selected by the team as its plant liaison. In addition to his other duties, he works with people elsewhere in the plant to resolve any production problems and achieve plant-wide quality objectives.

These three job design alternatives are identified in figure 15.2 as job simplification, job enlargement and rotation and job enrichment, respectively. Each varies in how specialised the division of labour becomes — that is, in how narrowly job tasks are defined. Although not every one of these designs may be a good choice to maximise Jackson White's performance and satisfaction, each has a role to play in the modern workplace.

	Job simplification	Job rotation and enlargement	Job enrichment
Job scope — number and variety of tasks	narrow	wide	wide
Job depth — extent of planning, controlling responsibility	low	low	high
Task specialisation — division of labour	high	moderate	low

Figure 15.2 ▸ A continuum of job-design alternatives

JOB SIMPLIFICATION

Job simplification involves standardising work procedures and employing people in well-defined and highly specialised tasks. This is an extension of the scientific management approach discussed in chapter 4. Simplified jobs are narrow in *job scope* — that is, the number and variety of different tasks a person performs. Jackson White's first job on the assembly line was highly simplified. He isn't alone. Many employees around the world earn their livings working at highly simplified tasks. The most extreme form of job simplification is **automation**, or the total mechanisation of a job.

The logic of job simplification is straightforward. Because the jobs don't require complex skills, workers should be easier and quicker to train, less difficult to supervise and easy to replace if they leave. Furthermore, because tasks are well defined, workers should become good at them while performing the same work over and over again. Consider the case of the fast-food sector. Of every dollar Australians spend on food, 33 cents is spent on fast food — significant, if still behind the US average of about 48 cents of every dollar. The fast-food sector is focused on minimising costs to ensure maximum efficiency. This occurs through a reliance on the principles of scientific management (see chapter 4) to ensure that every job is as simple as efficiency demands dictate. Jobs have been simplified to ensure that they can be filled by relatively low-skilled workers who are paid relatively low wages. Jobs in every McDonald's outlet, for instance, must conform to the requirements of station observation checklists (SOCs) that provide guidance on everything from the need for hygiene to the presentation of customer orders. Following these principles, the time needed to make a McDonald's hamburger was reduced from more than three minutes in 1980 to less than 40 seconds in 1999.[22]

Problems can arise in highly simplified jobs. Productivity can suffer as unhappy workers drive up costs through absenteeism and turnover, and through poor performance caused by boredom and alienation. Although simplified jobs appeal to some people, disadvantages can develop with the structured and repetitive tasks. For example, in the Datapoint case, Jackson White's social need is thwarted in Job 1 because the assembly line prevents interaction with coworkers. We would predict low satisfaction, occasional tardiness and absenteeism, and boredom, which may cause a high error rate. White's overall performance could be just adequate enough to prevent him from being fired. This is hardly sufficient for a computer maker trying to maintain a high-performance edge in today's competitive global economy.

JOB ROTATION AND JOB ENLARGEMENT

One way to move beyond simplification in job design is to broaden the scope through **job rotation** — increasing task variety by periodically shifting workers between jobs involving different task assignments. Job rotation can be done on a regular schedule; it can also be done periodically or occasionally. The latter approach is often used in training to broaden people's understanding of jobs performed by others. Another way to broaden scope is **job enlargement**, increasing task variety by combining two or more tasks that were previously assigned to separate workers. Often these are tasks done immediately before or after the work performed in the original job. Figure 15.3 shows how such *horizontal loading* — pulling pre-work and/or later work stages into the job — can be used to enlarge jobs. In this job design strategy the old job is permanently changed through the addition of new tasks.

Jackson White's second job on the modified assembly line is an example of job enlargement with occasional job rotation. Instead of doing only one task, he now does three. Also, he occasionally switches jobs to work on a different part of the assembly. Because job enlargement and rotation can reduce some of the monotony in otherwise simplified jobs, we

Job simplification employs people in clearly defined and very specialised tasks.

Automation is the total mechanisation of a job.

Job rotation increases task variety by periodically shifting workers between jobs involving different tasks.

Job enlargement increases task variety by combining into one job two or more tasks previously assigned to separate workers.

would expect an increase in White's satisfaction and performance. Satisfaction should remain only moderate, however, because the job still does not respond completely to his social needs. Although White's work quality should increase as boredom is reduced, some absenteeism is likely.

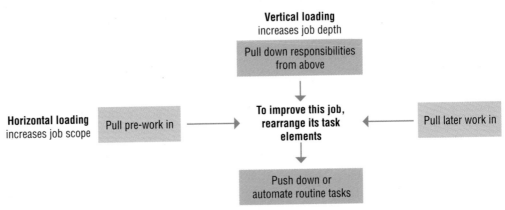

Figure 15.3 ▸ How to improve job design by horizontal and vertical loading

JOB ENRICHMENT

Frederick Herzberg, whose two-factor theory of motivation was discussed in chapter 14, questions the true value of horizontally loading jobs through enlargement and rotation. 'Why', he asks, 'should a worker become motivated when one or more meaningless tasks are added to previously existing ones or when work assignments are rotated among equally meaningless tasks?' By contrast, he says, 'If you want people to do a good job, give them a good job to do'.[23] He argues that this is best done through **job enrichment**, the practice of building more opportunities for satisfaction into a job by expanding its content.

In contrast to job enlargement and rotation, job enrichment focuses not just on job scope but also on *job depth* — that is, the extent to which task planning and evaluating duties are performed by the individual worker rather than the supervisor. As depicted in figure 15.3, changes designed to increase job depth are sometimes referred to as *vertical loading*. Herzberg's recommendations for enriching jobs through vertical loading are found in Manager's Notepad 15.1.[24] There are some elements of job enrichment in Job 3 in the Datapoint case. Jackson White works in a team responsible for task planning and evaluation, as well as actual product assembly. The job provides opportunities to satisfy his social needs, and allows for added challenge from acting as the team's plant liaison. Higher performance and satisfaction are the predicted results.

> **Job enrichment** increases job depth by adding work planning and evaluating duties normally performed by the supervisor.

MANAGER'S NOTEPAD 15.1

Job enrichment checklist

Check 1: Remove controls that limit people's discretion in their work.

Check 2: Grant people authority to make decisions about their work.

Check 3: Make people understand their accountability for performance results.

Check 4: Allow people to do 'whole' tasks or complete units of work.

Check 5: Make performance feedback available to those doing the work.

Some companies are seeking to re-enrich jobs that have long been progressively simplified. Westpac Bank chief executive David Morgan states that the bank realised that staff who are feeling positively about themselves and the company convey these same feelings to customers. The bank has therefore been using tools such as learning maps to show staff how their role relates to the roles of others and to the bank's broader vision. In addition, Morgan spends time discussing a range of issues with around 700 staff in groups of 70 during two around-Australia trips each year.[25]

DIRECTIONS IN JOB ENRICHMENT

Job enrichment is an important strategy with the potential to improve individual performance and satisfaction in the new workplace. But modern management theory takes job enrichment a step beyond the suggestions of Frederick Herzberg. Most importantly, it adopts a contingency perspective and recognises that job enrichment may not be best for everyone. Among the directions in job design, the core characteristics model developed by J. Richard Hackman and his associates offers a way for managers to create jobs, enriched or otherwise, that best fit the needs of people and organisations.[26]

Core characteristics model

The model described in figure 15.4 offers a diagnostic approach to job enrichment. Five core job characteristics are identified as task attributes of special importance. A job that is high in the core characteristics is considered enriched; the lower a job scores on the core characteristics, the less enriched it is.

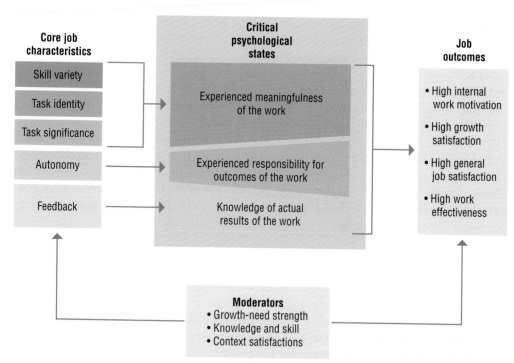

Figure 15.4 ▸ Job design and individual work outcomes using the core characteristics model

Source: J. Richard Hackman and Greg R. Oldham, *Work Redesign*
(Reading, MA: Addison-Wesley, 1980), p. 90.

Five core job characteristics

The *five core job characteristics* are as follows:

1. *Skill variety* — the degree to which a job requires a variety of different activities to carry out the work and involves the use of a number of different skills and talents of the individual.
2. *Task identity* — the degree to which the job requires completion of a 'whole' and identifiable piece of work, that is, one that involves doing a job from beginning to end with a visible outcome.
3. *Task significance* — the degree to which the job has a substantial impact on the lives or work of other people elsewhere in the organisation or in the external environment.
4. *Autonomy* — the degree to which the job gives the individual substantial freedom, independence and discretion in scheduling the work and in determining the procedures to be used in carrying it out.
5. *Feedback from the job itself* — the degree to which carrying out the work activities required by the job results in the individual obtaining direct and clear information on the results of his or her performance.

According to figure 15.4, this model of job design views job satisfaction and performance as being influenced by three critical psychological states of the individual: experienced meaningfulness of the work, experienced responsibility for the outcomes of the work, and knowledge of actual results of work activities. These psychological states, in turn, are influenced by the presence or absence of the five core job characteristics. In true contingency fashion, however, the core characteristics will not affect all people in the same way. Generally speaking, people who respond most favourably to enriched jobs will have strong higher-order needs and appropriate job knowledge and skills. They will also be otherwise satisfied with job context. One of the key contingency or moderator variables in the model

Growth-need strength is the desire to achieve psychological growth in one's work.

is **growth-need strength**, described in Alderfer's ERG theory (see chapter 14) as the degree to which an individual seeks psychological growth in his or her work. The expectation is that people with strong growth needs will respond most positively to enriched jobs.

When job enrichment is a good job design choice, Hackman and his colleagues recommend five ways to improve the core characteristics. First, you can *form natural units of work*. Make sure that the tasks people perform are logically related to one another and provide a clear and meaningful task identity. Second, try to *combine tasks*. Expand job responsibilities by pulling together into one larger job a number of smaller tasks previously done by others. Third, *establish client relationships*. Put people in contact with others who, as clients inside and/or outside the organisation, use the results of their work. Fourth, *open feedback channels*. Provide opportunities for people to receive performance feedback as they work and to learn how performance changes over time. Fifth, *practise vertical loading*. Give people more control over their work by increasing their authority to perform the planning and controlling previously done by supervisors.

Technology and job enrichment

A **sociotechnical system** integrates technology and human resources in high-performance systems.

An important issue of job enrichment involves the impact of technology on job design.[27] The managerial challenge is quite clear: job design should proceed with the goal of increasing productivity through integrated **sociotechnical systems**. These are job designs that use technology to best advantage while still treating people with respect and allowing their human talents to be applied to their fullest potential.[28] The continuing inroads made by computers into the workplace are changing structures, workflows and the mix of skills needed in many settings. Consider the special case of *robotics* — the use of computer-controlled machines to completely automate work tasks previously performed by hand.

Such automation of work is the most extreme form of job simplification and has both its limits and critics. On the positive side, technology offers an opportunity to take over many routine tasks previously assigned to individuals and thereby frees human talents for more enriched job assignments. In this and other ways, technology use and job enrichment can be complementary strategies.

Questions and answers on job enrichment

Is it expensive to implement job enrichment? Job enrichment can be costly. The cost grows as the required changes in technology, workflow and other facilities become more complex.

Will people demand more pay for doing enriched jobs? Herzberg believes that if people are being paid truly competitive wages (i.e. if pay dissatisfaction does not already exist), the satisfactions of performing enriched tasks will be adequate compensation for the increased work involved. But a manager must be cautious on this issue. Any job-enrichment program should be approached with recognition that pay may be an issue for the people involved.[29]

Should everyone's job be enriched? No, contingency counts. The people most likely to respond favourably to job enrichment are those seeking higher-order or growth-need satisfactions at work and who have the levels of training, education and ability required to perform the enriched job.

ALTERNATIVE WORK ARRANGEMENTS

Not only is the content of jobs changing for people in today's workplace, the context is changing too. Among the more significant developments is the emergence of a number of alternative ways for people to schedule their work time.[31] This is especially important as employers deal with work-life balance issues affecting today's highly diverse workforce. Many are finding that alternative work schedules can help attract and retain the best workers. It is popular in this sense to talk about a new and more 'flexible' workplace

in which alternative work schedules such as the compressed work week, flexible working hours, job sharing, telecommuting and part-time work are more and more common.

The compressed work week

A **compressed work week** is any work schedule that allows a full-time job to be completed in less than the standard five days of seven- to eight-hour shifts.[32] A common form is the '4–40' — that is, accomplishing 40 hours of work in four 10-hour days. One advantage of the 4–40 schedule is that the employee receives three consecutive days off from work

📀 A **compressed work week** allows a full-time job to be completed in less than five days.

each week. This benefits the individual through more leisure time and lower commuting costs. The organisation should also benefit through lower absenteeism and any improved performance that may result. Potential disadvantages include increased fatigue and family adjustment problems for the individual, as well as increased scheduling problems, possible customer complaints and union objections for the organisation.

In the Australian minerals and mining sector, many workers operate under a fly-in/fly-out (FIFO) system, which involves flying into the mines for an intense period of work before flying out for rest and to spend time with their families. The most common pattern is for workers to fly into a site and work 12-hour shifts on 14 consecutive days, then return home for a seven-day break before beginning the cycle again. The shifts during the 14 days of work are generally split between seven days of day shift and seven days of night shift. Though the work is paid well and many employees view this kind of remote work as a challenge, studies indicate that there is a high divorce rate among workers and there are often difficulties in maintaining relationships in such conditions.[33]

Flexible working hours

Flexible working hours give employees some choice in the pattern of daily work hours.

The term **flexible working hours**, also called *flexitime* or *flextime*, describes any work schedule that gives employees some choice in the pattern of their daily work hours. A sample flexible working schedule offers choices of starting and ending times, such as the program depicted in figure 15.5. Employees in this example work four hours of 'core' time, or the time they must be present at work. In this case, core time falls between 9 and 10 a.m. and 1 and 3 p.m. They are then free to choose another four work hours from 'flexitime' blocks. Such flexible schedules give employees greater autonomy while ensuring that they maintain work responsibility. Early risers may choose to come in earlier and leave earlier, while still completing an 8-hour day; late sleepers may choose to start later in the morning and leave later. In between these extremes are opportunities to attend to personal affairs, such as dental appointments, home emergencies, visits to children's schools and so on.

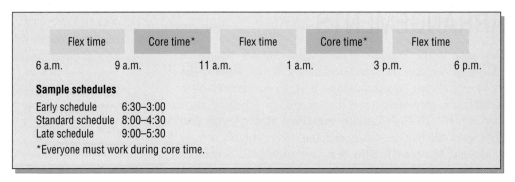

Figure 15.5 ▸ A sample flexible working hours schedule

The advantages of flexible working hours are especially important to members of a diverse workforce. By offering flexibility, organisations can attract and hold employees with special non-work responsibilities. The work schedule is important to many dual-career couples who face the complications of managing careers and other responsibilities, including parenting. Single parents with young children and employees with aged-care responsibilities also find it very attractive to have the option of adjusting work schedules to allow for other obligations to be met. The added discretion flexitime provides may also encourage workers to have more positive attitudes toward the organisation.

Job sharing

Another important development for today's workforce is **job sharing**, whereby one full-time job is split between two or more persons. Job sharing often involves each person working one half day, but it can also be done on weekly or monthly sharing arrangements. When it is feasible for jobs to be split and shared, organisations can benefit by employing talented people who would otherwise be unable to work. The qualified specialist who is also a parent may be unable to stay away from home for a full workday but may be able to work a half day. Job sharing allows two such persons to be employed as one. Although there are sometimes adjustment problems, the arrangement can be good for all concerned.

Job sharing is sometimes viewed skeptically by those who don't believe two workers can perform a shared job as productively as one person alone. However, when such concerns were investigated at Lotus Development Corporation early in the life of its job-sharing program, the results turned out to be just the opposite. When performance was studied, none of the initial nine teams of job sharers had to apologise to anybody. They were among the top performers in annual merit pay appraisals.[34]

Job sharing should not be confused with a more controversial concept called *work-sharing*. This involves an agreement between employees who face layoffs or terminations to cut back their work hours so they can all keep their jobs. Instead of losing 20 per cent of a firm's workforce to temporary layoffs in an unexpected business downturn, for example, a work-sharing program would cut everyone's hours by 20 per cent to keep them all employed. This allows employers to retain trained and loyal workers even when forced to temporarily economise by reducing labour costs. For employees whose seniority might otherwise protect them from layoff, the disadvantage is lost earnings. For those who would otherwise be terminated, however, it provides continued work — albeit with reduced earnings — and with a preferred employer. During the economic recession of the early 1990s, Sydney-based engineering consultants Tierney and Partners initiated a ten per cent cut in salaries across the company to preserve jobs. All employees accepted and received the cut, including the firm's managing partners. The decision ensured that the company survived a difficult period, and normal compensation was reinstated as soon as economic conditions improved.

Telecommuting

Another significant development in work scheduling is the growing popularity of a variety of ways for people to work away from a fixed office location. This includes alternatives ranging from self-employment and entrepreneurship based at home, to using the latest in computer and information technology to maintain a 'virtual' office that travels from point-to-point with you. **Telecommuting**, sometimes called *flexiplace*, is a work arrangement that allows at least a portion of scheduled work hours to be completed outside of the office, with *work-from-home* one of the options. Often this is facilitated by computer linkages to clients or customers and a central office. Although the number of telecommuters is rising, it has been estimated that only about one per cent of Australian employees telecommute on a regular basis.[36]

Telecommuting frees the jobholder from the normal constraints of commuting, fixed hours, special work attire and even direct contact with supervisors. It is popular, for example, among computer programmers and is found increasingly in such diverse areas as marketing, financial analysis and administrative support. New terms are becoming associated

Job sharing splits one job between two people.

www.ama.com.au

The Australian Medical Association is campaigning for new initiatives to create better jobs and help doctors avoid working shifts of up to 30 hours. Flinders Hospital in South Australia has developed a package of measures including flexitime, part-time employment, job sharing and compressed work weeks.[35]

Telecommuting or flexiplace involves working at home or other places using computer links to the office.

with telecommuting practices. We speak of *hotelling* when telecommuters come to the central office and use temporary office facilities; we are immersed in a world of *telemarketing* where customers are contacted and orders taken by service personnel working in diverse locations; and we often refer to *virtual offices* that include everything from an office at home to mobile workspace in cars and trucks.

Overall, there is no doubt that telecommuting is with us to stay as an important aspect of the continually developing new workplace.[37] Along with it, predictably, come potential advantages and disadvantages from a job design and management perspective. When asked what they like about these alternatives, telecommuters tend to report increased productivity, fewer distractions, the freedom to be your own boss and the benefit of having more time for themselves. On the negative side, they cite working too much, having less time to themselves, difficulty separating work and personal life, and having less time for family.[38] Other considerations for the individual include feelings of isolation and loss of visibility for promotion. Managers, in turn, may be required to change their routines and procedures to accommodate the challenges of supervising people from a distance. Such problems tend to be magnified in situations where employees feel forced into these work arrangements rather than opting for them voluntarily.[39] One telecommuter's advice to others is: 'You have to have self-discipline and pride in what you do, but you also have to have a boss that trusts you enough to get out of the way'.[40] Manager's Notepad 15.2 offers several guidelines for how to make telecommuting work for you.[41]

MANAGER'S NOTEPAD 15.2

How to make telecommuting work for you

- Treat telecommuting like any work day; keep regular hours.
- Limit non-work distractions; set up a private space dedicated to work.
- Establish positive routines and work habits; be disciplined.
- Report regularly to your boss and main office; don't lose touch.
- Seek out human contact; don't become isolated.
- Use technology: instant messaging, intranet links, net meetings.
- Keep your freedoms and responsibilities in balance.
- Reward yourself with time off; let flexibility be an advantage.

A recent study (undertaken by Margaret Lindorff of Monash University) of 79 telecommuters employed by large Australian organisations provides some interesting findings about the positive benefits and negative effects of telecommuting. In terms of the job characteristics model introduced earlier in this chapter, although the majority of those surveyed reported that they had some autonomy and flexibility in terms of their work schedule, only half of the employees thought that they had control of their workload, discretion in how they performed their work, and the ability to predict what they would be required to do from day to day. They generally believed their work to be significant, and viewed it as requiring skill, creativity, attention and awareness. Those surveyed also thought that they received appropriate feedback and reward for their efforts. Whereas most were comfortable with their working relationships, some felt psychologically isolated from their organisation and work colleagues. Work overload was a commonly identified problem for the telecommuters, resulting in difficulty in taking advantage of one of the key perceived benefits of telecommuting — achieving a balance between work and family responsibilities. In addition, many of the survey's respondents thought that telecommuting could impact negatively on their future career development. Lindorff concludes that while the study highlights the potential benefits of telecommuting, including flexibility and variety, the problems noted by some telecommuters such as overload, inappropriate supervision and poor work-family balance indicate that telecommuting 'cannot be seen as the ideal work form for all'.[42]

A recent study conducted in New Zealand found broadly similar results.[43] Interestingly, non-telecommuting staff were significantly more positive about the potential benefits of telecommuting than telecommuters. For instance, 75 per cent of non-telecommuters thought that telecommuting would improve their ability to balance work and family commitments; however, only 56 per cent of telecommuters were positive about telecommuting's ability to achieve this balance. The study's author, Phil Kerslake, recommends that those companies serious about integrating telecommuting should establish a formal work–personal life balance policy, undertake regular staff satisfaction surveys and implement training courses to help staff maximise the potential benefits of telecommuting. International business solutions company Ernst & Young typifies this approach, holding regular team functions and events, undertaking regular employee opinion surveys, and communicating with its people via e-mail, voicemail, face-to-face communication and traditional paper-based methods.[44]

Part-time and casual work

The growing use of part-time and casual workers is another striking employment trend. It is estimated that around 24 per cent of all employees in Australia are employed on a casual basis. About 20 per cent of the US workforce is in part-time positions and more than 30 per cent of the British workforce is casual or part-time.[45]

Part-time work is permanent employment, where the work is done on a schedule less than the standard work week and that does not qualify the individual as a full-time employee. Employees holding part-time positions have a continuing agreement of employment and are generally entitled to a proportion of salary and benefits consistent with the number of hours worked.[46]

Casual work is a type of part-time employment where there is no agreement or promise of ongoing employment or availability to work. Casual employees are often employed during peak times when an organisation's workload is too high for its permanent workforce, or may be hired during periods when permanent employees are ill or unavailable. Casual workers may work full-time hours during a particular period; however, most will work less than this, with availability of one to three days per week being common. Casual employees usually receive a salary loading in lieu of other benefits such as paid holidays and paid sick days.[47] Some employers use casual workers on a long-term basis to supplement the permanent workforce.

A number of industries rely heavily on part-time and casual workers. Retail outlets like Kmart employ an army of casual employees during the busy Christmas period as well as for stocktakes and sales, and during these times some of the casual workers might work full-time hours. Up to 90 per cent of workers in the fast-food sector are employed on a part-time or casual basis. This enables store managers to adjust labour costs according to demand (i.e. to have many workers on during the peak lunch and dinner periods, but not during the quiet periods in between).[48]

Part-time work is a form of permanent employment in which the worker works for less than the full-time work week.

Casual work is a type of part-time employment where there is no agreement or promise of ongoing work. Casual employees may be employed during peak business periods to supplement a permanent workforce and to provide management with greater flexibility in managing labour.

It is possible to hire on a part-time or casual basis everything from executive support, such as a chief financial officer, to such special expertise as engineering, computer programming and market research.

Because casual workers can be easily hired and/or terminated and their hours can be adjusted in response to changing needs, many employers like the flexibility to control costs and deal with cyclical demand. On the other hand, some employers worry that casual workers lack the commitment of permanent workers and may lower productivity. Perhaps the most controversial issue of the casualisation of the workforce relates to the different treatment that casual workers may receive from employers. They may miss out on important benefits available to permanent staff and may also miss out on some of the social aspects of work. Of course casual workers also lack security and stability of income. There is no doubt that many casual and part-time workers would like to achieve full-time status with their employers. On the other hand, some full-time workers would prefer to work fewer hours.

JOB STRESS

Stress is a state of tension experienced by individuals facing extraordinary demands, constraints or opportunities.

Flexibility in work scheduling can go a long way toward assisting with the pressures and tensions of achieving a satisfactory work-life balance. However, it is also necessary to recognise and consider an important fact of working life. The jobs that people are asked to perform, and the relationships and circumstances under which they have to do them, are often causes of significant stress. Formally defined, **stress** is a state of tension experienced by individuals facing extraordinary demands, constraints or opportunities.[49] Any look toward your future work career would be incomplete without considering stress as a challenge that you are sure to encounter along the way — and a challenge you must be prepared to help others learn to deal with.

With the ever-present and ever-changing demands of working in the new economy, it is not surprising that people are experiencing more stress in their daily lives. In his book *The Future of Success*, for example, Robert Reich says that even though the new economy gives us much to celebrate, its 'rewards are coming at the price of lives that are more frenzied, less secure, more economically divergent, more socially stratified'.[50] At centre stage in this milieu stand job stress and its implications for the managerial role. Consider this statement by a psychologist working with top-level managers who have alcohol abuse problems: 'All executives deal with stress. They wouldn't be executives if they didn't. Some handle it well, others handle it poorly.'[51]

There are high costs associated with handling stress poorly. Dr Rob Moodie, of the Victorian Health Department, has suggested that the cost of workplace stress in Australia exceeds $1.2 billion annually.[52] Researchers from Queen's University in Ireland studied 142 cases of suicide among young men and concluded that 45 per cent of the cases could be classified as 'executive stress', where the men were affected by severe workplace stress for which they had not sought medical help.[53]

Sources of stress

Stressors are the things that cause stress.

The things that cause stress are called **stressors**. Whether they originate directly in the work setting or emerge in personal and non-work situations, they all have the potential to influence one's work attitudes, behaviour and job performance.

Work factors have an obvious potential to create job stress. Some 46 per cent of workers in one survey reported that their jobs were highly stressful; 34 per cent said that their jobs were so stressful that they were thinking of quitting.[54] Today, we often experience such stress in long hours of work, excessive e-mails, unrealistic work deadlines, difficult bosses or coworkers, and unwelcome or unfamiliar work.[55] It is associated with excessively high or low task demands, role conflicts or ambiguities, poor interpersonal relations, or career progress that is too slow or too fast. A Melbourne-based management consultant, Gary Cox, notes that a great deal of stress can arise when there is a mismatch between people and their jobs and work environment. An introvert working in a job where outgoing, extroverted behaviour is required may quickly find the job to be highly stressful. Similarly, a work environment characterised by low morale and job insecurity could rapidly 'infect' employees who may otherwise be high performers.[56]

Stress tends to be high during periods of work overload, when office politics are common, and among persons working for organisations undergoing staff cutbacks and downsizing. This latter situation and lack of 'corporate loyalty' to the employee can be especially stressful to employees who view themselves as 'career' employees and who are close to retirement age. Two of the common work-related stress syndromes are: *set up to fail* — where the performance expectations are impossible or the support is totally inadequate to the task; and *mistaken identity* — where the individual ends up in a job that doesn't at all match talents or that he or she simply doesn't like.[57]

A variety of *personal factors* are also sources of potential stress for people at work. Such individual characteristics as needs, capabilities and personality can influence how one perceives and responds to the work situation. Researchers, for example, identify a **Type A personality** that is high in achievement orientation, impatience and perfectionism. Type A persons are likely to create stress in circumstances that others find relatively stress-free. In this sense, Type A people bring stress on themselves. The stressful behaviour patterns of Type A personalities include the following:[58]

 A **Type A personality** is a person oriented toward extreme achievement, impatience and perfectionism.

Characteristics of Type A personalities

- always moving, walking and eating rapidly
- acting impatient, hurrying others, disliking waiting
- doing, or trying to do, several things at once
- feeling guilty when relaxing
- trying to schedule more in less time
- using nervous gestures such as a clenched fist
- hurrying or interrupting the speech of others.

Finally, stress from *non-work factors* can have spillover effects that affect the individual at work. Stressful life situations including such things as family events (e.g. the birth of a new child), economics (e.g. a sudden loss of extra income) and personal affairs (e.g. a preoccupation with a bad relationship) are often sources of emotional strain. Depending on the individual and his or her ability to deal with them, preoccupation with such situations can affect one's work and add to the stress of work-life conflicts.

Consequences of stress

The discussion of stress so far may give the impression that it always acts as a negative influence on our lives. Stress actually has two faces — one constructive and one destructive.[59] Consider the analogy of a violin.[60] When a violin string is too loose, the sound produced by even the most skilled player is weak and raspy. When the string is too tight, however, the sound gets shrill and the string might even snap. But when the tension on the string is just right, neither too loose nor too tight, a most beautiful sound is created. With just enough stress, in other words, performance is optimised.

Constructive stress acts in a positive way to increase effort, stimulate creativity and encourage diligence in one's work.

The same argument tends to hold in the workplace. **Constructive stress** — sometimes called *eustress*, acts in a positive way for the individual and/or the organisation. It occurs in moderation and proves energising and performance enhancing.[61] The stress is sufficient to encourage increased effort, stimulate creativity and enhance diligence in one's work, while not overwhelming the individual and causing negative outcomes. Individuals with a Type A personality, for example, are likely to work long hours and to be less satisfied with poor performance. For them, challenging task demands imposed by a supervisor may elicit higher levels of task accomplishment. Even non-work stressors such as new family responsibilities may cause them to work harder in anticipation of greater financial rewards.

Destructive stress impairs the performance of an individual.

Job burnout is physical and mental exhaustion that can be incapacitating personally and in respect to work.

Workplace rage is overtly aggressive behaviour toward coworkers or the work setting.

Just like tuning the violin string, however, achieving the right balance of stress for each person and situation is difficult. The question is: When is a little stress too much stress? **Destructive stress**, or *distress*, is dysfunctional for the individual and/or the organisation. It occurs as intense or long-term stress that, as shown in figure 15.6, overloads and breaks down a person's physical and mental systems. Destructive stress can lead to **job burnout** — a form of physical and mental exhaustion that can be incapacitating both personally and in respect to one's work. Productivity can suffer as people react to very intense stress through turnover, absenteeism, errors, accidents, dissatisfaction and reduced performance. Today as well, there is increased concern for another job consequence of excessive stress, **workplace rage** — overtly aggressive behaviour toward coworkers and the work setting in general. Lost tempers are a common example — the unfortunate extremes are tragedies involving physical harm to others.[62]

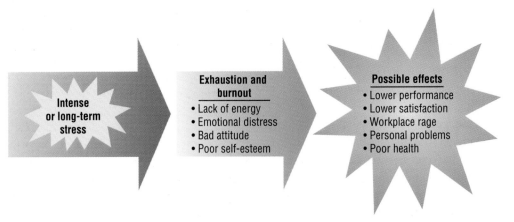

Figure 15.6 ▸ Potential negative consequences of a destructive job stress–burnout cycle

GET CONNECTED!

For ideas on how to understand your own stress levels and improve your responses, check out Mind Tools www.mindtools.com.

GET CONNECTED!

Medical research is also concerned that too much stress can reduce resistance to disease and increase the likelihood of physical and/or mental illness. It may contribute to health problems such as hypertension, ulcers, substance abuse, overeating, depression and muscle aches, among others.[63] Also important to understand is that excessive work stress can have spillover effects on one's personal life. A study of dual-career couples found that one partner's work experiences can have psychological consequences for the other — as one's work stress increases the partner is likely to experience stress too.[64] The bottom line here is that any stress we experience at work is contagious — it can affect one's spouse, family and friends. The wife of a company controller, for example, went through a time when her husband was stressed by a boss who was overly critical. 'He was angry, really angry when he came home', she says. His mood affected her and their young child and created what she called 'one of the worst times in our seven-year marriage'.[65]

Stress management strategies

There are at least four reasons that managers should also be skilled at dealing with workplace stress.[66] The first is humanitarianism. To the extent that managerial awareness and action can enhance employee health, managers have a humanitarian responsibility to do so. The second is productivity. Healthy employees are absent less often, make fewer errors and must be replaced less frequently than less healthy ones. The third is creativity. Persons in poor health tend to be less creative and are less likely to take reasonable risks than their healthy counterparts. The fourth is return on investment. When poor health reduces or removes the individual's contribution to the organisation, return on the time and money invested in human resources is lost.

Managers should obviously be alert to signs of excessive stress in themselves and the people with whom they work. The multiple and varied symptoms of excessive stress include changes in work attitudes and performance as well as personal restlessness, irritability and stomach upset. The best stress management alternative is to prevent it from ever reaching excessive levels in the first place. Stressors emerging from personal and non-work factors must be recognised so that action can be taken to prevent them from adversely affecting the work experience. Family difficulties may be relieved by a change of work schedule, or the anxiety they cause may be reduced by an understanding supervisor.

Among the work factors with the greatest potential to cause excessive stress are role ambiguities, conflicts and overloads. *Role clarification* through a management-by-objectives (MBO) approach can work to good advantage here. By bringing the supervisor and subordinate together in face-to-face task-oriented communications, MBO offers an opportunity to spot stressors and take action to reduce or eliminate them. Another issue is often a poor fit between individual abilities and aspirations and job demands. In this case job redesign may be helpful to better configure task requirements. Alternatively, changing jobs altogether can help achieve the desired person-job fit. People can also be encouraged to maintain adequate self-awareness and take a realistic approach to their responsibilities.

Sometimes others need help to combat the tendency of 'working too much'. They need to be reminded not to forgo holidays, or not to work excessive overtime, for example. Many organisations provide special help in the form of *employee assistance programs*. These programs help employees deal with special problems that may be adding excessive stress to their lives, such as personal financial problems, difficulties with child care or aged care, substance abuse and so forth. In organisations undergoing downsizing, layoffs or cutbacks, it is important to understand the *survivor syndrome* — stress experienced by persons who remain but fear for their jobs in the future. As more organisations experience this phenomenon, they are responding with programs to help those employees who remain employed to better cope after major staff cutbacks have occurred.

Personal wellness is a term used to describe the pursuit of one's physical and mental potential through a personal health-promotion program.[68] This form of *preventive stress management* recognises the individual's responsibility to enhance his or her personal health through a disciplined approach to such things as smoking, alcohol use, maintaining a nutritious diet, and engaging in a regular exercise and physical-fitness program. The essence of personal wellness is a lifestyle that reflects a true commitment to health.

Personal wellness makes a great deal of sense as a personal stress-management strategy. Those who aggressively maintain their personal wellness are better prepared to deal with the inevitable stresses of work and work-life conflicts. They may be able to deal with levels of workplace stress that are higher than others can tolerate; they may also have more insight into the personal wellness needs of their subordinates. Indeed, many organisations are now

When stress turns into workplace rage

There is a disturbing increase in the number of incidents of workplace rage. Ninety per cent of workers in a recent survey said they had witnessed an outburst by their boss or coworkers, and 16 per cent said that yelling and abuse are common in their office.[67]

How can managers help their workers deal with stress? What do you think are the causes of increased workplace rage?

Personal wellness is the pursuit of one's full potential through a personal-health promotion program.

formally sponsoring wellness programs for employees. Among the health-promotion activities typically offered are smoking control, health risk appraisals, back care, stress management, exercise/physical fitness, nutrition education, high blood pressure control and weight control. The expectations are that investments in such programs benefit both the organisation and its employees.

Blackmores, a leading provider of health products in the Asia–Pacific region, installed an in-house health and fitness facility in 1988. According to the company's CEO, Darin Walters, it is an investment that makes good sense.[69] 'We are a health company driven by strong values, and it was only natural that we should provide such a facility. Staff who are happier and healthier are good for the organisation and good for the Blackmores brand.' Two professional fitness instructors are employed in the facility, and the company also encourages its staff to achieve a balance between work and home life.

Ultimately the keys to personal stress management throughout a career rest with knowing how to help yourself. It is fitting, therefore, to end this discussion with Manager's Notepad 15.3 and its useful guidelines for coping with workplace stress.[70]

MANAGER'S NOTEPAD 15.3

Six ways to cope with workplace stress

1. *Take control of the situation.* Do your best, know your limits and avoid unrealistic deadlines.
2. *Pace yourself.* Plan your day to do high-priority things first, but stay flexible and try to slow down.
3. *Open up to others.* Discuss your problems, fears and frustrations with those who care about you.
4. *Do things for others.* Think about someone else's needs, and try to help satisfy those needs.
5. *Exercise.* Engage in regular physical activity as recommended by your doctor.
6. *Balance work and recreation.* Schedule time for recreation, including holidays from your work.

POINT ←

COUNTER ↑

Job satisfaction, stress and rewards

Many people think that having a higher income would make them happier and lead to reduced stress in their work lives. However, a recent Australian study found that employees earning more than $70 000 were more stressed than employees on lower incomes. Similarly, it is a common belief that workplace satisfaction levels should increase with age. With age, many of the problems of youth (such as the pressure to complete university or TAFE qualifications) should be over, and it is reasonable to think that our ability to find job satisfaction should improve over time. However, the same study found that workplace satisfaction appeared to decline with age.[71]

In your view, why do people with high incomes generally have higher levels of stress? What could they do to combat this problem?

CHAPTER 15
Study guide

The chapter 15 study guide helps you review the chapter content, prepare for examinations, apply what you have learned and further build your career readiness. The summary briefly answers the study questions posed at the start of the chapter. The list of key terms allows you to double-check your familiarity with basic concepts and definitions. The applied activities help you test your comprehension of chapter content. Suggestions offered as career readiness activities direct your attention to relevant sections of the Career Readiness Workbook where you can test and develop your career skills and apply what you have learned. The list of electronic resources suggests activities from the *Management: An Asia–Pacific Perspective* web site and, finally, the case for critical thinking helps you apply your new management knowledge.

SUMMARY

What is the meaning of work?

- Work is an activity that produces value for people; it is something people do to 'earn a living'.
- Work is an exchange of values between individuals who offer contributions such as time and effort to organisations that offer monetary and other inducements in return.
- A healthy psychological contract occurs when a person believes that his or her contributions and inducements are in balance. It is one component in a high quality of work life.
- Quality of work life (QWL) is an important issue in creating opportunities for positive work-life balance.

What are the issues in satisfaction, performance and job design?

- Job design is the process of creating or defining jobs by assigning specific work tasks to individuals and groups.
- Jobs should be designed so workers enjoy high levels of both job performance and job satisfaction.
- The high-performance equation states: Performance = Ability × Support × Effort.
- Job simplification creates narrow and repetitive jobs consisting of well-defined tasks with many routine operations, such as the typical assembly-line job.
- Job enlargement allows individuals to perform a broader range of simplified tasks. Job rotation allows individuals to transfer between different jobs of similar skill levels on a rotating basis.
- Job enrichment results in more meaningful jobs that involve more autonomy in decision making and broader task responsibilities.

How can jobs be enriched?

- The diagnostic approach to job enrichment involves analysing jobs according to five core characteristics: skill variety, task identity, task significance, autonomy and feedback.
- Jobs deficient in one or more of these core characteristics can be redesigned to improve their level of enrichment.

- Jobs can be enriched by forming natural work units, combining tasks, establishing client relationships, opening feedback channels and vertically loading to give workers more planning and controlling responsibilities.
- Job enrichment does not work for everyone. It works best for people with a high growth-need strength — the desire to achieve psychological growth in their work.

What are alternative work arrangements?

- Alternative work schedules can make work hours less inconvenient and enable organisations to respond better to individual needs and personal responsibilities.
- The compressed work week allows a full-time work week to be completed in fewer days.
- Flexible working hours allow people to adjust the starting and ending times of their daily schedules.
- Job sharing allows two people to share one job.
- Telecommuting allows people to work at home or in mobile offices through computer links with their employers and/or customers.
- An increasing number of people work on part-time schedules. More and more organisations are employing part-timers or casual workers to reduce their commitments to full-time positions.

How can job and workplace stress be managed?

- Stress occurs as the tension accompanying extraordinary demands, constraints or opportunities.
- Stress can be destructive or constructive — a moderate level of stress typically has a positive impact on performance.
- Stressors are found in a variety of work, personal and non-work situations.
- For some people, having a Type A personality creates stress as a result of continual feelings of impatience and pressure.
- Stress can be effectively managed through both prevention and coping strategies, including a commitment to personal wellness.

KEY TERMS

automation (p. 411)

casual work (p. 419)

compressed work week (p. 415)

constructive stress (p. 422)

destructive stress (p. 422)

flexible working hours (p. 416)

growth-need strength (p. 414)

job (p. 407)

job burnout (p. 422)

job design (p. 407)

job enlargement (p. 411)

job enrichment (p. 412)

job involvement (p. 407)

job performance (p. 408)

job rotation (p. 411)

job satisfaction (p. 407)

job sharing (p. 417)

job simplification (p. 411)

organisational commitment (p. 407)

part-time work (p. 419)

personal wellness (p. 423)

psychological contract (p. 405)

sociotechnical system (p. 414)

stress (p. 420)

stressors (p. 420)

telecommuting (p. 417)

Type A personality (p. 421)

workplace rage (p. 422)

APPLIED ACTIVITIES

Short-response questions

1. What is a 'healthy' psychological contract?
2. What difference does growth-need strength make in the job enrichment process?
3. Why is it important for a manager to understand the Type A personality?
4. Why might an employer not be interested in offering employees the option of working on a compressed work week schedule?

Application question

5. Graham Pilling has just attended a management development program in which the following 'high-performance equation' was discussed: Performance = Ability × Support × Effort. As a plant manager, he is interested in implementing the concept. He plans to hold a meeting for all of his team leaders to explain the implications of this equation. If you were Graham, how would you explain the importance of each performance factor — ability, support, effort — and how would you explain the significance of the multiplication signs in the equation?

CAREER READINESS ACTIVITIES

Recommended individual and group learning activities from the end-of-text Career Readiness Workbook for this chapter include:

Career advancement portfolio   **WB**

Update your career advancement portfolio to reflect your new skills and experiences. Include skills and personal insights you gain from the following projects and exercises.

Research and presentation project   **WB**

- Project 6 — Controversies in CEO pay — 'is it too high?'

Cross-functional integrative case   **WB**

Read the integrative case on Sarina Russo and answer the following questions:

15.1 Would you agree that Sarina Russo has a Type A personality? Justify your view.
15.2 The section on the meaning of work, in chapter 15, provides a rather negative perspective on the experience of work. Yet the federal government's Job Network has been set up to assist unemployed people find work, and in the case of those people who have been unemployed for extended periods, the government is prepared to pay considerable fees to Job Network providers to give them intensive assistance. In your view, is the service provided by Job Network enough? Should the service conclude with finding candidates a job?

Exercises in teamwork WB

- Exercise 7 — What do you value in work?
- Exercise 13 — The future workplace
- Exercise 22 — The case of the casual workforce

Management skills assessment WB

- Assessment 15 — Job design preference

ELECTRONIC RESOURCES

Don't forget to take full advantage of the online support for *Management: An Asia–Pacific Perspective* at www.johnwiley.com.au/highered/management: chapter 15 practice tests, e-flashcards, crossword puzzles, interactive management skills assessments, interactive cases, the online career advancement portfolio and much more!

CASE FOR CRITICAL THINKING

Read the following case for critical thinking on Com Tech. While you are reading the case keep in mind what you have learned in this chapter, then answer the questions.

CASE FOR CRITICAL THINKING
Com Tech:
focus on job design

Imagine working for a company that provides a challenging, stimulating environment, a great team and a sense of fun. Some may argue that such companies do not exist, but many in the IT sector view Com Tech Communications (now Dimension Data Australia) as *the* place to work. In fact one of its employees said: 'I work for the best company in the market'.

Com Tech's business is in providing complementary IT services, including technical training and network and systems solutions. It also resells hardware and software products to its corporate clients.

Founded by David Shein in 1987, Com Tech quickly established itself as one of the leading IT service companies in Australia and New Zealand. By 2001, the company employed more than 1400 staff and had annual revenues of more than $700 million. While many IT companies experienced stable or negative growth in the wake of the downturn in the IT sector in 2000 (the infamous 'tech wreck'), Com Tech continued to experience strong growth in the demand for its services.

The explanation for the company's success lies primarily with a strong, innovative culture, its people and their commitment to providing excellent customer service. Com Tech adopted an approach of empowering its employees to ensure they could make decisions to achieve 'legendary customer service'. According to general manager William Masson, 'staff have the freedom to do whatever they want to do, to excel and be innovative to get things done. Quite frankly, I don't think we pay enormous salaries; it is Com Tech's environment, culture, training and excellent technical reputation that attracts people.'

Unlike many of its competitors, the company looks beyond the technical skills of potential recruits. It believes it is important to recruit employees who are able to identify strongly with the goals of the company. In fact, in the selection process, it weights an individual's personality traits and values higher than technical knowledge and skills. It seeks to employ people who can perform at the highest levels within a culture that places a high value on commitment, teamwork and a strong customer focus. Com Tech then analyses the employee's skills and invests heavily in appropriate training so they can provide the high level of technical service the company is known for.

Com Tech's approach reflects the increasingly popular view that the real value of a company lies in its intangibles — its relationships with employers, customers and suppliers and its corporate culture.

The company's recent success in adapting to the needs of an important potential customer provides evidence of how this style of approach works in practice. Com Tech was one of five companies seeking to win a contract. Although all five of the competitors were competitively matched in terms of price and product offerings, only Com Tech could respond to the customer's request to submit the proposal within seven days. With more rigid, hierarchical structures, Com Tech's competitors needed closer to two weeks to develop and submit their proposals. According to William Masson: 'The customer was incredibly impressed with the autonomy and empowerment of the Com Tech staff as the team dealt with negotiations — within two hours we had closed the deal. There is no question that our people management processes give us a competitive edge.'

Teamwork is also considered a key to Com Tech's success. David Shein says of his employees: 'They are team orientated compared to individuals. They share information and have the view that knowledge is not power. A team player is obsessed with customer satisfaction, rather than someone who thinks they are indispensable.'

Not everything at Com Tech is perfect, however. The company experiences a relatively high turnover of staff in their first year of employment, particularly as new staff determine whether their style of working suits the empowered, challenging culture of Com Tech. In addition, the empowerment of employees has led some to view training as optional. Still, for those who remain, the company provides ongoing technical training and easy access to senior managers. Employees are encouraged to communicate with all levels of management, particularly when directions are unclear. Further, senior management supports employee decisions when they are challenged. The company also devotes resources to providing a comfortable and fun workplace.

Com Tech completed a merger with South Africa-based IT multinational Dimension Data in July 2001, the merged entity assuming the name Dimension Data Australia. Dimension Data employs more than 12 000 people and operates in over 30 countries. While David Shein insists the two companies are a strong fit, some staff naturally expressed some concern about the change.[72]

Source: Critical Examination of Strategic Behaviour at Com Tech–Dimension Data. James Mystakidis, John Hugh, Bill Martin, Patrick Paffard, Belinda Gibbons. Belinda Gibbons is Public Fundraising Director of Opportunity International Australia.

QUESTIONS

1. Describe the jobs at Com Tech in terms of their design and any relevant elements of the job characteristics model.

2. Do you think that employees at Com Tech would have a stronger psychological contract with the company than staff at other companies in this industry? Why or why not?

3. Can you identify any potential problems arising from Com Tech's approach and culture in the context of its continued growth and merger with Dimension Data? Are there other problems which might occur if the company's growth stalls or reverses?

4. What kinds of stress might exist for people working at Com Tech? Could any potential stressors be relieved by providing more flexible work options such as telecommuting?

CHAPTER 16

Teams and teamwork

CHAPTER 16 STUDY QUESTIONS

- How do teams contribute to organisations?

- What are current trends in the use of teams?

- How do teams work?

- How do teams make decisions?

- What are the challenges of high-performance team leadership?

GETTING @ CONNECTED

Hewlett-Packard Australia — managing virtual teams

Working at Hewlett-Packard Australia (HP) is like being part of a huge global family. If you are working in research and development, for instance, you might report to a local manager in Australia who is responsible for your HP branch office, as well as to a regional research and development manager located in Tokyo or Singapore. You might also be a member of a 'virtual' product design team made up of HP staff from across the world.

Although there are real challenges in building effective teams across different locations and cultures, HP believes that managing its organisation in this way is worth the effort. Such teams can take advantage of the best people available for a particular task, no matter where they reside, and team members can bring important local knowledge to the creation of global products.

Virtual teams do not suit everyone, however. Team members need to be self-motivated, able to work independently, and open to the idea of communicating with colleagues at unusual hours and in non-traditional ways. In particular, with videoconferencing, teleconferencing and e-mail being the primary means of communication, it goes without saying that team members need to be skilled and efficient communicators and IT-savvy.[1]

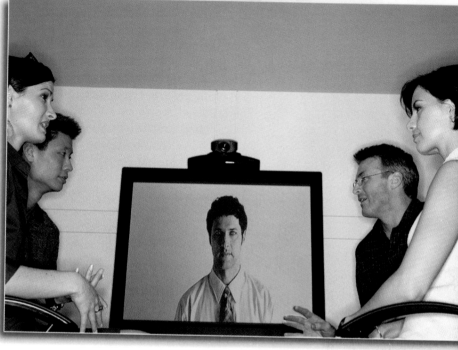

GET CONNECTED!

Check out the Hewlett-Packard web site www.jobs.hp.com to view information about the working environment at HP, and to read the stories of people working for HP around the globe.

GET CONNECTED!

People have the need to work in teams. There is a desire to work with others and enjoy the benefits of your work and your successes together... these satisfactions are as important today as they have ever been.[2]

Andy Grove, Chairman of Intel, Inc.

Prominent Australian management professors Doug Stace and Dexter Dunphy state that the use of teams is one of the features of work at leading organisations.

In organisations that have been hierarchical, there is now increasing and radical delegation to the team level... members have a high level of discretion in taking decisions relevant to the activities of their work unit.[3]

As these opening quotes suggest, the new workplace is rich in teams and teamwork. In building high-performance organisations driven by speed, innovation, efficiency, spontaneity and continuous change, harnessing the great potential of teams and teamwork is a part of the process. The overall goal is always to create work environments within which the full talents of people are enthusiastically mobilised in support of organisational goals. This critical human capital of organisations must be nurtured and developed both at the level of the individual contributor, the subject of the last chapter, and at the level of the work group or team, our present concern. But even as we recognise that finding the best ways to use teams as performance resources is an increasingly important managerial task, the ability to successfully lead through teamwork is not always easy to achieve.

Just the words *group* and *team* elicit both positive and negative reactions in the minds of many people. As noted by Australian writer Adele Ferguson, teams can represent the very best or the very worst, although most teams are probably somewhere between these two extremes.

Teams are appealing because they hold out the promise of something along the lines of the family unit: caring, sharing, loving and committed. The belief is that the ideal team is a miracle of autonomous cross-functional efficiency. It shares knowledge and creates solutions. It cuts costs and is close to the customer. Put simply, teams increase productivity, improve communication and improve processes. For these reasons the rules for work have been changing. Individuals are now being judged by how well they work in a team. This is translating into who will be hired, who will be promoted and who will be let go. But proponents of the dream team forget the dark side of the family unit: rivalry, bitchiness and the conflict between wanting to belong and wanting to be noticed as an individual. These darker elements subvert the dream team.[4]

TEAMS IN ORGANISATIONS

Most tasks in organisations are well beyond the capabilities of individuals alone — they can only be accomplished by people working together in teams. Especially in this age of intellectual capital and knowledge work, true managerial success will be earned in substantial part through success at mobilising, leading and supporting high-performing teams. The new organisational designs and cultures require it, as does any true commitment to empowerment and employee involvement.[5] There is no doubt that teams are indispensable to the new workplace. The question for managers and team leaders, and the guiding theme of this chapter, thus becomes: How do we make sure that teams and teamwork are utilised to everyone's best advantage?

Before proceeding, let's be specific about the terminology. A **team** is a small group of people with complementary skills, who work together to accomplish shared goals while holding themselves mutually accountable for performance results.[6] **Teamwork** is the process of people working together to accomplish these goals.

Challenges of teamwork

Figure 16.1 shows four important roles that managers must perform in order to fully master the challenges of teams and teamwork. These roles, along with examples, are: *supervisor* — serving as the appointed head of a formal work unit; *facilitator* — serving as the peer leader and networking hub for a special task force; *participant* — serving as a helpful contributing member of a project team; and *coach* — serving as the external convenor or sponsor of a problem-solving team staffed by others. In all of these settings, performance results will depend on both the understanding of how teams operate and actively helping them succeed.

Supervisor   Network facilitator   Helpful participant   External coach

How managers get involved with teams and teamwork

Figure 16.1 ▸ Team and teamwork roles for managers

Experience has taught all of us that teams and teamwork are not problem free. Who hasn't heard people complain about having to attend what they consider to be another 'time-wasting' meeting?[7] And who hasn't encountered **social loafing** — the presence of 'free-riders' who slack off because responsibility is diffused in teams and others are present to do the work?[8] Things don't have to be this way. The time we spend in groups can be productive and satisfying, but to make it so we must understand the complex nature of groups and their internal dynamics.[9]

An important skill is knowing *when* a team is the best choice for a task. Another is knowing *how* to work with and manage the team to best accomplish that task. Take social loafing as an example. What can a leader or other concerned team member do when someone is free-riding? It's not easy, but the problem can be handled. Actions can be taken to make individual contributions more visible, reward individuals for their contributions, make task assignments more interesting, and keep group size small so that free-riders are more visible and subject to peer pressure and leader evaluation.[10]

As we proceed, keep in mind other problems encountered when we work in teams. Personality conflicts are commonplace. Individual differences in personality and work style can disrupt the team. Tasks are not always clear. Ambiguous agendas and/or ill-defined problems can cause teams to work too long on the wrong things. Not everyone is always ready to work. Sometimes the issue is motivation, but it may be due to conflicts with other work deadlines and priorities. It may also be caused by a lack of team organisation and/or progress. Time is wasted when meetings lack purpose and when members come unprepared. These and other difficulties can turn the great potential of teams into frustration and failure. Clearly, teams are hard work. But, they are also worth it!

A **team** is a collection of people who regularly interact to pursue common goals.

Teamwork is the process of people actively working together to accomplish common goals.

Social loafing is the tendency of some people to avoid responsibility by 'free-riding' in groups.

Teams versus individualism

Cultures vary and so do their approaches to teams. People from cultures which are high in individualism may react negatively to the idea of team-based organisational structures.

Consider your openness to working in organisational teams and compare this to the views of class colleagues.

Synergy and the usefulness of teams

A major reason that teams are worth the effort is **synergy** — the creation of a whole that is greater than the sum of its parts. Teamwork in our society makes available everything from aircraft to the Internet to music videos. It all happens because of synergy, the bringing together of individual talents and efforts to create extraordinary things. Synergy occurs when a team uses its membership resources to the fullest and thereby achieves through collective action far more than could otherwise be achieved. This is obviously an important advantage for organisations facing the uncertainties and demands of increasingly complex operating environments.

Teams are also useful in other ways. They can be very beneficial for their members. Being part of a team can have a strong influence on individual attitudes and behaviours. When the experience is positive, working in and being part of a team helps satisfy important individual needs. Sometimes these are needs that may be difficult to meet in the regular work setting. Thus, teams can be very good for both organisations and their members. They are an indispensable human resource whose usefulness in the work setting includes the following:[11]

Usefulness of teams

- more resources for problem solving
- improved creativity and innovation
- improved quality of decision making
- greater commitments to tasks
- higher motivation through collective action
- better control and work discipline
- more individual need satisfaction.

Formal and informal groups

The teams officially recognised and supported by the organisation for specific purposes are **formal groups**. They are part of the formal structure and are created to fulfil a variety of essential operations. A good example is the work group consisting of a manager and subordinates, and responsible for the continuing performance of tasks important to the organisation. Work groups exist in various sizes and go by different labels. They may be called *departments* (e.g. market research department), *units* (e.g. product assembly unit), *teams* (e.g. customer service team) or *divisions* (e.g. office products division), among other possibilities. In all cases, they are the building blocks of organisation structures. Indeed, in Rensis Likert's classic view of organisations, they are interlocking networks of groups in which managers and leaders serve important 'linking pin' roles.[12] Each manager or leader serves both as a superior in one functional group and as a subordinate in the next-higher-level one. When the resulting vertical and horizontal linkages are well managed, they help integrate the diverse activities and accomplishments of teams throughout an organisation.

Standing in contrast to the formal groups just described are the **informal groups** that are also present and important in every organisation. These informal groups are not recognised on organisation charts and are not officially created to serve an organisational purpose. They emerge as part of the informal structure and from natural or spontaneous relationships among people. You might recognise these as *interest groups* in which workers band together to pursue a common cause or special position, such as a concern for poor working conditions. Some emerge as *friendship groups* that develop for a wide variety of personal reasons, including shared non-work interests. Others emerge as *support groups* in which the members basically help one another do their jobs.

Informal groups may also include people from outside the immediate organisation. For instance, increasingly complex Australian tax laws are encouraging accountants with small practices to develop informal alliances with friendly, often larger firms, who can share expertise and knowledge. For instance, small practices may use the services of a tax barrister based at a larger practice to provide written advice or representation for a client.[13] Two points about informal groups are especially important for managers to understand. First, informal groups are not necessarily bad. Indeed, they can have a positive impact on work performance. In particular, the relationships and connections made possible by informal groups may actually help speed the workflow or allow people to 'get things done' in ways not possible within the formal structure. Second, informal groups can help satisfy social needs that members find otherwise thwarted or not met in the formal work setting. Among other things, members of informal groups often find that the groups offer social satisfactions, security, support and a sense of belonging.

TRENDS IN THE USE OF TEAMS

The trend toward greater empowerment in organisations is associated with new developments that extend the use of teams beyond the formal group or work team described earlier.[14] In previous chapters, for example, we noted the growing use of cross-functional teams to improve integration. A variety of employee involvement teams, including quality circles, are also increasingly more commonplace as managers seek to expand opportunities for broadbased participation in workplace affairs. Developments in information technology are also creating further opportunities for people to work together in computer-mediated or virtual teams.

Committees

A **committee** brings people together outside of their daily job assignments to work in a small team for a specific purpose. The task agenda is typically narrow, focused and ongoing. Membership changes over time as the committee remains in existence. Committees are led by a designated head or chairperson, who is held accountable for performance results. Organisations usually have a variety of permanent or standing committees dedicated to a wide variety of concerns — diversity and compensation are two common examples.[15] At Marriott International, a committee of top executives meets several times each year to focus on human capital. The group reviews progress in hiring and retaining the best talent, and makes suggestions for future improvements.[16]

> A **committee** is a formal team designated to work on a special task on a continuing basis.

Project teams and task forces

Task forces or project teams perform important work for the organisation, but exist only temporarily. Importantly, the task assignments for project teams and task forces are very specific; completion deadlines are also clearly defined. Once the project or task is completed the team disbands. On long-running projects, the membership of the team may change over time. Creativity and innovation are very important. Project teams, for example, might be formed to develop a new product or service, redesign an office layout or provide specialised consulting for a client.[17] Like committees, project teams and task forces bring together people from various parts of an organisation to work on common problems. They bring to the team special skills and expertise critical to its purpose. In order to achieve the desired results, any project team or task force must be carefully established and then well run. Some guidelines for managing projects and task forces are found in Manager's Notepad 16.1.[18]

> **Task forces** are formal teams convened for a specific purpose and expected to disband when that purpose is achieved.

Guidelines for managing projects and task forces

- Select appropriate team members who will be challenged by the assignment, who have the right skills and who seem able to work well together.
- Clearly define the purpose of the team to ensure that members and important outsiders know what is expected, why, and on what timetable.
- Carefully select a team leader who has good interpersonal skills, can respect the ideas of others and is willing to do what needs to be done.
- Periodically review progress to ensure that all team members feel collectively accountable for results, and that they receive performance feedback.

Cross-functional teams

Organisational design today emphasises adaptation and horizontal integration.[19] It emphasises problem solving and information sharing. It also tries to eliminate the functional chimneys problem, described in chapter 10 as the tendency of workers to remain within their functions and restrict communication with other parts of an organisation. **Cross-functional teams**, whose members come from different functional units and parts of an organisation, are indispensable to fulfilment of these design goals.

🗹 **Cross-functional teams** bring together members from different functional departments.

Typically, the members of a cross-functional team come together to work on a specific problem or task and to do so with the needs of the whole organisation in mind. They are expected to share information, explore new ideas, seek creative solutions and meet project deadlines. Importantly, they are expected to not be limited by narrow functional concerns and demands. Rather, the team members collectively and individually are to think and act cross-functionally and in the best interests of the total system. At ABB Industrial Systems, Inc., cross-functional teams are specifically created to knock down the 'walls' separating departments within the firm. Representation on a team might consist, for example, of engineers, buyers, assemblers and shipping clerks.[20]

Employee involvement teams

🗹 **Employee involvement teams** meet on a regular basis to use their talents to help solve problems and achieve continuous improvement.

Another development in today's organisations is use of **employee involvement teams**. These are groups of workers who meet on a regular basis outside of their formal assignments, with the goal of applying their expertise and attention to important workplace matters. The general purpose of employee involvement teams is continuous improvement. Using a problem-solving framework, the teams try to bring the benefits of employee participation to bear on a wide variety of performance issues and concerns.

🗹 A **quality circle** is a group of employees who periodically meet to discuss ways of improving work quality.

Another popular form of employee involvement team is the **quality circle**, a group of workers that meets regularly to discuss and plan specific ways to improve work quality.[21] Usually it consists of 6–12 members from a work area. After receiving special training in problem solving, team processes and quality issues, members of the quality circle try to come up with suggestions that can be implemented to raise productivity through quality improvements. Quality circles became popular with some companies in Western countries, in part because of their place in Japanese management. Along with other types of involvement teams, they are now found in organisations where empowerment and participation are valued as keys to high performance.

National Library Board of Singapore •
www.lib.gov.sg

Teams helping to create a world-class library

In Asia, the importance of teamwork is on the rise. Whether coping with changing economic fortunes or working with partners in a merger or strategic alliance, the need for effective teamwork is taking on a new significance. At the National Library Board of Singapore, teamwork is viewed as one of the keys to creating a world-class library system and high-tech learning organisation. According to chief executive Christopher Chia: 'Once we can establish better group dynamics at the top, they can be transmitted down through the organisation so that all departments establish partnerships to work together'.[22]

Virtual teams

A newer form of group that is increasingly common in today's organisations is the **virtual team**, sometimes called a *computer-mediated group* or *electronic group network*.[23] This is a team of people who work together and solve problems largely through computer-mediated rather than face-to-face interactions. Chapter 3, on information and decision making, highlighted the role of new technology in today's organisations. Among the many developments, the sophistication of networking technologies and groupware programs is highly significant. As organisations become increasingly global in their operations and perspectives, the opportunity to use virtual teams whose members are physically dispersed, even among locations around the world, is highly advantageous.

The use of intranets and special software support for computerised meetings is changing the way many committees, task forces and other problem-solving teams function.[24] Working in virtual environments, team members consider problems and seek consensus on how to best deal with them. This is just like any team in respect to *what* gets done. *How* things get done, however, is different for virtual teams. This can be a source of both potential problems and advantages, which should be understood by managers considering the use of virtual teams in daily affairs.

Problems in virtual teamwork can occur when the members have difficulty establishing good working relationships. Relations among team members can become depersonalised as the lack of face-to-face interaction limits the role of emotions and non-verbal cues in the communication process.[25] But virtual teams also have many potential advantages. They can save time and travel expenses. They can allow members to work collectively in a time-efficient fashion, and without interpersonal difficulties that might otherwise occur — especially when the issues are controversial. A vice-president for human resources at Marriott, for example, once called electronic meetings 'the quietest, least stressful, most productive meetings you've ever had'.[26]

Members of a **virtual team** work together and solve problems through computer-based interactions.

Virtual teams can also be easily expanded to include additional experts as needed, and the discussions and information shared among team members can be stored on line for continuous updating and access.

Developing insights on virtual teams suggests that following some basic guidelines can help ensure that the advantages outweigh the disadvantages. The critical ingredients relate to the creation of positive impressions and the development of trust among team members who lack face-to-face meeting opportunities. First, virtual teams should begin with social messaging that allows the exchange of information about themselves to personalise the process. Second, virtual team members should be assigned clear roles so that they can focus while working alone and also know what others are doing. Third, virtual team members must join and engage the team with positive attitudes that support a willingness to work hard to meet team goals.[27]

International teams

International teams
are teams that include
members from at least two
different countries.

Employees are increasingly being asked to become members of **international teams**, particularly if they are undertaking an overseas assignment or working within a multinational company. International teams are comprised of members of different nationalities, and so the real challenge is to manage the cultural differences so that the team performs effectively.

International teams have arisen in response to a number of contemporary pressures on organisations. Globalisation has encouraged the view that companies in many industries, such as pharmaceuticals and motor vehicles, should take advantage of the opportunity to have a presence in international markets, and this usually requires that people work together across two or more countries. Many organisations are pursuing international strategic alliances, mergers, acquisitions or joint ventures. International teams are often established to help manage the new organisational structures created from these moves. In addition, the increased scientific and environmental complexities of many of the issues confronting today's organisations demand that the best expertise is used, no matter where it is located within the organisation, and the rise of better communications and IT makes interacting with colleagues in different locations far easier than in times past, as was noted in the previous discussion of virtual teams.

Issues arising from cultural differences can easily derail the performance of international teams, whether these differences involve language, understanding, communication styles, or the simple fact that members of the team may be located in different countries. For instance, a Hong Kong Chinese manager working in Hong Kong for a British-owned bank stated: 'When I went to Australia, I had to learn to interrupt or else I would never have spoken at all'.[28]

Few managers from 'doing' and 'action-oriented' cultures such as the American, British, Australian, New Zealander and Scandinavian cultures are comfortable with the reality that teams which work first on their personal interactions, start slowly, plan carefully and often speed up exponentially as they move further into their work. Managers from these cultures can easily become frustrated if they find their team colleagues working methodically and systematically when all they want to do is 'dive in' and move as quickly as possible.

Many companies use skilled facilitators to maximise the effectiveness of their international teams. These facilitators can help international teams move more quickly towards high performance by using appropriate support processes such as undertaking regular team reviews and helping teams to clearly specify their key goals and targets.[29]

Self-managing work teams

In a growing number of organisations the *functional team* consisting of a first-level supervisor and his or her immediate subordinates is disappearing. It is being replaced with a new organisational form built from the foundation of **self-managing work teams**. Sometimes called *autonomous work groups*, these are teams of workers whose jobs have been redesigned to create a high degree of task interdependence and who have been given authority to make many decisions about how they go about doing the required work.[30]

Self-managing teams operate with participative decision making, shared tasks and the responsibility for many of the managerial tasks performed by supervisors in more traditional settings. The 'self-management' responsibilities include planning and scheduling work, training members in various tasks, sharing tasks, meeting performance goals, ensuring high quality and solving day-to-day operating problems. In some settings, the team's authority may even extend to 'hiring' and 'firing' its members when necessary. A key feature is *multitasking*, in which team members each have the skills to perform several different jobs. As shown in figure 16.2, typical characteristics of self-managing teams are as follows:
- Members are held collectively accountable for performance results.
- Members have discretion in distributing tasks within the team.
- Members have discretion in scheduling work within the team.
- Members are able to perform more than one job on the team.
- Members train one another to develop multiple job skills.
- Members evaluate one another's performance contributions.
- Members are responsible for the total quality of team products.

 Members of **self-managing work teams** have the authority to make decisions about how they share and complete their work.

Characteristics of self-managing teams

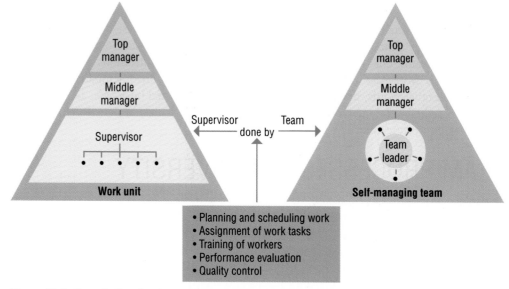

Figure 16.2 ▸ Organisational and management implications of self-managing work teams

The structural implications of self-managing teams are also depicted in figure 16.2. Members of a self-managing team report to higher management through a team leader rather than a formal supervisor, making the role of first-line supervisor unnecessary. This is an important change in the traditional structure. Each self-managing team handles the supervisory duties on its own, and each team leader handles the upward reporting relationships. High-level managers to whom self-managing teams report must learn to work with teams rather than individual subordinates.

This can be a difficult challenge for some managers who are used to more traditional operating methods. As the concept of self-managing teams spreads globally, researchers are also examining the receptivity of different cultures to self-management concepts.[31] Such cultural dimensions as high power distance and individualism, for example, may generate resistance that must be considered when implementing this and other team-based organisational practices.

Within a self-managing team the emphasis is always on participation. The leader and members are expected to work together not only to do the required work but also to make the decisions that determine how it gets done. A true self-managing team emphasises team decision making, shared tasks, high involvement and collective responsibility for accomplished results. The expected advantages include better performance, decreased costs and higher morale. Of course, these results are not guaranteed. Managing the transition to self-managing teams from more traditional work settings isn't always easy — the process requires leadership committed to both empowerment and a lot of support.

A study of self-managing teams in New Zealand found that the major benefits arising from their introduction were increased employee morale and motivation, increased employee knowledge gained from the experience of working in teams, improved quality and productivity and the development of better solutions for problems. There were a number of reasons for the success of self-managing teams, including the provision of appropriate resources and information, the use of effective communication, sponsorship from senior management and the use of empowerment to ensure that the teams were truly self-managing. Major problems encountered by self-managing teams included over-dependence on the leader by other team members, team members feeling that consensus was sometimes 'imposed', and complacency occurring when the team 'rested on its laurels'.[32]

The use of self-managing work teams appears to vary by industry sector and business size. As discussed in the case for critical thinking at the end of this chapter, travel company Flight Centre bases its entire business around self-managing teams. In contrast, a recent Australian study found that although most small and medium-sized Australian organisations have implemented teams, chiefly to enable employees to participate in decisions and in order to achieve higher workplace productivity, few had become more than semi-autonomous in operation. In other words, most teams in small and medium-sized businesses have emerged naturally based on existing work groups. Few have been deliberately designed to function as self-managing work teams.[33]

TEAM PROCESSES AND DIVERSITY

Regardless of its form and purpose, any team must achieve three key results — perform tasks, satisfy members and remain viable for the future.[34] On the *performance* side, a work group or team is expected to transform resource inputs (such as ideas, materials and objects) into product outputs (such as a report, decision, service or commodity) that have some value to the organisation. The members of a team should also be able to experience *satisfaction* from both these performance results and their participation in the process. And, in respect to *future viability*, the team should have a social and work climate that makes members willing and able to work well together in the future, again and again as needed.

What is an effective team?

An **effective team** is one that achieves and maintains high levels of both task performance and member satisfaction, and retains its viability for future action.[35] Figure 16.3 shows how any team can be viewed as an open system that transforms various resource inputs into

An **effective team** achieves high levels of both task performance and membership satisfaction.

these outcomes. Among the important inputs are such things as the organisational setting, the nature of the task, the team size and the membership characteristics.[36] Each of these factors plays a role in setting the stage for group performance.

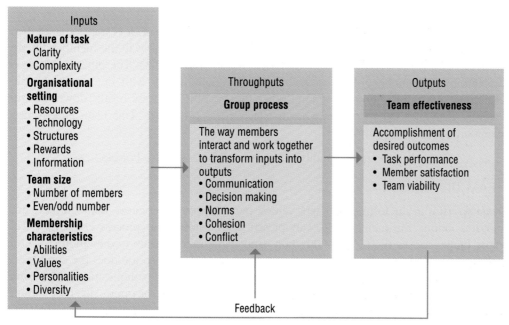

Figure 16.3 ▸ An open-systems model of work team effectiveness

GROUP INPUTS

The *nature of the task* is always important. It affects how well a team can focus its efforts and how intense the group process needs to be to get the job done. Clearly defined tasks make it easier for team members to focus their work efforts. Complex tasks require more information exchange and intense interaction than do simpler tasks. The *organisational setting* can also affect how team members relate to one another and apply their skills toward task accomplishment. A key issue is the amount of support provided in terms of information, material resources, technology, organisation structures, available rewards and spatial arrangements. Increasingly, for example, organisations are being architecturally designed to directly facilitate teamwork. At St Luke's Advertising Agency in London, the traditional office environment has been replaced in favour of a long desk in the centre of a large room. The desk has access for laptop computer connection and it provides a central focus at which open communication and the free flow of ideas are encouraged. There are some benches around the desk, as well as meeting rooms nearby; however, the company aims to eliminate the sense of hierarchy normally associated with the size, location and layout of offices and instead promote the type of creative thinking for which St Luke's has become famous.[37]

Team size affects how members work together, handle disagreements and reach agreements. The number of potential interactions increases geometrically as teams increase in size and communications become more congested. Teams larger than about six or seven members can be difficult to manage for the purpose of creative problem solving. When voting is required, teams with odd numbers of members are often preferred so as to prevent 'ties'. In all teams, the *membership characteristics* are important. Teams must have members with the right abilities, or skill mix, to master and perform tasks well. They must also have values, personalities and diversity appropriate to the task that are sufficiently compatible for everyone to work well together.

GROUP PROCESS

 Group process is the way team members work together to accomplish tasks.

Although having the right inputs available to a team is important, it is not a guarantee of effectiveness. What is called **group process** counts too. It is the way the members of any team actually work together as they transform inputs into outputs. The process aspects of any group or team include how well members communicate with one another, make decisions and handle conflicts, among other things. When process breaks down and the internal dynamics fail in any way, team effectiveness can suffer. This team effectiveness equation is a helpful reminder:

Team effectiveness equation

Team effectiveness = Quality of inputs + (Process gains − Process losses).

TEAM DIVERSITY

Team diversity, in the form of different values, personalities, experiences, demographics and cultures among the membership, can present significant group process challenges. The more homogeneous the team — the more similar the members are to one another — the easier it is to manage relationships. As team diversity increases, so too does the complexity of interpersonal relationships among members. But with the complications also come special opportunities. The more heterogeneous the team — the more diversity among members — the greater the variety of available ideas, perspectives and experiences that can add value to problem solving and task performance.

In teamwork, as with organisations at large, the diversity lesson is very clear. There is a lot to gain when membership diversity is valued and well managed. The process challenge is to maximise the advantages of team diversity while minimising its potential disadvantages. In the international arena, for example, research indicates that culturally diverse work teams have more difficulty learning how to work well together than do culturally homogeneous teams.[38] That is, they tend to struggle more in the early stages of working together. However, once the process challenges are successfully mastered, the diverse teams eventually prove to be more creative than the homogeneous ones.

Stages of team development

A synthesis of research on small groups suggests that there are five distinct phases in the life cycle of any team:[39]

Stages of team development

1. *Forming* — a stage of initial orientation and interpersonal testing
2. *Storming* — a stage of conflict over tasks and working as a team
3. *Norming* — a stage of consolidation around task and operating agendas
4. *Performing* — a stage of teamwork and focused task performance
5. *Adjourning* — a stage of task completion and disengagement.

FORMING STAGE

The forming stage involves the first entry of individual members into a team. This is a stage of initial task orientation and interpersonal testing. As individuals come together for the first time or two, they ask a number of questions: What can or does the team offer me? What will I be asked to contribute? Can my needs be met while my efforts serve the task needs of the team?

In the forming stage, people begin to identify with other members and with the team itself. They are concerned about getting acquainted, establishing interpersonal relationships, discovering what is considered acceptable behaviour and learning how others perceive the team's task. This may also be a time when some members rely on or become temporarily dependent on another member who appears 'powerful' or especially 'knowledgeable'. Such things as prior experience with team members in other contexts and individual impressions of organisation philosophies, goals and policies may also affect member relationships in new work teams. Difficulties in the forming stage tend to be greater in more culturally and demographically diverse teams.

STORMING STAGE

The storming stage of team development is a period of high emotionality. Tension often emerges between members over tasks and interpersonal concerns. There may be periods of outright hostility and infighting. Coalitions or cliques may form around personalities or interests. Subteams form around areas of agreement and disagreement involving group tasks and/or the manner of operations. Conflict may develop as individuals compete to impose their preferences on others and to become influential in the group's status structure.

Important changes occur in the storming stage as task agendas become clarified and members begin to understand one another's interpersonal styles. Here attention begins to shift toward obstacles that may stand in the way of task accomplishment. Efforts are made to find ways to meet team goals while also satisfying individual needs. Failure in the storming stage can be a lasting liability, whereas success in the storming stage can set a strong foundation for later team effectiveness.

NORMING STAGE

Cooperation is an important issue for teams in the norming stage. At this point, members of the team begin to become coordinated as a working unit and tend to operate with shared rules of conduct. The team feels a sense of leadership, with each member starting to play useful roles. Most interpersonal hostilities give way to a precarious balancing of forces as norming builds initial integration. Harmony is emphasised, but minority viewpoints may be discouraged.

In the norming stage, members are likely to develop initial feelings of closeness, a division of labour and a sense of shared expectations. This helps protect the team from disintegration. Holding the team together may become even more important than successful task accomplishment.

PERFORMING STAGE

Teams in the performing stage are more mature, organised and well functioning. This is a stage of total integration in which team members are able to deal in creative ways with both complex tasks and any interpersonal conflicts. The team operates with a clear and stable structure, and members are motivated by team goals.

The primary challenges of teams in the performing stage are to continue refining the operations and relationships essential to working together as an integrated unit. Such teams need to remain coordinated with the larger organisation and adapt successfully to changing conditions over time. A team that has achieved total integration will score high on the criteria of team maturity, such as those on the checklist in figure 16.4.[40]

	Very poor			Very good	
1. Trust among members	1	2	3	4	5
2. Feedback mechanisms	1	2	3	4	5
3. Open communications	1	2	3	4	5
4. Approach to decisions	1	2	3	4	5
5. Leadership sharing	1	2	3	4	5
6. Acceptance of goals	1	2	3	4	5
7. Valuing diversity	1	2	3	4	5
8. Member cohesiveness	1	2	3	4	5
9. Support for each other	1	2	3	4	5
10. Performance norms	1	2	3	4	5
	Where you don't want to be			Where you do want to be	

Figure 16.4 ▸ Criteria for assessing the maturity of a team

ADJOURNING STAGE

The final stage of team development is adjourning, when team members prepare to achieve closure and disband. It is especially common for temporary groups that operate in the form of committees, task forces and project teams. Ideally, the team disbands with a sense that important goals have been accomplished. Members are acknowledged for their contributions and the group's overall success. This may be an emotional time, and disbandment should be managed with this possibility in mind. For members who have worked together intensely for a period of time, breaking up the close relationships may be painful. In all cases, the team would like to disband with members feeling they would work with one another again sometime in the future.

Norms and cohesiveness

A **norm** is a behaviour, rule or standard expected to be followed by team members.

A **norm** is a behaviour expected of team members.[41] It is a 'rule' or 'standard' that guides their behaviour. When violated, a norm may be enforced with reprimands and other sanctions. In the extreme, violation of a norm can result in a member being expelled from a team or socially ostracised by other members. The *performance norm*, which defines the level of work effort and performance that team members are expected to contribute, is extremely important. It can have positive or negative implications for team performance and organisational productivity. In general, work groups and teams with positive performance norms are more successful in accomplishing task objectives than are teams with negative performance norms. Other important team norms relate to such things as helpfulness, participation, timeliness, quality and innovation.

Because a team's norms are largely determined by the collective will of its members, it is difficult for a manager or designated leader simply to dictate which norms will be adopted. Instead, the concerned manager or team leader must help and encourage members to develop norms that support organisational objectives. During forming and storming steps of development, for example, norms relating to membership issues such as expected attendance and levels of commitment are important. By the time the stage of performing is reached, norms relating to adaptability and change become most relevant. Guidelines for *how to build positive norms* are as follows:[42]

- Act as a positive role model.
- Reinforce the desired behaviours with rewards.
- Control results by performance reviews and regular feedback.
- Train and orient new members to adopt desired behaviours.
- Recruit and select new members who exhibit the desired behaviours.
- Hold regular meetings to discuss progress and ways of improving.
- Use team decision-making methods to reach agreement.

How to build positive norms

Norms vary in the degree to which they are accepted and adhered to by team members. Conformity to norms is largely determined by the strength of **cohesiveness**, defined as the degree to which members are attracted to and motivated to remain part of a team.[43] Persons in a highly cohesive team value their membership and strive to maintain positive relationships with other team members. They experience satisfaction from team identification and interpersonal relationships. Because of this, highly cohesive teams are good for their members. They can also be very good for organisations, but not always. It all depends on the performance norm that the cohesiveness is paired with.

⚙ **Cohesiveness** is the degree to which members are attracted to and motivated to remain part of a team.

A basic rule of group dynamics is: The more cohesive the team, the greater the conformity of members to team norms. This has important implications for team performance. Look at figure 16.5. When the performance norm of a team is positive, high cohesion and the resulting conformity to norms has a beneficial effect on overall team performance. This is a 'best-case' scenario for both the manager and the organisation. Competent team members work hard and reinforce one another's task accomplishments while experiencing satisfaction with the team. But when the performance norm is negative in a cohesive team, high conformity to the norm can have undesirable results. The figure shows this as a 'worst-case' scenario where team performance suffers from restricted work efforts by members. Between these two extremes are mixed situations of moderate to low performance.

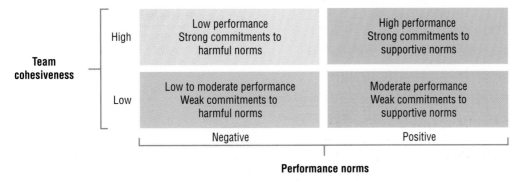

Figure 16.5 ▸ How cohesiveness and norms influence team performance

To achieve and maintain the best-case scenario shown in figure 16.5, managers should be skilled at influencing both the norms and cohesiveness of any team. They will want to build and maintain high cohesiveness in teams whose performance norms are positive. Guidelines on *how to increase cohesion* include the following:

How to increase team cohesiveness

- Induce agreement on team goals.
- Increase membership homogeneity.
- Increase interactions among members.
- Decrease team size.
- Introduce competition with other teams.
- Reward team rather than individual results.
- Provide physical isolation from other teams.

Task and maintenance needs

Task activities are actions taken by team members that directly contribute to the group's performance purpose.

Maintenance activities are actions taken by team members that support the emotional life of the group.

Research on the social psychology of groups identifies two types of activities that are essential if team members are to work well together over time.[44] **Task activities** contribute directly to the team's performance purpose, whereas **maintenance activities** support the emotional life of the team as an ongoing social system. Although a person with formal authority, such as a chairperson or supervisor, will often handle them, the responsibility for both types of activities should be shared and distributed among all team members. Any member can help lead a team by taking actions that help satisfy its task and maintenance needs. This concept of *distributed leadership in teams* thus makes every member continually responsible for recognising when task and/or maintenance activities are needed and then stepping in to provide them.

Figure 16.6 offers useful insights on distributed leadership in teams. Leading through task activities involves making an effort to define and solve problems and apply work efforts in support of accomplishing tasks. Without relevant task activities, such as initiating agendas, sharing information and others listed in the figure, teams will have difficulty accomplishing their objectives. Leading through maintenance activities, by contrast, helps strengthen and perpetuate the team as a social system. When the maintenance activities such as encouraging others and reducing tensions are performed well, good interpersonal relationships are achieved and the ability of the team to stay together over the longer term is ensured.

Distributed leadership roles in teams

Team leaders provide task activities		Team leaders provide maintenance activities	
• Initiating	• Elaborating	• Gatekeeping	• Following
• Information sharing	• Opinion giving	• Encouraging	• Harmonising
• Summarising			• Reducing tension

Team leaders avoid disruptive activities

• Being aggressive	• Competing
• Blocking	• Withdrawal
• Self-confessing	• Horsing around
• Seeking sympathy	• Seeking recognition

Figure 16.6 ▸ Distributed leadership helps teams meet task and maintenance needs.

Both team task and maintenance activities stand in distinct contrast to the *dysfunctional activities* also described in figure 16.6. Activities such as withdrawing and horsing around are usually self-serving to the individual member. They detract from, rather than enhance, team effectiveness. Unfortunately, very few teams are immune to dysfunctional behaviour by members. Everyone shares in the responsibility for minimising its occurrence and meeting the distributed leadership needs of a team by contributing functional task and maintenance behaviours.

Communication networks

Figure 16.7 depicts three interaction patterns and communication networks that are common in teams.[45] When teams are interacting intensively and their members are working closely together on tasks, close coordination of activities is needed. This need is best met by a **decentralised communication network** in which all members communicate directly with one another. Sometimes this is called the *all-channel* or *star communication network*. At other times and in other situations team members work on tasks independently, with the required work being divided up among them. Activities are coordinated and results pooled by a central point of control. Most communication flows back and forth between individual members and this hub or centre point. This creates a **centralised communication network** as shown in the figure. Sometimes this particular network is called a *wheel* or *chain communication structure*.

A **decentralised communication network** allows all members to communicate directly with one another.

In a **centralised communication network**, communication flows only between individual members and a hub or centre point.

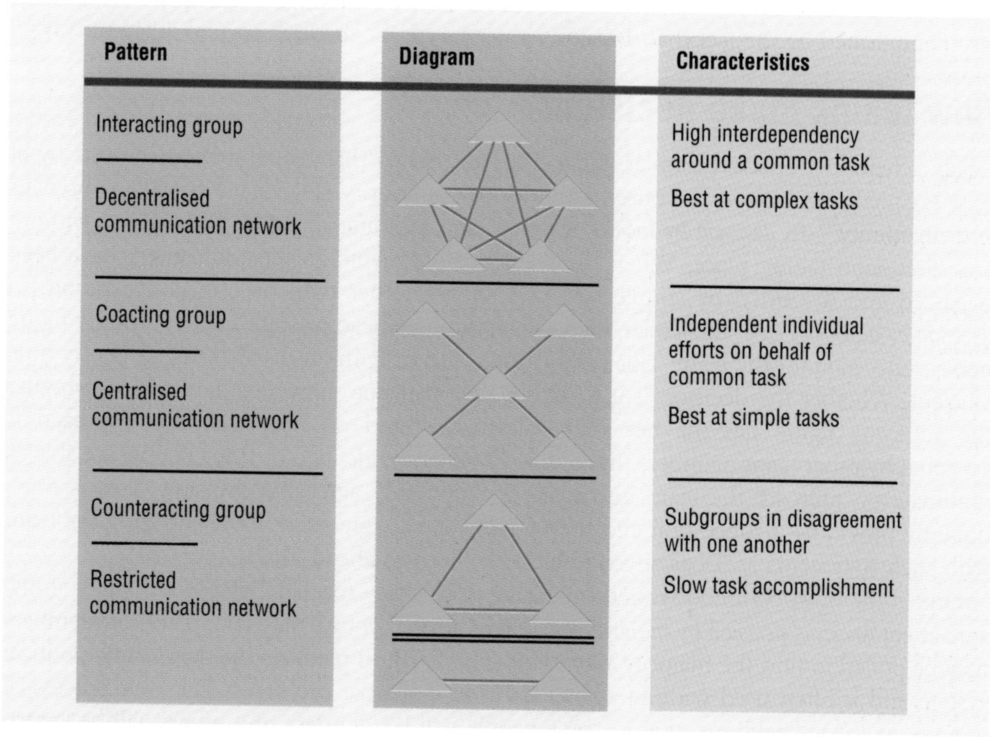

Pattern	Diagram	Characteristics
Interacting group Decentralised communication network		High interdependency around a common task Best at complex tasks
Coacting group Centralised communication network		Independent individual efforts on behalf of common task Best at simple tasks
Counteracting group Restricted communication network		Subgroups in disagreement with one another Slow task accomplishment

Figure 16.7 ▸ Interaction patterns and communication networks in teams

Source: © John R. Schermerhorn Jr, James G. Hunt and Richard N. Osborn, *Organizational Behavior*, 6th edn (New York: Wiley, 1997), p. 351. This material is used by permission of John Wiley & Sons, Inc.

When teams are composed of subgroups experiencing issue-specific disagreements, such as a temporary debate over the best means to achieve a goal, the resulting interaction pattern involves a *restricted communication network*. Here, the polarised subgroups contest one another and may engage in antagonistic relations. Communication between the subgroups is often limited and biased, with the result that problems can easily occur.

The best teams use communication networks in the right ways, at the right times, and for the right tasks. In general, centralised communication networks seem to work better on simple tasks.[46] These tasks require little creativity, information processing and problem solving, and lend themselves to more centralised control. They tend to be performed faster and more accurately by coacting groups. The reverse is true for more complex tasks, where interacting groups do better. Here, the decentralised networks work well since they are able to support the more intense interactions and information sharing required to perform under such task conditions. Interacting groups tend to be the top performers when tasks get complicated. When subgroups have difficulty communicating with one another, task accomplishment typically suffers for the short run at least. If the team is able to restore good communication between subgroups, it can benefit from the creativity and critical evaluation that typically accompanies conflict. If the subgroups drift further and further apart, negative dynamics set in and the team may suffer long-term damage.

DECISION MAKING IN TEAMS

🔘 **Decision making** is the process of making choices among alternative courses of action.

Decision making, discussed extensively in chapter 2, is the process of making choices among alternative possible courses of action. It is one of the most important group processes. It is also complicated by the fact that decisions in teams can be made in several different ways.

How teams make decisions

Edgar Schein, a respected scholar and consultant, notes that teams make decisions by at least six methods: lack of response, authority rule, minority rule, majority rule, consensus and unanimity.[47] In *decision by lack of response*, one idea after another is suggested without any discussion taking place. When the team finally accepts an idea, all others have been bypassed and discarded by simple lack of response rather than by critical evaluation. In *decision by authority rule*, the leader, manager, committee head or some other authority figure makes a decision for the team. This can be done with or without discussion and is very time efficient. Whether the decision is a good one or a bad one, however, depends on whether the authority figure has the necessary information and on how well this approach is accepted by other team members. In *decision by minority rule*, two or three people are able to dominate or 'railroad' the team into making a mutually agreeable decision. This is often done by providing a suggestion and then forcing quick agreement by challenging the team with such statements as 'Does anyone object? . . . Let's go ahead, then.'

One of the most common ways teams make decisions, especially when early signs of disagreement arise, is *decision by majority rule*. Here, formal voting may take place, or members may be polled to find the majority viewpoint. This method parallels the democratic political system and is often used without awareness of its potential problems. The very process of voting can create coalitions; that is, some people will be 'winners' and others will be 'losers' when the final vote is tallied. Those in the minority — the 'losers' — may feel left out or discarded without having had a fair say. They may be unenthusiastic about implementing the decision of the 'majority', and lingering resentments may impair team effectiveness in the future.

Teams are often encouraged to follow *decision by consensus*. This is a state of affairs whereby discussion leads to one alternative being favoured by most members and the other members agree to support it. When a consensus is reached, even those who may have

REALITY CHECK

Getting to group consensus

Everyone talks about group consensus, but we are often disappointed in our efforts to reach it. The reality is that consensus is only possible when the members of a team do the right things to make it possible.

What are some of the things you could do to help move a team toward consensus?

opposed the chosen course of action know that they have been heard and have had an opportunity to influence the decision outcome. Consensus, therefore, does not require unanimity. But it does require that team members be able to argue, engage in reasonable conflict, and yet still get along with and respect one another.[48] And it requires that there be the opportunity for any dissenting members to feel they have been able to speak — and that they have been listened to.

A *decision by unanimity* may be the ideal state of affairs. Here, all team members agree on the course of action to be taken. This is a 'logically perfect' method for decision making in teams, but it is also extremely difficult to attain in actual practice. One of the reasons that teams sometimes turn to authority decisions, majority voting or even minority decisions, in fact, is the difficulty of managing the team process to achieve consensus or unanimity.

POINT◄

COUNTER▲

Reward teams or reward individuals?

Associate Professor Ron Cacioppe of Curtin University in Western Australia argues that organisations should consider rewarding teams based on their stage of development. For instance, special individual salary increases, promotions and career development paths may assist in motivating people to join a team and begin its work (that is, during the 'forming' stage); whereas recognition rewards, such as praise, feedback and conference trips, and team rewards, such as gainsharing, team-focused merit pay and team spot bonuses, may make more sense during the 'performing' stage of team development.[49]

Can managers really be expected to 'fine tune' their reward systems to this degree? Won't individual differences still work against the effectiveness of this kind of approach?

Assets and liabilities of group decisions

The best teams do not limit themselves to just one decision-making method. Instead, they vary methods to best fit the problems at hand, in true contingency management fashion. A very important team leadership skill is the ability to help a team choose the 'best' decision method — one that provides for a timely and quality decision and one to which the members are highly committed. This reasoning is consistent with the Vroom–Jago leader-participation model discussed in chapter 13.[50] You should recall that this model describes how leaders should use the full range of individual, consultative and group decision methods as they resolve daily problems. To do this well, however, team leaders must understand the potential assets and potential liabilities of group decisions.[51]

The potential *advantages of group decision making* are significant. Because of this, the general argument is that team decisions should be sought whenever time and other circumstances permit. Team decisions make greater amounts of information, knowledge and expertise available to solve problems. They expand the number of action alternatives that are examined, and they help groups to avoid tunnel vision and tendencies to consider only a limited range of options. Team decisions increase the understanding and acceptance of outcomes by members. And importantly, team decisions increase the commitments of members to follow through to implement the decision once made. Simply put, team decisions can result in quality decisions that all members work hard to make successful.

The potential *disadvantages of group decision making* largely trace to the difficulties that can be experienced in group process. In a team decision there may be social pressure to conform. Individual members may feel intimidated or compelled to go along with the apparent wishes of others. There may be minority domination, where some members feel forced or 'railroaded' to accept a decision advocated by one vocal individual or small coalition. Also, the time required to make team decisions can sometimes be a disadvantage. As more people are involved in the dialogue and discussion, decision making takes longer. This added time may be costly, even prohibitively so, in certain circumstances.[52]

GROUPTHINK

A high level of cohesiveness can sometimes be a disadvantage during decision making. Members of very cohesive teams feel so strongly about the group that they may not want to do anything that might detract from feelings of goodwill. This may cause them to publicly agree with actual or suggested courses of action, while privately having serious doubts about them. Strong feelings of team loyalty can make it hard for members to criticise and evaluate one another's ideas and suggestions. Unfortunately, there are times when desires to hold the team together at all costs and avoid disagreements may result in poor decisions.

 Groupthink is a tendency for highly cohesive teams to lose their evaluative capabilities.

Symptoms of groupthink

Psychologist Irving Janis calls this phenomenon **groupthink**, the tendency for highly cohesive groups to lose their critical evaluative capabilities.[53] You should be alert to spot the following symptoms of groupthink when they occur in your decision-making teams:

- *Illusions of invulnerability.* Members assume the team is too good for criticism or beyond attack.
- *Rationalising unpleasant and disconfirming data.* Members refuse to accept contradictory data or to thoroughly consider alternatives.
- *Belief in inherent group morality.* Members act as though the group is inherently right and above reproach.
- *Stereotyping competitors as weak, evil and stupid.* Members refuse to look realistically at other groups.
- *Applying direct pressure to deviants to conform to group wishes.* Members refuse to tolerate anyone who suggests the team may be wrong.
- *Self-censorship by members.* Members refuse to communicate personal concerns to the whole team.
- *Illusions of unanimity.* Members accept consensus prematurely, without testing its completeness.
- *Mind guarding.* Members protect the team from hearing disturbing ideas or outside viewpoints.

If you encounter groupthink, Janis suggests taking action along the lines shown in Manager's Notepad 16.2.

MANAGER'S NOTEPAD 16.2

How to avoid groupthink

- Assign the role of critical evaluator to each team member; encourage a sharing of viewpoints.
- Do not, as a leader, seem partial to one course of action; do absent yourself from meetings at times to allow free discussion.
- Create subteams to work on the same problems and then share their proposed solutions.
- Have team members discuss issues with outsiders and report back on their reactions.
- Invite outside experts to observe team activities and react to team processes and decisions.
- Assign one member to play a 'devil's advocate' role at each team meeting.
- Hold a 'second-chance' meeting after consensus is apparently achieved to review the decision.

Creativity in team decision making

Among the potential benefits that teams can bring to organisations is increased creativity. Two techniques that are particularly helpful for creativity in decision making are brainstorming and the nominal team technique.[54] Both can now be pursued in computer-mediated or virtual team discussions, as well as in face-to-face formats.[55]

In *brainstorming*, teams of 5 to 10 members meet to generate ideas. Brainstorming teams typically operate within these guidelines:

- *All criticism is ruled out* — judgement or evaluation of ideas must be withheld until the idea-generation process has been completed
- *'Freewheeling' is welcomed* — the wilder or more radical the idea, the better
- *Quantity is important* — the greater the number of ideas, the greater the likelihood of obtaining a superior idea
- *Building on one another's ideas is encouraged* — participants should suggest how ideas of others can be turned into better ideas, or how two or more ideas can be joined into still another hybrid idea.

Rules for brainstorming

By prohibiting criticism, the brainstorming method reduces fears of ridicule or failure on the part of individuals. Ideally, this results in more enthusiasm, involvement and a freer flow of ideas among members. But there are times when team members have very different opinions and goals. The differences may be so extreme that a brainstorming meeting might deteriorate into antagonistic arguments and harmful conflicts. In such cases, a *nominal group technique* could help. This approach uses a highly structured meeting agenda to allow everyone to contribute ideas without the interference of evaluative comments by others. It allows for many alternatives to be generated and evaluated without risk of inhibitions or hostilities.

The basic steps for running a nominal group session are easy to implement. Participants are first asked to work alone and respond in writing with possible solutions to a stated problem. Ideas are then shared in round-robin fashion without any criticism or discussion; all ideas are recorded as they are presented. Ideas are next discussed and clarified in round-robin sequence, with no evaluative comments allowed. Next, members individually and silently follow a written voting procedure that allows for all alternatives to be rated or ranked in priority order. Finally, the last two steps are repeated as needed to further clarify the process.

How to run a nominal group

LEADING HIGH-PERFORMANCE TEAMS

When we think of the word 'team', sporting teams often come to mind. And we know these teams certainly have their share of problems. Members slack off or become disgruntled — even world-champion teams have losing streaks — and the most highly talented players sometimes lose motivation, quibble with other team members and lapse into performance slumps. When these things happen, the owners, managers and players are apt to take corrective action to 'rebuild the team' and restore what we have called team effectiveness. Work teams are teams in a similar sense. Even the most mature work team is likely to experience problems over time. When such difficulties arise, structured efforts at team building can help.

The team-building process

Team building is a sequence of planned activities used to gather and analyse data on the functioning of a team and to implement constructive changes to increase its operating effectiveness.[56] Most systematic approaches to team building follow the steps described in figure 16.8. The cycle begins with the awareness that a problem may exist or may develop within

 Team building is a sequence of collaborative activities to gather and analyse data on a team and make changes to increase its effectiveness.

the team. Members then work together to gather and analyse data so that the problem is finally understood. Action plans are made by members and collectively implemented. Results are evaluated in similar fashion by team members working together. Any difficulties or new problems that are discovered serve to recycle the team-building process. Consider this added detail in the case featured in figure 16.8.

The consultant received a call from the hospital's human resource manager. He indicated that a new hospital chief executive felt the top management team lacked cohesiveness and was not working well together as a team. The consultant agreed to facilitate a team-building activity that would include a day-long retreat at a nearby resort hotel. The process began when the consultant conducted interviews with the chief executive and other members of the executive team. During the retreat, the consultant reported these results to the team as a whole. He indicated that the hospital's goals were generally understood by all but that they weren't clear enough to allow agreement on action priorities. Furthermore, he reported that interpersonal problems between the director of nursing services and the director of administration were making it difficult for the team to work together comfortably. These and other issues were considered by the team at the retreat. Working sometimes in small subteams, and at other times together as a whole, they agreed first of all that action should be taken to clarify the hospital's overall mission and create a priority list of objectives for the current year. Led by the chief executive, activity on this task would involve all team members and was targeted for completion within a month. The chief executive asked that progress on the action plans be reviewed at each of the next three monthly executive staff meetings. Everyone agreed.

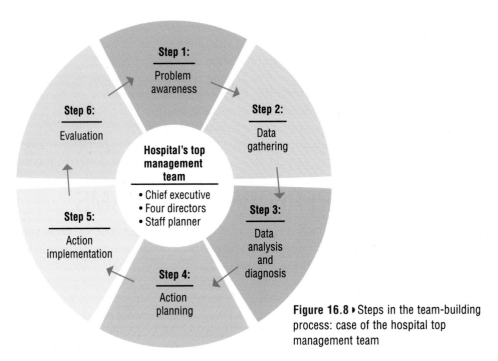

Figure 16.8 ▸ Steps in the team-building process: case of the hospital top management team

This actual example from the author's experience introduces team building as a way to assess a work team's functioning and take corrective action to improve its effectiveness. It can and should become a regular work routine. There are many ways to gather data on team functioning, including structured and unstructured interviews, questionnaires and team meetings. Regardless of the method used, the basic principle of team building remains the same. The process requires that a careful and collaborative assessment of the team's inputs, processes and results be made. All members should participate in data gathering, assist in data analysis and collectively decide on actions to be taken.

Sometimes teamwork can be improved when people share the challenges of unusual and even physically demanding experiences. Sydney-based company Bushsports provides team-building activities to a range of companies. For instance, in late 2001 more than 250 Commonwealth Bank staff participated in eight adventure sports; pharmaceutical company Novartis went abseiling; and superannuation and insurance giant AMP undertook a 'mini Olympics' at Sydney Olympic Park. Bushsports also offers team-building programs with themes such as 'survivor', 'wet 'n' wild', 'shipwrecked', 'mission: possible' and 'the mole'. Senior Qantas manager Gary Furlong attests to the benefit of such programs. After a team-building day involving abseiling and whitewater rafting, he said: 'I managed to take a lot away from the day and incorporate it into our two days of classroom training for the supervisors'.[57]

Team leadership challenges

Among the many developments in the workplace today, the continuing effort to refine and apply creative team concepts should be at the forefront of any progressive manager's action agendas. But harnessing the full potential of teams involves special leadership challenges. We know, for example, that high-performance teams generally share common character-istics. These include a clear and elevating goal, a task-driven and results-oriented structure, competent and committed members who work hard, a collaborative climate, high standards of excellence, external support and recognition, and strong and principled leadership.[58]

The last point on this list — the need for strong and principled leadership — may be the key to them all. In their book, *Teamwork: What Must Go Right, What Can Go Wrong*, Carl Larson and Frank LaFasto state: 'The right person in a leadership role can add tremendous value to any collective effort, even to the point of sparking the outcome with an intangible kind of magic'.[59] They further point out that leaders of high-performing teams share many characteristics with the 'transformational leader', examined in chapter 13.

Successful team leaders *establish a clear vision of the future*. This vision serves as a goal that inspires hard work and the quest for performance excellence — it creates a sense of shared purpose. Successful team leaders help to *create change*. They are dissatisfied with the status quo, influence team members toward similar dissatisfaction and infuse the team with the motivation to change in order to become better. Finally, successful team leaders *unleash talent*. They make sure the team is staffed with members who have the right skills and abilities. And they make sure these people are highly motivated to use their talents to achieve the group's performance objectives. Included in this responsibility is developing future leaders for the team. Peter Fahey, managing director of Yves Saint Laurent's Australasian operations and for-merly chief executive of YSL New Zealand, views his greatest challenge as building teams of people who have mutual respect and who can help develop the YSL business. Fahey is deeply involved in the selection of new people, arguing that it is critical to have teams of people who like working with each other. He works hard to empower his team members so that they can use their individual and collective skills to help YSL grow. He says: 'You don't do the job for them. You employ people that you trust and they do the job and you let them get on with it.'[60]

You don't get a high-performing team by just bringing a group of people together and giving them a shared name or title. Leaders of high-performance teams create supportive cli-mates in which team members know what to expect from the leader and each other, and know what the leader expects from them. They empower team members. By personal example they demonstrate the importance of setting aside self-interests to support the team's goals. And they view team building as an ongoing leadership responsibility. As said before, teams are hard work. But they are worth it.[61]

www.questgroup.com.au
www.footprint.co.nz

Companies like Quest Group Australia and Footprints in New Zealand offer team-building activities and tools for diagnosing problems and developing competencies among team members. Team members can, for instance, evaluate their progress, identify training needs and benchmark their performance against other teams.

What successful team leaders do

Study guide

The chapter 16 study guide helps you review the chapter content, prepare for examinations, apply what you have learned and further build your career readiness. The summary briefly answers the study questions posed at the start of the chapter. The list of key terms allows you to double-check your familiarity with basic concepts and definitions. The applied activities help you test your comprehension of chapter content. Suggestions offered as career readiness activities direct your attention to relevant sections of the Career Readiness Workbook where you can test and develop your career skills and apply what you have learned. The list of electronic resources suggests activities from the *Management: An Asia–Pacific Perspective* web site and, finally, the case for critical thinking helps you apply your new management knowledge.

SUMMARY

How do teams contribute to organisations?

- A team is a collection of people who work together to accomplish a common goal.
- Organisations operate as interlocking networks of formal work teams, which offer many benefits to the organisations and to their members.
- Teams help organisations through synergy in task performance, the creation of a whole that is greater than the sum of its parts.
- Teams help satisfy important needs for their members, providing various types of support and social satisfactions.
- Social loafing and other problems can limit the performance of teams.

What are current trends in the use of teams?

- Teams are important mechanisms of empowerment and participation in the workplace.
- Committees and task forces are used to facilitate operations and allow special projects to be completed with creativity.
- Cross-functional teams bring members together from different departments and help improve lateral relations and integration in organisations.
- Employee involvement teams, such as the quality circle, allow employees to provide important insights into daily problem solving.
- New developments in information technology are making virtual teams, or computer-mediated teams, more commonplace.
- Self-managing teams are changing organisations by allowing team members to perform many tasks previously reserved ofor their supervisors.

How do teams work?

- An effective team achieves high levels of task performance, member satisfaction and team viability.
- Important team input factors include the organisational setting, nature of the task, size and membership characteristics.

- A team matures through various stages of development, including forming, storming, norming, performing and adjourning.
- Norms are the standards or rules of conduct that influence the behaviour of team members. Cohesion is the attractiveness of the team to its members.
- In highly cohesive teams, members tend to conform to norms; the best situation for a manager or leader is a team with positive performance norms and high cohesiveness.
- Distributed leadership in serving a team's task and maintenance needs will help to achieve long-term effectiveness.
- Effective teams make use of alternative communication networks to best complete tasks.

How do teams make decisions?

- Teams can make decisions by lack of response, authority rule, minority rule, majority rule, consensus and unanimity.
- The potential advantages of team decision making include having more information available and generating more understanding and commitment.
- The potential liabilities to team decision making include social pressures to conform and greater time requirements.
- Groupthink is a tendency of members of highly cohesive teams to lose their critical evaluative capabilities and make poor decisions.
- Techniques for improving creativity in team decision making include brainstorming and the nominal group technique.

What are the challenges of high-performance team leadership?

- Team building helps team members develop action plans for improving the way they work together and the results they accomplish.
- The team-building process should be data based and collaborative, involving a high level of participation by all team members.
- High-performance work teams have a clear and shared sense of purpose as well as strong internal commitment to its accomplishment.

KEY TERMS

centralised communication network (p. 449)

cohesiveness (p. 447)

committee (p. 437)

cross-functional teams (p. 438)

decentralised communication network (p. 449)

decision making (p. 450)

effective team (p. 442)

employee involvement teams (p. 438)

formal groups (p. 436)

group process (p. 444)

groupthink (p. 452)

informal groups (p. 436)

international teams (p. 440)

maintenance activities (p. 448)

norm (p. 446)

quality circle (p. 438)

self-managing work teams (p. 441)

social loafing (p. 435)

synergy (p. 436)

task activities (p. 448)

task forces (p. 437)

team (p. 435)

team building (p. 453)

teamwork (p. 435)

virtual team (p. 439)

APPLIED ACTIVITIES

Short-response questions

1. How can a manager improve team effectiveness by modifying inputs?
2. What is the relationship between a team's cohesiveness, performance norm and performance results?
3. How would a manager know that his or her team was suffering from groupthink (give two symptoms) and what could he or she do about it (give two responses)?
4. What makes a self-managing team different from a traditional work team?

Application question

5. Mark Martin has just been appointed manager of a production team operating the 11 p.m. to 7 a.m. shift in a large manufacturing firm. An experienced manager, Mark is concerned that the team members really like and get along well with one another but they also appear to be restricting their task outputs to the minimum acceptable levels. What could Mark do to improve things in this situation and why should he do them?

CAREER READINESS ACTIVITIES

Recommended individual and group learning activities from the end-of-text Career Readiness Workbook for this chapter include:

Career advancement portfolio   **WB**

Update your career advancement portfolio to reflect your new skills and experiences. Include skills and personal insights you gain from the following projects and exercises.

Research and presentation project   **WB**

- Project 7 — Self-managing teams — 'how good are they?'

Cross-functional integrative case   **WB**

Read the integrative case on Sarina Russo and answer the following question:

What must Sarina Russo do to successfully manage the teams of people that she employs in her business?

Exercises in teamwork   **WB**

- Exercise 16 — Using teams
- Exercise 19 — Shelters for the homeless
- Exercise 24 — Creative solutions

Management skills assessment   **WB**

- Assessment 16 — Team leader skills

ELECTRONIC RESOURCES

Don't forget to take full advantage of the online support for *Management: An Asia–Pacific Perspective* at www.johnwiley.com.au/highered/management: chapter 16 practice tests, e-flashcards, crossword puzzles, interactive management skills assessments, interactive cases, the online career advancement portfolio and much more!

CASE FOR CRITICAL THINKING

Read the following case for critical thinking on Flight Centre. While you are reading the case keep in mind what you have learned in this chapter, then answer the questions.

In just 15 years, Flight Centre has become a major player in the international market for air travel, accommodation and tours. With more than 500 stores in five countries and net revenues of more than $1.8 billion, Flight Centre has achieved unparalleled success in an otherwise unattractive industry.

Fiercely competitive, the Australian travel industry generates slim profit margins of around 2 per cent. Low barriers to entry make the industry an easy target for new entrants. Price-sensitive consumers can easily shift allegiance between major travel agencies, such as Flight Centre, Traveland, Harvey World Travel and Jetset, and the suppliers of aeroplane seats and tours have significant power over the commissions they charge for their services. Yet, despite these forces, Flight Centre has remained profitable while taking large slabs of market share from its competitors.

Cofounder Graham Turner has achieved these outcomes by giving Flight Centre a radically different team-based organisational structure. It appears to deliver the results. Teams of three to seven people (usually the employees of a single store) are considered to be a *family*. Members of the family are encouraged to develop a high level of trust, acceptance and commitment so that they can together achieve the 'stretch' goals set for them, usually based around the company's philosophies of 'lowest prices, guaranteed' and 'the client is paramount'. At the next level, four or five families work together as a *village*. The village provides resources, support, mentoring and learning for its members, as well as being a place for healthy competition and rivalry. Next, the *country* serves as the grouping for two or three villages from the same *tribe*. The tribes represent the different brands used by Flight Centre, including Corporate Traveller and Student Flights. Each country is led by a country leader who is responsible for the country's performance. Citizens of each country get together at regular conferences to learn, compare stories and receive recognition for strong performance.

Flight Centre's systems encourage accountability and open communication. Every team holds a daily meeting to discuss goals, share information and consider current issues. Villages hold monthly 'buzz nights' after work, to help Flight Centre staff stay motivated and remain focused. Although fun, the purpose of buzz nights is serious — to review recent successes, zone in on new goals and share 'war stories' with colleagues from nearby stores. Buzz nights follow a carefully developed format to ensure that they meet their designated purposes. Villages and countries also hold conferences at enjoyable locations to enable wider participation in learning, sharing, recognising success and having fun. The entire organisation also gets together once a year for a conference, with several thousand people flying in to take part.

These ideas come from Turner's view of organisations in the 21st century. He believes that people have real needs for relationship and support in the workplace. Although companies can never replace families in totally satisfying this need, many organisations go too far in the opposite direction, providing workplaces which are impersonal, demotivating, and which become overly political as people strive to out-do each other. Turner states that:

> We try to look at the Australian Aborigines. Most people have a good understanding of how they lived as hunters and gatherers. If you didn't structure it that way you might end up with a structure that conflicts with what people have an inherent need for.[62]
>
> ...
>
> [The] workplace in modern society ... inevitably [has to] take over the inherent needs that humans have; that the villages, tribes and families used to provide.[63]

At Flight Centre, leadership is performed differently to most companies, whether in the travel industry or elsewhere. In conjunction with support managers who reside within countries and villages rather than at head office, teams run many of their own critical functions. Teams self-manage the hours to be worked, when leave is taken and who is recruited into the team. They are also responsible for financial issues and formulate their own profit and loss statements.

When recruiting new members, for instance, the team looks for people who are self-motivated and positive about joining a small, highly focused team working towards measurable business outcomes. Teams interview potential new 'family' members to see if they will fit into the team's culture and high-performance team norms.

Team leaders serve as 'captain–coaches' in which they perform support roles while continuing to serve as full team members. In addition, without the layers of 'back office' staff commonly found in growing and large organisations, Flight Centre retains a flat organisational structure with ready access between all elements of the structure, from the family through to the chief executive, Graham Turner.

Team members aim to ensure that potential new colleagues are comfortable with the performance-based pay systems operating at Flight Centre. Within this system, employees are paid a retainer equivalent to their 'cost of seat'. This figure represents the cost of the employee to the company in terms of his or her share of office rental costs, overheads, computers and the like. A system identifies when each team member is in 'profit' after these costs have been repaid, with the profits over and above these costs shared with the individual and also with the team as it achieves its targets. Team members thus remain extraordinarily goals-focused. They have a very clear understanding of the equation — work hard, provide great customer service, achieve your targets, and the rewards will follow.

Clearly, the rewards do follow. Graham Turner is estimated to have a net worth of more than $465 million from his stake in Flight Centre, and the company has created more than 50 millionaires among staff who have taken advantage of the company's share scheme. All staff are eligible to purchase shares, and the fact that more than 50 per cent have done so attests to the belief of Flight Centre's staff in the company's future. With the share price climbing from 75 cents at the time of its 1995 listing to more than $21 in January 2003, Graham Turner has shown that not only can he build an impressive business in a less-than-impressive industry, he is prepared to share the rewards with his family, village, country and tribe.[64]

QUESTIONS

1. What concepts discussed in the chapter seem relevant in explaining the success of Flight Centre?

2. Can you see any disadvantages or weaknesses with the Flight Centre approach? How could these be resolved?

3. Do you share Turner's view that organisations can meet the intrinsic needs of employees with this kind of approach? Why or why not?

CHAPTER 17

Communication and interpersonal skills

CHAPTER 17 STUDY QUESTIONS

- What is the communication process?

- How can communication be improved?

- How does perception influence communication?

- How can we deal positively with conflict?

- How can we negotiate successful agreements?

PricewaterhouseCoopers — treading the boards to improve communication

Imagine spending three days developing relationships with your customers. Nothing weird about that. Would you feel any different if you knew the customers were actually professional actors simply 'playing the part' of your customers?

That is precisely what occurs several times a year at accounting firm PricewaterhouseCoopers (PwC). Training officer Pat Blades runs an in-house theatrical program where actors are brought in to help PwC consultants improve their communication skills. Not only are the actors briefed on industry jargon and issues, they remain in character for negotiation sessions, presentations, lunches and cocktail functions, improvising as necessary.

Both PwC consultants and the actors involved report positive results from the program. According to one of the actors: 'You get the feeling that although a lot of their people are extremely smart and very good at their jobs, they really need help with the schmooze factor, which is obviously where deals can be won or lost. And because they have never seen you before, it is surprisingly easy for them to believe that you are exactly who you are purporting to be, even though they know in the back of their minds that you are just an actor.'[1]

The program has also been run successfully in Asia, with the emphasis moving from relationships with clients to managing cultural differences.

How strong are your communication skills? Would you like to participate in a program like the one described at PricewaterhouseCoopers? Try one of the communication skills assessments at www.queendom.com to check out your communication strengths and weaknesses.

GET CONNECTED!

Anyone heading into the new workplace must understand that the work of managers and team leaders is highly interpersonal and communication intensive. Whether you work at the top of the organisation, communicating strategies and building support for organisational goals, or at a lower level, interacting with others to support their work efforts and your own, communication and interpersonal skills are essential to your personal toolkit. Think back to the descriptions of managerial work by Henry Mintzberg, John Kotter and others as discussed in chapter 1. For Mintzberg, managerial success involves performing well as an information 'nerve centre', gathering information from and disseminating information to internal and external sources.[2] For Kotter, it depends largely on one's ability to build and maintain a complex web of interpersonal networks with insiders and outsiders, so as to implement work priorities and agendas.[3] Says Pam Alexander, CEO of Ogilvy Public Relations Worldwide: 'Relationships are the most powerful form of media. Ideas will only get you so far these days. Count on personal relationships to carry you further.'[4]

The ability to communicate well, both orally and in writing, is a critical managerial skill and the foundation of effective leadership.[5] Through communication, people exchange and share information with one another, and influence one another's attitudes, behaviours and understandings. Communication allows managers to establish and maintain interpersonal relationships, listen to others, and otherwise gain the information needed to create an inspirational workplace. No manager can handle conflict, negotiate successfully and succeed at leadership without being a good communicator. It is no wonder that 'communication skills' often top the list of attributes employers look for in job candidates. Any career portfolio should include adequate testimony to one's abilities to communicate well in interpersonal relationships, in various forms of public speaking and increasingly through the electronic medium of the computer. At Intel, Inc., for example, millions of e-mail messages a day move through the firm's computer networks. Some workers personally process as many as 300 per day; the average worker spends 2.5 hours per day 'communicating' with others via her or his computer.[6]

THE COMMUNICATION PROCESS

Communication is an interpersonal process of sending and receiving symbols with messages attached to them. In more practical terms, the key elements in the communication process are shown in figure 17.1. They include a *sender*, who is responsible for encoding an intended *message* into meaningful symbols, both verbal and non-verbal. The message is sent through a *communication channel* to a *receiver*, who then decodes or interprets its *meaning*. This interpretation, importantly, may or may not match the sender's original intentions. *Feedback*, when present, reverses the process and conveys the receiver's response back to the sender. Another way to view the communication process is as a series of questions. 'Who?' (sender) 'says what?' (message) 'in what way?' (channel) 'to whom?' (receiver) 'with what result?' (interpreted meaning).

What is effective communication?

Effective communication occurs when the intended message of the sender and the interpreted meaning of the receiver are one and the same. Although this should be the goal in any communication attempt, it is not always achieved. **Efficient communication** occurs at minimum cost in terms of resources expended. Time, in particular, is an important resource in the communication process. Picture your instructor taking the time to communicate individually with each student about this chapter. It would be virtually impossible. Even if it were possible, it would be costly. This is why managers often leave voice-mail

Communication is the process of sending and receiving symbols with meanings attached.

In **effective communication**, the intended meaning of the source and the perceived meaning of the receiver are identical.

Efficient communication occurs at minimum cost.

messages and interact by e-mail rather than visit their subordinates personally. Simply put, these alternatives are more efficient ways to communicate than through one-on-one and face-to-face communications.

One problem is that efficient communications are not always effective. A low-cost approach such as an e-mail note to a distribution list may save time, but it does not always result in everyone getting the same meaning from the message. Without opportunities to ask questions and clarify the message, erroneous interpretations are possible. By the same token, an effective comunication may not always be efficient. If a work team leader visits each team member individually to explain a new change in procedures, this may guarantee that everyone truly understands the change. But it may also be very costly in the demands it makes on the leader's time. A team meeting would be more efficient. In these and other ways, potential trade-offs between effectiveness and efficiency must be recognised in communication.

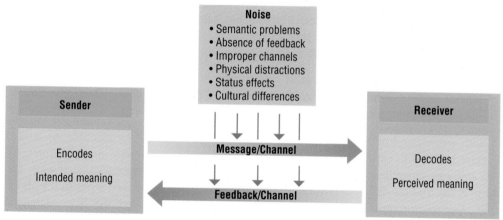

Figure 17.1 ▸ The process of interpersonal communication

Barriers to effective communication

Effective communication is a two-way process that requires effort and skill on the part of both the sender and the receiver. **Noise**, as figure 17.1 shows, is anything that interferes with the effectiveness of the communication process. For instance, translating from one language to another can often lead to a loss of intended meaning. Carolyn Blackman, vice-president of the Australia–China Chamber of Commerce and Industry, has witnessed many occurrences of this problem. To cite one example: a foreign executive touring shopping centres in China often said 'Is that so?' as he was shown around. The interpreter translated this to mean that the executive had no real interest in pursuing business in China. This interpretation was the opposite of the executive's intentions. Not only did he have considerable interest in doing business in China, his use of the phrase was merely intended to indicate that he was listening with interest.[7] In addition to these obvious problems when different languages are involved in a communication attempt, common sources of noise include poor choice of channels, poor written or oral expression, failure to recognise non-verbal signals, physical distractions and status effects.

Noise is anything that interferes with communication effectiveness.

POOR CHOICE OF CHANNELS

A **communication channel** is the medium through which a message is conveyed from sender to receiver. Good managers choose the right communication channel, or combination of channels, to accomplish their intended purpose in a given situation.[8] In general,

A **communication channel** is the medium through which a message is sent.

written channels are acceptable for simple messages that are easy to convey and for those that require extensive dissemination quickly. They are also important, at least as follow-up communications, when formal policy or authoritative directives are being conveyed. *Oral channels* work best for messages that are complex and difficult to convey, where immediate feedback to the sender is valuable. They are also more personal and can create a supportive, even inspirational, emotional climate.

POOR WRITTEN OR ORAL EXPRESSION

Communication will be effective only to the extent that the sender expresses a message in a way that can be clearly understood by the receiver. This means that words must be well chosen and properly used to express the sender's intentions. When they are not, semantic barriers to communication occur as encoding and decoding errors and as mixed messages. Consider the following gobbledegook found among some executive communications.

> *A business report said:* 'Consumer elements are continuing to stress the fundamental necessity of a stabilisation of the price structure at a lower level than exists at the present time.' (*Translation:* Consumers keep saying that prices must go down and stay down.)

> *A manager said:* 'Substantial economies were effective in this division by increasing the time interval between distribution of data-eliciting forms to business entities.' (*Translation:* The division was saving money by sending fewer questionnaires to suppliers.)

Both written and oral communication require skill. It isn't easy, for example, to write a concise letter or to express one's thoughts in a computer e-mail report. Any such message can easily be misunderstood. It takes practice and hard work to express yourself well. The same holds true for oral communication that takes place via the spoken word in telephone calls, face-to-face meetings, formal briefings, videoconferences and the like. Manager's Notepad 17.1 identifies guidelines for an important oral communication situation faced by managers — the executive briefing or formal presentation.[9]

MANAGER'S NOTEPAD 17.1

How to make a successful presentation

- *Be prepared.* Know what you want to say, know how you want to say it, and rehearse saying it.
- *Set the right tone.* Act audience centred, make eye contact, be pleasant and confident.
- *Sequence points.* State your purpose, make important points, follow with details, then summarise.
- *Support your points.* Give specific reasons for your points; state them in understandable terms.
- *Accent the presentation.* Use good visual aids and provide supporting 'handouts' when possible.
- *Add the right amount of polish.* Attend to details — have room, materials and arrangements ready to go.
- *Check your technology.* Check everything ahead of time; make sure it works and know how to use it.
- *Don't bet on the Internet.* Beware of plans to make real-time Internet visits; save sites on a disk and use a browser to open the file.
- *Be professional.* Be on time, wear appropriate attire, and act organised, confident and enthusiastic.

FAILURE TO RECOGNISE NON-VERBAL SIGNALS

Non-verbal communication takes place through such things as hand movements, facial expressions, body posture, eye contact and the use of interpersonal space. It can be a powerful means of transmitting messages. Eye contact or voice intonation can be used intentionally to accent special parts of an oral communication. The astute observer notes the 'body language' expressed by other persons. At times our body may be 'talking' for us even as we otherwise maintain silence. And when we do speak, our body may sometimes 'say' different things than our words convey. A **mixed message** occurs when a person's words communicate one message while his or her actions, body language, appearance or situational use of interpersonal space communicate something else. Watch how people behave in a meeting. A person who feels under attack may move back in a chair or lean away from the presumed antagonist, even while expressing verbal agreement. All of this is done quite unconsciously, but it sends a message to those alert enough to pick it up.

Non-verbal channels probably play a more important part in communication than most people recognise. One researcher indicates that gestures alone may make up as much as 70 per cent of communication.[10] In fact, a potential side effect of the growing use of electronic mail, computer networking and other communication technologies is that gestures and other non-verbal signals that may add important meaning to the communication event are lost.

Non-verbal communication takes place through gestures and body language.

A **mixed message** results when words communicate one message while actions, body language or appearance communicate something else.

ENTREPRENEURSHIP

Allan Pease • www.peasetraining.com

Communicating to the world

Management communicator Allan Pease has taken his ideas for better communication around the world. He conducts seminars in 30 countries and has written five best-selling books. One, *Body Language*, has been translated into 32 languages. He started selling rubber sponges door-to-door at age 10, and by 21 was the youngest salesperson in Australia to sell over $1 million in insurance in his first year. Translating his sales skills into easily understood ideas on communication, Pease has worked with employees in companies from IBM to McDonald's, and with universities, hospitals and the Australian Armed Forces. One of Pease's most valuable ideas is that we should learn to read body language in 'clusters' of actions, rather than trying to interpret one action in isolation from others. For instance, a man touching his nose while responding to a question might simply have an itchy nose; however, if he also rubs his eyes, looks down and tugs at his collar while answering, we may understandably view his response with some suspicion.[11]

www.geyer.com.au

Geyer is an Australian architectural firm that designs offices to encourage interactivity and open communication. Geyer's designs incorporate the latest technology, open-plan workstations and 'hot-desking' facilities (enabling people to move between desks), and allow for additional smaller meeting rooms.[12]

Filtering is the intentional distortion of information to make it appear more favourable to the recipient.

PHYSICAL DISTRACTIONS

Any number of physical distractions can interfere with the effectiveness of a communication attempt. Some of these distractions, such as telephone interruptions, drop-in visitors and lack of privacy, are evident in the following conversation between an employee, George, and his manager:

> Okay, George, let's hear your problem [phone rings, boss picks it up, promises to deliver a report 'just as soon as I can get it done']. Uh, now, where were we — oh, you're having a problem with your technician. She's [manager's secretary brings in some papers that need his immediate signature; secretary leaves] ... you say she's overstressed lately, wants to leave ... I tell you what, George, why don't you [phone rings again, lunch partner drops by] ... uh, take a stab at handling it yourself ... I've got to go now.[13]

Besides what may have been poor intentions in the first place, the manager in this example did not do a good job of communicating with George. This problem could be easily corrected. If George has something important to say, he should set aside adequate time for the meeting. Additional interruptions such as telephone calls and drop-in visitors could be eliminated by issuing appropriate instructions to the secretary. Many communication distractions can be avoided or at least minimised through proper planning.

STATUS EFFECTS

'Criticise my boss? I don't have the right to.' 'I'd get fired.' 'It's her company, not mine.' As suggested in these comments, the hierarchy of authority in organisations creates another potential barrier to effective communications. Consider the 'corporate cover-up' once discovered at an electronics company. Product shipments were being predated and papers falsified to meet unrealistic sales targets set by the president. His managers knew the targets were impossible to attain, but at least 20 persons in the organisation cooperated in the deception. It was months before the top found out. What happened in this case is **filtering** — the intentional distortion of information to make it appear favourable to the recipient.

The presence of such information filtering is often found in communications between lower and higher levels in organisations. Tom Peters, the popular management author and consultant, has called such information distortion 'Management Enemy Number 1'.[14] Simply put, it most often involves someone 'telling the boss what he or she wants to hear'. Whether the reason behind this is a fear of retribution for bringing bad news, an unwillingness to identify personal mistakes, or just a general desire to please, the end result is the same. The person receiving filtered communications can end up making poor decisions because of a biased and inaccurate information base.

IMPROVING COMMUNICATION

A number of things can be done to overcome barriers and improve the process of communication. They include active listening, body language, making constructive use of feedback, opening upward communication channels, understanding proxemics and the use of space, using technology, valuing diversity and using effective language.

Active listening

Managers must be very sensitive to their listening responsibility. When people 'talk', they are trying to communicate something. That 'something' may or may not be what they are saying. **Active listening** is the process of taking action to help the source of a message say exactly what he or she really means. There are five rules for becoming an active listener:[15]

1. *Listen for message content.* Try to hear exactly what content is being conveyed in the message.
2. *Listen for feelings.* Try to identify how the source feels about the content in the message.
3. *Respond to feelings.* Let the source know that her or his feelings are being recognised.
4. *Note all cues.* Be sensitive to non-verbal and verbal messages; be alert for mixed messages.
5. *Paraphrase and restate.* State back to the source what you think you are hearing.

Different responses to the following two questions contrast how a 'passive' listener and an 'active' listener might act in real workplace conversations. Put yourself in the position of the questioner in each case and then consider how you would react to each listener's response.

Rules for active listening

Active listening helps the source of a message say what he or she really means.

Question	Passive listener's response	Active listener's response
Don't you think employees should be promoted on the basis of seniority?	No, I don't.	It seems to you that they should, I take it?
What does the supervisor expect us to do about these out-of-date computers?	Do the best you can, I guess.	You're pretty disgusted with those machines, aren't you?

These examples should give you a sense of how the active listening approach can facilitate and encourage communication in difficult circumstances, rather than discourage it. Manager's Notepad 17.2, based on the work of prominent Australian social researcher Hugh Mackay, offers an additional set of useful guidelines for good listening.[16]

MANAGER'S NOTEPAD 17.2

Hugh Mackay's ten laws of human communication

1. It's not what our message does to the listener, but what the listener does with our message, that determines our success as communicators.
2. Listeners generally interpret messages in ways which make them feel comfortable and secure.
3. When people's attitudes are attacked head-on, they are likely to defend those attitudes and, in the process, to reinforce them.
4. People pay most attention to messages that are relevant to their own circumstances and point of view.
5. People who feel insecure in a relationship are unlikely to be good listeners.
6. People are more likely to listen to us if we also listen to them.
7. People are more likely to change in response to a combination of new experience and communication than in response to communication alone.
8. People are more likely to support a change that affects them if they are consulted before the change is made.
9. The message in what is said will be interpreted in the light of how, when, where and by whom it is said.
10. Lack of self-knowledge and an unwillingness to resolve our own internal conflicts make it harder for us to communicate with other people.

Body language

Since non-verbal communication is a critical element of face-to-face communication, it makes sense that you work to ensure that your body language reinforces your message and remains consistent with that message. Kris Cole, a well-known communications consultant in Australia, New Zealand and Asia, says that effective body language is SO CLEAR. **S** relates to how you *sit* or *stand* or use *space*. Open, less confrontational communication is more likely if you stand at an angle rather than directly opposite the person with whom you are communicating. You should also be aware not to infringe on the other person's 'personal space'. **O** stands for the *openness* of your movements and expression. Having your arms and legs crossed indicates that you are probably going to be defensive in your expression and responses. **C** is for how you *centre your attention* on the other person. Good communication demands that you focus your mind and eliminate distracting thoughts. **L** concerns how you *lean* towards the other person. Leaning towards someone can indicate interest; however, leaning too far can create undue pressure in the conversation. **E** stands for *eye contact*. In European cultures, eye contact indicates interest and engagement; although less eye contact may be appropriate if communicating with people from Asian cultures. **A** relates to how *appropriately you respond* to the speaker, with active listening being particularly important. **R** is about how *relaxed* you appear during communication. Being appropriately relaxed includes eliminating annoying habits such as jangling your keys or nibbling on a pen or pencil.[17]

Constructive feedback

Feedback is the process of telling someone else how you feel about something that person did or said.

The process of telling other people how you feel about something they did or said, or about the situation in general, is called **feedback**. The art of giving feedback is an indispensable skill, particularly for managers who must regularly give feedback to other people. Often this takes the form of performance feedback given as evaluations and appraisals. When poorly done, such feedback can be threatening to the recipient and cause resentment. When properly done, feedback — even performance criticism — can be listened to, accepted and used to good advantage by the receiver.[18] Managers at General Electric, for example, are evaluated on how they give performance feedback to employees. Each subordinate must be annually rated by the manager on a low–high performance curve; the weakest are advised to find jobs elsewhere. By the same token, GE managers are also evaluated on how well they receive feedback. Employees are encouraged to let their bosses know how they are performing, and they can do so anonymously if they prefer.[19]

There are ways to help ensure that feedback is useful and constructive rather than harmful. To begin with, the sender must learn to recognise when the feedback he or she is about to offer will really benefit the receiver and when it will mainly satisfy some personal need. A supervisor who berates a computer operator for data analysis errors, for example, actually may be angry about personally failing to give clear instructions in the first place. Also, a manager should make sure that any feedback is considered from the recipient's point of view as understandable, acceptable and plausible. Usefully accepted guidelines for giving 'constructive' feedback include:[20]

Constructive feedback guidelines

- Give feedback directly and with real feeling, based on trust between you and the receiver.
- Make sure that feedback is specific rather than general — use good, clear and preferably recent examples to make your points.
- Give feedback at a time when the receiver seems most willing or able to accept it.
- Make sure the feedback is valid and limit it to things the receiver can be expected to do something about.
- Give feedback in small doses — never give more than the receiver can handle at any particular time.

Use of communication channels

Channel richness is the capacity of a channel or communication medium to carry information in an effective manner.[21] Figure 17.2 shows that face-to-face communication, for example, is very high in richness, enabling personal two-way interaction and real-time feedback. At the other end of the continuum, posted e-mail or hard-copy bulletins are very low in richness, representing impersonal one-way interaction and largely insulated from quick feedback. In between, you can see how the other common channels of electronic and traditional letters and memos, as well as telephone conversations and voice-mail messages array themselves. Obviously managers need to understand the limits of a channel and choose wisely when using them to communicate various types of messages.

Channel richness is the capacity of a communication channel to effectively carry information.

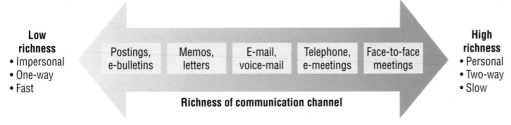

Low richness
• Impersonal
• One-way
• Fast

| Postings, e-bulletins | Memos, letters | E-mail, voice-mail | Telephone, e-meetings | Face-to-face meetings |

Richness of communication channel

High richness
• Personal
• Two-way
• Slow

Figure 17.2 ▸ Channel richness and the use of communication media

There are a number of steps that can be taken to keep communication channels open to reduce the harmful consequences of status effects and filtering, described earlier. A popular approach is called management by wandering around or **MBWA**. This means dealing directly with subordinates by regularly spending time walking around and talking with them about a variety of work-related matters. Instead of relying on less rich and more formal channels to bring information to your attention, MBWA involves finding out for yourself what is going on in a rich face-to-face communication channel. The basic objectives are to break down status barriers, increase the frequency of interpersonal contact and get more and better information from lower-level sources. Of course, this requires a trusting relationship. Patricia Gallup, CEO of PC Connection, is well known for her interactive style of leadership and emphasis on communication. She makes herself available by e-mail and greets employees by name as she walks the hallways. MBWA is clearly part of her style. She spends as much time as possible out of her office and on the floor where she can be close to workers in the various departments.[22]

Management practices designed to open channels and improve upward communications have traditionally involved *open office hours*, whereby busy senior executives like Gallup set aside time in their calendars to welcome walk-in visits during certain hours each week. Today this approach can be expanded to include *online discussion forums* and 'chat rooms' that are open at certain hours. Programs of regular *employee group meetings* are also helpful. Here, a rotating schedule of team meetings brings top managers into face-to-face contact with mixed employee groups throughout an organisation. In some cases, a comprehensive communications program includes an *employee advisory council* composed of members elected by their fellow employees. Such a council may meet with top management on a regular schedule to discuss and react to new policies and programs that will affect employees. Again, the face-to-face groups can be supplemented with a variety of *computer-mediated meetings* that serve similar purposes, overcoming the time and distance limitations that might otherwise make communication less frequent or intense.

In **MBWA**, managers spend time outside of their offices to meet and talk with workers at all levels.

www.flightcentre.com.au
www.flightcentre.co.nz

Flight Centre holds large meetings known as 'buzz nights' to thank employees for their work, to recognise the company's best performers, and to share information about success stories and learning experiences. The nights are designed to encourage openness and the widespread sharing of information.

CAREER

Communication

Can you handle criticism?

Few managers like criticising their staff, and fewer employees like to receive criticism. Yet, responding appropriately to criticism can contribute to learning from experience and can indicate maturity.

Poor and inappropriate responses to criticism include avoiding criticism, perhaps by changing the subject; denying that it applies to you; excusing criticism by downplaying its importance; or 'fighting fire with fire' — striking back at the critic. These kinds of responses are neither positive nor constructive.

A far healthier alternative is to ask for details, thus placing the responsibility on the critic to be specific rather than overly general in their criticism; to agree with any aspects of the criticism that are true; and to indicate your acceptance of the critic's right to an opinion (while maintaining your own position). This style of approach can disarm or neutralise your biggest critics, as long as you are committed to working on areas requiring genuine improvement.[24]

Questions

Can you identify any situations where you have not handled criticism appropriately?

Considering the above advice, what could you have done differently?

How can you respond more appropriately in the future?

When bosses suspect that they are having communication problems, *communication consultants* can be hired to conduct interviews and surveys of employees on their behalf.

Ingrid Jackson, for instance, consulted to a major Australian bank during a period of key strategic change at the organisation. Jackson coordinated a two-year communications strategy designed to involve and inform the bank's 23 000 retail staff in the change process. Moving away from the bank's traditional top-down communication processes, Jackson and an internal steering group applied a range of communication strategies to tackle the diversity of communication needs and styles present in such a large organisation, including:

- cascade briefings, which involved providing overhead transparencies and accompanying speaker notes so that regional, zone and branch managers could communicate effectively with their staff
- reverse cascades, so that questions that could not be answered at the cascade briefings were sent back up the line for a response
- visible executive leadership, in which key executives spent time travelling across Australia to speak to groups of staff
- staff booklets outlining the bank's new strategy and detailing the new organisation structures, roles and career streams
- national and State newsletters discussing the success of pilot projects and implementation across different States
- staff videos of ten minutes duration, provided monthly with discussion guides
- audio tapes for managers with interviews, discussions and questions and answers
- staff 'hot line' to respond to questions
- supervisor scripts, so that frontline managers could access appropriate form letters and implementation information.[23]

Another communication approach that seeks to broaden the awareness of 'bosses' regarding the feelings and perceptions of other people that they work closely with is 360° feedback, discussed in chapter 12.[25] This typically involves upward appraisals done by a manager's subordinates as well as additional feedback from peers, internal and external customers, and higher-ups. A self-assessment is also part of the process. Often this feedback is gathered through questionnaires in which respondents can remain anonymous. The goal of 360° feedback is to provide the manager with information that can be used for constructive improvement. Managers who have participated in the process often express surprise at what they learn. Some have found themselves perceived as lacking vision, having bad tempers, being bad listeners, lacking flexibility and the like.[26]

In addition to the more traditional use of financial and other quantitative indicators, the ANZ Banking Group uses 360° feedback to analyse the leadership qualities of its managers, as well as their ability to generally 'add value' to the corporation.[27]

Proxemics and space design

An important but sometimes neglected part of communication involves proxemics, or the use of interpersonal space.[28] The distance between people conveys varying intentions in terms of intimacy, openness and status; the proxemics or physical layout of an office is an often-overlooked form of non-verbal communication. See for yourself — offices with two or more chairs available for side-by-side seating, for example, convey different messages from those where the manager's chair sits behind the desk and those for visitors sit facing in front.

Office or workspace architecture is becoming increasingly recognised for its important influence on communication and behaviour. To support a new culture following the merger of computer companies Compaq, Digital and Tandem, Compaq (now merged with Hewlett-Packard) designed a new building in Auckland, New Zealand, around themes of openness and transparency. Walls have been replaced by glass, with the glass walls stretching through meeting rooms to allow views to the nearby Auckland harbour. Stairwells cut through floors, the space is totally flexible, and the corners have been removed from offices. The design is a deliberate attempt to encourage open communications among employees from different departments and from the different companies that joined in the merger.[29]

Technology use

Prerequisites to entry into just about any workplace with career value are basic computer literacy and a willingness to use the new technologies to maximum advantage. The new age of communication is one of e-mail, voice-mail, online discussions, videoconferencing, virtual or computer-mediated meetings, and more. A related and important development is the growing use of in-house or corporate intranets to provide opportunities for increased communication and collaboration. Progressive organisations use database programs such as Lotus Domino to host continuous online forums for internal communication and knowledge-sharing among employees. The purpose is to encourage fast and regular communication, and to provide a source of up-to-date information for problem solving and work implementation. When IBM surveyed its employees to find out how they learned what was going on at the company, executives were not surprised that coworkers were perceived as credible and useful sources. But they were surprised that the firm's intranet ranked equally high. IBM's internal web sites were ranked higher than news briefs, company memos and information from managers.[30]

The take-up of technology across the Asia–Pacific region is mixed. At one extreme, a recent survey found that 70 per cent of Asian consumers soon expect to use their mobile phones as the primary means of sending e-mails and getting news, with 61 per cent expecting to use their mobile phones as 'payment gateways'. At the other extreme, only 36 per cent of small businesses and 70 per cent of medium-sized businesses in western Sydney have their own Internet site or an Internet connection at all. Few of the businesses surveyed used information and communication technologies (ICT) for business-to-business transactions, invoicing, customer service or purchasing. In response to the ICT revolution, New Zealand-based children's clothing retailer Pumpkin Patch is seeking to promote better communication between its stores in Australia, New Zealand and the United Kingdom. With a broadband connection established between its stores and head office to create better e-mail, Internet and stock movement communication linkages, the company is looking to use wireless local area networks (LANs) in future ICT updates. This will enable portable handheld devices to be used for stocktakes, stock replenishment and customer 'serve yourself' sales.[31]

REALITY CHECK

How private is office communication?

In a recent survey by TMP Worldwide, 20 per cent of employees reported that their e-mails were regularly monitored by their employers, and more than 35 per cent reported that they received insufficient privacy in the workplace.[32]

Why do employers want to monitor employees' communications?

Valuing culture and diversity

Workforce diversity and globalisation are two of the most talked-about trends in modern society. Communicating under conditions of diversity, where the sender and receiver are part of different cultures, is certainly a significant challenge. Cross-cultural communication challenges were first discussed in chapter 5 on the global dimensions of management. Now, it is useful to recall that a major source of difficulty is **ethnocentrism**, the tendency to consider one's culture superior to any and all others. Ethnocentrism can adversely affect communication in at least three major ways: it may cause someone to *not* listen well to what others have to say; it may cause someone to address or speak with others in ways that alienate them; and it may lead to the use of inappropriate stereotypes when dealing with persons from another culture.[33]

For years, cultural challenges have been recognised by international travellers and executives. But as we know, you don't have to travel abroad to come face to face with communication and cultural diversity. Just going to work is a cross-cultural journey for most of us today. The workplace abounds with subcultures based on gender, age, ethnicity, race and other factors. As a result, the importance of cross-cultural communication skills applies at home just as much as it does in a foreign country. Remember, too, that cultural skills are gained by reaching out, crossing cultural boundaries and embracing differences.

Communications issues also arise because of gender differences. A recent study of female managers in Australian organisations found that the participants indicated that there were differences between their communication style and the style used by many male managers. Their views are captured in the following quotations.

> I think that there is a general recognition that I communicate in a different way within the executive team to the men and that I will get my message across in a different way. I probably am a little softer in some situations, but just as determined.

> My personal viewpoint is that it's style. Women are definitely less likely to be openly dogmatic: 'You will do this, you will do that'. I mean they're more likely to say: 'I think it would be a better idea if we did this', or 'Have you thought about that?'[34]

Language and organisational change

The words we choose can have a powerful impact on our effectiveness as communicators. In a study of two New Zealand organisations, it was found that the language used had a strong influence on how the organisations responded to environmental changes. In the case of multinational IT company Infotech (not its real name), the New Zealand office decided to pursue its own strategies while its parent company suffered heavy worldwide losses. These were viewed as its 'rebel' days. In responding to challenges, Infotech's managers saw the company's survival as a '1000-day journey' to recover faster than its competitors. They invoked a strongly positive view of 'the Kiwi way' as a motivator for the journey. As Infotech recovered, the managers referred to 'standing on our own two feet' to explain the New Zealand subsidiary's determination to succeed on its own terms. Then, as the parent company itself began to recover, managers used the word 'reglobalisation' to illustrate the parent company's desire to regain control over its New Zealand operation. The term became a rallying cry for employees keen to retain local control over Infotech operations.

Similarly, with reference to the world-changing events of 11 September 2001, when terrorists brought down the World Trade Center buildings in New York, well-known New Zealand manager Ian Clark argued that while a single organisation or manager can do little to influence world events, they do have control over how they respond in terms of their own area of influence. New strategies implemented in response to such events are much easier to carry out when managers pay ongoing attention to effectively managing communications within their companies. For Clark, 'the challenge is to give [employees] meaningful information without ringing alarm bells ... tell them what you are doing or planning to do about it [because] staff want the truth, leadership and plans for the future [rather than] misinformation, uncertainty, confusion and surprises'. As many staff give credibility to the views of their immediate supervisors, frontline managers and supervisors should assume a major role in any communication strategy.[35]

PERCEPTION

The process through which people receive and interpret information from the environment is called **perception**. It is the way we form impressions about ourselves, other people and daily life experiences and the way we process information into the decisions that ultimately guide our actions.[36]

As shown in figure 17.3, perception acts as a screen or filter through which information must pass before it has an impact on communication, decision making and action. The results of this screening process vary because individual perceptions are influenced by such things as values, cultural background and other circumstances of the moment. Simply put, people can and do perceive the same things or situations very differently. And, importantly, people behave according to their perceptions. Unless the potential for alternative perceptions is recognised and understood, this influence on individual behaviour may be neglected.

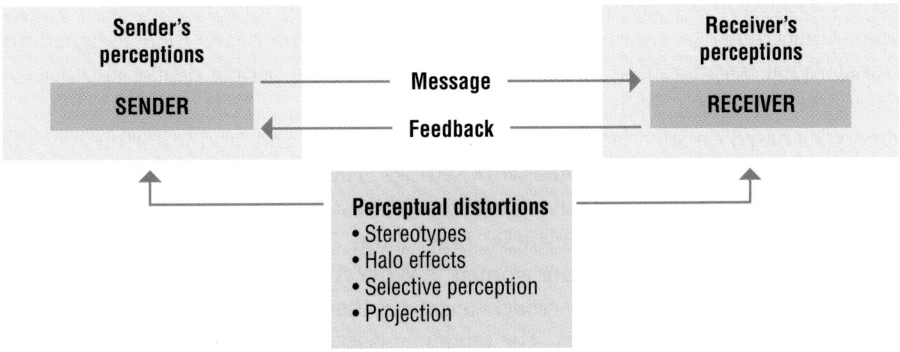

> **Perception** is the process through which people receive, organise and interpret information from the environment.

Figure 17.3 ▸ Perception and communication

Perception and attribution

It is natural for people to try to explain what they observe and the things that happen to them. This process of developing explanations for events is called *attribution*. The fact that people can perceive the same things quite differently has an important influence on attributions and their ultimate influence on behaviour. In social psychology, attribution theory describes how people try to explain the behaviour of themselves and other people.[37] One of its significant applications is in the context of people's performance at work.

Fundamental **attribution error** occurs when observers blame another person's performance failures more on internal factors relating to the individual than on external factors relating to the environment. In the case of someone who is producing poor-quality work,

> **Fundamental attribution error** overestimates internal factors and underestimates external factors as influences on someone's behaviour.

for example, a supervisor might blame a lack of job skills or laziness — an unwillingness to work hard enough. These internal explanations of the performance deficiency, moreover, are likely to lead the supervisor to try to resolve the problem through training, motivation or even replacement. The attribution error leads to the neglect of possible external explanations. They might suggest, for example, that the poor-quality work was caused by unrealistic time pressures or substandard technology. Opportunities to improve upon these factors through managerial action will thus be missed.

Another confounding aspect of perception and attribution is the **self-serving bias**. This occurs because individuals tend to blame their personal failures or problems on external causes, and attribute their successes to internal causes. In this instance, the individual may give insufficient attention to the need for personal change and development. Instead, he or she may be prone to take credit for successes and focus on the environment to explain away failures.

 **Self-serving bias** explains personal success by internal causes and personal failures by external causes.

 A **stereotype** is when attributes commonly associated with a group are assigned to an individual.

Perceptual tendencies and distortions

In addition to the attribution errors just discussed, a variety of perceptual distortions can also influence human behaviour in the workplace. Of particular interest are the use of stereotypes, halo effects, selectivity and projection.

STEREOTYPES

A **stereotype** occurs when someone is identified with a group or category, and then oversimplified attributes associated with the group or category are linked back to the individual. Common stereotypes are those of young people, old people, teachers, students, union members, males and females, among others. The phenomenon, in each case, is the same: a person is classified into a group on the basis of one piece of information, such as age, for example. Characteristics commonly associated with the group are then assigned to the individual. What is generalised about the group (e.g. 'Young people dislike authority') may or may not be true about the individual.

Stereotypes based on such factors as gender, age and race can, and unfortunately still do, bias the perceptions of people in some work settings. The *glass ceiling*, mentioned in chapter 1 as an invisible barrier to career advancement, still exists in some places.

In the world of international business, only about 7 per cent of expatriate managers working in the Asia–Pacific region are women.[38] Why? A Catalyst study of opportunities for women in global business points to *gender stereotypes* that place women at a disadvantage to men for these types of opportunities. The tendency is to assume they lack the ability and/or willingness for working abroad.[39] Although employment barriers caused by gender stereotypes are falling, women may still suffer from false impressions and biases imposed on them. Even everyday behaviour may be misconstrued based upon inaccurate perceptions. Consider this example: '*He's* talking with coworkers.' (*Interpretation:* He's discussing a new deal.); '*She's* talking with coworkers.' (*Interpretation:* She's gossiping.)[40]

Finally, *ability stereotypes* and *age stereotypes* also exist in the workplace. Their inappropriate use may place disabled and older workers at a disadvantage in various work situations. A worker with a disability may be overlooked in the hiring process because the recruiter assumes that someone with a disability would have a difficult time meeting a normal work schedule. A talented older worker may not be promoted to fill an important and challenging job, because a manager assumes older workers lack creativity, are cautious and tend to avoid risk. A recent study found that less than 11 per cent of recently hired staff in Australian organisations were aged 45 or older, while 47 per cent of organisations had no

REALITY CHECK

Age discrimination
The number of age discrimination complaints to the Human Rights and Equal Opportunity Commission tripled between 1999–2000 and 2000–2001. In fact, 70 per cent of Australian firms said they would retrench workers aged over 50 before others, because of their inflexibility and unwillingness to change. The same survey found, however, that 86 per cent of older workers were open to new opportunities and retraining.[41]

Have you experienced any form of age discrimination in a workplace or other organisation?

staff older than 55. With an ageing workforce, however, employers in some industries may have little choice but to employ older workers. It is estimated that by 2020 there will be as many people approaching retirement in Australia as there will be entering the workforce. As older workers can be just as productive and creative as younger employees, the pressure to employ more older staff is not necessarily a bad thing.[42]

HALO EFFECTS

A **halo effect** occurs when one attribute is used to develop an overall impression of a person or situation. When meeting someone new, for example, the halo effect may cause one trait, such as a pleasant smile, to result in a positive first impression. By contrast, a particular hairstyle or manner of dressing may create a negative reaction. Halo effects cause the same problem for managers as do stereotypes — that is, individual differences become obscured. This is especially significant with respect to a manager's view of subordinates' work performance. One factor, such as a person's punctuality, may become the 'halo' for a positive overall performance evaluation. Even though the general conclusion seems to make sense, it may or may not be true in a given circumstance.

> A **halo effect** occurs when one attribute is used to develop an overall impression of a person or situation.

SELECTIVITY

Selective perception is the tendency to single out for attention those aspects of a situation or person that reinforce or appear consistent with one's existing beliefs, values or needs.[43] What this often means in an organisation is that people from different departments or functions — such as marketing and manufacturing — tend to see things from their own points of view and tend not to recognise other points of view. Like the other perceptual distortions just discussed, selective perception can bias a manager's view of situations and individuals. One way to reduce its impact is to gather additional opinions from other people.

> **Selective perception** is the tendency to define problems from one's own point of view.

PROJECTION

Projection is the assignment of personal attributes to other individuals. A classic projection error is to assume that other persons share our needs, desires and values. Suppose, for example, that you enjoy a lot of responsibility and challenge in your work. Suppose, too, that you are the newly appointed supervisor for people whose work you consider dull and routine. You might move quickly to start a program of job enrichment to help them experience more responsibility and challenge. This may not be a good decision. Instead of designing jobs to best fit their needs, you have designed their jobs to fit *yours*. In fact, your subordinates may be quite satisfied and productive doing jobs that, to you, seem routine. Such projection errors can be controlled through self-awareness and a willingness to communicate and empathise with other persons — that is, to try to see things through their eyes.

> **Projection** is the assignment of personal attributes to other individuals.

COMMUNICATION AND CONFLICT MANAGEMENT

Communication and related interpersonal skills must be at the forefront of any attempt to develop managerial and leadership expertise. Among these essential skills, the ability to deal with interpersonal conflicts is critical. Formally defined, **conflict** is a disagreement between people on substantive or emotional issues.[44] Managers and leaders spend a lot of time dealing with conflicts of various forms. **Substantive conflicts** involve disagreements over

> **Conflict** is a disagreement over issues of substance and/or an emotional antagonism.
>
> **Substantive conflicts** involve disagreements over goals, resources, rewards, policies, procedures and job assignments.

such things as goals; the allocation of resources; the distribution of rewards, policies and procedures; and job assignments. **Emotional conflicts** result from feelings of anger, distrust, dislike, fear and resentment, as well as from personality clashes. Both forms of conflict can cause problems in the workplace. But when managed well, they can be helpful in promoting high performance, creativity and innovation.

Consequences of conflict

Whether or not conflict benefits people and organisations depends on two factors: the intensity of the conflict and how well the conflict is managed. The inverted 'U' curve depicted in figure 17.4 shows that conflict of moderate intensity can be good for performance. This **functional conflict**, or *constructive conflict*, stimulates people toward greater work efforts, cooperation and creativity. At very low or very high intensities **dysfunctional conflict**, or *destructive conflict*, occurs. Too much conflict is distracting and interferes with other more task-relevant activities; too little conflict may promote complacency and the loss of a creative, high-performance edge.

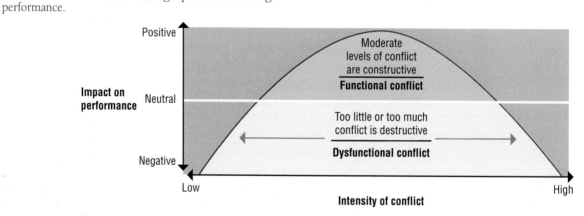

Figure 17.4 ▸ The relationship between conflict and performance

Causes of conflict

Conflict in organisations may arise for a variety of reasons. Indeed, the following antecedent conditions can make the eventual emergence of conflict very likely. *Role ambiguities* set the stage for conflict. Unclear job expectations and other task uncertainties increase the probability that some people will be working at cross-purposes, at least some of the time. *Resource scarcities* cause conflict. Having to share resources with others and/or compete directly with them for resource allocations creates a potential situation conflict, especially when resources are scarce. *Task interdependencies* cause conflict. When individuals or groups must depend on what others do to perform well themselves, conflicts often occur. *Competing objectives* are opportunities for conflict. When objectives are poorly set or reward systems are poorly designed, individuals and groups may come into conflict by working to one another's disadvantage. *Structural differentiation* breeds conflict. Differences in organisation structures and in the characteristics of the people staffing them may foster conflict because of incompatible approaches toward work. And *unresolved prior conflicts* tend to erupt in later conflicts. Unless a conflict is fully resolved, it may remain latent in the situation as a lingering basis for future conflicts over the same or related matters.

How to deal with conflict

When any one or more of these antecedent conditions is present, an informed manager expects conflicts to occur. And when they do, the conflicts then can either be 'resolved', in the sense that the sources are corrected, or 'suppressed', in that the sources remain but the conflict behaviours are controlled. Suppressed conflicts tend to fester and recur at a later time. They can also contribute to other conflicts over the same or related issues. True **conflict resolution** eliminates the underlying causes of conflict and reduces the potential for similar conflicts in the future.

Managers can try several approaches to restructure situations in order to resolve conflicts between individuals or groups. There are times when *appealing to superordinate goals* can focus the attention of conflicting parties on one mutually desirable end state. The appeal to higher-level goals offers all parties a common frame of reference against which to analyse differences and reconcile disagreements. Conflicts whose antecedents lie in the competition for scarce resources can also be resolved by *making more resources available* to everyone. Although costly, this technique removes the reasons for the continuing conflict. By *changing the people*, that is, by replacing or transferring one or more of the conflicting parties, conflicts caused by poor interpersonal relationships can be eliminated. The same holds true for *altering the physical environment* by rearranging facilities, work space or workflows to physically separate conflicting parties and decrease opportunities for them to come into contact with one another.

A variety of *integrating devices* or coordinating mechanisms, introduced in chapter 11 as ways to improve integration in organisations, can also be used with success in many settings. Implementing liaison personnel, special task forces and cross-functional teams, and even the matrix form of organisation, can change interaction patterns and assist in conflict management. *Changing reward systems* may reduce the competition between individuals and groups for rewards. Creating systems that reward cooperation can encourage behaviours and attitudes that promote teamwork and keep conflict within more constructive limits. *Changing policies and procedures* may redirect behaviour in ways that minimise the likelihood of unfortunate conflict situations. Finally, *training in interpersonal skills* can help prepare people to communicate and work more effectively in situations that are conflict prone.

Conflict management styles

Interpersonally, people respond to conflict through different combinations of cooperative and assertive behaviours.[45] *Cooperativeness* is the desire to satisfy another party's needs and concerns. *Assertiveness* is the desire to satisfy one's own needs and concerns. Figure 17.5 shows five interpersonal styles of conflict management that result from various combinations of the two. Briefly stated, these conflict management styles involve the following behaviours:

- **Avoidance** — being uncooperative and unassertive; downplaying disagreement, withdrawing from the situation and/or staying neutral at all costs.
- **Accommodation** or *smoothing* — being cooperative but unassertive; letting the wishes of others rule; smoothing over or overlooking differences to maintain harmony.
- **Competition** or *authoritative command* — being uncooperative but assertive; working against the wishes of the other party, engaging in win–lose competition and/or forcing through the exercise of authority.
- **Compromise** — being moderately cooperative and assertive, bargaining for 'acceptable' solutions in which each party wins a bit and loses a bit.

Conflict resolution is the removal of the substantial and/or emotional reasons for a conflict.

Avoidance pretends that a conflict doesn't really exist.

Accommodation, or smoothing, plays down differences and highlights similarities to reduce conflict.

Competition, or authoritative command, uses force, superior skill or domination to 'win' a conflict.

Compromise occurs when each party to the conflict gives up something of value to the other.

Five conflict management styles

Collaboration, or problem solving, involves working through conflict differences and solving problems so everyone wins.

- **Collaboration** or *problem solving* — being both cooperative and assertive; trying to fully satisfy everyone's concerns by working through differences; finding and solving problems so that everyone gains.[46]

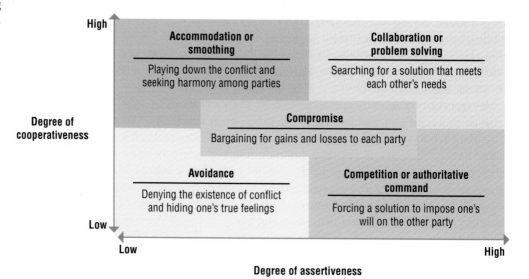

Figure 17.5 ▸ Alternative conflict management styles

The various conflict management styles can have quite different outcomes.[47] Thus they should be selected and used with caution, and with the requirements of each unique conflict situation carefully considered. Conflict management by *avoiding* or *accommodating* often creates **lose–lose conflict**. No one achieves her or his true desires and the underlying reasons for conflict often remain unaffected. Although a lose–lose conflict may appear settled or may even disappear for a while, it tends to recur in the future. Avoidance is an extreme form of non-attention. Everyone pretends that conflict doesn't really exist and hopes that it will simply go away. Accommodation plays down differences and highlights similarities and areas of agreement. Peaceful coexistence through a recognition of common interests is the goal. In reality, such smoothing may ignore the real essence of a conflict.

In **lose–lose conflict** no one achieves his or her true desires and the underlying reasons for conflict remain unaffected.

Competing and *compromising* tend to create **win–lose conflict**. Here, each party strives to gain at the other's expense. In extreme cases, one party achieves its desires to the complete exclusion of the other party's desires. Because win–lose methods fail to address the root causes of conflict, future conflicts of the same or a similar nature are likely to occur. In competition, one party wins, as superior skill or outright domination allows his or her desires to be forced on the other. This occurs in the form of authoritative command, where the forcing is accomplished by a higher-level supervisor who simply dictates a solution to subordinates. Compromise occurs when trade-offs are made such that each party to the conflict gives up and gains something of value. As a result, neither party is completely satisfied, and antecedents for future conflicts are established.

In **win–lose conflict** one party achieves its desires and the other party does not.

Collaborating in true problem solving tries to reconcile underlying differences and is often the most effective conflict management style. It is a form of **win–win conflict** whereby issues are resolved to the mutual benefit of all conflicting parties. This is typically achieved by confronting the issues and through the willingness of those involved to recognise that something is wrong and needs attention. Win–win conditions are created by eliminating the underlying causes of the conflict. All relevant issues are raised and discussed openly. Win–win methods are clearly the most preferred of the interpersonal styles of conflict management.

In **win–win conflict** the conflict is resolved to everyone's benefit.

According to Professor Susan Long, of Melbourne's Swinburne University of Technology, developing an organisational culture that encourages collaboration involves three key dimensions. First, establishing clear tasks and roles provides employees with a framework through which conflicts can be understood. Next, people in the workplace can be encouraged to learn from experience, therefore providing a shared base of knowledge and learning so that conflicts can be dealt with in mature ways. Finally, managers should create an environment in which employees are encouraged to raise concerns about tasks and roles, and ensure that these concerns are listened to and considered.[48]

NEGOTIATION

Put yourself in the following situations. How would you behave, and what would you do?
1. You have been offered a promotion and would really like to take it. However, the pay raise being offered is less than you hoped.
2. You have enough money to order one new computer for your department. Two of your subordinates have each requested a new computer for their individual jobs.[49]

These are but two examples of the many negotiation situations that involve managers and other people in the typical workplace.

Negotiation is the process of making joint decisions when the parties involved have different preferences. Stated a bit differently, it is a way of reaching agreement when decisions involve more than one person or group. People negotiate over such diverse matters as salary, merit raises and performance evaluations, job assignments, work schedules, work locations, special privileges and many other considerations. All such situations are susceptible to conflict and require exceptional communication skills.

Negotiation is the process of making joint decisions when the parties involved have different preferences.

Negotiation goals and approaches

There are two important goals in negotiation. *Substance goals* are concerned with outcomes — they are tied to the 'content' issues of the negotiation. *Relationship goals* are concerned with processes — they are tied to the way people work together while negotiating and how they (and any constituencies they represent) will be able to work together again in the future.

Effective negotiation occurs when issues of substance are resolved and working relationships among the negotiating parties are maintained or even improved in the process. The three criteria of effective negotiation are: *quality* — negotiating a 'wise' agreement that is truly satisfactory to all sides; *cost* — negotiating efficiently, using up minimum resources and time; and *harmony* — negotiating in a way that fosters, rather than inhibits, interpersonal relationships.[50] The way each party approaches a negotiation can have a major impact on these outcomes.[51]

Distributive negotiation focuses on 'claims' made by each party for certain preferred outcomes. This can take a competitive form in which one party can gain only if the other loses. In such 'win–lose' conditions, relationships are often sacrificed as the negotiating parties focus only on their respective self-interests. It may also become accommodative if the parties defer to one another's wishes simply 'to get it over with'.

Principled negotiation, often called **integrative negotiation**, is based on a 'win–win' orientation. The focus on substance is still important, but the interests of all parties are considered. The goal is to base the final outcome on the merits of individual claims and to try to find a way for all claims to be satisfied if at all possible. No one should 'lose', and relationships should be maintained in the process.

Distributive negotiation focuses on 'win–lose' claims made by each party for certain preferred outcomes.

Principled/integrative negotiation uses a 'win–win' orientation to reach solutions acceptable to each party.

Gaining integrative agreements

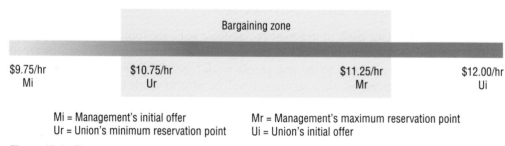

Four rules of principled negotiation

In their book *Getting to Yes*, Roger Fisher and William Ury point out that truly integrative agreements are obtained by following four negotiation rules:[52]

1. Separate the people from the problem.
2. Focus on interests, not on positions.
3. Generate many alternatives before deciding what to do.
4. Insist that results are based on some objective standard.

Proper attitudes and good information are important foundations for such integrative agreements. The attitudinal foundations of integrative agreements involve the willingness of each negotiating party to trust, share information with, and ask reasonable questions of the other party. The informational foundations of integrative agreements involve each party knowing what is really important to them and finding out what is really important to the other party. In addition, each should understand his or her personal best alternative to a negotiated agreement or **BATNA**. This is an answer to the question: What will I do if an agreement can't be reached?

BATNA is the best alternative to a negotiated agreement.

Figure 17.6 introduces a typical case of labour–management negotiations over a new contract and salary increase. This helps to illustrate elements of classic two-party negotiation as they occur in many contexts.[53] To begin, look at the figure and case from the labour union's perspective. The union negotiator has told her management counterpart that the union wants a new wage of $12.00 per hour. This expressed preference is the union's *initial offer*. However, she also has in mind a *minimum reservation point* of $10.75 per hour. This is the lowest wage rate that she is willing to accept for the union. But the management negotiator has a different perspective. His *initial offer* is $9.75 per hour, and his *maximum reservation point*, the highest wage he is prepared eventually to offer to the union, is $11.25 per hour.

Bargaining zone			
$9.75/hr Mi	$10.75/hr Ur	$11.25/hr Mr	$12.00/hr Ui

Mi = Management's initial offer
Ur = Union's minimum reservation point
Mr = Management's maximum reservation point
Ui = Union's initial offer

Figure 17.6 ▸ The bargaining zone in classic two-party negotiation

A **bargaining zone** is the area between one party's minimum reservation point and the other party's maximum reservation point.

In classic two-party negotiations of this type, the **bargaining zone** is defined as the zone between one party's minimum reservation point and the other party's maximum reservation point. The bargaining zone of $10.75 per hour to $11.25 per hour in this case is a 'positive' one, since the reservation points of the two parties overlap. If the union's minimum reservation point were greater than management's maximum reservation point, no room would exist for bargaining. Whenever a positive bargaining zone exists, there is room for true negotiation.

A key task for any negotiator is to discover the other party's reservation point. Until this is known and each party becomes aware that a positive bargaining zone exists, it is difficult to proceed effectively. When negotiation does move forward, each negotiator typically tries to achieve an agreement that is as close as possible to the other party's reservation point. Returning to figure 17.6, the union negotiator would like to get an offer as close to $12.00 per hour as possible. The management negotiator would like to get a contract for as close to $9.75 per hour as possible.

Avoiding negotiation pitfalls

The negotiation process is admittedly complex, and negotiators must guard against common mistakes. Four negotiator pitfalls that can be avoided by proper discipline and personal attention should be recognised. The first is the tendency of *falling prey to the myth of the 'fixed pie'*. This involves acting on the distributive assumption that in order for you to gain, the other person must give something up. Negotiating this way fails to recognise the integrative assumption that the 'pie' can sometimes be expanded and/or used to everyone's advantage. A second negotiation error is the *non-relational escalation of conflict*. The negotiator in this case becomes committed to previously stated 'demands' and allows concerns for 'ego' and 'face saving' to increase the perceived importance of satisfying these demands. The third error is *overconfidence and ignoring the other's needs*. The error here is becoming overconfident that your position is the only correct one and failing to see the needs of the other party and the merits in its position. The fourth error is the tendency to do *too much 'telling' and too little 'hearing'*. When committing the 'telling' problem, parties to a negotiation don't really make themselves understood to each other. When committing the 'hearing' problem neither party listens sufficiently to understand what the other is saying.[54]

It may not always be possible to achieve integrative agreements. When disputes reach the point of impasse, mediation and arbitration can be useful. **Mediation** involves a neutral third party who tries to improve communication between negotiating parties and keep them focused on relevant issues. The *mediator* does not issue a ruling or make a decision, but can take an active role in discussions. This may include making suggestions in an attempt to move the parties toward agreement. **Arbitration**, such as salary arbitration in professional sports, is a stronger form of dispute resolution. It involves a neutral third party, the *arbitrator*, who acts as a 'judge' and issues a binding decision. This usually includes a formal hearing in which the arbitrator listens to both sides and reviews all facets of the case before making a ruling. Some organisations formally provide for a process called *alternative dispute resolution*. This approach uses mediation and/or arbitration but only after direct attempts to negotiate agreements between the conflicting parties have failed. Often an *ombudsperson*, or designated neutral third party who listens to complaints and disputes, plays a key role in the process.

In **mediation**, a neutral party tries to help conflicting parties improve communication to resolve their dispute.

In **arbitration**, a neutral third party issues a binding decision to resolve a dispute.

Cross-cultural negotiation

Negotiating in other countries can bring particular challenges not normally faced in a manager's home country. Many such challenges can be traced to cultural differences. When negotiating in India, for example, an awareness of status differences is critical. Communication should be directed first to the most senior person in an organisation, and negotiators should be aware of the common practice of 'name dropping' during conversations, because the level and quality of the relationship between the person and his or her 'contact' may require additional investigation. As access to key players in the government bureaucracy is often critical to doing business in India, secretaries and assistants are often valuable sources of information and advice, and relationships with them should be cultivated where appropriate. Whereas Indian businesspeople will often take great pride in having Westerners to their homes for a meal, the Chinese will rarely invite foreigners to their home unless the relationship is very well developed. One of the major reasons for this is that the Chinese may view their dwellings as quite small in comparison to homes in many parts of the West. Another difference concerns the importance of time. Whereas Indians are 'habitually late' for appointments, the Chinese view punctuality as 'a positive asset in others'. Such cultural differences abound throughout the Asia–Pacific region, and the effective manager is well prepared for such differences.[55]

Ethical issues in negotiation

Managers, and anyone else involved in negotiation, should maintain high standards of ethical conduct even when they are personally engaged in a dynamic and challenging situation. The motivation to behave unethically sometimes arises from an undue emphasis on the profit motive. This may be experienced as a desire to 'get just a bit more' or to 'get as much as you can' from a negotiation. The motivation to behave unethically may also result from a sense of competition. This may be experienced as a desire to 'win' a negotiation just for the sake of it or as a misguided belief that someone else must 'lose' in order for you to gain.

When unethical behaviour occurs in negotiation, the persons involved sometimes attempt to rationalise or explain it away. We first discussed such rationalisations for unethical conduct in chapter 6. In a negotiation situation, the following comments may be indicative of inappropriate rationalising: 'It was really unavoidable', 'Oh, it's harmless', 'The results justify the means', or 'It's really quite fair and appropriate'.[56] Moral issues aside, tendencies to use or accept such explanations can be challenged by the possibility that any short-run gains may be accompanied by long-run losses. Unethical parties should also realise that they may be targeted for later 'revenge' from those disadvantaged by their tactics. Furthermore, once people behave unethically in one situation, they may consider such behaviour acceptable in similar circumstances in the future.

Visit the Conflict Resolution Network www.crnhq.org to access resources for dealing with conflict — from conflict between governments to conflict within organisations.

GET CONNECTED!

POINT←

↑COUNTER

Negotiations, bribes and culture

When negotiating in countries such as Australia and New Zealand, most managers are aware that the legal systems of these nations do not permit bribery or corrupt practices such as collusion. This is a grey area, however.

When does a gift become a bribe?
Paying for a meal and entertainment are common practices during negotiation.

What about providing front-row tickets to a theatre premiere or football grand final? If you are negotiating with someone visiting from another city, do you pay for the travel arrangements for his or her family? Is a bribe still a bribe if paid to a person overseas operating in a culture where 'grease payments' are seen as normal practice?

CHAPTER 17
Study guide

The chapter 17 study guide helps you review the chapter content, prepare for examinations, apply what you have learned and further build your career readiness. The summary briefly answers the study questions posed at the start of the chapter. The list of key terms allows you to double-check your familiarity with basic concepts and definitions. The applied activities help you test your comprehension of chapter content. Suggestions offered as career readiness activities direct your attention to relevant sections of the Career Readiness Workbook where you can test and develop your career skills and apply what you have learned. The list of electronic resources suggests activities from the *Management: An Asia–Pacific Perspective* web site and, finally, the case for critical thinking helps you apply your new management knowledge.

SUMMARY

What is the communication process?

- Communication is the interpersonal process of sending and receiving symbols with messages attached to them.
- Effective communication occurs when the sender and the receiver of a message both interpret it in the same way. Efficient communication occurs when the message is sent at low cost for the sender.
- Noise is anything that interferes with the effectiveness of communication. It occurs in the form of poor use of channels, poor written or oral expression, physical distractions and status effects, among other possibilities.

How can communication be improved?

- Active listening, through reflecting back and paraphrasing, can help overcome communication barriers.
- Upward communication may be improved through MBWA (managing by wandering around) and by the use of structured meetings, suggestion systems, advisory councils and the like.
- Space can be used and designed to improve communication in organisations.
- The appropriate use of information technology, such as e-mail and intranets, can improve communication in organisations.
- Greater cross-cultural awareness and sensitivity can help reduce the difficulties of communication and diversity.

How does perception influence communication?

- Perception acts as a filter through which all communication passes as it travels from one person to the next.
- Because people tend to perceive things differently, the same message may be interpreted quite differently by different people.
- Attribution is the process of assigning explanations to events.

- Attribution theory identifies tendencies toward fundamental attribution errors when judging the performance of others and self-serving bias when judging our own performance.
- Common perceptual distortions that may reduce communication effectiveness include stereotypes, projections, halo effects and selective perception.

How can we deal positively with conflict?

- Conflict occurs as disagreements over substantive or emotional issues.
- Managers should support functional conflict that facilitates a high-performance edge and creativity; they should avoid the harmful effects of too little or too much conflict that becomes dysfunctional.
- Conflict may be managed through structural approaches that involve changing people, goals, resources or work arrangements.
- Personal conflict management styles include avoidance, accommodation, compromise, competition and collaboration.
- True conflict resolution involves problem solving through a win–win collaborative approach.

How can we negotiate successful agreements?

- Negotiation is the process of making decisions in situations in which the participants have different preferences.
- Both substance goals, those concerned with outcomes, and relationship goals, those concerned with processes, are important in successful negotiation.
- Effective negotiation occurs when issues of substance are resolved and the process results in good working relationships.
- Distributive approaches to negotiation emphasise win–lose outcomes and are usually harmful to relationships.
- Integrative approaches to negotiation emphasise win–win outcomes and the interests of all parties.

KEY TERMS

accommodation (p. 479)

active listening (p. 469)

arbitration (p. 483)

attribution error (p. 475)

avoidance (p. 479)

bargaining zone (p. 482)

BATNA (p. 482)

channel richness (p. 471)

collaboration (p. 480)

communication (p. 464)

communication channel (p. 465)

competition (p. 479)

compromise (p. 479)

conflict (p. 477)

conflict resolution (p. 479)

distributive negotiation (p. 481)

dysfunctional conflict (p. 478)

effective communication (p. 464)

efficient communication (p. 464)

emotional conflicts (p. 478)

ethnocentrism (p. 474)

feedback (p. 470)

filtering (p. 468)

functional conflict (p. 478)

halo effect (p. 477)

lose–lose conflict (p. 480)

MBWA (p. 471)

mediation (p. 483)

mixed message (p. 467)

negotiation (p. 481)

noise (p. 465)

non-verbal communication (p. 467)

perception (p. 475)

principled/integrative negotiation (p. 481)

projection (p. 477)

selective perception (p. 477)

self-serving bias (p. 476)

stereotype (p. 476)

substantive conflicts (p. 477)

win–lose conflict (p. 480)

win–win conflict (p. 480)

APPLIED ACTIVITIES

Short-response questions

1. Briefly describe what a manager would do to be an 'active listener' when communicating with subordinates.

2. What is the difference between the halo effect and selective perception?

3. How do tendencies toward assertiveness and cooperativeness in conflict management result in win–lose, lose–lose and win–win outcomes?

4. What is the difference between substance and relationship goals in negotiation?

Application question

5. After being promoted to store manager for a new branch of a large department store chain, Harold Welsch was concerned about communication in the store. Six department heads reported directly to him, and 50 full-time and part-time sales associates reported to them. Given this structure, Harold worried about staying informed about all store operations, not just those coming to his attention as senior manager. What steps might Harold take to establish and maintain an effective system of upward communication in his store?

CAREER READINESS ACTIVITIES

Recommended individual and group learning activities from the end-of-text Career Readiness Workbook for this chapter include:

Career advancement portfolio   WB

Update your career advancement portfolio to reflect your new skills and experiences. Include skills and personal insights you gain from the following projects and exercises.

Research and presentation projects   WB

- Project 2 — Changing corporate cultures
- Project 5 — Affirmative action directions — 'where do we go from here?'

Cross-functional integrative case   WB

Read the integrative case on Sarina Russo and answer the following questions:

17.1 Imagine that you are (a) a prospective student of the Russo Institute of Technology, and (b) an employer seeking a new member of staff via Sarina Russo Job Access. Referring to the Sarina Russo Group web site www.sarinarusso.com.au, how effectively do you find it communicates its activities to you? What noise might interfere with the effectiveness of this communication?

17.2 Are there any ways in which Sarina Russo demonstrates the characteristics associated with a stereotype?

Exercises in teamwork *WB*

- Exercise 21 — A self-portrait of communication effectiveness
- Exercise 23 — How to give, and take, criticism

Management skills assessment *WB*

- Assessment 17 — Communication skills

ELECTRONIC RESOURCES

Don't forget to take full advantage of the online support for *Management: An Asia–Pacific Perspective* at www.johnwiley.com.au/highered/management: chapter 17 practice tests, e-flashcards, crossword puzzles, interactive management skills assessments, interactive cases, the online career advancement portfolio and much more!

CASE FOR CRITICAL THINKING

Read the following case for critical thinking on the United Nations. While you are reading the case keep in mind what you have learned in this chapter, then answer the questions.

The United Nations:
getting nations to work together

The United Nations is an historically unique organisation that strives for communication and cooperation across nations of the world. UN members are sovereign nations — the organisation is not a world government and does not make laws. Beginning on 24 October 1945 with 51 countries, it has grown into a collection of 191 countries (East Timor was admitted on 27 September 2002), who accept the obligations of the UN Charter, an international treaty that sets out basic principles of international relations. It is an organisation that truly embraces the concept of diversity and conflict resolution.[57]

A world order

The failure of the League of Nations following World War I left individual governments with no formalised world body to work out conflicts between nations. As a result, World War II materialised into a global conflict. At the conclusion of World War II, some leading nations chose to develop a successor to the League — the United Nations. The United Nations was meant to give all nations — large or small, rich or poor, and with differing political and economic systems — a voice and vote in the process of world politics.

The United Nations is made up of six main branches:

1. General Assembly — a 'parliament of nations' where each member has one vote
2. Security Council — with primary responsibility for maintaining international peace and security
3. Economic and Social Council — coordinating the economic and social work of the UN system
4. Trusteeship Council — responsible for international supervision of 11 Trust Territories to promote self-government. With this task completed in 1994, the body meets only when necessary.
5. Secretariat — headed by the Secretary-General, it handles the administrative work of the United Nations
6. International Court of Justice — located in The Hague, this body, also known as the World Court, is responsible for deciding disputes between countries.

While best known for its peacekeeping and humanitarian assistance, the United Nations — in cooperation with more than 30 affiliated organisations known together as the UN system — promotes human rights, protects the environment, fights disease, fosters economic development and reduces poverty.[58] Consistent with its Charter, the United Nations represents 'a centre for harmonizing the actions of nations'.[59]

The General Assembly considers a wide range of topics, from globalisation to the consolidation of new democracies. Its actions cannot be 'forced' onto any state, but its recommendations are an important indication of world opinion.

The Security Council is composed of 15 members. Five of these are permanent, including the USA, the United Kingdom, France, the Russian Federation and China. The other ten are elected for two-year terms. Decisions require nine 'yes' votes, and any permanent member can veto any decision. The Council has the power to enforce its decisions, including economic sanctions, arms embargos or, in rare occasions, 'all necessary means', which includes collective military force.

Where the United Nations offers the most opportunity is in its ability to marshal international public opinion. World conflicts are discussed on a world stage with a world audience. From the Cuban missile crisis in 1962 to restoring peace in the Balkans in the late 1990s, the United Nations helps prevent conflicts, and in post-conflict situations it lays the foundation for durable peace.

How does it work?

The UN General Assembly meets from September to December in regular session. All nations have an equal vote on a range of international issues.[60] When not in session, the Assembly's work is carried out by its committees and the Secretariat.

The Security Council has the primary responsibility for maintaining international peace and security. The Council may convene any time it is felt necessary and, under the Charter, all member states are required to carry out the Security Council's mandates.

The United Nations has many subunits that do not attract the same media attention as the General Assembly and Security Council. The UN system attempts to pool resources with autonomous organisations that are joined with the United Nations by special agreements. These groups work with the United Nations to advance world peace and prosperity.

Initiatives by the United Nations include:

- UN peacekeeping, recently involved in 15 operations, is staffed by 37 400 UN military and civilian personnel from 89 countries.
- The United Nations, along with the World Bank and the UN Development Programme, provides assistance worth more than US$30 billion per year.

- The World Food Programme provides about one-third of the world's food aid. Emergency food assistance helps feed more than 86 million people in 82 countries around the world.[61]
- A joint UNICEF – World Health Organization initiative has immunised 80 per cent of the world's children against six killer diseases.
- More international law has been developed through the United Nations in the past five decades than in all previous history.
- UN agencies aid and protect more than 25 million refugees and displaced persons around the world.

The UN's Universal Declaration of Human Rights, dating from 1948, argues that basic rights and freedoms exist for all men and women of the world. The High Commissioner for Human Rights coordinates all UN human rights activities, working with governments to promote their observance.

The United Nations provides an infrastructure system that transcends national borders, thereby encouraging international solutions to world problems. While many support its aims, the organisation is not without its detractors. Many smaller countries argue against domination from the larger nations, particularly from the Security Council's permanent membership. In response to pressure from a number of nations, including the USA, the United Nations launched a reform movement in the late 1990s. Discussions on financing, operations and the make-up of the Security Council continue — many times to the frustration of the smaller countries:

> If reform of the [Security] Council is to be truly comprehensive and consistent with the spirit and realities of our time, then we must seek to remove — or at least, as a first step, restrict — the use of the veto power. Democracy in the United Nations is a mockery if the voice of the majority is rendered meaningless by the narrow interests of the dominant few.[62]
>
> Minister for Foreign Affairs of Malaysia,
> HE Dato' Seri Abdullah bin Haji Ahmad Badawi

Others argue that the United Nations is too liberal and supports non-democratic regimes around the globe. The USA withheld its dues for a number of years in protest of UN policies and charges of administrative waste within its programs.

The future

The United Nations still represents the world's best opportunity to create a climate of communication and dispute resolution across national borders. It is an ongoing forum for disarmament negotiations, contributing to both the Treaty on the Non-Proliferation of Nuclear Weapons (1968) and the Comprehensive Nuclear Test-Ban Treaty in 1996.

UN Secretary-General Mr Kofi Annan states it best when he argues: 'Let it be remembered as a time when all of us joined forces and seized the opportunities created by the new era to revitalise our United Nations — this unique and universal instrument for concerted action in pursuit of the betterment of humankind'.[63]

QUESTIONS

1. What kinds of communication problems might occur at the UN?
2. Given the size and diversity of the UN, what could be done to promote clear communication between its member states?
3. Provide other examples of the ways in which other large organisations can ensure clear communication between different locations and levels of their operations.

Change leadership

CHAPTER 18 STUDY QUESTIONS

- What are the challenges of change?

- What is the nature of organisational change?

- How can planned organisational change be managed?

- What is organisation development?

- How do you build career readiness in a change environment?

Fisher & Paykel — smart innovation and technology leadership

GETTING @ CONNECTED

When it began manufacturing in the late 1930s, New Zealand-based Fisher & Paykel was making refrigerators and washing machines under licence from General Electric. It was not until the 1960s that the company began designing and manufacturing its own products. By the 1990s, it had developed in-house product technologies that had made it a household name in Australia and New Zealand and distinguished it as a whitegoods innovator and leader. These technologies include automatic washing machines with electronic controls and sensors, refrigerators that use microchips to control and monitor temperature and airflow, and dishwashers with a unique split cabinet design and electronic controls. Its production of hi-tech hospital humidifiers also gave the company a strong presence in healthcare.

Fisher & Paykel lists 'continuous improvement' among its core corporate values and this ideal encompasses every aspect of the company. In the company's own words: 'Everything we do must have a process focus that is measured in terms of quality, cost, delivery, safety and morale'.

The company works hard at product improvement and innovation. In addition to its products, though, Fisher & Paykel recognises there are a host of leadership and management challenges that it must meet to make the most of the opportunities its innovative technologies provide and to keep improving shareholder value. As managing director John Bongard said: 'Growth is only possible with continued investment in product development, new manufacturing systems and innovation'. Change at Fisher & Paykel is being driven by a strategy of simplification and the reshaping of nearly every aspect of its business, as it seeks to capitalise on the global opportunities its innovative technology has provided. In 2001, Fisher & Paykel split into standalone healthcare and appliances businesses, partly due to the increasing strategic importance of its healthcare division. The company is proud to say that its staff remained focused on their operational strategies and day-to-day goals despite the uncertainties the separation process created.[1]

GET CONNECTED!

Check out the Innovation DNA™ model on the InnovationNetwork web site www.thinksmart.com, and find out more about organisations that are truly innovative. Are you trained to participate in an innovation-driven and highly competitive global economy? Do you have good ideas? Can you help others to put their ideas into action? Build your plan for continued personal and professional development.

GET CONNECTED!

Top management at James Hardie, the Australian-based global building materials manufacturer, use brainstorming, team discussions and lateral-thinking techniques to develop new products, process technologies and management techniques.

When a group of Japanese students drove out of Tokyo one day, the event wouldn't have seemed remarkable to bystanders. But when they arrived some 900 kilometres later on the northern island of Hokkaido, Mitsubishi's president was very pleased. The students' car, powered by a new engine technology, had made the trip without refuelling! In fact, there was fuel to spare in the tank. It was an important breakthrough for the company. For a long time engineers had known the feat was technically possible, but they didn't know just how to do it. Finally, through hard work, a lot of information sharing and problem solving, and through learning, they found the answer.[2]

Finding answers to problems is what moves people, organisations and societies continuously ahead in our dynamic and very challenging world. We are living and working at a time when intellectual capital, knowledge management and learning organisations are taking centre stage. Rightfully so. Harvard scholars Michael Beer and Nitin Nohria observe: 'The new economy has ushered in great business opportunities and great turmoil. Not since the Industrial Revolution have the stakes of dealing with change been so high. Most traditional organisations have accepted, in theory at least, that they must either change or die.'[3] Speaking from the vantage point of a corporate leader always looking toward the future, John Chambers, CEO of Cisco Systems, would no doubt agree. 'Companies that are successful will have cultures that thrive on change', he says, 'even though change makes most people uncomfortable.'[4]

Creating positive change in organisations, as suggested by Chambers, is not an easy task. Change involves complexity, uncertainty, anxiety and risk. Leading organisations on the pathways of change takes great understanding, discipline and commitment to creativity and human ingenuity.[5] In his book *The Circle of Innovation*, consultant Tom Peters further warns that we must refocus the attention of managers and leaders away from past accomplishments and toward the role of innovation as the primary source of competitive advantage. Doing well in the past, simply put, is no guarantee of future success.[6]

The future is the issue in this final chapter of *Management: An Asia–Pacific Perspective* — organisational futures, managerial futures and your future. It is time to inquire once more into your managerial abilities to master the challenges of innovation and change and career readiness in the evolving new workplace. Take the opportunity to expand your portfolio of career skills to include the capacity for change leadership and self-renewal. As always, get connected!

CHALLENGES OF CHANGE

The World Economic Forum is a famous and futuristic think tank for global business, government and civic leaders. At the 2001 forum held in Davos, Switzerland, the popular buzzwords were 'business Webs', 'value networks', 'molecular organisations' and more. The following trends and possibilities were prominent among observations about the changing nature of business in the new economy.[7]

Companies that design and brand their own products, build and package them, and then deliver them to customers will soon no longer exist.

Companies [now] have the ability to strip down their business to its essence, to focus on where the greatest value creation (and profits) lies.

Extraneous functions can be eliminated through partnerships and newly supercharged forms of outsourcing.

Instead of one big monolithic entity, companies start to look like clusters of distributed capabilities.

There are those who might go so far as to say that the company as we have traditionally known it is dead, or at least dying.[8] The traditional forms, practices and systems of the past are being replaced by dramatic new developments driven by the forces of information technology and the relentless pressures of global competitiveness. And this is all happening very fast. No leader in any organisation, no matter how big or small and whether operating for-profit or not-for-profit, can fail to take notice. What lies ahead in the emerging digital and networked world of the 21st century is far too challenging for that.

ENTREPRENEURSHIP

Ballard Power Systems • www.ballard.com

Powering up the next generation of consumer products

Canadian fuel cell company Ballard Power Systems is rapidly expanding its presence in the Asia–Pacific region. The company is recognised as a world leader in zero-emission fuel cell technology. It is committed to continuous improvement of its products and processes. Like many companies, Ballard has recognised that to transform its technology into market success it will rely on close relationships with strategic partners, development partners and customers. It recently signed a collaboration agreement with Japan to commercialise residential fuel cell cogeneration units based on its proton exchange membrane technology. The units comprise a Ballard® fuel cell and a fuel-processing system manufactured by Ballard but based on a Tokyo gas fuel-processing technology. The company is also introducing a power module to the Japanese market, designed for integration into portable consumer products by Sony and Matsushita. Ballard's 'green' energy technologies are allowing manufacturers to produce more ecologically sustainable products such as self-powering mobile phones, personal stereos and video equipment that never require recharging.[9]

Strategic competitiveness

Although the points and details may differ, the conclusion reached by futurists is the same. The years ahead will be radically different from those past. We and our organisations must be prepared not only to change, but to change continuously and in the face of ever-present uncertainties. In earlier chapters we discussed the implications of this prospect to the benefits of **learning organisations** — ones that mobilise people, values and systems to achieve continuous change and performance improvements driven by the lessons of experience.[10] Scholar and consultant Peter Senge, author of the popular book *The Fifth Discipline*, advises managers to stimulate and lead change in ways that create true learning organisations in which everyone sets aside old ways of thinking, becomes self-aware and open to others, learns how the whole organisation works, understands and agrees to action plans and works together to accomplish the plans.[11]

Senge's learning organisation is the ideal — it is the target. It is what change leaders should strive for as they move organisations forward into the complicated world of tomorrow. This is a challenge of **strategic leadership**, defined by scholars Duane Ireland and Michael Hitt as the 'ability to anticipate, envision, maintain flexibility, think strategically and work with others to initiate changes that will create a viable future for the organisation'.[12] Strategic

Learning organisations continuously change and improve using the lessons of experience.

Strategic leadership enthuses people to continuously change, refine and improve strategies and their implementation.

leaders are change leaders that build learning organisations and keep them competitive even in difficult and uncertain times. The goal is to institutionalise as a core competency the ability to successfully and continuously change. Manager's Notepad 18.1 highlights strategic leadership components that best prepare managers to meet this challenge.[13]

Continuous innovation

Innovation is the process of taking a new idea and putting it into practice.

The 21st-century world of organisations will be driven by **innovation**, the process of creating new ideas and putting them into practice.[14] Management consultant Peter Drucker calls innovation 'an effort to create purposeful, focused change in an enterprise's economic or social potential'.[15] Said a bit differently, it is the act of converting new ideas into usable applications that ideally have positive economic or social consequences. Consider two very different examples.

Box & Dice Pty Ltd www.boxanddice.com.au. Founded in Sydney in the late 1980s, Box & Dice combines the expertise of traditional model making with state-of-the-art computer-aided technologies to produce prototypes of new products for clients from a range of industries — an important step in converting new ideas into real applications. In the company's own words: 'We make anything and everything … We bring ideas to life'. Products include the prototype of the official Olympic torch and a full-sized model of the official Olympic cauldron for the Sydney 2000 Olympics, presentation model tapware for the Australian bathroom products company Caroma Industries, and prototypes of the Focus Series and Super Dolphin flashlights for Eveready.[16]

GrameenPhone www.grameenphone.com. What happens when the digital age meets the developing world? Progress, at least if you are part of the Grameen Bank network in Bangladesh. Most of the country's 68 000 villages have no phone service; the average annual income is about A$360. That is changing through an innovative program. The bank makes loans to women entrepreneurs to allow them to buy and operate a mobile telephone, each typically serving an entire village. The bank's goal is twofold: to receive an economic return on its investment and to contribute to economic development. The Canadian International Development Agency praises the social impact, suggesting the model spread to serve the rural poor in other nations.[17]

Process innovations involve new or improved ways of manufacturing the product or service.

Product innovations involve the use of new or improved design principles or technologies for incorporation in products or services.

Innovation in and by organisations occurs in two broad forms: **process innovations**, which result in better ways of doing things; and **product innovations**, which result in the creation of new or improved goods and services. The management of both requires active encouragement and support for *invention* — the act of discovery, and for *application* — the act of use. Invention relates to the development of new ideas. Managers need to be concerned about building new work environments that stimulate creativity and an ongoing stream of new ideas. Application, on the other hand, deals with the use of inventions to take the best advantage of ideas. Here, managers must make sure that good ideas for new or modified work processes are actually implemented. They must also make sure that the commercial potential of ideas for new products or services is fully realised.

One way to describe the full set of leadership responsibilities for the innovation process is in these five steps, constituting what consultant Gary Hamel calls the *wheel of innovation*.[18]

Hamel's wheel of innovation

1. *Imagining* — thinking about new possibilities; making discoveries by ingenuity or communication with others; extending existing ways
2. *Designing* — testing ideas in concept; discussing them with peers, customers, clients or technical experts; building initial models, prototypes or samples
3. *Experimenting* — examining practicality and financial value through experiments and feasibility studies
4. *Assessing* — identifying strengths and weaknesses, potential costs and benefits, and potential markets or applications, and making constructive changes
5. *Scaling* — gearing up and implementing new processes; putting to work what has been learned; commercialising new products or services.

One of the major features of organisational innovation is that the entire process must be related to the needs of the organisation and its marketplace. New ideas alone are not sufficient to guarantee success in this setting — they must be implemented effectively in order to contribute to organisational performance.

Figure 18.1 uses the example of new product development to further highlight how the various steps of the innovation process contribute to something of great business significance, **commercialising innovation**.[19] This is the process of turning new ideas into products or processes that can make an economic difference in increased profits through higher sales or reduced costs. In Australasia and the Pacific Rim region, companies such as Fisher & Paykel, OneSteel, CSR, Proton, LG, Sony and Matsushita generate a substantial proportion of their revenue from new products embodying new technologies. Globally, Siemens, BP, Apple and 3M are pioneers of new product and process technologies. 3M, for example, generates over 30 per cent of its revenues from products that did not exist a few years ago. 3M is known globally for its Post-it® Notes and the Scotchguard™ stain repellent range. It also produces a large range of innovative computer-data storage technologies for industrial and consumer use. Many of these companies are able to successfully commercialise their knowledge through collaborativbe partnerships with other organisations that possess critical technology or knowledge. Often joint ventures allow companies to exploit their knowledge.[20]

☑️ **Commercialising innovation** turns ideas into products or processes with economic value added.

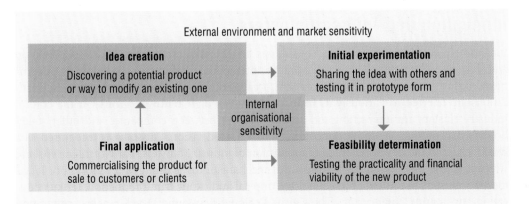

Figure 18.1 ▸ Process of innovation in organisations: the case of new product development

Characteristics of innovative organisations

Innovative organisations such as 3M and Fisher & Paykel mobilise talent and intellectual capital to support creativity and entrepreneurship. Their managers at all levels are masters at actively leading the innovative process. In highly innovative organisations, the *corporate strategy and culture support innovation*. The strategies of the organisation, the visions and values of senior management, and the framework of policies and expectations emphasise an entrepreneurial spirit. Innovation is expected, failure is accepted, and the organisation is willing to take risks. Highly deregulated industries often produce innovative organisations.[21]

In highly innovative organisations, *organisation structures support innovation*. More and more large organisations are trying to capture the structural flexibility of smaller ones. That is, they are striving for more organic operations with a strong emphasis on lateral communications and cross-functional teams and task forces. In particular, research and development, historically a separate and isolated function, is being integrated into a team setting. As Peter Drucker points out: 'Successful innovations ... are now being turned out by cross-functional teams with people from marketing, manufacturing and finance participating in research work from the very beginning'.[22] Innovative organisations are also reorganising to create many smaller divisions that allow creative teams to operate and to encourage 'intrapreneurial' new ventures.

In highly innovative organisations, *top management supports innovation*. In the case of 3M and Fisher & Paykel, for example, many top managers have been the innovators and product champions of the company's past. They understand the innovation process, are tolerant of criticisms and differences of opinion, and take all possible steps to keep the goals clear and the pressure on. The key, once again, is to allow the creative potential of people to operate fully.[23]

Innovation roles in organisations

In highly innovative organisations, *the organisation's staffing supports innovation* well. Organisations need different kinds of people to succeed in all stages of the innovation process. The *critical innovation roles* to be filled include the following:[24]

- *idea generators* — people who create new insights from internal discovery or external awareness, or both
- *information gatekeepers* — people who serve as links between people and groups within the organisation and with external sources
- *product champions* — people who advocate and push for change and innovation in general and for the adoption of specific product or process ideas in particular
- *project managers* — people who perform the technical functions needed to keep an innovative project on track with all the necessary resource support
- *innovation leaders* — people who encourage, sponsor and coach others to keep the innovation values and goals in place and channel energies in the right directions.

Innovation and industry clusters

⊘ Industry clusters or **learning regions** are groups of enterprises with common or complementary business interests, including the public and private entities on which they depend.

Increasingly, small to medium-sized businesses are realising the advantages of collaboration and information-sharing. These collaborative interactions within regions involving government, industry, research and development organisations, educational and academic institutions are referred to variously as **industry clusters** or **learning regions**. At the core of industry clusters are interaction and communication between companies and other stakeholders that produce learning, innovation and a shared vision. Australia is recognised as a world leader in the development and application of industry clusters. Far North Queensland was one of the first regions to establish this mechanism for learning and innovation. It has industry clusters in tourism, biotechnology, tropical and exotic fruit production, tertiary education and marine engineering. The Cairns Regional Economic Development Corporation (CREDC) has played a pivotal role in establishing and maintaining these clusters.

ORGANISATIONAL CHANGE

Change is intertwined with the processes of creativity and organisational innovation. Creativity fosters innovation and, according to Drucker, purposeful innovation should result in changes of positive economic or social consequence.[25] This all sounds quite positive and not very controversial. But what about the realities of trying to systematically change organisations and the behaviours of people within them? In Australia, New Zealand and eastern Asia, organisational change has often been promoted by governments and company managers. In New Zealand there were dramatic efforts aimed at changing behaviour in organisations, particularly those owned by the government. Many government businesses were privatised — railways, airlines, ports, telecommunications and postal services. Rules on foreign ownership were abolished, trade union and employee protection laws largely dismantled, and industries deregulated to allow new entrants. The country's free-market reforms aimed to kick-start major organisational change throughout the economy.

From the mid 1990s Australia has followed a similar reform agenda aimed at increasing organisational productivity. Successive federal and State governments deregulated industries, reduced trade union power and actively encouraged non-union workplaces.[26] The waterfront industry underwent dramatic organisational change, supported by the federal government, following attempts by employers to radically change operational and work practices. At the resource company Comalco, employees were offered staff contracts in exchange for agreeing to new flexible working practices. After a long industrial dispute at its Weipa operation, the company finally triumphed over trade union resistance and implemented substantial organisational change.

In Malaysia, the government is fostering wide-scale organisational change through its Vision 2020 initiative, which aims to make the country an economic powerhouse by 2020. Innovation, advanced technology, world-class productivity and high living standards, similar to those in neighbouring Singapore, are the government's goals. More muted attempts at microeconomic reform have been made in China, Korea and Japan. State-run industry bureaucrats in China have opposed changes to their organisations; whereas in Korea the trade unions have resisted reductions in pay and conditions. Japanese resistance to change, on the other hand, has come from private family-dominated industries, such as retailing, where they have considerable control and influence over their protected markets.

Change leadership

A **change agent** is a person or group who takes leadership responsibility for changing the existing pattern of behaviour of another person or social system. Change agents make things happen, and part of every manager's job is to act as a change agent in the work setting. This requires being alert to situations or to people needing change, being open to good ideas and being able to support the implementation of new ideas in actual practice. Figure 18.2 contrasts a *change leader* with a 'status quo manager'. The former is forward-looking, proactive and embraces new ideas; the latter is backward-looking, reactive and comfortable with habit. Obviously, the new workplace demands change leadership at all levels of management.

Models of change leadership

In chapter 16 on teams and teamwork, we discussed the concept of distributed leadership in teams. The point was that every team member has the potential to lead by serving group needs for task and maintenance activities. The same notion applies when it comes to change leadership in organisations. The responsibilities for change leadership are ideally distributed and shared top to bottom.

GET CONNECTED!

Check out resources available at the Change Management Resource Library at www.change-management.org.

GET CONNECTED!

A **change agent** tries to change the behaviour of another person or social system.

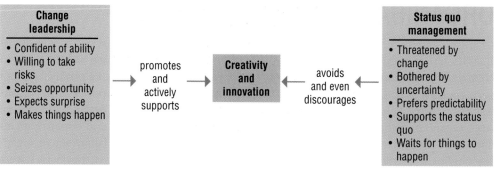

Figure 18.2 ▸ Change leadership versus status quo management

TOP-DOWN CHANGE

☞ In **top-down change**, the change initiatives come from senior management.

In **top-down change**, strategic and comprehensive changes are initiated with the goal of comprehensive impact on the organisation and its performance capabilities. This is the domain of strategic leadership as discussed earlier in the chapter. Importantly, however, reports indicate that some 70 per cent or more of large-scale change efforts actually fail.[27] The most common reason is poor implementation. The success of top-down change is usually determined by the willingness of middle-level and lower-level workers to actively support top-management initiatives. Change programs have little chance of success without the support of those who must implement them. Any change that is driven from the top runs the risk of being perceived as insensitive to the needs of lower-level personnel. It can easily fail if implementation suffers from excessive resistance and insufficient commitments to change. Thus, it is not enough to simply mandate change from the top — it must be supported by effective change leadership. Listed in Manager's Notepad 18.2 are several lessons learned from the study of successful large-scale transformational change in organisations.[28]

MANAGER'S NOTEPAD 18.2

How to lead transformational change

- Establish a sense of urgency for change.
- Form a powerful coalition to lead the change.
- Create and communicate a change vision.
- Empower others to move change forward.
- Celebrate short-term 'wins' and recognise those who help.
- Build on success — align people and systems with new ways.
- Stay with it — keep the message consistent, champion the vision.

☞ **Theory E change** is based on activities that increase shareholder or economic value.

A version of top-down change in business is called **Theory E change**, or change based on activities that increase shareholder or economic value as soon as possible.[29] Managers who pursue Theory E change use economic incentives, major restructuring and downsizing, and similar activities in the attempt to improve a firm's financial performance. The approach is very much top-down in nature and may carry heavy costs for employees and even corporate traditions. An example was the major restructuring of BHP Steel before its merger with Billiton. Thousands of production staff were retrenched when the Newcastle steelworks in Australia was closed and other operations were rationalised, prior to selling off the steel-making division. It is now an independent company trading as OneSteel. Financial markets responded favourably to the organisational change, with share values and dividends increasing. Similarly, Air New Zealand took staff reduction measures following the 11 September 2001 terrorist attacks in the USA, as it faced greatly reduced passenger demand and increasing costs. Theory E change, such as these examples, is driven from the top, emphasises changes in structures and systems, and tries to gain employee support through financial incentives. However, for those staff who are retrenched, this type of change is viewed quite negatively.

BOTTOM-UP CHANGE

Bottom-up change is also important in organisations. In such cases, the initiatives for change come from persons throughout an organisation and are supported by the efforts of middle-level and lower-level managers acting as change agents. Bottom-up change is essential to organisational innovation and is very useful in terms of adapting operations and technologies to the changing requirements of work. It is made possible by empowerment, involvement and participation as discussed in earlier chapters. For example, at the Malaysian car manufacturer Proton, workers contribute ideas on product and process change through suggestion boxes and workgroup meetings. Many of the solutions are adopted. The system is based on the Japanese *kaizen* concept that emphasises continuous improvement based on worker input. Proton strongly encourages workers to use their job knowledge, skills and practical expertise to improve products, productivity and the workplace.

A version of bottom-up change in business is called **Theory O change**, or change based on activities that increase organisational performance capabilities.[30] Change leaders pursuing the Theory O model try various approaches to improve organisational culture, and develop human capital to improve performance capabilities. Historical examples are The Body Shop, Fisher & Paykel and the Sony Corporation, all who focus organisational improvements around building employee commitment to new directions. Theory O change encourages participation from the bottom up, values employee attitudes, progresses step by step through experimentation and evolution, and tries to inspire support through employee involvement.

> In **bottom-up change**, change initiatives come from all levels in the organisation.

> **Theory O change** is based on activities that increase organisational performance capabilities.

INTEGRATED CHANGE LEADERSHIP

The most successful and enduring change leadership is that which can harness the advantages of both top-down and bottom-up change. Top-down initiatives may be needed to break traditional patterns and implement difficult economic adjustments; bottom-up initiatives are necessary to build institutional capability for sustainable change and organisational learning. An international example is the two-decade-long transformation efforts of Jack Welch at General Electric. When first taking over as CEO in 1981, he began an aggressive top-down E-type restructuring that led to major workforce cuts and a trimmer organisation structure. Once underway, however, this evolved into O-type change focusing on employee involvement.

A widely benchmarked US program called Work-Out is a good example. It actively involves all levels in a process of continuous reassessment and planned change.[31] In Work-Out sessions employees confront their managers in a 'town meeting' format, with the manager in front listening to suggestions for removing performance obstacles and improving operations. The managers are expected to respond immediately to the suggestions and support positive change initiatives raised during the session. The ability of the Work-Out design to stimulate bottom-up change has been widely praised as part of GE's efforts at continuous improvement.

REALITY CHECK

Why large-scale change efforts often fail

Most large-scale change efforts fail because senior executives fail to establish a sense of urgency throughout the organisation.

How could they do better?

Planned and unplanned change

⚙ **Planned change** occurs as a result of specific efforts by a change agent.

⚙ A **performance gap** is a discrepancy between the desired and actual state of affairs.

⚙ **Unplanned changes** occur spontaneously and without a change agent's direction.

We are particularly interested in **planned change** that occurs as a result of the specific efforts of a change agent. Planned change is a direct response to a person's perception of a **performance gap**, or a discrepancy between the desired and actual state of affairs. Performance gaps may represent problems to be resolved or opportunities to be explored. In each case, managers as change agents should be ever alert to performance gaps and take action to initiate planned changes to deal with them.

But, **unplanned changes** are important too. They occur spontaneously or randomly and without the benefit of a change agent's attention. Unplanned changes may be disruptive, such as a strike that results in a plant closure, or beneficial, such as an interpersonal conflict that results in a new procedure on interdepartmental relations. Catastrophic events such as the destruction of NASA's space shuttles *Challenger* in 1985 and *Columbia* in 2003 trigger unplanned change for organisations. These types of organisational failure produce immediate pressure for changes in structure, processes and practices to avoid reoccurrences. The appropriate goal in managing unplanned change is to act immediately once it is recognised in order to minimise negative consequences and maximise possible benefits.

TECHNOLOGY

Hoc Deng Agricultural

Appropriate technology for the developing world

Founded in the 1990s, Hoc Deng Agricultural, which is based in Kuala Lumpur, Malaysia, produces agricultural equipment for small-scale, independent farmers in South-East Asia. The company manufactures irrigation pumps, motorised ploughs and seed-sowing equipment. The emphasis is on simple, low-cost designs that can be maintained and repaired by farmers or local mechanics, unlike the costly equipment manufactured in developed countries. This approach has brought social and economic benefits for the local communities. The company is now also exporting to Latin America and Africa and employs over 50 production staff.[32]

Forces and targets for change

The impetus for organisational change can arise from a variety of external forces.[33] These include the global economy and market competition, local economic conditions, government laws and regulations, technological developments, market trends and social forces, among others. As an organisation's general and specific environments develop and change over time, the organisation must adapt as well. Internal forces for change are important too. Indeed, any change in one part of the organisation as a complex system — perhaps a change initiated in response to one or more of the external forces just identified — can often create the need for change in another part of the system.

The many targets for planned change are found among all the aspects of organisations already discussed in this book. All of them, including the following common *organisational targets for change* — tasks, people, culture, technology and structure — are highly interrelated.[34]

Organisational targets for change

• *Tasks* — the nature of work as represented by organisational mission, objectives and strategy, and the job designs for individuals and groups

- *People* — the attitudes and competencies of the employees and the human resource systems that support them
- *Culture* — the value system for the organisation as a whole and the norms guiding individual and group behaviour
- *Technology* — the operations and information technology used to support job designs, arrange workflows and integrate people and machines in systems
- *Structure* — the configuration of the organisation as a complex system, including its design features and lines of authority and communications.

MANAGING PLANNED CHANGE

Change is a complicated phenomenon in any setting, and human nature always stands at the heart of it. People tend to act habitually and in stable ways over time. They may not want to change even when circumstances require it. As a manager and change agent, you will need to recognise and deal with such tendencies in order to successfully lead planned change.

Phases of planned change

Kurt Lewin, a noted psychologist, recommends that any planned-change effort be viewed as the three-phase process shown in figure 18.3.[35] Lewin's three phases of planned change are *unfreezing* — preparing a system for change; *changing* — making actual changes in the system; and *refreezing* — stabilising the system after change.

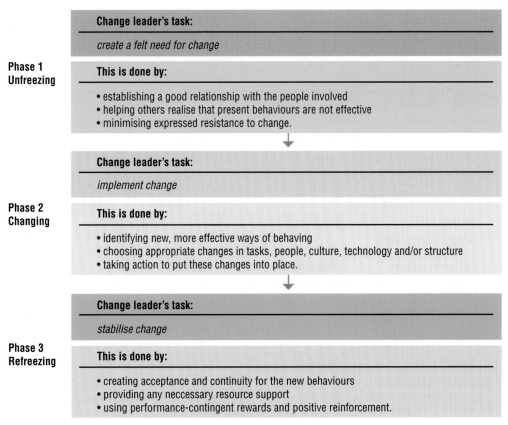

Phase 1 Unfreezing

Change leader's task:

create a felt need for change

This is done by:

- establishing a good relationship with the people involved
- helping others realise that present behaviours are not effective
- minimising expressed resistance to change.

Phase 2 Changing

Change leader's task:

implement change

This is done by:

- identifying new, more effective ways of behaving
- choosing appropriate changes in tasks, people, culture, technology and/or structure
- taking action to put these changes into place.

Phase 3 Refreezing

Change leader's task:

stabilise change

This is done by:

- creating acceptance and continuity for the new behaviours
- providing any neccessary resource support
- using performance-contingent rewards and positive reinforcement.

Figure 18.3 ▸ Lewin's three phases of planned organisational change

UNFREEZING

Unfreezing is the phase during which a situation is prepared for change.

In order for change to be successful, people must be ready for it. Planned change has little chance for long-term success unless people are open to doing things differently. **Unfreezing** is the stage in which a situation is prepared for change, and felt needs for change are developed. It can be facilitated in several ways: through environmental pressures for change, declining performance, the recognition that problems or opportunities exist, and through the observation of behavioural models that display alternative approaches. When handled well, conflict can be an important unfreezing force in organisations. It often helps people break old habits and recognise alternative ways of thinking about or doing things.

CHANGING

Changing is the phase where a planned change actually takes place.

In the **changing** phase, something new takes place in a system, and change is actually implemented. This is the point at which managers initiate changes in such organisational targets as tasks, people, culture, technology and structure. Ideally, all change is done in response to a good diagnosis of a problem and a careful examination of alternatives. However, Lewin believes that many change agents enter the changing phase prematurely, are too quick to change things, and therefore end up creating resistance to change. When managers implement change before people feel a need for it, consequently, there is an increased likelihood of failure.

REFREEZING

Refreezing is the phase at which change is stabilised.

The final stage in the planned-change process is **refreezing**. Here, the manager is concerned about stabilising the change and creating the conditions for its long-term continuity. Refreezing is accomplished by appropriate rewards for performance, positive reinforcement and providing necessary resource support. It is also important to evaluate results carefully, provide feedback to the people involved, and make any required modifications in the original change. When refreezing is done poorly, changes are too easily forgotten or abandoned with the passage of time. When it is done well, change can be more long lasting.

Choosing a change strategy

Managers use various approaches when trying to get others to adopt a desired change. Figure 18.4 summarises three common change strategies known as force-coercion, rational persuasion and shared power.[36] Each can have very different consequences for change agent and change target alike.

Change strategy	Power bases	Managerial behaviour
Force-coercion Using position power to create change by decree and formal authority	Legitimacy Rewards Punishments	*Direct forcing* and unilateral action *Political manoeuvring* and indirect action
Rational persuasion Creating change through rational persuasion and empirical argument	Expertise	*Informational efforts* using credible knowledge, demonstrated facts and logical argument
Shared power Developing support for change through personal values and commitments	Reference	*Participative efforts* to share power and involve others in planning and implementing change

Likely results

Fast — Temporary compliance

Slow — Longer term internalisation

Figure 18.4 ▸ Alternative change strategies and their leadership implications

FORCE-COERCION STRATEGIES

A **force-coercion strategy** uses the power bases of legitimacy, rewards and punishments as the primary inducements to change. A change agent that seeks to create change through force-coercion believes that people who run things are basically motivated by self-interest and by what the situation offers in terms of potential personal gains or losses.[37] This change agent believes that people change only in response to such motives, tries to find out where their vested interests lie, and then puts the pressure on. Once a weakness is found, it is exploited. The change agent is always quick to work 'politically' by building supporting alliances wherever possible. If the change agent has formal authority, she or he uses it along with whatever rewards and punishments are available. As figure 18.4 shows, the likely outcomes of force-coercion are immediate compliance but little commitment.

A **force-coercion strategy** pursues change through formal authority and/or the use of rewards or punishments.

Force-coercion can be pursued in at least two ways, both of which can be commonly observed in organisations. In a *direct forcing* strategy, the change agent takes direct and unilateral action to 'command' that change take place. This involves the exercise of formal authority or legitimate power, offering special rewards and/or threatening punishment. In *political manoeuvring* the change agent works indirectly to gain special advantage over other persons and thereby make them change. This involves bargaining, obtaining control of important resources, or granting small favours.

Regardless of the exact approach taken, the force-coercion strategy on its own produces limited results. Although it can be implemented rather quickly, most people respond to this strategy out of fear of punishment or hope for a reward. This usually results in only temporary compliance with the change agent's desires. The new behaviour continues only so long as the opportunity for rewards and punishments is present. For this reason, force-coercion is most useful as an unfreezing device that helps people break old patterns of behaviour and gain initial impetus to try new ones. The example of General Electric's Work-Out program, noted earlier, applies here.[38] Jack Welch started Work-Out to create a forum for active employee empowerment of continuous change. But, he didn't make the program optional. Like other change initiatives at the firm, participation in Work-Out was mandatory from the start. Welch used his authority as leader to initiate a new program that he felt confident would survive and prosper on its own — once it was experienced. Part of his commitment to change leadership was a willingness to use authority as needed to get things started.

RATIONAL PERSUASION STRATEGIES

Change agents using a **rational persuasion strategy** attempt to bring about change through persuasion backed by special knowledge, empirical data and rational argument. A change agent following this strategy believes that people are inherently rational and are guided by reason in their actions and decision making.[39] Once a specific course of action is demonstrated to be in a person's self-interest, the change agent assumes that reason and rationality will cause the person to adopt it. Thus, he or she uses information and facts to communicate the essential desirability of change.

A **rational persuasion strategy** pursues change through empirical data and rational argument.

The likely outcome of rational persuasion is eventual compliance with reasonable commitment. When successful, a rational persuasion strategy helps both unfreeze and refreeze a change situation. Although slower than force-coercion, it tends to result in longer lasting and internalised change. To be successful, a manager using rational persuasion must convince others that the cost–benefit value of a planned change is high and that it will leave them better off than before. This can come directly from the change agent if she or he has personal credibility as an 'expert'. If not, it can be obtained in the form of consultants and other outside experts, or from credible demonstration projects and benchmarks. The magic of Walt Disney World, for example, extends to more than family fun and holidays. Disney, the company, is widely respected globally for its business and management practices. Many firms use Disney to both benchmark and demonstrate to employees how change initiatives can improve their own operations. Rational persuasion strategies have been adopted by LG, Matsushita, Rio Tinto and Qantas, but with some minor local modifications to account for cultural differences between regions. Local management practices in the Asia–Pacific region are a fusion of global and home-grown approaches.

SHARED POWER STRATEGIES

A **shared power strategy** engages people in a collaborative process of identifying values, assumptions and goals from which support for change will naturally emerge. The process is slow, but it is likely to yield high commitment. Sometimes called a *normative re-educative strategy*, this approach is based on empowerment and is highly participative in nature. It relies on involving others in examining personal needs and values, group norms and operating goals as they relate to the issues at hand. Power is shared by the change agent and other persons as they work together to develop a new consensus to support needed change.

Managers using shared power as an approach to planned change need referent power and the skills to work effectively with other people in group situations. They must be comfortable allowing others to participate in making decisions that affect the planned change and the way it is implemented. Because it entails a high level of involvement, this strategy is often quite time consuming. But importantly, power sharing is likely to result in a longer-lasting and internalised change.

A change agent who shares power begins by recognising that people have varied needs and complex motivations.[40] He or she believes people behave as they do because of sociocultural norms and commitments to the expectations of others. Changes in organisations are understood to inevitably involve changes in attitudes, values, skills and significant relationships, not just changes in knowledge, information or intellectual rationales for action and practice. Thus, when seeking to change others, this change agent is sensitive to the way group pressures can support or inhibit change. In working with people, every attempt is made to gather their opinions, identify their feelings and expectations, and incorporate them fully into the change process.

The great 'power' of sharing power in the change process lies with unlocking the creativity and experience available from within the system, and often missed at the top. Unfortunately, many managers are hesitant to engage this process for fear of losing control of the strategic direction, or of having to compromise on important organisational goals. Harvard scholar Teresa M. Amabile, however, points out that managers and change leaders should have the confidence to

CAREER CONNECTION

Sustainability

Australian Conservation Foundation

Participative planning for a sustainable future

www.acfonline.org.au

Increased public concern for the natural environment is one of the biggest pressures for change facing businesses today. More than ever, people are paying attention to the environmental impact of the companies that are operating in their communities and trying to sell them goods and services. Managers of the future will need to run companies that are environmentally responsible. In many cases, this will require changes throughout their organisations. The Australian Conservation Foundation argues that, in the past, regional business development policy has tended to support companies and industries that were not always environmentally friendly, with a focus on the export of unprocessed commodities. Ecological degradation was overlooked as a necessary consequence of much of Australia's primary production, in the same way that pollution was seen as part of industrial development. Noting that change is necessary, the Australian Conservation Foundation recommends three management devices to encourage employees to become involved in developing sustainable long-term solutions: a *strategic framework* to define a shared vision for the future, identify critical local issues and set broad objectives; an *action plan* to set targets, identify costs and allocate responsibility; and a *monitoring framework* to monitor success and provide ongoing feedback.[41]

Questions

Would you work for an organistion that was not committed to environmental responsibility?
If some of the changes necessary to meet that commitment were costly or difficult to implement, how would you rise to the challenge?

share power regarding means and processes, but not overall goals. 'People will be more creative', she says, 'if you give them freedom to decide how to climb particular mountains. You needn't let them choose which mountains to climb.'[42]

Understanding resistance to change

Change typically brings with it resistance. When people resist change, furthermore, they are defending something important and that appears to them as threatened by the attempted change. Proposed changes to work arrangements in the Australian and New Zealand construction industry, involving more flexible working practices and performance-related pay, were viewed by the workforce as a threat to their occupational expertise and remuneration. In some companies there were industrial disputes and trade union membership increased. At Hansen Gills, a medium-sized construction firm, the company adopted a consultative approach to change. It used a committee, an innovative enterprise agreement and direct communication between management and the workforce to devise new work practices and effective ways to implement them. This approach avoided industrial disputes and created greater trust between management and workers.[43]

There are any number of reasons why people in organisations may resist planned change. Some of the more common ones are shown in Manager's Notepad 18.3. Such resistance is often viewed by change agents and managers as something that must be 'overcome' in order for change to be successful. This is not necessarily true. Resistance is better viewed as feedback that the informed change agent can use to constructively modify a planned change to better fit situational needs and goals. When resistance appears, it usually means that something can be done to achieve a better 'fit' between the planned change, the situation and the people involved.

MANAGER'S NOTEPAD 18.3

Why people may resist change

- *Fear of the unknown* — not understanding what is happening or what comes next
- *Disrupted habits* — feeling upset when old ways of doing things can't be followed
- *Loss of confidence* — feeling incapable of performing well under the new ways of doing things
- *Loss of control* — feeling that things are being done *to* you rather than *by* or *with* you
- *Poor timing* — feeling overwhelmed by the situation or that things are moving too fast
- *Work overload* — not having the physical or psychic energy to commit to the change
- *Loss of face* — feeling inadequate or humiliated because it appears that the 'old' ways weren't 'good' ways
- *Lack of purpose* — not seeing a reason for the change and/or not understanding its benefits.

Dealing with resistance to change

Once resistance to change is recognised and understood, it can be dealt with in various ways.[44] Among the alternatives for effectively managing resistance, the *education and communication* approach uses discussions, presentations and demonstrations to educate people beforehand about a change. *Participation and involvement* allows others to contribute

Footwear and clothing merchant Rivers involves its staff in group discussions to examine ways to improve management processes, staff productivity, the company's product range and the overall organisational climate. By involving all staff from the outset, coupled with a strong internal promotion system, Rivers is developing change leadership skills and expertise throughout the company.

ideas and help design and implement the change. The *facilitation and support* approach involves providing encouragement and training, actively listening to problems and complaints, and helping to overcome performance pressures. *Facilitation and agreement* provides incentives that appeal to those who are actively resisting or ready to resist. This approach makes trade-offs in exchange for assurances that change will not be blocked. *Manipulation and cooptation* tries to covertly influence others by providing information selectively and structuring events in favour of the desired change. *Explicit and implicit coercion* forces people to accept change by threatening resistors with a variety of undesirable consequences if they do not go along as planned. Obviously, the last two approaches carry great risk and potential for negative side effects.

Managing technological change

Technological change is common in today's organisations, but it also brings special challenges to change leaders. For the full advantages of new technologies to be realised, a good fit must be achieved with work needs, practices and people. This, in turn, requires sensitivity to resistance and continual gathering of information so that appropriate adjustments can be made during the time a new technology is being implemented. In this sense, the demands of managing technological change have been described using the analogy of contrasting styles between navigators from the Micronesian island of Truk and their European counterparts.[45]

> The European navigator works from a plan, relates all moves during a voyage to the plan, and tries to always stay 'on course'. When something unexpected happens, the plan is revised systematically, and the new plan followed again until the navigator finds the ship to be off course. The Trukese navigator, by contrast, starts with an objective and moves off in its general direction. Always alert to information from waves, clouds, winds, etc., the navigator senses subtle changes in conditions and steers and alters the ship's course continually to reach the ultimate objective.

Like the navigators of Truk, technological change may best be approached as an ongoing process that will inevitably require improvisation as things are being implemented. New technologies are often designed external to the organisation in which they are to be used. The implications of such a technology for a local application may be difficult to anticipate and plan for ahead of time. A technology that is attractive in concept may appear complicated to the new users; the full extent of its benefits and/or inadequacies may not become known until it is tried. This, in turn, means that the change leader and manager should be alert to resistance, should continually gather and process information relating to the change, and should be willing to customise the new technology to best meet the needs of the local situation.[46] The importance of appropriate new technology is well illustrated by the Hoc Deng Agricultural example in this chapter.

ORGANISATION DEVELOPMENT

Organisation development is a comprehensive effort to improve an organisation's ability to deal with its environment and solve problems.

Among consulting professionals, **organisation development** (OD) is known as a comprehensive approach to planned organisational change that involves the application of behavioural science in a systematic and long-range effort to improve organisational effectiveness.[47] Organisation development is supposed to help organisations cope with environmental and other pressures for change, while also improving their internal problem-solving capabilities. OD, in this sense, brings the quest for continuous improvement to the planned-change process.

There will always be times when the members of organisations should sit together and systematically reflect on strengths and weaknesses as well as performance accomplishments and failures. Organisation development is one way to ensure that this happens in a supportive and action-oriented environment. OD is an important avenue through which leaders can advance planned-change agendas, foster creativity and innovation, and more generally assist people and systems to continuously improve organisational performance. It often involves the assistance of an external consultant or an internal staff person with special training. But importantly, all managers should have the skills and commitment to use the various elements of OD in their continuous-improvement agendas. The notion of organisation development dovetails nicely with the popular concepts of total quality management (TQM) and employee involvement discussed throughout this book. In fact, the OD approach may offer added opportunities to use them to the best advantage.[48]

Organisation development goals

In organisation development, two goals are pursued simultaneously. The *outcome goals of OD* focus on task accomplishments, while the *process goals of OD* focus on the way people work together. It is this second goal that strongly differentiates OD from more general attempts at planned change in organisations. You may think of OD as a form of 'planned change plus', with the 'plus' meaning that change is accomplished in such a way that organisation members develop a capacity for continued self-renewal. That is, OD tries to achieve change while helping organisation members become more active and self-reliant in their ability to continue changing in the future. What also makes OD unique is its commitment to strong humanistic values and established principles of behavioural science. OD is committed to improving organisations through freedom of choice, shared power and self-reliance, and by taking the best advantage of what we know about human behaviour in organisations.

How organisation development works

Figure 18.5 presents a general model of OD and shows its relationship to Lewin's three phases of planned change. To begin the OD process successfully, any consultant or facilitator must first *establish a working relationship* with members of the client system. The next step is *diagnosis* — gathering and analysing data to assess the situation and set appropriate change objectives. This helps with unfreezing as well as pinpointing appropriate directions for action. Diagnosis leads to active *intervention*, wherein change objectives are pursued through a variety of specific interventions, a number of which will be discussed shortly.

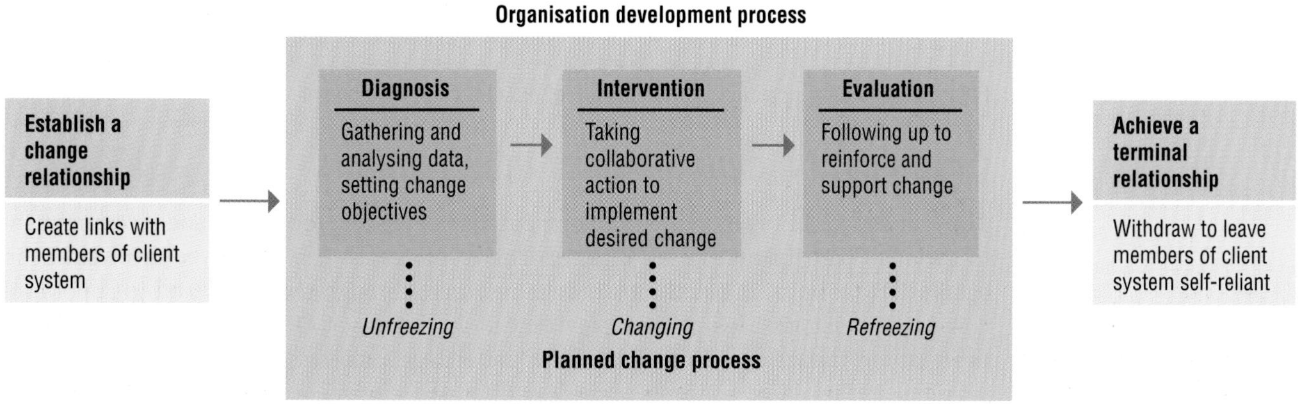

Organisation development process

Establish a change relationship	Diagnosis	Intervention	Evaluation	Achieve a terminal relationship
Create links with members of client system	Gathering and analysing data, setting change objectives	Taking collaborative action to implement desired change	Following up to reinforce and support change	Withdraw to leave members of client system self-reliant
	Unfreezing	*Changing*	*Refreezing*	

Planned change process

Figure 18.5 ▸ Organisation development and the planned change process

Essential to any OD effort is *evaluation*. This is the examination of the process to determine whether things are proceeding as desired and whether further action is needed. Eventually, the OD consultant or facilitator should *achieve a terminal relationship* that leaves the client able to function on its own. If OD has been well done, the system and its members should be better prepared to manage their ongoing need for self-renewal and development.

The success or failure of any OD program lies in part in the strength of its methodological foundations. As shown in figure 18.6, these foundations rest on **action research** — the process of systematically collecting data on an organisation, feeding it back to the members for action planning, and evaluating results by collecting more data and repeating the process as necessary. Action research is initiated when someone senses a performance gap and decides to analyse the situation to understand its problems and opportunities. Data gathering can be done in several ways. Interviews are a common means of gathering data in action research. Formal written surveys of employee attitudes and needs are also growing in popularity. Many such 'climate', 'attitude' or 'morale' questionnaires have been tested for reliability and validity. Some have even been used so extensively that norms are available so that one organisation can compare its results with those from a broad sample of counterparts.

> **Action research** is a collaborative process of collecting data, using it for action planning and evaluating the results.

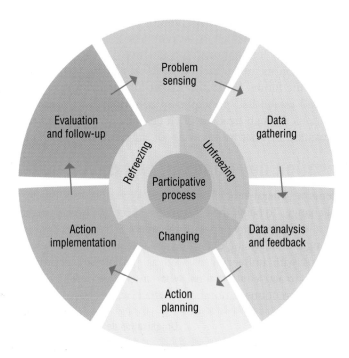

Figure 18.6 ▸ Action research is a foundation of organisation development

Organisation development interventions

The foundations of organisation development include respect for people and a commitment to their full participation in self-directed change processes. It is employee involvement in action. OD rallies an organisation's human resources through teamwork and in support of constructive change. This process is evident in the variety of **OD interventions** or activities that are initiated to directly facilitate the change processes. Importantly, these interventions are linked to concepts and ideas discussed elsewhere in this book and that are well represented in the practices and approaches of the new workplace.[49]

> **OD interventions** are structured activities that help create change in organisation development.

INDIVIDUAL INTERVENTIONS

Concerning individuals, organisation development practitioners generally recognise that the need for personal growth and development are most likely to be satisfied in a supportive and challenging work environment. They also accept the premise that most people are capable of assuming responsibility for their own actions and of making positive contributions to organisational performance. Based on these principles, some of the more popular OD interventions designed to help improve individual effectiveness include the following:

- *sensitivity training* — unstructured sessions (T-groups) where participants learn interpersonal skills and increased sensitivity to other people
- *management training* — structured educational opportunities for developing important managerial skills and competencies
- *role negotiation* — structured interactions to clarify and negotiate role expectations among people who work together
- *job redesign* — realigning task components to better fit the needs and capabilities of the individual
- *career planning* — structured advice and discussion sessions to help individuals plan career paths and programs of personal development.

Individual OD interventions

TEAM INTERVENTIONS

The team plays a very important role in organisation development (OD). OD practitioners recognise two principles in this respect. First, teams are viewed as important vehicles for helping people satisfy important needs. Second, it is believed that improved collaboration within and among teams can improve organisational performance. Selected OD interventions designed to improve team effectiveness include the following:

- *team building* — structured experiences to help team members set goals, improve interpersonal relations and become a better functioning team
- *process consultation* — third-party observation and advice on critical team processes (e.g. communication, conflict and decision making)
- *intergroup team building* — structured experiences to help two or more teams set shared goals, improve intergroup relations, and become better coordinated.

Team OD interventions

ORGANISATION-WIDE INTERVENTIONS

At the level of the total organisation, OD practitioners operate on the premise that any changes in one part of the system will also affect other parts. The organisation's culture is considered to have an important impact on member attitudes and morale. And it is believed that structures and jobs can be designed to bring together people, technology and systems in highly productive and satisfying working combinations. Some of the OD interventions often applied with an emphasis on organisational effectiveness include the following:

- *survey feedback* — comprehensive and systematic data collection to identify attitudes and needs, analyse results and plan for constructive action
- *confrontation meeting* — one-day intensive, structured meetings to gather data on workplace problems and plan for constructive actions
- *structural redesign* — realigning the organisation structure to meet the needs of environmental and contextual forces
- *management by objectives* — formalising MBO throughout the organisation to link individual, group and organisational objectives.

Organisation-wide OD interventions

www.singaporeair.com

Singapore Airlines (SIA) offers employees opportunities for academic training. University scholarships were created to bring out the high achievers and help staff realise their aspirations. Graduates are given challenging appointments to gain all-round experience or pursue mastery in a specialised area. The SIA Group spends over $100 million on training each year.

PERSONAL CHANGE AND CAREER READINESS

Now is the final chance for us to raise once again the issue of *you*, your continued personal and professional development and your career readiness.

Early career advice

In times like ours, where change is ever-present, fast-moving and often unpredictable, the management of your career and career development is extremely challenging. The challenges become even more magnified in the context of career entry, when you are beginning a new job with a new employer. In terms of early career advice, *lesson one* is clear: there is no substitute for performance. No matter what the assignment, you must work hard to quickly establish your credibility and value in any new job. The advice of *lesson two* is also undeniable: you must be and stay flexible. Don't hide from ambiguity; don't depend on structure. Instead, you must be always able and willing to adapt personally to reasonable new work demands, new situations and people, and new organisational forms. The demands of *lesson three* help keep the focus: you can't go forward without talent. You must commit to continuous learning and professional development. In order to get and stay ahead in a career during very competitive times, you must become a talent builder — someone who is always adding to and refining your talents to make them valuable to an employer. This requires discipline in continuously seeking the learning opportunities from your daily experiences, including the ones that present problems and prove difficult for you. The 'ability' to learn can only benefit you personally when accompanied by the 'willingness' to learn.

According to noted author and consultant Stephen Covey, the foundations for career success are within everyone's grasp. But, both the motivation and the effort required to succeed must come from within. Only you can make this commitment, and it is best made right from the beginning. Covey's advice is for you to take charge of your destiny, and to always move your career forward by showing initiative, seeking feedback on your performance continually, setting up your own mentoring systems, getting comfortable with teamwork, taking risks to gain experience and learn new skills, being a problem solver and keeping your life in balance.[50]

Building the brand called 'you'

The best career advice returns again and again to the same message — what happens is largely up to you. Don't let yourself down. Step forward and take charge of your continued learning and professional development. Build, refine and market what author and consultant Tom Peters refers to as the 'brand called "you"'. Peters advises each of us to continually work hard to create and maintain a unique and timely package of skills and capabilities with career potential. In Peters's words, your personal brand should be 'remarkable, measurable, distinguished and distinctive' relative to the competition — others like you.[51]

Sustaining career advantage

As with organisations that must innovate to achieve competitive advantage in their markets, you must be able to quickly adapt to the demands of an ever-changing workplace, economy and career environment. As shown in figure 18.7, this means that you must establish and maintain a **sustainable career advantage**. This is a combination of personal attributes — skills and capabilities — that allow you to consistently outperform others, that are continuously improving and that are always timely and relevant to the needs of employers.

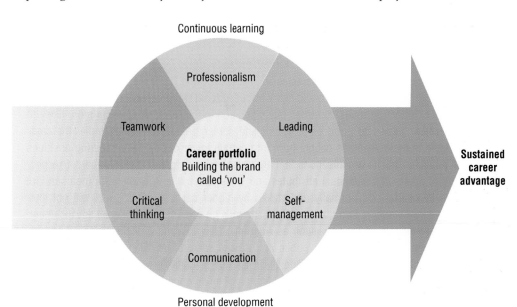

Figure 18.7 ▸ Building a career portfolio for sustainable career advantage

The Career Readiness Workbook is designed to help you begin the process of brand building and to prepare your credentials for sustainable career advantage in a world of dynamic employment opportunities. Hopefully you have already taken advantage of many learning activities offered in the workbook. Its many options are well worth serious attention.

Don't neglect the opportunity to build your personal career advancement portfolio to document your academic and personal accomplishments for external review. Of particular importance is a skill and outcome assessment that shows potential employers your capabilities in the important areas of professionalism, leadership, self-management, communication, teamwork and critical thinking. Talent that builds from these foundations is what today's employers are looking for, both among full-time employees and students on work experience.

Use your career portfolio to show important skills and outcomes gained from your management studies. Put the entire package on line as a means of further distinguishing yourself from the competition. Once started, your **electronic career portfolio** can be easily maintained as a continuing resource for self-assessment and personal development, as well as to communicate your talents to potential employers.

Management: An Asia–Pacific Perspective has been rich with insights into the new workplace, the nature of managerial work, and the great challenges organisations face in a highly competitive global economy. As you move forward in this exciting world of work, you must continue the process of brand building and continue to strengthen your potential for a satisfying lifelong career. You have to master the challenges of change without forgetting the goal — sustainable career advantage. Also, you can never forget that career development is a personal responsibility. Although many foundations have been set during your management course and other university studies, what happens next and in your career future is up to you.

There is no better time than the present to begin the process of career advancement. Make the commitment to move forward, right now. Get and stay connected!

POINT ←

The barriers to equal career opportunity

There are no genuine meritocracies in the world, and so it is not always the best-qualified or most suitable candidates who are offered good career advancement opportunities. In fact, in many countries one's position in the class structure is more likely to determine access to good employment and career prospects. For example, the caste system in India prohibits people born into certain lower castes from securing positions in public or private organisations that are preserved for higher caste members, irrespective of a person's individual attributes and skills. Even where lower caste members are able to secure jobs normally undertaken by higher caste members, this will not alter their social standing in Indian society — there is no opportunity for social advancement. In more developed nations, such as Australia, New Zealand and the United Kingdom, many senior positions in the public and private sectors are filled by people from the higher echelons of society, despite the existence of suitably qualified candidates from the middle or lower classes. The introduction of equal opportunity and affirmative action legislation in developed countries in the past thirty years has failed to substantially eradicate inequality and discrimination in the workplace.[52]

CHAPTER 18
Study guide

The chapter 18 study guide helps you review the chapter content, prepare for examinations, apply what you have learned and further build your career readiness. The summary briefly answers the study questions posed at the start of the chapter. The list of key terms allows you to double-check your familiarity with basic concepts and definitions. The applied activities help you test your comprehension of chapter content. Suggestions offered as career readiness activities direct your attention to relevant sections of the Career Readiness Workbook where you can test and develop your career skills and apply what you have learned. The list of electronic resources suggests activities from the *Management: An Asia–Pacific Perspective* web site and, finally, the case for critical thinking helps you apply your new management knowledge.

SUMMARY

What are the challenges of change?

- The future will be like our past — always unpredictable, very challenging and full of continuous change.
- A learning organisation is one in which people, values and systems support innovation and continuous change based on the lessons of experience.
- Organisations need strategic leaders who work with a strategic direction to initiate and successfully implement changes that help organisations perform well in changing environments.
- Innovation allows creative ideas to be turned into products and/or processes that benefit organisations and their customers.
- Highly innovative organisations tend to have supportive cultures, strategies, structures, staffing and top management.
- The possible barriers to innovation in organisations include a lack of top management support, excessive bureaucracy, short time horizons and vested interests.

What is the nature of organisational change?

- Change leaders are change agents who take responsibility for helping to change the behaviour of people and organisational systems.
- Managers should be able to spot change opportunities and lead the process of planned change in their areas of work responsibilities.
- Although organisational change can proceed with a top-down emphasis, inputs from all levels of responsibility are essential to achieve successful implementation.
- Theory E change seeks to improve economic performance through restructuring. Theory O change seeks to build organisational capability through improved culture and human resource development.
- The many possible targets for change include organisational tasks, people, cultures, technologies and structures.

How can planned organisational change be managed?

- Lewin identified three phases of planned change: unfreezing (preparing a system for change), changing (making a change) and refreezing (stabilising the system with a new change in place).

- Good change agents understand the nature of force-coercion, rational persuasion and shared power change strategies.
- People resist change for a variety of reasons, including fear of the unknown and force of habit.
- Good change agents deal with resistance positively and in a variety of ways, including education, participation, facilitation, manipulation and coercion.
- The special case of technological change requires an openness to resistance and willingness to improvise as implementation proceeds.

What is organisation development?

- Organisation development (OD) is a comprehensive approach to planned organisation change that uses principles of behavioural science to improve organisational effectiveness over the long term.
- OD has both outcome goals, with a focus on improved task accomplishment, and process goals, with a focus on improvements in the way people work together to accomplish important tasks.
- The OD process involves action research wherein people work together to collect and analyse data on system performance and decide what actions to take to improve things.
- OD interventions are structured activities that are used to help people work together to accomplish change; they may be implemented at the individual, group and/or organisational levels.

How do you build career readiness in a change environment?

- What happens in your career is up to you — take responsibility for building and maintaining a competitive 'brand called "you"'.
- Take charge of your learning — create a career portfolio that documents your career readiness at all times by displaying critical skills and accomplishments.
- Use the insights, examples and concepts from *Management: An Asia–Pacific Perspective* and your introductory management course as a strong foundation for lifelong personal development and career advancement.

KEY TERMS

action research (p. 510)

bottom-up change (p. 501)

change agent (p. 499)

changing (p. 504)

commercialising innovation (p. 497)

electronic career portfolio (p. 513)

force-coercion strategy (p. 505)

industry clusters (p. 498)

innovation (p. 496)

learning organisations (p. 495)

learning regions (p. 498)

OD interventions (p. 510)

organisation development (p. 508)

performance gap (p. 502)

planned change (p. 502)

process innovations (p. 496)

product innovations (p. 496)

rational persuasion strategy (p. 505)

refreezing (p. 504)

shared power strategy (p. 506)

strategic leadership (p. 495)

sustainable career advantage (p. 513)

Theory E change (p. 500)

Theory O change (p. 501)

top-down change (p. 500)

unfreezing (p. 504)

unplanned changes (p. 502)

Short-response questions

1. Identify and explain the importance of three internal targets for organisational change.
2. What are the three phases of change described by Lewin, and what do they mean?
3. What are the major differences in potential outcomes achieved by managers using the force-coercion, rational persuasion and shared power strategies of planned change?
4. What does the statement 'OD equals planned change plus' mean?

Application question

5. As a newly appointed manager in any work setting, you are liable to identify things that 'could be done better' and to have many 'new ideas' that you would like to implement. Based on the ideas presented in this chapter, how should you go about effecting successful planned change in such situations?

Recommended individual and group learning activities from the end-of-text Career Readiness Workbook for this chapter include:

Career advancement portfolio   *WB*

Update your career advancement portfolio to reflect your new skills and experiences. Include skills and personal insights you gain from the following projects and exercises.

Research and presentation project   *WB*

• Project 2 — Changing corporate cultures

Cross-functional integrative case   *WB*

Read the integrative case on Sarina Russo and answer the following questions:

18.1 It appears that 1998 was a significant year for Sarina Russo and her staff, with the establishment of Sarina Russo Job Access that evolved from the personnel division of The Office Business Academy. The business has subsequently grown rapidly. What are some of the possible change leadership actions that Sarina Russo took to ensure the success of this venture?

18.2 If you were planning the change described above, what change strategy might you use? What are your reasons for selecting this change strategy?

18.3 In what ways has Sarina Russo observed Tom Peters's advice to build the 'brand called "you"'? What could you do to build the 'brand called "you"'?

Exercise in teamwork   *WB*

• Exercise 13 — The future workplace

- Assessment 18 — Diagnosing change readiness

ELECTRONIC RESOURCES

Don't forget to take full advantage of the online support for *Management: An Asia–Pacific Perspective* at www.johnwiley.com.au/highered/management: chapter 18 practice tests, e-flashcards, crossword puzzles, interactive management skills assessments, interactive cases, the online career advancement portfolio and much more!

CASE FOR CRITICAL THINKING

Read the following case for critical thinking on the Walt Disney Company. While you are reading the case keep in mind what you have learned in this chapter, then answer the questions.

CASE FOR CRITICAL THINKING
The Walt Disney Company: Walt's legacy keeps growing

The Walt Disney Company has evolved from a wholesome family-oriented entertainment company into a massive multimedia conglomerate. With the purchase of the ABC Network in the USA in 1991, Disney moved beyond being a mere producer of media into the distribution of its and others' media products through a variety of channels. Has CEO Michael Eisner changed his mind from his earlier vision that 'content is king' to a realisation that control of distribution may be where the new value lies?

Disney through the years

After his first film business failed, artist Walt Disney and his brother Roy started a film studio in Hollywood in 1923. The first Mickey Mouse cartoon, *Plane Crazy*, was completed in 1928; the first cartoon with a soundtrack, *Steamboat Willie*, was their third production. The studio's first animated feature film was *Snow White* in 1937, followed by *Fantasia* and *Pinocchio* in the 1940s. Disneyland, the theme park developed largely by Walt, opened in 1955 in California. The original version of *The Mickey Mouse Club* television series was produced from 1955 to 1959, and the Disney weekly television series (under different names, including *The Wonderful World of Disney*) ran for 28 straight years.[53]

In 1966, Walt Disney died of lung cancer. Florida's Walt Disney World opened in 1971, the same year that Roy Disney died. His son, Roy E. Disney, took over the organisation, but without the creative leadership of brothers Walt and Roy Disney the firm fell on hard times. Walt's son-in-law, Ron Miller, became president in 1980. Many industry watchers felt that Disney had lost its creative energy and sense of direction because of lacklustre corporate leadership. In 1974, the Bass family, in alliance with Roy E. Disney, bought a controlling interest in the company. Their decision to bring in new CEO Michael Eisner, from Paramount, and a new president, Frank Wells, from Warner Brothers, ushered in a new era in the history of Disney.[54]

Work the brand

Michael Eisner has been involved in the entertainment industry from the start of his career. He demonstrates a knack for moving organisations from last place to first through a combination of hard work and timely decisions. After working at ABC, Eisner moved on to Paramount Pictures in 1976, which at the time was running last of the six major motion picture studios. During his reign as president, Paramount moved to first position with blockbusters such as *Raiders of the Lost Ark*, *Trading Places*, *Beverly Hills Cop*, and *Flying High!* (released in the USA as *Airplane!*). By applying lessons he learned in television to keep costs down, the average cost of a Paramount picture during his tenure was US$8.5 million, while the industry average was US$12 million.[55]

Eisner viewed Disney as a greatly under-utilised franchise identified by millions throughout the world. In addition to re-energising film production, Eisner wanted to extend the brand recognition of Disney products through a number of new avenues. Examples of his efforts included the cable Disney Channel, Tokyo Disneyland (Disney receives a management fee only), video distribution, Disney Stores, theatre shows and additional licensing arrangements for the Disney characters.

Disney represents movie production assets (Buena Vista Television, the Disney Channel, Miramax Film Company and Touchstone Pictures), theme parks, publication companies

(Disney Press, Mouse Works, Hyperion Press) and professional sports franchises in the USA (the Mighty Ducks hockey team and part of the California Angels baseball team).

However, in the early 1990s, problems began emerging for Disney. An attempt to build a park based on a Civil War theme was defeated by political pressure. EuroDisney, the firm's theme park in France, resulted in over US$500 million in losses for Disney due to miscalculations on attendance and concessions. In 1994, Eisner underwent emergency open-heart bypass surgery, and Frank Wells, long working in the shadow of his boss but increasingly viewed as integral for the success of Disney, died in a helicopter crash. Eisner's choice to succeed Wells, Michael Ovitz from Creative Artists Agency, did not work out and Ovitz soon left. Stories of Eisner's dictatorial management style brought succession worries to shareholders.

Capital Cities/ABC

In 1995, Eisner ushered in a new era at Disney by announcing the $19 billion takeover of television network Capital Cities/ABC. The deal came in the same week as Westinghouse Electric Corporation's US$5.4 billion offer for CBS Inc. Disney represents one of several consolidations of the media conglomerates that are increasingly controlling the distribution of entertainment programming in the USA.

Eisner appreciated the importance of both programming content and the distribution assets needed to deliver it.[56] As a result of many of his decisions, Disney has transformed from a sleepy film production studio into a major entertainment giant, with its revenues of over US$2 billion in 1987 increasing to US$22 billion in 1997.[57] Its share price has multiplied over 15 times, creating enormous wealth for both shareholders and executives of Disney.

One of the biggest questions arising from the ABC deal is whether Disney paid too dearly for declining network assets. Viewership among all the major networks continues to decline on a regular basis. Michael Jordan, the CEO of CBS, complains that 'the pure network television business is basically a low-margin to breakeven business'.[58] The networks are squeezed by having to pay extravagantly for programming and attracting an audience of older viewers who are scorned by advertisers.

However, another way to look at networks is as the lifeblood of the global, vertically integrated entertainment giants who own them as loss leaders that promote their parents' more lucrative operations. In this scenario, ABC acts as Disney's megaphone to tell the masses about Disney movies, theme parks, Disney-made shows and toys. Indeed, rather than shrinking, Rupert Murdoch's Fox, Paramount's UPN (United Paramount Network) and Time Warner's WB (Warner Bros.) are three of the newest networks.

Synergy is one key in today's network economies. ABC is able to turn 50 per cent profit margins on its ten network-owned stations and achieves a profit of over US$550 million, largely because of local news shows and syndicated shows like *Oprah* and *Wheel of Fortune*. The other big payday comes when networks own and syndicate a hit show, something they could not do before they were deregulated in the mid 1990s. By owning more of their own shows, the networks avoid increasing licence fees from the production companies.[59]

One risk in this strategy is that a network will miss out on a hit by favouring its own shows. Disney has blocked out certain parts of the week for its own shows. Fox and Disney appear best situated to exploit their platforms, with Fox injecting new life into an old brand, and Disney providing diverse production assets to feed its network.[60] This strategy works as long as networks remain big — since 1992, ABC and CBS have lost 25 per cent and 23 per cent of their viewers respectively. The networks have cushioned this problem by investing more in their cable holdings.

Not everything Disney touches turns to gold. In early 2001, the company was forced to downscale its Go.com web site as it continued to lose hundreds of millions of dollars. Disney's share price remains virtually unchanged since 1998.[61] Eisner, however, remains committed to integrating the ABC network into the greater Disney picture.

QUESTIONS

1. Examine the internal and external forces for change faced by Disney.
2. How have external forces in the entertainment industry affected Disney's need for change?
3. What changes do you foresee in the entertainment industry in the next five years?
4. Find four Internet sites discussing change management, stress management or the entertainment industry.

CONTENTS

CAREER READINESS WORKBOOK

Career advancement portfolio   W-4

Research and presentation projects   W-8

Cross-functional integrative case   W-15

Exercises in teamwork   W-20

Management skills assessments   W-32

Career advancement portfolio

WHAT IS A CAREER ADVANCEMENT PORTFOLIO®?

A career advancement portfolio (CAP) is a paper or electronic collection of documents that summarises your academic and personal accomplishments to potential employers. At a minimum, it will include:

Minimum components of a career advancement portfolio

• an up-to-date professional résumé
• a listing of courses in your degree or diploma
• a listing of your extracurricular activities and any leadership positions
• documentation of your career readiness in terms of skills and learning outcomes.

The CAP serves as an important means of communicating your résumé and credentials to potential employers. A professional and complete CAP allows these employers to easily review your background and range of skills and capabilities. It may convey your potential to a much greater depth and with a more positive impression than a traditional résumé.

Your CAP should document, in a progressive and developmental manner, your credentials and accomplishments as they build throughout your academic career. A few examples of the many different types of materials that you can include in your personal CAP, as testimonies to your academic accomplishments and career readiness, are actual samples of your use of spreadsheet software, your writing skills in the form of a short essay or research report, and a PowerPoint presentation.

As you progress through your degree or diploma, the CAP should be refined and materials added to display your most up-to-date skills, competencies and accomplishments. Use of the skill and outcome assessment framework, described below, will help you to do this.

Skill and outcome assessment framework

Skill and outcome assessment is an increasingly important part of management education. It allows you to document key academic accomplishments and career readiness for review by potential employers. The skill and outcome assessment framework focuses on these six areas of professional development: communication, leadership, teamwork, critical thinking, self-management and professionalism.

Skill and outcome assessment framework	
Communication Demonstrates ability to share ideas and findings clearly in written and oral expression • Writing • Oral presentation • Giving and receiving feedback • Technology utilisation	**Leadership** Demonstrates ability to influence and support others to perform complex and ambiguous tasks • Diversity awareness • Global awareness • Project management • Strategic leadership
Teamwork Demonstrates ability to work effectively as a team member and a team leader • Team contribution • Team leadership • Conflict management • Negotiation and consensus building	**Critical thinking** Demonstrates ability to gather and analyse information for creative problem solving • Problem solving • Judgement and decision making • Information gathering/interpretation • Creativity and innovation
Self-management Demonstrates ability to evaluate oneself, modify behaviour and meet obligations • Ethical understanding/behaviour • Personal flexibility • Tolerance for ambiguity • Performance responsibility	**Professionalism** Demonstrates ability to sustain a positive impression, instil confidence and advance in a career • Personal presence • Personal initiative • Career management • Unique 'value added'

Each of the learning resources and activities in the Career Readiness Workbook — projects, the cross-functional integrative case, exercises and self-assessments — are linked with one or more of these skills and outcome assessment areas. There is no better time than the present to start participating in the learning experiences and documenting your results and accomplishments in your CAP.

GETTING STARTED WITH YOUR CAREER ADVANCEMENT PORTFOLIO®

The supplementary resource materials available with this textbook support the development of your personal CAP in either paper or electronic versions. In both cases, the basic portfolio consists of a professional résumé and a compendium of coursework samples that display your career readiness skills and capabilities.

Paper portfolio format

The easiest way to organise a paper portfolio is with a binder. This binder should be professional in appearance and have an attractive cover page that clearly identifies it as your CAP. The binder should be indexed with dividers that allow a reader to easily browse the résumé and other materials to gain a complete view of your special credentials.

Electronic portfolio builder

In today's age of information technology and electronic communication, it is highly recommended that you develop an online or electronic career advancement portfolio. This format allows you to communicate easily and effectively through the Internet with employers offering job placements. An online version of your CAP can be displayed either on your personal web site or on one provided by your university, TAFE or polytechnic. Once you have created an electronic portfolio, it is easy to maintain. It is also something that will impress reviewers and help set you apart from the competition. At the very least, the use of an electronic CAP communicates to potential employers that you are a full participant in this age of information technology. Easy-to-use instructions and templates for building your personal and electronic CAP are available on the *Management: An Asia–Pacific Perspective* web site www.johnwiley.com.au/highered/management.

Résumé writing guide

The first thing that should go into your CAP is a professional résumé. Don't worry about how sophisticated or complete it is at first. The important things are to get it started and to continue to build it throughout your academic program of study. You'll be surprised at how complete it will become with systematic attention and a personal commitment to take full advantage of the professional development opportunities available to you.

We have provided a template, or résumé builder, on the *Management: An Asia–Pacific Perspective* web site www.johnwiley.com.au/highered/management. It shows both a professional format and the types of things that can and should be included.

Recommended portfolio project

A very good way to build on your personal CAP is by completing the following career development plan as part of your introductory management course. The objective of this project is to identify professional development opportunities that you can take advantage of while studying to advance your personal career readiness. Instructions for the project are available both here and in an online interactive version (refer to the *Management: An Asia–Pacific Perspective* web site www.johnwiley.com.au/highered/management).

CAREER DEVELOPMENT PLAN

Write a two-part memorandum and file it in your electronic or paper career advancement portfolio. This should be written in a professional format and addressed to your instructor or 'prospective employer'. The memorandum should do the following:

- **Part A.** Answer the question: What are my personal strengths and weaknesses as a potential manager? It is recommended that you use the skill and outcome assessment framework in structuring your analysis. It is also recommended that you support your answer in part by an analysis of scores and results from a selection of teamwork exercises and self-assessments, both in this workbook and on the *Management: An Asia–Pacific Perspective* web site. (You should also revisit this exercise once you've worked through more of the activities in the workbook.) You can also supplement the analysis with other relevant personal insights.
- **Part B.** Answer the question: How can I best take advantage of opportunities in my university, TAFE or polytechnic training to improve my managerial potential? Make this answer as specific as possible. Describe a clear plan of action that encompasses the time

available to you between now and graduation. This plan should include paid employment as well as academic and extracurricular experiences. Your goal should be to build a résumé and career portfolio through these activities that will best present you as a skilled and valuable candidate for the entry-level job that you would like in your chosen career field.

Your career development memorandum should be professional and error-free, and meet the highest standards of effective written communication. It should be sufficiently analytical in Part A to show serious consideration of your personal strengths and weaknesses in managerial potential at this point in time. It should be sufficiently detailed in Part B so that you can objectively evaluate your progress step by step between now and graduation. Overall, it should be a career development plan you can be proud to formally include in your CAP and share with potential employers interested in hiring you.

IMPROVING YOUR CAREER ADVANCEMENT PORTFOLIO®

Look back at the skill and outcome assessment framework. Throughout your study, you should concentrate on developing professional skills in:

- *Communication* — demonstrate an ability to share ideas and findings clearly in written and oral expression, and using technology if applicable
- *Leadership* — demonstrate an ability to influence and support others to perform complex and ambiguous tasks
- *Teamwork* — demonstrate an ability to work effectively as a team member and as a team leader
- *Critical thinking* — demonstrate an ability to gather and analyse information for creative problem solving
- *Self-management* — demonstrate an ability to evaluate yourself, modify behaviours and meet obligations
- *Professionalism* — demonstrate an ability to sustain a positive impression, instil confidence and advance in a career.

You can use all the activities in this Career Readiness Workbook to help your professional development. Use them to assess your strengths and weaknesses and to develop your career readiness.

Source: Adapted from David S. Chappell and John R. Schermerhorn Jr, *Career Advancement Portfolio*, Ohio University.

GET CONNECTED!

For tips on essay and report writing, and for preparing high quality presentations, visit the *Management: An Asia–Pacific Perspective* web site at www.johnwiley.com.au/highered/management.

GET CONNECTED!

Research and presentation projects

Project 1

DIVERSITY LESSONS — 'WHAT HAVE WE LEARNED?'

Diversity in the workplace is clearly the subject of significant attention. Managers and employers are being urged to recognise and value diversity, and many are pursuing active programs to improve the environment for diversity in the workplace. Yet 'glass ceilings' remain obstacles to career and personal accomplishment for too many women and minority groups.

Questions

1. What are the 'facts' in terms of progress for minority groups and women in the workplace?
2. What lessons of diversity have been learned?
3. What are the 'best' employers doing?

Instructions

Use research sources at your disposal to complete a brief report on the research questions. Specific topics for consideration might include the following:

- Case studies of employers reported as having strong diversity programs. What do they have in common? What do they do differently? Is there a basic 'model' that could be followed by managers in other settings?
- Investigation of diversity with specific reference to how well people of different racial, ethnic, gender and generational groups work together. What do we know about this, if anything? What are the common problems, if any? What concerns do managers and workers have?
- Analysis of survey reports on how the 'glass ceiling' may affect the careers of women and minority groups in various occupational settings. Get specific data, analyse them and develop the implications. Prepare a report that summarises your research.
- A critical look at the substance of diversity training programs. What do these programs try to accomplish, and how? Are they working or not, and how do we know? Is there a good model for diversity training that may be used by others?
- Look at where we go from here. What diversity issues lie ahead for the new managers of tomorrow?
- Case studies of women and minority groups who have started their own businesses. The following web sites may prove to be useful starting points:
  - Diversity@work Australia www.work.asn.au
  - New Zealand Equal Employment Opportunities Trust www.eeotrust.org.nz

- Equal Opportunity Practitioners in Higher Education Australasia www.eophea.anu.edu.au/diversity.html
- Victorian Department of Education, Employment and Training, 'Managing Diversity' web page www.sofweb.vic.edu.au/hrm/mandiv/managdiv.htm.

Project 2

CHANGING CORPORATE CULTURES

'Culture' is still a popular topic in management circles. Conventional wisdom holds that strong cultures can bond employees to a common sense of mission and reinforce work habits needed to serve customers well and maintain productivity. One aspect of organisational culture that is criticised today is lack of loyalty — loyalty of the organisation to employees and of employees to the organisation.

Questions

1. What do you think? Are organisational cultures changing?
2. If so, are they changing for the better or for the worse?

Instructions

Use research sources at your disposal to complete a brief report on these questions. Specific topics for consideration might include the following:

- Look for the latest thinking of management scholars and consultants on the role of 'corporate culture' in successful organisations. Many case examples and reports should be available on this topic. Look for success stories and try to interpret them in the context of the research question.

- Give special attention in your research to issues relating to loyalty. Try to access surveys of employees commenting on how they feel about job security, commitment to their organisation, for example.

- Make a list, from your research, of things that can be done to change the culture of an organisation or work group in a positive manner. Critically evaluate each of these items in terms of these action criteria: (a) feasibility of dealing with the item, (b) length of time needed to achieve impact on the item, and (c) the follow-up or reinforcement needed to maintain this impact. Review your entire analysis and answer this question: Can the recommended things really be accomplished by (a) a CEO, (b) a middle manager, and (c) a team leader?

- Place the issue of corporate culture in the context of the growing number of international mergers, joint ventures and strategic alliances found in the global economy. What is the importance of differences in 'corporate cultures' as organisations of different 'national cultures' try to work with one another? What do management consultants and scholars know or have to say about managing the problems of culture in this specific arena of business activity?

- The following web sites may prove to be useful starting points:
  - Asia Pacific Management Forum www.apmforum.com
  - BusinessCulture.com www.businessculture.com/newzealand.

Project 3

FOREIGN INVESTMENT IN AUSTRALASIA — 'WHAT ARE THE IMPLICATIONS?'

Foreign investment in Australasia is extensive, and on the increase. A large percentage of Australians and New Zealanders are employed by international companies, and the number continues to grow. In small cities, like Bundaberg or Geelong in Australia, or suburban Auckland or Palmerston North in New Zealand, the presence of an American or Japanese company has substantial implications for the local economy, and even for the local way of life. Indeed, some residents view the flourishing foreign investment as a cause for concern, not jubilation.

Questions

1. Which is it? Is foreign investment in Australasia a cause for concern, or is it something to be welcomed?
2. Do you believe there are reciprocal flows into other countries from Australia or New Zealand?

Instructions

Complete a brief report on these questions. Specific topics for consideration could include the following:

- The status of current foreign investment in the Asia–Pacific region. For example, how much is there, how fast is it growing, in what major industries is it found, and where is it located?
- The primary benefits and costs of this investment for the local communities and regions in which foreign companies operate. What do the communities gain from their presence? What price do you think they pay?
- How do Australians, New Zealanders and South-East Asians feel about working for foreign employers? Do they have opportunities for career advancement in foreign companies? Do the opportunities vary for men and women? Are foreign companies considered to be 'good' employers? Why or why not?
- The following web sites may prove to be useful starting points:
  - Trade New Zealand www.tradenz.govt.nz
  - Japanese Ministry of Foreign Affairs www.mofa.go.jp/region/asia-paci/australia and www.mofa.go.jp/region/asia-paci/nz
  - Invest Australia www.investaustralia.gov.au.

Project 4

CORPORATE SOCIAL RESPONSIBILITY — 'WHAT'S THE STATUS?'

An increasing range of business activities are being publicly scrutinised for their social responsibility implications. This scrutiny is imposed by both regulators (for example, Food Standards Australia New Zealand monitors food labelling to protect the public from inappropriate and misleading claims) and interest groups (for example, as part of Oxfam Community Aid Abroad's goal to 'build a fairer world', it works to promote economic and social justice through ethical trade and ethical investment).

Question

Where do businesses stand today with respect to the criteria for evaluating social responsibility discussed in the textbook?

Instructions

Complete a brief report on this question. Specific topics for consideration might include the following:

- Research and evaluate the 'status' of major organisations on a variety of social responsibility performance matters. How well are they doing? Would you use them as models of social responsibility for others to follow, or not?
- Conduct research to identify current examples of the 'best' and the 'worst' organisations in terms of performance or social responsibility criteria. Pursue this investigation on an international, national and/or local scale.
- Choose an issue such as environmental protection or product labelling. Conduct research to identify the 'best' and the 'worst' organisations in terms of performance in these specific areas. Again, consider looking at this issue on an international, national and/or local scale.
- Create a scale that could be used to measure the social responsibility performance of an organisation. Review the scholarly research in this area but use your own judgement. Test your scale by applying it to two or three local organisations.
- The following web sites may prove to be useful starting points:
  - Australian Human Rights and Equal Opportunity Commission www.humanrights.gov.au
  - Food Standards Australia New Zealand www.foodstandards.gov.au
  - Oxfam Community Aid Abroad www.caa.org.au and www.oxfam.org.nz.

Project 5

AFFIRMATIVE ACTION DIRECTIONS — 'WHERE DO WE GO FROM HERE?'

In a *Harvard Business Review* article ('From Affirmative Action to Affirming Diversity', March–April 1990), R. Roosevelt Thomas makes the following statement: 'Sooner or later, affirmative action will die a natural death'. He goes on to praise its accomplishments but then argues that it is time to 'move beyond affirmative action' and learn how to 'manage diversity'. There are a lot of issues that may be raised in this context — issues of equal employment opportunity, hiring quotas, positive discrimination and others.

Question

What is the status of affirmative action today?

Instructions

Complete a brief report on this question. Specific topics for consideration might include the following:

• Make sure you are clear on the term *affirmative action* and its legal underpinnings. Research the topic, identify the relevant laws, and make a history line to chart its development over time.
• Examine current debates on affirmative action at the level of national policy. What are the issues? How are the 'for' and 'against' positions being argued?
• Consider 'positive discrimination'. Is there any pattern to employment situations in which positive discrimination emerges as a management concern? Identify cases where positive discrimination has been charged. How have they been resolved and with what apparent human resource management implications?
• Examine controversies over *hiring quotas*. Is this what affirmative action is all about? What are the arguments, pro and con? What do the 'experts' say about it? Where do we seem to be headed in this area?
• Look at organisational policies that deal with diversity matters. Find what you consider to be the 'best' examples. Analyse them and identify the common ground. Prepare a summary that could be used as a policy development guideline for human resource managers who want to make sure their organisations truly support and value diversity in the workforce.
• Try to look at all of these issues and controversies from different perspectives. Talk to people of different 'majority' and 'minority' groups around your campus. Find out how they view these things, and why. What are the implications for human resource management today?
• The following web sites may prove to be useful starting points:
  – New Zealand Human Rights Commission www.hrc.co.nz
  – New Zealand Equal Employment Opportunities Trust www.eeotrust.org.nz
  – Equal Opportunity Commission of South Australia www.eoc.sa.gov.au
  – Australian Public Service Commission www.apsc.gov.au/publications/index.html.

Project 6

CONTROVERSIES IN CEO PAY — 'IS IT TOO HIGH?'

The high, sometimes extremely high, pay of CEOs in some Australian, New Zealander and international corporations has caught the public's eye. Many people aren't very happy with what they are discovering. For example, the Australian Institute of Management's national salary survey suggests the average Australian CEO earns a package worth more than a quarter of a million dollars. The top executives in Australia's biggest companies receive more than a million dollars a year. A recent report estimated that CEOs in the USA take home, on average, 160 times the pay of their employees. But it is not only the magnitude of the pay that is bothersome. Controversial too is the belief that the pay of some CEOs goes up even when their company's performance goes down.

Questions

1. What is happening in the area of executive compensation?
2. Are CEOs paid too much?
3. Are they paid for 'performance', or are they paid for something else?

Instructions

Use research sources at your disposal to complete a brief report on these questions. Specific topics for consideration might include the following:
- Check the latest reports on CEO pay. Try to get the facts. Prepare a briefing report as if you were writing a short informative article for a business magazine. The title of your article could be 'Status report: Where we stand today on CEO pay'.
- Consider the pay-for-performance issue. Do corporate CEOs get paid for performance or for something else? What do the researchers say? What do the business periodicals say? Find some examples to explain and defend your answers to these questions.
- Find some positive cases where you consider a CEO's pay to be justified. What criteria are you using to justify it?
- Take a position: Should a limit be set on CEO pay? If no, why not? If yes, what type of limit do we set? Should we deal with an absolute dollar limit, a multiple of what the lowest-paid worker in a firm earns, or some other guideline? Why? Who, if anyone, should set these limits — government, company boards of directors or someone else?
- Conduct a survey on campus. What do other students think about CEO pay? Do they think limits should be set? Take a poll in your local community. What does the public at large think? How does the public feel about limits to CEO pay? How about you — what is your conclusion? Is the attack on CEO pay justified?
- Check executive pay rates in a few countries around the Asia–Pacific region. How do they compare? How would you explain the differences?
- The following web sites may prove to be useful starting points:
  - BusinessWeek Online careers section www.businessweek.com/careers
  - Seek Executive http://executive.seek.com.au
  - The American Federation of Labor and Congress of Industrial Organizations www.aflcio.org.

Project 7

SELF-MANAGING TEAMS — 'HOW GOOD ARE THEY?'

In Geert Hofstede's framework for describing national cultures (see chapter 5), Australia is described as one of the most 'individualistic' countries in his research sample. This suggests Australians are a people motivated by self-interests and opportunities for personal accomplishment and gain. This seems somewhat contrary to the growing emphasis on 'teamwork' and the increasing use of self-managing teams and various types of employee involvement groups in organisations.

Questions

1. How well are self-managing teams working in the workplace in Australia and New Zealand?
2. What is the future of this approach?

Instructions

Use research sources at your disposal to complete a brief report on this question. Specific topics for consideration might include the following:

- Check the research on self-managing teams. Where have they been tried and with what success? Look for empirical data, not just theoretical arguments. Are there any patterns? What open questions remain to be answered?
- Look at the management guidelines for self-managing teams. What is the advice on how to ensure their success? What are the potential pitfalls in workplaces where one is changing *to* self-managing teams from other more traditional methods?
- Consider the individualism issue. Can self-managing teams work with highly individualistic workers? What advice is available on how to deal with this individualism issue if, indeed, it is an issue at all?
- Consider the organisation structure issue. How must an organisation's structure change in order to best support the activities of self-managing teams? What advice is available on handling these structural issues?
- Look more broadly at employee involvement groups in general. What do we know about the effectiveness of quality circles and other types of employee involvement groups? Are there any patterns that indicate when and under what conditions they tend to work best?
- Assume you have to give a formal briefing to a senior executive trying to decide if his or her organisation should try self-managing teams and employee involvement groups. Based on your research, what will you say?

Additional research and presentation projects are available on line at www.johnwiley.com.au/ highered/management.

GET CONNECTED!

Cross-functional integrative case

SARINA RUSSO WILL 'SEE YOU AT THE TOP!'

Janet Campbell

'I'll see you at the top' is the well-known catchcry of Brisbane businesswoman Sarina Russo. Since establishing her first business, The Office Business Academy, in 1979, Sarina Russo has sent thousands of young people on their own paths to the top. Today, she is the high-profile founder, managing director and CEO of a portfolio of successful businesses.

History

Sarina Russo was five in 1956 when, with her family, she left a small, impoverished Sicilian village for Australia. Responsibility came early to her. She had to learn English at school, and by the age of 13 was assisting her parents with their income tax returns and business interests. Despite this, she had difficulty with her studies, resulting in her having to repeat a grade and then leave school in Year 10. Yet the determination was there. She returned and, although failing English again in Year 12, continued her studies at university.

This resilience was also apparent in her early career. As a legal secretary in the late 1970s, Sarina Russo was fired from several roles for wearing a boob tube, for being five minutes late back from lunch, and for having a 'pushy' attitude. Though highly distressed by her sackings at the time, she now acknowledges their role both in setting her on the path that has led to today's successes and in making her sensitive to the plight of jobseekers.

She then took part-time work as a typing teacher — and was fired again! However, this time it was different. Her students wanted her back. 'It was an accident', Sarina Russo says. 'I was a dormant entrepreneur. I had no idea. I got fired from every legal [secretary] job in my life. Then I was a part-time typing teacher and they fired me and reinstated me, and that's when I recognised I was good at something, which was training.'[1]

In 1979 she took her savings of $2600, found cheap office space in Brisbane's CBD and convinced her bank manager to lend her enough money to cover her expenses while recruiting her first ten students. The Office Business Academy was in business — teaching typing, shorthand, bookkeeping, English and word processing, and offering a job placement service for its graduates. Family members assisted with making office furniture and painting the run-down offices. Sarina Russo's businesses continue to employ her family, including one niece, three nephews and her brother-in-law.

Twenty-four years later, the Sarina Russo Group represents six businesses: Russo Institute of Technology, Sarina Russo Job Access (Australia), Russo Recruitment, Russo Online, Russo Corporate Training and Sarina Investments. The businesses employ over 400 people, with offices in Queensland, New South Wales and Victoria.

The Office Business Academy has now evolved into the Russo Institute of Technology, which trains up to 3000 domestic and international students annually. It is recognised as one of the largest privately owned education-training institutes in Australia, employing up to 150 staff. The Russo Institute of Technology has developed a number of faculties to meet market needs including business, information technology, hospitality, tourism and English language.[2]

Partnerships to enhance student training and work experience opportunities have been established with industry leaders such as the Hilton Hotel and the Sheraton Hotel and Towers in Brisbane, Microsoft (the Russo Institute of Technology is a Microsoft Certified Solution Provider) and the Australian Federation of Travel Agents. A significant initiative is the alliance with the University of Southern Queensland — graduates of the Russo Institute of Technology are eligible for direct entry into the university's second year of undergraduate study. Students also have the facility to undertake courses through Russo Online, an online learning platform.

Sarina Russo takes a keen interest in commercial property. From her Brisbane CBD apartment, she regularly jogs through the city. While these runs are important for fitness and stress management, they also provide the opportunity to look for property acquisitions. Her first purchase in 1993 was a 12-level office building at 82 Ann Street for $2.05 million. This property became the headquarters of The Office Business Academy, taking her from paying rent of $300 000 annually to becoming a landlord.

'It was the biggest milestone in my life. I took a mortgage — the biggest in my life', Sarina Russo says. That mortgage changed her business perspective. 'First, it [the purchase] gave me an identity and took me on to another level. It took me to the "risk" zone. It made me look outside of my core business and also to look at the global aspects of my business.'[3]

Since that first purchase, there have been two more. Sarina Investments owns 457 Adelaide Street, purchased for $1.25 million in 1999, which is now home for the Russo Institute of Technology. While jogging one morning in 2001, she noticed 349 Queen Street was for sale, and by 8 p.m. that night had contracted to pay $4.3 million for the property. After $1 million in refurbishment, the Sarina Russo Plaza now houses the group's corporate training, administration and the Russo Consulting Group. It has also become headquarters for Sarina Russo Job Access.

Job Network provider

Of all her businesses, it is, arguably, Sarina Russo Job Access (Australia) that has contributed most to her increasingly high profile and business expansion in the last four years. Evolving from the personnel division of The Office Business Academy, Sarina Russo Job Access was established in early 1998 to capitalise on the federal government's Job Network initiative.

Job Network was created through the privatisation of the Commonwealth Employment Service (CES). The organisation is structured as a delivery system to provide government-funded employment services to jobseeker candidates and employers. The network comprises some 200 private, community and government organisations across Australia that successfully tendered to the federal government. Sarina Russo Job Access is one of these organisations.

Job Network providers earn fees from the federal government for finding positions for unemployed jobseekers. Their services are free to the prospective employers. Jobseekers are categorised by Centrelink (a federal government agency that delivers services, programs and payments on behalf of Australian government departments) according to their preparedness to start work. Fees for Job Network providers range from a few hundred dollars for those with adequate skills and experience to start work immediately, to several thousand dollars for those people, often long-term unemployed, deemed to need intensive assistance.

Employers register vacant positions with their local office of a Job Network provider. For example, a position can be registered at Sarina Russo Job Access Nundah (a Brisbane suburb) which then provides services such as:

- promotion of the position throughout its 30 eastern Australia Sarina Russo Job Access offices
- advertising of the position, on the Internet and in major daily newspapers
- screening and short-listing of individual candidates.

A star-rating system was introduced in 2001 to assess the performance of Job Network providers. In the first round of performance assessments, Sarina Russo Job Access scored one of the highest ratings — 4.5 out of a possible 5 stars — based in part on its performance in making 8431 job-match placements in 2000. This brought the total of people placed in work by the organisation since May 1998 to more than 25 000.

'We [Sarina Russo Job Access] take a very positive approach and provide intensive assistance [to candidates]...Each candidate is assessed and then we help them come up with the winning package — we have found that our clients, many of whom are large corporations, are very happy to take on our first choice candidates...If, in our assessment, we identify an issue that is preventing a candidate re-entering the workforce, we will address the barrier, be it through training or simply providing suitable clothing for the interview.'[4]

The success of Sarina Russo Job Access is also attributable to the contracts that Sarina Russo has established to provide staff to major employers such as the Queensland Government, Woolworths and Telstra. From an initial base of ten offices, Sarina Russo Job Access has rapidly expanded, and now provides employment and training services through a network of thirty locations in Queensland, northern New South Wales and Victoria. In addition to the government employment contract, Sarina Russo Job Access provides a range of customised permanent and temporary recruitment services to employers.[5]

Jobseekers approaching Sarina Russo Job Access for support may also be encouraged to undertake training through the Russo Institute of Technology to enhance their prospects. Ever the diplomat, Sarina Russo has been careful to publicly acknowledge the overall performance of the federal government's initiative: 'The new system is a success because of the excellent relationship between the government and private companies'.[6]

Ongoing study

While establishing and successfully managing businesses that focus on others' training and education, Sarina Russo has been careful not to neglect her own. She graduated from the three-year Harvard Business School Owner/President Management program in 1999 (the equivalent of an MBA), and returns to the USA each year for a refresher course, which also provides the opportunity to meet and renew acquaintance with owners, CEOs and presidents from leading organisations throughout the world.

'I've been studying all my life, I don't know anything else but lifetime learning so it was a natural progression to continue at Harvard Business School', said Sarina Russo. 'Knowledge is wealth, knowledge is value, knowledge brings confidence and is an integral part of life — we feed the body, so we should also feed the mind.

'It's by gaining knowledge that we gain the confidence to continue moving ahead in life no matter what challenges lie in the way, and we add to that knowledge by learning from our experiences in order to succeed.'[7] Sarina Russo also completed the Australian Institute of Company Directors' diploma course in 1997.

High profile

Setting up businesses, buying CBD property and taking a Harvard qualification — it's no wonder that Steve Vizard, a fellow republican delegate to the Australian Constitution Convention of 1998, describes Sarina Russo in his book, *Two Weeks in Lilliput*, as the 'smiling self-made Queensland businesswoman' who is 'permanently moving and shaking, a one-woman mardi gras float'.[8]

Ironically, Sarina Russo decided against using her own name for her first business, preferring instead 'The Office Business Academy'. She says: 'I thought it was a really cool name. Students could say, "I'm going back to *the office*"'.[9] These days the Sarina Russo brand is used for all Sarina Russo's businesses — an approach which complements her flair for self-publicity.

Often referred to by the print media as 'Porsche-driving', 'flamboyant' and, with tongue firmly in cheek, 'media shy', Sarina Russo is well-versed in the art of personal promotion — a valuable asset and a shrewd business development and branding strategy for her eponymously named businesses.

Sarina Russo provides great media attention — from the vandalism of her turquoise Porsche 911 at a charity golf event by an envious cyclist to her frequent and invariably positive comments about the potential of her business, clients and candidates. Responding to criticisms about Job Network, for example, she has been quoted as saying: 'We've [Job Network providers] got to unite, ignore the negative, stop blaming the government, take control, become competitive, develop a "branding"'[10], and, 'I think it's the individual attitude. We've got to be very careful that we stop blaming the federal or state governments for everything. We need to educate our kids to take responsibility for their own lives. This government is doing it well, saying "Don't be settled with the pension or unemployment benefit, do something with your life".'[11]

Few of her competitors are as well known, and Sarina Russo Job Access and the Russo Institute of Technology have achieved widespread awareness as highly effective job placement and training institutions. Her high profile also opens many doors, and she has established business relationships which must be the envy of her competitors — even hosting Queensland Premier Peter Beattie's 50th birthday party in November 2002 at her Brisbane CBD apartment.

Her attendance at 'A list' events leads to widespread reporting in the social columns. Arguably her greatest coup (to date, at least!) was taking naming rights for The Russo Group for a charity dinner in early 2002, at which former US president Bill Clinton was guest of honour, with Sarina hosting his table.

Recognition

Sarina Russo's ability to open key business and political doors is not just related to her prominence in the media — she has made a substantial commitment to community activities. These include board memberships of Queensland Education Training and International, Tourism Queensland and Austa Energy Corporation. Sarina Russo was appointed to the Queensland Premier's Business Advisory Board in 2000, and she is trustee and chairperson of the Jupiters Casino Community Benefit Fund. In addition, she was elected by Queensland voters as one of the Australian Republican Movement delegates to the Australian Constitution Convention in Canberra in February 1998.

Sarina Russo does not deny herself the symbols of success, including the Porsche, the penthouse CBD apartment overlooking the Brisbane River and her favourite clothing label,

Giorgio Armani, for which she shops in New York. From her students' perspective, she must present an inspirational image.

In addition to being regularly featured in the media, her success has been more formally recognised. She is an Honorary Ambassador for the City of Brisbane, appointed by Brisbane Lord Mayor Jim Soorley, and has been inducted into the Australian Businesswomen's Hall of Fame.

Sarina Russo received significant international recognition when she was honoured as one of the forty Leading Woman Entrepreneurs of the World for 2002, the most prestigious award in the world for women business owners. Previous Australian recipients include Janet Holmes à Court and Betty Byrne Henderson.

The future

Not content to rest on her laurels, Sarina Russo has many challenging future plans. The publication of her biography *Meet Me at the Top* in December 2002 calls for a busy schedule of public speaking engagements across Australia, and she wants to purchase more CBD property. There has also been a hint or two in the media that one day she may consider a political career. As a republican delegate at the Australian Constitution Convention, and regular commentator on public policy related to education and training, she has already demonstrated a keen interest in the issues of the day.

Her interest may not surprise Liberal Senator Santo Santoro and Federal Opposition parliamentarian Con Sciacca — they all hail from the same area in Sicily. Currently she does not publicly demonstrate a political affiliation, but contributes financially to both leading political parties.

Perhaps the dream currently closest to her heart is to establish her own university — not such a surprising prospect in view of the Russo Institute of Technology and the partnership with the University of Southern Queensland. She sees this ambition as being 'the ultimate recognition of her rise from a humble typing tutor'. 'It sounds funny, doesn't it, but that is my dream', Sarina Russo has said. 'I think it's [because of] my background. It's no longer a financial dream, it's a recognition of my community, my Italian heritage to be able to achieve that. I think that would be fantastic.'[12]

Of course, she also has the resources to retire comfortably. But this appears to be a highly unlikely prospect in the near future. When commenting on the future of her businesses, Sarina Russo notes: 'It's a journey of life. You become very committed to the company, to the people you work with. You owe it to them to give them a challenge and that's what makes a company successful.'[13]

Exercises in teamwork

Exercise 1

MY BEST MANAGER

Preparation

Working alone, make a list of the *behavioural attributes* that describe the *best* manager you have ever worked for. This could be someone you worked for in a full-time or part-time job, holiday job, volunteer job or student organisation. If you have trouble identifying an actual manager, make a list of behavioural attributes of the type of manager you would most like to work for in your next job.

Instructions

Form into groups as assigned by your instructor, or work with a classmate. Share your list of attributes and listen to the lists of others. Be sure to ask questions and make comments on items of special interest. Work together to create a master list that combines the unique attributes of the 'best' managers experienced by members of your group. Have a spokesperson share that list with the rest of the class.

Source: Adapted from John R. Schermerhorn Jr, James G. Hunt and Richard N. Osborn, *Managing Organizational Behavior*, 3rd edn (New York: Wiley, 1988), pp. 32–3. This material is used by permission of John Wiley & Sons, Inc.

Exercise 2

WHAT MANAGERS DO

Preparation

Think about the questions that follow. Record your answers in the spaces provided.

1. How much of a typical manager's time would you expect to be allocated to these relationships? (total should = 100%)
   ____% of time working with subordinates
   ____% of time working with boss
   ____% of time working with peers and outsiders
2. How many hours per week does the average manager work? ____ hours
3. What amount of a manager's time is typically spent in the following activities? (total should = 100%)
   ____% in scheduled meetings
   ____% in unscheduled meetings
   ____% doing desk work
   ____% talking on the telephone
   ____% walking around the organisation/work site

Instructions

Talk over your responses with a nearby classmate. Explore the similarities and differences in your answers. Be prepared to participate in a class discussion led by your instructor.

Exercise 3

DEFINING QUALITY

Preparation

Write your definition of the word *quality* here.
QUALITY = _____
_____

Instructions

Form groups as assigned by your instructor.

1. Have each group member present a definition of the word *quality*. After everyone has presented, come up with a consensus definition of *quality*. That is, determine and write down one definition of the word with which every member can agree.

2. Next, have the group assume the position of general manager in each of the following organisations. Use the group's *quality* definition to state for each a *quality objective* that can guide the behaviour of members in producing high-quality goods and/or services for customers or clients. Elect a spokesperson to share group results with the class. Organisations:

(a) A school of business administration
(b) A public hospital
(c) A retail sporting goods store
(d) A fast-food franchise restaurant
(e) A local post office
(f) A full-service bank branch
(g) A computer software manufacturing firm

Exercise 4

WHAT IS YOUR PROPENSITY FOR TAKING RISKS?

Preparation

Indicate how well each of the following statements reflects your attitudes or behaviour, using the following scale:

Very inaccurately = VI
Inaccurately = I
Moderately well = MW
Accurately = A
Very accurately = VA.

	VI	I	MW	A	VA
1. If I had a serious illness, I would purchase generic instead of brand-name drugs.	1	2	3	4	5
2. I invest (or would invest) much more money in bonds or certificates of deposit than in shares.	5	4	3	2	1
3. The thought of starting my own business appeals to me.	1	2	3	4	5
4. I am (or was) willing to go on blind dates frequently.	1	2	3	4	5

	VI	I	MW	A	VA
5. My career advice to young people is to pursue a well-established occupation with a high demand for newcomers to the field.	5	4	3	2	1
6. I would be willing to relocate to a city where I had no family or friends.	1	2	3	4	5
7. During the last few years, I have taken up a new sport, dance or foreign language on my own.	1	2	3	4	5
8. My preference is to have at least 90 per cent of my compensation based on guaranteed salary.	5	4	3	2	1
9. From time to time I buy jewellery, clothing or food from street markets.	1	2	3	4	5
10. The idea of piloting my own single-engine plane over the ocean appeals to me.	1	2	3	4	5

Scoring

Obtain your score by adding the numbers you have circled.

Interpretation

46–50   You are a heavy risk taker, bordering on reckless at times. You are most likely not assessing risk carefully enough before proceeding.

38–45   You probably are a sensible risk taker, and an adventuresome person in a way that enhances your leadership appeal to others.

5–37   You have a propensity to avoid risks. Your conservatism in this regard could detract from an entrepreneurial leadership style.

Instructions

Form into groups as assigned by the instructor. Share your responses and discuss how you would reconcile differences in risk-taking propensities among team members.

Source: Developed from Andrew DuBrin, *Leadership*, 3rd edn, p. 134. Copyright © Houghton Mifflin Company. Reprinted with permission.

Exercise 5

WHAT WOULD THE CLASSICS SAY?

Preparation

Consider this situation: Six months after being hired, Bob, a laboratory worker, is performing just well enough to avoid being fired. He was carefully selected and had the abilities required to do the job really well. At first Bob was enthusiastic about his new job, but now he isn't performing up to this high potential. Fran, his supervisor, is concerned and wonders what can be done to improve this situation.

Instructions

Assume the identity of one of the following persons: Frederick Taylor, Henri Fayol, Max Weber, Abraham Maslow, Chris Argyris. Assume that *as this person* you have been asked by Fran for advice on the management situation just described. Answer these questions as you think your assumed identity would respond. Be prepared to share your answers in class and to defend them based on the text's discussion of this person's views.

1. As [your assumed identity], what are your basic beliefs about good management and organisational practices?
2. As [your assumed identity], what do you perceive may be wrong in this situation that would account for Bob's low performance?
3. As [your assumed identity], what could be done to improve Bob's future job performance?

Exercise 6

THE GREAT MANAGEMENT HISTORY DEBATE

Preparation

Consider the question 'What is the best thing a manager can do to improve productivity in her or his work unit?'

Instructions

The instructor will assign you, individually or in a group, to one of the following positions. Complete the missing information as if you were the management theorist referred to. Be prepared to argue and defend your position before the class.

Position A: Mary Parker Follett offers the best insight into the question. Her advice would be to . . . [advice to be filled in by you or the group].

Position B: Max Weber's ideal bureaucracy offers the best insight into the question. His advice would be to . . . [advice to be filled in by you or the group].

Position C: Henri Fayol offers the best insight into the question. His advice would be to . . . [advice to be filled in by you or the group].

Position D: The Hawthorne Studies offer the best insight into the question. Elton Mayo's advice would be to . . . [advice to be filled in by you or the group].

Exercise 7

WHAT DO YOU VALUE IN WORK?

Preparation

The following nine items are from a survey conducted by Nicholas J. Beutell and O. C. Brenner. Order the nine items in terms of how important (9 = most important) they would be to you in a job.

How important is it to you to have a job that:
- is respected by other people? ____
- encourages continued development of knowledge and skills? ____
- provides job security? ____
- provides a feeling of accomplishment? ____
- provides the opportunity to earn a high income? ____
- is intellectually stimulating? ____
- rewards good performance with recognition? ____
- provides comfortable working conditions? ____
- permits advancement to high administrative responsibility? ____

Instructions

Form into teams as designated by your instructor, with each group consisting entirely of women or men. Each group should develop a consensus ranking of the items they think the opposite sex in the Beutell and Brenner survey ranked them. The reasons for the rankings should be shared and discussed so they are clear to everyone. A spokesperson for each group should then share the group's rankings with the class.

Source: Reprinted from Nicholas J. Beutell and O. C. Brenner, 'Sex Differences in Work Values', *Journal of Vocational Behavior*, vol. 28 (1986), pp. 29–41, with permission of Elsevier. Exercise adapted from Roy J. Lewicki, Donald D. Bowen, Douglas T. Hall and Francine S. Hall, *Experiences in Management and Organizational Behavior*, 3rd edn (New York: Wiley, 1988), pp. 261–7.

Exercise 8

CONFRONTING ETHICAL DILEMMAS

Preparation

Read and think about your response to each of the situations below.

1. Ron Jones, general manager of a large construction company, receives in the mail a large envelope marked 'personal'. It contains a competitor's cost data for a project that both companies will be bidding on shortly. The data are accompanied by a note from one of Ron's employees saying: 'This is the real thing!' Ron knows that the data could be a major advantage to his company in preparing a bid that can win the contract. *What should he do?*
2. Kay Smith is one of your top-performing staff members. She has shared with you her desire to apply for promotion to a new position just announced in a different division of the company. This will be tough on you since recent budget cuts mean you will be unable to replace anyone who leaves, at least for quite some time. Kay knows this and in all fairness has asked your permission before she submits an application. It is rumoured that the son of a good friend of your boss is going to apply for the job. Although his credentials are less impressive than Kay's, the likelihood is that he will get the job if she doesn't apply. *What will you do?*
3. Janine Drew got caught in a bind. She was pleased to represent her company as head of the local community

development committee. In fact, her supervisor's boss once held this position and told her in a hallway conversation: 'Do your best and give them every support possible'. Going along with this, Janine agreed to pick up the bill (several hundred dollars) for a dinner meeting with local community and business leaders. Shortly thereafter, her supervisor informed everyone that the entertainment budget was being eliminated in a cost-saving effort. Janine, not wanting to renege on supporting the community development committee, was able to charge the dinner bill to an advertising budget. Eventually, an internal auditor discovered the mistake and reported it to you, the personnel director. Janine is scheduled to meet with you in a few minutes. *What will you do?*

Instructions

Working alone, make the requested decisions in each of these incidents. Think carefully about your justification for the decision. Meet in a group assigned by your instructor. Share your decisions and justifications in each case with other group members. Listen to theirs. Try to reach a group consensus on what to do in each situation and why. Be prepared to share the group decisions, and any dissenting views, in general class discussion.

Exercise 9

BEATING THE TIME WASTERS

Preparation

1. Make a list of all the things you need to do tomorrow. Prioritise each item in terms of *how important it is to create outcomes that you can really value*. Use this classification scheme:
   Most important, top priority = A
   Important, not top priority = B
   Least important, low priority = C
2. Look again at all the activities you have classified as B. Reclassify any that are really A's or C's. Look at your list of A's. Reclassify any that are really B's or C's. Double-check to make sure you are comfortable with your list of C's.
3. Make a list of all the 'time wasters' that often interfere with your ability to accomplish everything you want to on any given day.

Instructions

Form into groups as assigned by the instructor. Have all group members share their lists and their priority classifications. Members should politely 'challenge' each other's classifications to make sure that only truly 'high-priority' items receive an A rating. They might also suggest that some C items are of such little consequence that they might not be worth doing at all. After each member of the group revises his or her 'to do' list based on this advice, go back and discuss the time wasters identified by group members. Develop a master list of time wasters and discuss what to do about them. Have a group spokesperson be prepared to share discussion highlights and tips on beating common time wasters with the rest of the class.

Source: Developed from Roy J. Lewicki, Donald D. Bowen, Douglas T. Hall and Francine S. Hall, *Experiences in Management and Organizational Behavior*, 3rd edn (New York: Wiley, 1988), pp. 314–16. This material is used by permission of John Wiley & Sons, Inc.

Exercise 10

PERSONAL CAREER PLANNING

Preparation

Complete the following three activities and bring the results to class. Your work should be in a written form suitable for your instructor's review.

1. *Strengths and weaknesses inventory.* Different occupations require special talents, abilities and skills if people are to excel in their work. Each of us has a repertoire of existing strengths and weaknesses that are 'raw materials' we presently offer a potential employer. Of course, actions can (and should!) be taken over time to further develop current strengths and to turn weaknesses into strengths. Make a list identifying your most important strengths and weaknesses at the moment in relation to the career direction you are most likely to pursue upon graduation. Place an asterisk next to each item you consider most important to deal with in your courses and student activities *before* graduation.

2. *Five-year career objectives.* Make a list of 3–5 career objectives that are appropriate given your list of personal strengths and weaknesses. Limit these objectives to ones that can be accomplished within five years of completing your degree or diploma.

3. *Five-year career action plans.* Write a specific action plan for accomplishing each of the five objectives. State exactly what you will do, and by when, in order to meet each objective. If you will need special support or assistance, identify it *and* state how you will obtain it. Remember, an outside observer should be able to read your action plan for each objective and end up feeling confident that he or she knows exactly what you are going to do, and why.

Instructions

Form into groups as assigned by the instructor. Share your career-planning analysis with the group; listen to those of others. Participate in a discussion that examines any common patterns and major differences among group members. Take advantage of any opportunities to gather feedback and advice from others. Have one group member be prepared to summarise the group discussion for the class as a whole. Await further class discussion led by the instructor.

Source: Developed in part from Roy J. Lewicki, Donald D. Bowen, Douglas T. Hall and Francine S. Hall, *Experiences in Management and Organizational Behavior*, 3rd edn (New York: Wiley, 1988), pp. 261–7. This material is used by permission of John Wiley & Sons, Inc.

Exercise 11

ESSENTIALS OF MOTIVATION

Preparation

This exercise will help you better understand your own motivators. Using your present role as a student, or, if you are employed, your role as an employee in your workplace, consider factors that would motivate you to work harder and perform better. List these factors under a heading of 'motivators'. Looking at the theories of motivation discussed in the chapter, decide which theory best describes the method you used to describe your list of motivators. Explain why this theory best describes the method you used.

Instructions

Form into groups of three or four and discuss the various ways in which each group member arrived at their list of motivators. Which theory was most commonly used? Why? Pay attention to the differences between content and process theories in your discussion. Using the list of motivators you have made, think about how your employer/manager (remember this can be your instructor) can empower you in the tasks for which you have responsibility.

Source: Adapted from Jack Wood, Joseph Wallace, Rachid M. Zeffane, John R. Schermerhorn, James G. Hunt and Richard N. Osborn, *Organisational Behaviour: A Global Perspective*, 2nd edn (Brisbane: John Wiley & Sons, 2001), p. 162.

Exercise 12

THE MBO CONTRACT

Preparation

Listed below are performance objectives from a management by objectives (MBO) contract for a plant manager.

1. Increase deliveries to 98% of all scheduled delivery dates.
2. Reduce waste and spoilage to 3% of all raw materials used.
3. Reduce lost time due to accidents to 100 workdays per year.
4. Reduce operating costs to 10% below budget.
5. Install a quality-control system at a cost of less than $53 000.
6. Improve production scheduling and increase machine use time to 95% capacity.
7. Complete a management development program this year.
8. Teach a TAFE or polytechnic course in human resource management.

Instructions

1. Study this MBO contract. In the margin write one of the following symbols to identify each objective as an improvement, maintenance or personal development objective.

Improvement objective   = I
Maintenance objective   = M
Personal development objective = P

2. Assume that this MBO contract was actually developed and implemented under the following circumstances. After each statement, write 'yes' if the statement reflects proper MBO procedures and write 'no' if it reflects poor MBO procedures.
   (a) The general manager drafted the eight objectives and submitted them to the plant manager for review. ___
   (b) The general manager and the plant manager thoroughly discussed the eight objectives in proposal form before they were finalised. ___
   (c) The general manager and the plant manager scheduled a meeting in six months time to review progress on the objectives. ___
   (d) The general manager did not discuss the objectives with the plant manager again until the scheduled meeting was held. ___
   (e) The general manager told the plant manager that his or her annual pay rise would depend entirely on the extent to which these objectives were achieved. ___
3. Share and discuss your responses to steps 1 and 2 of the exercise with a nearby classmate. Reconcile any differences of opinion by referring back to the chapter discussion of MBO. Await further class discussion.

Exercise 13

THE FUTURE WORKPLACE

Instructions

Form groups as assigned by the instructor. Brainstorm to develop a master list of the major characteristics you expect to find in the future workplace in the year 2020. Use this list as background for completing the following tasks:

1. Write a one-paragraph description of what the typical 'workplace 2020 manager's' workday will be like.
2. Draw a 'picture' representing what the 'workplace 2020 organisation' will look like.
3. Choose a spokesperson to share your results with the class and explain their implications for the class members.

Exercise 14

DOTS AND SQUARES PUZZLE

Instructions

1. Shown here is a collection of 16 dots. Study the figure to determine how many 'squares' can be created by connecting the dots.
2. Draw as many squares as you can find in the figure while making sure a dot is at every corner of every square. Count the squares and write this number in the margin to the right of the figure.
3. Share your results with those of a classmate sitting nearby. Indicate the location of squares missed by either one of you.
4. Based on this discussion, redraw your figure to show the maximum number of possible squares. Count them and write this number to the left of the figure.
5. Await further class discussion led by your instructor.

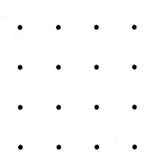

Exercise 15

INTERVIEWING JOB CANDIDATES

Preparation

Make a list of the 'generic' questions you think any potential employer should ask any job candidate, regardless of the specific job or situation. Then, place a tick next to those of the following items you think represent additional important questions to ask.

____ How old are you?
____ Where were you born?
____ Where are you from?
____ What religion are you?
____ Are you married, single or divorced?
____ If not married, do you have a partner?
____ Do you have any dependent children or elderly parents?

Instructions

Form work groups as assigned by your instructor. Share your responses with other group members, and listen to theirs. Develop a group consensus on a list of 'generic' interview questions you think any manager should be prepared to ask of job candidates. Also develop a group consensus on which of the items on the preceding list represent questions that an interviewer should ask. Elect a spokesperson to present the group's results to the class, along with the reasons for selecting these questions.

Exercise 16

USING TEAMS

Instructions

This exercise will help you understand your own attitudes towards the use of teams in organisations. For each statement below, decide which of the following responses best fits you.

Strongly agree   = 4
Somewhat agree   = 3
Somewhat disagree = 2
Strongly disagree   = 1

1. Each individual in a work team should have a clear assignment so that individual accountability can be maintained. _____
2. For a team to function effectively, the team must be given complete authority over all aspects of the task. _____
3. One way to get teams to work is simply to assemble a group of people, tell them in general what needs to be done and let them work out the details. _____

4. Once a team 'gets going', management can turn its attention to other matters. _____

5. To ensure that a team develops into a cohesive working unit, managers should be especially careful not to intervene in any way during the initial start-up period. _____

6. Training is not critical to a team because the team will develop any needed skills on its own. _____

7. It's easy to provide teams with the support they need because they are basically self-motivating. _____

8. Teams need little or no structure to function effectively. _____

9. Teams should set their own direction, with managers determining the means to the selected end. _____

10. Teams can be used in any organisation. _____

Scoring

To obtain your score, total your responses to all statements.

Interpretation

Based on research conducted by J. Richard Hackman and others, all of the statements are false.

1. An emphasis on individual accountability essentially undermines any effort to develop a team.
2. Complete authority is likely to lead to anarchy. Limits should be set.
3. Teams should be kept small, have clear boundaries and have an enabling structure that ensures member motivation.
4. Teams need coaching, counselling and support at certain intervals during their functioning.
5. The start-up period is critical, which is why managers must spend time and energy coaching and counselling the team during this period. Once the team gets going, the manager should pull back until it reaches a natural break or completes a performance cycle.
6. Training is absolutely critical and should be done before the team is assembled or shortly thereafter. If the needed skills and knowledge change, management should be ready to assist in training to help the team quickly learn the new skills and knowledge.
7. Providing support for teams is difficult. A reward system must recognise and reinforce team performance, an educational system must provide needed skills and knowledge, an information system must provide necessary information, and physical and fiscal resources must be available as needed.

8. Teams need some structure to work effectively.
9. The opposite is true. Managers should set the direction and establish wide limits on constraints with the means to the end determined by the team.
10. Teams cannot be used effectively in organisations that have strong individualistic cultures.

Source: © Adapted from J. Richard Hackman (ed.), *Groups That Work (And Those That Don't)* (San Francisco: Jossey-Bass, 1990). This material is used by permission of John Wiley & Sons, Inc.

Exercise 17

COMPENSATION AND BENEFITS DEBATE

Preparation

Consider the following quotations.

On *compensation*: 'A basic rule of thumb should be — pay at least as much, and perhaps a bit more, in base wage or salary than what competitors are offering'.

On *benefits*: 'When benefits are attractive or at least adequate, the organisation is in a better position to employ highly qualified people'.

Instructions

Form groups as assigned by the instructor. Each will be given *either* one of the preceding position statements *or* one of the following alternatives.

On *compensation*: Given the importance of controlling costs, organisations can benefit by paying as little as possible for labour.

On *benefits*: Given the rising cost of healthcare and other benefit programs and the increasing difficulty many organisations have staying in business, it is best to minimise paid benefits and let employees handle more of the cost on their own.

Each group should prepare to debate a counterpoint group on its assigned position. After time is allocated to prepare for the debate, each group will present its opening positions. Each will then be allowed one rebuttal period to respond to the other group. General class discussion on the role of compensation and benefits in the modern organisation will follow.

Exercise 18

SOURCES AND USES OF POWER

Preparation

Consider the way you behaved in each of the situations described below. They may be from a full-time or part-time job, student organisation or class group or sports team. If you do not have an experience of the type described, try to imagine yourself in one; think about how you would expect yourself to behave.

1. You needed to get a peer to do something you wanted that person to do but were worried he or she didn't want to do it.
2. You needed to get a subordinate to do something you wanted her or him to do but were worried the subordinate didn't want to do it.
3. You needed to get your boss to do something you wanted him or her to do but were worried the boss didn't want to do it.

Instructions

Form into groups as assigned by the instructor. Start with situation 1 and have all members of the group share their approaches. Determine what specific sources of power (see chapter 13) were used. Note any patterns in group members' responses. Discuss what is required to be successful in this situation. Do the same for situations 2 and 3. Note any special differences in how situations 1, 2 and 3 should be or could be handled. Choose a spokesperson to share results in general class discussion.

Exercise 19

SHELTERS FOR THE HOMELESS

Instructions

This exercise should take about one hour; it can be done inside or outside of class. Organise the class into teams of about six people. Each team takes on the assignment of formulating plans for building temporary shelters for the homeless. The dwellings you plan to build, for example, might be two-room cottages with electricity and indoor plumbing. During the time allotted to the task, formulate plans for going ahead with shelters for the homeless. Consider dividing up work by assigning certain roles to each team member. Sketch out tentative answers to the following questions:

1. How will you obtain funding for your venture?
2. Which homeless people will you help?
3. Where will your shelters be?
4. Who will do the actual construction?

After your plan is completed, evaluate the quality of the teamwork that took place within the group. Search the chapter for techniques you might have used to improve it.

Source: Carol Dalglish and Andrew DuBrin, *Leadership: An Australasian Focus* (Brisbane: John Wiley & Sons, 2002).

Exercise 20

GENDER DIFFERENCES IN MANAGEMENT

Preparation

The question is: Do women or men make better managers? A research study by the Foundation for Future Leadership examined the management abilities of 645 men and 270 women in terms of supervisor, peer and self-evaluations. Among the management skills studied were those listed below.

Skills	Women higher	Men higher	No difference
Problem solving	____	____	____
Planning	____	____	____
Controlling	____	____	____
Managing self	____	____	____
Managing relationships	____	____	____
Leading	____	____	____
Communicating	____	____	____

Instructions

1. Indicate in the space provided whether you believe women scored higher on the average than men for each skill, men scored higher than women, or no difference in scores was found.
2. Meet in your discussion groups to share results and the rationale for your choices. Try to arrive at a group consensus regarding the likelihood of differences between women and men. Ask questions of one another:
   - What is your experience with men as managers?
   - What is your experience with women as managers?
   - Why exactly do you think women or men would score better on each dimension?
   - Is it useful to try and identify gender differences in management?
   - Why is gender even relevant when it comes to questions about management skills?
3. Be prepared to summarise your results and participate in further class discussion led by the instructor.

Exercise 21

A SELF-PORTRAIT OF COMMUNICATION EFFECTIVENESS

Instructions

The statements below relate to various aspects of communication effectiveness. Indicate whether each of the statements is mostly true or mostly false, even if the most accurate answer would depend somewhat on the situation. Asking another person in your class who is familiar with your communication behaviour to help you answer the questions will enhance the accuracy of your answers.

	True	False
1. When I begin to speak in a group, most people stop talking, turn toward me, and listen.	____	____
2. I receive compliments on the quality of my writing.	____	____
3. The reaction to the outgoing message on my answering machine has been favourable.	____	____
4. I welcome the opportunity to speak in front of a group.	____	____
5. I have published something, including a letter to the editor, an article for the school newspaper, or a comment in a company newsletter.	____	____
6. I have my own web site.	____	____
7. The vast majority of my written projects in school have received a grade of B or A.	____	____
8. People generally laugh when I tell a joke or make what I think is a witty comment.	____	____
9. I stay informed by reading newspapers, watching news on television, or logging on to news information.	____	____
10. I have heard such terms as 'enthusiastic', 'animated', 'colourful' or 'dynamic' applied to me.	____	____
Total:	____	____

Scoring and interpretation

If eight or more of the above statements are true in relation to you, it is most likely that you are an effective communicator. If three or fewer statements are true, you may need substantial improvement in your communication skills. Keep in mind also that scores on the quiz you just took are probably highly correlated with charisma.

Source: Carol Dalglish and Andrew DuBrin, *Leadership: An Australasian Focus* (Brisbane: John Wiley & Sons, 2002).

Exercise 22

THE CASE OF THE CASUAL WORKFORCE

Preparation

Casual work is a rising percentage of total employment in Australia and New Zealand. Go to the library and read about the current use of casual workers in business and industry. Ideally, go to the Internet, enter a government database, and locate some current statistics on the size of the casual labour force, the proportion that is self-employed and part-time, and the proportion of casuals who are voluntary and involuntary.

Instructions

In your assigned work group, pool the available information on the casual workforce. Discuss the information. Discuss one another's viewpoints on the subject as well as its personal and social implications. Be prepared to participate in a classroom 'dialogue session' in which your group will be asked to role-play one of the following positions:

(a) Human resources manager of a large discount retailer hiring casual workers

(b) Owner of a local specialty music shop hiring casual workers

(c) Recent college or university graduate working as a casual employee at the discount retailer in (a)

(d) Single parent with two children in primary school, working as a casual employee of the music shop in (b).

The question to be answered by the (a) and (b) groups is: What does the casual force mean to me? The question to be answered by the (c) and (d) groups is: What does being a casual worker mean to me?

Exercise 23

HOW TO GIVE, AND TAKE, CRITICISM

Preparation

The 'criticism session' may well be the toughest test of a manager's communication skills. Picture Setting 1 — you and an employee meeting to review a problem with the employee's performance. Now picture Setting 2 — you and your boss, meeting to review a problem with *your* performance. Both situations require communication skills in giving and receiving feedback. Even the most experienced person can have difficulty, and the situations can end as futile gripe sessions that cause hard feelings. The question is: How can such 'criticism sessions' be handled in a positive manner that encourages improved performance... and good feelings?

Instructions

Form into groups as assigned by the instructor. Focus on either Setting 1 or Setting 2, or both, as also assigned by

the instructor. First, answer the question from the perspective assigned. Second, develop a series of action guidelines that could best be used to handle situations of this type. Third, prepare and present a mini-management training session to demonstrate the unsuccessful and successful use of these guidelines.

If time permits, outside of class prepare a more extensive management training session that includes a videotape demonstration of your assigned criticism setting being handled first poorly and then very well. Support the videotape with additional written handouts and an oral presentation to help your classmates better understand the communication skills needed to successfully give and take criticism in work settings.

Exercise 24

CREATIVE SOLUTIONS

Instructions

Complete these two tasks while working alone. Be prepared to present and explain your responses in class.

1. Without lifting your pencil from the paper, draw no more than four straight lines that cross through all of the following dots.

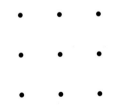

2. Turn the following into words.
    (a) _____program
    (b) r\e\a\d\i\n\g
    (c) ECNALG
    (d)   j
             u
          yousme
             t
    (e)   stand
             i

Optional instructions

After working alone, share your responses with a nearby classmate or with a group. See if you can develop different and/or better solutions based on this exchange of ideas.

Source: Adapted from Russell L. Ackoff, *The Art of Problem Solving* (New York: Wiley, 1978). This material is used by permission of John Wiley & Sons, Inc.

Exercise 25

FORCE-FIELD ANALYSIS

Instructions

1. Form into your class discussion groups.
2. Review the concept of force-field analysis — the consideration of forces driving in support of a planned change and forces resisting the change.

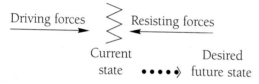

3. Use this force-field analysis worksheet in the assignment:

   List of driving forces (those supporting the change)
   -
   -
   - ... list as many as you can think of

List of resisting forces (those working against the change)
-
-
- ... list as many as you can think of

4. Apply force-field analysis and make your lists of driving and resisting forces for one of the following situations:
   (a) Due to rapid advances in web-based computer technologies, the possibility exists that the course you are presently taking could be in part offered on line. This would mean a reduction in the number of required class sessions, but an increase in students' responsibility for completing learning activities and assignments through computer mediation.
   (b) A new owner has just taken over a small walk-in-and-buy-by-the-slice pizza shop near a university. There are presently eight employees, three of whom are full-time and five of whom are part-time. The shop is presently open 7 days a week from 10.30 a.m. to 10.30 p.m. each day. The new owner believes there is a market niche available for late-night pizza and would like to stay open each night until 2 a.m.
   (c) A situation assigned by the instructor.
5. Choose the three driving forces that are most significant to the proposed change. For each force develop ideas on how it could be further increased or mobilised in support of the change.
6. Choose the three resisting forces that are most significant to the proposed change. For each force develop ideas on how it could be reduced or turned into a driving force.
7. Be prepared to participate in class discussion led by the instructor.

Management skills assessments

Assessment 1

SKILLS OF EFFECTIVE MANAGERS

Instructions

Indicate the extent to which the following statements describe you. Circle the number that best represents your self-evaluation.

Very much like me = VM
Somewhat like me   = SW
Occasionally like me = O
Seldom like me   = S
Nothing like me   = N

	VM	SW	O	S	N
1. I am at ease in written and oral communication, including listening.	1	2	3	4	5
2. I handle stress well and seldom have time management problems.	1	2	3	4	5
3. I have no trouble making decisions that affect me and/or others.	1	2	3	4	5
4. I can identify, analyse and solve problems effectively.	1	2	3	4	5
5. I am effective at getting others to perform at high levels.	1	2	3	4	5
6. I delegate tasks to others to help them learn more and to involve them in the activity at hand.	1	2	3	4	5
7. I set goals and establish a long-term vision for everything I do, and can help others do the same.	1	2	3	4	5

	VM	SW	O	S	N
8. I am keenly aware of my own strengths and weaknesses.	1	2	3	4	5
9. I work well with groups and can help others develop into effective teams.	1	2	3	4	5
10. I handle conflict well and am able to help others resolve their differences.	1	2	3	4	5

Scoring

Sum the numbers you have circled.

Interpretation

The lower the total, the more you believe that you have the skills characteristic of effective managers. Next, examine each response. Any response of 3 or 4 suggests skills that you need to develop. You should focus your outside-of-lecture assignments and time in such a way as to improve your skills in those areas.

Source: Based on table 1, 'The most frequently cited skills of effective managers', from David A. Whetton and Kim S. Cameron, *Developing Management Skills*, 2nd edn (New York: HarperCollins, 1991). © Reprinted by permission of Pearson Education, Inc., Upper Saddle River, NJ.

Assessment 2

CROSS-CULTURAL SKILLS AND ATTITUDES

Instructions

Listed below are various skills and attitudes that various employers and cross-cultural experts think are important for relating effectively to coworkers in a culturally diverse environment. Indicate whether or not each statement applies to you.

	Applies to me now	Not there yet
1. I have spent some time in another country.	_____	_____
2. At least one of my friends is deaf, blind or uses a wheelchair.	_____	_____
3. Currency from other countries is as real as the currency from my own country.	_____	_____
4. I can read in a language other than my own.	_____	_____
5. I can speak in a language other than my own.	_____	_____
6. I can write in a language other than my own.	_____	_____
7. I can understand people speaking in a langauge other than my own.	_____	_____
8. I use my second langauge regularly.	_____	_____
9. My friends include people of races different than my own.	_____	_____
10. My friends include people of different ages.	_____	_____
11. I feel (or would feel) comfortable having a friend with a sexual orientation different from mine.	_____	_____
12. My attitude is that although another culture may be very different from mine, that culture is equally good.	_____	_____
13. I would be willing to (or already do) hang art from different countries in my home.	_____	_____
14. I would accept (or have already accepted) a work assignment of more than several months in another country.	_____	_____
15. I have a passport.	_____	_____

Scoring and interpretation

If you answered 'Applies to me now' to ten or more of the above questions, you most likely function well in a multicultural work environment. If you answered 'Not there yet' to ten or more of the above questions, you need to develop more cross-cultural awareness and skills to work effectively in a multicultural work environment. You will notice that being bilingual gives you at least five points on this quiz.

Source: Developed from Andrew DuBrin, *Leadership*, 3rd edn, pp. 348–9. Copyright © Houghton Mifflin Company. Reprinted with permission. Several ideas for statements on this quiz are derived from Ruthann Dirks and Janet Buzzard, 'What CEOs Expect of Employees Hired for International Work', *Business Education Forum*, April 1997, pp. 3–7; Gunnar Beeth, 'Multicultural Managers Wanted', *Management Review*, May 1997, pp. 17–21.

Assessment 3

DECISION-MAKING BIASES

Instructions

How good are you at avoiding potential decision-making biases? Test yourself by answering the following questions:
1. Which is riskier?
   (a) Driving a car on a 1000 km trip
   (b) Flying on a 1000 km commercial airline flight
2. Are there more words in the English language:
   (a) that begin with 'r'?
   (b) that have 'r' as the third letter?
3. Mark is finishing his MBA at a prestigious university. He is very interested in the arts and at one time considered a career as a musician. Is Mark more likely to take a job:
   (a) in the management of the arts?
   (b) with a management consulting firm?
4. You are about to hire a new central-region sales director for the fifth time this year. You predict that the next director should work out reasonably well since the last four were poor performers and the odds favour hiring at least one good sales director in five tries. Is this thinking:
   (a) correct?
   (b) incorrect?
5. A newly hired engineer for a computer company in Auckland has four years experience and good all-round qualifications. When asked to estimate the starting salary for this employee, a chemist with very little knowledge about the profession or industry guessed an annual salary of $35 000. What is your estimate?
   $_____ per year

Scoring

Your instructor will provide answers and explanations for the assessment questions.

Interpretation

Each of the preceding questions examines your tendency to use a different judgemental heuristic. In his book *Judgment in Managerial Decision Making*, 3rd edn (New York: Wiley, 1994), pp. 6–7, Max Bazerman calls these heuristics 'simplifying strategies, or rules of thumb' used in making decisions. He states: 'In general, heuristics are helpful, but their use can sometimes lead to severe errors ... If we can make managers aware of the potential adverse impacts of using heuristics, they can then decide when and where to use them.' This assessment offers an initial insight into your use of such heuristics. An informed decision maker understands the heuristics, is able to recognise when they appear, and eliminates any that may inappropriately bias decision making.

Test yourself further. Before hearing from your instructor, go back and write next to each item the name of the judgemental heuristic (see chapter 3 text discussion) that you think applies.

Then write down a situation that you have experienced in which some decision-making bias may have occurred. Be prepared to share and discuss this incident with the class.

Source: Adapted from Max H. Bazerman, *Judgment in Managerial Decision Making*, 3rd edn (New York: Wiley, 1994), pp. 13–14. This material is used by permission of John Wiley & Sons, Inc.

Assessment 4

A 21ST-CENTURY MANAGER

Instructions

Rate yourself on the following personal characteristics. Use this scale.

Strong, I am very confident with this one = S
Good, but I still have room to grow = G
Weak, I really need work on this one = W
Unsure, I just don't know = U

1. *Resistance to stress* — the ability to get work done even under stressful conditions
2. *Tolerance for uncertainty* — the ability to get work done even under ambiguous and uncertain conditions
3. *Social objectivity* — the ability to act free of racial, ethnic, gender and other prejudices or biases

4. *Inner work standards* — the ability to personally set and work to high performance standards
5. *Stamina* — the ability to sustain long work hours
6. *Adaptability* — the ability to be flexible and adapt to changes
7. *Self-confidence* — the ability to be consistently decisive and display one's personal presence
8. *Self-objectivity* — the ability to evaluate personal strengths and weaknesses and to understand one's motives and skills relative to a job
9. *Introspection* — the ability to learn from experience, awareness and self-study
10. *Entrepreneurism* — the ability to tackle problems and take advantage of opportunities for constructive change

Scoring

Give yourself one point for each S, and half a point for each G. Do not give yourself points for W and U responses. Total your points and enter the result here as PMF = ____.

Interpretation

This assessment offers a self-described *profile of your management foundations (PMF)*. Are you a perfect 10, or is your PMF score something less than that? There shouldn't be too many 10s around. Ask someone who knows you to assess you on this instrument. You may be surprised at the differences between your PMF score as you described it and your PMF score as described by someone else. Most of us, realistically speaking, must work hard to grow and develop continually in these and related management foundations. This list is a good starting point as you consider where and how to further pursue the development of your managerial skills and competencies. The items on the list are recommended by the American Assembly of Collegiate Schools of Business (AACSB) as the skills and personal characteristics that should be nurtured in college and university students of business administration. Their success — and yours — as 21st-century managers may well rest on an initial awareness of the importance of these basic management foundations and a willingness to strive continually to strengthen them throughout the work career.

Source: Outcome Measurement Project, Phase I and Phase II Reports (St. Louis: © AACSB International — The Association to Advance Collegiate Schools of Business, 1986 and 1987).

Assessment 5

GLOBAL AWARENESS

Instructions

This assessment helps you assess your comprehension of strategic management and your readiness to perform as a strategic manager. For each statement below, decide which of the following responses best fits you.

Strongly agree   = 4
Somewhat agree   = 3
Somewhat disagree = 2
Strongly disagree   = 1

1. Some areas of Malaysia are very much like Indonesia.
2. Although aspects of behaviour such as motivation and attitudes within organisational settings remain diverse across cultures, organisations themselves appear to be increasingly similar in terms of design and technology.
3. Spain, France, Japan, Singapore, Mexico, Brazil and Indonesia have cultures with a strong orientation towards authority.
4. Japan and Austria define male–female roles more rigidly and value qualities like forcefulness and achievement more than Norway, Sweden, Denmark and Finland.
5. Some areas of Malaysia are very much like Brunei.
6. Australia, Great Britain, the Netherlands, Canada and New Zealand have cultures that view people first as individuals and place a priority on their own interests and values; whereas Colombia, Pakistan, Taiwan, Peru, Singapore, Mexico, Greece and Hong Kong have cultures in which the good of the group or society is considered the priority.
7. The USA, Israel, Austria, Denmark, Ireland, Norway, Germany and New Zealand have cultures with a low orientation towards authority.
8. The same manager may behave differently in different cultural settings.
9. Denmark, Canada, Norway, Singapore, Hong Kong and Australia have cultures in which employees tolerate a high degree of uncertainty, but such levels of uncertainty are not well tolerated in Israel, Austria, Japan, Italy, Argentina, Peru, France and Belgium.
10. Some areas of Malaysia are very much like the Philippines.

Scoring

To obtain your score, sum the results for all statements.

Interpretation

All of the statements are true, so your score should be close to 40. The closer your score is to 40, the more you understand the global context of organisational environments. The closer your score is to 10, the less you understand the global context. For developmental purposes, you should note items for which you scored 1 or 2 and concentrate on improving your knowledge in those areas.

Source: Paul Davidson and Ricky W. Griffin, *Management: An Australasian Perspective,* 2nd edn (Brisbane: John Wiley & Sons, 2002), p. 205.

Assessment 6

THE ETHICAL REASONING INVENTORY

Instructions

Describe how well you agree with each of the following statements. Use the following scale:

Disagree strongly = DS
Disagree   = D
Neutral   = N
Agree   = A
Agree strongly   = AS

	DS	D	N	A	AS
1. When applying for a job, I would cover up the fact that I had been fired from my most recent job.	5	4	3	2	1

	DS	D	N	A	AS

2. Cheating just a few dollars in one's favour on an expense account is okay if a person needs the money. 5 4 3 2 1

3. Employees should inform on each other for wrongdoing. 1 2 3 4 5

4. It is acceptable to give approximate figures for expense account items when one does not have all the receipts. 5 4 3 2 1

5. I see no problem with conducting a little personal business on company time. 5 4 3 2 1

6. Just to make a sale, I would stretch the truth about a delivery date. 5 4 3 2 1

7. I would fix up a purchasing agent with a date just to close a sale. 5 4 3 2 1

8. I would flirt with my boss just to get a bigger salary increase. 5 4 3 2 1

9. If I received $300 for doing some odd jobs, I would report it on my income tax return. 1 2 3 4 5

10. I see no harm in taking home a few office supplies. 5 4 3 2 1

11. It is acceptable to read the e-mail messages and faxes of other workers, even when not invited to do so. 5 4 3 2 1

12. It is unacceptable to call in sick in order to take a day off, even if only done once or twice a year. 1 2 3 4 5

13. I would accept a permanent, full-time job even if I knew I wanted the job for only six months. 5 4 3 2 1

14. I would first check company policy before accepting an expensive gift from a supplier. 1 2 3 4 5

	DS	D	N	A	AS

15. To be successful in business, a person usually has to ignore ethics. 5 4 3 2 1

16. If I felt physically attracted toward a job candidate, I would hire that person over a more qualified candidate. 5 4 3 2 1

17. On the job, I tell the truth all the time. 1 2 3 4 5

18. If a student is very pressed for time, it would be acceptable either to have a friend write the paper or purchase one. 5 4 3 2 1

19. I would authorise accepting an office machine on a thirty-day trial period, even if I knew we had no intention of buying it. 5 4 3 2 1

20. I would never accept credit for a coworker's ideas. 1 2 3 4 5

Scoring

Add the numbers you have circled to obtain your total score.

Interpretation

90–100 You are a strongly ethical person who may take a little ribbing from coworkers for being too strait-laced.

60–89 You show an average degree of ethical awareness, and therefore should become more sensitive to ethical issues.

40–59 Your ethics are underdeveloped, but you at least have some awareness of ethical issues. You need to raise your level of awareness about ethical issues.

20–39 Your ethical values are far below contemporary standards in business. Begin a serious study of business ethics.

Source: Developed from Andrew DuBrin, *Leadership*, 3rd edn, pp. 219–20. Copyright © Houghton Mifflin Company. Reprinted with permission.

Assessment 7

TIME MANAGEMENT PROFILE

Instructions

Complete the following questionnaire by indicating 'Y' (yes) or 'N' (no) for each item. Force yourself to respond yes or no. Be frank and allow your responses to create an accurate picture of how you tend to respond to these kinds of situations.

1. When confronted with several items of similar urgency and importance, I tend to do the easiest one first. _____

2. I do the most important things during that part of the day when I know I perform best. _____

3. Most of the time I don't do things someone else can do — I delegate this type of work to others. _____

4. Even though meetings without a clear and useful purpose upset me, I put up with them. _____

5. I skim documents before reading them and don't complete any that offer a low return on my time investment. _____

6. I don't worry much if I don't accomplish at least one significant task each day. _____

7. I save the most trivial tasks for that time of day when my creative energy is lowest. _____

8. My workspace is neat and organised. _____

9. My office door is always 'open' — I never work in complete privacy. _____

10. I schedule my time completely from start to finish every workday. _____

11. I don't like 'to do' lists, preferring to respond to daily events as they occur. _____

12. I 'block' a certain amount of time each day or week that is dedicated to high-priority activities. _____

Scoring

Count the number of 'Y' responses to items 2, 3, 5, 7, 8 and 12. Enter that score here ____. Count the number of 'N' responses to items 1, 4, 6, 9, 10 and 11. Enter that score here ____. Add together the two scores.

Interpretation

The higher the total score, the closer your behaviour matches recommended time management guidelines. Reread those items where your response did not match the desired one. Why don't they match? Do you have reasons why your behaviour in this instance should be different from the recommended time management guideline? Think about what you can do (and how easily it can be done) to adjust your behaviour to be more consistent with these guidelines.

Source: Suggested by a discussion in © Robert E. Quinn, Sue R. Faerman, Michael P. Thompson and Michael R. McGrath, *Becoming a Master Manager: A Competency Framework* (New York: Wiley, 1990), pp. 75–6. This material is used by permission of John Wiley & Sons, Inc.

Assessment 8

ARE YOU A STRATEGIC MANAGER?

Instructions

This assessment helps you assess your comprehension of strategic management and your readiness to perform as a strategic manager. For each statement below, decide which of the following responses best fits you.

Strongly agree = 4
Somewhat agree = 3
Somewhat disagree = 2
Strongly disagree = 1

Strategic managers:
1. tend to be well informed about the wide range of decisions being made in the organisation _____
2. frequently push programs in a piecemeal fashion _____
3. are good personal time managers _____
4. are not personally involved in all decisions _____

5. prefer to build consensus for ideas rather than use their authority to get things done _____

6. are skilful organisational politicians _____

7. know when to delegate and to whom to delegate _____

8. are considered expert at being imprecise _____

9. seem to convey a sense of direction without actually committing themselves publicly to precise objectives _____

10. develop sources of information aside from the formal channels to find out what is going on in the organisation _____

Scoring

To obtain your score, total the results for all statements.

Interpretation

All of the statements are true, so your score should be close to 40. The closer your score is to 40, the more you understand strategic management and the closer you are to performing effectively as a strategic manager. The closer your score is to 10, the less you understand strategic management and the less ready you are to perform as a strategic manager. For developmental purposes, you should note items for which you scored 1 or 2 and concentrate on improving your knowledge in those areas.

Source: Paul Davidson and Ricky W. Griffin, *Management: An Australasian Perspective*, 2nd edn (Brisbane: John Wiley & Sons, 2002), p. 272.

Assessment 9

AN ENTREPRENEURIAL QUIZ

Instructions

Place a tick in the box next to the response that best represents your self-evaluation.

1. Are you a self-starter?
   - ☑ I do things on my own. Nobody has to tell me to get going.
   - ☐ If someone gets me started, I keep going all right.
   - ☐ I take things easy. I don't push myself until I have to.

2. How do you feel about other people?
   - ☑ I like people. I can get along with just about anybody.
   - ☐ I have plenty of friends — I don't need anybody else.
   - ☐ Most people irritate me.

3. Can you lead others?
   - ☑ I can get most people to go along with me when I start something.
   - ☐ I can give the orders if someone tells me what we should do.
   - ☐ I let someone else get things moving. Then I go along if I feel like it.

4. Can you take responsibility?
   - ☐ I like to take charge of things and see them through.
   - ☑ I'll take over if I have to, but I'd rather let someone else be responsible.
   - ☐ There are always eager beavers around wanting to show how smart they are. I let them.

5. How good an organiser are you?
   - ☐ I like to have a plan before I start. I'm usually the one to get things lined up when the group wants to do something.
   - ☑ I do all right unless things get too confused. Then I quit.
   - ☐ You can get everything organised and then something comes along and presents too many problems, so I just take things as they come.

6. How good a worker are you?
   - ☑ I can keep going as long as I need to. I don't mind working hard for something I want.
   - ☐ I'll work hard for a while, but when I've had enough, that's it.
   - ☐ I can't see that hard work gets you anywhere.

7. Can you make decisions?
   - ☑ I can make up my mind in a hurry if I have to. It usually turns out okay, too.
   - ☐ I can if I have plenty of time. If I have to make up my mind fast, I change my mind later.
   - ☐ I don't like to be the one who has to decide things.

8. Can people trust what you say?
   - ☑ Yes, I don't say things I don't mean.
   - ☐ I try to be honest most of the time, but sometimes I just say what's easiest.
   - ☐ Why bother if the other person doesn't know the difference?

9. Can you stick with what you decide to do?
- ☑ If I make up my mind to do something, I don't let anything stop me.
- ☐ I usually finish what I start — if it goes well.
- ☐ If it doesn't go well right away, I quit. Why beat your brains out?

10. How good is your health?
- ☐ I *never* run down!
- ☑ I have enough energy for most things I want to do.
- ☐ I run out of energy sooner than most of my friends.

Scoring

You will note that the response boxes for each question have been arranged in three columns. Total the number of ticks in each column in the three boxes below.

☐   ☐   ☐

Interpretation

If most of your marks are in the first column, you probably have what it takes to run a business. If not, you are likely to have more trouble than you can handle by yourself. You should look for a partner who is strong on the points on which you are weak. If most marks are in the third column, not even a good partner will be able to shore you up. Now go back and answer the first question on the quiz.

Source: © Donald Dible, *Business Start-up Basics* (Upper Saddle River, NJ: Prentice Hall, 1978), pp. 9–10.

Assessment 10

MANAGERIAL ASSUMPTIONS

Instructions

Read the following statements. Use the space to the right to write 'Yes' if you agree with the statement, or 'No' if you disagree with it. Force yourself to take a 'yes' or 'no' position. Do this for every statement.

1. Are good pay and a secure job enough to satisfy most workers? _____

2. Should a manager help and coach employees in their work? _____

3. Do most people like real responsibility in their jobs? _____

4. Are most people afraid to learn new things in their jobs? _____

5. Should managers let staff control the quality of their own work? _____

6. Do most people dislike work? _____

7. Are most people creative? _____

8. Should a manager closely supervise and direct the work of subordinates? _____

9. Do most people tend to resist change? _____

10. Do most people work only as hard as they have to? _____

11. Should workers be allowed to set their own job goals? _____

12. Are most people happiest off the job? _____

13. Do most workers really care about the organisation they work for? _____

14. Should a manager help staff members advance and grow in their jobs? _____

Scoring

Count the number of 'yes' responses to items 1, 4, 6, 8, 9, 10 and 12. Write that number here as X = ____. Count the number of 'yes' responses to items 2, 3, 5, 7, 11, 13 and 14. Write that score here as Y = ____.

Interpretation

This assessment sheds insight into your orientation toward Douglas McGregor's Theory X (your 'X' score) and Theory Y (your 'Y' score) assumptions. You should review the discussion of McGregor's thinking in chapter 4 and consider further the ways in which you are likely to behave toward other people at work. Think, in particular, about the types of 'self-fulfilling prophecies' you are likely to create.

Assessment 11

ORGANISATIONAL DESIGN PREFERENCES

Instructions

To the right of each item, write the number from the following scale that shows the extent to which the statement accurately describes your views.

Strongly agree   = 5
Agree somewhat   = 4
Undecided   = 3
Disagree somewhat = 2
Strongly disagree   = 1

I prefer to work in an organisation where:

1. goals are defined by those in higher levels   _____
2. work methods and procedures are specified   _____
3. senior management makes important decisions   _____
4. my loyalty counts as much as my ability to do the job   _____
5. clear lines of authority and responsibility are established   _____
6. senior management is decisive and firm   _____
7. my career is pretty well planned out for me   _____
8. I can specialise   _____
9. my length of service is almost as important as my level of performance   _____
10. management is able to provide the information I need to do my job well   _____
11. a chain of command is well established   _____
12. rules and procedures are adhered to equally by everyone   _____
13. people accept the authority of a leader's position   _____
14. people are loyal to their boss   _____
15. people do as they have been instructed   _____
16. people clear things with their boss before going over his or her head   _____

Scoring

Total your scores for all statements.

Interpretation

This assessment measures your preference for working in an organisation designed along 'organic' or 'mechanistic' lines (see chapter 11). The higher your score (above 64), the more comfortable you are with a mechanistic design; the lower your score (below 48), the more comfortable you are with an organic design. Scores between 48 and 64 can go either way. This organisational design preference represents an important issue in the new workplace. Indications are that today's organisations are taking on more and more organic characteristics. Presumably, those of us who work in them will need to be comfortable with such designs.

Source: © Organisational Preference Inventory. John F. Veiga and John N. Yanouzas, *The Dynamics of Organization Theory: Gaining a Macro Perspective*, 1st edn (St. Paul, MN: West, 1979), pp. 158–60. Used by permission.

Assessment 12

PERFORMANCE APPRAISAL ASSUMPTIONS

Instructions

In each of the following pairs of statements, circle the statement that best reflects your assumptions about performance evaluation.

Performance evaluation is:

1. (a) a formal process that is done annually
   (b) an informal process done continuously

2. (a) a process that is planned for employees
   (b) a process that is planned with employees

3. (a) a required organisational procedure
   (b) a process done regardless of requirements

4. (a) a time to evaluate employees' performance
   (b) a time for employees to evaluate their manager

5. (a) a time to clarify standards
   (b) a time to clarify the employees' career needs

6. (a) a time to confront poor performance
   (b) a time to express appreciation

7. (a) an opportunity to clarify issues and provide direction and control
   (b) an opportunity to increase enthusiasm and commitment

8. (a) only as good as the organisation's forms
   (b) only as good as the manager's coaching skills

Scoring

There is no formal scoring for this assessment, but there may be a pattern to your responses. Check them again.

Interpretation

In general, the 'a' responses represent a more traditional approach to performance appraisal that emphasises its *evaluation* function. This role largely puts the supervisor in the role of documenting an employee's performance for control and administrative purposes. The 'b' responses represent a more progressive approach that includes a strong emphasis on the *counselling* or *development* role. Here, the supervisor is concerned with helping the employee do better and with learning from the employee what he or she needs to be able to do better. There is more of an element of reciprocity in this role. It is quite consistent with new directions and values emerging in today's organisations.

Source: Developed in part from © Robert E. Quinn, Sue R. Faerman, Michael P. Thompson and Michael R. McGrath, *Becoming a Master Manager: A Competency Framework* (New York: Wiley, 1990), p. 187. This material is used by permission of John Wiley & Sons, Inc.

Assessment 13

LEAST-PREFERRED COWORKER SCALE

Instructions

Think of all the different people with whom you have ever worked — in jobs, in social clubs or in student projects. Next think of the *one person* with whom you could work *least* well — that is, the person with whom you had the most difficulty getting a job done. This is the one person — a peer, boss or subordinate — with whom you would least want to work.

Describe this person by circling numbers at the appropriate points on each of the following pairs of bipolar adjectives. Work rapidly. There are no right or wrong answers.

Pleasant	8 7 6 5 4 3 2 1	Unpleasant
Friendly	8 7 6 5 4 3 2 1	Unfriendly
Rejecting	1 2 3 4 5 6 7 8	Accepting
Tense	1 2 3 4 5 6 7 8	Relaxed
Distant	1 2 3 4 5 6 7 8	Close
Cold	1 2 3 4 5 6 7 8	Warm
Supportive	8 7 6 5 4 3 2 1	Hostile
Boring	1 2 3 4 5 6 7 8	Interesting
Quarrelsome	1 2 3 4 5 6 7 8	Harmonious
Gloomy	1 2 3 4 5 6 7 8	Cheerful
Open	8 7 6 5 4 3 2 1	Guarded
Backbiting	1 2 3 4 5 6 7 8	Loyal
Untrustworthy	1 2 3 4 5 6 7 8	Trustworthy
Considerate	8 7 6 5 4 3 2 1	Inconsiderate
Nasty	1 2 3 4 5 6 7 8	Nice
Agreeable	8 7 6 5 4 3 2 1	Disagreeable
Insincere	1 2 3 4 5 6 7 8	Sincere
Kind	8 7 6 5 4 3 2 1	Unkind

Scoring

This is called the 'least-preferred coworker scale' (LPC). Compute your LPC score by totalling all the numbers you circled. Enter that score here as LPC = ____.

Interpretation

The LPC scale is used by Fred Fiedler to identify a person's dominant leadership style (see chapter 13). Fiedler believes that this style is a relatively fixed part of one's personality and is therefore difficult to change. This leads Fiedler to his contingency views, which suggest that the key to leadership success is finding (or creating) good 'matches' between style and situation. If your score is 73 or above, Fiedler considers you a 'relationship-motivated' leader. If your score is 64 and below, he considers you a 'task-motivated' leader. If your score is between 65 and 72, Fiedler leaves it up to you to determine which leadership style is most like yours.

Source: Fred E. Fiedler and Martin M. Chemers, *Improving Leadership Effectiveness: The Leader Match Concept*, 2nd edn (New York: Wiley, 1984). Used by permission.

Assessment 14

TWO-FACTOR PROFILE

Instructions

On each of the following dimensions, distribute a total of ten points between the two options. For example:

Summer weather (_7_) . . . . (_3_) Winter weather

1. Very responsible job (_ _) . . . . (_ _) Job security

2. Recognition for work accomplishments (_ _) . . . . (_ _) Good relations with coworkers

3. Advancement opportunities at work (_ _) . . . . (_ _) A boss who knows his or her job well

4. Opportunities to grow and learn on the job (_ _) . . . . (_ _) Good working conditions

5. A job that I can do well (_ _) . . . . (_ _) Supportive rules, policies of employer

6. A prestigious or high-status job (_ _) . . . . (_ _) A high base wage or salary

Scoring

Summarise your total scores for all items in the *left-hand column* and write it here: MF = ____.
Summarise your total scores for all items in the *right-hand column* and write it here: HF = ____.

Interpretation

The MF score indicates the relative importance that you place on motivating or satisfier factors in Herzberg's two-factor theory. This shows how important job content is to you. The HF score indicates the relative importance that you place on hygiene or dissatisfier factors in Herzberg's two-factor theory. This shows how important job context is to you.

Assessment 15
JOB DESIGN PREFERENCE

Instructions

People differ in what they like and dislike about their jobs. Listed below are 12 pairs of jobs. For each pair, indicate which job you would prefer. Assume that everything else about the jobs is the same — pay attention only to the characteristics actually listed for each pair of jobs. If you would prefer the job in Column A, indicate how much you prefer it by putting a tick in a blank to the left of the Neutral point. If you prefer the job in Column B, check one of the blanks to the right of Neutral. Check the Neutral blank only if you find the two jobs equally attractive or unattractive. Try to use the Neutral blank sparingly.

Column A		Column B
1. A job that offers little or no challenge.	Strongly prefer A — Neutral — Strongly prefer B	A job that requires you to be completely isolated from coworkers.
2. A job that pays well.	Strongly prefer A — Neutral — Strongly prefer B	A job that allows considerable opportunity to be creative and innovative.
3. A job that often requires you to make important decisions.	Strongly prefer A — Neutral — Strongly prefer B	A job in which there are many pleasant people to work with.
4. A job with little security in a somewhat unstable organisation.	Strongly prefer A — Neutral — Strongly prefer B	A job in which you have little or no opportunity to participate in decisions that affect your work.
5. A job in which greater responsibility is given to those who do the best work.	Strongly prefer A — Neutral — Strongly prefer B	A job in which greater responsibility is given to loyal employees who have the most seniority.
6. A job with a supervisor who sometimes is highly critical.	Strongly prefer A — Neutral — Strongly prefer B	A job that does not require you to use much of your talent.
7. A very routine job.	Strongly prefer A — Neutral — Strongly prefer B	A job in which your coworkers are not very friendly.
8. A job with a supervisor who respects you and treats you fairly.	Strongly prefer A — Neutral — Strongly prefer B	A job that provides constant opportunities for you to learn new and interesting things.
9. A job that gives you a real chance to develop yourself personally.	Strongly prefer A — Neutral — Strongly prefer B	A job with excellent vacation and fringe benefits.
10. A job in which there is a real chance you could be laid off.	Strongly prefer A — Neutral — Strongly prefer B	A job that offers very little chance to do challenging work.
11. A job that gives you little freedom and independence to do your work in the way you think best.	Strongly prefer A — Neutral — Strongly prefer B	A job with poor working conditions.
12. A job with very satisfying teamwork.	Strongly prefer A — Neutral — Strongly prefer B	A job that allows you to use your skills and abilities to the fullest extent.

Interpretation

People differ in their need for psychological growth at work. This instrument measures the degree to which you seek growth-need satisfaction. Score your responses as follows:

For items 1, 2, 7, 8, 11 and 12 give yourself the following points for each item:

1	2	3	4	5	6	7
Strongly prefer A			Neutral			Strongly prefer B

For items 3, 4, 5, 6, 9 and 10 give yourself the following points for each item.

7	6	5	4	3	2	1
Strongly prefer A			Neutral			Strongly prefer B

Add up all of your scores and divide by 12 to find the average. If you score above 4.0 your desire for growth-need satisfaction through work tends to be high and you are likely to prefer an enriched job. If you score below 4.0 your desire for growth-need satisfaction through work tends to be low and you are likely to not be satisfied or motivated with an enriched job.

Source: Reprinted by permission from © J. R. Hackman and G. R. Oldham, *The Job Diagnostic Survey: An Instrument for the Diagnosis of Jobs and the Evaluation of Job Redesign Projects, Technical Report 4* (New Haven, CT: Yale University, Department of Administrative Sciences, 1974).

Assessment 16

TEAM LEADER SKILLS

Instructions

Consider your experience in groups and work teams, and ask yourself: 'What skills do I bring to team leadership situations?' Then, complete the following inventory by rating yourself on each item using this scale:

Almost never = 1
Seldom = 2
Sometimes = 3
Usually = 4
Almost always = 5

1. I facilitate communications with and among team members between team meetings. 1 2 3 4 5

2. I provide feedback/coaching to individual team members on their performance. 1 2 3 4 5

3. I encourage creative and 'out-of-the-box' thinking. 1 2 3 4 5

4. I continue to clarify stakeholder needs/expectations. 1 2 3 4 5

5. I keep team members' responsibilities and activities focused within the team's objectives and goals. 1 2 3 4 5

6. I organise and run effective and productive team meetings. 1 2 3 4 5

7. I demonstrate integrity and personal commitment. 1 2 3 4 5

8. I have excellent persuasive and influence skills. 1 2 3 4 5

9. I respect and leverage the team's cross-functional diversity. 1 2 3 4 5

10. I recognise and reward individual contributions to team performance. 1 2 3 4 5

11. I use the appropriate decision-making style for specific issues. 1 2 3 4 5

12. I facilitate and encourage border management with the team's key stakeholders. 1 2 3 4 5

13. I ensure that the team meets its team commitments. 1 2 3 4 5

14. I bring team issues and problems to the team's attention and focus on constructive problem solving. 1 2 3 4 5

15. I provide a clear vision and direction for the team. 1 2 3 4 5

Scoring

The inventory measures seven dimensions of team leadership. Add your scores for the items listed next to each dimension below to get an indication of your potential strengths and weaknesses.

1, 9	Building the team
2, 10	Developing people
3, 11	Team problem solving/decision making
4, 12	Stakeholder relations
5, 13	Team performance
6, 14	Team process
7, 8, 15	Providing personal leadership

Interpretation

The higher the score, the more confident you are on the particular skill and leadership capability. When considering the score, ask yourself if others would rate you the same way. Consider giving this inventory to people who have worked with you in teams and have them rate you. Compare the results to your self-assessment. Also, remember that it is doubtful that any one team leader is capable of exhibiting all the skills listed above. More and more, organisations are emphasising 'top management teams' that blend a variety of skills, rather than depending on the vision of the single, heroic leader figure. As long as the necessary leadership skills are represented within the membership it is more likely that the team will be healthy and achieve high performance. Of course, the more skills you bring with you to team leadership situations the better.

Source: Developed from © Lynda McDermott, Nolan Brawley and William Waite, *World-Class Teams: Working Across Borders* (New York: Wiley, 1998). This material is used by permission of John Wiley & Sons, Inc.

Assessment 17

COMMUNICATION SKILLS

Instructions

Analyse the communication in two of your relationships — one that is very painful and one that is very pleasant. Next, analyse how your communication behaviour varies in the two relationships and what areas of communication

you might need to work on. Answer the questions by using the following scale:

| Minimal problem | 1 | 2 | 3 | 4 | 5 | 6 | 7 | Great problem |

	Painful		Pleasant	
	Other	Self	Other	Self
1. Expresses ideas in unclear ways	——	——	——	——
2. Tries to dominate conversations	——	——	——	——
3. Often has a hidden agenda	——	——	——	——
4. Is formal and impersonal	——	——	——	——
5. Does not listen well	——	——	——	——
6. Is often boring, uninteresting	——	——	——	——
7. Is withdrawn and uncommunicative	——	——	——	——
8. Is overly sensitive, too easily hurt	——	——	——	——
9. Is too abstract and hard to follow	——	——	——	——
10. Is closed to the ideas of the other	——	——	——	——
Total score	——	——	——	——

Scoring

Total each column to obtain your score.

Interpretation

Review your answers. What patterns do you see?

Source: © Robert E. Quinn, Sue R. Faerman, Michael P. Thompson and Michael R. McGrath, *Becoming a Master Manager: A Competency Framework* (New York: Wiley, 1990), p. 38. This material is used by permission of John Wiley & Sons, Inc.

Assessment 18

DIAGNOSING CHANGE READINESS

Instructions

Choose an organisation with which you are familiar. It could be the organisation where you work, the university or some other organisation. This exercise will assess the organisation's readiness for change. Assume that the senior management team of the organisation wants to introduce change and will be driving the change process (that is, the senior management team is the change agent). On the following Helpscores chart, rate each potential problem for your organisation. Circle the number that best describes current conditions in the organisation.

Helpscores identifies ten potential problem areas — one for each letter that can help or hinder change. Circle the number that best describes current conditions in the organisation.

H ____ Rate: *Similarity* between the change agent and organisation members (homophily)

1	2	3	4	5	6	7
little similarity			moderate similarity			great similarity

E ____ Rate: *Understanding* of one another by change agent and organisation members (empathy)

1	2	3	4	5	6	7
little understanding			some understanding			much understanding

L ____ Rate: Extent of *collaboration* between change agent and organisation members (link)

1	2	3	4	5	6	7
to no extent			to some extent			to a great extent

P ____ Rate: *Accessibility* of organisation members and change agent to one another (proximity)

1	2	3	4	5	6	7
low access			moderate access			high access

S ____ Rate: Clarity of *planning and organisation* by change agent and organisation members (structuring)

1	2	3	4	5	6	7
not at all clear			moderately clear			extremely clear

C ____ Rate: Amount of financial, human and other *resources* available for change (capacity)

1	2	3	4	5	6	7
almost none available			some available			a great deal available

O ____ Rate: Willingness to be *influenced* by the change agent and organisation members (openness)

1	2	3	4	5	6	7
not at all open			somewhat open			very open

R ____ Rate: Potential *benefit* of the change for change agent and organisation members (reward)

1	2	3	4	5	6	7
very low reward potential			moderate reward potential			very high reward potential

E ____ Rate: Amount of *effort and enthusiasm* of the change agent and organisation members (energy)

1	2	3	4	5	6	7
very little energy			some energy			a great deal of energy

S ____ Rate: *Variety* of people and resources involved in the change effort (synergy)

1	2	3	4	5	6	7
very little variety			some variety			a great deal of variety

Scoring

To score this instrument, simply add up the ten numbers circled. Scores can range from 10 to 70.

Interpretation

10–20 Do not attempt change in this system. A lot of initial groundwork is needed prior to any effort to make changes or introduce innovations.

21–40 The first steps in creating change should involve work on those Helpscores variables that rated particularly low.

41–60 Change or innovations have a strong potential for success.

61–70 The success of change or innovation is very likely.

Source: Adapted from Marshal Shashkin and William C. Morris, *Organizational Behavior: Concepts and Experiences* (© Virginia: Reston Publishing, 1984), pp. 410–11. Prentice Hall.

ENDNOTES

Chapter 1 notes

1 Information from SEEK web site www.seek.com.au.

2 Fast Company web site www.fastcompany.com.

3 Hewitt Associates, 'Best Employers to Work for in Australia: 2001', http://was.hewitt.com/bestemployersaustralia/results/index.htm, viewed 12 November 2002.

4 Charles O'Reilly III and Jeffrey Pfeffer, *Hidden Value: How Great Companies Achieve Extraordinary Results with Ordinary People* (Boston: Harvard Business School Publishing, 2000), p. 2.

5 For a research perspective see Denise M. Rousseau, 'Organizational Behavior in the New Organizational Era', *Annual Review of Psychology*, vol. 48 (1997), pp. 515–46; for a consultant's perspective see Tom Peters, *The Circle of Innovation* (New York: Knopf, 1997); and Joan Magretta, *Managing in the New Economy* (Boston: Harvard Business School Press, 1999).

6 See Kevin Kelly, *New Rules for a New Economy: 10 Radical Strategies for a Connected World* (New York: Penguin, 1999).

7 Information from Thomas A. Stewart, 'Brain Power', *Fortune* (17 March 1997), p. 107; John A. Byrne, 'Jack: A Close-Up Look at How America's #1 Manager Runs GE', *Business Week* (8 June 1998), pp. 91–111; Robert Slater, *Jack Welch and the G.E. Way: Management Insights and Leadership Secrets of the Legendary CEO* (New York: McGraw-Hill, 1998).

8 James C. Sarros and Oleh Butchatsky, *Leadership — Australia's Top CEOs: Finding Out What Makes Them the Best* (Sydney: HarperCollins, 1998).

9 Corporate Research Foundation, *The Best Companies to Work for in Australia* (Sydney: HarperCollins, 1999); Australian Centre for Industrial Relations Research and Training, *Australia at Work: Just Managing?* (Sydney: Prentice Hall, 1999), p. 92.

10 Thomas A. Stewart, *Intellectual Capital: The Wealth of Organizations* (New York: Bantam, 1998).

11 See Peter F. Drucker, *The Changing World of the Executive* (New York: T. T. Times Books, 1982), and *The Profession of Management* (Cambridge, MA: Harvard Business School Press, 1997); and Francis Horibe, *Managing Knowledge Workers: New Skills and Attitudes to Unlock the Intellectual Capital in Your Organization* (New York: Wiley, 1999).

12 Kenichi Ohmae's books include *The Borderless World: Power and Strategy in the Interlinked Economy* (New York: Harper, 1989); *The End of the Nation State* (New York: Free Press, 1996); *The Invisible Continent: Four Strategic Imperatives of the New Economy* (New York: Harper, 1999).

13 For a discussion of globalisation see Thomas L. Friedman, *The Lexus and the Olive Tree: Understanding Globalization* (New York: Bantam Doubleday Dell, 2000); and John Micklethwait and Adrian Woolridge, *A Future Perfect: The Challenges and Hidden Promise of Globalization* (New York: Crown, 2000).

14 Michael E. Porter, *The Competitive Advantage of Nations: With a New Introduction* (New York: Free Press, 1998).

15 Information from BRL Hardy web site www.brlhardy.com.au and Chris Milne, 'BRL Takes on America with a Robust Blend', *BRW* (28 March–3 April 2002), p. 35.

16 See, for example, Carl Shapiro and Hal R. Varian, *Information Rules: A Strategic Guide to the Network Economy* (Cambridge, MA: Harvard Business School Press, 1998).

17 Australian Bureau of Statistics, 'Use of the Internet by Householders, Australia' (Canberra: ABS, 16 February 2001), www.afpwebworks.com, viewed 24 August 2002. Statistics New Zealand, 'Information Technology', www.stats.govt.nz, viewed 12 February 2003.

18 Linley Hartman, 'Managing the New Workforce: The Challenge of Mixed Employment Relationships', in Retha Wiesner and Bruce Millett (eds), *HRM: Issues and Future Directions* (Brisbane: John Wiley & Sons, 2002). Statistics New Zealand, 'New Zealand Labour Force Projections 1996(Base)–2051', www.stats.govt.nz, viewed 12 February 2003.

19 See Richard D. Bucher, *Diversity Consciousness: Opening Our Minds to People, Cultures, and Opportunities* (Upper Saddle River, NJ: Prentice Hall, 2000).

20 For a discussion of diversity issues see R. Roosevelt Thomas Jr, 'From Affirmative Action to Affirming Diversity', *Harvard Business Review* (November–December 1990), pp. 107–17; and *Beyond Race and Gender: Unleashing the Power of Your Total Workforce by Managing Diversity* (New York: AMACOM, 1992).

21 Quotations from Thomas, op. cit. (1990); and *Business Week* (8 August 1990), p. 50.

22 Robin Kramar, 'Managing Diversity: Challenges and Future Directions', in Retha Wiesner and Bruce Millett (eds), *Management and Organisational Behaviour: Contemporary Challenges and Future Directions* (Brisbane: John Wiley & Sons, 2001).

23 Fiona Krautil, 'Managing Diversity in Esso Australia', in E. M. Davis and C. Harris (eds), *Making the Link, No. 6* (Sydney: Affirmative Action Agency and the Labour Management Studies Foundation, 1995), pp. 22–8.

24 For discussions of the glass ceiling effect, see: Ann M. Morrison, Randall P. White and Ellen Van Velso, *Breaking the Glass Ceiling* (Reading, MA: Addison-Wesley, 1987); Anne E. Weiss, *The Glass Ceiling: A Look at Women in the Workforce* (New York: Twenty First Century, 1999); Debra E. Meyerson and Joyce K. Fletcher, 'A Modest Manifesto for Shattering the Glass Ceiling', *Harvard Business Review* (January–February 2000).

25 Judith B. Rosener, 'Women Make Good Managers, So What?', *Business Week* (11 December 2000), p. 24.

26 See, for example, Clarence Walton, *The Moral Manager* (New York: Harper Business, 1990).

27 Brad Howarth, 'Failure: After One.Tel', *BRW* (15 June 2001).

28 R. W. Judy and C. D'Amico, *Workforce 2020: Work and Workers in the 21st Century* (Indianapolis: Hudson Institute, 1997).

29 Credo selection from www.jnj.com.

30 Charles Handy, *The Age of Unreason* (Cambridge, MA: Harvard Business School Press, 1990).

31 See the issue feature 'Free Agent Nation', *Fast Company* (December 1997).

32 'Is Your Job Your Calling?', *Fast Company* (February–March 1998), p. 108.

33 Tom Peters, 'The New Wired World of Work', *Business Week* (28 August 2000), pp. 172–3.

34 Robert Reich, 'The Company of the Future', *Fast Company* (November 1998), pp. 124 ff.

35 Developed from Peters, op. cit. (2000).

36 For an overview of organisations and organisation theory, see W. Richard Scott, *Organizations: Rational, Natural and Open Systems* (Upper Saddle River, NJ: Prentice Hall, 1997).

37 Sarros and Butchatsky, op. cit., p. 246.

38 For a discussion of organisations as systems, see Lane Tracy, *The Living Organization* (New York: Quorum Books, 1994).

39 'Measuring People Power', *Fortune* (2 October 2000), p. 186.

40 Developed from Jay A. Conger, *Winning 'em Over: A New Model for Managing in the Age of Persuasion* (New York: Simon & Schuster, 1998), pp. 180–1; Stewart D. Friedman, Perry Christensen and Jessica DeGroot, 'Work and Life: The End of the Zero-Sum Game', *Harvard Business Review* (November–December 1998), pp. 119–29; Chris Argyris, 'Empowerment: The Emperor's New Clothes', *Harvard Business Review* (May–June 1998), pp. 98–105; John A. Byrne, 'Management by Web', *Business Week* (28 August 2000), pp. 84–98.

41 Philip B. Crosby, *Quality Is Still Free: Making Quality Certain in Uncertain Times* (New York: McGraw-Hill, 1995). For a comprehensive review see Robert E. Cole and W. Richard Scott (eds), *The Quality Movement & Organization Theory* (Thousand Oaks, CA: Sage, 2000).

42 Jeffrey Pfeffer and John F. Veiga, 'Putting People First for Organizational Success', *Academy of Management Executive*, vol. 13 (May 1999), pp. 37–48; and Jeffrey Pfeffer, *The Human Equation: Building Profits by Putting People First* (Boston: Harvard Business School Press, 1998).

43 Henry Mintzberg, 'The Manager's Job: Folklore and Fact', *Harvard Business Review*, vol. 53 (July–August 1975), p. 61. See also his book *The Nature of Managerial Work* (New York: Harper & Row, 1973, and HarperCollins, 1997).

44 Hal Lancaster, 'Middle Managers Are Back — But Now They're "High-Impact" Players', *Wall Street Journal* (14 April 1998), p. B1.

45 Sarros and Butchatsky, op. cit., p. 237.

46 Lancaster, op. cit.

47 For a perspective on the first-level manager's job, see Leonard A. Schlesinger and Janice A. Klein, 'The First-Line Supervisor: Past, Present and Future', in Jay W. Lorsch (ed.), *Handbook of Organizational Behavior* (Englewood Cliffs, NJ: Prentice Hall, 1987), pp. 370–82. Research reported in 'Remember Us?', *The Economist* (1 February 1992), p. 71.

48 Friedman, Christensen and DeGroot, op. cit.

49 Craig Donaldson, 'Flexible Working Hours', *Human Resources* (October 2001), p. 3. Statistics New Zealand, 'Labour Market (Employment and Unemployment)', www.stats.govt.nz, viewed 12 February 2003.

50 Anne Fisher, 'Six Ways to Supercharge Your Career', *Fortune* (13 January 1997), pp. 46–57.

51 Information from Marc Weingarten, 'The Next Napster', *Smart Business* (March 2001), pp. 48–9.

52 For a classic study see Thomas A. Mahoney, Thomas H. Jerdee and Stephen J. Carroll, 'The Job(s) of Management', *Industrial Relations*, vol. 4 (February 1965), pp. 97–110.

53 This running example is developed from information from 'Accountants Have Lives, Too, You Know', *Business Week* (23 February 1998), pp. 88–90, and the Ernst & Young web site www.ey.com.

54 'Adecco Appoints New COO', *Human Resources* (October 2001).

55 Amanda Gome and Emily Ross, 'The Top 5', *BRW* (3–10 October 2002), p. 56.

56 Mintzberg, op. cit. (1973), p. 30.

57 See for example, John R. Veiga and Kathleen Dechant, 'Wired World Woes: www.help', *Academy of Management Executive*, vol. 11 (August 1997), pp. 73–9.

58 See Mintzberg, op cit. (1973); and Henry Mintzberg, 'Covert Leadership: The Art of Managing Professionals', *Harvard Business Review* (November–December 1998), pp. 140–7.

59 'Australia's Most Female-friendly CEO Named', *Human Resources* (November 2001).

60 Mintzberg, op. cit. (1973), p. 60.

61 For research on managerial work see Morgan W. McCall Jr, Ann M. Morrison and Robert L. Hannan, *Studies of Managerial Work: Results and Methods, Technical Report #9* (Greensboro, NC: Center for Creative Leadership, 1978), pp. 7–9. See also John P. Kotter, 'What Effective General Managers Really Do', *Harvard Business Review* (November–December 1982), pp. 156–7.

62 Kotter, op. cit., p. 164. See also his book, *The General Managers* (New York: Free Press, 1986); and David Barry, Catherine Durnell Crampton and Stephen J. Carroll, 'Navigating the Garbage Can: How Agendas Help Managers Cope with Job Realities', *Academy of Management Executive*, vol. 11 (May 1997), pp. 43–56.

63 See Handy, op. cit., and *Beyond Certainty: The Changing Worlds of Organizations* (Cambridge, MA: Harvard Business School Press, 1997).

64 Robert L. Katz, 'Skills of an Effective Administrator', *Harvard Business Review* (September–October 1974), p. 94.

65 Hendrie Weisinger, *Emotional Intelligence at Work* (San Francisco: Jossey-Bass, 2000).

66 See Daniel Goleman's books *Emotional Intelligence* (New York: Bantam Books, 1995) and *Working with Emotional Intelligence* (New York: Bantam Books, 1998); and his articles 'What Makes a Leader', *Harvard Business Review* (November–December 1998), pp. 93–102, and 'Leadership that Gets Results', *Harvard Business Review* (March–April 2000), pp. 79–90, quote from p. 80.

67 Richard E. Boyatzis, *The Competent Manager: A Model for Effective Performance* (New York: Wiley, 1982).

68 Adapted from Apple History, www.apple-history.com/history. html, viewed 29 November 2002.

69 ibid.

70 ibid.

71 ibid.

72 ibid.

73 ibid.

74 Pui-Wing Tam 'Apple Seeks New Image as Producer of "Killer Apps"', *Wall Street Journal* (5 January 2001), pp. B1, B4.

75 Apple History, op. cit.

Chapter 2 notes

1 Information from Agilent Technologies web site www. agilent.com.au and www.jobs.agilent.com/locations/australia.html.

2 James Hunt, 'The Future of Work', in Retha Wiesner and Bruce Millett (eds), *Management and Organisational Behaviour:* *Contemporary Challenges and Future Directions* (Brisbane: John Wiley & Sons, 2001).

3 Quote from *The New Blue* (IBM Annual Report, 1997), p. 8.

4 Robert Reich, *The Future of Success* (New York: Knopf, 2001), p. 7.

5 See Michael E. Porter, *Competitive Strategy: Techniques for Analyzing Industries and Competitors* (New York: Free Press, 1980) and *Competitive Advantage: Creating and Sustaining Superior Performance* (New York: Free Press, 1986); also Richard A. D'Aveni, *Hyper-Competition: Managing the Dynamics of Strategic Maneuvering* (New York: Free Press, 1994).

6 Kath Walters, 'Fast 100 Focus: Blueprint Management Group', *BRW*, vol. 22, no. 47 (2000). John Stensholt, 'Fast 100: How the Top Ten Got There: Customcall', *BRW*, vol. 23, no. 44 (2001).

7 James C. Sarros and Oleh Butchatsky, *Leadership — Australia's Top CEOs: Finding Out What Makes Them the Best* (Sydney: HarperCollins, 1998).

8 Michael E. Porter, *The Competitive Advantage of Nations* (New York: Free Press, 1989).

9 The Institution of Engineers, Australia, www.ieaust.org.au/ events/aeea/2001/aeea_entrants/aeea_entrantdetails25.html, viewed 13 November 2002.

10 See Richard D. Bucher, *Diversity Consciousness: Opening Our Minds to People, Cultures, and Opportunities* (Upper Saddle River, NJ: Prentice Hall, 2000), p. 201.

11 James D. Thompson, *Organizations in Action* (New York: McGraw-Hill, 1967), and Robert B. Duncan, 'Characteristics of Organizational Environments and Perceived Environmental Uncertainty', *Administrative Science Quarterly*, vol. 17 (1972), pp. 313–27. For discussion of the implications of uncertainty see Hugh Courtney, Jane Kirkland and Patrick Viguerie, 'Strategy Under Uncertainty', *Harvard Business Review* (November–December 1997), pp. 67–79.

12 Quotation from a discussion by Richard J. Shonberger and Edward M. Knod Jr, *Operations Management: Serving the Customer*, 3rd edn (Plano, TX: Business Publications, 1988), p. 4.

13 Quote from *The Vermont Teddy Bear Company Gazette*, vol. 4 (summer 1993), p. 3.

14 Information from 'How Marriott Never Forgets a Guest', *Business Week* (21 February 2000), p. 74.

15 Amanda Gome, 'The Big Issues: Leonie Clyne', *BRW*, vol. 24, no. 8 (28 February 2002).

16 Roger D. Blackwell and Kristina Blackwell, 'The Century of the Consumer: Converting Supply Chains into Demand Chains', *Supply Chain Management Review* (fall 1999).

17 See Michael Dell, *Direct from Dell: Strategies that Revolutionized an Industry* (New York: Harper Business, 1999).

18 See Joseph M. Juran, *Quality Control Handbook*, 3rd edn (New York: McGraw-Hill, 1979) and 'The Quality Trilogy: A Universal Approach to Managing for Quality', in H. Costin (ed.), *Total Quality Management* (New York: Dryden, 1994); W. Edwards Deming, *Out of Crisis* (Cambridge, MA: MIT Press, 1986) and 'Deming's Quality Manifesto', *Best of Business Quarterly*, vol. 12 (winter 1990–91), pp. 6–10. See also Howard S. Gitlow and Shelly J. Gitlow, *The Deming Guide to Quality and Competitive Position* (Englewood Cliffs, NJ: Prentice Hall, 1987); Joseph M. Juran, 'Made in U.S.A.: A Renaissance in Quality', *Harvard Business Review* (July–August 1993), pp. 42–50.

19 Philip B. Crosby, *Quality is Free* (New York: McGraw-Hill, 1979); *The Eternally Successful Organization* (New York: McGraw-Hill, 1988); and *Quality Is Still Free: Making Quality Certain in Uncertain Times* (New York: McGraw-Hill, 1995).

20 Christopher Knowlton, 'What America Makes Best', *Fortune* (28 March 1988), pp. 40–54; Roger L. Hale, Douglas R. Hoelscher and Ronald E. Kowal, *Quest for Quality* (Minneapolis, MN: Tennant Company, 1989); and Roger L. Hale, Donald D. Carlton, Ronald E. Kowal and Tim K. Sehnert, *Made in the USA: How One American Company Helps Satisfy Customer Needs through Strategic Supplier Quality Management* (Minneapolis, MN: Tennant Company, 1991).

21 Rafael Aguay, *Dr. Deming: The American Who Taught the Japanese about Quality* (New York: Free Press, 1997).

22 See W. Edwards Deming, *Out of Crisis*, op. cit.

23 See Edward E. Lawler III, Susan Albers Mohrman and Gerald E. Ledford Jr, *Employee Involvement and Total Quality Management: Practices and Results in Fortune 1000 Companies* (San Francisco: Jossey-Bass, 1992).

24 Edward E. Lawler III and Susan Albers Mohrman, 'Quality Circles After the Fad', *Harvard Business Review* (January–February 1985), pp. 65–71.

25 Quotes from Arnold Kanarick, 'The Far Side of Quality Circles', *Management Review*, vol. 70 (October 1981), pp. 16–17.

26 See B. Joseph Pine II, Bart Victor and Andrew C. Boynton, 'Making Mass Customization Work', *Harvard Business Review* (September–October 1993), pp. 108–19; and 'The Agile Factory: Custom-made, Direct from the Plant', *Business Week*, special report on '21st Century Capitalism' (23 January 1995), pp. 158–9; and Justin Martin, 'Give 'Em *Exactly* What They Want', *Fortune* (10 November 1997), p. 283.

27 Tom Peters, *The Circle of Innovation* (New York: Knopf, 1997), p. 429.

28 Martin, op. cit. (1997).

29 Edgar H. Schein, 'Organizational Culture', *American Psychologist*, vol. 45 (1990), pp. 109–19. See also Schein's *Organizational Culture and Leadership*, 2nd edn (San Francisco: Jossey-Bass, 1997); and *The Corporate Culture Survival Guide* (San Francisco: Jossey-Bass, 1999).

30 James C. Collins and Jerry I. Porras, *Built to Last: Successful Habits of Visionary Companies* (New York: Harper Business, 1997).

31 Schein, op. cit. (1997); Terrence E. Deal and Allan A. Kennedy, *Corporate Cultures: The Rites and Rituals of Corporate Life* (Reading, MA: Addison-Wesley, 1982); Ralph Kilmann, *Beyond the Quick Fix* (San Francisco: Jossey-Bass, 1984).

32 In their book *Corporate Culture and Performance* (New York: Macmillan, 1992), John P. Kotter and James L. Heskett make the point that strong cultures have the desired effects over the long term only if they encourage adaptation to a changing environment. See also Collins and Porras, *Built to Last*, op. cit. (1997).

33 This is a simplified model developed from Schein, *Organizational Culture and Leadership*, op. cit. (1997).

34 Danielle Townsend, 'Getting a Life', *HR Monthly* (November 2000), p. 18.

35 'Australia Post's Red-Letter Day', *The Sydney Morning Herald* (22 October 2001), http://old.smh.com.au/news/specials/natl/reputation2001/, viewed 1 November 2002.

36 Ralph H. Kilmann, Mary J. Saxton and Roy Serpa, 'Issues in Understanding and Changing Corporate Culture', *California Management Review*, vol. 28 (1986), pp. 87–94.

37 Information from Lend Lease web site, www.lendlease.com.au.

38 See Mary Kay Ash, *Mary Kay: You Can Have It All* (Roseville, CA: Prima Publishing, 1995).

39 Lee Gardenswartz and Anita Rowe, *Managing Diversity: A Complete Desk Reference and Planning Guide* (Chicago: Irwin, 1993).

40 R. Roosevelt Thomas Jr, *Beyond Race and Gender: Unleashing the Power of Your Total Workforce by Managing Diversity* (New York: AMACOM, 1992), p. 10; see also R. Roosevelt Thomas Jr, 'From Affirmative Action to Affirming Diversity', *Harvard Business Review* (November–December 1990), pp. 107–17; R. Roosevelt Thomas Jr with Marjorie I. Woodruff, *Building a House for Diversity* (New York: AMACOM, 1999).

41 Gardenswartz and Rowe, op. cit., p. 220 ff.

42 Taylor Cox Jr, *Cultural Diversity in Organizations* (San Francisco: Berrett-Koehler, 1994).

43 Joseph A. Raelin, *Clash of Cultures* (Cambridge, MA: Harvard Business School Press, 1986).

44 Geert Hofstede, *Culture's Consequences: Comparing Values, Behaviors, Institutions and Organizations Across Nations* (Beverly Hills: Sage, 1981).

45 For examples of role model approaches see Anthony Robbins and Joseph McClendon III, *Unlimited Power: A Black Choice* (New York: Free Press, 1997) and Augusto Failde and William Doyle, *Latino Success: Insights from America's Most Powerful Latino Executives* (New York: Free Press, 1996).

46 Australian Institute of Management, 'Leadership & Trust', www.aimwa.com/whatsnew.cfm?mode=details&newsid=55, press release, viewed 25 August 2002.

47 Barbara Benedict Bunker, 'Appreciating Diversity and Modifying Organizational Cultures: Men and Women at Work', in Suresh Srivastva and David L. Cooperrider, *Appreciative Management and Leadership: The Power of Positive Thought and Action in Organizations* (San Francisco: Jossey-Bass, 1990), pp. 127–49.

48 See Gary N. Powell, *Women & Men in Management* (Thousand Oaks, CA: Sage, 1993) and Cliff Cheng (ed.), *Masculinities in Organizations* (Thousand Oaks, CA: Sage, 1996). For added background, see also Sally Helgesen, *Everyday Revolutionaries: Working Women and the Transformation of American Life* (New York: Doubleday, 1998).

49 Anti-Discrimination Commission Queensland, 'Disability Discrimination: Your Rights and Responsibilities', www.adcq.qld.gov.au/pubs/disfin.html#1, viewed 25 August 2002.

50 Australian Human Rights and Equal Opportunity Commission, 'Pregnant and Productive: It's a Right Not a Privilege to Work While Pregnant', www.hreoc.gov.au/sex_discrimination/pregnancy/report.html, viewed 25 August 2002. EEO Trust, www.eeotrust.org.nz, viewed 13 February 2003.

51 Information from 'The Bugs in Microsoft Culture', *Fortune* (8 January 2001), p. 128.

52 Office of the Director of Equal Opportunity in Public Employment, 'People with a Disability — Comparative Tables 2000 — NSW Public Sector' www.eeo.nsw.gov.au/stats/pwd00.htm, viewed 25 August 2002.

53 This section is based on ideas set forth by R. Roosevelt Thomas Jr, in *Beyond Race and Gender*, op. cit.; and Thomas and Woodruff, *Building a House for Diversity*, op. cit.

54 Alan Barron, 'Submission to The Affirmative Action Agency', www.endeavourforum.org.au/feb9.html, viewed 19 November 2002.

55 Thomas, *Beyond Race and Gender*, op. cit., p. 17.

56 Lucent Technologies, www.lucent.com.au/intl/au/en/work/benefits.html, viewed 28 March 2003.

57 Thomas and Woodruff, *Building a House for Diversity*, op. cit., pp. 211–26.

58 Based on ibid., pp. 11–12.

59 'Diversity Today: Corporate Recruiting Practices in Inclusive Workplaces', *Fortune* (12 June 2000), p. S4.

60 John Hey, 'The World's Best Brand', *Fortune* (31 May 1993), p. 46.

61 Michael McCarthy, 'Soft Drink Firms Search for Answers as Volumes Drop', *Wall Street Journal* (27 July 1992).

62 Maria Mallory, 'Behemoth on a Bear', *Business Week* (3 November 1994) p. 54.

63 Elizabeth Lesley, 'Does Snapple Have the Juice to Go National?', *Business Week* (18 January 1993), pp. 52–3.

64 Mallory, op. cit., p. 55.

65 Maria Mallory, 'At Coke, Marketing Is It', *Business Week* (21 February 1994), p. 39.

66 Maria Mallory, 'The Cola Wars Go to College', *Business Week* (19 September 1994), p. 42.

67 Bill Saporito, 'How U.S. Soccer Hopes to Score', *Fortune* (27 June 1994), p. 127.

68 Joyce Barnathan, 'Destination, Vietnam', *Business Week* (14 February 1994), pp. 26–7; John Templeton, 'Nestle: A Giant in a Hurry', *Business Week* (22 March 1993), p. 50.

69 Nikhil Deogun, 'Ivester Sees Rise in Sales, Opportunity for Coke in Asia's Turmoil', *Wall Street Journal* (11 December 1997), p. A4.

70 Nikhil Deogun, 'Coca-Cola May Purchase Orangina', *Wall Street Journal* (22 December 1997), pp. B1, B8.

71 CNNfn.com, 'Coke Reports Flat 3Q', http://cnnfn.com/hotstories/companies/9810/15/coke/ (15 October 1998).

72 Douglas Herbert, 'Coke Mops up the Mess', CNNfn, http://money.cnn.com/1999/06/24/worldbiz/coke_damage/ (25 June 1999).

73 CNNfn, 'Coke CEO Ivestor Resigns', http://money.cnn.com/1999/12/06/companies/coke/ (6 December 1999).

74 CNNfn, 'A Coke and a Smile?', http://money.cnn.com/2000/12/04/deals/coke/index.htm (4 December 2000).

75 'New Formula Coke', *The Economist* (1 February 2001), www.economist.com.

76 Justin Bachman, 'Coca-Cola Buys Bottled Coffee Company Planet Java', *Business Wire* (12 January 2001).

Chapter 3 notes

1 Ching Yee Tan, Making the Digital Transformation a Reality, paper presented at 15th CIO Workshop, Raffles Hotel, Singapore (1 August 2002), www.ida.gov.sg, viewed 26 August 2002; David T. E. Lim, Growing the Asian ICT Market, paper presented at iX2002, Suntec City (17 June 2002), www.ida.gov.sg, viewed 26 August 2002.

2 See Alvin Toffler, *Powershift* (New York: Bantam Books, 1990) and www.tofflerassociates.com/index1.htm.

3 Information from 'E-Meetings Redefine Productivity', *Fortune*, special advertising section (5 February 2001), p. S2.

4 Peter F. Drucker, Esther Dyson, Charles Handy, Paul Daffo and Peter M. Senge, 'Looking Ahead: Implications of the Present', *Harvard Business Review* (September–October 1997), pp. 18–32.

5 Thomas A. Stewart, *Intellectual Capital: The Wealth of Organizations* (New York: Doubleday, 1997).

6 Paul Roberts, 'Humane Technology — PeopleSoft', *Fast Company* (April–May 1998), p. 122.

7 See Susan G. Cohen and Don Mankin, 'The Changing Nature of Work: Managing the Impact of Information Technology', chapter 6 in Susan Albers Mohrman, Jay R. Galbraith, Edward E. Lawler III and Associates, *Tomorrow's Organization: Crafting Winning Capabilities in a Dynamic World* (San Francisco: Jossey-Bass, 1998), pp. 154–78.

8 Information from example in 'Management by Web', *Business Week* (28 August 2000), p. 88.

9 Efraim Turban, R. Kelly Rainer Jr and Richard E. Potter, *Introduction to Information Technology* (New York: Wiley, 2001).

10 Information from Robert W. Bly, 'Does Your "Second Generation" Site Get a Passing Grade?' (8 September 2000), www.mcknightpartners.com/whatyouneedtoknow.htm.

11 Drucker et al., op. cit., p. 22.

12 Information from John A. Byrne, 'Visionary vs. Visionary', *Business Week* (28 August 2000), pp. 210–14.

13 The article by Dorothy Leonard-Barton and John J. Sviokla, 'Putting Expert Systems to Work', *Harvard Business Review* (March–April 1988), pp. 91–8, provides a practical overview of expert systems and their management applications. See also Barbara Garson, *The Electronic Sweatshop* (New York: Viking Penguin, 1989).

14 Mary J. Cronin, 'Ford's Intranet Success', *Fortune* (30 March 1998), p. 158; and Steven V. Brull, 'Networks That Do New Tricks', *Business Week* (6 April 1998), p. 100.

15 IBM case study, 'The Wesley Private Hospital Computerises Clinical Information System', www-8.ibm.com/solutions/au/publicsector/downloads/Wesley.pdf, viewed 28 March 2003.

16 Jaclyn Fierman, 'Winning Ideas from Maverick Managers', *Fortune* (6 February 1995), pp. 66–80.

17 Henry Mintzberg, *The Nature of Managerial Work* (New York: Harper & Row, 1973, and HarperCollins, 1997).

18 Information from Peter Burrows, 'Sun's Bid to Rule the Web', *Business Week* (24 July 2000), pp. EB31–42.

19 For scholarly reviews, see Dean Tjosvold, 'Effects of Crisis Orientation on Managers' Approach to Controversy in Decision Making', *Academy of Management Journal*, vol. 27 (1984), pp. 130–8; and Ian I. Mitroff, Paul Shrivastava and Firdaus E. Udwadia, 'Effective Crisis Management', *Academy of Management Executive*, vol. 1 (1987), pp. 283–92.

20 See David Greising, *I'd Like to Buy the World a Coke: The Life and Leadership of Roberto Goizueta* (New York: Wiley, 1998).

21 See Hugh Courtney, Jane Kirkland and Patrick Viguerie, 'Strategy Under Uncertainty', *Harvard Business Review* (November–December 1997), pp. 67–79.

22 For a good discussion, see Watson H. Agor, *Intuition in Organizations: Leading and Managing Productively* (Newbury Park, CA: Sage, 1989); Herbert A. Simon, 'Making Management Decisions: The Role of Intuition and Emotion', *Academy of Management Executive*, vol. 1 (1987), pp. 57–64; Orlando Behling and Norman L. Eckel, 'Making Sense Out of Intuition', *Academy of Management Executive*, vol. 5 (1991), pp. 46–54.

23 Agor, op. cit., p. 11.

24 Daniel J. Isenberg, 'How Senior Managers Think', *Harvard Business Review*, vol. 62 (November–December 1984), pp. 81–90.

25 The Yellow Pages® Business Ideas Grants, www.yellowpages.com.au/big/past.htm, viewed 25 August 2002; and Café Bones, www.cafebones.com.au, viewed 4 December 2002.

26 Daniel J. Isenberg, 'The Tactics of Strategic Opportunism', *Harvard Business Review*, vol. 65 (March–April 1987), pp. 92–7.

27 See George P. Huber, *Managerial Decision Making* (Glenview, IL: Scott, Foresman, 1975). For a comparison, see the steps in Xerox's problem-solving process as described in David A. Garvin, 'Building a Learning Organization', *Harvard Business Review* (July–August 1993), pp. 78–91.

28 'Heinz Wattie's Completes Reorganisation: Corporate Office Consolidates from Auckland to Melbourne', media release, www.heinz.com.au/cda/hwa_page/1,2601,1014,00.html, viewed 25 August 2002. © Heinz Watties.

29 Peter F. Drucker, *Innovation and Entrepreneurship: Practice and Principles* (New York: Harper & Row, 1985).

30 James C. Sarros, Judy H. Grey and Iain L. Densten, *Key Findings: Australian Business Leadership Survey* (Melbourne: Australian Institute of Management, 2002). Available www.aim.com.au.

31 For a sample of Simon's work, see Herbert A. Simon, *Administrative Behavior* (New York: Free Press, 1947); James G. March and Herbert A. Simon, *Organizations* (New York: Wiley, 1958); Herbert A. Simon, *The New Science of Management Decision* (New York: Harper, 1960).

32 This presentation is based on the work of R. H. Hogarth, D. Kahneman, A. Tversky and others, as discussed in Max H. Bazerman, *Judgment in Managerial Decision Making*, 3rd edn (New York: Wiley, 1994).

33 Barry M. Staw, 'The Escalation of Commitment to a Course of Action', *Academy of Management Review*, vol. 6 (1981), pp. 577–87; Barry M. Staw and Jerry Ross, 'Knowing When to Pull the Plug', *Harvard Business Review*, vol. 65 (March–April 1987), pp. 68–74.

34 The classic work is Norman R. F. Maier, 'Assets and Liabilities in Group Problem Solving', *Psychological Review*, vol. 74 (1967), pp. 239–49.

35 ibid.

36 Peter F. Drucker, 'The Future That has Already Happened', *Harvard Business Review*, vol. 75 (September–October 1997), pp. 20–4.

37 Drucker et al., op. cit.

38 See, for example, Thomas H. Davenport and Laurence Prusak, *Working Knowledge: How Organizations Manage What They Know* (Cambridge, MA: Harvard Business School Press, 1997).

39 Hal Lancaster, 'Contributors to Pools of Company Know-How Are Valued Employees', *Wall Street Journal* (9 December 1997), p. B1; Thomas A. Stewart, 'Is This Job Really Necessary?', *Fortune* (12 January 1998), pp. 154–5.

40 Richard Waters, 'Own Words: Jack Welch, General Electric', *Financial Times* (1 October 1997).

41 Steven E. Prokesch, 'Unleashing the Power of Learning', *Harvard Business Review* (September–October 1997), pp. 147–68.

42 Peter Senge, *The Fifth Discipline* (New York: Harper, 1990).

43 ibid.

44 Prokesch, op. cit.

45 Waters, op. cit.

46 Ken Orr, Stowe Boyd, Dave Higgins, Michael Kull, Bob Puccinelli, Karl Wiig, et al., *Knowledge Management: Tools and Strategies for Real-Time Collaboration and Exchange* (Arlington, MA: Cutter Consortium, 2001).

47 Robert D. Hof, Steve Hamm and Ira Sager, 'Is the Center of the Computing Universe Shifting?', *Business Week* (19 January 1999), pp. 64–72.

48 Miguel Helft, 'Sun Succeeds with Market Savvy, Pragmatism', *San Jose Mercury News* (6 December 1998).

49 Hof, Hamm and Sager, op. cit.

50 ibid.

51 ibid.

52 ibid.

53 ibid.

54 Helft, op. cit.

55 Amy Merrick, 'Companies Go the Extra Mile to Retain Employees', *R&D* (September 1998), p. S3.

56 Hof, Hamm and Sager, op. cit.

57 ibid.

58 Information from Sun Microsystems, www.sun.com.

59 Hof, Hamm and Sager, op. cit.

60 Helft, op. cit.

61 Hof, Hamm and Sager, op. cit.

62 Helft, op. cit.

63 Hof, Hamm and Sager, op. cit.

64 Information from Ira Sager, Catherine Yang, Linda Himelstein and Neil Gross, 'Power Play: AOL–Netscape–Sun', *Business Week* (7 December 1998).

65 J. Taschek, 'This Just In: The World Revolves Around Sun', *PC Week* (4 January 1999), p. 48.

66 ibid.

67 John McFarlane, 'Whose Webtone is It, Anyway?', www.sun.com, viewed May 1998. © John McFarlane, Sun Microsystems.

68 Helft, op. cit.

Chapter 4 notes

1 Advertising Distribution Services web site www.adservices. com.au; CommercialWare press release, 'CommercialWare Signs On Coles Myer. Solution Being Used for Olympics Fulfilment', press release (19 September 2000), www.commercial ware.com/news/articles/Article43.asp, viewed 9 December 2002.

2 Pauline Graham, *Mary Parker Follett — Prophet of Management: A Celebration of Writings from the 1920s* (Boston: Harvard Business School Press, 1995).

3 For a timeline of 20th-century management ideas see '75 Years of Management Ideas and Practice: 1922–1997', *Harvard Business Review*, supplement (September–October 1997).

4 A thorough review and critique of the history of management thought, including management in ancient civilisations, is provided by Daniel A. Wren, *The Evolution of Management Thought*, 4th edn (New York: Wiley, 1993).

5 See '75 Years of Management Ideas and Practice: 1922–1997', op. cit.

6 Elite Lobby Group, 'Best Business Hotels in Asia Awards in Singapore', October 2000, www.ritzcarlton.com/hotels/singapore/ overview/press_room.html, viewed 9 December 2002.

7 For a sample of this work see Henry L. Gantt, *Industrial Leadership* (Easton, MD: Hive, 1921; Hive edition published in 1974); Henry C. Metcalfe and Lyndall Urwick (eds), *Dynamic Administration: The Collected Papers of Mary Parker Follett* (New York: Harper & Brothers, 1940); James D. Mooney, *The Principles of Administration*, rev. edn (New York: Harper & Brothers, 1947); Lyndall Urwick, *The Elements of Administration* (New York: Harper & Brothers, 1943) and *The Golden Book of Management* (London: N. Neame, 1956).

8 References on Taylor's work are from Frederick W. Taylor, *The Principles of Scientific Management* (New York: W. W. Norton, 1967), originally published by Harper & Brothers in 1911. For a criticism, see Charles W. Wrege and Amedeo G. Perroni, 'Taylor's Pig-Tale: A Historical Analysis of Frederick W. Taylor's Pig-Iron Experiments', *Academy of Management Journal*, vol. 17 (March 1974), pp. 6–27. See Edwin A. Locke, 'The Ideas of Frederick W. Taylor: An Evaluation', *Academy of Management Review*, vol. 7 (1982), p. 14, for an examination of the contemporary significance of Taylor's work. See also the recent biography by Robert Kanigel, *The One Best Way* (New York: Viking, 1997).

9 Kanigel, op cit.

10 See Frank B. Gilbreth, *Motion Study* (New York: Van Nostrand, 1911).

11 Simon Jeffery, 'Call Centres', *The Guardian* (20 February 2001), www.guardian.co.uk/netnotes/article/0,6729,440567,00.html, viewed August 2002.

12 Available in the English language as Henri Fayol, *General and Industrial Administration* (London: Pitman, 1949); subsequent discussion is based on M. B. Brodie, *Fayol on Administration* (London: Pitman, 1949).

13 M. P. Follett, *Freedom and Coordination* (London: Management Publications Trust, 1949). Eulogy from Richard C. Cabot, *Encyclopedia of Social Work*, vol. 15, s.v., 'Follett, Mary Parker', p. 351.

14 Judith Garwood, 'A Review of *Dynamic Administration: The Collected Papers of Mary Parker Follett*', *New Management*, vol. 2 (1984), pp. 61–2.

15 Mallesons Stephen Jaques, 'Work-related Stress: Employer Liability', press release, www.mallesons.com/news/articles/5501647W.htm, viewed 15 November 2002.

16 Gayle Bryant, 'Call Centres Connect with Staff', *BRW* (30 May– 5 June 2002).

17 A. M. Henderson and Talcott Parsons (eds and trans), *Max Weber: The Theory of Social Economic Organization* (New York: Free Press, 1947).

18 ibid., p. 337.

19 The Hawthorne Studies are described in detail in F. J. Roethlisberger and William J. Dickson, *Management and the Worker* (Cambridge, MA: Harvard University Press, 1966) and G. Homans, *Fatigue of Workers* (New York: Reinhold, 1941). For an interview with three of the participants in the relay assembly test-room studies, see R. G. Greenwood, A. A. Bolton and R. A. Greenwood, 'Hawthorne a Half Century Later: "Relay Assembly Participants Remember"', *Journal of Management*, vol. 9 (1983), pp. 217–31.

20 Philip Rennie, 'Get-smart Charity', *BRW* (6–12 June 2002), p. 47.

21 The criticisms of the Hawthorne Studies are detailed in Alex Carey, 'The Hawthorne Studies: A Radical Criticism', *American Sociological Review*, vol. 32 (1967), pp. 403–16; H. M. Parsons, 'What Happened at Hawthorne?', *Science*, vol. 183 (1974), pp. 922–32; B. Rice, 'The Hawthorne Defect: Persistence of a Flawed Theory', *Psychology Today*, vol. 16 (1982), pp. 70–4. See also Wren, op. cit.

22 This discussion of Maslow's theory is based on Abraham H. Maslow, *Eupsychian Management* (Homewood, IL: Richard D. Irwin, 1965), and Abraham H. Maslow, *Motivation and Personality*, 2nd edn (New York: Harper & Row, 1970).

23 Douglas McGregor, *The Human Side of Enterprise* (New York: McGraw-Hill, 1960).

24 Information from 'About AIMD', American Institute for Managing Diversity web site: www.aimd.org/about_aimd.htm.

25 Department of Employment and Workplace Relations, 'Workplace Diversity Strategy 1999–2002', available www.dewrsb.gov.au/publications/workplaceDiversityStrategy/default.asp, viewed 27 August 2002.

26 Chris Argyris, *Personality and Organization* (New York: Harper & Row, 1957).

27 The ideas of Ludwig von Bertalanffy contributed to the emergence of this systems perspective on organisations. See his article, 'The History and Status of General Systems Theory', *Academy of Management Journal*, vol. 15 (1972), pp. 407–26. This viewpoint is further developed by Daniel Katz and Robert L. Kahn in their classic book, *The Social Psychology of Organizations* (New York: Wiley, 1978). For an integrated systems view, see Lane Tracy, *The Living Organization* (New York: Quorum Books, 1994). For an overview, see W. Richard Scott, *Organizations: Rational, Natural and Open Systems*, 4th edn (Upper Saddle River, NJ: Prentice Hall, 1998).

28 Chester I. Barnard, *Functions of the Executive* (Cambridge, MA: Harvard University Press, 1938).

29 See discussion by Scott, op. cit., pp. 66–8.

30 Peter F. Drucker, 'The Future That has Already Happened', *Harvard Business Review,* vol. 75 (September–October 1997), pp. 20–4.

31 For an overview, see Scott, op. cit., pp. 95–7.

32 For the classics see: W. Edwards Deming, *Quality, Productivity and Competitive Position* (Cambridge, MA: MIT Press, 1982); Joseph M. Juran, *Quality Control Handbook*, 3rd edn (New York: McGraw-Hill, 1979).

33 Jay R. Galbraith, 'Designing the Networked Organization: Leveraging Size and Competencies' in Susan Albers Mohrman, Jay R. Galbraith, Edward E. Lawler III and Associates, *Tomorrow's Organization: Crafting Winning Capabilities in a Dynamic World* (San Francisco: Jossey-Bass, 1998), pp. 76–102.

34 Thomas J. Peters and Robert H. Waterman Jr, *In Search of Excellence: Lessons from America's Best-Run Companies* (New York: Harper & Row, 1982).

35 William Ouchi, *Theory Z: How American Businesses Can Meet the Japanese Challenge* (Reading, MA: Addison-Wesley, 1981); Richard Tanner Pascale and Anthony G. Athos, *The Art of Japanese Management: Applications for American Executives* (New York: Simon & Schuster, 1981).

36 Ouchi, op. cit.; see also the review by J. Bernard Keys, Luther Tray Denton and Thomas R. Miller, 'The Japanese Management Theory Jungle — Revisited', *Journal of Management*, vol. 20 (1994), pp. 373–402.

37 The classic work is Peter Senge, *The Fifth Discipline* (New York: Harper, 1990).

38 John Gardner, *No Easy Victories* (New York: Harper & Row, 1968).

39 Peter F. Drucker, Esther Dyson, Charles Handy, Paul Daffo and Peter M. Senge, 'Looking Ahead: Implications of the Present', *Harvard Business Review* (September–October, 1997), pp. 18–32.

40 Quote from Ralph Z. Sorenson, 'A Lifetime of Learning to Manage Effectively', *Wall Street Journal* (28 February 1983), p. 18.

41 Japan Airlines Fact Sheet, www.japanair.com/Company/Fact_Sheet/default.htm, viewed 9 December 2002.

42 Japan Airlines Fact Sheet, 'Japan Airlines: America's Best Customer for 29 Years', www.japanair.com/company/fact/default.html, viewed 5 March 2000.

43 Deborah Ancona, Thomas Kochan, Maureen Scully, John Van Maanen and D. Eleanor Westney, 'Changing Models in the Corporation', in *Managing for the Future: Organizational Behavior and Processes* (Cincinnati, OH: South-Western College Publishing, 1996), pp. 3–17.

44 Japan Airlines, 'JAL Subsidiary Airlines', press release (20 January 2000), www.jal.jp/en, viewed 17 April 2000.

45 I. Kaneko, 'Take Off For Profits', press release (13 November 1998), www.japanair.com/company/press/98speech.html, viewed 5 March 2000.

46 ibid.

47 Cyborg, 'Court Ruling and Reasons', www.cyborg.ne.jp/~jfu/english/Reason.html, viewed 5 March 2000.

48 A. Anderson, 'Topic 1: Japan at a Glance', www.anderson.ucla.edu/research/japan/pointers/part1.html, viewed 15 April 2000.

49 Y. Funabashi, 'Japan Searching For a Model For Its New Birth', *Asahi Evening News* (24 April 2000), p. 6.

50 Personal communication, crew member, 28 April 2000.

51 Kaneko, op. cit.

52 Stephen P. Robbins, Bruce Millett, Ron Cacioppe and Terry Waters-Marsh, *Organisational Behaviour: Leading and Managing in Australia and New Zealand*, 2nd edn (Sydney: Prentice Hall, 2001).

Chapter 5 notes

1 Information from 'NTT DoCoMo Flies Past the Milestones', *Fortune* (24 July 2000), advertisement; and corporate web site www.nttdocomo.com.

2 David James, 'The World is Going Global: What Will It Look Like?', *BRW* (4 August 2000).

3 See Kenichi Ohmae, *The Evolving Global Economy* (Cambridge, MA: Harvard Business School Press, 1995).

4 Rosabeth Moss Kanter, *World Class: Thinking Locally in the Global Economy* (New York: Simon & Schuster, 1995), preface.

5 For a discussion of globalisation see Thomas L. Friedman, *The Lexus and the Olive Tree: Understanding Globalization* (New York: Bantam Doubleday Dell, 2000); and John Micklethwait and Adrian Woolridge, *A Future Perfect: The Challenges and Hidden Promise of Globalization* (New York: Crown, 2000).

6 For a discussion of issues, see James H. Mittleman, *The Globalization Syndrome* (Princeton, NJ: Princeton University Press, 2000).

7 Quote from Jeffrey E. Garten, 'The Mind of the CEO', *Business Week* (5 February 2001), p. 106.

8 Australian Department of Foreign Affairs and Trade, 'Asia-Pacific Economic Cooperation (APEC) and Australia' overview, www.dfat.gov.au/apec/, viewed 30 August 2002.

9 Australian Department of Foreign Affairs and Trade, 'Australia and the OECD', www.dfat.gov.au/oecd/index.html, viewed 30 August 2002.

10 Australian Department of Foreign Affairs and Trade, 'Annual Report 2000–2001: North Asia', www.dfat.gov.au/dept/annual_reports/00_01/s02/02_1-1-1.html, viewed 30 August 2002.

11 Mark Vaile, Minister for Trade, Australia, 'Australia New Zealand Trade Ministers' Meeting', Christchurch, New Zealand, joint communique, 29–30 August 2002, www.dfat.gov.au/geo/new_zealand/aus_nz_tade_ministers_meeting_2002.html, viewed 10 December 2002.

12 The *Economist* is a good weekly source of information on Europe. See www.economist.com.

13 For an overview see 'Europe's Mid-Life Crisis', *The Economist: A Survey of the European Union* (31 May 1997).

14 A monthly publication that covers the *maquiladora* industries is the *Twin Plant News* (El Paso, Texas); see web site at www.twin-plant-news.com.

15 Australian Department of Foreign Affairs and Trade 'Annual Report 2000–2001: Americas and Europe', www.dfat.gov.au/dept/annual_reports/00_01/s02/02_1-1-3.html, viewed 30 August 2002.

16 ibid. See also New Zealand Ministry of Foreign Affairs & Trade, 'United States – New Zealand: Economic Relationship', www.mft.govt.nz, viewed 14 February 2003.

17 'Annual Report 2000–2001: Americas and Europe', op. cit.

18 ibid.

19 Adapted from China Internet Information Center, 'China's WTO Updates', www.china.org.cn/english/40525.htm, viewed 10 December 2002.

20 The *Economist* is a good weekly source of information on Africa. See www.economist.com.

21 Mort Rosenblum, 'Turnaround: Once a Basket Case, Mozambique Now a Free-Market Example', *Columbus Dispatch* (14 December 1997), p. 4c.

22 MBendi Information for Africa web site www.mbendi.co.za/orsadc.htm.

23 James A. Austin and John G. McLean, 'Pathways to Business Success in Sub-Saharan Africa', *Journal of African Finance and Economic Development*, vol. 2 (1996), pp. 57–76.

24 Information from 'International Business: Consider Africa', *Harvard Business Review*, vol. 76 (January–February 1998), pp. 16–18.

25 See 'Inside View: South Africa', *The New York Times* (18 September 2000), pp. A15–A17.

26 Australian Department of Foreign Affairs and Trade, 'South Africa Country Brief', www.dfat.gov.au/geo/south_africa/south_africa_country_brief.html, viewed 9 December 2002.

27 New Zealand Ministry of Foreign Affairs & Trade, 'South Africa — August 2002', www.mft.govt.nz, viewed 14 February 2003.

28 Quote from John A. Byrne, 'Visionary vs. Visionary', *Business Week* (28 August 2000), p. 210.

29 For research discussions of privatisation and transitional economies, see R. Duane Ireland, Shaker A. Zahra, Isabel Gutierrez and Michael A. Hitt (special issue editors), 'Special Topic Forum on Privatization and Entrepreneurial Transformation', *Academy of Management Review*, vol. 25 (July 2000), pp. 509–669.

30 'Annual Report 2000–2001: Americas and Europe', op. cit.

31 Michael E. Porter, 'How to Kick Global Goals', *BRW* (28 March–3 April 2002), p. 55.

32 Business for Social Responsibility, 'Discrimination', white paper, www.bsr.org/BSRResources/WhitePaperDetail.cfm?DocumentID=520#leader, viewed 10 December 2002.

33 Sylvia Ann Hewlett, 'The Boundaries of Business: The Human Resource Deficit', *Harvard Business Review*, (July–August 1991), pp. 131–3. See also William B. Johnston, 'Global Workforce 2000: The New World Labor Market', *Harvard Business Review*, (March–April 1991), pp. 115–27.

34 Austrade, 'Export Market Development Grants', www2.austrade.gov.au/exportassistance/page20326.asp, viewed 2 November 2002. Trade New Zealand, 'About the Trade New Zealand Export Awards', www.tradenz.govt.nz, viewed 14 February 2003.

35 Developed from Anthony J. F. O'Reilly, 'Establishing Successful Joint Ventures in Developing Nations: A CEO's Perspective', *Columbia Journal of World Business* (spring 1988), pp. 65–71; and 'Best Practices for Global Competitiveness', *Fortune* (30 March 1998), pp. S1–S3, special advertising section.

36 See Peter F. Drucker, 'The Global Economy and the Nation-State', *Foreign Affairs*, vol. 76 (September–October 1997), pp. 159–71.

37 This framework is introduced in David P. Rutenberg, *Multinational Management* (Boston: Little Brown, 1982).

38 Adapted from R. Hall Mason, 'Conflicts between Host Countries and Multinational Enterprise', *California Management Review*, vol. 17 (1974), pp. 6, 7.

39 For a good overview, see Randall E. Stross, *Bulls in the China Shop and Other Sino-American Business Encounters* (New York: Pantheon, 1991); as well as John Studdard and James G. Shiro, *The New Silk Road: Secrets of Business Success in China Today* (New York: Wiley, 2000).

40 For an interesting discussion of one company's experience in China, see Jim Mann, *Beijing Jeep: A Case Study of Western Business in China* (Boulder, CO: Westview Press, 1997).

41 Craig Smith, 'Foreign Investors Break Free From Chinese Partners', *Wall Street Journal* (11 June 1998), p. A17.

42 Information from corporate web site: www.nikeBiz.com/labor/toc_monitoring.shtml.

43 'An Industry Monitors Child Labor', *The New York Times* (16 October 1997), pp. B1, B9; and Rugmark International web site: www.rugmark.de/english/index.htm.

44 Definition from World Commission on Environment and Development, *Our Common Future* (Oxford: Oxford University Press, 1987); reported on International Institute for Sustainable Development web site: www.iisd.org.

45 Examples reported in Neil Chesanow, *The World-Class Executive* (New York: Rawson Associates, 1985).

46 Based on Barbara Benedict Bunker, 'Appreciating Diversity and Modifying Organizational Cultures: Men and Women at Work', in Suresh Srivastva and David L. Cooperrider, *Appreciative Management and Leadership: The Power of Positive Thought and Action in Organizations* (San Francisco: Jossey-Bass, 1990), pp. 127–49.

47 For a good overview of the practical issues, see Philip R. Harris and Robert T. Moran, *Managing Cultural Differences*, 2nd edn (Houston: Gulf Publishing, 1987); and Martin J. Gannon, *Understanding Global Cultures* (Thousand Oaks, CA: Sage, 1994).

48 Information from Ronald B. Lieber, 'Flying High, Going Global', *Fortune* (7 July 1997), pp. 195–7.

49 See Gary P. Ferraro, 'The Need for Linguistic Proficiency in Global Business', *Business Horizons* (May–June 1996), pp. 39–46; quote from Carol Hymowitz, 'Companies Go Global, But Many Managers Just Don't Travel Well', *Wall Street Journal* (15 August 2000), p. B1.

50 Edward T. Hall, *Beyond Culture* (New York: Doubleday, 1976).

51 Edward T. Hall, *The Silent Language* (New York: Anchor Books, 1959); *The Hidden Dimension* (New York: Anchor Books, 1969).

52 Hall, *The Silent Language*, op. cit.

53 Lady Borton, 'Working in the Vietnamese Voice', *Academy of Management Executive*, vol. 14 (December 2000), pp. 20–31.

54 Edward T. Hall, *Hidden Differences* (New York: Doubleday, 1990).

55 Business for Social Responsibility, 'Religion in the Workplace', white paper, www.bsr.org/BSRResources/WhitePaperDetail.cfm?Document ID=528#leader, viewed 10 December 2002.

56 Personal communication with Australian project manager, interviewed by Retha Wiesner, 10 April 2002.

57 Geert Hofstede, *Culture's Consequences: Comparing Values, Behaviors, Institutions and Organizations Across Nations* (Beverly Hills: Sage, 1981). Hofstede and Michael H. Bond further explore Eastern and Western perspectives on national culture in their article 'The Confucius Connection: From Cultural Roots to Economic Growth', *Organizational Dynamics*, vol. 16 (1988), pp. 4–21, which presents comparative data from Bond's 'Chinese Values Survey'.

58 For an introduction to the fifth dimension, see Hofstede and Bond, op. cit.

59 Michael Schuman, 'How Interbrew Blended Disparate Ingredients in Korean Beer Venture', *Wall Street Journal* (24 July 2000), pp. A1, A6.

60 Fons Trompenaars, *Riding the Waves of Culture: Understanding Cultural Diversity in Business* (London: Nicholas Brealey Publishing, 1993).

61 See Robert B. Reich, 'Who Is Them?', *Harvard Business Review* (March–April 1991), pp. 77–88.

62 'Going International: Willett Systems Limited', *Fortune* (16 February 1998), p. S6, special advertising section.

63 Mark Clifford and Majeet Kripalani, 'Different Countries, Adjoining Cubicles', *Business Week* (28 August 2000), pp. 182–4.

64 For a perspective on the role of women in expatriate managerial assignments, see Marianne Jelinek and Nancy J. Adler, 'Women: World-Class Managers for Global Competition', *Academy of Management Executive* (February 1988), pp. 11–19.

65 Information from Gail Edmondson, 'See the World, Erase its Borders', *Business Week* (28 August 2000), pp. 113–14.

66 SingTel, 'Community Role', http://welcome.singtel.com/about_singtel/community_role/communityrole.asp, viewed 9 December 2002.

67 Geert Hofstede, 'Motivation, Leadership, and Organization: Do American Theories Apply Abroad?', *Organizational Dynamics* (summer 1980), p. 43. See also Hofstede's 'Cultural Constraints in Management Theories', *Academy of Management Review*, vol. 7 (1993), pp. 81–94.

68 The classics are William Ouchi, *Theory Z: How American Businesses Can Meet the Japanese Challenge* (Reading, MA: Addison-Wesley, 1981) and Richard Tanner Pascale and Anthony G. Athos, *The Art of Japanese Management: Applications for American Executives* (New York: Simon & Schuster, 1981).

69 For a good discussion, see chapters 4 and 5 in Miriam Erez and P. Christopher Early, *Culture, Self-Identity and Work* (New York: Oxford University Press, 1993).

70 J. Bernard Keys, Luther Tray Denton and Thomas R. Miller, 'The Japanese Management Theory Jungle — Revisited', *Journal of Management*, vol. 20 (1994), pp. 373–402.

71 See Yumiko Ono and Bill Spindle, 'Standing Alone: Japan's Long Decline Makes One Thing Rise — Individualism', *Wall Street Journal* (29 December 2000), pp. A1, A4.

72 Quote from Kenichi Ohmae, 'Japan's Admiration for U.S. Methods is an Open Book', *Wall Street Journal* (10 October 1983), p. 21. See also his book *The Borderless World: Power and Strategy in the Interlinked Economy* (New York: Harper, 1989).

73 Geert Hofstede, 'A Reply to Goodstein and Hunt', *Organizational Dynamics*, vol. 10 (summer 1981), p. 68.

74 Cadbury Schweppes, 'Company Subsidiaries', www.cadbury schweppes.com/contact/company_subsidiaries/index.html, viewed 10 December 2002.

75 Cadbury Schweppes, 'Strategy', www.cadburyschweppes.com/com pany_information/business_strategy/index.html, viewed 10 December 2002.

76 Cadbury Schweppes, 'Annual Report 2000', www.cadbury schweppes.com/pdfs/annual_reports/2000ar_description_of_business. pdf, viewed 10 December 2002.

77 Personal communication with international manager at Cadbury Schweppes plc, April 2001; Helen Deresky, *International Management*, 3rd edn (Reading, MA: Addison-Wesley, 2000); Cottee's web site, www.cottees.com.au, viewed 25 October 2002; Cadbury Schweppes, 'Strategy', op. cit.

Chapter 6 notes

1 Information from *Philanthropy News Digest*, vol. 5 (21 April 1999); Jim Carlton, 'Environmentalists to Fight Globalization', *Wall Street Journal* (17 July 2000), p. A2; and Goldman Foundation web site: www.goldman prize.org.

2 See Joel Makower, *Beyond the Bottom Line: Putting Social Responsibility to Work for Your Business and the World* (New York: Simon & Schuster, 1994).

3 See a variety of information at Business for Social Responsibility web site: www.bsr.org.

4 Information and quotes from 'The Socially Correct Corporate', *Fortune*, special advertising section (24 July 2000), pp. S32–S34.

5 Lend Lease, 'Community: Our Commitment', www.lend lease.com.au/llweb/llc/main.nsf/all/all_community_overview, viewed 16 December 2002.

6 Reported in Adam Smith, 'Wall Street's Outrageous Fortunes', *Esquire* (April 1987), p. 73.

7 Desmond Tutu, 'Do More Than Win', *Fortune* (30 December 1991), p. 59.

8 For an overview, see Francis Joseph Aguilar, *Managing Corporate Ethics: Learning from America's Ethical Companies*

How to Supercharge Business Performance (New York: Oxford, 1994); and Linda K. Trevino and Katherine A. Nelson, *Managing Business Ethics* (New York: Wiley, 1995).

9 Department of Immigration & Multicultural & Indigenous Affairs, 'Abolition of the "White Australia" Policy', fact sheet, www.immi.gov.au/facts/08abolition.htm, viewed 3 November 2002.

10 Trevino and Nelson, op. cit., p. 15.

11 See Gerald F. Cavanagh, Dennis J. Moberg and Manuel Velasquez, 'The Ethics of Organizational Politics', *Academy of Management Review*, vol. 6 (1981), pp. 363–74; Justin G. Longenecker, Joseph A. McKinney and Carlos W. Moore, 'Egoism and Independence: Entrepreneurial Ethics', *Organizational Dynamics* (winter 1988), pp. 64–72; Justin G. Longenecker, Joseph A. McKinney and Carlos W. Moore, 'The Generation Gap in Business Ethics', *Business Horizons* (September–October 1989), pp. 9–14.

12 Raymond L. Hilgert, 'What Ever Happened to Ethics in Business and in Business Schools', *The Diary of Alpha Kappa Psi* (April 1989), pp. 4–8.

13 Jerald Greenburg, 'Organizational Justice: Yesterday, Today, and Tomorrow', *Journal of Management*, vol. 16 (1990), pp. 399–432; and Mary A. Konovsky, 'Understanding Procedural Justice and its Impact on Business Organizations', *Journal of Management*, vol. 26 (2000), pp. 489–511.

14 Interactional justice is described by Robert J. Bies, 'The Predicament of Injustice: The Management of Moral Outrage', in L. L. Cummings and B. M. Staw (eds), *Research in Organizational Behavior*, vol. 9 (Greenwich, CT: JAI Press, 1987), pp. 289–319. The example is from Carol T. Kulik and Robert L. Holbrook, 'Demographics in Service Encounters: Effects of Racial and Gender Congruence on Perceived Fairness', *Social Justice Research*, vol. 13 (December 2000), pp. 375–402.

15 Robert D. Haas, 'Ethics: A Global Business Challenge', *Vital Speeches of the Day* (1 June 1996), pp. 506–9.

16 Thomas Donaldson, 'Values in Tension: Ethics Away from Home', *Harvard Business Review*, vol. 74 (September–October 1996), pp. 48–62.

17 Thomas Donaldson and Thomas W. Dunfee, 'Towards a Unified Conception of Business Ethics: Integrative Social Contracts Theory', *Academy of Management Review*, vol. 19 (1994), pp. 252–85.

18 Developed from Donaldson, op. cit.

19 Reported in Barbara Ley Toffler, 'Tough Choices: Managers Talk Ethics', *New Management*, vol. 4 (1987), pp. 34–9. See also Barbara Ley Toffler, *Tough Choices: Managers Talk Ethics* (New York: Wiley, 1986).

20 See discussion by Trevino and Nelson, op. cit., pp. 47–62.

21 Information from Steven N. Brenner and Earl A. Mollander, 'Is the Ethics of Business Changing?', *Harvard Business Review*, vol. 55 (January–February 1977).

22 Saul W. Gellerman, 'Why "Good" Managers Make Bad Ethical Choices', *Harvard Business Review*, vol. 64 (July–August 1986), pp. 85–90.

23 The Body Shop came under scrutiny over the degree to which its business practices actually live up to this charter and the company's selfpromoted green image. See, for example, John Entine, 'Shattered Image', *Business Ethics* (September–October 1994), pp. 23–8.

24 Information on this case from William M. Carley, 'Antitrust Chief Says CEOs Should Tape all Phone Calls to Each Other', *Wall Street Journal* (15 February 1983), p. 23; 'American Air, Chief End Antitrust Suit, Agree Not to Discuss Fares with Rivals', *Wall Street Journal* (15 July 1985), p. 4; 'American Airlines Loses Its Pilot', *The Economist* (18 April 1998), p. 58.

25 The Body Shop, 'Values Reporting', www.thebodyshop.com/web/tbsgl/values_rep.jsp, viewed 11 December 2002.

26 Alan L. Otten, 'Ethics on the Job: Companies Alert Employees to Potential Dilemmas', *Wall Street Journal* (14 July), p. 17; and 'The Business Ethics Debate', *Newsweek* (25 May 1987), p. 36.

27 Whistleblowers Australia, www.uow.edu.au/arts/sts/bmartin/dissent/contacts/au_wba/info.html, viewed 11 December 2002.

28 See 'Whistle-Blowers on Trial', *Business Week* (24 March 1997), pp. 172–8; 'NLRB Judge Rules for Massachusetts Nurses in Whistle-Blowing Case', *American Nurse* (January–February 1998), p. 7.

29 For a review of whistleblowing, see Marcia P. Micelli and Janet P. Near, *Blowing the Whistle* (Lexington, MA: Lexington Books, 1992); see also Micelli and Near, 'Whistleblowing: Reaping the Benefits', *Academy of Management Executive*, vol. 8 (August 1994), pp. 65–72.

30 Information from James A. Waters, 'Catch 20.5: Mortality as an Organizational Phenomenon', *Organizational Dynamics*, vol. 6 (spring 1978), pp. 3–15.

31 Robert D. Gilbreath, 'The Hollow Executive', *New Management*, vol. 4 (1987), pp. 24–8.

32 Developed from recommendations of the Government Accountability Project reported in 'Blowing the Whistle without Paying the Piper'.

33 All reported in Charles D. Pringle and Justin G. Longenecker, 'The Ethics of MBO', *Academy of Management Review*, vol. 7 (April 1982), p. 309. See also Barry Z. Posner and Warren H. Schmidt, 'Values and the American Manager: An Update', *California Management Review*, vol. 26 (spring 1984), pp. 202–16.

34 Information from corporate web site: www.gapinc.com.

35 See Thomas Donaldson and Lee Pres-ton, 'The Stakeholder Theory of the Corporation', *Academy of Management Review*, vol. 20 (January 1995), pp. 65–91.

36 For a good review see Robert H. Miles, *Managing the Corporate Social Environment* (Englewood Cliffs, NJ: Prentice Hall, 1987).

37 Information from 'The Socially Correct Corporate', op. cit.; David Kirkpatrick, 'Looking for Profits in Poverty', *Fortune* (5 February 2001), pp. 174–6.

38 Developed from a discussion in Makower, op cit., pp. 17–18.

39 The historical framework of this discussion is developed from Keith Davis, 'The Case for and against Business Assumption of Social Responsibility', *Academy of Management Journal* (June 1973), pp. 312–22; Keith Davis and William Frederick, *Business and Society: Management: Public Policy, Ethics*, 5th edn (New York: McGraw-Hill, 1984). The debate is also discussed by Makower, op. cit., pp. 28–33. See also, 'Civics 101', *The Economist* (11 May 1996), p. 61.

40 The Friedman quotation is from Milton Friedman, *Capitalism and Freedom* (Chicago: University of Chicago Press, 1962); the Samuelson quotation is from Paul A. Samuelson, 'Love That Corporation', *Mountain Bell Magazine* (spring 1971). Both are cited in Davis, 'The Case for and Against'.

41 Davis and Frederick, op. cit.

42 Ernst & Young, 'Corporate Social Responsibility: Unlocking the Value', executive summary, www.ey.com.au, viewed 1 November 2002. *Corporate Social Responsibility: A Survey of Global Companies.* © Ernst & Young, 2002.

43 See Makower, op. cit., pp. 71–5; and Sandra A. Waddock and Samuel B. Graves, 'The Corporate Social Performance — Financial Performance Link', *Strategic Management Journal* (1997), pp. 303–19.

44 Davis, op. cit.

45 Archie B. Carroll, 'A ThreeDimensional Model of Corporate Performance', *Academy of Management Review*, vol. 4 (1979), pp. 497–505.

46 Elizabeth Gatewood and Archie B. Carroll, 'The Anatomy of Corporate Social Response', *Business Horizons*, vol. 24 (September–October 1981), pp. 9–16.

47 For the other side of this issue and the support available through government sources for small businesses, see 'When Bureaucrats Are a Boon', *Business Week*, enterprise issue (1 September 1997), pp. ENT 4–6.

48 Alan Nankervis, Robert Compton and Marian Baird, *Strategic Human Resource Management*, 4th edn (Melbourne: Nelson Thomson Learning, 2002), p. 492; New Zealand's Health and Safety Net, www.osh.dol.govt.nz.

49 Raymond J. Stone, *Human Resource Management*, 3rd edn (Brisbane: John Wiley & Sons, 1998), p. 693.

50 Asia Pacific Consumer Law, www.ciroap.org/apcl.

51 Various articles on HIH can be found at www.news.com.au/indexa/0,7141,hih,00.html, accessed 12 December 2002.

52 © Lucinda Schmidt, 'Warnings Were Ignored', *BRW* (15 June 2001). By permission of Journalists Copyright.

53 ibid.

54 ibid.

55 Melissa Fyfe, 'HIH Chiefs Accused', www.theage.com.au/news/national/2001/05/25/FFXBI7HE3NC.html, viewed 12 March 2002.

56 ibid.

57 ibid.

58 ibid.

59 ibid.

60 James C. Sarros and Oleh Butchatsky, *Leadership — Australia's Top CEOs: Finding Out What Makes Them the Best* (Sydney: HarperCollins, 1998), p. 242.

61 Jim Clemmer, 'Balancing Technology, Management and Leadership', www.clemmer.net/excerpts/balancingtech.shtml, viewed 7 March 2002.

Chapter 7 notes

1 Quote from 'Today's Companies Won't Make It, and Gary Hamel Knows Why', *Fortune* (4 September 2000), pp. 386–7.

2 Gary Hamel, *Leading the Revolution* (Boston: Harvard Business School Press, 2000).

3 Henry Mintzberg, 'The Manager's Job: Folklore and Fact', *Harvard Business Review*, vol. 53 (July–August 1975), pp. 54–67; Henry Mintzberg, 'Planning on the Left Side and Managing on the Right', *Harvard Business Review*, vol. 54 (July–August 1976), pp. 46–55.

4 Quote from Stephen Covey and Roger Merrill, 'New Ways to Get Organized at Work', *USA Weekend* (6–8 February 1998), p. 18. Books by Stephen R. Covey include: *The 7 Habits of Highly Effective People: Powerful Lessons in Personal Change* (New York: Fireside, 1990), and Stephen R. Covey and Sandra Merril Covey, *The 7 Habits of Highly Effective Families: Building a Beautiful Family Culture in a Turbulent World* (New York: Golden Books, 1996).

5 For a classic study, see Stanley Thune and Robert House, 'Where Long-Range Planning Pays Off', *Business Horizons*, vol. 13 (1970), pp. 81–7. For a critical review of the literature, see Milton Leontiades and Ahmet Teel, 'Planning Perceptions and Planning Results', *Strategic Management Journal*, vol. 1 (1980), pp. 65–75; J. Scott Armstrong, 'The Value of Formal Planning for Strategic Decisions', *Strategic Management Journal*, vol. 3 (1982), pp. 197–211. For special attention to the small business setting, see Richard B. Robinson Jr, John A. Pearce II, George S. Vozikis and Timothy S. Mescon, 'The Relationship between Stage of Development and Small Firm Planning and Performance', *Journal of Small Business Management*, vol. 22 (1984), pp. 45–52; Christopher Orphen, 'The Effects of Long-Range Planning on Small Business Performance: A Further Examination', *Journal of Small Business Management*, vol. 23 (1985), pp. 16–23. For an empirical study of large corporations, see Vasudevan Ramanujam and N. Venkatraman, 'Planning and Performance: A New Look at an Old Question', *Business Horizons*, vol. 30 (1987), pp. 19–25.

6 For more information on Dyson, see John Campling, *Managing in the Global Economy*, video documentary series (Brisbane: John Wiley & Sons, 2001).

7 Quotes from *Business Week* (8 August 1994), pp. 78–86.

8 See William Oncken Jr and Donald L. Wass, 'Management Time: Who's Got the Monkey?', *Harvard Business Review*, vol. 52 (September–October 1974), pp. 75–80, and featured as an HBR classic, *Harvard Business Review*, (November–December 1999).

9 Covey and Merrill, op. cit., p. 18.

10 For more information on Ocean Spirit Cruises see Campling, *Managing in the Global Economy*, op. cit.

11 See Elliot Jaques, *The Form of Time* (New York: Russak & Co., 1982). For an executive commentary on his research, see Walter Kiechel III, 'How Executives Think', *Fortune* (21 December 1987), pp. 139–44.

12 See Henry Mintzberg, 'Rounding Out the Manager's Job', *Sloan Management Review* (fall 1994), pp. 1–25.

13 For a thorough review of forecasting, see J. Scott Armstrong, *Long-Range Forecasting*, 2nd edn (New York: Wiley, 1985).

14 See, for example, Robert C. Camp, *Business Process Benchmarking* (Milwaukee: ASQ Quality Press, 1994); Michael J. Spendolini, *The Benchmarking Book* (New York: AMACOM, 1992); and Christopher E. Bogan and Michael J. English, *Benchmarking for Best Practices: Winning Through Innovative Adaptation* (New York: McGraw-Hill, 1994).

15 'How Classy Can 7-Eleven Get?', *Business Week* (1 September 1997), pp. 74–5; and, Kellie B. Gormly, '7-Eleven Moving Up a Grade', *Columbus Dispatch* (3 August 2000), pp. C1–C2.

16 Frederick W. Taylor, *The Principles of Scientific Management* (New York: W. W. Norton, 1967), originally published by Harper & Brothers in 1911.

17 See 'Acer Chief Plays Cards Carefully', *The Australian* (10 October 2001), p. 25.

18 John Campling, Technological Change and Decision-Making Processes in Organisations: Opportunities for Change, paper submitted to the British Academy of Management for 2002 Conference, London, http://home.hccnet.nl/22.sas/, viewed 12 July 2002; 'Heroes to Order', *The Guardian* (5 October 2001), p. 25; http://www.specialforces.co.uk/home.htm, viewed 12 July 2002.

19 For more information on Skyrail see Campling, *Managing in the Global Economy*, op. cit.

20 Thomas J. Peters and Robert H. Waterman Jr, *In Search of Excellence: Lessons from America's Best-Run Companies* (New York: Basic Books, 1984).

21 Toddi Gutner, 'Better Your Business: Benchmark It', *Business Week*, enterprise issue (27 April 1998), pp. ENT4–6.

22 Based on discussion by Harold Koontz and Cyril O'Donnell, *Essentials of Management* (New York: McGraw-Hill, 1974), pp. 362–5; see also Rob Cross and Lloyd Baird, 'Technology is Not Enough: Improving Performance by Building Organizational Memory', *Sloan Management Review* (spring 2000), pp. 69–78.

23 See John F. Love, *McDonald's: Behind the Arches* (New York: Bantam Books, 1986); Ray Kroc and Robert Anderson, *Grinding It Out: The Making of McDonald's* (New York: St. Martin's Press, 1990).

24 Douglas McGregor, *The Human Side of Enterprise* (New York: McGraw-Hill, 1960).

25 International Labour Organization, *Breaking Through The Glass Ceiling: Women in Management* (2001); Boardroom Partners, *Talking at the Table* (2001); John Campling, 'International Economic Restructuring, Enterprise Bargaining and Gender Outcomes: Predictions for Australia', *The International Journal of Comparative Labour Law and Industrial Relations*, vol. 10, no. 1 (spring 1994), pp. 36–54.

26 Cited in Peter F. Drucker, *Management: Tasks, Responsibilities, Practices* (New York: Harper & Row, 1973), p. 797.

27 Eric L. Harvey, 'Discipline vs. Punishment', *Management Review*, vol. 76 (March 1987), pp. 25–9.

28 The 'hot stove rules' are developed from R. Bruch McAfee and William Poffenberger, *Productivity Strategies: Enhancing Employee Job Performance* (Englewood Cliffs, NJ: Prentice Hall, 1982), pp. 54–5. They are originally attributed to Douglas McGregor, 'Hot Stove Rules of Discipline', in G. Strauss and L. Sayles (eds), *Personnel: The Human Problems of Management* (Englewood Cliffs, NJ: Prentice Hall, 1967).

29 For more information see Campling, *Managing in the Global Economy*, op. cit.

30 See Dale D. McConkey, *How to Manage by Results*, 3rd edn (New York: AMACOM, 1976); Stephen J. Carroll Jr and Henry J. Tosi Jr, *Management by Objectives: Applications and Research* (New York: Macmillan, 1973); and Anthony P. Raia, *Managing by Objectives* (Glenview, IL: Scott, Foresman, 1974).

31 Douglas McGregor, op. cit.

32 The work on goal setting and motivation is summarised in Edwin A. Locke and Gary P. Latham, *Goal Setting: A Motivational Technique That Works!* (Englewood Cliffs, NJ: Prentice Hall, 1984).

33 For a discussion of research, see Carroll and Tosi, op. cit.; Raia, op. cit.; Steven Kerr, 'Overcoming the Dysfunctions of MBO', *Management by Objectives*, vol. 5, no. 1 (1976).

34 'Skyrail Wins Major International Eco-tourism Award', *The Skyrail Newsletter*, issue 7 (2000), p. 1.

35 'Green Globe 21 Presentation', *SkyNews: The Skyrail Newsletter* (July 2002), p. 1.

36 Campling, 'Skyrail' in *Managing in the Global Economy*, op. cit.

Chapter 8 notes

1 Based on interviews with Cairns-based Virgin Blue management (9 April 2002) and Cairns Chamber of Commerce (July 2002); www.virginblue.com.au/about/wwcf.html; www.virginblue.com.au/about/cabcrew.html; 'Virgin Wants to Keep Itself Nice and Single', *The Australian* (12 October 2001), p. 22.

2 Interview with the Seven Television Network's General Manager, Media and Investment (May 2001).

3 Michael T. Hannan and John Freeman, 'The Population Ecology of Organizations', *American Journal of Sociology*, vol. 82 (1977), pp. 929–64.

4 Ernst Von Weizsacker, Amory B. Lovins and L. Hunter Lovins, *Factor 4: Doubling Wealth, Halving Resource Use* (Sydney: Allen & Unwin, 1997); John Campling, A Strategy for Sustainable Industry and Regional Economic Development in Far North Queensland, occasional paper (Townsville: James Cook University School of Business, 2003). See also Adrian Wilkinson, Malcolm Hill and Paul Gollan, 'The Sustainability Debate', *International Journal of Operations and Production Management*, vol. 21, no. 12 (2001), p. 1492.

5 Masahiro Ota, 'Cutting Edge: The Zero Emission Challenge', *Aichi Voice*, vol. 9 (1998), www.pref.aichi.jp/voice/9_cutting_edge.html.

6 Campling, op. cit.; N. Hooper, 'Recycled Rubber Hits the Road to Success', *BRW* (3 August 1998), www.brw.com.au/content/030898/brw12.html.

7 Campling, op. cit.

8 ibid. See also S. Banerjee, 'Managerial Perceptions of Corporate Environmentalism: Interpretations from Industry and Strategic Implications for Organisations', *Journal of Management Studies*, vol. 38, no. 4 (2001), pp. 479–513; M. Polansky, 'Incorporating the Natural Environment in Corporate Strategy: A Stakeholder Approach', *Journal of Business Strategy*, vol. 12, no. 2 (1995), pp. 152–5; H. Tibbs, 'Industrial Ecology: An Environmental Agenda for Industry', *Whole Earth Review* (September–October 1995), pp. 120–34.

9 Campling, op. cit.

10 IKEA www.ikea.co.uk/about_ikea/social/environment.asp; and interview with managers of IKEA Australia.

11 Henry Mintzberg, 'Patterns in Strategy Formation', *Management Science*, vol. 24 (1978), pp. 327–36.

12 Gary Hamel and C. K. Prahalad, 'Strategic Intent', *Harvard Business Review* (May–June 1989), pp. 63–76.

13 Information and quotes from Marcia Stepanek, 'How Fast Is Net Fast?', *Business Week E-Biz* (1 November 1999), pp. EB52–EB54.

14 Keith H. Hammond, 'Michael Porter's Big Ideas', *Fast Company* (March 2001).

15 Michael A. Hitt, R. Duane Ireland and Robert E. Hoskisson, *Strategic Management: Competitiveness and Globalization* (Minneapolis: West, 1997), p. 5.

16 Michael E. Porter, *Competitive Strategy: Techniques for Analyzing Industries and Competitors* (New York: Free Press, 1980); Michael E. Porter, 'Clusters and the New Economics of Competition', *Harvard Business Review* (November–December 1998), pp. 77–90.

17 Richard A. D'Aveni, *Hyper-Competition: Managing the Dynamics of Strategic Maneuvering* (New York: Free Press, 1994).

18 Peter F. Drucker, 'Five Questions', *Executive Excellence* (6 November 1994), pp. 6–7.

19 Peter F. Drucker, *Management: Tasks, Responsibilities, Practices* (New York: Harper & Row, 1973), p. 122.

20 ibid.

21 See Laura Nash, 'Mission Statements: Mirrors and Windows', *Harvard Business Review* (March–April 1988), pp. 155–6. James C. Collins and Jerry I. Porras, 'Building Your Company's Vision', *Harvard Business Review* (September–October 1996), pp. 65–77; James C. Collins and Jerry I. Porras, *Built to Last: Successful Habits of Visionary Companies* (New York: Harper Business, 1997).

22 Gary Hamel, *Leading the Revolution* (Boston, MA: Harvard Business School Press, 2000), pp. 72–3.

23 © Foster's Group Limited www.fosters.com.au.

24 Fisher & Paykel www.fisherpaykel.co.nz.

25 Interviews with former Comalco management staff and CFMEU officials.

26 Information from corporate web site www.merck.com.

27 Terrence E. Deal and Allan A. Kennedy, *Corporate Cultures: The Rites and Rituals of Corporate Life* (Reading, MA: Addison-Wesley, 1982), p. 22. For more on organisational culture see Edgar H. Schein, *Organizational Culture and Leadership*, 2nd edn (San Francisco: Jossey-Bass, 1997).

28 Peter F. Drucker's views on organisational objectives are expressed in his classic books, *The Practice of Management* (New York: Harper & Row, 1954), and *Management: Tasks, Responsibilities, Practices*, op. cit. See also his article 'Management: The Problems of Success', *Academy of Management Executive*, vol. 1 (1987), pp. 13–19.

29 C. K. Prahalad and Gary Hamel, 'The Core Competencies of the Corporation', *Harvard Business Review* (May–June 1990), pp. 79–91; see also, Hitt et al., op. cit., pp. 99–103.

30 For a discussion of Michael Porter's approach to strategic planning, see his books *Competitive Strategy*, op. cit. and *Competitive Advantage: Creating and Sustaining Superior Performance* (New York: Free Press, 1986); his article, 'What Is Strategy?', *Harvard Business Review* (November–December 1996), pp. 61–78; and Richard M. Hodgetts' interview 'A Conversation with Michael E. Porter: A Significant Extension Toward Operational Improvement and Positioning', *Organizational Dynamics* (summer 1999), pp. 24–33.

31 See the discussion by Hitt et al., op. cit., pp. 66–7.

32 The four grand strategies were originally described by William F. Glueck, *Business Policy: Strategy Formulation and Management Action*, 2nd edn (New York: McGraw-Hill, 1976).

33 Hitt et al., op. cit., p. 197.

34 See William McKinley, Carol M. Sanchez and A. G. Schick, 'Organizational Downsizing: Constraining, Cloning, Learning', *Academy of Management Executive*, vol. 9 (August 1995), pp. 32–44.

35 Kim S. Cameron, Sara J. Freeman and A. K. Mishra, 'Best Practices in White-Collar Downsizing: Managing Contradictions', *Academy of Management Executive*, vol. 4 (August 1991), pp. 57–73.

36 Michael E. Porter and Mark B. Fuller,' Coalitions and Global Strategy', in Michael E. Porter (ed.), *Competition in Global Industries* (Cambridge, MA: Harvard University Press, 1986).

37 John Campling, Organisational and Locational Change in the Canadian Automotive Industry: A Proposed Framework for Industrial Analysis, unpublished Master's Thesis, Queen's University, Canada (1984).

38 Sun Tzu, *The Art of War* (New York: Delacorte Press, 1983).

39 Information from Michael Rappa, 'Business Models on the Web', www.ecommerce.ncsu.edu/business_models.html, viewed 6 February 2001.

40 D'Aveni, op. cit., pp. 13–16, 21–4.

41 ibid.

42 ibid.

43 See the discussion in Thomas L. Wheelen and J. David Hunger, *Strategic Management & Business Policy*, 7th edn (Upper Saddle River, NJ: Prentice Hall, 2000), pp. 133–47.

44 Porter, op. cit. (1980, 1986, 1996).

45 Information from www.polo.com.

46 John Campling, 'International Economic Restructuring, Enterprise Bargaining and Gender Outcomes: Predictions for Australia', *The International Journal of Comparative Labour Law and Industrial Relations*, vol. 10, no. 1 (spring 1994), pp. 36–54.

47 Information from Suzanne Steel, 'Quality in Bloom', *Business Today* (22 August 1994), pp. 1–2.

48 Richard G. Hamermesh, 'Making Planning Strategic', *Harvard Business Review*, vol. 64 (July–August 1986), pp. 115–20; Richard G. Hamermesh, *Making Strategy Work* (New York: Wiley, 1986).

49 See Gerald B. Allan, 'A Note on the Boston Consulting Group Concept of Competitive Analysis and Corporate Strategy', Harvard Business School, Intercollegiate Case Clearing House, ICCH9-175-175 (Boston: Harvard Business School, June 1976).

50 Hamermesh, op. cit. (1986).

51 The adaptive model is described in Raymond E. Miles and Charles C. Snow's book, *Organizational Strategy, Structure, and Process* (New York: McGraw-Hill, 1978); and their articles, 'Designing Strategic Human Resources Systems', *Organizational Dynamics*, vol. 13 (summer 1984), pp. 36–52, and 'Fit, Failure, and the Hall of Fame', *California Management Review*, vol. 26 (spring 1984), pp. 10–28.

52 John T. Campling and Paul J. Gollan, *Bargained Out: Negotiating Without Unions in Australia* (Sydney: Federation Press, 1999); John T. Campling, 'Workplace Bargaining in Non Unionised Firms', *International Journal of Employment Studies*, vol. 6, no. 1 (April 1998), pp. 59–82; John T. Campling, 'Enterprise Bargaining in Lightly and Non-Unionised Firms: Comparative Australian Case Study Evidence', *The International Journal of Comparative Labour Law and Industrial Relations*, vol. 12, no. 4 (winter 1996), pp. 315–36.

53 James Brian Quinn, 'Strategic Change: Logical Incrementalism', *Sloan Management Review*, vol. 20 (fall 1978), pp. 7–21.

54 Henry Mintzberg, *The Nature of Managerial Work* (New York: Harper & Row, 1973, and HarperCollins, 1997); John P. Kotter, *The General Managers* (New York: Free Press, 1986).

55 Henry Mintzberg, 'Planning on the Left Side and Managing on the Right', *Business Review*, vol. 54 (July–August 1976), pp. 46–55; Henry Mintzberg and James A. Waters, 'Of Strategies, Deliberate and Emergent', *Strategic Management Journal*, vol. 6 (1985), pp. 257–72; Henry Mintzberg, 'Crafting Strategy', *Harvard Business Review*, vol. 65 (July–August 1987), pp. 66–75.

56 For research support, see Daniel H. Gray, 'Uses and Misuses of Strategic Planning', *Harvard Business Review*, vol. 64 (January–February 1986), pp. 89–97.

57 For a discussion of corporate governance issues, see Hugh Sherman and Rajeswararao Chaganti, *Corporate Governance and the Timeliness of Change* (Westport, CT: Quorum Books, 1998).

58 H. Chen and T. J. Chen, 'Governance Structures in Strategic Alliances: Transaction Cost Versus Resource-based Perspective', *Journal of World Business*, vol. 38, no. 1 (2003), pp. 1–14.

59 See R. Duane Ireland and Michael A. Hitt, 'Achieving and Maintaining Strategic Competitiveness in the 21st Century', *Academy of Management Executive*, vol. 13 (1999), pp. 43–57.

60 Matt Murray, 'As Huge Companies Keep Growing, CEOs Struggle to Keep Pace', *Wall Street Journal* (8 February 2001), p. A6.

61 ibid.

62 Hammond, op. cit.

63 Murray, op. cit., p. A6.

64 P&G home page www.pg.com, viewed 1 March 2001.

65 ibid.

66 R. Tomkins and S. Voyle, 'Revenge of the Proctoids: The Ousting of Durk Jager', *Financial Times (London)* (12 June 2000), p. 22.

67 ibid.

68 ibid.

69 Kayte VanScoy, 'Can the Internet Hot-Wire P&G?', *SmartBusinessMag.com* (January 2001), pp. 69–79.

70 ibid.

71 ibid.

72 ibid.

73 ibid.

74 ibid.

75 ibid.

76 ibid.

77 ibid.

78 ibid.

Chapter 9 notes

1 Interview with local Wizard branch manager, Sydney; www.wizard.com.au; Sue Lecky, 'A Wizard Idea Still Calls for a Magic Touch', *The Sydney Morning Herald* (3 November 2001).

2 Information from the corporate web sites and from The Entrepreneur's Hall of Fame: www.ltbn.com/halloffame.html.

3 See www.dicksmith.com.au; *Who's Who Australia* (2000).

4 Information from www.poppy.com.au, viewed June–July 2002.

5 *Business Sunday* (Channel 9); *Business Report* (Channel 7).

6 For a review and discussion of the entrepreneurial mind see Jeffry A. Timmons, *New Venture Creation: Entrepreneurship for the 21st Century* (New York: Irwin/McGraw-Hill, 1999), pp. 219–25.

7 See the review by Robert D. Hisrich and Michael P. Peters, *Entrepreneurship*, 4th edn (New York: Irwin/McGraw-Hill, 1998), pp. 67–70.

8 Based on research summarised by Hisrich and Peters, op. cit., pp. 70–4.

9 Timothy Butler and James Waldroop, 'Job Sculpting: The Art of Retaining Your Best People', *Harvard Business Review* (September–October 1999), pp. 144–52.

10 This list is developed from Timmons, op. cit., pp. 47–8; and Hisrich and Peters, op. cit., pp. 67–70.

11 Interviews with Tjapukai management, 2001, 2003.

12 Council of Small Business Organisations of Australia, 2001.

13 Australian Bureau of Statistics, Small Business Series (2002).

14 See www.adacel.com.au; 'Aussies Grab Spot on Global Flight Path', *The Australian* (28 November 2001), p. 3.

15 David C. Michael and Greg Sutherland, *Asia's Digital Dividends* (New York: Wiley, 2001).

16 Information from Kevin Ferguson, 'To B2B or Not B2B', *Business Week Frontier* (14 August 2000), pp. F36–F42.

17 Statistics from Family Business Australia, 2001; Australian Bureau of Statistics, 2001.

18 Quote from the case 'Am I my Uncle's Keeper?' by Paul I. Karofsky (Northeastern University Center for Family Business) and published at www.fambiz.com, viewed 17 February 2003.

19 *Survey of Small and Mid-Sized Businesses: Trends for 2000* (Arthur Andersen, 2000).

20 ibid.

21 Family Business Australia www.fambiz.com.au.

22 Based on Norman M. Scarborough and Thomas W. Zimmer, *Effective Small Business Management* (Englewood Cliffs, NJ: Prentice Hall, 2000), pp. 25–30; and Scott Clark, 'Most Small-Business Failures Tied to Poor Management', *Business Journal* (10 April 2000).

23 See www.vitasoy.com; interview with Vitasoy (Australia) management, 2002.

24 See, for example, John L. Nesheim, *High Tech Start Up* (New York: Free Press, 2000).

25 Developed from William S. Sahlman, 'How to Write a Great Business Plan', *Harvard Business Review* (July–August 1997), pp. 98–108.

26 Discussion based on 'The Life Cycle of Entrepreneurial Firms', in Ricky Griffin, *Management*, 6th edn (New York: Houghton Mifflin, 1999), pp. 309–10; and Neil C. Churchill and Virginia L. Lewis, 'The Five Stages of Small Business Growth', *Harvard Business Review* (May–June 1993), pp. 30–50.

27 See ibid.; Linda Pinson and Jerry Jinnett, *Anatomy of a Business Plan: A Step-By-Step Guide to Starting Smart, Building the Business, and Securing Your Company's Future*, 4th edn (Chicago: Dearborn Trade, 1999).

28 Paul Reynolds, 'The Truth about Start-Ups', *Inc.* (February 1995), p. 23.

29 Standard components of business plans are described in many text sources such as Pinson and Jinnett, op. cit., and Scarborough and Zimmerer, op. cit.; and on web sites such as: American Express Small Business Services, Business Town.com and BizPlanIt.com.

30 Gifford Pinchot III, *Intrapreneuring, or Why You Don't Have to Leave the Corporation to Become an Entrepreneur* (New York: Harper & Row, 1985).

31 Kazuhiro Asakawa and Mark Lehrer, 'Managing Local Knowledge Assets Globally: The Role of Regional Innovation Relays', *Journal of World Business*, vol. 38, no. 1 (2002), pp. 31–42.

32 Interviews with Troppo Architects senior designers; various issues of *Architecture Australia*, 1997–2002.

33 See www.masportpump.com/earlydays.htm.

34 See www.masportfoundries.com/castings.html.

35 See www.garden-aids.co.nz/masport.html.

36 See www.masportfoundries.com/potbellies.html.

37 Telephone interviews with Masport managers, October–November 2002.

Chapter 10 notes

1 Henry Mintzberg and Ludo Van der Heyden, 'Organigraphs: Drawing How Companies Really Work', *Harvard Business Review* (September–October 1999), pp. 87–94.

2 John T. Campling and Grant Michelson, 'A Strategic Choice — Resource Dependence Analysis of Trade Union Mergers in the British and Australian Television Broadcasting and Film Industries', *Journal of Management Studies*, vol. 35, no. 5 (September 1998), pp. 1–23; John T. Campling and Grant Michelson, 'Trade Union Mergers in British and Australian Television Broadcasting', *The British Journal of Industrial Relations*, vol. 35, no. 2 (June 1997), pp. 215–42.

3 John T. Campling and Paul J. Gollan, *Bargained Out: Negotiating Without Unions in Australia* (Sydney: Federation Press, 1999).

4 The classic work is Alfred D. Chandler Jr, *Strategy and Structure: Chapters in the History of the Industrial Enterprise* (Cambridge, MA: MIT Press, 1962).

5 See Alfred D. Chandler Jr, 'Origins of the Organization Chart', *Harvard Business Review* (March–April 1988), pp. 156–7.

6 Information from Maggie Jackson, 'Work's Lessons Occurring in Unexpected Places', *Rockland Journal News* (7 January 1998), pp. 4A, 4E.

7 See Kenneth Noble, 'A Clash of Styles: Japanese Companies in the U.S', *New York Times* (25 January 1988), p. 7.

8 For a discussion of departmentalisation, see H. I. Ansoff and R. G. Bradenburg, 'A Language for Organization Design', *Management Science*, vol. 17 (August 1971), pp. B705–B731; Mariann Jelinek, 'Organization Structure: The Basic Conformations', in Mariann Jelinek, Joseph A. Litterer, and Raymond E. Miles (eds), *Organizations by Design: Theory and Practice* (Plano, TX: Business Publications, 1981), pp. 293–302; Henry Mintzberg, 'The Structuring of Organizations', in James Brian Quinn, Henry Mintzberg and Robert M. James (eds), *The Strategy Process: Concepts, Contexts and Cases* (Englewood Cliffs, NJ: Prentice Hall, 1988), pp. 276–304.

9 Robert L. Simison, 'Jaguar Slowly Sheds Outmoded Habits', *Wall Street Journal* (26 July 1991), p. A6; and Richard Stevenson, 'Ford Helps Jaguar Get Back Old Sheen', *International Herald Tribune* (14 December 1994), p. 11.

10 These alternatives are well described by Mintzberg, 'The Structuring of Organizations', op. cit.

11 See www.clubmed.com; www.gm.com.

12 See www.bhpbilliton.com; *BHP Billiton Annual Report 2000–01*.

13 See www.3m.com.

14 The focus on process is described in Michael Hammer, *Beyond Reengineering* (New York: Harper Business, 1997).

15 ibid.

16 Excellent reviews of matrix concepts are found in Stanley M. Davis and Paul R. Lawrence, *Matrix* (Reading, MA: Addison-Wesley, 1977); Paul R. Lawrence, Harvey F. Kolodny and Stanley M. Davis, 'The Human Side of the Matrix', *Organizational Dynamics*, vol. 6 (1977), pp. 43–61; Harvey F. Kolodny, 'Evolution to a Matrix Organization', *Academy of Management Review*, vol. 4 (1979), pp. 543–53.

17 Davis and Lawrence, op. cit.

18 See Mintzberg and Van der Heyden, op. cit.

19 Developed from Frank Ostroff, *The Horizontal Organization: What the Organization of the Future Looks Like and How it Delivers Value to Customers* (New York: Oxford University Press, 1999).

20 The nature of teams and teamwork is described in Jon R. Katzenbach and Douglas K. Smith, 'The Discipline of Teams', *Harvard Business Review* (March–April 1993), pp. 111–20.

21 Susan Albers Mohrman, Susan G. Cohen and Allan M. Mohrman Jr, *Designing Team-Based Organizations: New Forms for Knowledge Work* (San Francisco: Jossey-Bass, 1995).

22 See Glenn M. Parker, *Cross-Functional Teams* (San Francisco: Jossey-Bass, 1995).

23 See Ron Ashkenas, Dave Ulrich, Todd Jick and Steve Kerr, *The Boundaryless Organization: Breaking the Chains of Organizational Structure* (San Francisco: Jossey-Bass, 1996); Rupert F. Chisholm, *Developing Network Organizations: Learning from Practice and Theory* (Reading, MA: Addison-Wesley, 1998).

24 Information from William Bridges, 'The End of the Job', *Fortune* (19 September 1994), pp. 62–74; Alan Deutschman, 'The Managing Wisdom of High-Tech Superstars', *Fortune* (17 October 1994), pp. 197–206.

25 Cathryn Jimenez, 'Clean-out at Goodman Fielder', *The Australian* (12 December 2001); www.goodmanfielder.com.au.

26 See the discussion by Jay R. Galbraith, 'Designing the Networked Organization: Leveraging Size and Competencies', in Susan Albers Mohrman, Jay R. Galbraith, Edward E. Lawler III and Associates, *Tomorrow's Organizations: Crafting Winning Capabilities in a Dynamic World* (San Francisco: Jossey-Bass, 1998), pp. 76–102.

27 Ashkenas et al., op. cit.

28 Robert Slater, *Jack Welch and the GE Way: Management Insights and Leadership Secrets of the Legendary CEO* (New York: McGraw-Hill, 1998); 'Jack the Job-Killer Strikes Again', *Business Week* (12 February 2001), p. 12. See also E. F. Cabrera, J. Ortega and A. Cabrera, 'An Exploration of the Factors that Influence Employee Participation in Europe', *Journal of World Business*, vol. 38, no. 1 (2003), pp. 43–54.

29 Slater, op. cit.

30 See the collection of articles by Cary L. Cooper and Denise M. Rousseau (eds), *Trends in Organizational Behavior, Volume 6, The Virtual Organization* (New York: Wiley, 2000).

31 David Van Fleet, 'Span of Management Research and Issues', *Academy of Management Journal*, vol. 26 (1983), pp. 546–52.

32 Developed from Roger Fritz, *Rate Your Executive Potential* (New York: Wiley, 1988), pp. 185–6; Roy J. Lewicki, Donald D. Bowen, Douglas T. Hall and Francine S. Hall, *Experiences in Management and Organizational Behavior*, 3rd edn (New York: Wiley, 1988), p. 144.

33 See George P. Huber, 'A Theory of Effects of Advanced Information Technologies on Organizational Design, Intelligence, and Decision Making', *Academy of Management Review*, vol. 15 (1990), pp. 67–71.

34 'Ready for October Launch', *The Sydney Morning Herald* (9 September 2002); Cairns Chamber of Commerce, interview on Australian Airlines, 2002.

35 'Ready for October Launch', op. cit.

36 'Not To Be a Low-Fare Carrier', Associated Press News Service (11 April 2002).

Chapter 11 notes

1 LG Annual Reports, 1999–2000 and 2000–01; www.lge.com.au.

2 Jessica Lipnack and Jeffrey Stamps, *The Age of the Network: Organizing Principles for the 21st Century* (Essex Junction, VT: Omneo, 1994).

3 For a discussion of organisation theory and design, see W. Richard Scott, *Organizations: Rational, Natural, and Open Systems*, 4th edn (Upper Saddle River, NJ: Prentice Hall, 1998).

4 For a classic work see Jay R. Galbraith, *Organizational Design* (Reading, MA: Addison-Wesley, 1977).

5 This framework is based on Harold J. Leavitt, 'Applied Organizational Change in Industry: Structural, Technological and Humanistic Approaches', in James G. March (ed.), *Handbook of Organizations* (Chicago: Rand McNally, 1965), pp. 1144–70; and Edward E. Lawler III, *From the Ground Up: Six Principles for Building the New Logic Corporation* (San Francisco: Jossey-Bass, 1996), pp. 44–50.

6 A. M. Henderson and Talcott Parsons (eds and trans), *Max Weber: The Theory of Social Economic Organization* (New York: Free Press, 1947).

7 For classic treatments of bureaucracy, see Alvin Gouldner, *Patterns of Industrial Bureaucracy* (New York: Free Press, 1954); Robert K. Merton, *Social Theory and Social Structure* (New York: Free Press, 1957).

8 Tom Burns and George M. Stalker, *The Management of Innovation* (London: Tavistock, 1961; republished by Oxford University Press, London, 1994).

9 See Henry Mintzberg, *Structure in Fives: Designing Effective Organizations* (Englewood Cliffs, NJ: Prentice Hall, 1983).

10 Information from Thomas Petzinger Jr, 'Self-Organization Will Free Employees to Act Like Bosses', *Wall Street Journal* (3 January 1997), p. B1.

11 See Rosabeth Moss Kanter, *The Changing Masters* (New York: Simon & Schuster, 1983). Quotation from Rosabeth Moss Kanter and John D. Buck, 'Reorganizing Part of Honeywell: From Strategy to Structure', *Organizational Dynamics*, vol. 13 (winter 1985), p. 6.

12 See, for example, Jay R. Galbraith, Edward E. Lawler III and Associates, *Organizing for the Future* (San Francisco: Jossey-Bass, 1993); Susan Albers Mohrman, Jay R. Galbraith, Edward E. Lawler, III and Associates, *Tomorrow's Organization: Crafting Winning Capabilities in a Dynamic World* (San Francisco: Jossey-Bass, 1998).

13 Peter Senge, *The Fifth Discipline: The Art and Practice of the Learning Organization* (New York: Doubleday, 1994).

14 A classic treatment of environment and organisational design is found in James D. Thompson, *Organizations in Action* (New York: McGraw-Hill, 1967). See also Scott, op. cit., pp. 264–9.

15 Alfred D. Chandler Jr, *Strategy and Structure: Chapters in the History of the American Industrial Enterprise* (Cambridge, MA: MIT Press, 1962).

16 See, for example, Danny Miller, 'Configurations of Strategy and Structure: Towards a Synthesis', *Strategic Management Journal*, vol. 7 (1986), pp. 233–49.

17 Joan Woodward, *Industrial Organization: Theory and Practice* (London: Oxford University Press, 1965; republished by Oxford University Press, 1994).

18 This classification is from Thompson, op. cit.

19 See Peter M. Blau and Richard A. Schoennerr, *The Structure of Organizations* (New York: Basic Books, 1971); and Scott, op. cit., pp. 259–63.

20 D. E. Gumpert, 'The Joys of Keeping the Company Small', *Harvard Business Review* (July–August 1986), pp. 6–8, 12–14.

21 John R. Kimberly and Robert H. Miles, *The Organizational Life Cycle* (San Francisco: Jossey-Bass, 1980).

22 Kim Cameron, Sarah J. Freeman and Naneil K. Mishra, 'Best Practices in White-Collar Downsizing: Managing Contradictions', *Academy of Management Executive*, vol. 5 (August 1991), pp. 57–73.

23 See Gifford Pinchot III, *Intrapreneuring: Or Why You Don't Have to Leave the Corporation to Become an Entrepreneur* (New York: Harper & Row, 1985).

24 See Jay Lorsch and John Morse, *Organizations and Their Members: A Contingency Approach* (New York: Harper & Row, 1974); and Scott, op. cit., pp. 263–4.

25 'The Rebirth of IBM', *The Economist* (6 June 1998), pp. 65–8.

26 Paul R. Lawrence and Jay W. Lorsch, *Organizations and Environment* (Boston: Division of Research, Graduate School of Business Administration, Harvard University, 1967).

27 Burns and Stalker, op. cit.

28 See Galbraith, op. cit.; and Susan Albers Mohrman, 'Integrating Roles and Structure in the Lateral Organization', chapter 5 in Galbraith et al., op. cit.

29 For a good discussion of coordination and integration approaches, see Scott, op. cit., pp. 231–9.

30 Michael Hammer and James Champy, *Reengineering the Corporation: A Manifesto for Business Revolution*, rev. edn (New York: Harper Business, 1999).

31 Michael Hammer, *Beyond Reengineering* (New York: Harper Business, 1997).

32 Hammer, op. cit., p. 5; see also the discussion of processes in Gary Hamel, *Leading the Revolution* (Boston, MA: Harvard Business School Press, 2000).

33 Thomas M. Koulopoulos, *The Workflow Imperative* (New York: Van Nostrand Reinhold, 1995); Hammer, op. cit.

34 Ronni T. Marshak, 'Workflow Business Process Reengineering', special advertising section, *Fortune* (1997).

35 A similar example is found in Hammer, op. cit., pp. 9, 10.

36 Hammer, op. cit., pp. 28–30.

37 Hammer, op. cit., p. 29.

38 'Stings in E-tailing', *The Australian* (11 October 2001), p. 30.

39 Hammer, op. cit., p. 27.

40 Quote from Hammer and Company web site www.hammerandco.com.

41 Reed Abelson, 'Two of the Big Six in Accounting Plan to Form New No. 1', *New York Times* (19 September 1997), p. A1.

42 Thor Caldmanis, 'Price Waterhouse, Coopers to Merge', *USA Today* (19 September 1997), p. 1B.

43 ibid.

44 Barnet Wolf, 'Merger of Accountants to Shrink Big Six by One', *Columbus Dispatch* (19 September 1997), p. 1F.

45 'Accounting: The Big Five?', *The Economist* (20 September 1997), pp. 69–70.

46 'Professional Business Services', in *U.S. Industry and Trade Outlook* (New York: McGraw-Hill, 1998), pp. 49-1 to 49-9.

47 ibid.

48 Ernst & Young 2002 global results at www.ey.com/global/content. nsf/International/Press_Release_-_Ernst_&_Young_Fiscal_Year_2002_ Global_Revenues, viewed 28 March 2003.

49 'Accounting: The Big Five?', op. cit., pp. 69–70.

50 ibid.

51 Abelson, op. cit., p. A1.

Chapter 12 notes

1 Information from the web sites of the Australian Human Resources Institute www.ahri.com.au and AstraZeneca www.astrazeneca.com.au.

2 Nancy J. Perry, 'The Workers of the Future', *Fortune*, vol. 123, no. 12 (spring–summer 1991), pp. 68–72.

3 Robert Reich, *The Future of Success* (New York: Knopf, 2001), p. 15.

4 Quote from John A. Byrne, 'Visionary vs. Visionary', *Business Week* (28 August 2000), pp. 210–14.

5 Simon Lloyd, 'Branding From the Inside Out', *BRW* (14 March 2002), www.brw.com.au.

6 A good overview is provided by Robert Reich, 'The Company of the Future', *Fast Company* (November 1998), pp. 124 ff.

7 See, for example, 'Rethinking Work', *Business Week*, special report (17 October 1994), pp. 74–87.

8 Jeffrey Pfeffer and John F. Veiga, 'Putting People First for Organizational Success', *Academy of Management Executive*, vol. 13 (May 1999), pp. 37–48.

9 Jeffrey Pfeffer, *The Human Equation: Building Profits by Putting People First* (Boston: Harvard Business School Press, 1998).

10 James N. Baron and David M. Kreps, *Strategic Human Resources: Frameworks for General Managers* (New York: Wiley, 1999), pp. 4–6.

11 Baron and Kreps, op. cit., pp. 471–502.

12 Robin Kramer, HRM in the 1990s: Management's Dream Come True?, paper presented at the ANZAM 2000 Conference, Sydney (3–6 December 2000).

13 Tim Treadgold, 'Love in a Hot Climate', *BRW* (17–23 January 2002), pp. 52–5, www.brw.com.au.

14 John Kavanagh, 'Human Frailty', *BRW* (7 March 2002), www.brw.com.au.

15 Sherrill Nixon, 'Traditional Notion of Job Alters As More Work Nights and Part Time', *The Sydney Morning Herald* (5 June 2002), p. 4.

16 R. Roosevelt Thomas Jr, *Beyond Race and Gender: Unleashing the Power of Your Total Workforce by Managing Diversity* (New York: AMACOM, 1992), p. 4.

17 ibid.

18 AstraZeneca web site www.astrazeneca.com.au.

19 Information from McDonald's web sites www.mcdonalds.com.au and www.mcdonalds.co.nz.

20 'Forget Jobs Vacant', *Asian Business* (August 2001), p. 66.

21 James C. Sarros and Rosetta J. Moors, *Right From The Top: Profiles in Australian Leadership* (Sydney: McGraw-Hill, 2001), p. 123.

22 Robert Skeffington, 'Appearances: The Beautiful People Get More Pay', *BRW* (20 September 2001), www.brw.com.au.

23 Raymond J. Stone, *Human Resource Management*, 4th edn (Brisbane: John Wiley & Sons, 2002), p. 99.

24 ibid.

25 ibid.

26 Stone, op. cit., pp. 100–1.

27 Stone, op. cit., pp. 100–3.

28 Stone, op. cit., pp. 693–4.

29 Stone, op. cit., p. 191.

30 ibid.

31 Stone, op. cit., p. 693.

32 Stone, op. cit., p. 699.

33 ibid.

34 Lynne Bennington and Ruth Wein, Employer Discrimination Thrives Despite Legislation, paper presented at the ANZAM 1999 Conference, Hobart (December 1999).

35 Lynne Bennington and Ruth Wein, 'Circumnavigating the CV', *Management Today* (March 2000), pp. 24–5.

36 David James and Andrew Heathcote, 'Race Gets the Silent Treatment', *BRW* (11 April 2002), www.brw.com.au. Statistics New Zealand www.stats.govt.nz.

37 Stone, op. cit., p. 642.

38 ibid.

39 ibid.

40 Stone, op. cit., p. 645.

41 Stone, op. cit., pp. 646–51.

42 Stone, op. cit., p. 643.

43 Stone, op. cit., pp. 536–57.

44 ibid.

45 ibid.

46 Kathryn Bartol, David Martin, Margaret Tein and Graham Matthews, *Management — A Pacific Rim Focus* (Sydney: McGraw-Hill, 2001), p. 333.

47 New Zealand Department of Labour www.ers.dol.govt.nz/act/changes.html.

48 Stone, op. cit., p. 745.

49 Stone, op. cit., pp. 748–9.

50 Peter J. Dowling, Denice E. Welch and Randall S. Schuler, *International Human Resource Management*, 3rd edn (Ohio: South-Western, 1999), pp. 4–10.

51 ibid.

52 S. Treloar, The ANZAC Mentality: Expatriate Management in Australian-based Companies, unpublished Masters thesis, University of Western Sydney (1997), p. 35; Alan Nankervis, Robert Compton and Marian Baird, *Strategic Human Resource Manage-ment*, 4th edn (Melbourne: Nelson Thomson Learning, 2002), p. 635.

53 Nick Foster, Another 'Glass-Ceiling'?: The Experiences of Women Professionals and Managers on International Assignments, paper presented at the ANZAM 2000 Conference, Sydney (3–6 December 2000).

54 See Baron and Kreps, op. cit.

55 See Boris Yavitz, 'Human Resources in Strategic Planning', in Eli Ginzberg (ed.), *Executive Talent: Developing and Keeping the Best People* (New York: Wiley, 1988), p. 34.

56 Information from Thomas A. Stewart, 'In Search of Elusive Tech Workers', *Fortune* (16 February 1998), pp. 171–2.

57 See Ernest McCormick, 'Job and Task Analysis', in Marvin Dunnette (ed.), *Handbook of Industrial and Organizational Psychology* (Chicago: Rand McNally, 1976), pp. 651–96.

58 Nicholas Way, 'Recruiting: Star Search', *BRW* (18 August 2000), www.brw.com.au.

59 Michelle Hannen, 'Shop Tactics', *BRW* (6–12 June 2002), pp. 58–61.

60 Information from Gautam Naik, 'India's Technology Whizzes find Passage to Nokia', *Wall Street Journal* (1 August 2000), p. B1.

61 See David Greising, *I'd Like to Buy the World a Coke: The Life and Leadership of Roberto Goizueta* (New York: Wiley, 1998).

62 Gayle Bryant, 'Nets Catch the Right People For the Job', *BRW* (4 April 2002), www.brw.com.au.

63 ibid.

64 Way, op. cit.

65 See John P. Wanous, *Organizational Entry: Recruitment, Selection, and Socialization of Newcomers* (Reading, MA: Addison-Wesley, 1980), pp. 34–44.

66 Tony Thomas, 'Recruitment: The Battle for Talent', *BRW* (12 April 2001), www.brw.com.au.

67 See 'Key to Success: People, People, People', *Fortune* (27 October 1997), p. 232.

68 See Dale Yoder and Herbert G. Heneman (eds), *ASPA Handbook of Personnel and Industrial Relations*, vol. 1 (Washington: Bureau of National Affairs, 1974), pp. 152–4; Walter Kiechel III, 'How to Pick Talent', *Fortune* (8 December 1986), pp. 201–3; *HRM Magazine* (April 1991), pp. 42–3.

69 E. Vaughn and J. McLean, 'A Survey and Critique of Management Selection Practices in Australian Business Firms', *Asia Pacific Human Resource Management*, vol. 27, no. 4. (November 1989), p. 20, cited in Stone, op. cit., p. 225.

70 Stone, op. cit., p. 220.

71 Stone, op. cit., p. 243.

72 Reported in 'Would You Hire This Person Again?', *Business Week*, enterprise issue (9 June 1997), pp. ENT32.

73 Stone, op. cit., p. 236.

74 Information from William M. Bulkeley, 'Replaced by Technology: Job Interviews', *Wall Street Journal* (22 August 1994), pp. B1, B4.

75 For a scholarly review, see John Van Maanen and Edgar H. Schein, 'Toward a Theory of Socialization', in Barry M. Staw (ed.) *Research in Organizational Behavior*, vol. 1 (Greenwich, CT: JAI Press, 1979), pp. 209–64; for a practitioner's view, see Richard Pascale, 'Fitting New Employees into the Company Culture', *Fortune* (28 May 1984), pp. 28–42.

76 This involves the social information processing concept as discussed in Gerald R. Salancik and Jeffrey Pfeffer, 'A Social Information Processing Approach to Job Attitudes and Task Design', *Administrative Science Quarterly*, vol. 23 (June 1978), pp. 224–53.

77 'Mad Dogs and Expatriates', *The Economist* (3 March 1984), p. 67, cited in Stone, op. cit., p. 769.

78 Sherrill Nixon, 'Checkers Sniff Out CV Porkies As Companies Flee Fraud Stings', *The Sydney Morning Herald* (9 September 2002), p. 3.

79 Doug Davies, Lawson Savery and Ruth Taylor, The Effectiveness of Training in Improving Staff Relations and Reducing Turnover in Services Industries, paper presented at the ANZAM 2000 Conference, Sydney (3–6 December 2000).

80 Kenneth R. Bartlett, The Relationship between Training and Organizational Commitment in the Health Care Field: A US–New Zealand Comparison, paper presented at the ANZAM 2000 Conference, Sydney (3–6 December 2000).

81 *Fortune*, 'Key to Success', op. cit.

82 Dick McCann and Nikki Mead, 'E-learning: Part of the Solution', *Management Today* (April 2002), p. 40.

83 See Larry L. Cummings and Donald P. Schwab, *Performance in Organizations: Determinants and Appraisal* (Glenview, IL: Scott, Foresman, 1973).

84 See Mark R. Edwards and Ann J. Ewen, *360-Degree Feedback: The Powerful New Tool for Employee Feedback and Performance Improvement* (New York: AMACOM, 1996).

85 Emily Ross, 'Take a Number, and Fret', *BRW* (1 November 2001), www.brw.com.au.

86 Lisa Bradley and Neil Ashkanasy, Performance Appraisal in Australia: Does It Serve Its Purpose?, paper presented at the ANZAM 1998 Conference, Adelaide (6–9 December 1998).

87 Charles Handy, *The Age of Unreason* (Cambridge, MA: Harvard Business School Press, 1990), p. 55.

88 Leon Gettler, 'Career Management', *Management Today* (April 2002), p. 5.

89 See Thomas P. Ference, James A. F. Stoner and E. Kirby Warren, 'Managing the Career Plateau', *Academy of Management Review*, vol. 2 (October 1977), pp. 602–12.

90 Gettler, ibid.

91 Timothy Butler and James Waldroop, 'Job Sculpting: The Art of Retaining Your Best People', *Harvard Business Review* (September–October 1999), pp. 144–52.

92 Danielle Townsend, 'Getting a Life', *HR Monthly* (November 2000), p. 18, www.ahri.com.au.

93 Jill McLean and Margaret Lindorff, Work-Family Balance Among Dual-Career Parents, paper presented at the ANZAM 2000 Conference, Sydney (3–6 December 2000).

94 Michael Laurence, 'The Bucks Stop Here', *BRW* (30 May–5 June 2002), pp. 46–52.

95 Andrew Cornell, 'Wage Case', *AFR Boss* (March 2002), pp. 56–9.

96 Jan Eakin, 'Top Bosses Face Life on $700 000', *The Sydney Morning Herald* (10 May 2002), p. 7.

97 Laurence, ibid.

98 Jarek Czechowicz, 'Where There's an Incentive...', *Management Today* (March 2002), pp. 10–11.

99 Stone, op. cit, pp. 799–801.

100 Jay Finegan, 'Unconventional Wisdom', *Inc.* (1 December 1994), pp. 44–56.

101 'Outback's Approach to Success: More Support, Less Bureaucracy', *Nation's Restaurant News*, vol. 29, no. 13 (27 March 1995), p. 33.

102 ibid.

103 The following section draws heavily from Jay Finegan's *Inc.* article that gave Outback the Entrepreneurs of the Year Award.

Chapter 13 notes

1 Tim Treadgold, 'Wesfarmers' Winning Ways' *BRW* (13–19 September 2001), pp. 47–9.

2 Philip Rennie, 'Conglomerates: Farmers Hit Paydirt', *BRW* (27 April 2001), www.brw.com.au; Tim Treadgold, 'Unfashionably Patient', *BRW* (22 June 2001), www.brw.com.au; Treadgold, 'Wesfarmers' Winning Ways', op. cit.; Stuart Washington, 'Mr Consistency', *BRW* (29 August–4 September 2002), pp. 58–61.

3 See Jean Lipman-Blumen, *Connective Leadership: Managing in a Changing World* (New York: Oxford University Press, 1996), pp. 3–11.

4 Two periodicals that follow current leadership topics in a variety of organisational settings are *Non-Profit Management and Leadership* and *Leader to Leader*, both published by Jossey-Bass.

5 James M. Kouzes and Barry Z. Posner, 'The Leadership Challenge', *Success* (April 1988), p. 68. See also their books *The Leadership Challenge: How to Get Extraordinary Things Done in Organizations* (San Francisco: Jossey-Bass, 1987); *Credibility: How Leaders Gain and Lose It, Why People Demand It* (San Francisco: Jossey-Bass, 1996); and *Encouraging the Heart: A Leader's Guide to Rewarding and Recognizing Others* (San Francisco: Jossey-Bass, 1999).

6 Burt Nanus, *Visionary Leadership: Creating a Compelling Sense of Vision for Your Organization* (San Francisco: Jossey-Bass, 1992).

7 Quotation from General Electric Company Annual Report 1997, p. 5. For more on Jack Welch's leadership approach at GE see Robert Slater, *Jack Welch and the GE Way: Management Insights and Leadership Secrets of the Legendary CEO* (New York: McGraw-Hill, 1998).

8 See Kouzes and Posner, op. cit. (1988); and James C. Collins and Jerry I. Porras, 'Building Your Company's Vision', *Harvard Business Review* (September–October 1996), pp. 65–77.

9 Rosabeth Moss Kanter, 'Power Failure in Management Circuits', *Harvard Business Review* (July–August 1979), pp. 65–75.

10 For a good managerial discussion of power, see David C. McClelland and David H. Burnham, 'Power Is the Great Motivator', *Harvard Business Review* (March–April 1976), pp. 100–10.

11 The classic treatment of these power bases is John R. P. French Jr and Bertram Raven, 'The Bases of Social Power', in Darwin Cartwright (ed.), *Group Dynamics: Research and Theory* (Evanston, IL: Row, Peterson, 1962), pp. 607–13. For managerial applications of this basic framework, see Gary Yukl and Tom Taber, 'The Effective Use of Managerial Power', *Personnel*, vol. 60 (1983), pp. 37–49; and Robert C. Benfari, Harry E. Wilkinson and Charles D. Orth, 'The Effective Use of Power', *Business Horizons*, vol. 29 (1986), pp. 12–16. Gary A. Yukl, *Leadership in Organizations*, 4th edn (Englewood Cliffs, NJ: Prentice Hall, 1998), includes 'information' as a separate, but related, power source.

12 Ria Voorhaar, 'Local Boys Make Good', *BRW* (11 May 2001), www.brw.com.au; Bill Tuckey, 'Ford's Charger Forced to Retreat', *BRW* (16–22 August 2001), p. 36. See also Alex Taylor III, 'The Fiasco at Ford', *Fortune* (4 February 2002), www.fortune.com.

13 Based on David A. Whetten and Kim S. Cameron, *Developing Management Skills*, 2nd edn (New York: HarperCollins, 1991), pp. 281–97.

14 ibid., p. 282.

15 James Thomson, 'Life is Short', *BRW* (8–14 August 2002), pp. 32–4.

16 Chester I. Barnard, *Functions of the Executive* (Cambridge, MA: Harvard University Press, 1938).

17 Quoted in Peter Stephenson, *Naked Leadership* (Frenchs Forest: Prentice Hall, 2002), p. 209.

18 Stephenson, op. cit., p. 215.

19 Jay A. Conger, 'Leadership: The Art of Empowering Others', *Academy of Management Executive*, vol. 3 (1989), pp. 17–24.

20 For example, see Esther Wachs Book, 'Leadership for the Millennium', *Working Woman* (March 1998), pp. 29–34; Charles Garfield, 'Innovation Imperative', *Executive Excellence* (21 November 2000) from www.pcconnection.com/scripts/about/story03.asp.

21 The early work on leader traits is well represented in Ralph M. Stogdill, 'Personal Factors Associated with Leadership: A Survey of the Literature', *Journal of Psychology*, vol. 25 (1948), pp. 35–71. See also Edwin E. Ghiselli, *Explorations in Management Talent* (Santa Monica, CA: Goodyear, 1971), and Shelley A. Kirkpatrick and Edwin A. Locke, 'Leadership: Do Traits Matter?', *Academy of Management Executive* (1991), pp. 48–60.

22 See also John W. Gardner, 'The Context and Attributes of Leadership', *New Management*, vol. 5 (1988), pp. 18–22; John P. Kotter, *The Leadership Factor* (New York: Free Press, 1988); and Bernard M. Bass, *Stogdill's Handbook of Leadership* (New York: Free Press, 1990).

23 Kirkpatrick and Locke, op. cit.

24 James B. Hunt, Senior Executive Leadership Profiles: An Analysis of 54 Australian Top Managers, paper presented to the ANZAM 2000 Conference, Sydney (3–6 December 2000).

25 See, for example, Jan P. Muczyk and Bernie C. Reimann, 'The Case for Directive Leadership', *Academy of Management Review*, vol. 12 (1987), pp. 637–47.

26 Bass, op. cit.

27 Robert R. Blake and Jane Srygley Mouton, *The New Managerial Grid III* (Houston: Gulf Publishing, 1985).

28 For a good discussion of this theory, see Fred E. Fiedler, Martin M. Chemers and Linda Mahar, *The Leadership Match Concept* (New York: Wiley, 1978). Fiedler's current contingency research with the cognitive resource theory is summarised in Fred E. Fiedler and Joseph E. Garcia, *New Approaches to Effective Leadership* (New York: Wiley, 1987).

29 Amanda Gome, 'How the Top 10 Got There', *BRW* (8–14 November 2001), pp. 54–5.

30 Paul Hersey and Kenneth H. Blanchard, *Management and Organizational Behavior* (Englewood Cliffs, NJ: Prentice Hall, 1988). For an interview with Paul Hersey on the origins of the model, see John R. Schermerhorn Jr, 'Situational Leadership: Conversations with Paul Hersey', *Mid-American Journal of Business* (fall 1997), pp. 5–12.

31 See Claude L. Graeff, 'The Situational Leadership Theory: A Critical View', *Academy of Management Review*, vol. 8 (1983), pp. 285–91.

32 Gayle C. Avery, 'Situational Leadership Preferences in Australia: Congruity, Flexibility and Effectiveness', *Leadership & Organization Development Journal*, vol. 22, no. 1 (2000), pp. 11–21.

33 See, for example, Robert J. House, 'A Path–Goal Theory of Leader Effectiveness', *Administrative Sciences Quarterly*, vol. 16 (1971), pp. 321–38; and Robert J. House and Terence R. Mitchell, 'Path–Goal Theory of Leadership', *Journal of Contemporary Business* (autumn 1974), pp. 81–97. The path–goal theory is reviewed by Bass, op. cit., and Yukl, op. cit. A supportive review of research is offered in Julie Indvik, 'Path–Goal Theory of Leadership: A Meta-Analysis', in John A. Pearce II and Richard B. Robinson Jr (eds), *Academy of Management Best Paper Proceedings* (1986), pp. 189–92.

34 See the discussions of path–goal theory in Yukl, op. cit.; and Bernard M. Bass, 'Leadership: Good, Better, Best', *Organizational Dynamics* (winter 1985), pp. 26–40.

35 See Steven Kerr and John Jermier, 'Substitutes for Leadership: Their Meaning and Measurement', *Organizational Behavior and Human Performance*, vol. 22 (1978), pp. 375–403; Jon P. Howell and Peter W. Dorfman, 'Leadership and Substitutes for Leadership among Professional and Nonprofessional Workers', *Journal of Applied Behavioral Science*, vol. 22 (1986), pp. 29–46.

36 Victor H. Vroom and Arthur G. Jago, *The New Leadership: Managing Participation in Organizations* (Englewood Cliffs, NJ: Prentice Hall, 1988). This is based on earlier work by Victor H. Vroom, 'A New Look in Managerial Decision-Making', *Organizational Dynamics* (spring 1973), pp. 66–80; and Victor H. Vroom and Phillip Yetton, *Leadership and Decision-Making* (Pittsburgh: University of Pittsburgh Press, 1973).

37 For a good discussion see Edgar H. Schein, *Process Consultation Revisited: Building the Helping Relationship* (Reading, MA: Addison-Wesley, 1999).

38 See the discussion by Victor H. Vroom, 'Leadership and the Decision Making Process', *Organizational Dynamics*, vol. 28 (2000), pp. 82–94.

39 James R. Meindl, 'On Leadership: An Alternative to the Conventional Wisdom', in Barry M. Staw and Larry L. Cummings (eds), *Research in Organizational Behavior*, vol. 12 (London: JAI Press, 1990); in Jack Wood, Joseph Wallace, Rachid M. Zeffane, John R. Schermerhorn, James G. Hunt and Richard N. Osborn, *Organisational Behaviour: A Global Perspective*, 2nd edn (Brisbane: John Wiley & Sons, 2001).

40 For a review see Yukl, op. cit.

41 Among the popular books addressing this point of view are Warren Bennis and Burt Nanus, *Leaders: The Strategies for Taking Charge* (New York: Harper Business 1997); Max DePree, *Leadership Is an Art* (New York: Doubleday, 1989); Kotter, *The Leadership Factor*, op. cit. (1988); and Kouzes and Posner, op. cit.

42 See, for example, Jay A. Conger, 'Inspiring Others: The Language of Leadership', *Academy of Management Executive*, vol. 5 (1991), pp. 31–45.

43 The distinction was originally made by James McGregor Burns, *Leadership* (New York: Harper & Row, 1978) and was further developed by Bernard Bass in *Leadership and Performance Beyond Expectations* (New York: Free Press, 1985) and 'Leadership: Good, Better, Best', op. cit.

44 This list is based on Kouzes and Posner, op. cit., and Gardner, op. cit.

45 James C. Sarros and Rosetta J. Moors, *Right From The Top: Profiles in Australian Leadership* (Sydney: McGraw-Hill, 2001), pp. 20–52; John Kavanagh, 'We Love Your Work', *BRW* (13–19 September 2001), pp. 52–6.

46 Mark Storey, 'Executive of the Year: Keith McLaughlin', *New Zealand Management* (December 2001), pp. 20–1.

47 Daniel Goleman, 'Leadership that Gets Results', *Harvard Business Review* (March–April 2000), pp. 78–90. See also his books *Emotional Intelligence* (New York: Bantam Books, 1995) and *Working with Emotional Intelligence* (New York: Bantam Books, 1998).

48 Daniel Goleman, 'What Makes a Leader?', *Harvard Business Review*, (November–December 1998), pp. 93–102.

49 Goleman, op. cit. (1998).

50 Sarros and Moors, op. cit. (2001), pp. 36–141; Michelle Hannen and Emily Ross, 'Leaders for All Seasons', *BRW* (10–16 January 2002), pp. 51–5.

51 A. H. Eagly, S. J. Daran and M. G. Makhijani, 'Gender and the Effectiveness of Leaders: A Meta-Analysis', *Psychological Bulletin*, vol. 117 (1995), pp. 125–45.

52 Research on gender issues in leadership is reported in Sally Helgesen, *The Female Advantage: Women's Ways of Leadership* (New York: Doubleday, 1990); Judith B. Rosener, 'Ways Women Lead', *Harvard Business Review*, (November–December 1990), pp. 119–25; and Alice H. Eagly, Steven J. Karau and Blair T. Johnson, 'Gender and Leadership Style among School Principals: A Meta Analysis', *Administrative Science Quarterly*, vol. 27 (1992), pp. 76–102. See also the discussion of women leaders in chapter 11, Jean Lipman-Blumen, op. cit.

53 James Dunn, 'The Stuff of Leadership', *Management Today* (May 1998), pp. 14–18; Voohaar, op. cit. (2001); Kavanagh, op. cit. (2001).

54 Vroom, op. cit. (2000).

55 Rosener, op. cit. (1990).

56 For debate on whether some transformational leadership qualities tend to be associated more with female than male leaders, see 'Debate: Ways Women and Men Lead', *Harvard Business Review* (January–February 1991), pp. 150–60.

57 Quote from 'As Leaders, Women Rule', *Business Week* (20 November 2000), pp. 75–84. Rosabeth Moss Kanter is the author of *Men and Women of the Corporation*, 2nd edn (New York: Basic Books, 1993).

58 Peter F. Drucker, 'Leadership: More Doing than Dash', *Wall Street Journal* (6 January 1988), p. 16. For a compendium of writings on leadership sponsored by the Drucker Foundation, see Frances Hesselbein, Marshall Goldsmith and Richard Beckhard, *Leader of the Future* (San Francisco: Jossey-Bass, 1997).

59 Thomson, op. cit. (2002), p. 34.

60 General Electric Company Annual Report 1997, p. 5.

61 Gardner, op. cit.

62 See Steven R. Covey, *Principle-Centered Leadership* (New York: Free Press, 1992); and Lee G. Bolman and Terrence E. Deal, *Leading With Soul* (San Francisco: Jossey-Bass, 1995).

63 Sarros and Moors, op. cit., p. 59.

64 Sarros and Moors, op. cit., p. 3.

65 Sarros and Moors, op. cit., p. 17.

66 Sarros and Moors, op. cit., pp. 1–17. See also Maureen Murrill, 'Listing: Aussie's Next Challenge', *BRW* (29 March 1999); Tim Treadgold, 'Strategy: Passing the Buck', *BRW* (17 January 2002).

Chapter 14 notes

1 Nicholas Way, 'Staffing: The Kings of Culture', *BRW*, vol. 22, no. 13 (7 April 2000), www.brw.com.au.

2 Danielle Townsend, 'Getting a Life', *HR Monthly* (November 2000), p. 18.

3 Frank Blount and Bob Joss, *Managing in Australia* (Sydney: Lansdowne Publishing, 1999), p. 201.

4 © James C. Sarros and Rosetta J. Moors, *Right From The Top: Profiles in Australian Leadership* (Sydney: McGraw-Hill, 2001), p. 7.

5 Example taken from Kevin Kelley, 'I'm the Boss, That's Why', *Business Week*, enterprise issue (9 June 1997), p. ENT 32.

6 For a comprehensive treatment of extrinsic rewards, see Bob Nelson, *1001 Ways to Reward Employees* (New York: Workman Publishing, 1994).

7 For a research perspective, see Edward Deci, *Intrinsic Motivation* (New York: Plenum, 1975); and Edward E. Lawler III, 'The Design of Effective Reward Systems', in Jay W. Lorsch (ed.), *Handbook of Organizational Behavior* (Englewood Cliffs, NJ: Prentice Hall, 1987), pp. 255–71.

8 Michael Maccoby's book, *Why Work: Leading the New Generation* (New York: Simon & Schuster, 1988), deals extensively with this point of view.

9 Information from Ellen Graham, 'Work May Be a Rat Race, But It's Not a Daily Grind', *Wall Street Journal*, (19 September 1997), pp. R1, R4. The story of Starbucks is told in Howard Schulz and Dori Jones Yang, *Pour Your Heart Into It: How Starbucks Built a Company One Cup at a Time* (New York: Hyperion, 1999).

10 Information from www.ibm.com.au.

11 See Abraham H. Maslow, *Eupsychian Management* (Homewood, IL: Richard D. Irwin, 1965); Abraham H. Maslow, *Motivation and Personality*, 2nd edn (New York: Harper & Row, 1970). For a research perspective, see Mahmoud A. Wahba and Lawrence G. Bridwell, 'Maslow Reconsidered: A Review of Research on the Need Hierarchy', *Organizational Behavior and Human Performance*, vol. 16 (1976), pp. 212–40.

12 Raymond J. Stone, *Human Resource Management*, 4th edn (Brisbane: John Wiley & Sons, 2002), p. 741.

13 See Clayton P. Alderfer, *Existence, Relatedness, and Growth* (New York: Free Press, 1972).

14 The complete two-factor theory is in Frederick Herzberg, Bernard Mausner, and Barbara Block Synderman, *The Motivation to Work*, 2nd edn (New York: Wiley, 1967); Frederick Herzberg, 'One More Time: How Do You Motivate Employees?', *Harvard Business Review* (January–February 1968), pp. 53–62, and reprinted as an **HBR classic** (September–October 1987), pp. 109–20.

15 Critical reviews are provided by Robert J. House and Lawrence A. Wigdor, 'Herzberg's Dual-Factor Theory of Job Satisfaction and Motivation: A Review of the Evidence and a Criticism', *Personnel Psychology*, vol. 20 (winter 1967), pp. 369–89; Steven Kerr, Anne Harlan and Ralph Stogdill, 'Preference for Motivator and Hygiene Factors in a Hypothetical Interview Situation', *Personnel Psychology*, vol. 27 (winter 1974), pp. 109–24.

16 Frederick Herzberg, 'Workers' Needs: The Same Around the World', *Industry Week* (21 September 1987), pp. 29–32.

17 Anne Marie Francesco and Barry Allen Gold, *International Organizational Behaviour* (New Jersey: Prentice Hall, 1998), pp. 90–1.

18 For a collection of his work, see David C. McClelland, *The Achieving Society* (New York: Van Nostrand, 1961); 'Business Drive and National Achievement', *Harvard Business Review*, vol. 40 (July–August 1962), pp. 99–112; David C. McClelland and David H. Burnham, 'Power Is the Great Motivator', *Harvard Business Review* (March–April 1976), pp. 100–10; David C. McClelland, *Human Motivation* (Glenview, IL: Scott, Foresman, 1985); and David C. McClelland and Richard E. Boyatsis, 'The Leadership Motive Pattern and Long-Term Success in Management', *Journal of Applied Psychology*, vol. 67 (1982), pp. 737–43.

19 Information from www.paulhanna.com.au.

20 Developed originally from a dis-cussion in Edward E. Lawler III, *Motivation in Work Organizations* (Monterey, CA: Brooks/Cole Publishing, 1973), pp. 30–6.

21 'Smart Motivating', *New Zealand Management* (October 2000), p. 19.

22 Allison Ashby, 'Staff: How to Land, and Retain, the Elusive Generation X', *BRW* (2 June 2000), www.brw.com.au; Nick Way, 'Battle of the Chromosomes', *Management Today* (August 2000), pp. 14–18.

23 See, for example, J. Stacy Adams, 'Toward an Understanding of Inequity', *Journal of Abnormal and Social Psychology*, vol. 67 (1963), pp. 422–36; J. Stacy Adams, 'Inequity in Social Exchange', in L. Berkowitz (ed.), *Advances in Experimental Social Psychology* (New York: Academic Press, 1965), pp. 267–300.

24 See, for example, J. W. Harder, 'Play for Pay: Effects of Inequity in a Pay-for-Performance Context', *Administrative Science Quarterly*, vol. 37 (1992), pp. 321–35.

25 Australian Council of Trade Unions, '50 Years On, Women Short-Changed $166', press release (29 June 2001), www.actu.asn.au/news/1022639603_3965.html.

26 See Philip Rennie, 'Strategy: King of the Aisles', *BRW* (6 December 2001), www.brw.com.au.

27 Jan Eakin, 'Top Bosses Face Life on $700 000', *The Sydney Morning Herald* (10 May 2002), p. 7.

28 Victor H. Vroom, *Work and Motivation* (New York: Wiley, 1964; republished by Jossey-Bass, 1994).

29 The work on goal-setting theory is well summarised in Edwin A. Locke and Gary P. Latham, *Goal Setting: A Motivational Technique That Works!* (Englewood Cliffs, NJ: Prentice Hall, 1984). See also Edwin A. Locke, Kenneth N. Shaw, Lisa A. Saari and Gary P. Latham, 'Goal Setting and Task Performance 1969–1980', *Psychological Bulletin*, vol. 90 (1981), pp. 125–52; Mark E. Tubbs, 'Goal Setting: A Meta-Analytic Examination of the Empirical Evidence', *Journal of Applied Psychology*, vol. 71 (1986), pp. 474–83; and Terence R. Mitchell, Kenneth R. Thompson and Jane George-Falvy, 'Goal Setting: Theory and Practice', chapter 9 in Cary L. Cooper and Edwin A. Locke (eds), *Industrial and Organizational Psychology: Linking Theory with Practice* (Malden, MA: Blackwell Business, 2000), pp. 211–49.

30 Gary P. Latham and Edwin A. Locke, 'Self-Regulation Through Goal Setting', *Organizational Behavior and Human Decision Processes*, vol. 50 (1991), pp. 212–47.

31 See Tony Thomas, 'Goals: Climb Every Mountain', *BRW* (12 April 2001), www.brw.com.au.

32 E. L. Thorndike, *Animal Intelligence* (New York: Macmillan, 1911), p. 244.

33 See B. F. Skinner, *Walden Two* (New York: Macmillan, 1948); *Science and Human Behavior* (New York: Macmillan, 1953); and *Contingencies of Reinforcement* (New York: Appleton-Century-Crofts, 1969).

34 OB Mod is clearly explained in Fred Luthans and Robert Kreitner, *Organizational Behavior Modification* (Glenview, IL: Scott, Foresman, 1975) and Fred Luthans and Robert Kreitner, *Organizational Behavior Modification and Beyond* (Glenview, IL: Scott, Foresman, 1985); see also Fred Luthans and Alexander D. Stajkovic, 'Reinforce for Performance: The Need to Go Beyond Pay and Even Rewards', *Academy of Management Executive*, vol. 13 (1999), pp. 49–57.

35 Information from www.tupperware.com.au/dir063/webtupp.nsf/pages/careerpath.

36 For a good review, see Lee W. Frederickson (ed.), *Handbook of Organizational Behavior Management* (New York: Wiley–Interscience, 1982); Luthans and Kreitner, op. cit. (1985); and Alexander D. Stajkovic and Fred Luthans, 'A Meta-Analysis of the Effects of Organizational Behavior Modification on Task Performance 1975–95', *Academy of Management Journal*, vol. 40 (1997), pp. 1122–49.

37 Edwin A. Locke, 'The Myths of Behavior Mod in Organizations', *Academy of Management Review*, vol. 2 (October 1977), pp. 543–53.

38 For a discussion of compensation and performance, see Rosabeth Moss Kanter, 'The Attack on Pay', *Harvard Business Review*, vol. 65 (March–April 1987), pp. 60–7; and Edward E. Lawler III, *Strategic Pay* (San Francisco: Jossey-Bass, 1990).

39 Karthryn M. Bartol and Cathy C. Durham, 'Incentives: Theory and Practice', chapter 1 in Cooper and Locke, op. cit. (2000).

40 Anne Davies and Jeni Porter, 'Poor Little Rich Kids', *The Sydney Morning Herald* (2 June 2001), www.smh.com.au.

41 Information from Jaclyn Fierman, 'The Perilous New World of Fair Pay', *Fortune* (13 June 1994), pp. 57–61.

42 Alex Kennedy, 'Pizzas with Pizzazz', *BRW* (9 June 1997), www.brw.com.au.

43 Tove Helland Hammer, 'New Developments in Profit Sharing, Gain Sharing, and Employee Ownership', chapter 12 in John P. Campbell and Richard J. Campbell (eds), *Productivity in Organizations: New Perspectives from Industrial and Organizational Psychology* (San Francisco: Jossey-Bass, 1988).

44 Edward E. Lawler III, *From the Ground Up: Six Principles for Building the New Logic Corporation* (San Francisco: Jossey-Bass, 1996), pp. 217–18. See also Lawler's *Rewarding Excellence* (San Francisco: Jossey-Bass, 2000).

45 Information from ACT Public Service, www.psm.act.gov.au/strategic.htm.

46 James Thomson, 'Remuneration: Value for Money', *BRW* (20 December 2001), www.brw.com.au.

47 Hewitt Associates, 'Best Employers to Work For in Australia: 2001', www.bestemployersaustralia.com/results/casestudy.asp; Emily Ross, 'Staff: Love the Job', *BRW* (2 February 2001),www.brw.com.au.

48 Tony Thomas, 'How the Big Firms Divide the Cake', *BRW* (30 April 1999), www.brw.com.au.

49 Stone, op. cit., p. 483.

50 Denise Knight, 'The Loyalty Lure', *HR Monthly* (October 2000), p. 18; Darryl Blake, *Skroo The Rules: What the World's Most Productive Workplace Does Differently* (Melbourne: Information Australia, 2001), p. 7.

51 Susan Pulliam, 'New Dot-Com Mantra: "Just Pay Me in Cash, Please"', *Wall Street Journal* (28 November 2000), p. C1.

52 Charles Eiskmeyer, 'The Saturn Enthusiast's Page' (1998), www.erols.com/core/.

53 Charles Child and Peter Brown, 'Possibilities for Saturn Include SUV, Hybrid, Light Truck', *Automotive News* (9 February 1998), p. 6.

54 'Saturn Cuts Output; Will Not Resort to Incentives', *Ward's Automotive News* (October 1997), p. 35.

55 Don Bohl, 'Saturn Corporation', *American Management Association Compensation and Benefits Review* (21 November 1997), p. 51.

56 ibid, p. 52.

57 ibid, p. 53.

58 Robyn Meredith, 'Saturn Union Votes to Retain Its Cooperative Company Pact', *The New York Times* (12 March 1998), section D, p. 1.

59 Child and Brown, op. cit., p. 7.

60 Bohl, op. cit., p. 53.

61 ibid, p. 53.

62 ibid, p. 53.

Chapter 15 notes

1 Jeffrey Pfeffer and John F. Veiga, 'Putting People First for Organizational Success', *Academy of Management Executive*, vol. 13 (May 1999), pp. 37–48; see also Jeffrey Pfeffer, *The Human Equation: Building Profits by Putting People First* (Boston: Harvard Business School Press, 1998).

2 See Mary Williams Walsh, 'Luring the Best in an Unsettled Time', *The New York Times* (30 January 2001).

3 Charles O'Reilly III and Jeffrey Pfeffer, *Hidden Value: How Great Companies Achieve Extraordinary Results Through Ordinary People* (Boston: Harvard Business School Publishing, 2000), quotes from p. 2.

4 Catherine C. Junia, 'Enterprisers: Laughter is the Best Medicine', *Businessworld* (24 May 2001), accessed at ProQuest database May 2002.

5 Lyrics from '9 to 5' by Dolly Parton. Published by Velvet Apple/Fox Fanfare Music, Inc. © 1980 Velvet Apple Music & Warner-Tamerlane Publishing Corp. All rights reserved. Used by permission.

6 John P. Kotter, 'The Psychological Contract: Managing the Joining Up Process', *California Management Review*, vol. 15 (spring 1973), 91–9; Denise Rousseau (ed.), *Psychological Contracts in Organizations* (San Francisco: Jossey-Bass, 1995); Denise Rousseau, 'Changing the Deal While Keeping the People', *Academy of Management Executive*, vol. 10 (1996), pp. 50–9; and Denise Rousseau and Rene Schalk (eds), *Psychological Contracts in Employment: Cross-Cultural Perspectives* (San Francisco: Jossey-Bass, 2000).

7 Linda Grant, 'Unhappy in Japan', *Fortune* (13 January 1997), p. 142.

8 Tim Baker, 'The New Employment Co-Dependency', *Management Today*, (October 2000), pp. 6–7; see also David M. Noer, *Breaking Free: A Prescription for Personal and Organisational Change* (San Francisco: Jossey-Bass, 1997), pp. 214–17.

9 For a thought provoking discussion of this issue, see Ben Hamper, *Rivethead: Tales from the Assembly Line* (New York: Warner, 1991).

10 Studs Terkel, *Working* (New York: Avon Books, 1975).

11 'Making the Right Call on Health', *The Age* (26 April 2001), p. 10.

12 Sue Shellenbarger, 'In Real Life, Hard Choices Upset Any Balancing Act', *Wall Street Journal* (19 April 1995), p. B1.

13 For an overview, see Paul E. Spector, *Job Satisfaction* (Thousand Oaks, CA: Sage, 1997); and Timothy A. Judge and Allan H. Church, 'Job Satisfaction: Research and Practice', chapter 7 in Cary L. Cooper and Edwin A. Locke (eds), *Industrial and Organizational Psychology: Linking Theory with Practice* (Malden, MA: Blackwell Business, 2000).

14 Amanda Sinclair, 'A Feeling for Business', *BRW* (22 February 1999), www.brw.com.au, viewed 28 March 2002.

15 Jim O'Rourke, 'We Like Our Work But Also a Whinge', *Sun-Herald* (14 April 2002), p. 38.

16 Anne Fellowes, 'Can't Buy Me Love', *Management Today* (November–December 1999), pp. 20–1.

17 Leon Gettler, 'Do You Get What You Pay For?', *Management Today* (November–December 2000), pp. 4–5.

18 Norman F. Ramion, 'Satisfaction Guaranteed', *Asian Business*, vol. 35, no. 6 (1999), pp. 61–2; Norman F. Ramion, 'Weathering the Storm', *Asian Business*, vol. 35, no. 7 (1999), pp. 56–7, accessed at ProQuest database May 2002.

19 Ramion, 'Satisfaction Guaranteed', op. cit.

20 See Melvin Blumberg and Charles D. Pringle, 'The Missing Opportunity in Organizational Research: Some Implications for a Theory of Work Motivation', *Academy of Management Review*, vol. 7 (1982), pp. 560–9.

21 Based on an example in Edward E. Lawler III, *Motivation in Work Organizations* (Monterey, CA: Brooks/Cole, 1973), pp. 154–5.

22 Cameron Allan, Greg J. Bamber, Nils Timo, The McDonaldisation of Employment Relations: A Case Study of Fast Food in Australia, paper presented at the ANZAM 2000 Conference, Sydney (3–6 December 2000).

23 See Frederick Herzberg, Bernard Mausner and Barbara Block Synderman, *The Motivation to Work*, 2nd edn (New York: Wiley, 1967). The quotation is from Frederick Herzberg, 'One More Time: How Do You Motivate Employees?', *Harvard Business Review* (January–February 1968), pp. 53–62, and reprinted as an HBR classic (September–October 1987), pp. 109–20.

24 Herzberg, op. cit. (1987).

25 John Breusch, 'Makeover Man', *AFR Boss* (March 2002), pp. 16–22.

26 For a complete description of the core characteristics model, see J. Richard Hackman and Greg R. Oldham, *Work Redesign* (Reading, MA: Addison-Wesley, 1980).

27 See Richard E. Walton, *Up and Running: Integrating Information Technology and the Organization* (Boston, MA: Harvard Business School Press, 1989).

28 Richard Walton, 'From Control to Commitment in the Workplace', *Harvard Business Review* (March–April 1985), pp. 77–94; and William A. Pasmore, *Designing Effective Organizations: A Sociotechnical Systems Perspective* (New York: Wiley, 1988).

29 Paul J. Champagne and Curt Tausky, 'When Job Enrichment Doesn't Pay', *Personnel*, vol. 3 (January–February 1978), pp. 30–40.

30 Noel Waite, 'Women are Doing Things *Differently* for Themselves', *Management Today* (September 2000), pp. 20–2.

31 Barney Olmsted and Suzanne Smith, *Creating a Flexible Workplace: How to Select and Manage Alternative Work Options* (New York: American Management Association, 1989).

32 See Allen R. Cohen and Herman Gadon, *Alternative Work Schedules: Integrating Individual and Organizational Needs* (Reading, MA: Addison-Wesley, 1978), p. 125; Simcha Ronen and Sophia B. Primps, 'The Compressed Work Week as Organizational Change: Behavioral and Attitudinal Outcomes', *Academy of Management Review*, vol. 6 (1981), pp. 61–74.

33 Lisa Phillips, 'Long Distance Commuting', *Management Today* (September 2000), p. 23.

34 'Networked Workers', *Business Week* (6 October 1997), p. 8; and Diane E. Lewis, 'Flexible Work Arrangements as Important as Salary to Some', *Columbus Dispatch* (25 May 1998), p. 8.

35 Annabel Crabb, 'Trainee Doctors are Looking for Lifestyle', *The Age* (6 December 2001), p. 8.

36 D. Lamond, P. Standen and P. Daniels, 'Contexts, Cultures and Forms of Teleworking', in G. Griffin (ed.), *Management Theory & Practice* (Melbourne: Macmillan, 1998), pp. 145–57, quoted in Margaret Lindorff, 'Home-based Telework and Telecommuting in Australia: More Myth than Modern Work Form', *Asia Pacific Journal of Human Resources*, vol. 38, no. 3 (2000), pp. 1–11.

37 For a review see Wayne F. Cascio, 'Managing a Virtual Workplace', *Academy of Management Executive*, vol. 14 (2000), pp. 81–90.

38 ibid.

39 See Sue Shellenbarger, 'Overwork, Low Morale Vex the Mobile Office', *Wall Street Journal* (17 August 1994), pp. B1, B7.

40 Quote from Phil Porter, 'Telecommuting Mom Is Part of a National Trend', *Columbus Dispatch* (29 November 2000), pp. H1, H2.

41 These guidelines are collected from a variety of sources, including: The Southern California Telecommuting Partnership www.socalcommute.org/telecom.htm; and ISDN Group www.isdnzone.com.

42 Margaret Lindorff, Closing the Divide Between Work and Home: The Case of Teleworking, paper presented at the ANZAM 2001 Conference, Auckland (5–8 December 2001).

43 Phil Kerslake 'Is the Grass Greener on the Other Side?', *New Zealand Management* (May 2001), pp. 30–2.

44 Tim Pegler, 'How Do You Manage Workers Who are Not on Site?', *Management Today* (November–December 2001), pp. 6–7.

45 Raymond J. Stone, *Human Resource Management*, 4th edn (Brisbane: John Wiley & Sons, 2002), p. 59.

46 Alan Nankervis, Robert Compton and Marian Baird, *Strategic Human Resource Management*, 4th edn (Melbourne: Nelson Thomson Learning, 2002), p. 232.

47 ibid.

48 Allan et al., op. cit.

49 See Arthur P. Brief, Randall S. Schuler and Mary Van Sell, *Managing Job Stress* (Boston: Little, Brown, 1981), pp. 7, 8.

50 Robert Reich, *The Future of Success* (New York: Knopf, 2000), p. 8.

51 Michael Weldholz, 'Stress Increasingly Seen as Problem with Executives More Vulnerable', *Wall Street Journal*, (28 September 1982), p. 31.

52 Stephen Dabkowski, 'Working Themselves into the Grave', *BRW* (1997), www.brw.com.au, viewed May 2002.

53 Michael Atkinson, 'A Stress of the Imagination?', *Management Today* (June 1999), p. 42.

54 Sue Shellenbarger, 'Do We Work More or Not? Either Way, We Feel Frazzled', *Wall Street Journal* (30 July 1997), p. B1.

55 See, for example, 'Desk Rage', *Business Week* (27 November 2000), p. 12.

56 Peter Kelleher, 'Let Me Stress', *Management Today* (August 1999), pp. 14–19.

57 Carol Hymowitz, 'Impossible Expectations and Unfulfilling Work Stress Managers, Too', *Wall Street Journal* (16 January 2001), p. B1.

58 The classic work is Meyer Friedman and Ray Roseman, *Type A Behavior and Your Heart* (New York: Knopf, 1974).

59 See Hans Selye, *Stress in Health and Disease* (Boston: Butterworth, 1976).

60 Carol Hymowitz, 'Can Workplace Stress Get Worse?', *Wall Street Journal* (16 January 2001), pp. B1, B3.

61 See Steve M. Jex, *Stress and Job Performance* (San Francisco: Jossey-Bass, 1998).

62 Reported in Sue Shellenbarger, 'Finding Ways to Keep a Partner's Job Stress from Hitting Home', *Wall Street Journal* (29 November 2000), p. B1; Daniel Costello, 'Incidents of "Desk Rage" Disrupt America's Offices', *Wall Street Journal* (16 January 2001), pp. B1, B3.

63 See Daniel C. Ganster and Larry Murphy, 'Workplace Interventions to Prevent Stress-Related Illness: Lessons from Research and Practice', chapter 2 in Cooper and Locke (eds), op. cit.

64 ibid.

65 The extreme case of 'workplace violence' is discussed by Richard V. Denenberg and Mark Braverman, *The Violence-Prone Workplace* (Ithaca, NY: Cornell University Press, 1999).

66 See John M. Ivancevich and Michael T. Matteson, 'Optimizing Human Resources: A Case for Preventive Health and Stress Management', *Organizational Dynamics*, vol. 9 (autumn 1980), pp. 6–8. See also John M. Ivancevich, Michael T. Matteson and Edward P. Richards III, 'Who's Liable for Stress on the Job?', *Harvard Business Review* (March–April 1985), pp. 60–71.

67 TMP, 'Desk Rage on the Rise', press release (April 2002), http://au.tmp.com/press/april2002h.asp, viewed 29 August 2002.

68 Robert Kreitner, 'Personal Wellness: It's Just Good Business', *Business Horizons* (May–June 1982), pp. 28–35.

69 Tamara Rapoport, 'Taking the Pressure Down', *Management Today* (March 2001), pp. 6–7.

70 Developed from Kreitner, 'Personal Wellness'; and 'Plain Talk about Stress', National Institute of Mental Health Publication (Rockville, MD: US Department of Health and Human Services).

71 O'Rourke, op. cit.

72 Adapted from the work of James Mystakidis, Tracey Gawthorne, Belinda Gibbons, John Hugh, Bill Martin and Patrick Paffard — students of the Macquarie Graduate School of Management, 2001.

Chapter 16 notes

1 James C. Sarros and Rosetta J. Moors, *Right from the Top: Profiles in Australian Leadership* (Sydney: McGraw-Hill, 2001), pp. 149–58.

2 See John A. Bryne, 'Visionary vs. Visionary', *Business Week* (28 August 2000), pp. 210–14.

3 Doug Stace and Dexter Dunphy, *Beyond the Boundaries*, 2nd edn, (Sydney: McGraw-Hill, 2001), p. 202.

4 Adele Ferguson, 'A World of Shifting Goalposts', *Management Today* (January–February 1999), pp. 14–19.

5 See, for example, Edward E. Lawler III, Susan Albers Mohrman and Gerald E. Ledford Jr, *Employee Involvement and Total Quality Management: Practices and Results in Fortune 1000 Companies* (San Francisco: Jossey-Bass, 1992); Susan Albers Mohrman, Susan G. Cohen and Allan M. Mohrman Jr, *Designing Team-based Organizations: New Forms for Knowledge Work* (San Francisco: Jossey-Bass, 1995).

6 Jon R. Katzenbach and Douglas K. Smith, *The Wisdom of Teams: Creating the High Performance Organization* (Boston: Harvard Business School Press, 1993).

7 For insights on how to conduct effective meetings, see Mary A. De Vries, *How to Run a Meeting* (New York: Penguin, 1994).

8 A classic work is Bib Latane, Kipling Williams and Stephen Harkins, 'Many Hands Make Light the Work: The Causes and Consequences of Social Loafing', *Journal of Personality and Social Psychology*, vol. 37 (1978), pp. 822–32.

9 See Marvin E. Shaw, *Group Dynamics: The Psychology of Small Group Behavior*, 2nd edn (New York: McGraw-Hill, 1976); Harold J. Leavitt, 'Suppose We Took Groups More Seriously', in Eugene L. Cass and Frederick G. Zimmer (eds), *Man and Work in Society* (New York: Van Nostrand Reinhold, 1975), pp. 67–77.

10 John M. George, 'Extrinsic and Intrinsic Origins of Perceived Social Loafing in Organizations', *Academy of Management Journal* (March 1992), pp. 191–202; and W. Jack Duncan, 'Why Some People Loaf in Groups While Others Loaf Alone', *Academy of Management Executive*, vol. 8 (1994), pp. 79–80.

11 See Leavitt, op. cit.

12 The 'linking pin' concept is introduced in Rensis Likert, *New Patterns of Management* (New York: McGraw-Hill, 1962).

13 John Stensholt, 'Tax: Teamwork Beats the Trauma', *BRW* (4 October 2001) www.brw.com.au, viewed 30 May 2002.

14 See discussion by Susan G. Cohen and Don Mankin, 'The Changing Nature of Work: Managing the Impact of Information Technology', chapter 6 in Susan Albers Mohrman, Jay R. Galbraith, Edward E. Lawler III and Associates, *Tomorrow's Organization: Crafting Winning Capabilities in a Dynamic World* (San Francisco: Jossey-Bass, 1998), pp. 154–78.

15 Information from 'Diversity: America's Strength', *Fortune*, special advertising section (23 June 1997); American Express corporate communication (1998).

16 Example in Sue Shellenbarger, 'Companies are Finding Real Payoffs in Aiding Employee Satisfaction', *Wall Street Journal* (11 October 2000), p. B1.

17 See Susan D. Van Raalte, 'Preparing the Task Force to Get Good Results', *S.A.M. Advanced Management Journal*, vol. 47 (winter 1982), pp. 11–16; Walter Kiechel III, 'The Art of the Corporate Task Force', *Fortune* (28 January 1991), pp. 104–6.

18 Developed from ibid.

19 Mohrman et al., op. cit.

20 Ron Carter, 'Team Concept Puts Workers and Bosses in Same Boat', *Columbus Dispatch* (27 October 1997), pp. 8, 9.

21 For a good discussion of quality circles, see Edward E. Lawler III and Susan Albers Mohrman, 'Quality Circles After the Fad', *Harvard Business Review* (January–February 1985), pp. 65–71; Edward E. Lawler III and Susan Albers Mohrman, 'Employee Involvement, Reengineering, and TQM: Focusing on Capability Development', in Mohrman et al., op. cit. (1998), pp. 179–208.

22 Steve Morris, 'Teaming up', *Asian Business*, vol. 35, no. 8 (1999), pp. 58–9.

23 See Wayne F. Cascio, 'Managing a Virtual Workplace', *Academy of Management Executive*, vol. 14 (2000), pp. 81–90.

24 Wanda J. Orlikowski and J. Debra Hofman, 'An Improvisational Model for Change Management: The Case of Groupware Technologies', *Sloan Management Review* (winter 1997), pp. 11–21.

25 R. Brent Gallupe and William H. Cooper, 'Brainstorming Electronically', *Sloan Management Review* (fall 1993), pp. 27–36; Cascio, op. cit.

26 William M. Bulkeley, 'Computerizing Dull Meetings Is Touted as an Antidote to the Mouth That Bored', *Wall Street Journal* (28 January 1992), pp. B1, B2.

27 Cascio, op. cit.

28 Example from Sue Canney Davison and Karen Ward, *Leading International Teams* (London: McGraw-Hill, 1999).

29 ibid.

30 See, for example, Paul S. Goodman, Rukmini Devadas and Terri L. Griffith Hughson, 'Groups and Productivity: Analyzing the Effectiveness of Self-Managing Teams', chapter 11 in John P. Campbell and Richard J. Campbell (eds), *Productivity in Organizations: New Perspectives from Industrial and Organizational Psychology* (San Francisco: Jossey-Bass, 1988); Jack Orsbrun, Linda Moran, Ed Musslewhite and John H. Zenger, with Craig Perrin, *Self-Directed Work Teams: The New American Challenge* (Homewood, IL: Business One Irwin, 1990); Dale E. Yeatts and Cloyd Hyten, *High Performing Self-Managed Work Teams* (Thousand Oaks, CA: Sage, 1997).

31 Bradley L. Kirkman and Debra L. Shapiro, 'The Impact of Cultural Values on Employee Resistance to Teams: Toward a Model of Globalized Self-Managing Work Team Effectiveness', *Academy of Management Review*, vol. 22 (1997), pp. 730–57.

32 Antonias Vitalis, David Tweed and Ngai Weng Low, New Zealand Managers' Perceptions of Success Factors in the Implementation of Selfmanaging Teams: An Exploratory Study, paper presented at the ANZAM 2001 Conference, Auckland (5–8 December 2001).

33 Stephanie Miller, Real Teams in Small Australian Firms, paper presented at the ANZAM 2001 Conference, Auckland (5–8 December 2001).

34 For a discussion of effectiveness in the context of top management teams, see Edward E. Lawler III, David Finegold and Jay A. Conger, 'Corporate Boards: Developing Effectiveness at the Top', in Mohrman et al., op. cit. (1998), pp. 23–50.

35 For a review of research on group effectiveness, see J. Richard Hackman, 'The Design of Work Teams', in Jay W. Lorsch (ed.), Handbook of Organizational Behavior (Englewood Cliffs, NJ: Prentice Hall, 1987), pp. 315–42; and J. Richard Hackman, Ruth Wageman, Thomas M. Ruddy and Charles L. Ray, 'Team Effectiveness in Theory and Practice', chapter 5 in Cary L. Cooper and Edwin A. Locke (eds), Industrial and Organizational Psychology: Linking Theory with Practice (Malden, MA: Blackwell Business, 2000).

36 ibid; Lawler et al., op. cit. (1998).

37 Adapted from a BBC for business training video, 'Solving Problems and Thinking Creatively', 20 Steps to Better Management, episode 19, (London: BBC, 1996).

38 See Warren Watson, 'Cultural Diversity's Impact on Interaction Process and Performance', Academy of Management Journal, vol. 16 (1993); and Christopher Earley and Elaine Mosakowski, 'Creating Hybrid Team Structures: An Empirical Test of Transnational Team Functioning', Academy of Management Journal, vol. 5 (February 2000), pp. 26–49.

39 J. Steven Heinen and Eugene Jacobson, 'A Model of Task Group Development in Complex Organizations and a Strategy of Implementation', Academy of Management Review, vol. 1 (1976), pp. 98–111; Bruce W. Tuckman, 'Developmental Sequence in Small Groups', Psychological Bulletin, vol. 63 (1965), pp. 384–99; Bruce W. Tuckman and Mary Ann C. Jensen, 'Stages of Small-Group Development Revisited', Group & Organization Studies, vol. 2 (1977), pp. 419–27.

40 See for example, Edgar Schein, Process Consultation (Reading, MA: Addison-Wesley, 1988); and Linda C. McDermott, Nolan Brawley and William A. Waite, World-Class Teams: Working Across Borders (New York: Wiley, 1998).

41 For a good discussion, see Robert F. Allen and Saul Pilnick, 'Confronting the Shadow Organization: How to Detect and Defeat Negative Norms', Organizational Dynamics (spring 1973), pp. 13–16.

42 See Schein, op. cit., pp. 76–9.

43 Shaw, op. cit.

44 A classic work in this area is Kenneth D. Benne and P. Sheets, 'Functional Roles of Group Members', Journal of Social Issues, vol. 2 (1948), pp. 42–7; see also, Likert, op. cit., pp. 166–9; Schein, op. cit., pp. 49–56.

45 Based on John R. Schermerhorn Jr, James G. Hunt and Richard N. Osborn, Organizational Behavior, 7th edn (New York: Wiley, 2000), pp. 345–6.

46 Research on communication networks is found in Alex Bavelas, 'Communication Patterns in Task-Oriented Groups', Journal of the Acoustical Society of America, vol. 22 (1950), pp. 725–30; Shaw, op. cit.

47 Schein, op. cit., pp. 69–75.

48 See Kathleen M. Eisenhardt, Jean L. Kahwajy and L. J. Bourgeois III, 'How Management Teams Can Have a Good Fight', Harvard Business Review (July–August 1997), pp. 77–85.

49 Information from Ron Cacioppe, 'Using Individual and Team Reward–Recognition Strategies to Achieve Organisational Success', in Retha Wiesner and Bruce Millett (eds), Management and Organisational Behaviour: Contemporary Challenges and Future Directions (Brisbane: John Wiley & Sons, 2001), pp. 72–85.

50 Victor H. Vroom and Arthur G. Jago, The New Leadership: Managing Participation in Organizations (Englewood Cliffs, NJ: Prentice Hall, 1988); Victor H. Vroom, 'A New Look in Managerial Decision-Making', Organizational Dynamics (spring 1973), pp. 66–80; Victor H. Vroom and Phillip Yetton, Leadership and Decision-Making (Pittsburgh: University of Pittsburgh Press, 1973).

51 Norman R. F. Maier, 'Assets and Liabilities in Group Problem Solving', Psychological Review, vol. 74 (1967), pp. 239–49.

52 ibid.

53 See Irving L. Janis, 'Groupthink', Psychology Today (November 1971), pp. 43–6; Victims of Groupthink, 2nd edn (Boston: Houghton Mifflin, 1982).

54 These techniques are well described in Andre L. Delbecq, Andrew H. Van de Ven and David H. Gustafson, Group Techniques for Program Planning (Glenview, IL: Scott, Foresman, 1975).

55 Gallupe and Cooper, op. cit.

56 A very good overview is provided by William D. Dyer, Team-Building (Reading, MA: Addison-Wesley, 1977).

57 Information from Bushsports web site www.bushsports.com.au.

58 Information from Jennifer Scott, 'Working Better Together Is the Challenge', Columbus Dispatch (3 November 1997), pp. 10–11.

59 Carl E. Larson and Frank M. J. LaFasto, *Team Work: What Must Go Right, What Can Go Wrong* (Newbury Park, CA: Sage, 1990).

60 Damon Birchfield, 'How YSL's Peter Fahey Developed a "Nose" for Managing', *New Zealand Management* (February 2002), pp. 44–5.

61 See Jon R. Katzenbach, 'The Myth of the Top Management Team', *Harvard Business Review*, vol. 75 (November–December 1997), pp. 83–91.

62 Darryl Blake, *Skroo the Rules: What the World's Most Productive Workplace Does Differently* (Melbourne: Information Australia, 2001), p. 89.

63 ibid, p. 91.

64 Information from: 'Rich 200: Graham Turner', *BRW* (23 May 2002); Blake, op. cit.; Elizabeth Johnston, 'Elf Boys', *AFR Boss* (8 June 2001), p. 26; Richard Dunford and Ian Palmer, Achieving High Performance in Unattractive Industries: The Case of Flight Centre, paper presented at the ANZAM 2000 Conference, Sydney (3–6 December 2000); Murray Massey, 'Travel Agency Succeeds by Going Tribal', *BRW* (22 March 1999); Garry West, 'An Apple Orchard Lad Worth $100 Million', *Australian Financial Review* (8 March 1999).

Chapter 17 notes

1 See Lachlan Colquhoun, 'Scenes From a Client Call', *BRW* (24–30 January 2002), pp. 70–3.

2 Henry Mintzberg, *The Nature of Managerial Work* (New York: Harper & Row, 1973, and HarperCollins, 1997).

3 John P. Kotter, 'What Effective General Managers Really Do', *Harvard Business Review* (November–December 1982), pp. 156–7; and *The General Managers* (New York: Free Press, 1986).

4 'Relationships Are the Most Powerful Form of Media', *Fast Company* (March 2001), p. 100.

5 See Mintzberg, op. cit.; Kotter, op. cit.

6 Alison Overholt, 'Intel's Got (Too Much) Mail', *Fast Company* (March 2001), pp. 56–8.

7 Carolyn Blackman, *Negotiating China* (Sydney: Allen & Unwin, 1997), p. 64.

8 See Robert H. Lengel and Richard L. Daft, 'The Selection of Communication Media as an Executive Skill', *Academy of Management Executive*, vol. 2 (August 1988), pp. 225–32.

9 See also Eric Matson, 'Now That We Have Your Complete Attention', *Fast Company* (February–March 1997), pp. 124–32.

10 David McNeill, *Hand and Mind: What Gestures Reveal about Thought* (Chicago: University of Chicago Press, 1992).

11 Allan Pease and Alan Garner, *Talk Language* (Sydney: Pease Training, 1999), pp. 133–5.

12 Rebecca Crawley, 'Smart Work in New-style Offices', *BRW* (1997), www.brw.com.au, viewed 20 August 2002.

13 Adapted from Richard V. Farace, Peter R. Monge and Hamish M. Russell, *Communicating and Organizing* (Reading, MA: Addison-Wesley, 1977), pp. 97–8.

14 Tom Peters and Nancy Austin, *A Passion for Excellence* (New York: Random House, 1985).

15 This discussion is based on Carl R. Rogers and Richard E. Farson, 'Active Listening' (Chicago: Industrial Relations Center of the University of Chicago, n.d.).

16 Hugh Mackay, extract from *The Good Listener* (Sydney: Pan Macmillan, 1998), pp. 332–3. Reprinted by permission of Pan Macmillan Australia Pty Ltd. Copyright © Mackay Research Pty Limited, 1994.

17 © Kris Cole, *Crystal Clear Communication*, 2nd edn (Sydney: Prentice Hall, 2000. Penguin Books Australia), pp. 94–100.

18 A useful source of guidelines is John J. Gabarro and Linda A. Hill, 'Managing Performance', Note 9-96-022 (Boston, MA: Harvard Business School Publishing, n.d.).

19 Information from Carol Hymowitz, 'How to Tell Employees All the Things They Don't Want to Hear', *Wall Street Journal* (22 August 2000), p. B1.

20 Developed from John Anderson, 'Giving and Receiving Feedback', in Paul R. Lawrence, Louis B. Barnes and Jay W. Lorsch (eds), *Organizational Behavior and Administration*, 3rd edn (Homewood, IL: Richard D. Irwin, 1976), p. 109.

21 See Lengel and Daft, op. cit.

22 Information from Esther Wachs Book, 'Leadership for the Millennium', *Working Woman* (March 1998), pp. 29–34.

23 © Ingrid Jackson, 'Change Riffles Bank Notes', *Management Today* (April 1999), pp. 36–8. Ingrid Jackson is the director of Sydney consulting firm Executive Management Solutions.

24 Pease and Garner, op. cit., pp. 103–21.

25 Richard Lepsinger and Anntoinette D. Lucia, *The Art and Science of 360° Feedback* (San Francisco: Jossey-Bass, 1997).

26 See Brian O'Reilly, '360° Feedback Can Change Your Life', *Fortune* (17 October 1994), pp. 93–100.

27 Richard Walsh, *Executive Material* (Sydney: Allen & Unwin, 2002), p. 140.

28 A classic work on proxemics is Edward T. Hall's book, *The Hidden Dimension* (Garden City, NY: Doubleday, 1986).

29 Sherrill Tapsell, 'Creating a Can-do Culture', *New Zealand Management* (May 2001), pp. 17–21.

30 Information from Susan Stellin, 'Intranets Nurture Companies from the Inside', *New York Times* (21 January 2001), p. C4.

31 Vikki Bland, 'ET Phone the Office: Managing Evolving Telecommunications', *New Zealand Management* (April 2002), pp. 48–53; 'Wired, Wired West', *Edge: New Thinking from the University of Western Sydney* (February 2002), pp. 24–5.

32 'Privacy at Work Still an Issue', *Illawarra Mercury* (20 October 2001), p. 9.

33 See Edward T. Hall, *The Silent Language* (New York: Doubleday, 1973).

34 © James C. Sarros and Rosetta J. Moors, *Right from the Top: Profiles in Australian Leadership* (Sydney: McGraw-Hill, 2001), pp. 136–7.

35 Richard Dunford and Deborah Jones, Managers as Sense-givers: Narrative in Strategic Change, paper presented at the ANZAM 2000 Conference, Sydney (3–6 December); Ian Clark, 'Spreading the Right Word', *New Zealand Management*, vol. 48, no. 11 (2001), pp. 115–16.

36 See H. R. Schiffman, *Sensation and Perception: An Integrated Approach*, 3rd edn (New York: Wiley, 1990).

37 A good review is E. L. Jones (ed.), *Attribution: Perceiving the Causes of Behavior* (Morristown, NJ: General Learning Press, 1972). See also John H. Harvey and Gifford Weary, 'Current Issues in Attribution Theory and Research', *Annual Review of Psychology*, vol. 35 (1984), pp. 427–59.

38 ECA, *Managing Mobility Survey: Asian Region Interim Report* (London, 1996) quoted in Alan Nankervis, Robert Compton and Marian Baird, *Strategic Human Resource Management*, 4th edn (Melbourne: Nelson Thomson Learning, 2002), p. 636.

39 Information from 'Misconceptions About Women in the Global Arena Keep Their Numbers Low', Catalyst study, www.catalystwomen.org.

40 These examples are from Natasha Josefowitz, *Paths to Power* (Reading, MA: Addison-Wesley, 1980), p. 60. For more on gender issues see Gary N. Powell (ed.), *Handbook of Gender and Work* (Thousand Oaks, CA: Sage, 1999).

41 Sev Ozdowski, 'Age Shall Not Weary Valuable Workers', *Newcastle Herald* (5 December 2001), p. 9.

42 James Thomson, 'The Rise of Grey Labour', *BRW* (21 March 2002), www.brw.com.au, viewed 30 May 2002.

43 The classic work is Dewitt C. Dearborn and Herbert A. Simon, 'Selective Perception: A Note on the Departmental Identification of Executives', *Sociometry*, vol. 21 (1958), pp. 140–4. See also, J. P. Walsh, 'Selectivity and Selective Perception: Belief Structures and Information Processing', *Academy of Management Journal*, vol. 24 (1988), pp. 453–70.

44 Richard E. Walton, *Interpersonal Peacemaking: Confrontations and Third-Party Consultation* (Reading, MA: Addison-Wesley, 1969), p. 2.

45 See Kenneth W. Thomas, 'Conflict and Conflict Management', in M. D. Dunnett (ed.), *Handbook of Industrial and Organizational Behavior* (Chicago: Rand McNally, 1976), pp. 889–935.

46 See Robert R. Blake and Jane Strygley Mouton, 'The Fifth Achievement', *Journal of Applied Behavioral Science*, vol. 6 (1970), pp. 413–27; Alan C. Filley, *Interpersonal Conflict Resolution* (Glenview, IL: Scott, Foresman, 1975).

47 This discussion is based on Filley, op. cit.

48 Susan Long, 'Cooperation and Conflict: Two Sides of the Same Coin', in Retha Wiesner and Bruce Millett (eds), *Management and Organisational Behaviour: Contemporary Challenges and Future Directions* (Brisbane: John Wiley & Sons, 2001), pp. 95–107.

49 Portions of this treatment of negotiation originally adapted from John R. Schermerhorn Jr, James G. Hunt and Richard N. Osborn, *Managing Organizational Behavior*, 4th edn (New York: Wiley, 1991), pp. 382–7. Used by permission.

50 See Roger Fisher and William Ury, *Getting to Yes: Negotiating Agreement Without Giving In* (New York: Penguin, 1983); James A. Wall Jr, *Negotiation: Theory and Practice* (Glenview, IL: Scott, Foresman, 1985); and William L. Ury, Jeanne M. Brett and Stephen B. Goldberg, *Getting Disputes Resolved* (San Francisco: Jossey-Bass, 1997).

51 Fisher and Ury, op. cit.

52 ibid.

53 Developed from Max H. Bazerman, *Judgment in Managerial Decision Making*, 4th edn (New York: Wiley, 1998), chapter 7.

54 Fisher and Ury, op. cit.

55 Sanjyot P. Dunung, *Doing Business in Asia*, 2nd edn (San Francisco: Jossey-Bass, 1998).

56 Roy J. Lewicki and Joseph A. Litterer, *Negotiation* (Homewood, IL: Irwin, 1985).

57 United Nations, 'The UN in Brief', www.un.org/Overview/brief.html, viewed 15 March 2001.

58 ibid.

59 United Nations, 'What is the United Nations?', www.un.org/geninfo/ir/ch1/ch1.htm, viewed 15 March 2001.

60 United Nations, 'The UN in Brief', op. cit.

61 ibid.

62 Global Policy Forum, 'Selected Quotations on the Subject of UN Reform', www.globalpolicy.org/reform/quotes.htm, viewed 15 March 2001.

63 ibid.

Chapter 18 notes

1 Information from Fisher & Paykel, www.fisherpaykel.co.nz and www.fisherpaykel.com/Corporate/.

2 Information from 'On the Road to Innovation', in special advertising section, 'Charting the Course: Global Business Sets Its Goals', *Fortune* (4 August 1997).

3 Michael Beer and Nitin Nohria, 'Cracking the Code of Change', *Harvard Business Review* (May–June 2000), pp. 133–41.

4 Quote from John A. Byrne, 'Visionary vs. Visionary', *Business Week* (28 August 2000), p. 210.

5 See Peter F. Drucker, 'The Discipline of Innovation', *Harvard Business Review* (November–December 1998), pp. 3–8.

6 Tom Peters, *The Circle of Innovation* (New York: Knopf, 1997).

7 Quotes from David Kirkpatrick, 'From Davos, Talk of Death', *Fortune* (5 March 2001), pp. 180–2.

8 ibid.

9 Information from Ballard Power Systems, www.ballard.com; Sony Consumer Products Update, 2002.

10 Peter Senge, *The Fifth Discipline* (New York: Harper, 1990).

11 ibid.; see also Brian Dumaine, 'Mr. Learning Organization', *Fortune* (17 October 1994), pp. 147–57.

12 R. Duane Ireland and Michael A. Hitt, 'Achieving and Maintaining Strategic Competitiveness in the 21st Century: The Role of Strategic Leadership', *Academy of Management Executive*, vol. 13 (February 1999), pp. 43–57.

13 ibid.

14 See, for example, Roger von Oech, *A Whack on the Side of the Head* (New York: Warner Books, 1983) and *A Kick in the Seat of the Pants* (New York: Harper & Row, 1986).

15 Cited in Peter F. Drucker, *Management: Tasks, Responsibilities, Practices* (New York: Harper & Row, 1973), p. 797.

16 Box & Dice www.boxanddice.com.au.

17 Information from 'Providing Rural Phone Service Profitably in Poor Countries', *Business Week* (18 December 2000), special advertising section.

18 Based on Edward B. Roberts, 'Managing Invention and Innovation', *Research Technology Management* (January–February 1988), pp. 1–19; and Gary Hamel, *Leading the Revolution* (Boston, MA: Harvard Business School Press, 2000).

19 Based on Hamel, op. cit., pp. 293–5

20 Iris Berdrow and Henry W. Lane, 'International Joint Ventures: Creating Value through Successful Knowledge Management', *Journal of World Business*, vol. 38, no. 1 (2003), pp. 15–30.

21 This discussion is stimulated by James Brian Quinn, 'Managing Innovation Controlled Chaos', *Harvard Business Review*, vol. 63 (May–June 1985); and John T. Campling, Competitive Shock and the Employment Relationship: A Study of the Transformation of Employee Relations in UK Commercial Television, 1985 to 1991, unpublished Doctoral Thesis, University of Cambridge (1992).

22 Peter F. Drucker, 'Best R&D Is Business Driven', *Wall Street Journal* (10 February 1988), p. 11.

23 Developed in part from Quinn, op. cit.

24 See Roberts, op. cit.

25 Drucker, op. cit. (1998).

26 John T. Campling and Paul J. Gollan, *Bargained Out: Negotiating Without Unions in Australia* (Sydney: Federation Press, 1999).

27 Beer and Nohria, op. cit.; and 'Change Management, An Inside Job', *The Economist* (15 July 2000), p. 61.

28 Based on John P. Kotter, 'Leading Change: Why Transformation Efforts Fail', *Harvard Business Review* (March–April 1995), pp. 59–67.

29 The model is described by Beer and Nohria, op. cit.

30 ibid.

31 ibid.

32 Information from Institute of Development Studies Project Manager, Malaysia.

33 See Edward E. Lawler III, 'Strategic Choices for Changing Organizations', chapter 12 in Allan M. Mohrman Jr, Susan Albers Mohrman, Gerald E. Ledford Jr, Thomas G. Cummings, Edward E. Lawler III and Associates, *Large Scale Organizational Change* (San Francisco: Jossey-Bass, 1989).

34 The classic description of organisations on these terms is by Harold J. Leavitt, 'Applied Organizational Change in Industry: Structural, Technological and Humanistic Approaches', in James G. March (ed.), *Handbook of Organizations* (Chicago: Rand McNally, 1965), pp. 1144–70.

35 Kurt Lewin, 'Group Decision and Social Change', in G. E. Swanson, T. M. Newcomb and E. L. Hartley (eds), *Readings in Social Psychology* (New York: Holt, Rinehart, 1952), pp. 459–73.

36 This discussion is based on Robert Chin and Kenneth D. Benne, 'General Strategies for Effecting Changes in Human Systems', in Warren G. Bennis, Kenneth D. Benne, Robert Chin and Kenneth E. Corey (eds), *The Planning of Change*, 3rd edn (New York: Holt, Rinehart, 1969), pp. 22–45.

37 The change agent description is developed from an exercise reported in J. William Pfeiffer and John E. Jones, *A Handbook of Structured Experiences for Human Relations Training*, vol. 2 (La Jolla, CA: University Associates, 1973).

38 Ram N. Aditya, Robert J. House and Steven Kerr, 'Theory and Practice of Leadership: Into the New Millennium', chapter 6 in Cary L. Cooper and Edwin A. Locke (eds), *Industrial and Organizational Psychology: Linking Theory with Practice* (Malden, MA: Blackwell Business, 2000).

39 Pfeiffer and Jones, op. cit.

40 Pfeiffer and Jones, op. cit.

41 Australian Conservation Foundation, *Natural Advantage: Sustainability in Our Regions* (ACF: Sydney, 2001).

42 Teresa M. Amabile, 'How to Kill Creativity', *Harvard Business Review* (September–October, 1998), pp. 77–87.

43 Campling and Gollan, op. cit.

44 John P. Kotter and Leonard A. Schlesinger, 'Choosing Strategies for Change', *Harvard Business Review*, vol. 57 (March–April 1979), pp. 109–12.

45 Wanda J. Orlikowski and J. Debra Hofman, 'An Improvisational Model for Change Management: The Case of Groupware Technologies', *Sloan Management Review* (winter 1997), pp. 11–21.

46 ibid.

47 Overviews of organisation development are provided by W. Warner Burke, *Organization Development: A Normative View* (Reading, MA: Addison-Wesley, 1987); William Rothwell, Roland Sullivan and Gary N. McLean, *Practicing Organization Development* (San Francisco: Jossey-Bass, 1995); and Wendell L. French and Cecil H. Bell Jr, *Organization Development*, 6th edn (Englewood Cliffs, NJ: Prentice Hall, 1998).

48 See, for example, Edward E. Lawler III, Susan Albers Mohrman and Gerald E. Ledford Jr, *Employee Involvement and Total Quality Management: Practices and Results in Fortune 1000 Companies* (San Francisco: Jossey-Bass, 1992).

49 See French and Bell, op. cit.

50 Stephen Covey, 'How to Succeed in Today's Workplace', *USA Weekend* (29–31 August 1997), pp. 4–5.

51 Tom Peters, 'The Brand Called "You"', *Fast Company* (August–September 1997).

52 John Campling, 'International Economic Restructuring, Enterprise Bargaining and Gender Outcomes: Predictions for Australia', *The International Journal of Comparative Labour Law and Industrial Relations*, vol. 10, no. 1 (spring 1994), pp. 36–54.

53 'Disney' in *Hoover's Handbook of American Business* (Austin, TX: Hoover's Business Press, 1997).

54 ibid.

55 Academy of Achievement Lobby, 'Michael Eisner's Biography', www.achievement.org/autodoc/page/eis0bio-1.

56 See Michael O'Neal, 'Disney's Kingdom', *Business Week* (14 August 1995), pp. 30–4.

57 Seth Lubove and Robert La Franco, 'Why Mickey Isn't Doing Much Talking These Days', *Forbes* (25 August 1997), pp. 45–6.

58 'Disney', Value Line Investment Survey, 1998.

59 Marc Gunther, 'What's Wrong with This Picture?', *Fortune* (12 January 1998), pp. 106–14.

60 ibid.

61 ibid.

Career Readiness Workbook notes

Sarina Russo will 'See you at the top!'

1 Mark Phillips, 'Russo Works on Bold Ambitions', *Herald Sun* (15 May 2001), p. 23.

2 Russo Institute of Technology, www.russo.qld.edu.au.

3 Graeme James, '$4m Office Buy Tops Up Russo Brisbane Property Investment', *The Courier-Mail* (6 September 2001), p. 75.

4 Claire Dargan, 'Greater Access to Network of Jobs', *The Courier-Mail* (9 October 1999), p. E59.

5 Sarina Russo Group, www.sarinarusso.com.au.

6 Dargan, op. cit.

7 'Harvard Advice on Corporate Survival', *The Courier-Mail* (3 October 2001), p. C23.

8 D. Atkins, 'Taking a Swing at the Premier', *The Courier-Mail* (22 October 1998), p. 16.

9 Sarina Russo and Russ Gleeson, excerpt from draft of *Meet Me at the Top* (Melbourne: Crown Content, 2002).

10 Michelle Grattan, 'Job Network: Outside Review Is Necessary', *Australian Financial Review* (12 October 1998), p. 19.

11 Deborah Cassrels, 'See You at the Top', *The Courier-Mail* (5 February 2001), p. 16.

12 Phillips, op. cit.

13 Vanessa Williams, 'Attitude Points Way to the Top' *Herald Sun* (30 August 2000), p. 23.

GLOSSARY

A

Above-average returns exceed what could be earned from alternative investments of equivalent risk.   p. 212

Accommodation, or smoothing, plays down differences and highlights similarities to reduce conflict.   p. 479

An **accommodative strategy** accepts social responsibility and tries to satisfy prevailing economic, legal and ethical performance criteria.   p. 161

Accountability is the requirement to show performance results to a supervisor.   p. 17

Action research is a collaborative process of collecting data, using it for action planning and evaluating the results.   p. 510

Active listening helps the source of a message say what he or she really means.   p. 469

Adaptive organisations operate with a minimum of bureaucratic features and encourage worker empowerment and teamwork.   p. 299

Administrators are managers who work in public or not-for-profit organisations.   p. 17

Affirmative action commits the organisation to hiring and advancing minority groups and women.   pp. 51, 322

An **after-action review** formally examines results to identify lessons learned in a completed project or special operation.   p. 189

An **angel investor** is a wealthy individual willing to invest in return for equity in a new venture.   p. 256

In **arbitration**, a neutral third party issues a binding decision to resolve a dispute.   p. 483

An **assessment centre** examines how job candidates handle simulated work situations.   p. 332

Fundamental **attribution error** overestimates internal factors and underestimates external factors as influences on someone's behaviour.   p. 475

An **authority decision** is a decision made by the leader and then communicated to the group.   p. 364

Automation is the total mechanisation of a job.   p. 411

Avoidance pretends that a conflict doesn't really exist.   p. 479

B

A **bargaining zone** is the area between one party's minimum reservation point and the other party's maximum reservation point.   p. 482

Base compensation is a salary or hourly wage paid to an individual.   p. 339

BATNA is the best alternative to a negotiated agreement.   p. 482

The **BCG matrix** analyses business opportunities according to market growth rate and market share.   p. 227

The **behavioural decision model** describes decision making with limited information and bounded rationality.   p. 78

A **behaviourally anchored rating scale** uses specific descriptions of actual behaviours to rate various levels of performance.   p. 336

Benchmarking uses external comparisons to gain insights for planning.   p. 183

In **bottom-up change**, change initiatives come from all levels in the organisation.   p. 501

A **boundaryless organisation** eliminates internal boundaries among parts and external boundaries with the external environment.   p. 281

Budgets are plans that commit resources to projects or activities.   p. 181

A **bureaucracy** is a rational and efficient form of organisation founded on logic, order and legitimate authority.   p. 99

Business associations represent the interests of organisations in an industry or region.   p. 324

A **business incubator** offers space, shared services and advice to help small businesses get started.   p. 257

A **business plan** describes the direction for a new business and the financing needed to operate it.   p. 254

A **business strategy** identifies how a division or strategic business unit will compete in its product or service domain.   p. 219

C

A **career** is a sequence of jobs that constitute what a person does for a living.   p. 338

Career planning is the process of systematically matching careers goals and individual capabilities with opportunities for their fulfilment.   p. 339

A **career plateau** is a position from which someone is unlikely to move to a higher level of work responsibility.   p. 339

Casual work is a type of part-time employment where there is no agreement or promise of ongoing work. Casual employees may be employed during peak business periods to supplement a permanent workforce and to provide management with greater flexibility in managing labour.   p. 419

Centralisation is the concentration of authority for most decisions at the top level of an organisation.   p. 286

In a **centralised communication network**, communication flows only between individual members and a hub or centre point.   p. 449

Certain environments offer complete information on possible action alternatives and their consequences.   p. 74

The **chain of command** links all persons with successively higher levels of authority.   p. 283

A **change agent** tries to change the behaviour of another person or social system.   p. 499

Changing is the phase where a planned change actually takes place.   p. 504

Channel richness is the capacity of a communication channel to effectively carry information.   p. 471

Charismatic leaders develop special leader–follower relationships and inspire followers in extraordinary ways.   p. 366

Child labour is the full-time employment of children for work otherwise done by adults.   p. 129

The **classical decision model** describes decision making with complete information.   p. 78

Coaching involves an experienced person offering performance advice to a less-experienced person.   p. 334

Codes of ethics are written guidelines that state values and ethical standards intended to guide the behaviour of employees.   p. 157

Coercive power is the capacity to punish or withhold positive outcomes as a means of influencing other people.   p. 354

Cohesiveness is the degree to which members are attracted to and motivated to remain part of a team.   p. 447

Collaboration, or problem solving, involves working through conflict differences and solving problems so everyone wins.   p. 480

Commercialising innovation turns ideas into products or processes with economic value added.   p. 497

A **committee** is a formal team designated to work on a special task on a continuing basis.   p. 437

Communication is the process of sending and receiving symbols with meanings attached.   p. 464

A **communication channel** is the medium through which a message is sent.   p. 465

A **company** is a legal entity that exists separately from its owners.   p. 255

Comparative management studies how management practices differ among countries and cultures.   p. 134

Competition, or authoritative command, uses force, superior skill or domination to 'win' a conflict.   p. 479

A **competitive advantage** allows an organisation to deal with market and environmental forces better than its competitors.   pp. 36, 206

A **compressed work week** allows a full-time job to be completed in less than five days.   p. 415

Compromise occurs when each party to the conflict gives up something of value to the other.   p. 479

Computer competency is the ability to understand and use computers to advantage.   p. 64

Growth through **concentration** is within the same business area.   p. 219

A **conceptual skill** is the ability to think analytically and solve complex problems.   p. 24

Concurrent controls focus on what happens during the work process.   p. 190

Conflict is a disagreement over issues of substance and/or an emotional antagonism.   p. 477

Conflict resolution is the removal of the substantial and/or emotional reasons for a conflict.   p. 479

A **conglomerate** is an organisation with a diverse range of business units spanning a wide variety of industries.   p. 296

Constructive stress acts in a positive way to increase effort, stimulate creativity and encourage diligence in one's work.   p. 422

A **consultative decision** is a decision made by a leader after receiving information, advice or opinions from group members.   p. 364

Contingency planning identifies alternative courses of action for use if and when circumstances change with time.   p. 183

Contingency thinking tries to match management practices with situational demands.   p. 107

Continuous improvement involves always searching for new ways to improve operations quality and performance.   p. 43

In **continuous-process production** raw materials are continuously transformed by an automated system.   p. 302

Controlling is the process of measuring performance and taking action to ensure desired results.   pp. 20, 185

Core competencies are special strengths that give an organisation a competitive advantage.   p. 216

Core values are underlying beliefs shared by members of the organisation and that influence their behaviour.   p. 46

Corporate governance is the system of control and performance monitoring of top management.   p. 230

Corporate social responsibility is the obligation of an organisation to act in ways that serve the interests of its stakeholders.   p. 158

A **corporate strategy** sets long-term direction for the total enterprise.   p. 218

Corruption involves illegal practices to further one's business interests.   p. 128

Cost-benefit analysis involves comparing the costs and benefits of each potential course of action.   p. 77

A **cost leadership strategy** seeks to operate with lower costs than competitors.   p. 225

A **crisis** is an unexpected problem that can lead to disaster if not resolved quickly and appropriately.   p. 73

The **critical-incident technique** keeps a log of someone's effective and ineffective job behaviours.   p. 336

Cross-functional teams bring together members from different functional departments.   pp. 277, 438

Cultural relativism suggests there is no one right way to behave; ethical behaviour is determined by its cultural context.   p. 150

Culture is a shared set of beliefs, values and patterns of behaviour common to a group of people.   p. 129

Culture shock is the confusion and discomfort a person experiences when in an unfamiliar culture.   p. 129

Customer relationship management (CRM) strategically tries to build lasting relationships and add value to customers.   p. 41

Customer structures group together people and jobs that serve the same customers or clients.   p. 274

A **cybernetic control system** is self-contained in its performance-monitoring and correction capabilities.   p. 187

D

Debt financing involves borrowing money that must be repaid over time with interest.   p. 255

Decentralisation is the dispersion of authority to make decisions throughout all levels of the organisation.   p. 286

A **decentralised communication network** allows all members to communicate directly with one another.   p. 449

A **decision** is a choice among possible alternative courses of action.   p. 73

Decision making is the process of making choices among alternative courses of action.   pp. 76, 450

A **decision support system** allows a computer to help organise and analyse data for problem solving.   p. 70

A **defensive strategy** seeks to protect the organisation by doing the minimum legally required to satisfy social expectations.   p. 161

Delegation is the process of distributing and entrusting work to other persons.   p. 285

Departmentalisation is the process of grouping together people and jobs into work units.   p. 271

Destructive stress impairs the performance of an individual.   p. 422

Differentiation is the degree of difference between subsystems in an organisation.   p. 305

A **differentiation strategy** offers products that are unique and different from the competition.   p. 225

Discipline is the act of influencing behaviour through reprimand.   p. 192

Discrimination occurs when someone is denied a job or a job assignment for reasons not job relevant.   pp. 9, 321

Distributive justice is concerned that people are treated the same regardless of individual characteristics.   p. 150

Distributive negotiation focuses on 'win–lose' claims made by each party for certain preferred outcomes.   p. 481

Growth through **diversification** is by acquisition of or investment in new and different business areas.   p. 220

The term **diversity** describes race, gender, age and other individual differences.   p. 47

Diversity management involves identifying and managing those employee characteristics likely to have a significant impact on the organisation's ability to achieve its strategic objectives.   p. 323

Divestiture sells off parts of the organisation to focus attention and resources on core business areas.   p. 221

A **divisional structure** groups together people working on the same product, in the same area, with similar customers, or on the same processes.   p. 273

Downsizing decreases the size of operations with the intent to become more streamlined.   p. 221

Dysfunctional conflict is destructive and hurts task performance.   p. 478

E

An **e-business strategy** strategically uses the Internet to gain competitive advantage.   p. 222

Inventory control by **economic order quantity** orders replacements whenever inventory level falls to a predetermined point.   p. 194

In **effective communication**, the intended meaning of the source and the perceived meaning of the receiver are identical.   p. 464

An **effective team** achieves high levels of both task performance and membership satisfaction.   p. 442

Efficient communication occurs at minimum cost.   p. 464

An **electronic career portfolio** documents academic and personal accomplishments on line for external review.   p. 513

Electronic commerce is buying and selling goods and services through use of the Internet.   p. 66

Emergent strategies develop over time as managers learn from and respond to experience.   p. 230

Emotional conflicts result from feelings of anger, distrust, dislike, fear and resentment as well as from personality clashes.   p. 478

Emotional intelligence is the ability to manage ourselves and our relationships effectively.   pp. 24, 367

Employee involvement teams meet on a regular basis to use their talents to help solve problems and achieve continuous improvement.   p. 438

Empowerment distributes decision-making power throughout an organisation.   p. 356

Enterprise-wide networks use IT to move information quickly and accurately within an organisation.   p. 70

An **entrepreneur** is willing to pursue opportunities in situations others view as problems or threats.   p. 242

Entrepreneurship is dynamic, risk-taking, creative and growth-oriented behaviour.   p. 242

Environmental uncertainty is a lack of complete information about the environment.   p. 39

Equal employment opportunity is the right to employment and advancement without regard to race, sex, religion, colour or national origin.   p. 321

Equity financing involves exchanging ownership shares for outside investment monies.   p. 255

Escalating commitment is the continuation of a course of action even though it is not working.   p. 80

Ethical behaviour is accepted as 'right' or 'good' in the context of a government moral code.   p. 148

An **ethical dilemma** is a situation that although offering potential benefit or gain is also unethical.   p. 152

Ethical imperialism is an attempt to impose one's ethical standards on other cultures.   p. 151

Ethics sets standards as to what is good or bad, or right or wrong in one's conduct.   p. 148

Ethics training seeks to help people understand the ethical aspects of decision making and to incorporate high ethical standards into their daily behaviour.   p. 155

Ethnocentrism is the tendency to consider one's culture as superior to others.   pp. 129, 474

The **euro** is the new common European currency.   p. 120

The **European Union (EU)** is a political and economic alliance of European countries.   p. 119

Expatriates live and work in a foreign country.   p. 135

Expectancy is a person's belief that working hard will result in high task performance.   p. 387

Expert power is the capacity to influence other people because of specialised knowledge.   p. 354

Expert systems allow computers to mimic the thinking of human experts for applied problem solving.   p. 70

In **exporting**, local products are sold abroad.   p. 125

External control occurs through direct supervision or administrative systems such as rules and procedures.   p. 191

Extinction discourages a behaviour by making the removal of a desirable consequence contingent on its occurrence.   p. 390

Extranets are computer networks for communication between the organisation and its environment.   p. 71

Extrinsic rewards are provided by someone else.   p. 379

F

Family businesses are owned and controlled by family members.   p. 250

Feedback is the process of telling someone else how you feel about something that person did or said.   p. 470

Feedback controls take place after an action is completed.   p. 191

Feedforward controls ensure that directions and resources are right before the work begins.   p. 190

Filtering is the intentional distortion of information to make it appear more favourable to the recipient.   p. 468

A **first-mover advantage** comes from being first to exploit a niche or enter a market.   p. 253

Flexible benefits programs allow employees to choose from a range of benefit options.   p. 340

Flexible working hours give employees some choice in the pattern of daily work hours.   p. 416

A **focused cost leadership strategy** seeks the lowest costs of operations within a special market segment.   p. 225

A **focused differentiation strategy** offers a unique product to a special market segment.   p. 225

A **force-coercion strategy** pursues change through formal authority and/or the use of rewards or punishments.   p. 505

A **forecast** is an attempt to predict future outcomes.   p. 182

Formal groups are officially recognised and supported by the organisation.   p. 436

Formal structure is the official structure of the organisation.   p. 269

A **franchise** is when one business owner sells to another the right to operate the same business in another location.   p. 248

Franchising provides the complete 'package' of support needed to open a particular business.   p. 125

Fringe benefits are non-monetary compensation in the form of health insurance, retirement plans, etc.   p. 340

The **functional chimneys problem** is a lack of communication and coordination across functions.   p. 272

Functional conflict is constructive and helps task performance.   p. 478

Functional managers are responsible for one area of activity, such as finance, marketing, production, human resources, accounting or sales.   p. 17

A **functional strategy** guides activities within one specific area of operations.   p. 219

Functional structures group together people with similar skills who perform similar tasks.   p. 271

G

The **GE Business Screen** analyses business strength and industry attractiveness for strategy formulation.   p. 228

The **general environment** is comprised of cultural, economic, legal–political and educational conditions.   p. 37

General managers are responsible for complex organisational units that include many areas of functional activity.   p. 17

Geographical structures group together people and jobs performed in the same location.   p. 274

The **glass ceiling effect** is an invisible barrier limiting the advancement of women and minority groups.   p. 9

In the **global economy**, resources, markets and competition are worldwide in scope.   p. 118

A **global manager** is culturally aware and well informed on international affairs.   p. 119

In **global sourcing**, materials or services are purchased around the world for local use.   p. 125

Globalisation is the worldwide interdependence of resource flows, product markets and business competition.   pp. 6, 118

A **graphic rating scale** uses a checklist of traits or characteristics to evaluate performance.   p. 336

A **group decision** is a decision made with the full participation of all group members.   p. 364

Group process is the way team members work together to accomplish tasks.   p. 444

Groupthink is a tendency for highly cohesive teams to lose their evaluative capabilities.   p. 452

Growth strategies involve expansion of the organisation's current operations.   p. 219

Growth-need strength is the desire to achieve psychological growth in one's work.   p. 414

H

A **halo effect** occurs when one attribute is used to develop an overall impression of a person or situation.   p. 477

The **Hawthorne effect** is the tendency of persons singled out for special attention to perform as expected.   p. 102

Heuristics are strategies for simplifying decision making.   p. 80

High-context cultures rely on non-verbal and situational cues as well as spoken or written words in communication.   p. 131

Higher-order needs are esteem and self-actualisation needs in Maslow's hierarchy.   p. 380

The **human relations movement** suggests that managers using good human relations will achieve productivity.   p. 102

Human resource management is the process of attracting, developing and maintaining a quality workforce.   p. 321

Human resource planning analyses staffing needs and identifies actions to fill those needs.   p. 327

A **human skill** is the ability to work well in cooperation with other people.   p. 24

Hygiene factors are found in the job context, such as working conditions, interpersonal relations, organisational policies and salary.   p. 381

I

Importing is the process of acquiring products abroad and selling them in domestic markets.   p. 125

The **individualism view** considers ethical behaviour as that which advances long-term self-interests.   p. 149

Industrial relations is the process of negotiation and bargaining between employers and employees.   p. 324

Industry clusters or **learning regions** are groups of enterprises with common or complementary business interests, including the public and private entities on which they depend.   p. 498

Informal groups are unofficial and emerge from relationships and shared interests among members.   p. 436

The **informal structure** is the set of unofficial relationships among an organisation's members.   p. 270

Information is data made useful for decision making.   p. 64

Information competency is the ability to use computers and information technology to locate, retrieve, evaluate, organise and analyse information for decision making.   p. 64

Information systems use IT to collect, organise and distribute data for use in decision making.   p. 68

Information technology (IT) is computer hardware, software, networks and databases supporting information use.   p. 64

An **initial public offering (IPO)** is an initial selling of shares of stock to the public and for trading on a stock exchange.   p. 256

Innovation is the process of taking a new idea and putting it into practice.   p. 496

Innovation groups or **skunkworks** are teams allowed to work creatively together, free of constraints from the larger organisation.   p. 257

Input standards measure work efforts that go into a performance task.   p. 188

Instrumentality is a person's belief that various outcomes will occur as a result of task performance.   p. 387

Integration is the level of coordination achieved among subsystems in an organisation.   p. 305

Integrity in leadership is honesty, credibility and consistency in putting values into action.   p. 370

Intellectual capital is the collective brain power or shared knowledge of a workforce.   pp. 5, 64

Intensive technology focuses the efforts and talents of many people to serve clients.   p. 302

Interactional justice is the degree to which others are treated with dignity and respect.   p. 150

Internal control occurs through self-discipline and self-control.   p. 191

International businesses conduct commercial transactions across national boundaries.   p. 123

International management involves managing operations in more than one country.   p. 119

International teams are teams that include members from at least two different countries.   p. 440

Intranets are computer networks used for communication and data sharing within an organisation.   p. 70

Intrapreneurship is entrepreneurial behaviour displayed by people or subunits within large organisations.   pp. 257, 303

Intrinsic rewards occur naturally during job performance.   p. 379

Intuitive thinking approaches problems in a flexible and spontaneous fashion.   p. 75

ISO 14000 offers a set of certification standards for responsible environmental policies.   p. 129

ISO certification indicates conformance with a rigorous set of international quality standards.   p. 42

J

A **job** is the collection of tasks a person performs in support of organisational objectives.   p. 407

Job analysis studies job requirements and facts that can influence performance.   p. 327

Job burnout is physical and mental exhaustion that can be incapacitating personally and in respect to work.   p. 422

A **job description** details the duties and responsibilities of a job holder.   p. 327

Job design is the allocation of specific work tasks to individuals and groups.   p. 407

Job enlargement increases task variety by combining into one job two or more tasks previously assigned to separate workers.   p. 411

Job enrichment increases job depth by adding work planning and evaluating duties normally performed by the supervisor.   p. 412

Job involvement is defined as the extent to which an individual is dedicated to a job.   p. 407

Job performance is the quantity and quality of task accomplishment by an individual or group.   p. 408

Job rotation increases task variety by periodically shifting workers between jobs involving different tasks.   p. 411

Job satisfaction is the degree to which an individual feels positively or negatively about a job.   p. 407

Job sharing splits one job between two people.   p. 417

Job simplification employs people in clearly defined and very specialised tasks.   p. 411

A **job specification** lists the qualifications required of a job holder.   p. 327

Joint ventures establish operations in a foreign country through joint ownership with local partners.   p. 126

The **justice view** considers ethical behaviour as that which treats people impartially and fairly according to guiding rules and standards.   p. 150

Just-in-time (JIT) scheduling minimises inventory by routing materials to work stations 'just in time' to be used.   p. 195

K

A **keiretsu** is a group of Japanese manufacturers, suppliers and finance firms with common interests.   p. 137

Knowledge management is the processes using intellectual capital for competitive advantage.   p. 82

A **knowledge worker** is someone whose knowledge is a critical asset to employers.   p. 5

L

The **law of effect** states that behaviour followed by pleasant consequences is likely to be repeated; behaviour followed by unpleasant consequences is not.   p. 389

Leadership style is the recurring pattern of behaviours exhibited by a leader.   p. 358

Leading is the process of arousing enthusiasm and directing efforts toward organisational goals. pp. 20, 352

A **learning organisation** continuously changes and improves using the lessons of experience. pp. 82, 109, 300, 495

Legitimate power is the capacity to influence other people by virtue of formal authority, or the rights of office. p. 354

A **licensing agreement** occurs when a firm pays a fee for the rights to make or sell another company's products. p. 125

Lifelong learning is continuous learning from daily experiences and opportunities. p. 23

Line managers directly contribute to the production of the organisation's basic goods or services. p. 16

Lobbying expresses opinions and preferences to government officials. p. 163

In **long-linked technology** a client moves from point to point during service delivery. p. 302

In **lose–lose conflict** no one achieves his or her true desires and the underlying reasons for conflict remain unaffected. p. 480

Low-context cultures emphasise communication via spoken or written words. p. 130

Lower-order needs are physiological, safety and social needs in Maslow's hierarchy. p. 380

M

Maintenance activities are actions taken by team members that support the emotional life of the group. p. 448

Management is the process of planning, organising, leading and controlling the use of resources to accomplish performance goals. p. 19

Management by exception focuses managerial attention on substantial differences between actual and desired performance. p. 189

Management by objectives (MBO) is a process of joint objective setting between a superior and subordinate. p. 195

Management development is training to improve knowledge and skills in the management process. p. 335

A **management information system** uses IT to meet the information needs of managers in daily decisions. p. 72

Management science uses mathematical techniques to analyse and solve management problems and support. p. 105

A **managerial competency** is a skill-based capability for high performance in a management job. p. 24

Managers are responsible for and support the work of others. p. 15

Managing diversity is building an inclusive work environment that allows everyone to reach their full potential. p. 51

Mass production manufactures a large number of uniform products with an assembly-line type of system. p. 302

A **matrix structure** combines functional and divisional approaches to emphasise project or program teams. p. 275

In **MBWA**, managers spend time outside of their offices to meet and talk with workers at all levels. p. 471

Mechanistic designs are centralised with many rules and procedures, a clear-cut division of labour, narrow spans of control and formal coordination. p. 299

Mediating technology links together people in a beneficial exchange of values. p. 302

In **mediation**, a neutral party tries to help conflicting parties improve communication to resolve their dispute. p. 483

Mentoring assigns early-career employees as protégés to more senior ones. p. 334

Merit pay awards pay increases in proportion to performance contributions. p. 392

Middle managers oversee the work of large departments or divisions. p. 16

The **mission** is the organisation's reason for existence in society. p. 214

A **mixed message** results when words communicate one message while actions, body language or appearance communicate something else. p. 467

Modelling demonstrates through personal behaviour the job performance expected of others. p. 334

In **monochronic cultures** people tend to do one thing at a time. p. 131

The **moral-rights view** considers ethical behaviour as that which respects and protects fundamental rights. p. 149

Motion study is the science of reducing a task to its basic physical motions.   p. 98

Motivation accounts for the level, direction and persistence of effort expended at work.   p. 378

A **multicultural organisation** is based on pluralism and operates with respect for diversity.   p. 48

Multiculturalism involves pluralism and respect for diversity.   p. 47

A **multinational corporation (MNC)** is a business with extensive operations in more than one foreign country.   p. 126

Multiperson comparisons compare one person's performance with that of others.   p. 337

N

NAFTA is the North American Free Trade Agreement linking Canada, the USA and Mexico in a regional economic alliance.   p. 120

Need for achievement (nAch) is the desire to do something better, to solve problems, or to master complex tasks.   p. 383

Need for affiliation (nAff) is the desire to establish and maintain good relations with people.   p. 383

Need for power (nPower) is the desire to control, influence, or be responsible for other people.   p. 383

Needs are unfulfilled physiological or psychological desires.   pp. 102, 379

Negative reinforcement strengthens a behaviour by making the avoidance of an undesirable consequence contingent on its occurrence.   p. 390

Negotiation is the process of making joint decisions when the parties involved have different preferences.   p. 481

A **network structure** uses IT to link with networks of outside suppliers and service contractors.   p. 279

Noise is anything that interferes with communication effectiveness.   p. 465

Non-programmed decisions apply specific solutions crafted for a unique problem.   p. 73

Non-verbal communication takes place through gestures and body language.   p. 467

A **norm** is a behaviour, rule or standard expected to be followed by team members.   p. 446

O

Objectives are specific results that one wishes to achieve.   p. 174

An **obstructionist strategy** avoids social responsibility and reflects mainly economic priorities.   p. 161

OD interventions are structured activities that help create change in organisation development.   p. 510

Open systems transform resource inputs from the environment into product outputs.   pp. 12, 106

Operant conditioning is the control of behaviour by manipulating its consequences.   p. 389

Operating objectives direct activities toward key and specific performance results.   p. 216

Operational plans define specific activities to implement strategic plans.   p. 180

An **optimising decision** chooses the alternative giving the absolute best solution to a problem.   p. 78

Organic designs are decentralised with fewer rules and procedures, open divisions of labour, wide spans of control and more personal coordination.   p. 299

An **organisation** is a collection of people working together in a division of labour to achieve a common purpose.   p. 11

An **organisation chart** describes the arrangement of work positions within an organisation.   p. 269

Organisation development is a comprehensive effort to improve an organisation's ability to deal with its environment and solve problems.   p. 508

Organisation structure is a system of tasks, workflows, reporting relationships and communication linkages.   p. 269

Organisational behaviour is the study of individuals and groups in organisations.   p. 102

Organisational behaviour modification (OB Mod) is the application of operant conditioning to influence human behaviour at work.   p. 389

Organisational commitment is defined as the loyalty of an individual to the organisation.   p. 407

Organisational culture is the system of shared beliefs and values that develops within an organisation and guides the behaviour of its members.   pp. 45, 216

Organisational design is the process of creating structures that best serve mission and objectives.   p. 296

In the **organisational life cycle** an organisation passes through different stages from birth to maturity.   p. 302

Organisational stakeholders are directly affected by the behaviour of the organisation and hold a stake in its performance.   p. 158

Organisational synergy is obtained when a combination of ideas and knowledge from different parts of an organisation creates improvements in the productive processes and outputs throughout the organisation.   p. 296

Organising is the process of assigning tasks, allocating resources and arranging activities to implement plans.   pp. 20, 268

Orientation familiarises new employees with jobs, coworkers and organisational policies and services.   p. 333

Output standards measure performance results in terms of quantity, quality, cost or time.   p. 188

P

Participatory planning includes the people who will be affected by plans and/or whose help is needed to implement them.   p. 184

A **partnership** is when two or more people agree to contribute resources to start and operate a business together.   p. 255

Part-time work is a form of permanent employment in which the worker works for less than the full-time work week.   p. 419

Perception is the process through which people receive, organise and interpret information from the environment.   p. 475

Performance appraisal is the process of formally evaluating performance and providing feedback to a job holder.   p. 335

Performance effectiveness is an output measure of task or goal accomplishment.   p. 13

Performance efficiency is a measure of resource cost associated with goal accomplishment.   p. 13

A **performance gap** is a discrepancy between the desired and actual state of affairs.   p. 502

A **performance management system** sets standards, assesses results and plans for performance improvements.   p. 335

Personal staff are 'assistant-to' positions that support senior managers.   p. 286

Personal wellness is the pursuit of one's full potential through a personal-health promotion program.   p. 423

A **plan** is a statement of intended means for accomplishing objectives.   p. 175

Planned change occurs as a result of specific efforts by a change agent.   p. 502

Planning is the process of setting objectives and determining how to accomplish them.   pp. 19, 174

A **policy** is a standing plan that communicates broad guidelines for decisions and action.   p. 181

Political risk is the possible loss of investment or control over a foreign asset because of political changes in the host country.   p. 135

Political-risk analysis forecasts how political events may impact foreign investments.   p. 135

In **polychronic cultures** time is used to accomplish many different things at once.   p. 131

A **portfolio planning** approach seeks the best mix of investments among alternative business opportunities.   p. 227

Positive reinforcement strengthens a behaviour by making a desirable consequence contingent on its occurrence.   p. 389

Power is the ability to get someone else to do something you want done or to make things happen the way you want.   p. 353

Prejudice is the display of negative, irrational attitudes toward women or minority groups.   p. 9

Principled/integrative negotiation uses a 'win–win' orientation to reach solutions acceptable to each party.   p. 481

Privatisation is the selling of state-owned enterprises into private ownership.   p. 124

A **proactive strategy** meets all the criteria of social responsibility, including discretionary performance.   p. 161

Problem solving involves identifying and taking action to resolve problems.   p. 73

Procedural justice is concerned that policies and rules are fairly administered.   p. 150

Procedures or **rules** precisely describe actions that are to be taken in specific situations.   p. 181

Process innovations involve new or improved ways of manufacturing the product or service.   p. 496

Process reengineering systematically analyses work processes to design new and better ones.   p. 306

A **process structure** groups jobs and activities that are part of the same processes.   p. 275

Process value analysis identifies and evaluates core processes for their performance contributions.   p. 307

Product innovations involve the use of new or improved design principles or technologies for incorporation in products or services.   p. 496

Product life cycle is the series of stages a product or service goes through in the 'life' of its marketability.   p. 226

Product structures group together people and jobs working on a single product or service.   p. 274

Productivity is the quantity and quality of work performance, with resource utilisation considered.   p. 12

Programmed decisions apply solutions from past experience to a routine problem.   p. 73

Progressive discipline is the process of tying reprimands to the severity and frequency of misbehaviour.   p. 192

Project managers coordinate complex projects with task deadlines and people with many areas of expertise.   p. 16

Project schedules are single-use plans for accomplishing a specific major project.   p. 181

Project teams are convened for a particular task or project and disband once it is completed.   p. 277

Projection is the assignment of personal attributes to other individuals.   p. 477

Protectionism is a call for tariffs and favourable treatments to protect domestic firms from foreign competition.   p. 124

A **psychological contract** is the set of expectations held by an individual about working relationships with the organisation.   p. 405

Punishment discourages a behaviour by making an unpleasant consequence contingent on its occurrence.   p. 390

Q

A **quality circle** is a group of employees who periodically meet to discuss ways of improving work quality.   pp. 43, 438

Quality control checks processes, materials, products and services to ensure that they meet high standards.   p. 195

Quality of work life (QWL) is the overall quality of human experiences in the workplace.   p. 17

R

A **rational persuasion strategy** pursues change through empirical data and rational argument.   p. 505

Realistic job previews provide job candidates with all pertinent information about a job and the organisation.   p. 330

Recruitment is a set of activities designed to attract a qualified pool of job applicants.   p. 328

Referent power is the capacity to influence other people because of their desire to identify personally with you.   p. 355

Refreezing is the phase at which change is stabilised.   p. 504

Reliability means a selection device measures consistently over repeated uses.   p. 331

Restructuring changes the scale and/or mix of operations to gain efficiency and improve performance.   p. 220

A **retrenchment strategy** involves reducing the scale of current operations.   p. 220

Reward power is the capacity to offer something of value as a means of influencing other people.   p. 354

A **risk environment** lacks complete information, but offers 'probabilities' of the likely outcomes for possible action alternatives.   p. 74

S

Satisficing decisions choose the first satisfactory alternative that comes to your attention.   p. 78

Satisfier factors are found in job content, such as a sense of achievement, recognition, responsibility, advancement and personal growth.   p. 381

Scenario planning identifies alternative future scenarios and makes plans to deal with each.   p. 174

Scientific management emphasises careful selection and training of workers, and supervisory support.   p. 97

Selection is choosing from a pool of the best-qualified job applicants.   p. 330

Selective perception is the tendency to define problems from one's own point of view.   p. 477

Self-fulfilling prophecies occur when people act in ways that confirm another's expectations.   p. 103

Members of **self-managing work teams** have the authority to make decisions about how they share and complete their work.   p. 441

Self-serving bias explains personal success by internal causes and personal failures by external causes.   p. 476

Sexual harassment occurs as behaviour of a sexual nature that affects a person's employment situation.   p. 321

Shaping is positive reinforcement of successive approximations to the desired behaviour.   p. 391

A **shared power strategy** pursues change by participation in assessing values, needs and goals.   p. 506

Simultaneous systems operate when mechanistic and organic designs operate together in an organisation.   p. 303

A **skill** is the ability to translate knowledge into action that results in desired performance.   p. 23

Skills-based pay is a system of paying workers according to the number of job-relevant skills they master.   p. 394

Small-batch production manufactures a variety of products crafted to fit customer specifications.   p. 302

A **small business** has fewer than 100 employees, is independently owned and operated and is normally one of many competitors in its industry. Small businesses are common in the restaurant, building, retailing and personal services sectors.   p. 247

A **social audit** is a systematic assessment of an organisation's accomplishments in areas of social responsibility.   p. 160

Social loafing is the tendency of some people to avoid responsibility by 'free-riding' in groups.   p. 435

Socialisation systematically changes the expectations, behaviour and attitudes of new employees.   p. 333

A **sociotechnical system** integrates technology and human resources in high-performance systems.   p. 414

A **sole proprietorship** is an individual pursuing business for a profit.   p. 255

Span of control refers to the number of subordinates directly reporting to a manager.   p. 284

Specialised staff provide technical expertise for other parts of the organisation.   p. 286

The **specific environment** includes the people and groups with whom an organisation interacts.   p. 38

Staff managers use special technical expertise to advise and support line workers.   p. 16

Stakeholders are the individuals, groups and institutions directly affected by an organisation's performance.   pp. 38, 215

A **stereotype** is when attributes commonly associated with a group are assigned to an individual.   p. 476

In **strategic alliances** organisations join together in partnership to pursue an area of mutual interest.   p. 221

A **strategic business unit (SBU)** is a major business area that operates with some autonomy.   p. 219

Strategic human resource management involves attracting, developing and maintaining a quality workforce to implement organisational strategies.   p. 327

Strategic intent focuses and applies organisational energies on a unifying and compelling goal.   p. 211

Strategic leadership enthuses people to continuously change, refine and improve strategies and their implementation.   pp. 231, 495

Strategic management is the process of formulating and implementing strategies.   p. 211

Strategic opportunism focuses on long-term objectives while being flexible in dealing with short-term problems.   p. 76

Strategic plans define long-term needs and set action directions for the organisation.   p. 180

A **strategy** is a pattern in a stream of organisational decisions.   p. 211

Strategy formulation is the process of creating strategies.   p. 213

Strategy implementation is the process of putting strategies into action. p. 214

Stress is a state of tension experienced by individuals facing extraordinary demands, constraints or opportunities. p. 420

Stressors are the things that cause stress. p. 420

Subcultures are common to groups of people with similar values and beliefs based on shared work responsibilities and personal characteristics. p. 48

Substantive conflicts involve disagreements over goals, resources, rewards, policies, procedures and job assignments. p. 477

Substitutes for leadership are factors in the work setting that direct work efforts without the involvement of a leader. p. 364

A **subsystem** is a smaller component of a larger system. pp. 106, 304

A **succession plan** describes how the leadership transition and related financial matters will be handled. p. 251

The **succession problem** is the issue of who will run the business when the current head leaves. p. 251

Supply chain management strategically links all operations dealing with resource supplies. p. 42

Sustainable career advantage is a combination of personal attributes that allows you to consistently outperform others in meeting needs of employers. p. 513

Sustainable development meets the needs of the present without hurting future generations. p. 129

Sweatshops employ workers at very low wages, for long hours, and in poor working conditions. p. 128

A **SWOT analysis** examines organisational strengths and weaknesses and environmental opportunities and threats. p. 216

A **symbolic leader** uses symbols to establish and maintain a desired organisational culture. p. 47

Synergy is the creation of a whole greater than the sum of its individual parts. p. 436

A **system** is a collection of interrelated parts working together for a purpose. p. 106

Systematic thinking approaches problems in a rational and analytical fashion. p. 75

T

Task activities are actions taken by team members that directly contribute to the group's performance purpose. p. 448

Task forces are formal teams convened for a specific purpose and expected to disband when that purpose is achieved. p. 437

A **team** is a collection of people who regularly interact to pursue common goals. p. 435

Team building is a sequence of collaborative activities to gather and analyse data on a team and make changes to increase its effectiveness. p. 453

Team leaders or **supervisors** report to middle managers and directly supervise non-managerial workers. p. 16

Team structures use permanent and temporary cross-functional teams to improve lateral relations. p. 277

Teamwork is the process of people actively working together to accomplish common goals. p. 435

A **technical skill** is the ability to use a special proficiency or expertise in one's work. p. 23

The **technological imperative** states that technology is a major influence on organisation structure. p. 302

Technology includes equipment, knowledge and work methods that transform inputs into outputs. p. 302

Telecommuting or flexiplace involves working at home or other places using computer links to the office. p. 417

Theory E change is based on activities that increase shareholder or economic value. p. 500

Theory O change is based on activities that increase organisational performance capabilities. p. 501

Theory X assumes people dislike work, lack ambition, are irresponsible and prefer to be led. p. 103

Theory Y assumes people are willing to work, accept responsibility, are self-directed and creative. p. 103

Theory Z describes a management framework emphasising long-term employment and teamwork. p. 109

360° feedback includes in the appraisal process superiors, subordinates, peers and even customers. p. 337

In **top-down change**, the change initiatives come from senior management. p. 500

Top managers guide the performance of the organisation as a whole or of one of its major parts. p. 15

Total quality management (TQM) is managing with commitment to continuous improvement, product quality and customer satisfaction.   pp. 14, 42

Training provides learning opportunities to acquire and improve job-related skills.   p. 334

Transactional leadership is leadership that directs the efforts of others through tasks, rewards and structures.   p. 366

Transformational leadership is inspirational leadership that gets people to do more in achieving high performance.   p. 366

Transnational corporations are MNCs that operate worldwide on a borderless basis.   p. 127

A **Type A personality** is a person oriented toward extreme achievement, impatience and perfectionism.   p. 421

U

An **uncertain environment** lacks so much information that it is difficult to assign probabilities to the likely outcomes of alternatives.   p. 74

Unfreezing is the phase during which a situation is prepared for change.   p. 504

Unions represent the interests of employees in an industry, occupation or organisation.   p. 324

Universalism suggests ethical standards apply across all cultures.   p. 151

Unplanned changes occur spontaneously and without a change agent's direction.   p. 502

The **upside-down pyramid** puts customers at the top, served by workers whose managers support them.   p. 282

The **utilitarian view** considers ethical behaviour that which delivers greatest good to the most people.   p. 149

V

Valence is the value a person assigns to work-related outcomes.   p. 387

Validity means a selection device has a demonstrated link with future job performance.   p. 331

A **value chain** is the sequence of activities that transform materials into finished products.   p. 108

Values are broad beliefs about what is or is not appropriate behaviour.   p. 149

Venture capitalists make large investments in new ventures in return for an equity stake in the business.   p. 256

Growth through **vertical integration** is by acquiring suppliers or distributors.   p. 220

A **virtual organisation** is a shifting network of strategic alliances that are engaged as needed.   p. 282

Members of a **virtual team** work together and solve problems through computer-based interactions.   p. 439

Vision is a term used to describe a clear sense of the future.   p. 353

Visionary leadership brings to the situation a clear sense of the future and an understanding of how to get there.   p. 353

W

Whistleblowers expose the misdeeds of others in organisations.   p. 156

A **wholly owned subsidiary** is a local operation completely owned by a foreign firm.   p. 126

In **win–lose conflict** one party achieves its desires and the other party does not.   p. 480

In **win–win conflict** the conflict is resolved to everyone's benefit.   p. 480

Workflow is the movement of work from one point to another in a system.   p. 307

Workforce diversity describes differences among workers in gender, race, age, ethnic culture, able-bodiedness, religious affiliation and sexual orientation.   p. 8

Work-life balance involves balancing career demands with personal and family needs.   p. 339

Workplace rage is overtly aggressive behaviour toward coworkers or the work setting.   p. 422

A **work process** is a related group of tasks that together create a value for the customer.   p. 306

In the **World Trade Organization (WTO)**, member nations agree to negotiate and resolve disputes about tariffs and trade restrictions.   p. 124

Z

A **zero-based budget** allocates resources to a project or activity as if it were brand new.   p. 181

INDEX